I0418996

Edvard Munch
in the National Museum

A comprehensive overview

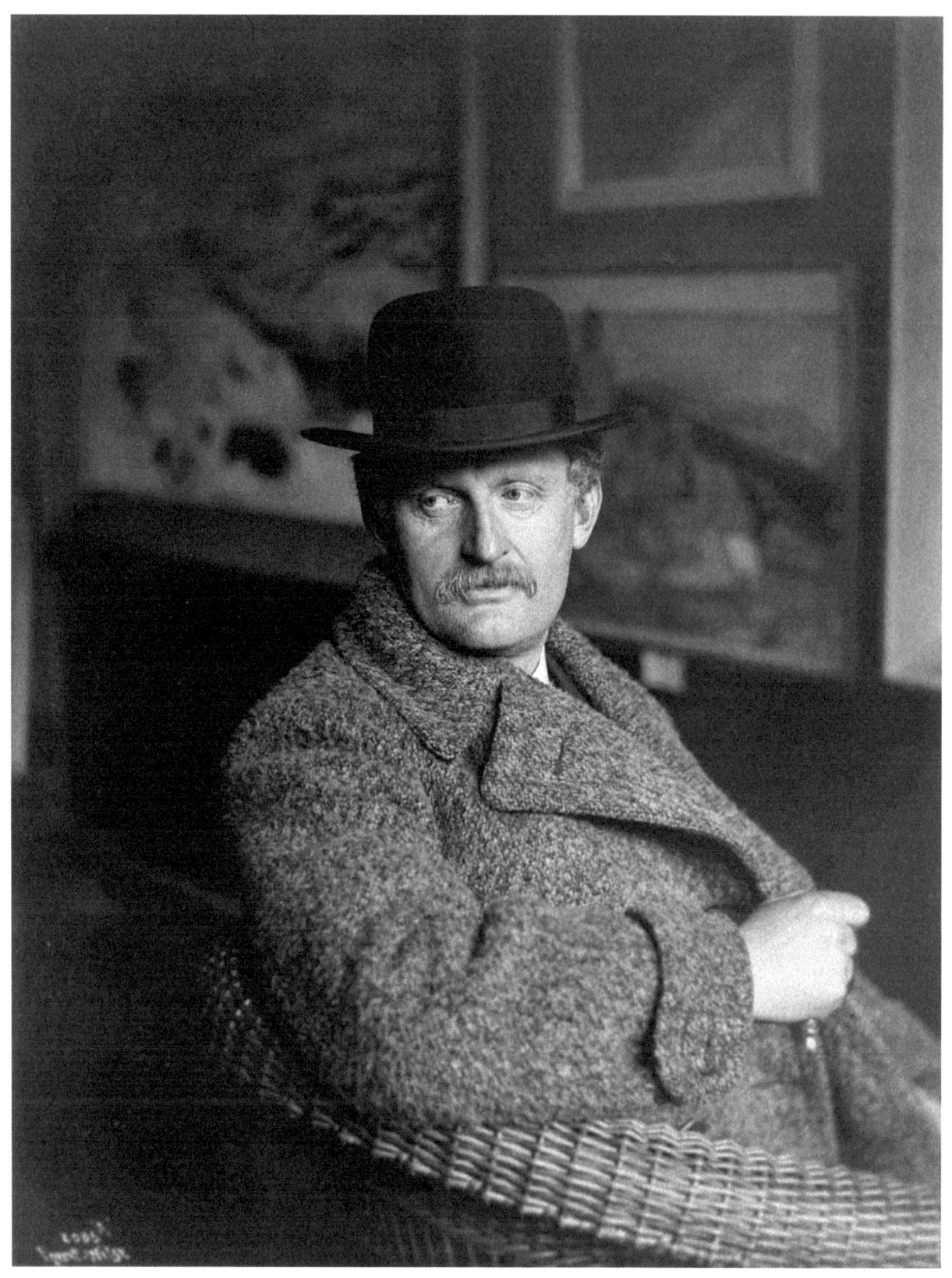

Edvard Munch, 1912
Norsk Folkemuseum
NF.09060-016
Photo: Anders Beer Wilse

Contents

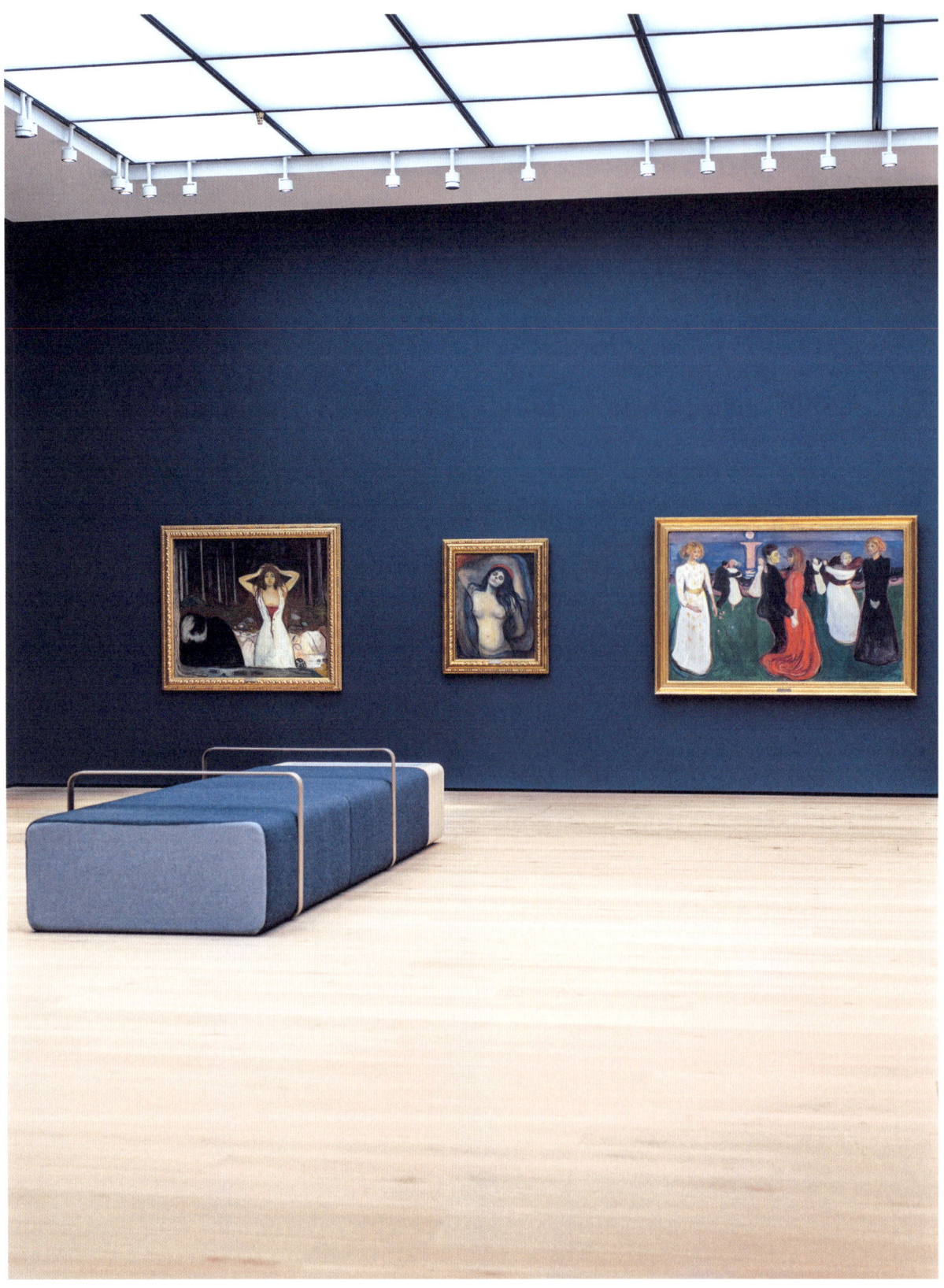

The Munch room in the new National Museum, 2022.
Photo: Nasjonalmuseet / Annar Bjørgli

Foreword

Edvard Munch (1863-1944) is without doubt Norway's most famous artist. His painting *The Scream*, with its powerful depiction of human vulnerability, is recognised by people around the world. It is one of very few works of art to have been rendered as an emoji, now available to billions of smartphone users. But Munch was so much more than just *The Scream*.

Munch helped to change pictorial art. Thanks to his ability to formulate deep, existential themes in a new and modern idiom, he became an important contributor to symbolism, expressionism, and early modernism. The moods Munch captures on canvas, card, and paper are as relevant today as they were when he created his works. He probes some of our deepest feelings.

The long tradition of dedicating a room to Munch's art has been continued in the new National Museum. On display in the new Munch room are a number of the artist's best known and most significant works.

Paintings from the so-called Frieze of Life form the core of the new presentation. In this series, Munch depicts the emotional life of the modern soul in iconic pictures such as *The Scream*, *Madonna*, *Ashes*, *The Dance of Life*, and *Death in the Sickroom*. The Munch room gives visitors the opportunity to get up close to some of the artist's defining works, to reflect on what he wants to convey, and to notice their own feelings in response to the situations he depicts.

Further paintings by Munch can also be seen in some of the museum's other exhibition rooms, where they are set in their art historical context.

How the museum acquired these seminal works and how the idea of a dedicated Munch room evolved at the National Gallery are just two of the stories this publication seeks to tell. The book is first and foremost a catalogue of the museum's holdings, a comprehensive overview of all the works by Edvard Munch currently in the National Museum's collection. But it also aims to highlight various aspects of the relationship between the artist and the institution. It is well established that the National Gallery played a crucial role in Munch's career.

The first Munch work to be acquired by the National Gallery's purchasing committee was the painting *Night in Nice*, created and purchased in 1891. Most of the Munch works now held by the museum entered the National Gallery's collection during the artist's lifetime, with Munch himself often playing an active part in the process that led to the acquisition. Among the many Munch donations, two stand out as exceptional because of their size. The first, from Olaf Schou, made primarily in the period 1909-1910, consisted of no fewer than twelve paintings. This was followed some years later by the gift from Charlotte and Christian Mustad, which eventually amounted to fifteen paintings, transferred to the museum between its centenary year of 1937 and 1970. In addition, the collection has over the years benefited from numerous smaller yet no less important and generous donations from individuals. Notable donors include the German art connoisseur Julius Meier-Graefe and Munch himself.

As of 2021, the museum has built up a collection of 57 paintings, 164 graphic works, 14 drawings, four original prints in books and four posters.

In order to elucidate the institutional history behind the works and the various aspects of the relationship between Munch and the institution, we have engaged a cast of experts. We wish to thank our former colleagues Nils Messel and Sidsel Helliesen, both of whom have been involved in the project since its inception and who have contributed illuminating texts that demonstrate their extensive knowledge and expertise. Further, it has been our priority to draw on the resources of the museum's own staff in this work. Marianne Yvenes and Øystein Ustvedt have served as editors. The museum's conservator Thierry Ford is represented with a summary of relevant conservation history, curator Mai Britt Guleng with an article that addresses the Frieze of Life and the establishment of the Munch room. The work of the editors has been supported by a team that included senior curator Wenche Volle and curator Vibeke Waallann Hansen. Volle, Waallann Hansen, and Ustvedt have all contributed texts and information concerning the cataloguing of individual paintings. Helle Ravn, Trine Nordkvelle, and Ida Hove Solberg have participated with additional research, quality checks, and various cataloguing tasks.

We are deeply grateful for external assistance from the Munch expert Frank Høifødt, who has read and quality-checked texts, and from former senior curator at the Munch Museum, Gerd Woll, who has cooperated with Sidsel Helliesen in reviewing the museum's holdings of Munch's works on paper. We also wish to acknowledge the importance of our dialogue and exchanges with the Munch Museum. In this respect, the Munch Museum's library deserves particular mention, as do also senior curator of painting Petra Pettersen and art historian Nina Else Lystad. And last but not least, we wish to thank the library of the National Museum and the National Library of Norway.

We hope this book will be a source of joy to a large audience and will encourage further study of Munch's work.

Karin Hindsbo
Director, The National Museum

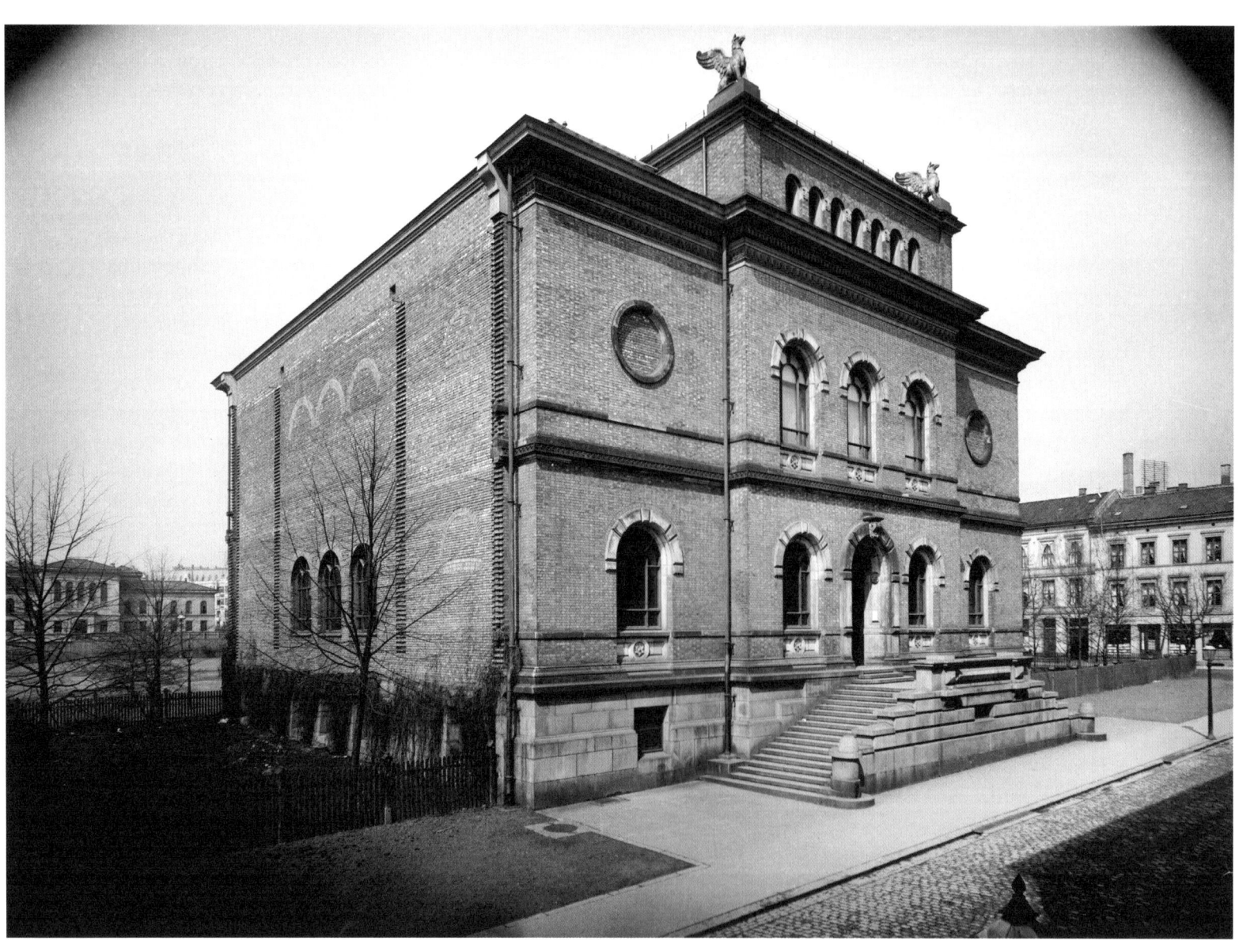

The sculpture museum, later the National Gallery.
Probably between 1890 and 1900.
Photo: Norsk Teknisk Museum / Severin Worm-Petersen

Nils Messel

Edvard Munch and the National Gallery

In the vast literature about Edvard Munch, scholars have been seeking to interpret the artist and his work since the early 1890s. That literature is of course full of variations, depending on time, place and the personal preferences of each author. However, one common denominator in much of what has been written over the years seems to be the considerable scepticism that Munch supposedly encountered in his younger years. It would appear that the dramatic impetus in most of these stories lies in the idea of a brutal clash between the lonely genius and a blinkered world. For some, it is as if the conflict between the artist and the public only reaches resolution long after the artist's death.

In the case of Edvard Munch and the National Gallery, we get to view a very different reality. No other Norwegian artist has been treated with a similar level of attentiveness and interest by the nation's own museum. His pictures were acquired to an extent that other artists could only ever dream of. Even before World War I, plans were in place for something as unusual as a room devoted to the work of the great master. Spectacular Munch exhibitions were arranged, and the museum's staff published a slew of texts, including the first detailed biography of the artist, authored by the museum's long-standing director, Jens Thiis.

It is impossible to say exactly when the National Gallery became aware of the unusual new talent that had appeared on the Norwegian art scene. But when, in the spring of 1884, the name of the twenty-year-old Edvard Munch cropped up on the list of applicants for Customs Treasurer Schäffer's two-year travel grant, recipients of which were chosen on the advice of the National Gallery's board, it would seem that he was already well-known.

Frits Thaulow had recently offered him a private scholarship to help him to travel to Paris.[1] If he could add to that a contribution from the Schäffer fund, then the finances for his journey would be secured. The addition of a few warm words from older colleagues would also expedite the application. "In allowing myself to recommend Mr. Edv. Munch to be considered for an allowance from the revenues of the Schäffer endowment," wrote Christian Krohg, "I declare it to be the firm conviction of myself and my colleagues' that among the younger artists, he is the one who, thanks to his rare colouristic ability, his artistic sensibility and his originality, inspires the most hope and deserves the greatest encouragement."[2] On 16 June 1884, member of the board Julius Middelthun addressed a letter to Munch on behalf of the museum: "I am pleased to inform you that yesterday evening the Board of Directors of the National Gallery placed you top of the list of candidates to receive 400 kroner from Customs Treasurer Schæffer's endowment fund." A member of the board since 1869, Middelthun had taught the young Munch at the Royal School of Design and considered him his best student. With money from both the Schäffer fund and from Thaulow, Munch was at last ready to embark on his first study trip abroad. He set out just after New Year 1885.

A few years later, in 1889, with recommendations from a number of admirers, Munch was again placed first on the list of candidates for a state travel scholarship. Here again the nominations were made by the board of the National Gallery, in cooperation with the artists' organisation. Thus for example Erik Werenskiold wrote: "It is my pleasure to recommend Munch for the State Scholarship. There can be no doubt, in my view, as to his considerable gifts. He has the eye of a painter and is well advanced with respect to tone; his draughtsmanship has been neglected, despite his obvious talent; for his abilities to unfold their full promise, he would benefit from going abroad to receive rigorous training."[3] Munch received this scholarship three years in a row (instead of the usual two), having been prevented by illness from studying for part of the time. Once again his destination was Paris.

Few doubted that Edvard Munch was destined to become the master of tomorrow. And his more established fellow artists took pleasure in hanging the pictures of this talented youth on their own walls.[4] The challenge now was to get him represented on the walls of the National Gallery.

The first purchases

Safely back from his state-funded foreign travels, in 1891 Munch submitted three smaller paintings to the National Annual Autumn Exhibition. For the seven members of the National Gallery's board, the pressing task was to agree on what to buy from the exhibition.[5] Erik Werenskiold proposed the atmospheric *Night in Nice* (cat. 15). The catalogue price was 300 kroner. An initial straw poll resulted in a decision *not* to buy the painting. Only Eilif Peterssen, Mathias Skeibrok and Werenskiold voted in favour. A final decision was postponed until the next meeting. When Werenskiold came with the news that the picture could now be had for just 200 kroner, a majority favoured the purchase, albeit with three people still opposing the idea: chairman C.F. Larsen, C.W. Barth and P.N. Arbo. Werenskiold could therefore inform Munch:

> Dear Munch, perhaps you already know that your picture – *Night in Nice* – has been bought for the gallery for 200 kroner. I took responsibility for the price, thinking that you would rather accept a lower price than not get the picture into the gallery. Jeanniot's landscape was also bought, after lengthy discussion. Arbo and Barth are the worst people we could have on the gallery board, and it is a scandal that two such fools should have a say in the disposal of public funds. Whenever something good is suggested, they are almost inevitably opposed to it; but if it's something bad, then they say it should be purchased.[6]

1891 was the last year Munch participated in the Autumn Exhibition. By that point, several art dealers had set up shop in the Norwegian capital in cooperation with whom artists could arrange exhibitions, in addition to which there were simpler venues suitable for displaying art that could be rented at a reasonable price. Solo exhibitions were the strategy of choice for those with ambition.

In the autumn of 1893, Munch was preparing to send a number of pictures to Berlin. He had plans for a new exhibition at a venue at Unter den Linden 19. Before the pictures were dispatched to Berlin, Gerhard Munthe suggested to the other members of the board that the museum should purchase *The Storm* (Woll M 324), a dramatic picture of ominous darkness that Munch had painted at Åsgårdstrand that summer. The price was 600 kroner. But Erik Werenskiold was the only one willing to back Munthe's proposal, and without a majority there could be no purchase.[7]

Several opportunities arose when in autumn 1895 Munch presented a new exhibition in Kristiania, this time at Blomqvist kunsthandel on Karl Johans gate. The artist offered the museum four works. Both *The Sick Child* (cat. 8) and *Spring* (cat. 12) could be regarded as old regulars from the many exhibitions he had now had abroad. Of the works on offer at Blomqvist that autumn, "Soloppgang" (Sunrise) may well be identical with *Sunrise at Åsgårdstrand* (Woll M 314), painted a few years earlier, while *Self-Portrait with Cigarette* (cat. 32) was entirely new.

After several caustic reviews, Munch's good friend Thorolf Holmboe wrote a positive piece in Munch's defence, in which he encouraged the National Gallery not to miss the opportunity. "Allow me to suggest the large, excellent work on the room's main wall entitled Spring, his 'Self-Portrait' and 'Sunrise', and, for the Department of Prints and Drawings, every one of the etchings."[8] Gerhard Munthe formally proposed the purchase of the self-portrait, and this time he was backed by a solid majority. For the artist, the sale of *Night in Nice* (cat. 15)

four years earlier represented an important breakthrough, but for the National Gallery, the acquisition of *Self-Portrait with Cigarette* was even more significant. For with this the museum took possession of its first major work by Munch. Andreas Aubert also recommended the purchase of *Spring*, a proposal that was rejected. For now the kitty was empty.[9] Whether or not the museum purchased some of the graphic works from the exhibition, as Holmboe had suggested, is difficult to know. As Helliesen and Woll write in the current catalogue, the inventorying of drawings and graphics wasn't as detailed as it was for paintings. When Jens Thiis took over as director around New Year 1909, the museum owned "some 70 prints".[10] Most of these were probably acquired before and just after the turn of the century.

Following an exhibition at the Diorama venue in autumn 1897, Munch offered the museum four portraits.[11] These were a "large portrait of a woman", identical with *Inger in Black and Violet* (cat. 20), *Hans Jæger* (cat. 13), *Gunnar Heiberg* (Woll M 253) and "the other portrait of a woman" (which today cannot be identified). If the museum were to buy the first three as a job lot, then Munch would offer a discount of 500 kroner, i.e. he would sell all three for 2,200 kroner. The museum restricted itself to *Hans Jæger*, a portrait that had first been shown at the Autumn Exhibition in 1889, and subsequently at a number of exhibitions in Germany.[12]

A new attempt to sell the full-length portrait of Munch's sister, Inger, was presented to the board just over a year later, at its meeting of 5 December 1898. This time the price was 1,500 kroner. Further, the ten-year-old *Spring* was still available, now with a price tag of 2,500 kroner. The fact that both pictures lacked frames and that *Spring* was in a poor state of repair did little to dampen the board's interest. At their first meeting of 1899, the board resolved to buy both.

In autumn 1901, Munch had a new and larger exhibition in Kristiania, this time in the former premises of the Museum of Decorative Arts and Design in Stortingsgate 14, "Hollendergården". The exhibition catalogue listed seventy-two paintings and thirty-four prints. On top of which, as was often the case, a number of works were added at the last minute, after the catalogue had gone to press, one of which was *The Scream* (cat. 23). After visiting the exhibition, the irrepressibly enthusiastic Gerhard Munthe informed Munch of his plans:

> Dear Edvard Munch, I would be grateful to you if you could let me know by return of post the price for your picture "Evening" (the three girls on the bridge) and likewise for your "Moonlight" (which hangs, or hung, beside the former). For the moment, I am uncertain of the National Gallery's status and of the mood of board, but I wish to suggest the purchase of one or the other (or

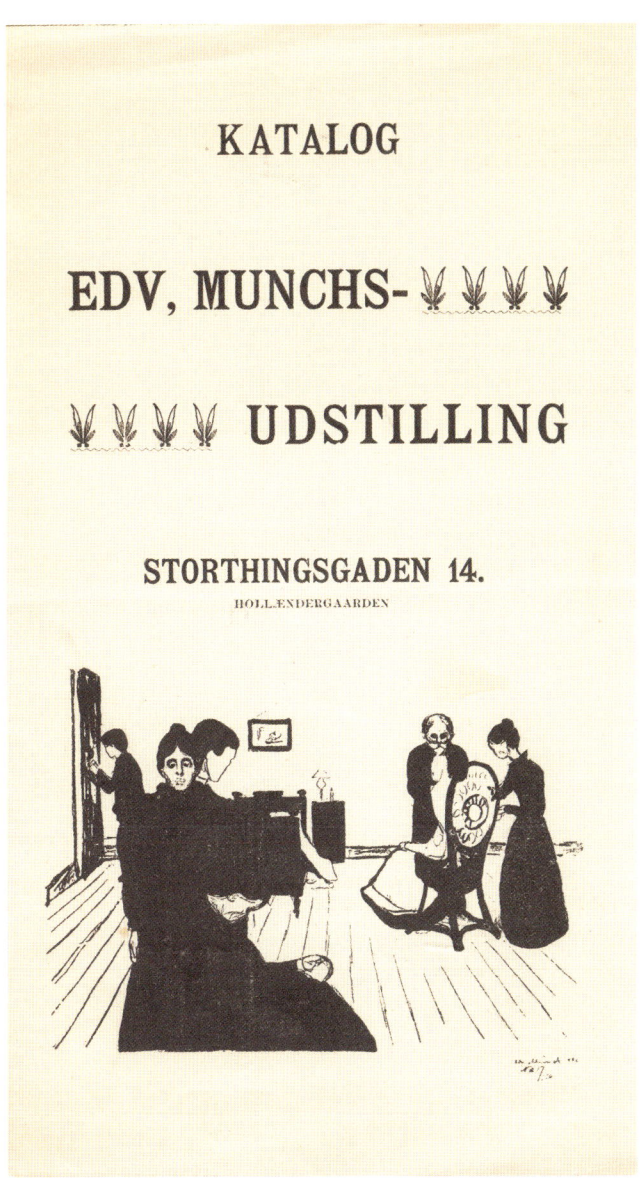

KATALOG

EDV, MUNCHS- ✹✹✹✹

✹✹✹✹ UDSTILLING

STORTHINGSGADEN 14.

HOLLENDERGAARDEN

The National Gallery's board/purchasing committee could only vote on proposed acquisitions if they had seen the pictures with their own eyes. This effectively limited opportunities for purchasing to exhibitions in the capital. No other young artist arranged as many major solo exhibitions as Munch. The exhibition in Hollendergården in autumn 1901 was the sixth in little more than ten years.

both) of these pictures. I would also be interested to hear if you would be willing to exchange your purchased Winter picture if we made up the difference. (You never know what ideas might arise – and I imagine such a condition might be needed for the purchase of, say, the Moonlight picture.) Finally, we also wish to ask what you want for the "Scream" picture, or for the other one, which you call "Angst". Could I ask you, once the exhibition is over (or at reasonably short notice), to have these four pictures sent to the Gallery for closer inspection?[13]

Since other members of the board, such as chairman Elling Holst and Andreas Aubert, also had their favourites, eventually as many as seven works were sent to the museum for further discussion.[14]

At several board meetings during the autumn, the focus was on one or more Munch purchases. As always, the problem was the "National Gallery's status", i.e. the shortage of funds that prevented the purchase of more than one, or possibly two works, together with the fact that not everyone on the board was equally enthusiastic. Aubert and Thorolf Holmboe were tasked with discussing prices and the possibility of a part swap for previously purchased works. When the board met on 29 October, they were able to report "that Mr. Munch had agreed to pass on to the gallery the pictures 'White Night' and 'Summer Night' (the three girls on the bridge) for 2,000 kroner and pledged not to take 'The Scream' abroad and further to grant first-refusal for the work to either the National Gallery or Mr Olaf Schou."[15] Munch had also expressed a willingness to take back *Night in Nice* for the sum he had originally received for it, 200 kroner. The final outcome of the negotiations was the purchase of just one picture, the large canvas of Nordstrand in winter with a frozen, moonlit fjord, *White Night* (cat. 41) for 1,200 kroner.[16]

By the end of 1901, the thirty-eight-year-old Munch was represented with eight paintings and a considerable number of print works in the National Gallery. This was more than any of his older colleagues could boast. Neither Krohg, Werenskiold, Munthe nor Peterssen could claim a similar representation in the national art collection.

Between 1901 and 1909 no new purchases were made, despite energetic attempts by certain members of the board. In November 1904, Gustav Vigeland had suggested the purchase of *Moonlight* (cat. 21), when it was shown at the exhibition Munch held at the Diorama venue.[17] Shortly before Christmas 1907, after a visit to the art collector Ernest Thiel in Stockholm, the sculptor proposed that the National Gallery should commission a copy of *The Sick Child*: "After seeing Edv. Munch's picture of the sick girl in Thiel's gallery, I take this opportunity to suggest that the board ask Edv. Munch whether he would be willing to paint a replica of the picture with the sick girl. The 1st picture is now owned by the lawyer Nørregaard, the 2nd by the brewery owner Olaf Schou and the 3rd is in Thiel's gallery."[18] Somewhat impatiently, the artist repeated his proposal in a new letter the following day:

> I reiterate my suggestion that the board should approach Edv. Munch to execute a replica of "Sick Girl", since I am convinced that the picture that Munch would produce in such an event will be an object of particular interest beside the picture that Olaf Schou has stated shall eventually accrue to the Art Museum. For many – artists included – this picture based on the old theme, painted as Munch now paints, will be more instructive than one that might be acquired from Munch with a wholly new subject.[19]

It would appear that Vigeland's proposal was never discussed at a full session of the board.

1909 – "You will have the best and finest wall all to yourself"

Since its founding in 1837, the National Gallery had been run by a board that worked for free and was made up of artistically knowledgeable lay people and artists. After merging with the municipal Sculpture Museum in 1903, the lack of a professional director became an increasingly urgent problem. In 1908, funding was at last secured to finance such a position, and the thirty-eight-year-old curator from the National Museum of Decorative Arts in Trondheim, Jens Thiis (1870–1942), was appointed as its first incumbent. He took up the post around New Year 1909.

Few if any could compete with the new director when it came to engaging with Edvard Munch. The two had known each other since the early 1890s. Thiis had lauded his friend in countless lectures and articles. In his seminal work on art history *Norske malere og billedhuggere* (Norwegian Painters and Sculptors) published in 1907, he gave prominence to Munch, boldly characterising him as "the most gifted of all the painters who have seen the light of day in Norway."[20] "I considered it one of my first and most important tasks to expand, either through purchase or donation, the gallery's Munch collection," he later recalled.[21]

One of the first tasks Thiis addressed as director was the reorganisation of the permanent collection. In the Square Room, the finest space in the gallery's south wing, the works of older romantic painters, from J.C. Dahl to Hans Gude, were taken down. Here Thiis wanted to show the masters of today and tomorrow: "I am in the process of organising a delightful large top-lit hall as a kind of elite space for Norwegian painting," he wrote to Munch

in Copenhagen in early March. "It has four walls, of which you will have the best and finest all to yourself. Werenskiold, Krohg, Peterssen, Munthe, Heyerdahl etc. will have to make do with two of the others to present the best of their work; the 4th is reserved for Gauguin, Monet, Rafaelli, Josephson etc."[22] In making such a flattering offer, the newly appointed director was probably hoping to acquire some works from a Munch exhibition that was about to open in Kristiania, the first there in many years.

In the early years of the century, Munch had spent most of his time in Germany, where opportunities for commissions and sales to a wealthy middle class were plentiful. The idea of a new exhibition in Norway had begun to take shape in autumn 1908. Blomqvist's venue on Karl Johans gate would be available in March 1909, his friend Jappe Nilssen informed him.[23] At the time, Munch was in Copenhagen, undergoing treatment at Dr. Jacobson's private clinic for anxiety and alcohol abuse. Shortly after New Year he received a new, encouraging message from Nilssen, who had recently visited the National Gallery's new director:

> I went over there in connection with your exhibition here. He asked me to write to you saying that he wants you to send *everything, all* the paintings you own, to him up there so that he, Thiis, and I can choose a selection of them. He wants there to be an elite exhibition. The gallery is sure to make a substantial purchase. He asked me to write in particular that you must send the portrait of the Frenchman Archimart [...] *That* he must have for the gallery at any price. But in addition, at least one more, maybe several. A big one, he said, the bigger the better. It's imperative for them to acquire some pictures from your recent period. But also some older ones. [...] Further, the gallery wishes to buy the naked girl that Nørregaard has from you but which is still your property.[24]

The agreement with Blomqvist was for an exhibition in two parts. The first, to open on 3 March, would show print works, while the second, to open on 16 March, would consist of paintings. When the prints went on show, Thiis was among the first through the door. Full of enthusiasm, he wrote to Munch in Copenhagen:

> Your exhibition of black-and-white art seems overwhelming in its richness and diverse beauty. It is a long time since art has had a similar impact on me. On the first day, I immediately selected the best – in my estimation – to fill the gaps in the Prints and Drawings Collection [–] 16 items. Together with the 70-odd items that we already had, they will form a truly representative collection of your art in this field. Fortunately for the

Prints and Drawings Collection, I was able to buy independently without asking anyone's permission; I needed only Gundersen to approve my choice. So, I got the items I wanted, and was free to act without hesitation.[25]

It was still a while until the exhibition of paintings would open. Thiis asked Blomqvist to have several of the pictures sent round to the museum so that they could be studied in better light and alongside the Munch pictures the museum already owned. He had his eye on five works in particular: *Starry Night* (Woll M 321) *Ashes* (cat. 30), *Vampire* (Woll M 349), *Puberty* (cat. 26) and *The Frenchman* (cat. 46). A telegram was sent to Copenhagen: Would Munch consider selling these to the National Gallery if the Ministry of Church and Education gave its consent? And if so, would he be willing to give the museum a good price, if possible 10,000 kroner? Munch telegraphed his positive reply the following day: "The pictures for 10,000 kroner, will hold for 4 days." His one condition was that he be allowed to borrow *Vampire* and *Ashes* for a short time in order to copy them.[26]

When the National Gallery created the position of director, the old system for purchasing work by means of a board majority was abandoned. The Ministry of Church and Education and the artists' organisation, BKS, felt that purchases should still be overseen by various "purchasing committees", where most of the members were artists. In March 1909, the bureaucrats were still working on the new statutes. The exhibition of Munch's paintings was due to open on 16 March. So where was the purchasing committee? Thiis was desperate. In a long letter to the ministry, he pleaded to be allowed to make purchases on his own. It would be "an unforgivable and irreparable failing" if this opportunity to buy Munch's older pictures were missed. "It could be many years before he shows an exhibition of similar importance here, by which time, one can safely predict, all the older and much of the best work will be in the hands of other owners. Foreign collectors and galleries are vying to acquire his pictures."[27] At the same time, Thiis asked the ministry for permission to use 10,000 kroner from the Houen Fund for the acquisition.

While the ministry approved Thiis' request to use up to 10,000 kroner from the Houen Fund, it was unwilling to let him act alone. In all haste, a temporary purchasing committee was appointed, which after a little negotiation consisted of the painters Harriet Backer, Halfdan Strøm, Arne Kavli and Anders Svarstad. In the event, however, the committee did not entirely share the director's opinion about the pictures. There was agreement about *Puberty*, *Ashes* and *The Frenchman*. But instead of *Vampire* they voted for *The Day After* (cat. 27) and instead of *Starry Night* they wanted to buy *On the Veranda* (cat. 45). And so it was. Thiis had to accept the committee's preferences. Even so, the purchase was still a spectacular triumph for both

Munch and Thiis, who had now made his mark as Scandinavia's most radical museum director, a decisive advocate for the new and unconventional.

Admittedly there was some tentative criticism about the choice of pictures, the fact that most were from the 1890s, and that consequently the artist's recent shift to a more vivid palette was not so well represented.[28] Munch himself was worried that people wouldn't understand just how experimental he had now become as a colourist. "Posterity will not get an impression of what I've been aiming at and experimenting with when it comes to colour intensity and unity," he complained to Jappe Nilssen.[29] And in a draft letter to Thiis, he cautiously expressed something similar: "Dear Thiis! Perhaps it's silly of me to interfere with the Gallery's purchase - I would say that this aspect of my production is large - where my colour experiments and colour intensity are shown to their best - that isn't represented by the pictures that the Gallery is currently acquiring."[30]

Jappe Nilssen felt that Thiis' selection was the best, without the changes made by the purchasing committee. "But it's good as it is," he wrote to Munch; "[...] Now you'll have your own wall up there, the best in the building, and for years [to come], my dear old Munch, and I hope it won't be all that long before you have your own hall, the Munch room, which will have two stars in Baedeker."[31]

Olaf Schou's donations

No sooner were the five new paintings from Blomqvist hanging on the gallery's wall, than Thiis received an effusive letter from the art collector Olaf Schou (1861-1925), inviting him to visit Schou at his home at Sinsen in order to select art for the National Gallery from the magnate's large private collection.

In July 1909, a proud Thiis was able to inform the Ministry of Church and Education about the gift: "I have the honour to inform the worthy Ministers that Mr. Olaf Schou of Sinsen, has allowed me to select from his collection whatever may be suitable for incorporation into the National Gallery, and that accordingly he has dispatched 82 paintings and studies as a gift to the art museum."[32] Roughly one week later, on 2 August, Thiis reported that a further thirty-four pictures had been sent down from Sinsen![33]

The immensely wealthy Schou had been in contact with Munch since the late 1880s. Whenever the artist was short of funds, he could always depend on the generous art collector for help. It had long been known that the unmarried Schou intended to entrust his pictures to the National Gallery at some point in the future. On several occasions, Schou had bought Munch paintings that the National Gallery had been eager to acquire, but which it had been forced to forgo either due to lack of funds or because of difficulties with board members. At least if they ended up with Schou, one could breathe a little easier. For in time they were sure to end up on the gallery's walls.[34]

Of the more than one hundred works that Schou gifted to the museum in the summer of 1909, seven were by Munch: *Betzy Nilsen* (cat. 10), *Moonlight by the Mediterranean* (cat. 18), *Madonna* (cat. 29), *Young Woman Washing* (cat. 33), *The Sick Child* (1896 version, Woll M 392), *Mother and Daughter* (cat. 35) and *The Girls on the Bridge* (cat. 42). Apart from the small portrait study *Betzy Nilsen*, Thiis found space for all the new pictures from Schou in the "Young Painters' Room". With the pictures in place, Thiis called in the photographer Væring to immortalise the new Munch wall. The resulting photograph became one of the earliest postcards we know of to feature the interior of the National Gallery.

Encouraged by the great success of his March 1909 exhibition, Munch was soon preparing a sequel. This time he wanted to hire the Diorama venue on Karl Johans gate. It was to be a truly massive exhibition. The catalogue lists 111 paintings, 25 drawings and no less than 170 prints. It opened in March 1910, and like the year before, Thiis was involved in both the selection and the hanging of the works. There were three works in particular that he wanted for the museum: *Death in the Sickroom* (cat. 22), *Madonna* (cat. 29) and *The Scream* (cat. 23).

The National Museum's own purchasing budget offered no scope for a deal, and it can safely be assumed that, after the sizeable pay-out of the previous year, little could be hoped for from the Houen Fund. But perhaps Olaf Schou could help! Schou was no longer actively collecting and had since moved abroad. Nonetheless he was favourably disposed to Thiis' appeal. "Olaf Schou has now given me a response," Thiis wrote to Munch. "He is willing to acquire 'Death in the Sickroom' and 'The Dance of Life' and at the same time to hang onto 'The Scream' in order to donate these 3 pictures to the National Gallery - provided he can get them for 6,000 kroner."[35] Thus, three new and highly important Munch works could be sent straight from the exhibition to the National Gallery - where, for the time being, they went into storage in the cellar. Schou wanted to avoid publicity for his gift - "since for private reasons he does not wish to be perceived as a buyer or donor of art at present." But soon enough it was decided that the wall was where they belonged, and that required some rearranging of the existing display.

Munch's wall in the Square Room - the "elite room" - now held (from the left) *Death in the Sickroom*, *Puberty*, *Spring*, *Inger in Black and Violet*, and *The Sick Child* (1896 version). In the Young painters' room, space was found for *The Dance of Life* and *The Scream*, as can be seen from a new photo by Væring, taken in the spring of 1912.[36] The portrait *Julius Meier-Graefe* (cat. 25) is already hanging on the short wall to the left. It had arrived in the spring of 1912 as a gift from its subject, the German art critic

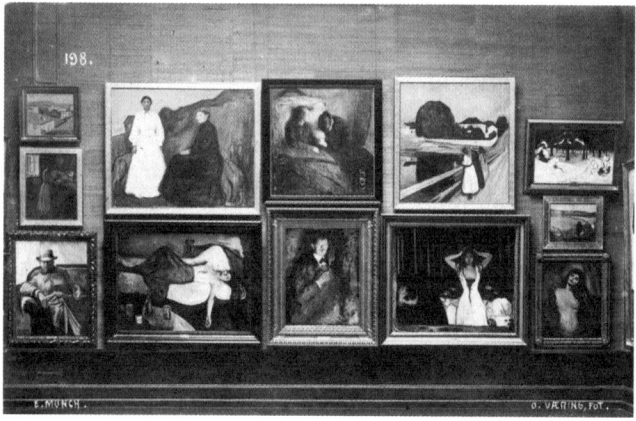

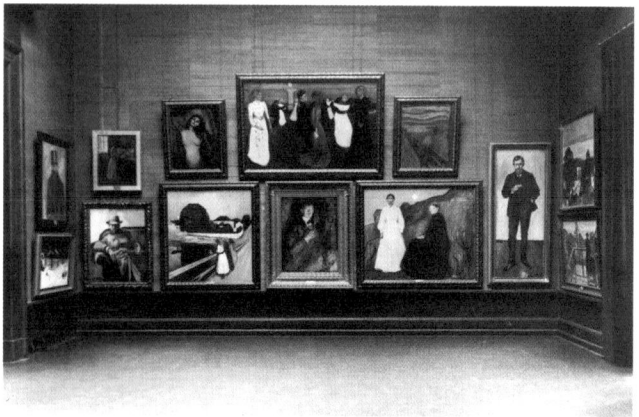

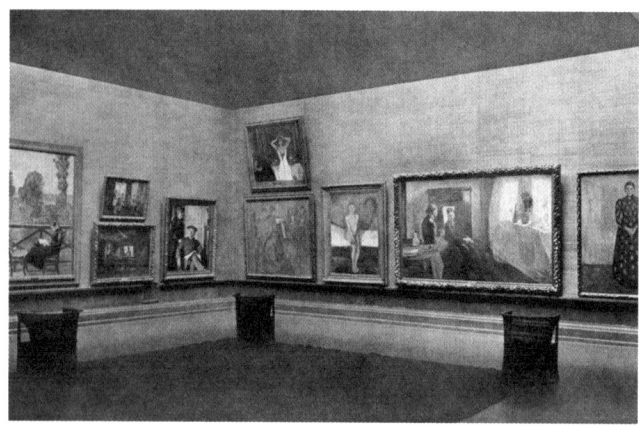

The wall devoted to Munch in the "Young painters' room", photographed in autumn 1909, after the addition of the new acquisitions from Blomqvist and the first gifts from Olav Schou. Photo: O. Væring. The National Museum's documentation archive.

The main wall in the "Young painters' room", photographed in 1912, after the addition of Olav Schous's gifts *The Dance of Life* (cat. 40) and *The Scream* (cat. 23), and the transfer of *The Sick Child* (cat. 8) and *The Day After* (cat. 27) to the Square room. Photo: O. Væring. The National Museum's documentation archive.

In the museum's Square room, often referred to as the "Hall of Fame", the main wall was reserved for Munch. In a photo from 1912, one can see to the right *Inger in Black and Violet* (cat. 20). The wall concludes with *The Day After* (cat. 27) mounted above *The Sick Child* (cat. 8). Photo: O. Væring. The National Museum's documentation archive.

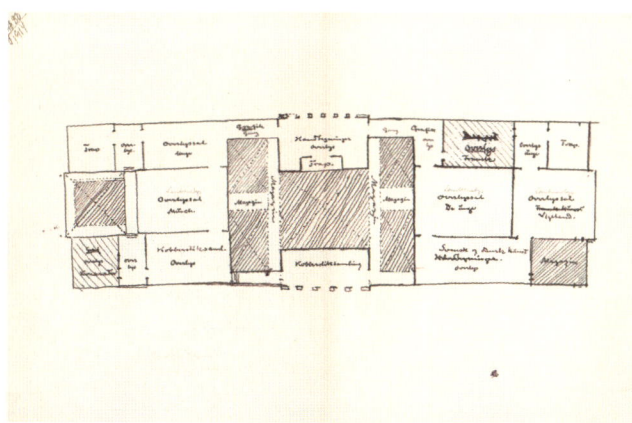

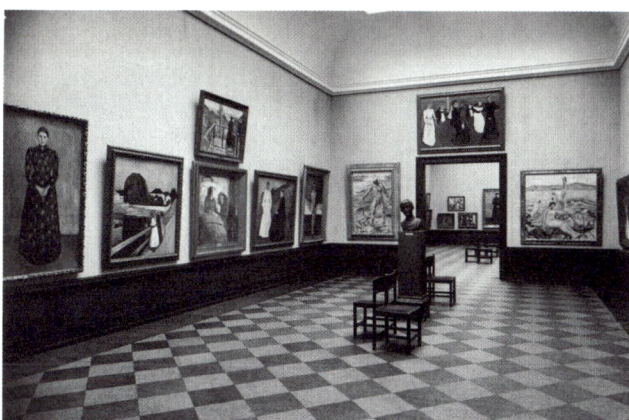

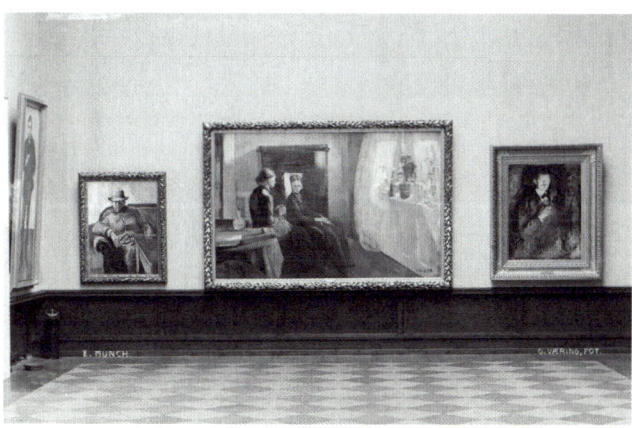

Even before World War I, Jens Thiis had plans for a room devoted to Edvard Munch, initially a top-lit hall on the upper floor. This plan from the National Museum's documentation archive is from 1913.

With the inauguration of the National Gallery's north wing in spring 1924, Edvard Munch at last had a hall of his own, in the photograph here in its newly renovated state in spring 1930. On the main wall one sees *Spring* (cat. 12) flanked by *Hans Jæger* (cat. 13) and *Self-Portrait with Cigarette* (cat. 32). Photo: O. Væring. The National Museum's documentation archive.

and author, who became a close friend and supporter of Munch during his tumultuous years in Berlin before the turn of the century.

During the first three years of Jens Thiis' time as director, the National Gallery was enriched by no fewer than fifteen new Munch paintings, all of them acquired with the help of external funds or as generous gifts.

A large picture of sunbathing women, *Midsummer* (cat. 51), was purchased from Munch's exhibition at Blomqvist in the autumn of 1915. It had been painted in the summer of that year and with its bright and bold palette it was a good example Munch's modern, experimental approach to colour. Here again, the museum failed to fund the purchase from its own budget, and had to rely on the ever generous Olav Schou, who bought the picture as a gift to the museum. By that point the benefactor himself had left Norway for good, but he continued to spread his largesse - even after his death. For his will stipulated that revenue from an endowment fund set up in his name should go to, among other things, the purchase of art for the National Gallery.[37] It is a provision that has so far enabled the purchase of a further four Munch paintings.[38]

1924 - Munch gets his own room

The expansion of the museum building took time. After completion of a new south wing in 1907, the next phase was to add a north wing. By the spring of 1924, this too was ready for use. With almost double the exhibition space (twenty-five new rooms and cabinets), the permanent collection could now be rehung in its entirety.

Christian Langaard's sizeable bequest of older foreign art was moved into a beautiful top-lit hall. So too were the many pictures purchased by the Friends of the National Gallery, which were assigned to the north-wing's Square Room. And finally, Edvard Munch could have a room to himself. The overcrowded Munch wall in the Young painters' room and the somewhat chaotic hanging on the feature wall of the south-wing's Square Room were things of the past. Time and again, especially in the years after World War I, it had been necessary to take down the permanent display to make room for the temporary exhibitions of French art that were shown on an annual basis.[39] Henceforth, Munch's pictures would hang in peace. The northwest transverse room was earmarked for him and him alone. At the time, the National Gallery was virtually the only national art museum worldwide to devote an entire room of its permanent exhibition to a living artist.

Evidently for Thiis it was a long-held view that Munch should have his own room. As early as May 1913, on a floor plan for the "The completed National Gallery" (which he thought would be finished in 1916), Thiis had earmarked a large top-lit hall on the top floor for Munch - much as Jappe Nilssen had predicted back in the spring of 1909.[40]

It is interesting to note that already in this draft plan Thiis had sacrificed the south-wing's inner courtyard for a top-lit Munch room – albeit on the top floor rather than the first floor, which would be the solution adopted in 1937.

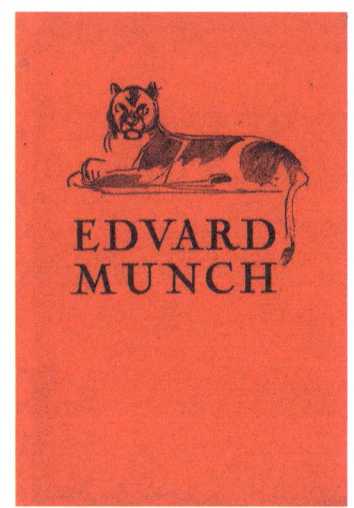

1927 – The Great Munch Exhibition

After World War I, Munch's fame grew internationally. At Ekely in Skøyen he received a steady stream of invitations, not least from Germany. The Germans were inclined to regard the Norwegian as providing a Nordic-Germanic alternative to sensual French Impressionism and as an ideal among the growing family of German Expressionists. Munch's triumphs in Germany peaked with an invitation from Berlin's Nationalgalerie to mount a solo exhibition in the magnificent Kronprinzenpalais in the spring of 1927. In 1919, the palace had been converted into a museum for modern art.

While the exhibition was going on in Berlin and the newspapers were full of enthusiastic reviews, Jens Thiis was busy writing "Malerkunsten i det 19. og 20. Aarhundre" (The Art of Painting in the 19th and 20th Centuries), his contribution to the new *Norsk kunsthistorie* (A History of Norwegian Art), published by Gyldendal forlag. After many flattering remarks about Munch's earlier triumphs in Germany, he wrote the following:

> But all the earlier honours that Germany has lavished on Munch pale in comparison to the event that is on-going as I write – the vast exhibition at *Berlin's National Gallery*, where he fills every room on all three floors of the Crown Prince's Palace on Unter den Linden. [...] It is my hope that it will be possible to arrange for the exhibition in its entirety to be shown in our own National Gallery before its works are dispersed and returned to their owners.[41]

With his habitual energy and determination, Thiis succeeded in the shortest possible time in arranging for the exhibition to be shown in Norway. It was, however, by no means identical with the event in Berlin. Many German collectors were reluctant to extend the loans of the works they owned. Thiis scoured Oslo for new pictures. Ultimately, he was able to pull together a larger number of works than had been shown in Germany. The catalogue ran to 289 paintings, with a few more added at the last minute, after the catalogue had gone to press. Also on show were a selection of drawings and watercolours, most of them loaned from the artist himself, and the roughly 100 graphic works that the National Gallery owned at the time. Unfortunately, the time was too short to catalogue the works on paper.

Such an ambitious exhibition project was something entirely new in the history of the National Gallery. Solo

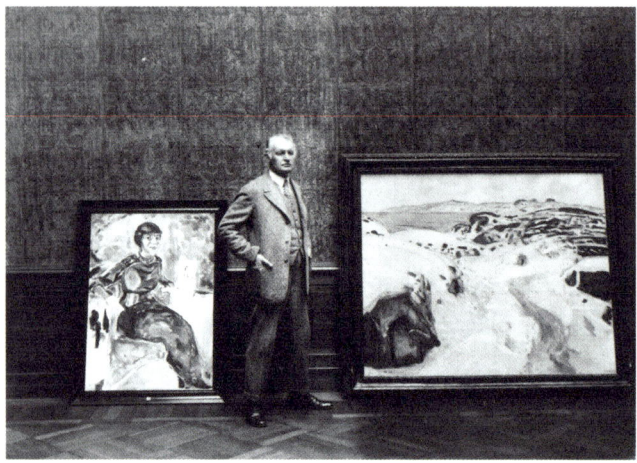

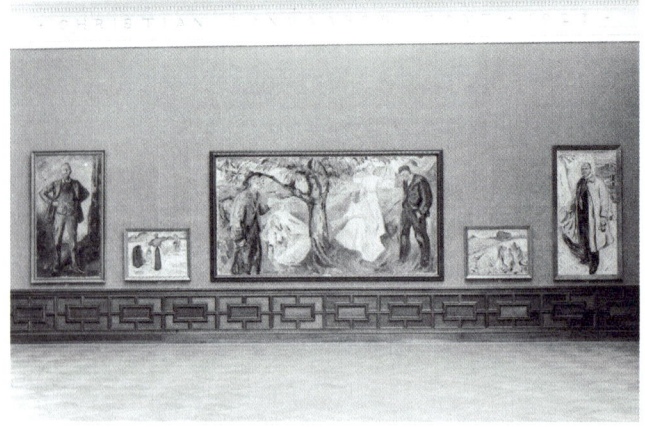

The catalogue of the Munch exhibition in the National Gallery in summer 1927 lists nearly 300 paintings. Also on show were several drawings, watercolours, and some 100 prints.

Edvard Munch visiting during preparations for the exhibition in summer 1927. Jens Thiis personally took charge of the hanging, assisted by academy professor Axel Revold. Photo: The National Museum's documentation archive.

The official opening of the 1927 Munch exhibition took place in the Langaard Room, which had been emptied of its old masters for the occasion. On the main wall one sees *Life*, recently purchased by Dresdener Gemäldegalerie. To the right is *Christian Gierløff*, on loan from the Gothenburg Museum of Art, and to the left *Daniel Jacobson*, which Jens Thiis hoped Munch would donate to the museum after the exhibition. It remained at the National Gallery until after World War II, when it was handed over to Oslo Municipality. Photo: O. Væring. The National Museum's documentation archive.

exhibitions were usually the preserve of Kunstforeningen, Kunstnerforbundet or Blomqvist, which, since 1914, had at its disposal a new and modern exhibition venue in Tordenskjoldsgate. But everyone agreed that in the field of Norwegian art, Munch was in a class of his own. Thiis received the ministry's permission to make the necessary preparations, such as emptying the first floor of the entire permanent collection! The unusual costs of mounting such an exhibition could not, however, be carried by the public. The National Gallery was obliged to work within its budget. The exhibition would have to be arranged so as "not to incur expenses for the gallery and without impairing similar exhibitions in the future".[42] That presented something of a dilemma. Luckily, "an art-loving private gentleman offered to stand as guarantor for the considerable costs of shipping and insurance," as Thiis put it in the catalogue. It was an open secret that that private gentleman was the banker and art enthusiast Johannes Sejersted Bødtker. In the event, the exhibition made a substantial profit.[43]

To help with the hanging of the nearly 300 paintings in the seven top-lit rooms and twenty cabinets on the first floor, Thiis called in Axel Revold, professor at the Academy of Fine Arts. As far as possible, they wanted the presentation to be chronological, but with thematic digressions. For example, one room was devoted to sketch versions of the paintings for the Aula at Oslo University, another to self-portraits, and so on. Munch called in during the preparations and was pleased with what he saw. "[...] I find the impression overwhelmingly good. It works much better than it did in Berlin, more unified, more coherent. And then I find it richer. And the light is so beautiful. Especially in the Langaard Room. And many of my pictures are so dependent on the lighting."[44]

The official opening took place at noon in the Langaard Room on 8 June 1927. "Everyone" was present. Thiis gave a speech, and the President of Parliament, Carl J. Hambro, had the honour of declaring the exhibition open. But Munch was conspicuous in his absence. He was no fan of such exclusive gatherings.

The crowds poured in. One thousand visitors on the first day! The final day was Sunday 24 July. By that point, the exhibition had been seen by as many as 31,000 people.[45] That was more than had seen it in Berlin, a city with a population of several million. Extra trains were laid on, with the national railway offering a 25% discount. The ticket to the exhibition also gave access to the artist's monumental paintings in the University Aula. The comprehensive illustrated catalogue, with the text of Thiis' opening speech as a preface and a greeting from Ludwig Justi, director of the Nationalgalerie in Berlin, was so popular that many extra batches had to be ordered from the printers.

As a thank you for the exhibition in Berlin, Munch had given the Nationalgalerie the exhibited painting *Snow Shovellers* (Woll M 1092) and seven prints.[46] Hitherto the artist had not been represented in this major German collection, and they wanted to buy something in addition. But getting Munch to sell was a near impossibility, as even the powerful Justi had to admit.[47] For the National Gallery in Oslo, it was reasonable to assume that they too could expect a gift, even though everyone knew how difficult Munch found it to part with his pictures. For the past ten years he hadn't sold a single work, he admitted in a newspaper interview in connection with the exhibition. He needed them around him.[48]

Jens Thiis dropped some heavy hints about *Daniel Jacobson* (Woll M 822), the full-length portrait of the Danish neurologist who had treated Munch as a patient at his private clinic in Copenhagen from October 1908 to April 1909. "[...] I am awfully keen on the portrait of the famous Jacobsen," he confessed to *Dagbladet*.[49] But Munch was slow to respond. It wasn't until the summer of 1928 that he wrote: "I'm sending the portrait to see how it looks [...] I still haven't decided which picture I shall give, though it will probably be this – but only if I receive an assurance that I can borrow it for exhibitions – I feel I need permission for this since these men's portraits form a bodyguard for my art [...] Along with it I am also sending the bathing man – which I still need."[50]

Together with the alternative work, *Bathing Man* (cat. 54), the doctor's portrait was registered in the National Gallery's inventory as "a gift from the artist as a thank you for the exhibition at the museum in 1927". This was corrected in the new collection catalogue *Norsk malerkunst i Nasjonalgalleriet* (Norwegian Painting in the National Gallery) in 1933. Whereas *Bathing Man* was again described in the latter as a gift, *Daniel Jacobson* was recorded as "Deposited by the artist 1927". For the time being, the depiction was a superb eye-catcher among Munch's portraits at the National Gallery. But after World War II, the City of Oslo made a claim to the picture. The dispute did not end in the National Gallery's favour. Accordingly, the portrait was transferred to the City of Oslo Art Collection.

The exhibition of 1927 prompted a debate about improving the facilities for showing Munch's art. Soon, the idea that he should have a museum of his own, like the one recently granted to Gustav Vigeland, was doing the rounds. "Open a Munch Museum!" Was the peremptory headline in *Norges Kommunistblad* on 9 June. Munch himself provided arguments. It had been his dream for many years, not least because he wanted to show his Frieze of Life as a whole, rather than have it broken up or scattered to the four winds.[51]

Of course, Thiis also wanted more exhibition space for Munch. If the National Gallery was fortunate enough to acquire more Munch pictures, it would be difficult to display them. The museum was full to capacity. In the longer term, the museum needed to expand onto the Tullinløkka site. But the only addition of space that could be achieved quickly and at manageable cost involved filling in the inner courtyard of the south wing. It was a solution that would add several rooms, including a spacious and imposing top-lit hall for Munch.[52] At the time, Thiis was sticking to the proposal he had made back in 1913, that the new Munch room should be on the second floor: "We have the courtyard at the National Gallery, which is currently unused, but which, if filled in, would provide space for three magnificent halls the size of Langaard room [...] The uppermost one could become a Munch room with beautiful skylights, etc. Beneath it there would be space for two halls with artificial lighting."[53]

The National Gallery was, however, in poor repair and desperately short of funds. The priority was the renovation of the central section. This was suffering from water leaks and the floors were rotten. For several years, parts of the ground floor had been closed because the roof was sagging and had to be supported by scaffolding. On the first floor, the stucco mouldings on the ceiling were crumbling, posing a hazard to visitors below. Munch would have to remain in his "old" room for several years to come. By the spring of 1930, the central building had been refurbished. It was reopened with a modern reinforced concrete ceiling (without the heavy lateral beams of its original state), with skylights and extra electrical lighting above the glass. The faded Japanese tatami wallcoverings had been replaced with a lighter sail-cloth alternative. "One notes with great interest the new burlap wallcovering that is quite in keeping with the wishes of Edvard Munch."[54]

1933 – How to mark a seventieth birthday

On 12 December 1933, Munch turned seventy. Preparations had been underway for a long time in the Department of Prints and Drawings. The large top-lit hall on the second floor was cleared of the Swedish and Danish art that it usually held. It was here that curator Eli Ingebretsen Greve would open a major exhibition of Munch's graphic work on his birthday. On show would be some eighty works, most of them selected from the prints in the museum's own collection.[55] In addition, Greve had managed to persuade Munch to loan ten recent lithographs. "These were works the National Gallery desperately wanted, but which the scarcity of funds prevented us from buying."[56] They would remain in the museum, as a gift from the artist. To judge from an article in *Aftenposten* on 7 June 1934, the exhibition must have remained in place until the summer of that year, for the newspaper wrote at that point that Munch's new gift was still "on display in the Munch exhibition on the second floor". For several years, Greve had been hoping the artist would donate some of his recent lithographs to the Department of Prints and Drawings. She had become particularly aware of the lack of recent works in the autumn of 1931, while writing a

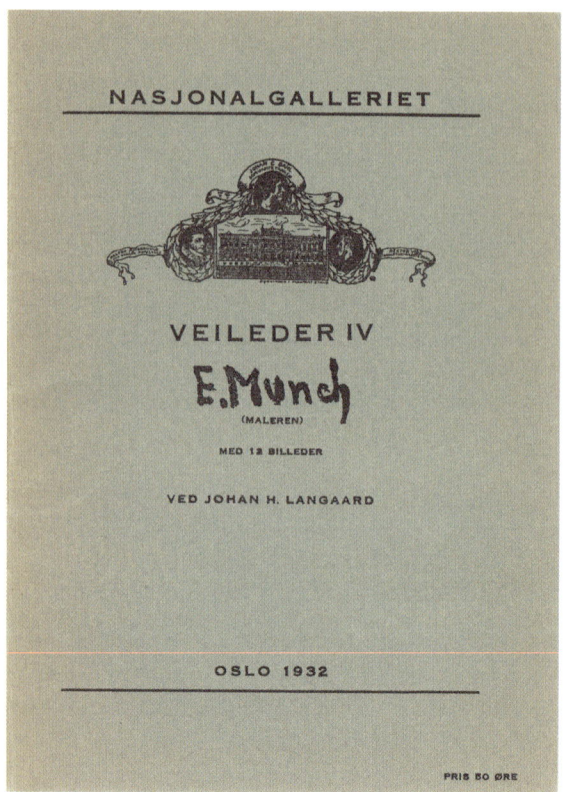

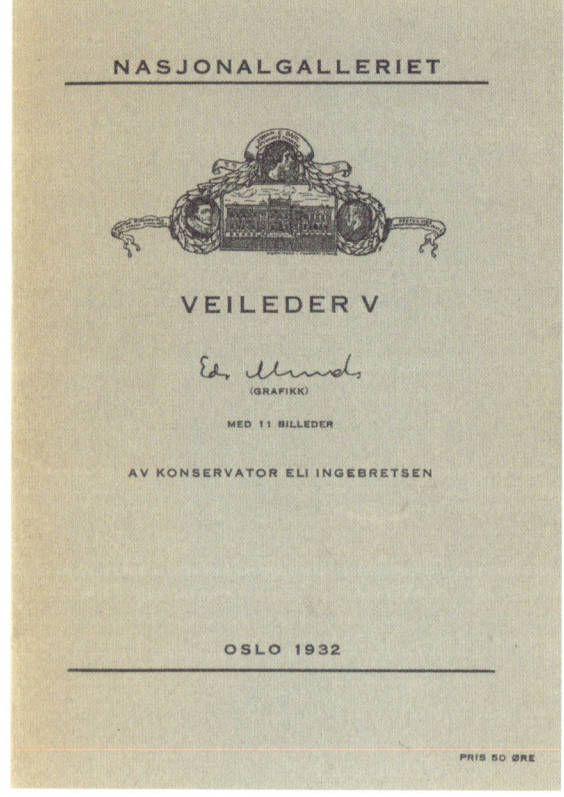

Raising awareness for Edvard Munch's art was a priority for the museum, but public funding did not always match ambitions. In 1932, funds donated by the City of Oslo enabled the publication of two "guides" about Munch, as a painter and a printmaker. The printmaker guide was written by Eli Ingebretsen Greve, curator at the Department of Prints and Drawings. This was the first Norwegian publication about Munch's graphic art.

Edv. Munch gir Nasjonalgalleriet en verdifull gave.

Fra Nasjonalgalleriets Munch-utstilling. En rekke av litografiene som gaven omfatter sees på denne vegg.

Edvard Munch har skjenket Nasjonalgalleriets kobberstikk- og håndtegningssalon 10 grafiske hovedarbeider fra de siste 20 år.

Arbeidene er utstillet på Munch-utstillingen i galleriets 3. etasje.

— Det er arbeider som Nasjonalgalleriet hårdt trengte, men som de knappe bevilgninger vel aldri ville ha tillatt oss å kjøpe, sier bestyreren

av kobberstikksamlingen, konservator Eli Ingebretsen. Samtlige arbeider som gaven omfatter blev utlånt av Edv. Munch selv under den store utstilling i galleriet i anledning av kunstnerens 70 års dag.

Den periode som arbeidene gjelder var tidligere absolutt ikke representert i Nasjonalgalleriet. Gaven består bl. a. av det berømte Schreiner-portrett og de store Ildebrands-billedene. Alle arbeidene er litografier fra hans senere år, og det var nettop dette vi trengte sårt — tresnittene og raderingene fra hans tidligere år har vi nemlig et relativt fyldig utvalg av. Det er en storslagen gave!

The Department of Prints and Drawings marked Munch's 70th birthday with a major exhibition of his prints. Lacking works from the past twenty years, the museum loaned ten recent lithographs from the artist, which, shortly afterwards, it was able to inventory as a gift. Facsimile from *Aftenposten*, 7 June 1934.

monograph about the artist's graphic work, "albeit only [about] what is in the museum's collection, which, as you know, contains nothing of your graphic work from the last 20 years", she had written to him, somewhat plaintively.[57]

The exhibition of prints opened on Munch's actual birthday. Rather unusually, it was also announced that the works could be viewed on opening day in the evening from 6 to 8pm. As a finale to the day's event, the director would present one of his highly popular lecture-slide shows about Munch. It is likely that Thiis used the opportunity to mention the important meeting he had chaired in the National Gallery the day before, for which he had convened some twenty people from artist organisations and the cultural sphere to discuss the creation of a separate museum for the artist.[58] A working committee had been appointed to develop the plan. In addition to Jens Thiis, that committee consisted of Munch's good friend and confidant Sigurd Høst, art historian and member of the National Gallery's board Henrik Grevenor, and Johan H. Langaard from the National Gallery's administration.

Further, Thiis had taken the initiative to nominate Munch for the Grand Cross of the Order of St. Olav.[59] And finally, the director could at last announce the publication of *Edvard Munch og hans samtid. Slekten, livet og kunsten, geniet* (Edvard Munch and his era. Family, life and art, genius.) He had started writing the book in 1927, after the Great Munch Exhibition. The work had gone on sale just before the current anniversary.

1936 - The National Gallery's centenary and a new hall for Munch

As a worthy way to commemorate the first hundred years of its history, the museum had for many months been preparing a large exhibition about "the father of Norwegian painting", Johan Christian Dahl. But then, in 1936, the government approved extraordinary funding to build over the courtyard of the museum's south wing, as Thiis had long dreamed of. If the construction work was to be finished in time for the centenary celebrations in the spring of 1937, then they might even have to cancel the Dahl event. Fortunately, the directors of Kunstnernes Hus offered their own institution as a venue for the Dahl exhibition, allowing it to go ahead as envisaged.[60] The National Gallery's centenary celebration was scheduled for 29 April. For much of the winter the museum was closed while the builders did their work. By the time they were finished, the courtyard had been filled with a large new top-lit hall on the first floor, two smaller exhibition rooms on the ground floor and an extensive storage facility in the basement. Everything was now ready to welcome guests from home and abroad, from the Royal Palace, the government and civil service, from the art and culture community, and from the major museums of other Nordic countries. After speeches and

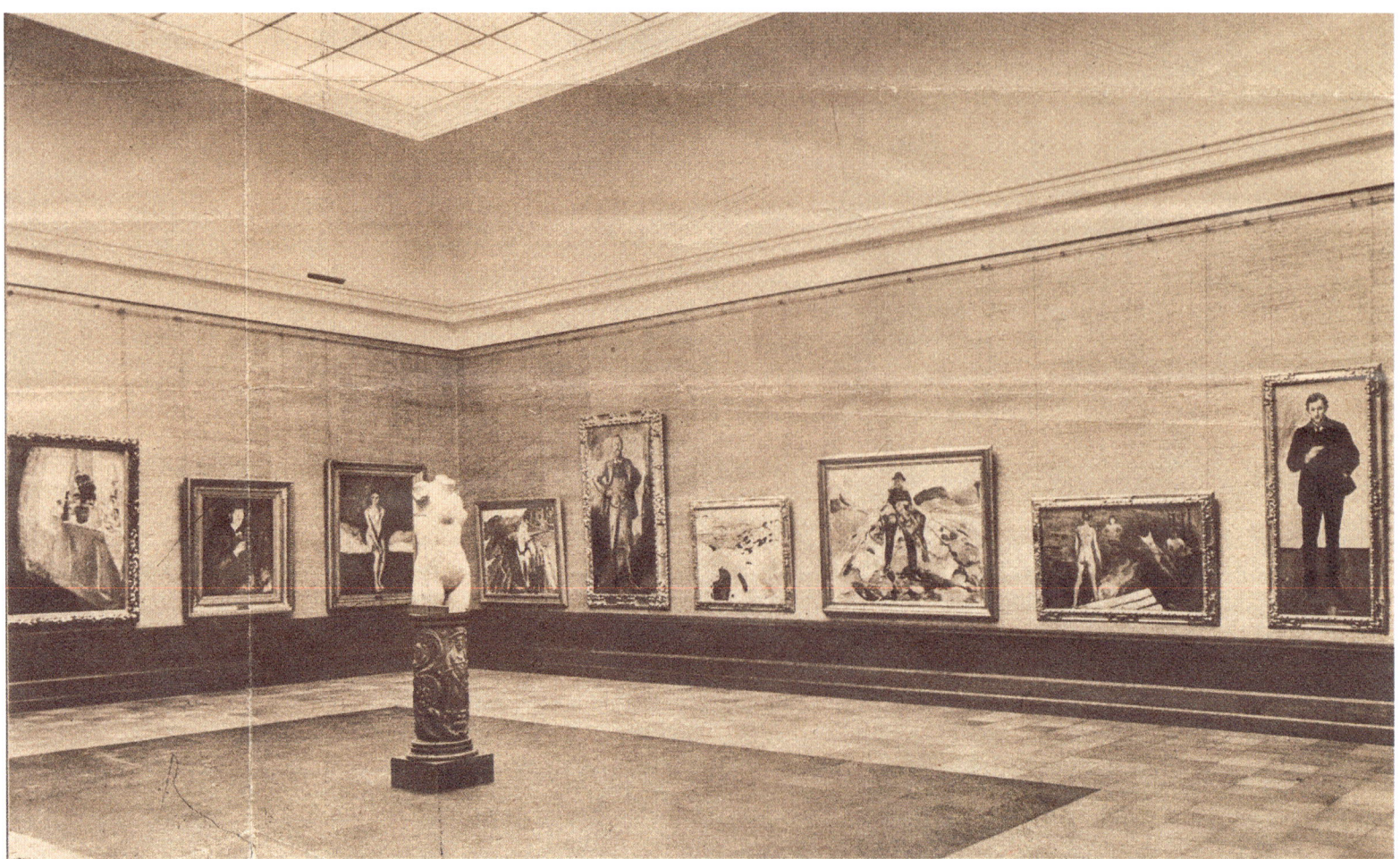

orchestral music in the University Aula, His Majesty King Haakon and director Thiis led the guests in procession over to the museum and up into the new top-lit hall in the south wing. There it was revealed that the hall was devoted to the art of Edvard Munch. The king gave a short welcome speech and wished the museum well on its anniversary and with its newly acquired rooms.

For a while, it seems, Thiis had been considering another use for the space. According to Sigurd Willoch's *Nasjonalgalleriet gjennem hundre år* (National Gallery through a Hundred Years), a commemorative volume written to mark the anniversary, the new top-lit hall was originally conceived as "a hall in honour of the art of the 1880s", while the square anteroom would be reserved for Munch![61] The probable reason for the last-minute reassignment of the rooms was a magnificent but spatially demanding donation received as just one of many gifts that poured into the museum in the run-up to the centenary opening. The donation was a set of Munch paintings from the private Mustad collection.

Christian and Charlotte Mustad from the Madserud estate were among Oslo's foremost Munch collectors. They had loaned thirteen paintings for the 1927 exhibition, and now they had given seven to the museum for keeps: *Inger Munch in Black* (cat. 6), *Bathing Boys* (cat. 28), *Two Nudes* (cat. 44), *Winter on the Fjord* (cat. 50), *Man in the Cabbage-Field* (cat. 52), *Self-Portrait with the Spanish Flu* (cat. 55) and *Autumn Ploughing* (cat. 56). These were simply

For the museum's 100th anniversary in 1937, the Norwegian government approved funding for the National Gallery to expand its exhibition space by filling in the courtyard of the south wing. The anniversary was formally inaugurated by King Haakon in the new top-lit hall on the upper floor, which was dedicated to Edvard Munch's paintings. Facsimile from *Oslo Illustrerte*, 15 May 1937.

more than the square anteroom could contain, whereas there was sufficient space for them in the new top-lit hall. Here Thiis was able to display six of the seven pictures received from the Mustads.[62] And with that, Munch had his new hall.

No one was surprised that the artist, never a fan of large crowds, did not attend the centenary event in person. After the hubbub had died down, Thiis sent Munch an invitation to come and inspect his new hall: "You will surely have read in the papers about the museum's reorganisation and the centenary celebrations, about the King's opening of the rebuilt and restructured museum with its Munch room, and how everyone, foreign guests and people from our own city, including its artists, were impressed and pleased with the reorganisation, and especially the Munch room. [...] When will you, chère maître, come and see your work in its new setting and the rest of the National Gallery?"[63] We cannot be sure whether Munch ever came to view the new hall. On this, our sources are silent.

Over in Germany, 1937 was the year when Edvard Munch's paintings were removed from the country's museums. As with so many other modern artists, the Nazis condemned his work as "entartet" (degenerate). Thanks to the efforts of Norwegian art dealers, however, most of these pictures found their way to Norway, where they were sold at auction in 1938 and 1939. The failure of the National Gallery to bid for these works in January and February 1939 should not necessarily be attributed to moral scruples. For the Norwegian public, the "repatriation" of Munch's works amounted almost to a heroic rescue operation. Rather, the National Gallery's omission was a consequence - as usual - of a lack of money. In the autumn of 1938, at an auction following the death of Munch's good friend, Supreme Court lawyer Harald Nørregaard, it had at last been possible to acquire *Moonlight* (cat. 21), the atmospheric painting of a woman in front of a white picket fence, and the early *Self-Portrait* (cat. 9).[64] A price of 9,000 kroner was paid for the former, 7,000 for the latter. The purchase was made possible with a contribution from the Olaf Schou Endowment Fund. Following that, it is easy to understand how difficult it would have been to find several thousand kroner for new Munch paintings just a few months later. For the time being, Schou's endowment fund had nothing to spare.

1940-1945 - Munch in the National Gallery during the war

On 1 September 1939, the day Germany invaded Poland, the National Gallery's board convened to discuss how best to safeguard the museum's pictures in the event of the war coming to Norway: "[...] I now have just one thing to think about," Thiis wrote to Munch, "the possibility that bombs may start falling on us and we must hurry to save from our National Gallery what we call our national treasures, J.C. Dahl, Fearnley, Krohg, Munch. The larger pictures, including *Spring*, will be evacuated from the museum immediately."[65] Formally, Jens Thiis continued as director of the National Gallery until the summer of 1941. But suffering from cancer, he was often absent from his post and had to entrust much of the museum's routine management to Johan H. Langaard. On 1 August 1941 he was officially replaced by the painter Søren Onsager, the candidate imposed by the new, Nazi-aligned Ministry of Culture and Enlightenment. Eli Ingebretsen Greve, curator of the Department of Prints and Drawings, resigned her position on 30 January 1942.

A proposal to organise an exhibition along the lines of Germany's popular "Entartete Kunst" events was put forward by Gulbrand Lunde, minister of culture under Norway's pro-Nazi party, Nasjonal Samling, and director of national propaganda. However, Onsager wanted to do things a little differently. He wanted to include good art in the exhibition. "I see no other way to create a reasonably interesting exhibition on this theme. Degenerate art should be seen against the background of good material, for it is only then one recognises its wretchedness. *Heil og Sæl*."[66]

The exhibition "Art and Non-Art in the National-Gallery Cleansing, April 1942" was mounted on the first floor of the south wing. Here Munch was represented with four of his most important works: *Inger Munch in Black* (cat. 6), *Spring* (cat. 12), *The Girls on the Bridge* (cat. 42) and *White Night* (cat. 41). Onsager had the ministry's permission to retrieve the works from their out-of-town storage. But contrary to what one might expect given Nazi Germany's attitude to Munch, in Norway the artist was still regarded with the utmost reverence and esteem. Accordingly, he was presented not among the intolerable modernists of the degenerate art section, but rather as the pinnacle of what Onsager described as the most respected national idiom. Alongside Werenskiold, Munthe, Krohg and Peterssen, Munch's paintings were shown in the south-wing's Square Room, on the very wall where Thiis had hung them as part of the new arrangement of 1909 - "the best and finest wall". Even for the National Gallery's Nazi-sympathising director, Munch was still the nation's most important artist, no matter what people thought of him in Germany. "There are many who wish to place Munch among the degenerate artists. Nothing is more absurd, I would say. There is nothing in Munch's art that could be described as degenerate or corrupting. Quite the contrary, even his tiniest sketch is full of power and intuition."[67] With Munch approaching his eightieth birthday, Onsager asked the artist whether he would countenance an exhibition of his graphic works.[68] Munch declined the invitation.[69]

A new Munch exhibition in the summer of peace, 1945

By the time of liberation in May 1945, the museum was almost empty of art. The building was dishevelled, but in reasonably good condition. In the skylights, many broken panes of glass had been covered with boards to prevent leaks. The collection of plaster casts still occupied the halls on the ground floor, while the original sculptures were buried under sandbags in the basement. Most of the picture collection was stashed away in 246 containers in the old silver mines at Kongsberg, with several other transport crates held at Hadeland Folk Museum and the local museum at Bagn.

Former curator and now acting director, Johan H. Langaard, was eager to reopen the museum as soon as possible. But it would take time to fetch the National Gallery's collection home. Furthermore, a new hanging of the permanent exhibition should be postponed until a new director had been appointed. According to the statutes, it was the director alone who was responsible for hanging the collection.[70] In the event, it would not be possible to reopen the Munch room before September 1946.[71] Various proposals for loaned exhibitions were considered, but ultimately it was two other ideas that found approval: an exhibition of work from Edvard Munch's artistic estate and an exhibition of Munch prints "facilitated by private loans if the gallery's own portfolios cannot be retrieved".[72]

Langaard got in touch with Oslo's municipal authorities. Munch had died in January 1944. In his will he had bequeathed his entire art collection, consisting of more than a thousand paintings, 3,000 drawings and watercolours, and 18,000 graphic works, to the City of Oslo.[73] The municipality responded positively to the proposal.

Langaard selected around 340 of the best-preserved paintings from among the works found at Ekely, the artist's home at Skøyen to the west of Oslo.[74] It was also the intention to show a selection of prints. As in 1927, the entire first floor was again dedicated to Munch. In the first room, visitors were greeted by a large series of self-portraits – nearly twenty of them. Turning to the right, one entered the "red hall", or Dahl room, an elongated space with the deep red wallcoverings from the early 1930s. Here one found Munch's graphic works displayed in the old reusable frames of the Department of Prints and Drawings.

The exhibition covered all the periods of Munch's long life. The paintings were mounted uncleaned, without frames, and several had holes and other damage. Due to the lack of time and funds there was no catalogue, and nothing was labelled. While there was no chronology to the exhibition, some effort had been made to impose a thematic order. For example, the many versions of a theme were grouped together so as to highlight the artist's stylistic phases and development.

The exhibition opened on 10 July 1945 in the presence

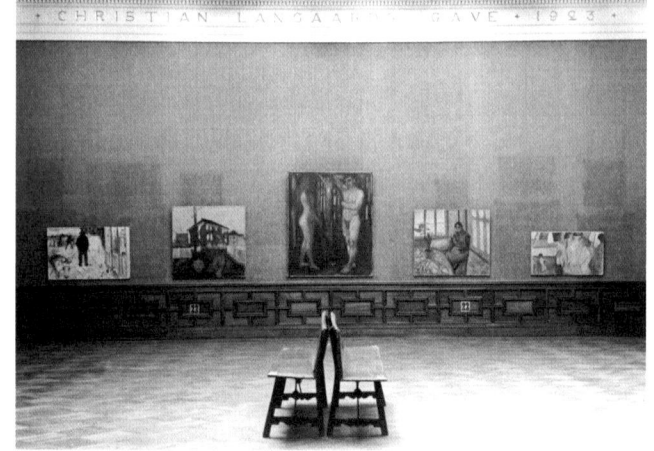

During World War II, the National Gallery's collections were evacuated. In the summer of 1945, following the declaration of peace, the museum reopened with a large Munch exhibition. The entire upper floor remained filled with 340 paintings and a number of prints, all from the artist's testamentary gift to the city of Oslo, until January 1946. Photo: O. Væring. The National Museum's documentation archive.

of the Crown Prince Couple. Oslo's mayor, Rolf Stranger, gave a formal speech, in which he reiterated the intention to build a museum for the artist as a worthy and appropriate thank you for his magnificent bequest.

The choice of a Munch exhibition to reopen the National Gallery in the 1945 summer of peace proved a great success both for the museum and for Munch's enduring reputation. It was overwhelmingly well received, attracting visitors in their tens of thousands.[75] But despite the enthusiasm, a few points still came in for criticism: the opening hours were far too short (Sunday, Tuesday and Wednesday from 12 noon to 3pm, Thursday and Friday from 5 to 8pm), and the lack of labelling and a catalogue were lamented. During the autumn the weather turned cold, and with it the museum. Electrical power was intermittent and little else was functioning.

"On the final Sunday of the National Gallery's exhibition of Munch's testamentary gift, it received around 3,000 visitors," curator Eli Ingebretsen Greve would later recall. She herself was present to stand guard over the works.

> January the 20th 1946 was a dark, foggy day. At around 2pm, the lights went out in the exhibition halls, but still the visitors could not tear themselves away. By closing time at 3pm, dusk was falling, yet many people demanded that we stay open a little longer. The pictures took on a strange, independent life in the winter twilight. New colour effects emerged in the darkness. The gloom brought out new qualities in the paintings. People didn't want to leave, and it proved impossible to close the museum at the usual time. It was as if the dense, black crowd moving through the halls was clinging to something enduring and essential that mattered to them personally and which they couldn't bear to lose. A human message, a view of life that summarised, exposed, or confirmed their own problems.[76]

Thanks to its success, this large Munch exhibition was soon followed by another, this time featuring many of the woodcuts from Munch's estate. (The museum's own Munch prints were still in the silver mines at Kongsberg.) This time it was Eli Ingebretsen Greve who contacted the municipality and secured their cooperation. The exhibition opened on 19 March 1946 and would continue to the end of April. The National Gallery's new director, Sigurd Willoch, presided over the opening. Few people knew Munch's "Nachlass" better than he did.[77] Greve, who had also prepared a catalogue for the exhibition, was widely praised for her excellent presentation of the exhibited material. During the six weeks of the exhibition, the curator was enthusiastically assisted on her guided tours by the artist Henrik Finne, whose own colour woodcut technique acquired new sophistication during this period.

The success of the woodcut exhibition inspired Greve to intensify her scholarly work. But due to illness and premature death she never saw the publication of her *Edvard Munch. Liv og verk i lys av tresnittene* (Edvard Munch. His life and work in light of the woodcuts). The book appeared posthumously, in 1963, the centenary of Munch's birth and the year the Munch Museum opened. In 1950, Willoch's extensive catalogue of Edvard Munch's etchings was published as a leather-bound deluxe volume in folio format, paid for by the City of Oslo on the occasion of the city's 900th anniversary.[78]

As early as 8 April 1946, a large commemorative exhibition had opened in Copenhagen's City Hall. For this, the new director of the municipal Munch Collection, Johan H. Langaard, had selected close to a hundred paintings from the exhibition in the National Gallery, which had just come to an end. Also on display were 125 graphic works. In 1947 it was the turn of Stockholm and Gothenburg. This marked the beginning of a hectic period of marketing the artist abroad, a task undertaken primarily by the new City of Oslo Art Collection, an institution created to manage Munch's substantial testamentary gift.[79]

Although the establishment of this new institution took the pressure off the National Gallery when it came to presenting and promoting Munch, it soon became clear that in the international arena the participation of the National Gallery remained indispensable, not least because the museum (together with the Rasmus Meyer Collection in Bergen) held many of the most important works from the 1880s and 1890s, a period that was somewhat underrepresented in the municipal collection.

The first major international presentation under the auspices of the National Gallery was at the Venice Biennale in 1954. Of the forty-three paintings in the exhibition, senior curator Leif Østby, the exhibition's commissioner, had selected fourteen from the National Gallery, including *Inger in Black and Violet, The Scream, Moonlight* (1893), *Madonna, Puberty, The Girls on the Bridge, Bathing Man* and *Self-Portrait with the Spanish Flu*. While the excitement in Venice was palpable, the same cannot be said for tourists in Oslo, since many of the Munch room's best-known works were absent for months. Indeed, this would become a serious problem for the museum as Munch's international fame grew, prompting ever more requests for the loan of seminal works.

Prior to its showing in Venice in the summer of 1954, *The Scream*, for example, had not been seen outside the National Gallery since 1910, the year it was gifted to the museum. But between 1954 and 1993, the iconic picture visited as many as forty museums and galleries around the world! And then, shortly after its return from a Munch exhibition in the former Winter Olympics town of Sapporo, *The Scream* was stolen from the National Gallery in the early hours of 12 February 1994, the day Norway's own Winter Olympics were due to open in Lillehammer. The picture was recovered a few months after this spectacular theft. But the incident marked the end of the picture's travels. It was duly bolted to the wall of the Munch room, which thus became the obligatory destination for hundreds of thousands of foreign visitors every year.

The very first painting Munch ever showed in an exhibition, "The Norwegian Industrial and Art Exhibition" at Tullinløkka in the summer of 1883, was *Study of a Head* (cat. 4). This was also the last Munch work the museum was able to purchase, which it did in 1964. In some respects this acquisition is the exception that proves the rule. Prices for the artist's pictures had long since outstripped what the museum itself could afford to pay.

The last Munch donation to the museum (to date) happened back in 1970. In that year, the National Gallery received a further ten paintings from Charlotte and Christian Mustad as a testamentary gift. These included *The Kiss* (cat. 17), *Melancholy* (cat. 19) and *Moonlight* (cat. 31).[80] Together with the seven paintings the couple had given in 1937, on the occasion of the museum's centenary, this was one of the most significant donations the museum had ever received from a private collector. In his letter of thanks, director Sigurd Willoch estimated that the gift was equivalent to "half a century's worth of the purchasing support the National Gallery had received from the Norwegian state".[81] Willoch had to rearrange several of the smaller adjacent rooms to accommodate the gift. The Munch room was long since full to capacity.

Since the start of the 20th century, almost no public funds had been used to purchase Munch pictures. The fact that the Munch collection could grow to such a size is due almost entirely to the generosity of private individuals and independent foundations. Of the museum's fifty-seven paintings, only eleven were bought with money from the ordinary purchasing fund. The other forty-six have come to the museum as gifts or with support from endowment funds.

Another memorable year in the story of Munch and the National Gallery, which in 2003 had become part of the National Museum, was 2013, the 150th anniversary of the artist's birth. The exhibition "Munch 150", a collaboration between the National Museum and the Munch Museum, lasted from 2 June to 13 October. It was seen by around 485,000 visitors. The National Gallery focused on Munch's art up to the year 1904, the Munch Museum on the latter forty years of his life. A joint catalogue covered 271 paintings, drawings and graphic works, and included many scholarly articles to illuminate his prolific career. As in 1927, and again in 1945, the National Gallery's first floor was cleared to make way for the master's work.

Back in 1909, Jens Thiis had promised Munch the museum's finest space. It is a promise that has now been kept for more than a century. And it is hard to imagine the contract between the artist and the museum being broken at any point in the foreseeable future.

Notes

1 Lasse Jacobsen, "Edvard Munchs søknader til legatene og til Statens kunstnerstipend", www.emunch.no.

2 MM K 1411, Munchmuseet. Dated 9 May 1884. Letter from Krohg to the Ministry of Church and Education (visited 29 June 2021).

3 MM K 1221, Munchmuseet. Dated 11 June 1888. Letter from Werenskiold to the Ministry of Church and Education (visited 29 June 2021).

4 At the National Annual Autumn Exhibition in 1884, Thaulow purchased *Morning* (Woll M 110). The following year he also wanted to buy the full-length portrait *Karl Jensen-Hjell* (Woll M 122). For several years *The Sick Child* (Woll M 130) hung in the home of Krohg, while in 1889 Erik Werenskiold purchased *Summer Night. Inger on the Beach* (Woll M 182) from that year's Autumn Exhibition.

5 According to the National Gallery's new statutes, adopted in 1884, the museum's board of directors should consist of a chairman and "at least" four members. It was considered desirable that the members should be practising artists, and should include representatives for painting, sculpture and architecture. As for the chairman, the ministry was to appoint "a man thoroughly acquainted with scholarship in the theory and history of art". The first chairman under the new statutes was the professor of art history Lorentz Dietrichson. In January 1891, having served six years in the position, he was replaced by the medical doctor Carl Frederik Larsen, regarded by the ministry as a highly capable chairman of Kunstforening from 1874 to 1885, but known by younger artists as a rather headstrong and conservative figure. In 1891, the ministry also opted to increase the number of board members from four to six. In addition to Larsen, the board now consisted of the history painter Peter Nicolai Arbo, the maritime painter and former naval officer, Carl Wilhelm Barth, the architect Holm Munthe, the sculptor Mathias Skeibrok, Eilif Peterssen and Erik Werenskiold, the latter as deputy for the art critic Andreas Aubert.

6 MM K 1224, Munchmuseet. Dated 14 December 1891. Letter from Werenskiold to Munch (visited 29 June 2021). Werenskiold also suggested a landscape by a French guest exhibitor, Pierre-Georges Jeanniot. His suggestion was approved, albeit without the support of maritime painter Barth and history painter Arbo.

7 *The Storm* is now owned by the Museum of Modern Art, New York.

8 Thorolf Holmboe, "Edv. Munchs Udstilling", *Morgenbladet*, 16 October 1895.

9 In 1895, the National Gallery also received its first donation of a Munch painting, a portrait Munch had painted in 1885 of his good friend and fellow artist, Jørgen Sørensen (cat. 7). The picture was given to the museum by Nikolai J. Sørensen in memory of a beloved younger brother who had died young in the autumn of 1894.

10 MM K 1182, Munchmuseet. Undated [March 1909]. Letter from Thiis to Munch (visited 29 June 2021).

11 See Minutes of Proceedings 1893-1905, Meeting of 11 November 1897, Item 2, NMFK/NG-1000/A/Aa/L0003, The National Museum's documentation archive.

12 See Minutes of Proceedings 1893-1905, Meeting of 18 November 1897, Item 3, NFMK/NG-1000/A/Aa/L0003, The National Museum's documentation archive.

13 MM K 720, Munchmuseet. Dated 14 October 1901. Letter from Munthe to Munch (visited 29. juni 2021). The "purchased winter picture" that Munthe refers to, *Winter in the Woods* (cat. 37), was purchased in the spring of 1901 directly from the artist.

14 The following were submitted: *Evening on Karl Johan* (Woll M 290), *Moonlight* (cat. 21), *The Scream* (cat. 23), *The Day After* (cat. 27), *White Night* (cat. 41), *The Girls on the Bridge* (cat. 42) and *The Girls on the Bridge* (oblong format, Woll M 484).

15 See Minutes of Proceedings 1893-1905, Meeting of 29 November 1901, Item 4, NFMK/NG-1000/A/Aa/L0003, The National Museum's documentation archive.

16 "Summer Night", now known as *The Girls on the Bridge* (cat. 42), was purchased by the art collector Olaf Schou, who gifted the picture to the National Gallery in 1909. *The Scream* spent a few months at the National Gallery before Munch told Aubert that he wanted it back (letter, 18 March 1902, NB correspondence collection 32, letter to Andreas Aubert). He wanted to display it at the prestigious Secession Exhibition in Berlin, as one element in his twenty-two-picture frieze depicting stages of life, described in the catalogue as "Darstellung einer Reihe von Lebensbildern". *The Scream* was acquired by Schou at a later date and was included in his 1910 donation to the National Gallery. The "moonlight picture" that Munthe was so eager to acquire ended up with Munch's good friend Harald Nørregaard and was only purchased for the museum in 1938.

17 Vigeland to the chairman of the board, Elling Holst, 7 November 1904, Journal no. 84/1904, NFMK/NG-1000/D/Da/L0007, The National Museum's documentation archive.

18 Vigeland to the board, 9 December 1907, Journal no. 106/1907, NFMK/

19 NG-1000/D/Da/L0008, The National Museum's documentation archive.

19 Vigeland to the board, 10 December 1907, Journal no. 107/1907, NFMK/NG-1000/D/Da/L0008, The National Museum's documentation archive.

20 Jens Thiis, *Norske malere og billedhuggere*, Vol. 2, *Fransk malerkunst* (Bergen: J. Griegs forlag, 1907), 428.

21 Jens Thiis, *Edvard Munch og hans samtid* (Oslo: Gyldendal, 1933), 290.

22 MM K 1182, Munchmuseet. Undated [March 1909]. Letter from Thiis to Munch (visited 29 June 2021).

23 Nilssen to Munch, November 1908, quoted here from Erna Holmboe Bang, *Edvard Munchs kriseår* (Oslo: Gyldendal, 1963), 30.

24 Nilssen to Munch, undated [January 1909], quoted here from Erna Holmboe Bang, *Edvard Munchs kriseår* (Oslo: Gyldendal, 1963), 37-38. The "naked girl" is probably identical with *Puberty* (cat. 26).

25 MM K 1182, Munchmuseet. Undated [March 1909]. Letter from Thiis to Munch (visited 29 June 2021). According to an older provision, the purchase of graphic works and drawings should be undertaken by the chairman of the board (now the director) in consultation with the collection's curator, who at that point was Fredrik Gundersen.

26 See Thiis to the Ministry of Church and Education, 15 March 1909, quoted here from Copybook 1898-1920, NFMK/NG-1000/B/L0003, p. 506, The National Museum's documentation archive.

27 Thiis to the Ministry of Church and Education, 11 March 1909, quoted here from Copybook 1898-1920, NFMK/NG-1000/B/L0003, p. 502-503, The National Museum's documentation archive.

28 See Hans Dedekam, "Edvard Munch", *Morgenbladet*, 27 March 1909.

29 NB correspondence collection 604, Munch to Nilssen, 24 March 1909.

30 MM N 2079, Munchmuseet. Undated [March 1909]. Letter draft, Munch to Thiis (visited 29 June 2021).

31 Nilssen to Munch, undated [late March 1909], quoted here from Erna Holmboe Bang, *Edvard Munchs kriseår* (Oslo: Gyldendal, 1963), 68-69. The "Baedeker" was Europe's most widely used series of travel guides.

32 Thiis to the Ministry of Church and Education, 23 July 1909, quoted here from Copybook 1898-1920, NFMK/NG-1000/B/L0003, p. 529, The National Museum's documentation archive.

33 Thiis to the Ministry of Church and Education, 2 August 1909, quoted here from Copybook 1898-1920, NFMK/NG-1000/B/L0003, p. 535, The National Museum's documentation archive.

34 See Tone Skedsmo, *Olav Schous gaver til Nasjonalgalleriet* (Oslo: National Gallery, 1987). The exhibition with the same title was an important event in the National Gallery's 150th anniversary celebrations.

35 MM K 1446, Munchmuseet. Dated 2 April 1910. Letter from Thiis til Munch (visited 29 June 2021).

36 Photo used in *Norsk malerkunst i Nationalgalleriet: Halvhundrede gjengivelser av norske maleres arbeider* (Kristiania: Mittet, 1912).

37 Skedsmo, 184-188.

38 In 1933 *Rue Lafayette* (cat. 16), in 1938 *Moonlight* (cat. 21) and *Self-Portrait* (cat. 9), and in 1958 the very early *From Vestre Aker* (cat. 1).

39 The Society for French Art was assigned the Square Room in the south wing for the following exhibitions: Corot 1919, Degas 1920, Renoir 1921, Manet 1922, Courbet 1923, Matisse 1924, Gauguin 1927, French painting from David to Courbet 1928.

40 Jens Thiis, "Det fuldførte Nationalgalleri. År 1916", 12 May 1913, journal no. 80/1914, NFMK/NG-1000/D/da/L0010, The National Museum's documentation archive.

41 Jens Thiis, "Malerkunsten i det 19. og 20. aarhundre", in *Norsk kunsthistorie*, Vol. 2 (Oslo: Gyldendal, 1927), 505.

42 Thiis' wording in the preface to the exhibition catalogue, *Edvard Munch* (Oslo: National Gallery, 1927), 4.

43 The profits came from admission charges and catalogue sales. It was suggested that the revenue should be used to purchase a work by Munch, an idea the artist opposed. In 1929 the money was used to purchase Henrik Sørensen's *Inferno* (NG.M.01601).

44 From an interview in *Oslo Aftenavis*, 9 June 1927.

45 Report in *Dagbladet*, 25 July 1927.

46 See MM K 3582, Munchmuseet. Dated 14 September 1927. Letter from Nationalgalerie Berlin to Munch (visited 29 June 2021).

47 "[...] ein Ankauf eines Bildes vom Künstler selbst ist ein hoffnungslose Fall, da er sich von keinem Bilde trennen kann," wrote Justi to a private collector on 27 April 1927. See Uwe M. Schneede and Dorothee Hansen, *Munch und Deutschland* (Stuttgart: Hatje, 1994), 130.

48 *Norges Kommunistblad*, 16 June 1927.

49 "Munch skjenker malerier til Berlin og Oslo", *Dagbladet*, 12 September 1927.

50 Munch to Thiis, undated, received 3 July 1928, Journal no. 89/1928, NFMK/NG-1000/D/da/L0013, The National Museum's documentation archive.

51 "Kunstneren og hans verk", *Norges Kommunistblad*, 16 June 1927.

52 "Nationalgalleriet er overfyldt", *Tidens Tegn*, 15 June 1927.

53 "En æressal for Munch?", *Morgenposten*, 10 June 1927.

54 *Oslo Aftenavis*, 9 April 1930.

55 As of 1932, the Department of Prints and Drawings had 108 graphic works by Munch, according to Ingebretsen Greve, *Edvard Munch (grafikk)* (Oslo: Nasjonalgalleriet, 1932), 12.

56 "Edv. Munch gir Nasjonalgalleriet en verdifull gave", *Aftenposten*, 7 June 1934.

57 MM K 1451, Munchmuseet. Dated 23 November 1931. Letter from Ingebretsen Greve to Munch (visited 29 June 2021).

58 "Munch og Nasjonalgalleriet: Et viktig møte idag angående et Munch-museum", *Aftenposten*, 11 December 1933.

59 Thiis to the Chapter of the Order of the Royal Norwegian Order of Saint Olav, copy of letter, Journal no. 197/1933, NFMK/NG-1000/D/Da/L0017, The National Museum's documentation archive.

60 Organised by Johan H. Langaard, the exhibition lasted from 27 April to 20 June. Having worked several years as a volunteer, Langaard was given a position as combined secretary and librarian in 1929, before finally being appointed as a curator in late autumn 1936.

61 Sigurd Willoch, *Nasjonalgalleriet gjennem hundre år* (Oslo: Gyldendal, 1937), 184. The National Gallery did not itself have the funds to finance a centenary publication. For the preparation of the manuscript, Willoch received a grant from the Nansen Foundation, while the printing of the book was financed by Oslo Sparebank.

62 There was no space for *Two Nudes* (cat. 44).

63 MM K 1172, Munchmuseet. Dated 8 May 1937. Letter from Thiis to Munch (visited 29 June 2021).

64 As early as 1935, two Munch paintings were gifted to the museum from Harald Nørregaard's collection: *Aase Nørregaard* (cat. 38) and the double portrait *Aase and Harald Nørregaard* (cat. 39).

65 Thiis to Munch, 13 September 1939, NFMK/NG-1000/D/Da/L0021, The National Museum's documentation archive.

66 Onsager to the Ministry, 15 April 1942, journal no. 118/1942, NFMK/NG-1000/D/Da/L0023, The National Museum's documentation archive. "Heil og Sæl" was a nazi greeting.

67 Søren Onsager, "Ved Edvard Munchs død", *Aftenposten*, 25 January 1944.

68 Onsager to Munch, 6 July 1943, Journal no. 272/1943, NFMK/NG-1000/D/Da/L0024, The National Museum's documentation archive.

69 Munch to Onsager, 15 July 1943, Journal no. 299/1943, NFMK/NG-1000/D/Da/L0024, The National Museum's documentation archive.

70 Contrary to many rumours, Johan H. Langaard did not become the museum's new director, but rather Sigurd Willoch PhD, who was appointed by the state cabinet on 4 February 1946. On 7 March 1946, Langaard was appointed director of the municipal "Munch Collection" in Oslo, soon to be renamed the Oslo Municipal Art Collections. Leif Østby MA was appointed to replace Langaard as curator in the summer of 1946.

71 "Nasjonalgalleriet i går, i dag og i morgen", *Arbeiderbladet*, 17 August 1946.

72 "Møte i Nasjonalgalleriets råd lørdag 19 mai 1945", note by Johan Langaard, Journal no. 89/1945, NFMK/NG-1000/D/Da/L0029, The National Museum's documentation archive.

73 See Arne Eggum, *Munch i Munchmuseet* (Oslo: Messel Forlag, 1998), 8.

74 Langaard was assisted by a young curator from the Norwegian Museum of Cultural History, Reidar Revold, and art history student Knut Berg, who later became director of the National Gallery.

75 The exhibition received 71,000 visitors in the six months that it was open, according to an interview with Langaard; "Munchgalleriet vil bli en severdighet av internasjonal rang", *Dagbladet*, 12 March 1946.

76 Eli Ingebretsen Greve, *Edvard Munch: Liv og verk i lys av tresnittene* (Oslo: J.W. Cappelens forlag, 1963), 1.

77 Together with the painter Jean Heiberg, Willoch had been engaged by the City of Oslo as early as 1944 to provide an initial assessment of the scope and value of the bequest; see Sigurd Willoch, "Edvard Munchs gave i Nasjonalgalleriet", *Morgenbladet*, 19 July 1945.

78 Sigurd Willoch, *Edvard Munchs raderinger* (Oslo: Johan Grundt Tanum, 1950). The catalogue was based largely on the inventory of the bequest that Willoch had prepared in 1944-1945.

79 It was not until 1963 that the Munch Museum in Oslo's eastern suburb of Tøyen was ready for use.

80 *Andreas Reading* (cat. 3), *Around the Paraffin Lamp* (cat. 5), *The Kiss* (cat. 17), *Melancholy* (cat. 19), *Ragnhild Bäckström* (cat. 24), *Moonlight* (cat. 31), *Seated Nude* (cat. 34), *Mrs. Schwarz* (cat. 48), *Seated Nude* (cat. 49), and *Workers Returning Home* (cat. 57).

81 Willoch to Mustad's lawyer Øystein Thommessen, 27 October 1970/Munch, Edv. NFMK/NG-1000/Ea/L0036, The National Museum's documentation archive.

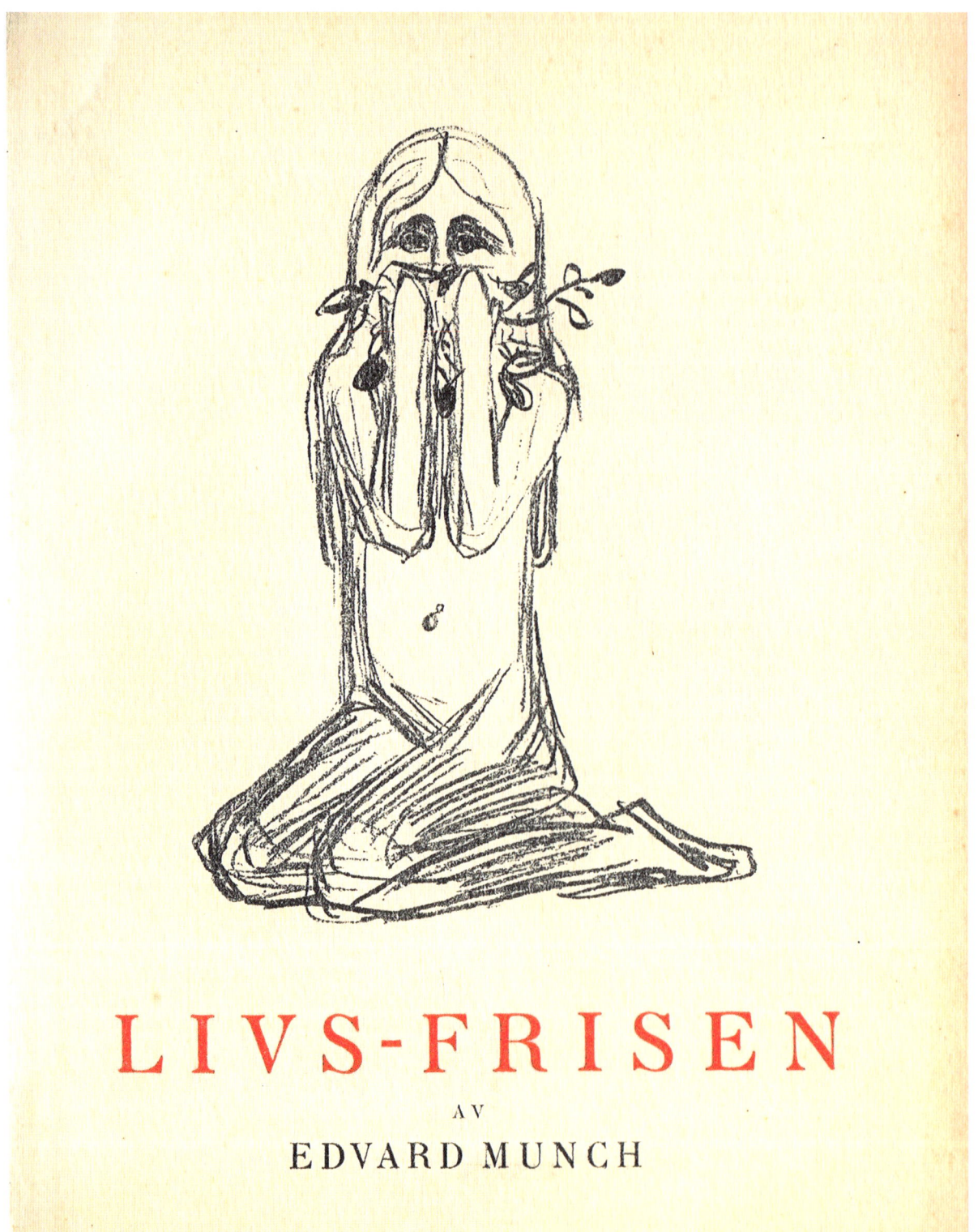

LIVS-FRISEN

AV

EDVARD MUNCH

The front cover of Munch's booklet *Livs-frisen*
(The Frieze of Life), 1919, Blomqvist Kunsthandel.
Photo: Munchmuseet

Mai Britt Guleng

In the beginning was the picture series. Edvard Munch's "Frieze of Life" and the National Gallery

Exhibiting paintings in series was an important element of Edvard Munch's artistic practice. The picture series that came to be known as The Frieze of Life contained paintings which, Munch felt, belonged together.[1] These included seven works that are now in the collection of the National Museum: *The Kiss* (cat. 17), *Melancholy* (cat. 19), *Death in the Sickroom* (cat. 22), *The Scream* (cat. 23), *Madonna* (cat. 29), *Ashes* (cat. 30) and *The Dance of Life* (cat. 40).

However, the links between the picture series and the museum go far beyond these seven individual works. Jens Thiis, the first director of the National Gallery, applied a number of approaches to forge a close connection between Munch's artistic ambitions and the institution he led. His reasons and methods in this regard form one of the themes of this article.

What was it about Munch's picture series that motivated the National Gallery's deep interest in them? What did The Frieze of Life say about the artist Edvard Munch that could not be conveyed in other ways? To shed light on these questions, it is essential to understand how Munch's picture series evolved over time and the vision he nurtured for a permanently mounted Frieze of Life. Let us start by stepping back in time, to his first picture series.

The first series

Two of the National Museum's paintings, *Melancholy* and *The Scream*, featured in Munch's first series, which he presented as part of an exhibition in Berlin in 1893. This series consisted of six paintings, grouped together in the catalogue under the title "Study for a Series 'Love'".[2]

Thanks to Munch's friend, the writer Stanisław Przybyszewski, we know which pictures the series included. In a publication from 1894, Przybyszewski describes the individual paintings and interprets the connections between them.[3] Addressing them in the order they are given in the catalogue, he traces a story that develops from the first to the last.

According to Przybyszewski, the first painting of the love series, *Summer Night's Dream* (*Summer Night's Dream. The Voice*, Museum of Fine Arts, Boston), is an evocative

and mysterious representation of longing. The next three pictures, *The Kiss*, *Love and Pain*, and *The Madonna Face*, were about the fulfillment of love and the power struggle between man and woman. *The Kiss* (Munch Museum) shows the merging of two individuals as they surrender to desire.[4] In *Love and Pain*, we see a woman bending over a man's neck. For Przybyszewski, this was a depiction of a bloodthirsty woman sucking the life force from a man, and Munch later renamed the painting *Vampire* (Gothenburg Museum of Art). *The Madonna Face* (now lost), he tells us, is the image of a woman in a state of erotic passion.

Passion is followed by jealousy, symbolically represented in the National Museum's painting *Melancholy*. The sixth and final painting, *Despair*, is identical with the National Museum's *The Scream*. Przybyszewski describes this picture as a landscape with some kind of bridge on which a strange creature stands with his mouth wide open. Here, he exclaims, "nature screamed for a new incarnation". As the final tableau of the series, Przybyszewski tells us, the painting depicts the angst-ridden struggle between a person's intellect and sex drive. Thus, the narrative of the love series shows the story of a man's suffering as lust runs its course, taking us from longing through to its painful conclusion. In other words, the series was interpreted as based on an idea, amounting to a narrative with a beginning and an end, which could be read from the paintings when viewed in sequence.

For Munch, however, the content was not definitively fixed. For his second picture series, "Kärlek" (Love), shown at an exhibition in Stockholm in 1894, he made several changes.[5] This latter presentation differed from the Berlin series in several respects.

An evolving series

Here Munch included several new paintings. The number of pictures grew from six to fifteen, while the number of motifs doubled to twelve. Three of the motifs were represented in two different versions; The Kiss, Woman Making Love, and Vampire. This duplication served to emphasise the importance of the image within the suggested plot: The Kiss, The Kiss – Woman Making Love,

1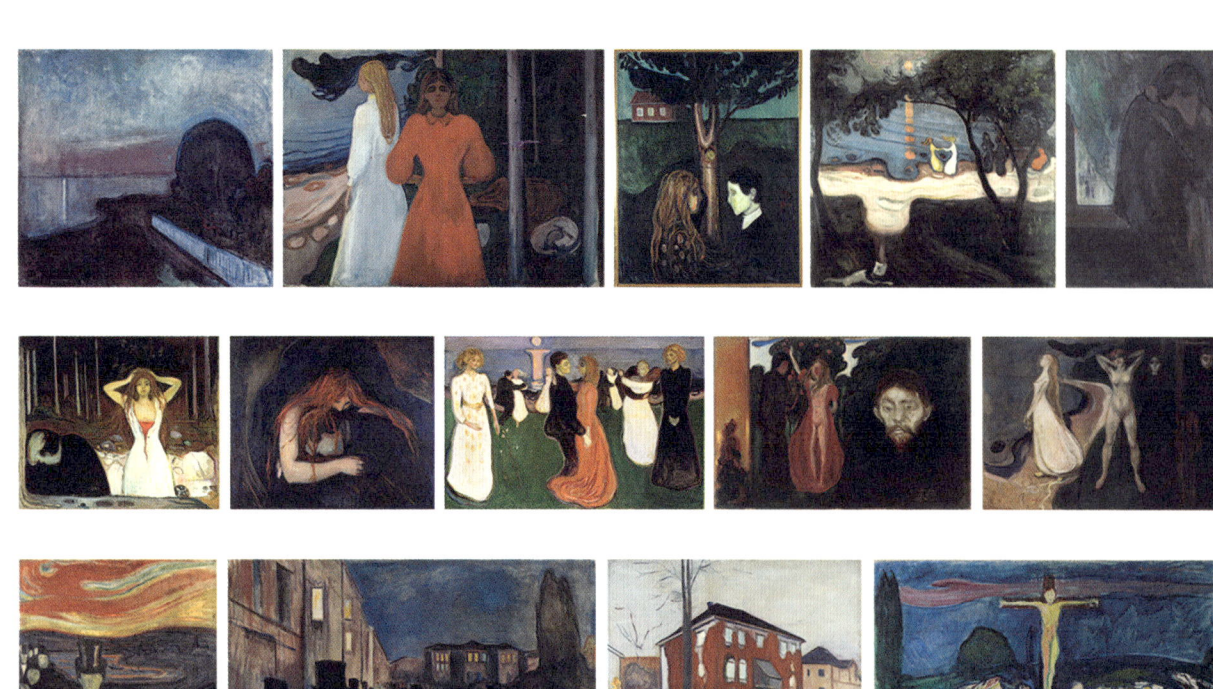

2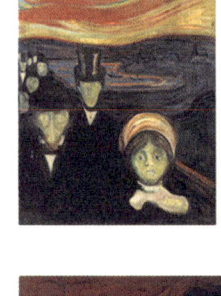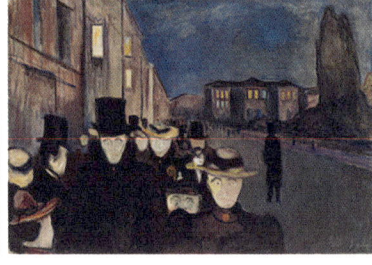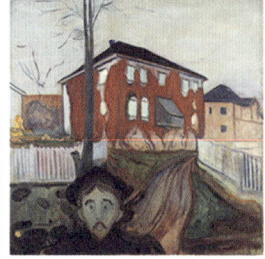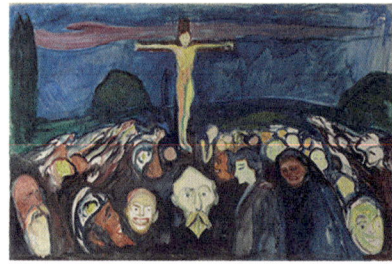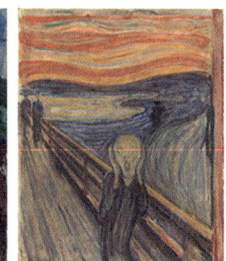

3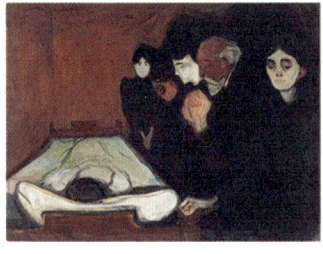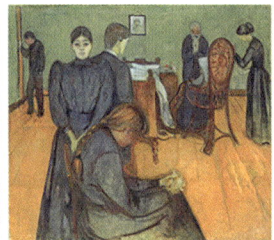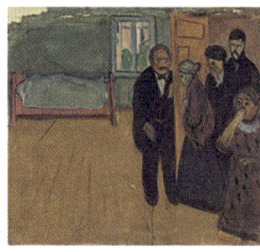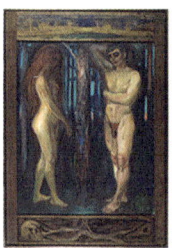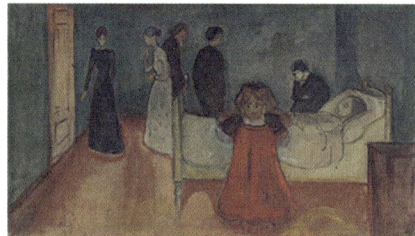

4

The Picture Series "A Presentation of a Number of Images from Life", Berlin Secession, 1902.

Woman Making Love - Vampire, Vampire. One of the two paintings referred to as *Woman Making Love* is now the National Museum's *Madonna*. It is also possible that one of the two *The Kiss* paintings is the one now in the museum's collection (cat. 17).

One important change is that one of the paintings was given both a new title and position. In the Berlin exhibition, *Vampire* had the title *Love and Pain*. Munch later insisted that the painting was meant to depict a woman tenderly kissing a man on the neck.[6] Nevertheless, he adopted Przybyszewski's interpretation of the woman as a dangerous, blood-sucking creature. Accordingly, he moved the picture to later in the series - further along the progression from love's inception to its decay. This changed the meaning of both the painting and the series as a whole.

Munch's open-minded approach demonstrates that, for him, neither the paintings nor the series were defined once and for all. They carried the potential for a range of stories, which he continued to experiment with in new permutations over the years that followed.

The indeterminacy of the content allowed Munch to add a new theme in 1902. Up until then, the series had been about the growth and decay of love, followed by existential anxiety. But in the exhibition at the Berlin Secession in 1902, he introduced the sub-theme of sickness and death. This time the series had the title "Presentation of a Series of Pictures of Life". It consisted of twenty-two paintings distributed across all four walls of the exhibition space. Each wall had its own subtitle. Under the heading "The Germ of Love", the six paintings on the left wall included the National Museum's *The Kiss* and *Madonna*.[7] The theme for the main wall was "Love's Flowering and Fall", where the paintings included, among others, *Ashes* and *The Dance of Life*. As love wanes, it is followed by suffering and jealousy, which leads in turn to "Anxiety". One of the five pictures brought together under this heading on the third wall, on the right, was *The Scream*.

The fourth and final theme, "Death", was represented by five works on the back wall of the exhibition space. One of the works in this set was the National Museum's *Death in the Sickroom*. This was the first time that Munch included images relating to sickness and death in his series. Now the story that begins with amorous attraction ends not in existential anxiety, but with the end of life itself.

In his picture series, Munch varied the themes he wanted to emphasise. Even so, certain motifs retained a closer association with the picture series than others. Two of these are the National Museum's *The Scream* and *Madonna*.

Conceived as part of a whole

Both *The Scream* and *Madonna* were displayed as elements in picture series from the time of their comple-

tion through until they entered the museum's collection in 1909 and 1910 respectively. It is difficult to determine whether or not they were actually conceived for a larger context. Both paintings evolved over a lengthy period of time. Did the idea for the whole only arise once the paintings stood finished on the easel? Although it is impossible to say what came first in the creative process, Munch's exhibition practice shows the importance of these works for the picture series.[8]

Munch's reason for showing the pictures as a series was the connections that arise between them. In a letter to a friend, he explained that he wanted to make the pictures easier to understand. Paintings that might otherwise appear "rather incomprehensible" thus became easier to grasp.[9] The works give meaning to each other.

This is not to say that these series were the key to understanding the works, not even for the artist. Each arrangement suggested a new pictorial narrative. In the years from 1893 to 1918, Munch exhibited between ten and twelve picture series of related content, but each slightly different from the last. The number of works varied, from a minimum of six to a maximum of twenty-two. While no single painting featured in all of the series, five motifs were always present: The Kiss, Madonna, Vampire, Melancholy, and The Scream. Munch also experimented with different hangings, from showing the pictures individually at the conventional eye-level, through to placing them as a frieze high up under the ceiling, as he did in Berlin in 1902 and Leipzig in 1903 (ill. 2). Despite the variation in their titles, the picture series invariably addressed the themes of *love*, *the stages of life*, and *the condition of the modern soul*. Sometimes he hung his own reflective texts beside the pictures.[10]

Munch always considered his creative experiments with different variations of the picture series as important. But in 1918 he took a further step. He wanted to see the picture series, now called The Frieze of Life permanently mounted.

The Frieze of Life - permanently housed

Munch put forward his idea for a permanent Frieze of Life in conjunction with an exhibition at Blomqvist Kunsthandel in 1918. As a foretaste of what such a frieze might look like, he showed twenty paintings mounted high on the wall, against a textile wall covering.[11] As Munch explained in the exhibition catalogue, collectively, the paintings would form a "poem about life, about love and death". He wanted to see the pictures permanently mounted in a "suitable architectural setting". Such a space would require a patron with appropriate premises, preferably a public institution.

Munch's initiative at the Blomqvist exhibition did not result in a public commission. One reason may have been

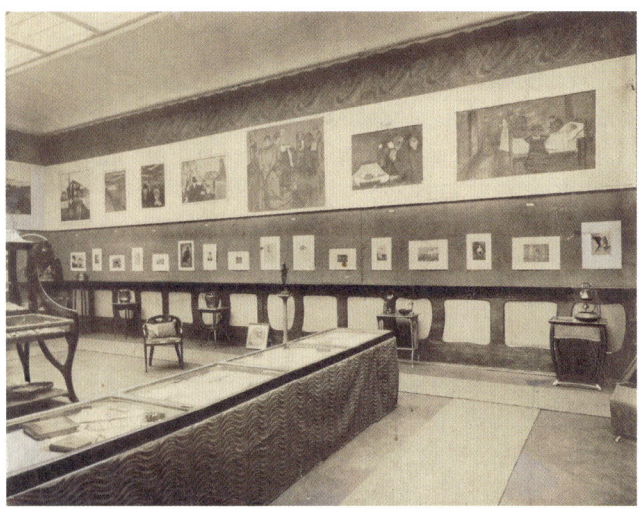

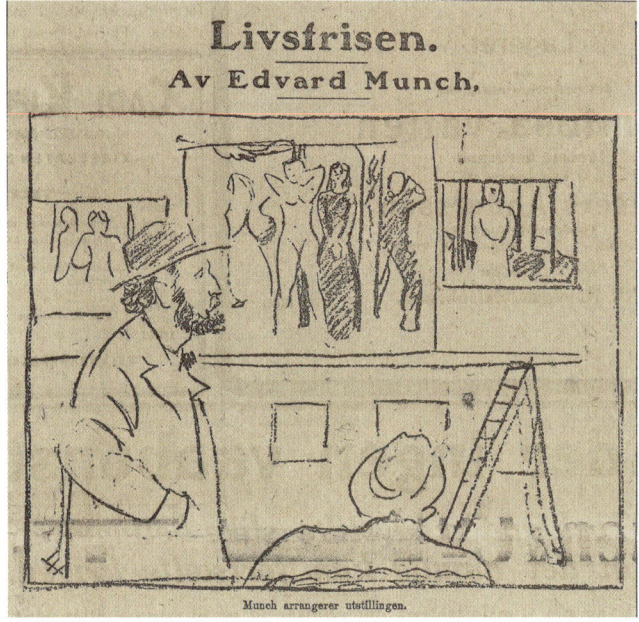

Edvard Munch's frieze at P.H. Beyer & Sohn,
Leipzig, 1903.
MM.D.01100-01
Photo: Munchmuseet

The Frieze of Life at Blomqvist Kunsthandel. *Tidens
Tegn*, 15 October 1918.
Photo: Nasjonalbiblioteket

the criticism he received. The works had been painted at
different times, from the 1890s onwards. As a whole they
appeared somewhat disparate, it was claimed. Munch
addressed this negative reception by publishing an article
entitled "Kritiken over 'Livsfrisen'" (The Criticism of "The
Frieze of Life") in the booklet *Livs-frisen* (1919). In this, he
explained that a permanent series would consist of new
paintings with formats adapted to the architecture of the
space.[12]

Ten years on, Munch was still clinging to the idea. In
1929, he published his own notes on art written over the
years since the late 1880s, the time, he tells us, when he
first began to develop the idea of The Frieze of Life.[13] It
was absolutely crucial that The Frieze of Life should hang
alone, without works by other artists. Since many of the
paintings that had previously featured in the series had
since been sold far and wide, Munch would have to paint
new versions. In the 1920s, he produced new versions
of, among others, *Ashes* and *The Dance of Life*.[14] But still
Munch was not offered a permanent home for the works.

The National Gallery owned seven of the best known
paintings from the series. The museum's director Jens
Thiis decided to acknowledge that fact in a decisive way.

Munch in the National Gallery

Thiis began to explore the possibility of building a separate hall for Munch's paintings as early as 1913 (see Nils
Messel's article in this publication). Nothing came of the
idea. But in 1924, Thiis was able to push through a plan
to devote an entire hall to Munch on the museum's upper
floor. The National Gallery began purchasing works by
Munch as far back as the 1890s. As director, Thiis worked
diligently to secure further acquisitions from private collectors, not least from Olaf Schou. In 1937, he was able to
add a major donation from the Mustad family. Thanks
largely to this latter acquisition, Thiis was able to justify
a new and larger space for Munch's work later that same
year, in the top-lit hall on the upper floor of the south wing.

For Thiis, the idea of displaying Munch alone in a separate hall – without other artists – was a continuation of the
artist's own exhibition practice. Given the subjective turn
in Munch's art that happened around 1890, Thiis found
it perfectly understandable that the artist had stopped
participating in group exhibitions in Norway. Solo exhibitions became his ideal format, Thiis claimed in his book
*Edvard Munch og hans samtid. Slekten, livet og kunsten,
geniet* (Edvard Munch and his era. Family, life and art,
genius), from 1933.[15] The Munch room was effectively the
museum's version of a solo exhibition.

In his book, Thiis devotes an entire chapter to the
Frieze of Life. Just seven years younger than Munch, Thiis
had been acquainted with the picture series ever since
1895, when it was presented in Berlin under the title "Die

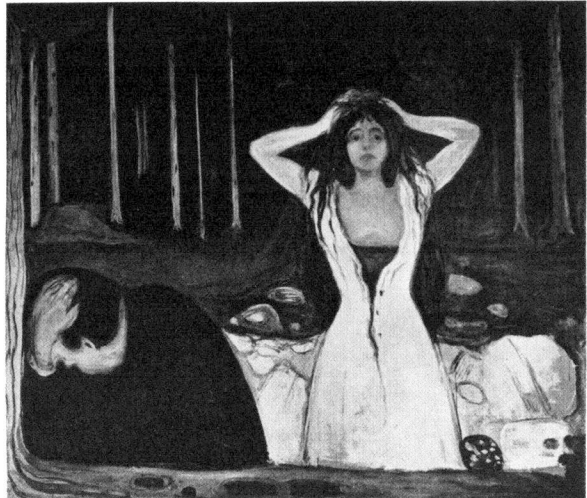

MUNCH: Aske (1894). Tilhører «Livsfrisen». Nasjonalgalleriet

Liebe".[16] He had also visited the Berlin Secession in 1902, where he viewed the large frieze of twenty-two paintings hung high on the wall, which made "a powerful impression" on him.[17] In addition, Thiis had seen the exhibitions that featured the series in Kristiania (Oslo), most recently in 1918.

According to Thiis, it is impossible to say where the Frieze of Life begins and where it ends. It runs "like a thread through Munch's entire production", both his painted works and his prints. Apart from the portraits and landscapes, the artist's work constitutes an unbroken "frieze" of life.[18] Thus Thiis explains that, for him, virtually everything in the Munch room could be viewed as a Frieze of Life.

Thiis took over Munch's unfulfilled ambition to find a permanent home for his picture series and transferred it to the National Gallery.[19] Here he was probably thinking of both Munch and the National Gallery. He considered it almost shameful that in 1918 Munch had been forced to publically defend "the great artistic idea of his career" in written form. The Frieze of Life was Munch's child of pain, the distillate of his work.[20] As Munch's younger friend, he emphasises his close personal relationship with the artist, especially in the chapter "In the Company of Munch". Over the years, the director of the National Gallery had come "to know and to love this great man, and I learned to understand, even adore his art!"[21]

By detailing the links between the Frieze of Life and the National Gallery, Thiis also clarified the museum's role as guardian of Munch's art. In the captions to several of the paintings in his book, Thiis follows the work titles with, "Part of 'The Frieze of Life' in the National Gallery". Where the painting was not owned by the National Gallery, he only adds an "From 'The Frieze of Life'". It was probably Thiis himself who penned the review of his book that appeared in *Sandefjords Blad*. Here as well, the caption to *The Dance of Life* includes the remark that the picture belongs to the Frieze of Life in the National Gallery.[22]

The series in the National Museum

Picking up the baton from Munch, the director of the National Gallery, Jens Thiis, developed his own version of the artist's dream of a permanent Frieze of Life. In doing so, he staked a claim for the National Gallery as the institution that was safeguarding Munch's artistic heritage. The inherent, conceptual content of the pictures and their interconnections could only become apparent if they were assembled in a single space of their own.

Thiis was not alone in considering the picture series as central to Munch's art. This was demonstrated in 2013 when the National Museum and the Munch Museum celebrated the 150th anniversary of Edvard Munch's birth with the joint exhibition *Munch150*. Both the National Gallery

From Jens Thiis' book *Edvard Munch og hans samtid*, 1933.

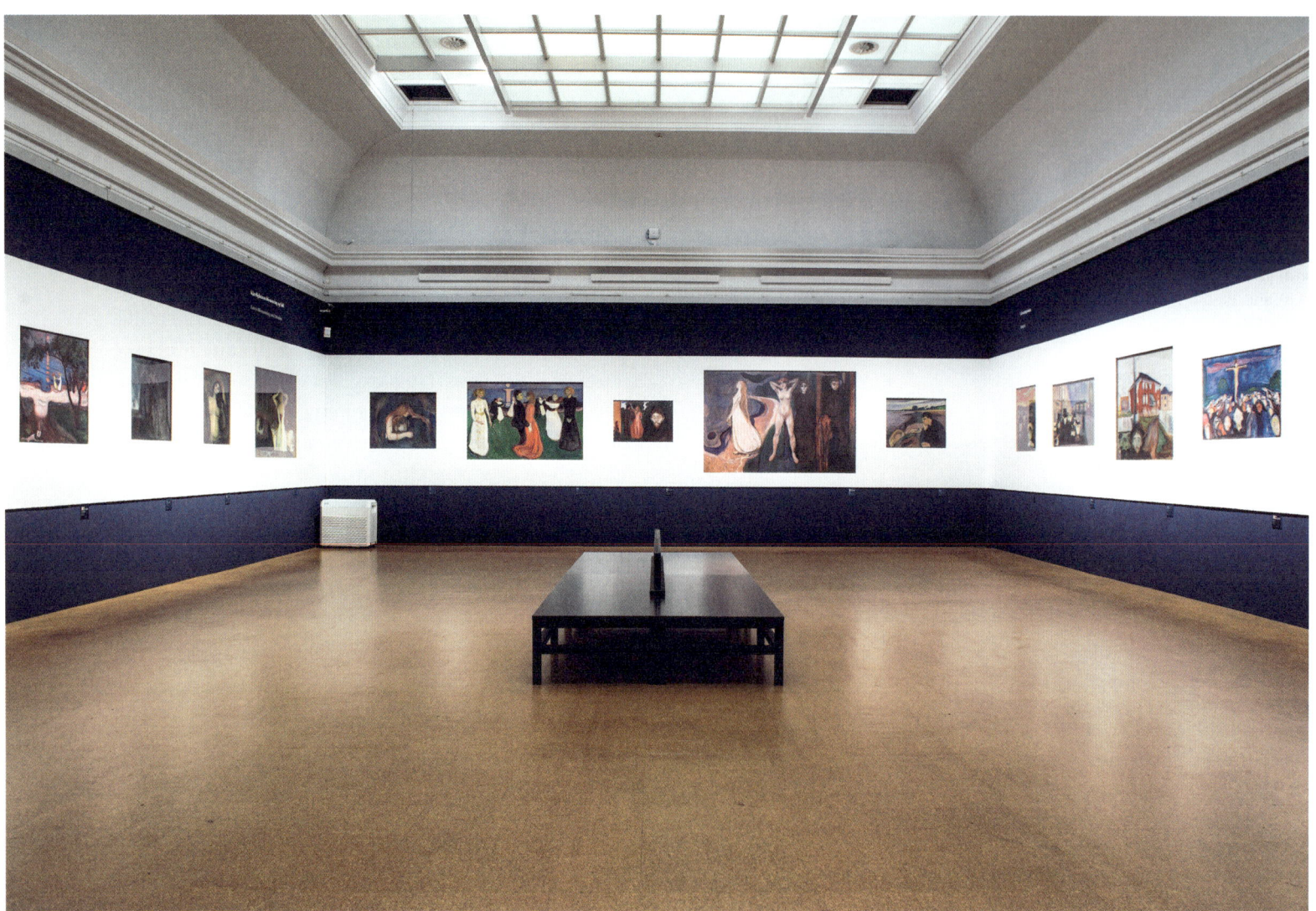

and the Munch Museum mounted reconstructed picture series. At the National Gallery we showed both Munch's first series on the theme of love from Berlin in 1893, and the frieze devised for the Berlin Secession in 1902. The Munch Museum displayed the Reinhardt Frieze and the Linde Frieze.

The tradition of showing Munch in a hall of his own is preserved in the new National Museum, where a large room with a single entrance is dedicated to his art. Further works by Munch are on display in other rooms in the context of other artists.

Munch publically defended his Frieze of Life on many occasions. Over several decades, he experimented with various combinations of works in series, which he presented under various titles in various exhibitions, thus demonstrating how his paintings acquired meaning depending on their juxtaposition with other works. His paintings were conceived to be shown in conjunction with others, not exclusively as independent works. In the beginning was the picture series.

A reconstruction of the Berlin 1902 exhibition was shown at Nasjonalgalleriet on the occasion of the Munch 150-year anniversary exhibition in 2013.
Photo: Nasjonalmuseet / Børre Høstland

Notes

1 Munch uses "Livsfrisen" (The Frieze of Life) as the title for a series for the first time in 1918, in connection with an exhibition at Blomqvist Kunsthandel. Edvard Munch, *Blomqvists kunstudstilling* (exhibition catalogue), Kristiania, [October] 1918. Contains: *Livsfrisen og annet* (first printed in *Tidens Tegn* 15.10. and 29.10.1918). Munch Museum, MM UT 22. This and subsequent archive references of this kind to Munch's printed catalogues and texts can be used to access the respective materials at www.eMunch.no.

2 Edvard Munch, *Eduard Munch Gemälde-Ausstellung* (exhibition catalogue), Berlin. Unter den Linden 19, [03.12.1893-?]. The six paintings in the series "Studie zu einer Serie 'Die Liebe'" were collected under cat. nos. 4a–f.

3 Stanisław Przybyszewski, *Freie Bühne*, February 1894; reprinted in Stanisław Przybyszewski (et al.), *Das Werk des Edvard Munch. Vier Beiträge* (Berlin: S. Fischer Verlag, 1894), 11–31.

4 For the reasoning behind the identification of the six paintings in the series, see Mai Britt Guleng, "The Narratives of *The Frieze of Life*. Edvard Munch's Picture Series", in Mai Britt Guleng, Birgitte Sauge, Jon-Ove Steihaug (eds.), *Edvard Munch 1863-1944* (Milan: Skira Editore, 2013), (catalogue for the exhibition *Munch150* at the National Museum and the Munch Museum, 02.06.-13.10.2013), 129-139.

5 Edvard Munch, *Förteckning öfver Edvard Munch Utställningen*. Konstföreningens Lokal, Stockholm, 1894, (Galerie Blanch. 01.10.-31.10.1894), cat. nos. 55-69 (15 paintings). The catalogue contains, among other things, excerpts from Przybyszewski's descriptions in Swedish translation.

6 Per Faxneld, "Blood, Sperm and Astral Energy-Suckers: Edvard Munch's Vampire", in Mai Britt Guleng (ed.), *eMunch. no - Text and Image* (Oslo: Unipub, 2011) (catalogue for exhibition at Munch Museum 21.01.-25.04.2011), 187-198; Mai Britt Guleng, "Edvard Munch - The Narrator", ibid., 219-236.

7 The identification of the specific paintings shown in Berlin in 1902 is based on Jan Kneher, *Edvard Munch in seinen Ausstellungen zwischen 1892 und 1912: eine Dokumentation der Ausstellungen und Studie zur Rezeptionsgeschichte von Munchs Kunst* (Worms: Wernersche Verlagsgesellschaft, 1994), 427-428; work details in Gerd Woll, *Edvard Munch. Complete Paintings*, Vols. 1-4 (Oslo: Cappelen Damm, 2008 B).

8 Other works, such as *Melancholy* (cat. 19), *The Kiss* (cat. 17) and *Death in the Sickroom* (cat. 22) were initially exhibited as independent works, but later included in series.

9 Letter, Munch to Johan Rohde, [end of March 1893], transcript in Munch Museum, MM PN 21.

10 "Mine Ord dertil" ("My words on this"), Munch Museum, MM.T.2759, leaf 6r, [after 1903].

11 Exhibition catalogue, Edvard Munch, *Blomqvists kunstudstilling*, 1918, ibid.

12 Edvard Munch, *Livs-Frisen*, published in connection with the exhibition at Blomqvist Kunsthandel, Kristiania, [October] 1919. Munch Museum, MM UT 23.

13 Edvard Munch, *Edvard Munch utstilling: Blomqvist Kunsthandel*, Oslo, [15.03.-?.1929], (Oslo: Blomqvist Kunsthandel, 1929). Contains: "1889-1929: Små utdrag fraa min dagbok", 1-2. Munch Museum, MM UT 24. Munch claimed that the frieze had its origins in his "Bohemian period" in the late 1880s, and that it took on clearer form in 1889-90, during his study visit to Paris; see Munch, draft letter to Ragnar Hoppe, Munch Museum, MM N 2273, 4; Edvard Munch, *Livsfrisens tilblivelse* (booklet without cover) (Oslo, 1928), Munch Museum, MM UT 13. See Lasse Jacobsen, "Edvard Munch's Own Publications", in Mai Britt Guleng (ed.), *eMunch.no - Text and Image* (Oslo: Unipub, 2011) (catalogue for exhibition at Munch Museum 21.01.-25.04.2011), 109-120.

14 Munch is recorded as making a copy of his own paintings *The Dance of Life* and *Ashes* in 1925 in the National Gallery's copyist register.

15 Jens Thiis, *Edvard Munch og hans samtid. Slekten, livet og kunsten, geniet* (Oslo: Gyldendal norsk forlag, 1933).

16 *Sonder-Ausstellung des Edv. Munch og Axel Gallén*, Ugo Barroccio, Unter den Linden 16, 3. bis 24. März 1895. Thiis, ibid., 215.

17 Thiis, ibid., 257.

18 Ibid., 260. Thiis traces the origins of the Frieze of Life to the diary entries made at Saint-Cloud in 1889; ibid., 258.

19 A few years earlier, Thiis had been somewhat less positive about Munch's picture series. Concerning the frieze that Munch showed at Blomqvist in 1907, he wrote that he himself found it difficult to see how the pictures constituted a series, although he admits that this could be his own failing. Jens Thiis, "Edvard Munch. Et foredrag holdt i anledning af en udstilling af kunstnerens arbeider i Kristiania", in *I Ord och Bild*, 16th year, 10th issue, Kungl. Hofboktryckeriet, Iduns tryckeri A-B: Stockholm, 1907, special edition, 533-545, here 534.

20 Jens Thiis, *Edvard Munch og hans samtid*, 262.

21 Ibid., 220.

22 "Julens Bøker", *Sandefjords Blad*, 20 December 1933, no. 295, 43rd year.

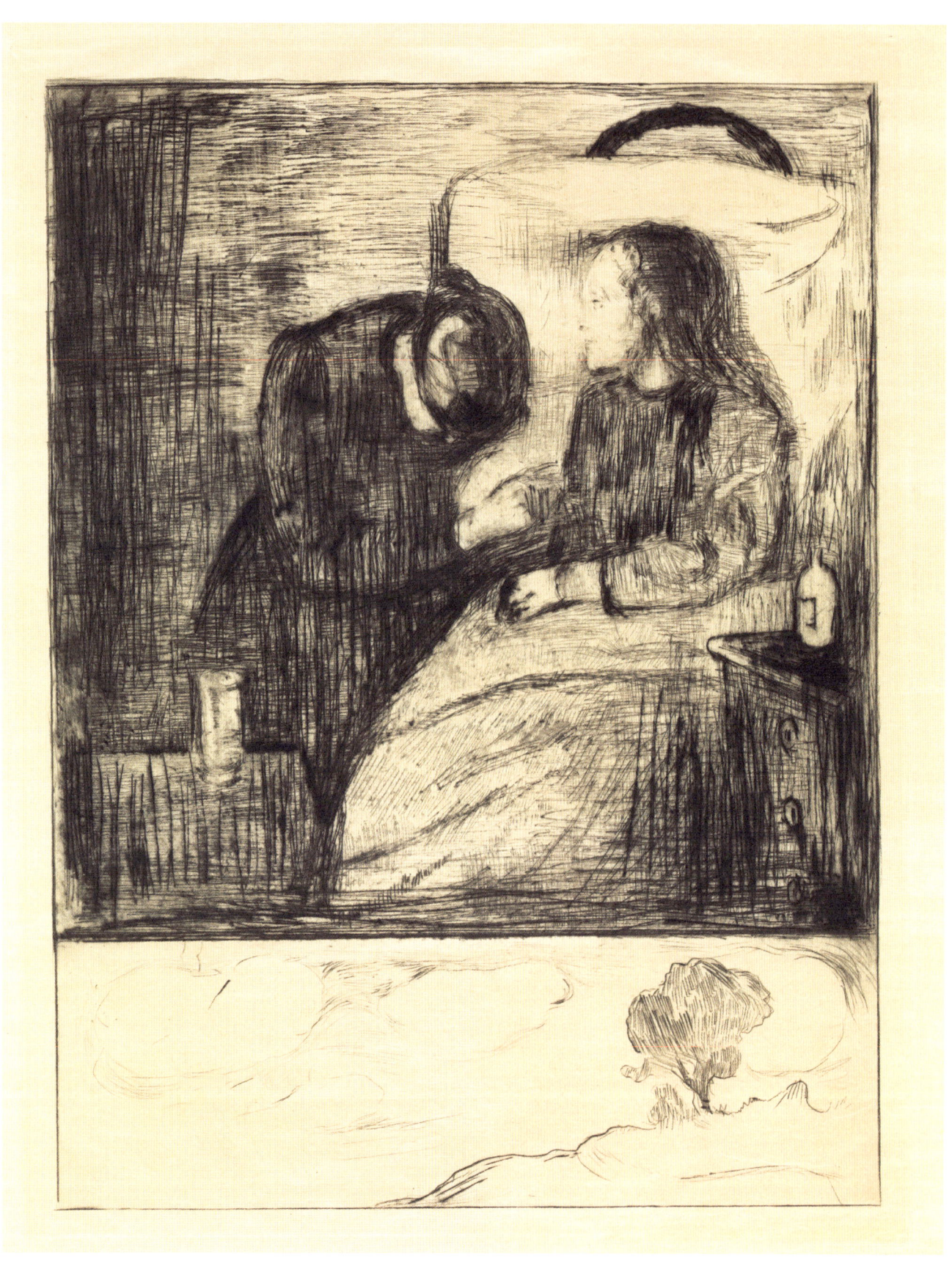

Edvard Munch: *The Sick Child*, (1894 or 1895)
Intaglio, Japan paper, 387 × 291 mm
NG.K&H.A.19054, cat. 64
Photo: Nasjonalmuseet / Dag A. Ivarsøy

Sidsel Helliesen

The printmaker and the collection

An international pioneer with a broad and varied oeuvre

Edvard Munch is best known as a painter, yet his graphic works are by no means inferior to his paintings. The spectrum is broad and varied. Gerd Woll's authoritative catalogue raisonné of the graphic works (Woll 2001/2012) encompasses 748 entries.[1] Of these, 203 are intaglios, 398 lithographs, and 147 woodcuts.[2] In other words, he used all three traditional printmaking techniques – intaglio, planographic and relief. Nevertheless, Munch's practice as a graphic artist was far from conventional. Today he has a prominent position in the history of modern graphic art. He was a pioneer and has indeed been recognised as one of the great masters of printmaking. In terms of both technique and style he was an innovator, and several of his works are among the most appreciated in the field.

Munch began working with prints in late autumn 1894, creating some of his most important statements within just a few years. The work was done in Berlin, Paris and later Kristiania (Oslo). At that time, however, printmaking in Norway was in its infancy, and it would be several decades before the medium gained broad recognition in the Norwegian art community.[3] From the perspective of graphic art in Norway, Munch is effectively an outsider.

Whether living abroad or at home, Munch retained his international orientation and contacts to the end of his life. Both printers and exhibition opportunities in foreign countries were central to his activities. Which is not to say that he had no profile in his home country. He exhibited prints frequently in Norway and also used Norwegian printers. But he was not a central figure in the printmaking scene that was beginning to emerge in Norway.[4] Nonetheless, no other Norwegian comes anywhere close to the recognition that Munch achieved – and has retained – internationally as a graphic artist.

Reference work and introduction

Gerd Woll's catalogue raisonné[5] has been the foundation for the work behind this catalogue of Munch's graphic works held in the National Museum. The catalogue is conceived primarily as a reference work, with the consequence that certain information is repeated in several of the entries, and many details will only be of interest to specialists. Although this introduction contains consider-able detailed information, it is also intended for readers who have no specialist knowledge of Munch or graphic art. The aim of this introduction, taken in conjunction with the catalogue, is to provide an insight into Munch's work as a printmaker and to familiarise the reader with the museum's collection. It is also our hope that it will stimulate a deeper interest in graphic art in general and that of Munch in particular, and possibly even in museum collections more widely, their character and history.

The National Gallery collection

The National Museum currently holds 160 of Munch's graphic works. In addition, the catalogue describes four lost works,[6] four original works in printed publications, and four original graphic posters (Appendices 1 and 2). The selection covers the years from 1894 to 1930. The National Museum's collection includes many important works from Munch's most creative periods, several of which are examples of early impressions. But there are also later reprints and reworked versions. Accordingly, the collection highlights important aspects of Munch's work with printmaking.

With the exception of the four posters, the current holdings were formerly the property of the National Gallery. The first works were acquired in 1898/1899, the most recent in 1997. Unfortunately, dates of acquisition and provenance are only known for a limited number of impressions.[7] Efforts to establish detailed provenance for Munch's graphic works have been ongoing for many years, but with only modest success. The main reason for this is that acquired material was not consistently inventoried with pertinent information about earlier owner(s) and dates of acquisition.[8] Regrettably, it would appear that many records are also missing in the museum's archives.[9] Considerable material exists, but there are many gaps. After assessing the investigations done so far and the resources invested relative to the meagre results, we have chosen to curtail this aspect of our research.

Fredrik Gundersen, who was the curator at the Collection of Prints and Drawings from 1883 to 1927, was by all accounts a thorough and conscientious museum professional. Yet he inventoried only three works by Munch,[10] despite the fact that the museum must have acquired many during his time. His successor, Eli Ingebretsen (Greve from 1939),[11] inventoried 45 prints by Munch according to date of acquisition between 1927 and 1947.[12] Most of these entries contain provenance information. She also registered Munch's graphic works in a supplementary record entitled "Norsk grafikk I" (Norwegian Graphics I), which contains a total of 160 entries. The record includes all the Munch prints in the collection as of 1949.[13] The entries follow the numbering in Gustav Schiefler's catalogue published in two volumes in 1907 and 1928 respectively.[14] In the case of the woodcuts that Munch produced after Schiefler had completed his catalogue, Greve refers to her own catalogue for the 1946 exhibition "Edvard Munch's Woodcuts" at the National Gallery (see p. 41). The entries contain various acquisition details from Ingebretsen Greve's time as curator.[15] The inventorying of Munch's works was revised during an exhaustive audit of the National Gallery's collection of prints and drawings in 1969-70,[16] although resources at that point did not allow an investigation of the works' provenance. In 1970, a brief overview of Norwegian graphics held in the collection was published, based on the recently completed audit.[17]

Dating - a challenge

For an account of the system and contents of the entries in the holdings catalogue, we refer to "Prints and drawings - User's guide", p. 189-192. We would, however, like to point out the problem of dating the individual impressions. This is a challenging exercise for a number of reasons. For one thing, Munch dated his impressions only relatively rarely. Moreover, the few dates that he does supply are not always reliable. Further, Munch often pulled prints from the plate(s) or stone(s) at different times, in many cases at intervals of several years and using different printers. This makes the dating of the individual impressions both important and interesting. Although Munch's own datings are not always reliable, we have adopted them here, with a commentary where relevant. In the case of the undated works, we have included probable dates based on various criteria such as paper type, the quality and condition of the impression, and other information, such as biographical factors, the period when the printer worked for Munch, exhibitions, catalogues etc. Even so, we have often had to settle for fairly generous time spans.

The first prints

Munch produced his first graphic works in Berlin in the autumn of 1894.[18] By the end of 1895 he had probably completed 45 prints. Of these, 30 are found in the National Museum's collection.[19] His very first works are generally considered to be two portraits in drypoint, *Richard Mengelberg* (cat. 58) and *Portrait of a Young Woman* (cat. 59). These were followed by various figurative compo-

sitions, for which, in addition to drypoint, he used various intaglio techniques such as line etching, aquatint and open-bite (cat. 60-69). Around the same time, he also made his first lithograph, *Puberty* (cat. 70).

In June 1895, the critic and author Julius Meier-Graefe published a portfolio with eight of Munch's prints, plus an essay by Meier-Graefe himself.[20] A member of the circle of intellectuals and artists who frequented the café "Zum schwarzen Ferkel", Meier-Graefe was one of the founders of the magazine *PAN*. The Munch portfolio was published in two editions. One was a deluxe edition of only ten, printed on Japan paper before the plates were steel faced, signed and numbered by the artist. The other was an edition of 55, containing unsigned impressions printed on wove paper from steel-faced plates. The National Museum has six of the eight images contained in the Meier-Graefe portfolio,[21] although only one is from the portfolio itself: *Tête-à-Tête* (cat. 66). *The Day After* (cat. 67) is signed and was dated by the artist the same year as the portfolio was published. *The Sick Child* (cat. 64) is undated but is probably also an impression from 1895. *Two People. The Lonely Ones* (cat. 69) is dated 1896, while *Kristiania Bohemians I* (cat. 71) and *Dr. Max Asch* (cat. 77) were printed by O. Felsing, a printshop that Munch probably used from 1902 to 1914.[22] The portfolios were printed at Angerer Kunstanstalt. According to Schiefler, Munch also used Carl Sabo during his early days in Berlin. The six prints in the museum's collection with images that are also in the portfolio illustrate Munch's practice of pulling prints from the plates on several occasions, often using different printers, and sometimes at intervals of several years.

States

The early works in the museum's collection also include examples of different "states". The term "state" denotes any particular stage in the artist's development of the matrix. For example, the museum's impression of *The Sick Child*, is the fourth of seven recorded states (indicated as IV/VII in the catalogue). First, Munch depicted the sick girl and the woman as a mirror version of his painting of 1895-96 (see cat. 8). In addition to minor changes and additions to depicted figures, he added a landscape below the main image (in state III). Later, this part of the plate was cut off, presumably after 1906. At different points in time, impressions were pulled by the artist himself, Sabo, Angerer and Felsing, and Scheel in Kristiania. In the case of the *Bathing Women*, the plate for which Munch first prepared in 1895, the museum has two impressions, one dated 1895 (cat. 72), the other undated and printed at O. Felsing's (cat. 73). The two impressions are examples not just of an early and a late pull from the plate, but also of two different states, albeit with relatively modest changes in a plate that we know to have been printed in as many as 15 states.

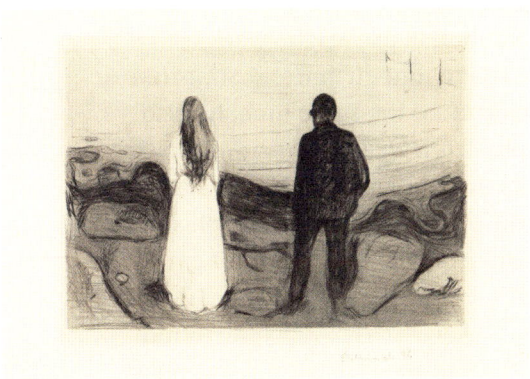

cat. 69

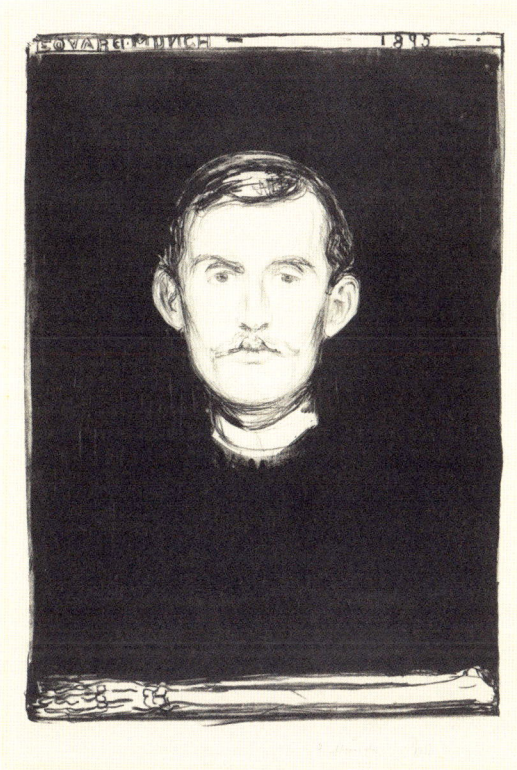

cat. 84

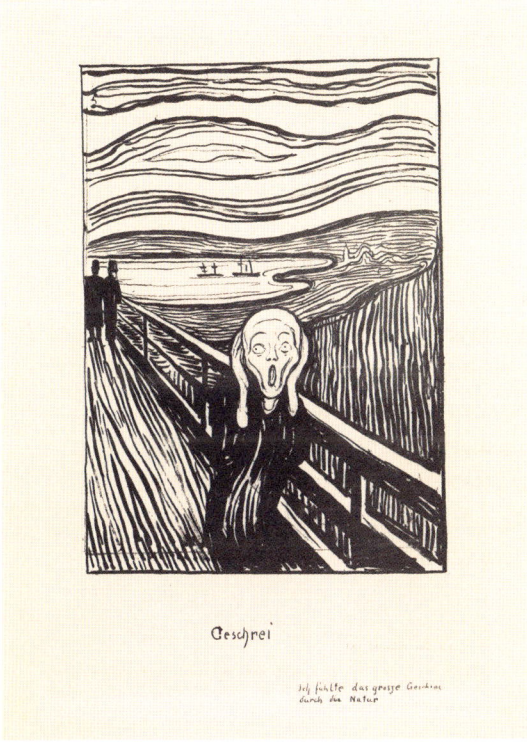

cat. 85

Most of Munch's early intaglio prints, and not least the prints in the Meier-Graefe portfolio, can reasonably be described as mature and successful works that show varied and subtle use of the characteristic qualities of the techniques. A good example in this respect is *Two People. The Lonely Ones* (cat. 69). In giving visual expression to the poignant loneliness of a man and a woman, Munch demonstrates a superb command of drypoint's rich black-and-white register and its potential for soft lines and texturing effects, and an equally expert sense of balance between areas of different tone.

A superb command of intaglio and lithography

Munch mastered lithography as quickly as he mastered the intaglio techniques. His earliest lithographs include such outstanding works as *Self-Portrait*, *The Scream* and *Madonna*, all executed in 1895. In *Self-Portrait* (cat. 84), the outline of the head and the facial features together with the framing elements at the upper and lower edges are drawn with lithographic crayon, while lithographic tusche is used for the dark surrounding. In addition, a number of careful scratches in the stone to either side of the head have produced fine white streaks on the print. The condensed composition and the balanced but expressive handling of the aspect ratio and the use of contrasts are prominent qualities of this black-and-white print. The picture is reminiscent of a stela and is often cited as an example of Munch's preoccupation with death as a theme. One prominent feature of *The Scream* (cat. 85) is the bold, sweeping brushstrokes. The landscape - the path with the railing, the water, hills and sky - are represented as patterns of rhythmically repeated lines that effectively serve to amplify the almost de-materialised, terror-stricken figure in the foreground. Compared to the painting of two years earlier (see cat. 23), the powerful black-and-white effect of the lithograph, with its simplification of the motif and more succinct idiom, seems only to enhance the expressive force of the theme. *Madonna* (cat. 86) is similarly a black-and-white lithograph repeating an image Munch had already developed as a painting (see cat. 29). Here again, lithography's intense tonal contrasts and more concise description of the subject serve to heighten the expressivity. At the same time, Munch has retained here a softness in the idiom and execution that captures the ambiguous sensuality of the subject. The concentration on the naked torso and face of the female figure as she arches her back, her eyes closed, her head encircled by her heavy, undulating hair, has obvious erotic connotations of pleasure, yearning and suffering, but there are also religious and more broadly symbolist overtones.

Why make prints?

By 1894, Munch was a mature and famous painter, and there has been some speculation about why he turned to printmaking and who it was who inducted him into the medium. Little can be said with any certainty.[23] The speed with which he mastered the techniques and harnessed their expressive potential is remarkable, albeit not unique in the history of graphic art. For a gifted and experienced artist such as Munch, a little help would have gone a long way. Initially, that help probably came from the printers in Berlin. It is reasonable to suppose that Munch the painter saw printmaking as an opportunity to create publicity and improve his income. The fact that so many of his prints are based on subjects he had previously developed as paintings does not necessarily imply a lack of new ideas. At the same time, in the many prints Munch made based on earlier paintings, the graphic treatment of the image has little in common with so-called reproduction prints.[24] Although he retains the defining elements of a motif, he invariably exploits the distinctive possibilities and formats of the graphic medium. So even if it was the potential of that medium to spread his artistic visions to a broader audience that initially attracted Munch, it seems clear that printmaking also fascinated him as an autonomous means of artistic expression. This is confirmed by his exploratory approach to graphic techniques and by the results he eventually achieved using plates of metal, stone and eventually also wood.

To the metropolis of printmaking

Plans to continue working with prints were probably an important motivation for Munch to travel to Paris in February 1896. In the 1890s, Paris was a lively centre of activity for all aspects of graphic art. Munch soon found himself in the thick of it, so to speak, and the results were impressive. The year and a half that he spent in the art metropolis proved remarkably productive. But far more importantly, it was a period of discovering technical and artistic solutions that represented innovations and successes in their own right and which also laid the foundations for further development.

Among the intaglio prints Munch produced in Paris, a group of mezzotints, some in black and white, some in colour, constitute an intermezzo in his production, insofar as he generally showed little interest in this particular technique. Even so, some of the colour prints are very beautiful. Sadly, the museum possesses only one of these works, a late black-and-white impression (*Model with Hood and Collar*, cat. 123). It was lithography, and later woodcuts, rather than intaglio techniques, that interested Munch most during this period. In this respect, his acquaintance with the lithographer Auguste Clot was of major importance. Not only did Clot provide the skills of a master printer, he also introduced Munch to much of the best that was happening on the city's rich graphic scene. In Paris, Munch was invited to contribute to Ambroise Vollard's portfolio *Les peintres graveurs*, the 22 prints of which were printed by Clot.[25] Although we do not know when Munch acquired the prints by Toulouse-Lautrec that were in his estate, it is worth noting that he owned the series *Elles*, a major work by the French artist, produced in 1896 and probably printed by Clot.[26] Munch also used Lemercier & Cie, one of the largest printing firms in Paris, and Alfred Porcabeuf of the Atelier Alfred Salmon. It is unclear, however, when and for which works Munch used the various printers, although it is known that Clot was responsible for most of the seminal works from 1896 and 1897.[27]

Experiments with colour

For example, we know that it was Clot who printed the two-colour lithograph *Angst* (Woll G 63) in *Les peintres graveurs*. Here, both the lower black section of the composition and the red of the sky were printed in a single pull from one and the same stone. This simplification of the printing process is a foretaste of Munch's later innovations with colour woodcuts. Meanwhile, the bold brushwork is an extension of the idiom of *The Scream*. During his early days in Paris, Munch also continued to explore the lithographic style of *Self-Portrait* with its characteristic interplay of opaque black and unworked white surfaces combined with a subtle use of chalk and fine scratches. One excellent example in this respect is *Death in the Sick-room*[28] an early impression of which is in the National Museum's collection (cat. 100). Other examples in the collection are *The Urn* (cat. 103), *Jealousy I* (cat. 105), *Jealousy II* (cat. 106), and *On the Waves of Love* (cat. 112).

At the same time, Munch was keen to work with multiple colours. On the one hand, it was a prospect that presumably appealed to him as a painter, on the other, it reflected a trend of the period. Perhaps as a preliminary exercise, he coloured some of his black-and-white prints by hand,[29] in other cases, he used dyed paper. In addition to the experimental approach that we see in *Angst*, while in Paris he also got to grips with the more traditional method for making multicolour prints by using a number of matrices. One early example is a portrait of August Strindberg.[30] The museum has both a black-and-white impression (in which Strindberg's name is misspelled, dated 1896; cat. 101), and one printed in black and blue (with the name corrected; cat. 102). It is assumed that both were printed by Clot.

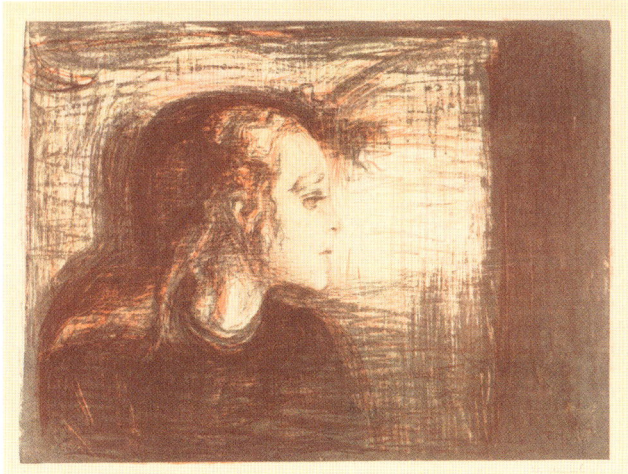

cat. 108

A colour-lithographic masterpiece

Munch's most famous colour lithograph from his time in Paris is *The Sick Child I*, which he developed in a range of colour combinations and states.[31] The National Museum owns two impressions: a rare early version in black and grey, dated 1896 and numbered 3 of 50 by the artist[32] (cat. 107), and a multicolour version, in a hitherto undescribed state, in red, grey and yellow (cat. 108). The print shows a section of the painting *The Sick Child* (Woll M 392; see cat. 8). During the time that Munch was in Paris, Olaf Schou ordered a replica of the painting, and it was probably in connection with this commission that Munch made the lithograph. In this work the artist concentrates on the head of the sick young girl, which is rendered with remarkable sensitivity. The torsion of the neck, the soft hair, the delicate profile and the introverted expression are formulated with a tremulous interaction of texture and tone, together with transparent inks in the colour versions. With empathy, Munch captures the physical and mental condition of the mortally ailing girl. In terms of both its pictorial and its technical qualities, *The Sick Child I* is considered one of Munch's most important print works and widely admired as one of the finest achievements of modern graphic art.

The lithograph has the same orientation as the painting, which it also closely resembles in terms of size and detail, indicating that the image was probably drawn on paper and then transferred to the lithographic stone.[33] While Munch may have encountered this method in Berlin,[34] his first documented use of it is in collaboration with Clot. One illustrative example is *Separation II*, of which the museum owns a monochrome impression in blue (cat. 110). The method simplifies the work process, and Munch used it frequently in his later lithographic work. However, transfer lithography is often regarded less as an authentic form of graphic art and more as a "finer" form of reproduction, a criticism Pola Gauguin directed at Munch when he submitted four transfer lithographs for the first exhibition at the Association of Norwegian Printmakers, in 1922.[35]

Groundbreaking woodcuts

In addition to the lithographic work Munch did in Paris in 1886, he also began an innovative and fruitful exploration of the possibilities of wood as a matrix, a form of expression that would later mean much to him. It was especially as a woodcut artist that he earned his reputation as a pioneer and master. In Schiefler's catalogue, five woodcuts are recorded under the year 1896 and five under 1897.[36] Since no woodcuts were included in Munch's exhibition at Siegfried Bing's gallery in May 1896 (see note 29), we can assume that at that point he still had not completed any. The fact that he was working in the medium by the late autumn of 1896, however, is documented in a letter from Alfred Hauge.[37] There was a revival of interest in the woodcut technique at around this time. Major exponents include Felix Vallotton and Paul Gauguin. It would appear that Clot's innovative printing workshop was also conducive to Munch's work.[38]

There are good reasons to believe that *Angst* is one of the first woodcuts Munch produced. The image is a reversed version of the lithograph in the Vollard portfolio (Woll G 63), on which it seems directly based (the Vollard print was in its own right an inverted version of a painting Munch had done in 1894, Woll M 363). In the woodcut, Munch has left the marks of the gouges and chisels unrefined, a woodcut style that in some respects became his trademark. In *Angst*, the crudeness of the cutting somewhat compromises the clarity of the depicted forms, an observation that corroborates the hypothesis that this is one of Munch's first works in the medium. The impression owned by the National Museum (cat. 121) is an early impression in black and white.

A simplification of depicted forms combined with a crudeness of the cutting is also noticeable in *Man's Head in Woman's Hair* (cat. 118). The National Museum's impression of this work is one of only two known impressions of a four-colour version, in which the red of the woman's face and hair, the green of the man's face and the just discernible blue elements are all printed from a single plate that was cut into pieces using a jigsaw. The pieces were inked up separately, reassembled and printed in a single pulling. This is a highly economical way to print multicolour woodcuts. It is often described as Munch's jigsaw-puzzle method and is regarded as one of his personal contributions to the development of the modern woodcut.[39]

The first planned colour woodcuts

Among Munch's early colour woodcuts, *Moonlight I* (cat. 119) is particularly interesting - and pictorially effective. Once again, the image is based on a section of a painting (see cat. 21). The special mood of a summer night, of longing and eroticism are as evident in the woodcut as in the painting. This is the only one of Munch's early colour woodcuts that was planned as a colour print, insofar as the image presupposes printing from two plates, in this case from the front and backside of the same piece of wood. In addition, there exist a number of interesting hand-coloured impressions printed from several woodblocks that illustrate Munch's approach to complex colour woodcuts. The museum's impression is printed from the front of the key-block (black), from the back of the same woodblock (pale grey), and from a colour woodblock that was cut into three pieces (inked brown, grey-blue and grey-green respectively). Following Schiefler, it is believed that Munch made the key-block while in Paris and pulled a few impressions at Clot's or Lemercier's. We do not know when he added the colour woodblock nor when he segmented it. Munch also varied the combination of colours in different impressions. Accordingly, *Moonlight I* exists in a number of variants.

So too does *Towards the Forest I* (cat. 127). The key-block for this work, of which there exist a few monochrome impressions, was apparently developed while Munch was living in Paris. The National Museum has an early impression from the key-block plus a colour woodblock that was divided into three sections (inked blue, green and reddish-brown respectively). Munch continued to refine both *Moonlight I* and *Towards the Forest I*; he added new blocks and changed the use of those he already had.

According to Schiefler, *Evening. Melancholy I* also dates from Munch's time in Paris. The version in the National Museum (cat. 120) is an impression from the key-block after it was cut into two sections (both printed in black), combined with a colour block that was also cut in two (inked bluish-green and ochre respectively). It would seem, however, that this impression was printed not in Paris, but somewhat later in Berlin by Lassally. It is yet another example of Munch's practice of getting different printers to pull prints from his plates at different times. As mentioned, sometimes he modified the existing plates, sometimes he added new ones. *Evening. Melancholy I*, *Two Women on the Shore* from 1898 (cat. 133) and *Encounter in Space*, also from 1898 (cat. 135), are all typical examples of the so-called jigsaw-puzzle technique. In *Two Women on the Shore*, the two women account for one piece, the sea for another and the landscape for a third. In *Encounter in Space*, each of the figures accounts for a single piece, the background for another. It would appear that these impressions were also printed at Lassally's in Berlin after 1906.

Did the jigsaw-puzzle technique start in Paris?

The jigsaw-puzzle technique is integral to Munch's exploratory approach to multicolour printmaking, which he first started working on while in Paris. It is possible, however, that he only began experimenting with cutting up the woodblocks - a move that radically simplifies the printing process - after his return to Norway in 1897. He had in his home a carpenter's bench and a jigsaw, tools he was familiar with from early in life.[40] Since he didn't include any colour woodcuts in the exhibition at the Dioramalokalet in Kristiania, which opened on 15 September 1897, it is reasonable to assume that he didn't complete any colour prints from segmented plates before the autumn of 1897 at the earliest.

It would appear that the only colour woodcut that was included at Dioramalokalet was *Mystical Shore* (see cat. 129), which was printed from both sides of a single plate. One feature of this work is the coarseness of the cutting,

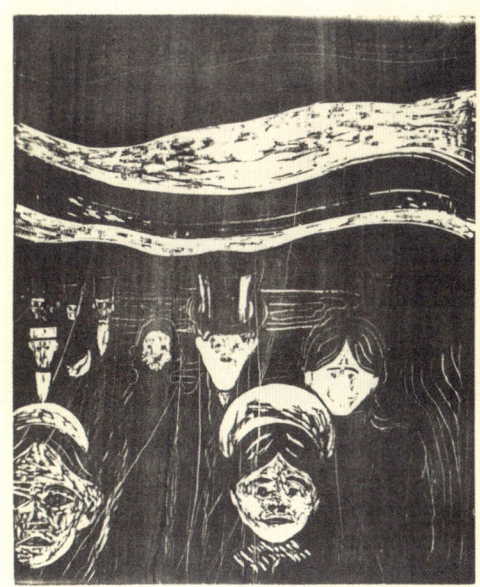

cat. 121

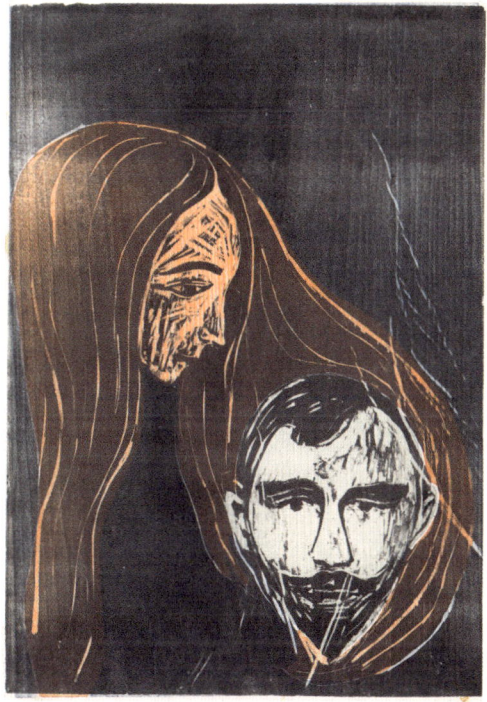

cat. 118

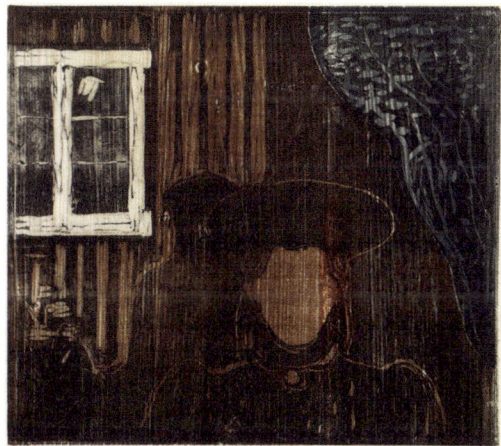

cat. 119

which produces clear traces of the tools in the print. This cutting style is equally evident in the black-and-white woodcut *Old Fisherman* (cat. 128), which was apparently also produced shortly after Munch's return from Paris and was included in the exhibition at Dioramalokalet. It is also present in *Winter Landscape* (cat. 134) from 1898 and *Nude* from 1897. The National Museum owns an impression of the *Nude* that was probably pulled by the artist himself in 1913 (cat. 131). In addition, the museum has four of the woodcuts Munch made in 1899 (all of them later impressions). Two of these are executed in the coarse black-and-white cutting style: *Woman's Head* (cat. 137) and *Man and Woman* (cat. 139). *Two People. The Lonely Ones* (cat. 140), with the same subject as the drypoint of 1894 (cat. 69), was produced in a number of multicolour versions, sometimes at intervals of several years and using stencils in addition to segmented woodblocks. The National Museum's impression has just two colours (black and greyish-blue), a palette that evokes a more intimate mood. In the museum's impression of *Woman's Head against the Shore* (cat. 138), the segmenting of the plate is somewhat less conspicuous, not least because of the diffuseness of the colours, which adds to the soft mood of the picture and gives an impression of hand-colouring. The effect is unusual but not unique. The number of lithographs that Munch produced in 1899 is small, but among them, *Ashes II* is a significant work. The National Museum owns an early impression printed on blue paper by Petersen and Waitz in Kristiania (cat. 136).

Reworked versions

In late autumn 1901 Munch travelled to Berlin in the hope of achieving an international breakthrough as a graphic artist.[41] According to Schiefler, the following year he produced colour versions of the lithographs *Madonna* and *Vampire II* by superimposing colours from new matrices on impressions pulled from the original stones. In both cases the process involved the use of woodcuts. In the case of *Madonna* (cat. 87), it is unclear how this was achieved. In *Vampire II* (cat. 89), the green, blue and ochre tones are printed from a single segmented plate. Believing that one of the crates containing matrices that should have been sent to Berlin was lost, Munch made new matrices for several important works, including the subjects "Melancholy", "The Kiss" and "Moonlight". *Melancholy III* (cat. 159) is a mirror version of the original woodcut (cat. 120). The museum's impressions of both versions were, however, printed by Lassally in 1902 or later. The museum's impression of the woodcut version of "The Kiss", a subject Munch returned to on many occasions, is from the woodblocks he produced in 1902 (*The Kiss IV*, cat. 160). This is a typical and highly effective example of Munch's characteristic use of the grain of the woodblock to produce a richly textured background. In addition to the jigsaw-puzzle technique, Munch's coarse cutting style and his use of the wood grain were pioneering features for which he is now famous and which have inspired younger generations of woodcut artists. Munch created three new woodcuts in 1902, two of which are represented in the National Museum's collection. Further, in the case of *Old Man Praying*, the museum has two impressions. One of these appears to be an early impression (cat. 161), the other probably from after 1906 (cat. 162). The museum's impression of the powerful *Head of an Old Man with Beard* (cat. 163) is one of two impressions that we know of with a red background.

A deluge of lithographs and intaglios

Compared with the relatively small number of woodcuts that he made, the quantity of lithographs and intaglios printed by both Lassally and Felsing was considerable. With the latter, Munch maintained a close working relationship right up until the outbreak of war in 1914. A number of lithographs and intaglios from 1902 are represented in the museum's collection. One in particular stands out: *Nude. The Sin* (cat. 156). Munch produced both monochrome and multicolour versions of this subject, the latter combining red, yellow and blue. The museum has an early black-and-white impression. The following year, he was far less active in terms of printmaking. Even so, the lithographs *The Brooch. Eva Mudocci* (cat. 167) and *Salome* (cat. 168) remain among his best-known works. The museum has an early impression of the latter, while its impression of *The Brooch. Eva Mudocci* is pulled from a new stone prepared in Kristiania in 1915. For this, he used transfer paper to take an imprint from the original stone, which was in the keeping of Lassally in Berlin. Anton Peder Nielsen assisted Munch with the transfer and printing.

Bringing the plates and stones home to Norway

We can assume that Munch began his extensive collaboration with the lithographer Anton Peder Nielsen (Kildeborg) shortly after his return home in 1909. Nielsen became an invaluable support to Munch in his later work on lithographs and woodcuts.[42] On the outbreak of war in 1914, Munch asked for all the woodblocks and metal plates he had in Berlin to be sent to him in Norway, plus probably the stones he had had transferred from Paris in 1904. In 1917, he took delivery of five of the stones from Lassally, together with transfer imprints of the others that would allow him to produce duplicate stones in Norway. Munch set up print workshops both in his house at Hvitsten and at Ekely, where he lived from 1916, with all he needed in terms of presses, plates and paper. Over the years he had

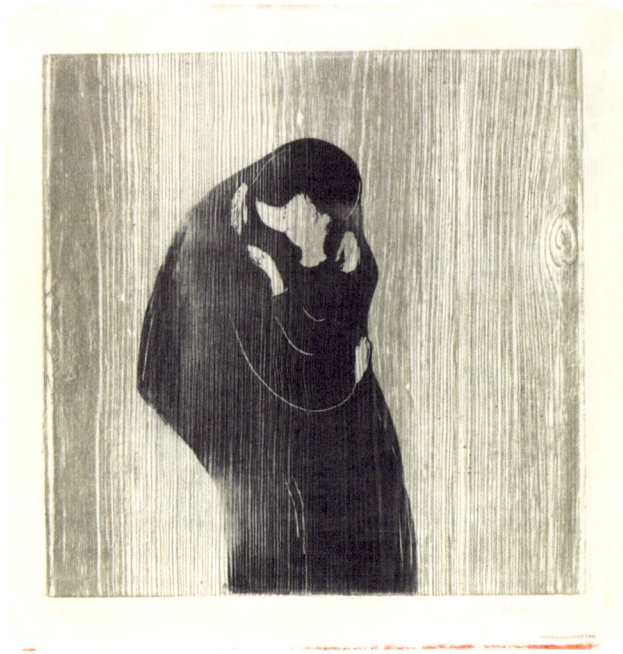

cat. 160

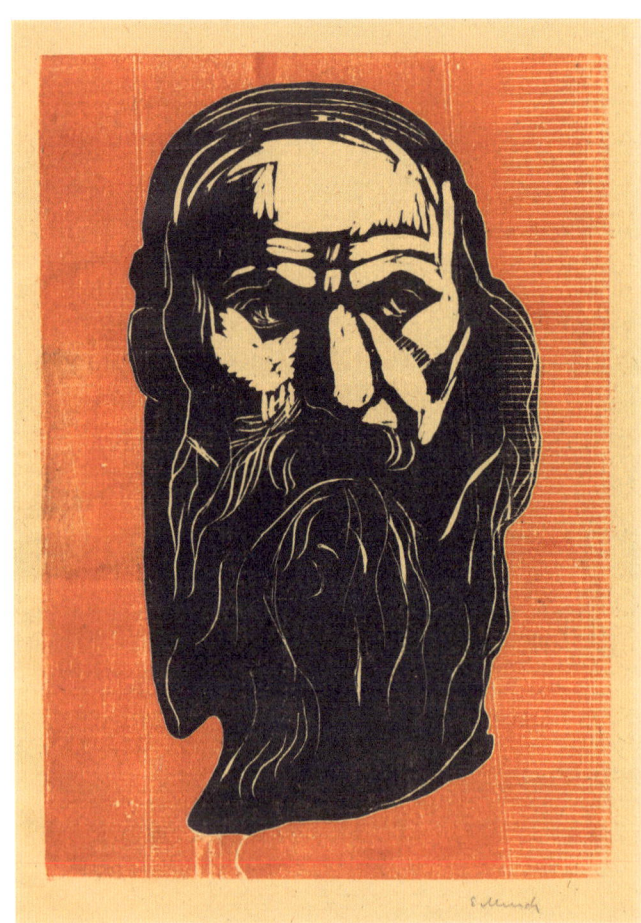

cat. 163

several highly productive periods, although they brought only a limited renewal of his idiom. The exception is a number of woodcuts, none of which, unfortunately, has found their way into the National Museum's collection. It has to be acknowledged that the prints the museum has from Munch's last decade have few distinguishing features.

A retrospective woodcut exhibition at the National Gallery

Edvard Munch bequeathed his artistic estate to the City of Oslo. After the artist's death in January 1944, his works were registered by the art historian Sigurd Willoch and the painter Jean Heiberg in conjunction with winding up the estate. They concluded that the graphic work amounted to 15,391 impressions registered under 714 catalogue numbers.[43] In the autumn of 1945, around 300 of the paintings were exhibited in the National Gallery, while some 250 woodcuts were put on display the following spring. Opening on 19 March, the latter exhibition was too big for the ground-floor gallery usually used by the Department of Prints and Drawings and had to be mounted on the museum's upper floor instead. It was organised by Eli Ingebretsen Greve, who had shown particular interest in Munch's graphics and especially his woodcuts. For the exhibition, she prepared a detailed catalogue with a view to publication, a plan that unfortunately never came to fruition.[44] Where there were variants of the catalogue's 140 items, several impressions were shown, some of them trial proofs and some hand-coloured. All were described in detail. The exhibition also included a number of woodblocks. It was impressively prepared, and Greve was widely praised for her work. The newspaper reviews give a vivid impression of just how overwhelming the presentation of Munch's woodcuts was. Although many of the works were known from earlier exhibitions, a lot of the material had never been shown before and was greeted with enthusiasm. Of particular interest was the "discovery" of Munch's jigsaw-puzzle method. Pola Gauguin and Håkon Stenstadvold, both of whom were familiar with the woodcut medium, emphasised the innovative aspect of this technique.[45] All in all, a broad audience was fascinated by the insights into Munch's way of working that the plates and print variations provided. As Stenstadvold wrote, the exhibition placed the viewer "close up to genius and hence also in more intimate contact with the artist and his working methods."

Notes

1 Gerd Woll, *Edvard Munch. The Complete Graphic Works* (London: Philip Wilson Publishers 2001)/*Edvard Munch. Samlede grafiske verk* (revised edition) (Oslo: Orfeus, 2012), referred to here as Woll G and Woll 2001/2012.

2 For a brief description of intaglio, lithographic and woodcut techniques, see p. 189-190.

3 Sidsel Helliesen, *Norsk grafikk gjennom 100 år* (Oslo: Aschehoug, 2000).

4 Although he helped to initiate Norske Grafikere (the Association of Norwegian Printmakers), which held its constitutive assembly on 15 November 1919, and contributed four works to the association's inaugural exhibition in 1922 (Woll 2012, 23), Munch was not active in this scene.

5 See note 1.

6 Cat. 62, *The Girl at the Window* (Woll G 5); cat. 104, *The Urn* (Woll G 67); cat. 170, *Amanda* (Woll G 249); cat. 183, *The Storm* (Woll G 371).

7 See overview p. 190-191.

8 A few years after the Christiania Collection of Prints and Drawings was established in 1877, a portion of the early acquisitions was inventoried. It would appear that subsequent cataloguing was carried out retrospectively in batches, with quantities of material remaining unregistered. The inventorying made use of two parallel numbering systems, one of which (the A series) comprises works acquired by the Department of Prints and Drawings, while the other (the B series) consisted of works acquired by the National Gallery (see note 9). It wasn't until the late 1950s that the department adopted a single consistent numbering system. In 1969-70 the entire collection (with minor exceptions) was reviewed and the inventory completed. The parallel A and B series were continued. The extent to which acquisition details were recorded varies; tracing information within the archives was not a priority at the time of the extensive retrospective inventorying.

9 This is partly due to the complex history of the Christiania Collection of Prints and Drawings. The collection was established in 1877 on a private initiative and as an independent institution. In 1883, the collection was deposited at the National Gallery (which took over its administration), before it was ultimately incorporated into the National Gallery as a separate department in 1908. For its part, the National Gallery traces its origins to a government resolution of 28 December 1836, approving the establishment of a national art collection. In 1881, the museum moved into the new museum building at Tullinløkka. In 1883, the Collection of Prints and Drawings was accommodated in rooms on the top floor. In 1903, the status of the Sculpture

Museum, which was also housed in the same building, changed from municipal to state ownership and the building's three collections were brought together under the common name of Statens Kunstmuseum (the State Art Museum). The Department of Prints and Drawings continued to be treated as a separate entity within the National Gallery until 2003, when the National Gallery was incorporated into the National Museum of Art, Architecture and Design.

10 *August Strindberg* NG.K&H.A.09239, cat. 101; *August Strindberg* NG.K&H.A.09238, cat. 102; *Hans Jæger I* NG.K&H.A.09240, cat. 115. These entries are in the supplementary record "A II", which was compiled retrospectively. The first part, which includes the Munch prints, was compiled around 1900.

11 Eli Ingebretsen (1896-1949; from 1939, Eli Greve) became assistant to Fredrik Gundersen in 1919. After Gundersen's death in 1927, she was appointed curator. During the Nazi occupation, she resigned her position in 1942. She returned in 1945 and, with some interruptions due to illness, continued in the post until 1949.

12 In supplementary record "B I", which was partly compiled retrospectively, first by Gundersen, then by Eli Ingebretsen Greve. In her Munch entries in "B I", several works from one and the same acquisition are entered under a single inventory number. The works were distinguished during the audit of 1969-70 and given new inventory numbers. The Munch entries in "B I" are: NG.K&H.B.00357: cat. 197; NG.K&H.B.00358: cat. 171; NG.K&H.B.00577: cat. 195; NG.K&H.B.00611: cat. 206, 208, 209, 217, 218; NG.K&H.B.00612: cat. 210, 211, 212, 213, 215; NG.K&H.B.00613: cat. 66, 91, 122, 130, 131, 137, 139, 140, 141, 143, 165, 168, 180, 182, 184, 185, 189, 196, 200, 203, 204, 205, 207, 214, 219, 220; NG.K&H.B.00614: cat. 149; NG.K&H.B.00615: cat. 119; NG.K&H.B.00616: cat. 88; NG.K&H.B.00816: cat. 167. Most of the Munch entries in "B I" contain details about provenance, although unfortunately it has not been possible to verify all of them.

13 P. 35-40. "Norsk grafikk I" (Norwegian Graphics I) is one of several supplementary records that list parts of the collection sorted by artist. These were compiled in parallel with, and apparently in some cases instead of, inventories. The handwriting suggests that the registering of Munch's prints was interrupted after entry no. 105; the latest piece of information is from 1947, which gives a *terminus post quem* for the latter series of entries (cat. 106-160). A *terminus ante quem* is provided by the year of Ingebretsen Greve's death in 1949.

14 Gustav Schiefler, *Verzeichnis des graphischen Werks Edvard Munchs bis 1906* (Berlin: Bruno Cassirer, 1907), and *Edvard Munch. Das graphische Werk 1906-1926*, (Berlin: Euphorion Verlag, 1928). (Facsimile edition, Oslo: Cappelen, 1974), here referred to as Sch and Schiefler 1907, 1928.

15 It has not been possible to confirm all the details in Eli Ingebretsen Greve's entries and in the notes in the supplementary records compiled by other curators at the Department of Prints and Drawings.

16 Entered in a supplementary record established as a continuation of the A series inventory.

17 Liv I. Jones, *Norsk grafikk til 1970* (Oslo: Nasjonalgalleriet, 1971).

18 In a letter to Karen Bjølstad, 14.11.1894, he writes that he has "started etching in order perhaps to release a small collection later," (MM N 807, Munchmuseet).

19 Further, the impression of *The Girl at the Window* is lost (cat. 62), while the museum has two impressions of *Bathing Women* (cat. 72 and 73). There are also two impressions of both *Madonna* and *Vampire* (cat. 86 and 87, and cat. 88 and 89, respectively), one with, the other without, colour plate. See below for details.

20 Meier-Graefe's article is reproduced in German and Norwegian translation in Gerd Woll, *Edvard Munch 1895 - første år som grafiker* (Oslo: Munchmuseet, 1995), n.p. [27-40].

21 One impression is lost, see cat. 62.

22 See Woll 2012, 19, and note 60, 27.

23 See Gerd Woll in *Edvard Munch 1895 - første år som grafiker* (Oslo: Munchmuseet, 1995), 10 ff.

24 In the case of such prints, the aim of reproducing a picture that exists in some other medium significantly influences the idiom and choice of graphic technique. In time, various techniques were developed and used for such reproduction purposes, while at the same time most of those same techniques were soon explored as potential media by artists. In the late 19th century, reproduction prints were usurped by photo-mechanical reproduction techniques.

25 The publisher and gallerist Ambroise Vollard was a central figure in the art boom that Paris experienced around the turn of the century. The National Museum has a copy of *Les peintres graveurs* in its collection (NG.K&H.A.16518-A.16528). Unfortunately, Munch's lithograph is missing. The museum also owns a copy of the portfolio that Vollard published the following year, *L'Album d'estampes originales de la Galerie Vollard*, which contained 32 prints (NG.K&H.A.16539 - A.16569, A.16762 [two impressions of Georges Auriol's *Tête d'enfant*, whereas Pierre Bonnard's

Le Canotage is lacking]). The portfolio's provenance is unknown, and it is also unknown whether the prints that are now missing were present when the portfolio was acquired.

26 A series of ten, plus title page. The National Gallery acquired *Elles* in 1947 (NG.K&H.A.16751-16762), together with six other lithographs by Toulouse-Lautrec (NG.K&H.A.16763-16767), from Munch's estate.

27 In addition to Clot, Lemercier also printed Munch's lithographs. This is confirmed by William Molard, who in a letter dated 23.02.1899 (MM K 1900) assured Munch that Lemercier had received 30 francs from him and that the stones were in good condition. On 20.01.1904 (MM K 431) Ludvig Karsten could also reassure Munch that the stones were still "in safe keeping" at Lemercier's, despite the fact that the workshop had changed owner. Lithographic stones usually remained the property of the printer, and receipts from Clot dated 30.08.1897 (MM K 4169) and 01.03.1898 (MM K 4170) attest that he had received 25 francs from Munch for the use of lithographic stones. With regard to the four lithographs on zinc plate that Munch made in 1897, Gustav Schiefler remarks that they were printed at Lemercier's. Regarding the first woodcuts from 1896-97, Schiefler notes that some were hand-printed by the artist and some printed in Paris by Clot or Lemercier, while in most cases Lemercier is specified as the professional printer. This is confirmed by several letters from Tulla Larsen, who was asked to arrange the printing of both woodcuts and lithographs at Lemercier's on Munch's behalf in the summer of 1899. However, where the printing of intaglios is concerned, Lemercier's role is less clear. Lemercier & Cie. was essentially a printing company for lithographs, yet Schiefler states that several of the intaglio works from 1896-97 were printed there. This would appear to be confirmed by a letter that came to light in 1983 in the archives of Atelier Leblanc, a successor to Atelier Salmon, owned by Alfred Porcabeuf, which makes it clear that the majority of the intaglio works must have been printed there. (This note was provided by Gerd Woll.)

28 *Death in the Sickroom* can be dated to the spring of 1896 as it was one of two lithographs produced in Paris that were shown in an exhibition at Siegfried Bing in May 1896. Munch took part with paintings and prints. Woll 1996, 11.

29 At the same time, he showed hand-coloured impressions in exhibitions (including at Bing's in May 1896), indicating that he regarded these as valid works, and he continued to hand-colour prints throughout his active life.

30 Completed in June 1896, Woll 1996, 11-12. *The Urn* (cat. 103) and *Jealousy I* (cat. 104) are printed from the other side of the stone (MM P 156).

31 The fact that *The Sick Child I* was not included in the exhibition at Bing in May 1896 indicates that this work was probably completed later (Woll 1996, 14). For the different versions of *The Sick Child I*, Munch probably prepared a total of six stones (a key-stone, see next note, and five colour stones, of which up to five would have been used for one impression). The limestone blocks used for lithography were usually the property of the printer and were generally repolished after printing ready for reuse. This is what happened with the stones for *The Sick Child I*. In the case of other stones Munch had used at Clot's workshop, he paid rent for them after having returned home in May 1897. It would appear that he later bought them and had them sent to Lemercier. In 1904, the stones in Lemercier's keeping were sent to Lassally in Berlin, and in 1914 Munch had them shipped to Norway, together with a number of impressions on transfer paper (see note 33), which would allow the motif to be transferred to new stones and printed in new editions. Woll 2012, 15; Woll G 72; Woll 2008 B, 7.

32 In those days it was not yet common to number the individual impressions of an edition. Neither would it have been entirely practical given Munch's practice of pulling varying numbers of new impressions at different times.

33 The impressions of the key-stone, i.e. all the monochrome impressions of *The Sick Child I*, are transfer lithographs. A transfer lithograph is made by painting or drawing the motif with a grease-based medium on a sheet of paper and transferring it to the stone (by pressing or rubbing against the stone surface). A specially prepared paper is often used for this purpose. In a note from 1922, Munch mentions that at Clot's workshop he used a paper Clot had prepared himself (see note 35).

34 Woll 2012, 12.

35 *Tidens Tegn*, 22.09.1922. In a draft response, Munch writes that at Clot's he used an excellent transfer paper prepared with albumen and that he finds "the grainy [transfer paper] thoroughly tedious - [...] I found that, despite all the protests of the printers and reprinters, [...] that in some cases it was [better] to use plain paper - preferably [...] newsprint - I found it more convenient to use. It was readily available - it produced a livelier [...] and softer print. - For uses that didn't require the finest grain - it was good -". MM.N.290, emunch.no

36 1896: Sch 62 *Angstgefühl*, Sch 80 *Männerkopf in Frauenhaar*, Sch 81 *Mondschein*, Sch 82 *Abend (Melancholi: Am Strand)*, Sch 83 *Sommernacht*; 1897: Sch 98 *Im männlichen Gehirn*, Sch 99 *Weibliche Akt*, Sch 100 *Zum Walde*, Sch 101 *Badende Frauen*, Sch 102 *Der Kuss*. In general, Schiefler grouped the works for each year according to technique, and did not attempt to order them chronologically within any one year. For the woodcuts of 1896 and 1897, Schiefler discusses the states that he was aware of as of October 1906 (when the first volume of his catalogue was completed), without further remarks on whether all the states, including where relevant the segmenting of plate(s), were produced during the year under which they were listed. The one exception is *Der Kuss*, for which he knew of a number of states involving the use of different woodblocks; here he records that the latest state (Sch 102 D) dates from 1902. See Woll G 114, 115, 124 and 102 (cat. 160).

37 To Thorvald Erichsen, undated, but can be dated to November; transcript by the Munch Museum. Woll 2012, 14.

38 Woll 2012, 19.

39 For discussions concerning contemporary sources of inspiration for Munch's woodcuts, Richard S. Field's claim about the significance of Paul Gauguin for Munch's woodcut technique, Ferdinand Willumsen's use of segmented plates, which Munch probably knew about, and the possibility of Munch knowing that Norges Geografiske Opmaaling (the Norwegian mapping authority) used a similar technique in the production of maps, see Woll 1992, 261-268. Concerning the discussion about technical methods, see Sidsel Helliesen, *Norske grafikk gjennom 100 år* (Oslo: Aschehoug, 2000), 309, note 69.

40 Woll 2012, 15.

41 Woll 2012, 19.

42 Woll 2012, 12, 21. Nielsen visited Munch, who had the necessary equipment for printing, at his home at Hvitsten, and from 1916 at Ekely. Nielsen was Danish by birth, but settled in Norway in 1903. In 1922, after many years of employment at Hagen and Halvorsen & Larssen, Nielsen set up his own printing company, Litografia. Apparently, for a while, Munch's lithographs were printed in the National Gallery.

43 The number was adjusted later, Woll 2012, 8, note 2.

44 *Edvard Munchs tresnitt* (Oslo: Nasjonalgalleriet, 1946). Eli Ingebretsen Greve's book *Edvard Munch. Liv og verk i lys av tresnittene* was published posthumously (Oslo: Cappelen, 1963). The book is illustrated throughout (selection and texts probably by Arve Moen) and includes the exhibition catalogue (161-192).

45 P. Gauguin, "Edvard Munchs tresnitt i Nasjonalgalleriet", *Verdens Gang*, 26.03.1946; H. Stenstadvold, "Munchs tresnitt i Nasjonalgalleriet", *Aftenposten*, 27.03.1946. Other reviews: "Edvard Munchs tresnitt i Nasjonalgalleriet", *Dagbladet*, 18.03.1946; "Munch saget fargeplatene", *Aftenposten*, 18.03.1946; "Edvard Munchs tresnitt i Nasjonalgalleriet", *Morgenbladet*, 19.03.1946; F.N[ielssen], "Insisterende utstilling av Edvard Munchs tresnittverk", *Dagbladet*, 22.03.1946.

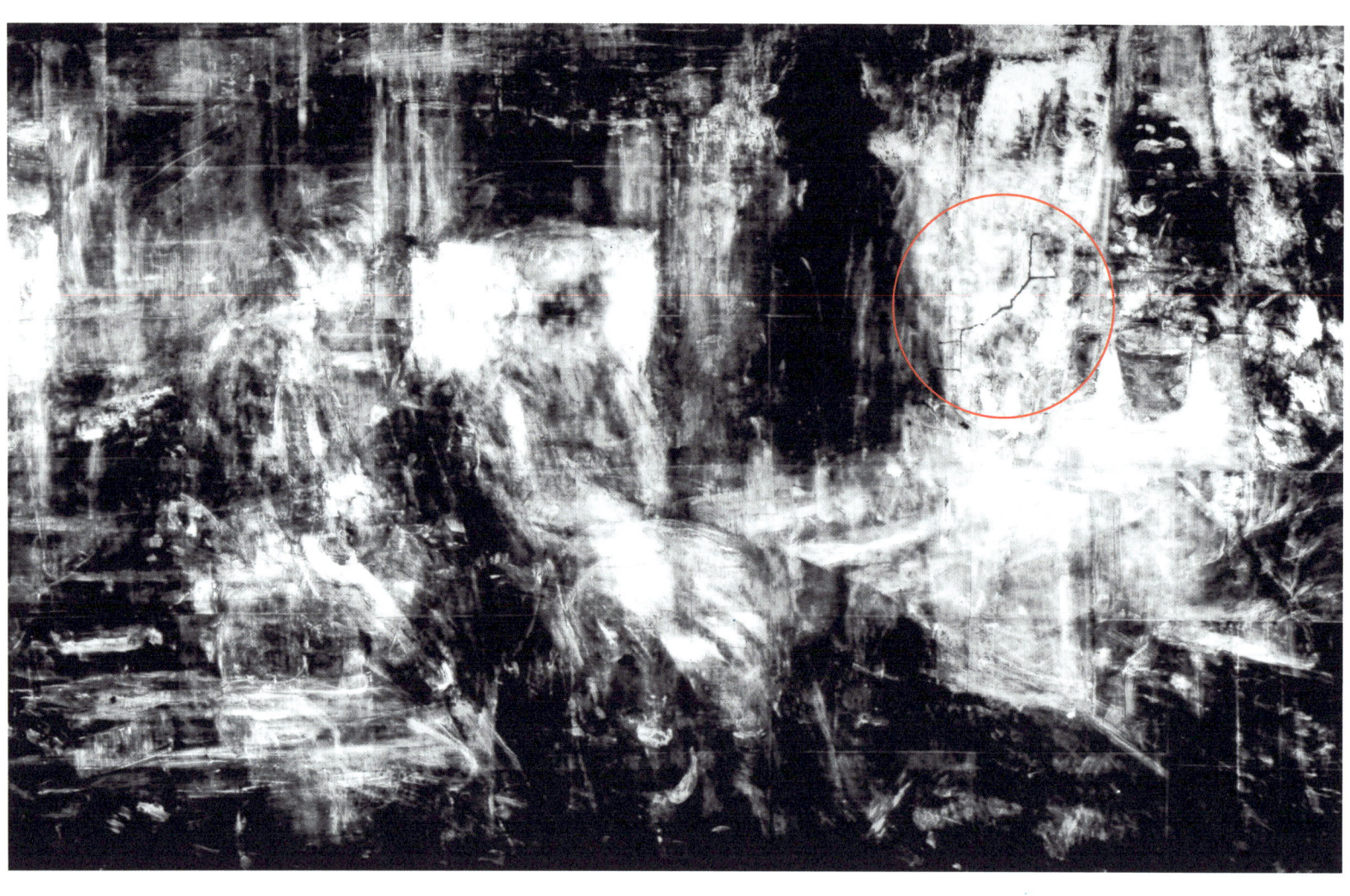

Composite X-ray of *Spring* (cat. 12) showing large tear
damage, top right, 1973.
Photo: Nasjonalmuseet / Leif Einar Plahter

The conservation history of the fifty-seven Munch paintings at the National Museum (Nasjonalmuseet) is crucial, as conservation represents one of the five defining tasks of a museum,[1] and the Munch paintings are at the core of Nasjonalmuseet's collections. The significance of tracing the conservation histories of these paintings as a group and their relation to the Munch room is that it produces a broader historic context and a better understanding of the Nasjonalmuseet's past conservation and working practices. The fifty-seven Munch paintings are arguably the best-known part of the museum's paintings collection but are also the most controversial in terms of restoration history. In addition, Munch's paintings have presented custodians and conservators with complex preservation challenges which have often resulted in disagreements with regard to best practices.[2] Due to the artist's tendency to experiment with different types of support and painting techniques (thinly diluted paint, the alternation between thick and thin layers, and different paint media), many of his paintings are fragile and in need of regular care and treatment.[3] Nasjonalmuseet has had a long history of collection care and painting conservation, which began with its founding in 1837.[4] Drawing on the statements of visitors and the press, and sources relating to acquisition policies, display legacies, restoration and conservation activities, this article seeks to chart Nasjonalmuseet's changing practices and attitudes towards the Munch collection throughout the 20th century and up to the present.

The establishment of conservation

Christen Brun (employed 1870–1905) was the first official conservator-restorer of paintings to be appointed by the museum, following a long tradition of using local artist-restorers stretching back to 1837.[5] Having received some training abroad, Christian Brun was also the first to work on Munch paintings in Norway, beginning with Nasjonalmuseet's earliest acquisition, *Night in Nice* (cat. 15), which came under his care in 1891. However, it was not until 1899 and the acquisition of Nasjonalmuseet's largest Munch painting, *Spring* (cat. 12), that any specific reference is made relating to conservation. The artist Erik Werenskiold (1855–1938) recalled the commotion that arose during a viewing of the painting in the basement of Nasjonalgalleriet prior to a meeting of the museum's acquisition committee in 1899.[6] He describes the

museum's secretary, Fredrik Gundersen, as agitated and shocked. The large unframed canvas (169 × 264 cm) was in poor condition with a large tear running diagonally across the right-hand part. Munch had temporarily repaired the damage with a strongly adhesive medical tape. But when Werenskiold found Munch happily enjoying a drink in the café at the Grand Hotel and confronted him with the situation, Munch appeared indifferent to the painting's condition. In his view, the damage was not disfiguring, so long as the main composition (the two figures) remained intact. Munch even suggested that the painting could be cropped a little. The painting was eventually purchased and repaired by Christen Brun. This repair was confirmed in 1973 using X-ray imaging, which revealed the presence of a large tear beneath later retouches in the region of the window curtain.[7] Otherwise, information about the early conservation of the Munch paintings remains sparse prior to the requirement for written documentation of restoration treatments that was introduced in 1949.

Conservation controversies

Despite the lack of conservation reports pre-1949, controversies concerning restoration practices, and the scandals and conflicts between the newly appointed director Jens Thiis (directorship 1908–1941) and succeeding conservator-restorer, Harald Brun (employed 1905–1921), give a good insight into the early conservation history of the Munch paintings.[8] The period was essentially characterised by the acquisition and display policies of the director, and restoration interventions appear to have been closely linked to the presentation and exhibition of the Munch paintings. This culminated with the creation of a permanent Munch room in 1937.[9] Frames were changed and the paint surfaces cleaned and varnished, of which the latter attracted criticism.

Varnishing

Since the 1860s, it had become established practice to periodically clean and varnish all the works in the painting collection.[10] However, when Nasjonalgalleriet's new south wing was reopened in the summer of 1909, the museum became embroiled in a restoration controversy concerning the varnishing of some of the newly acquired Munch

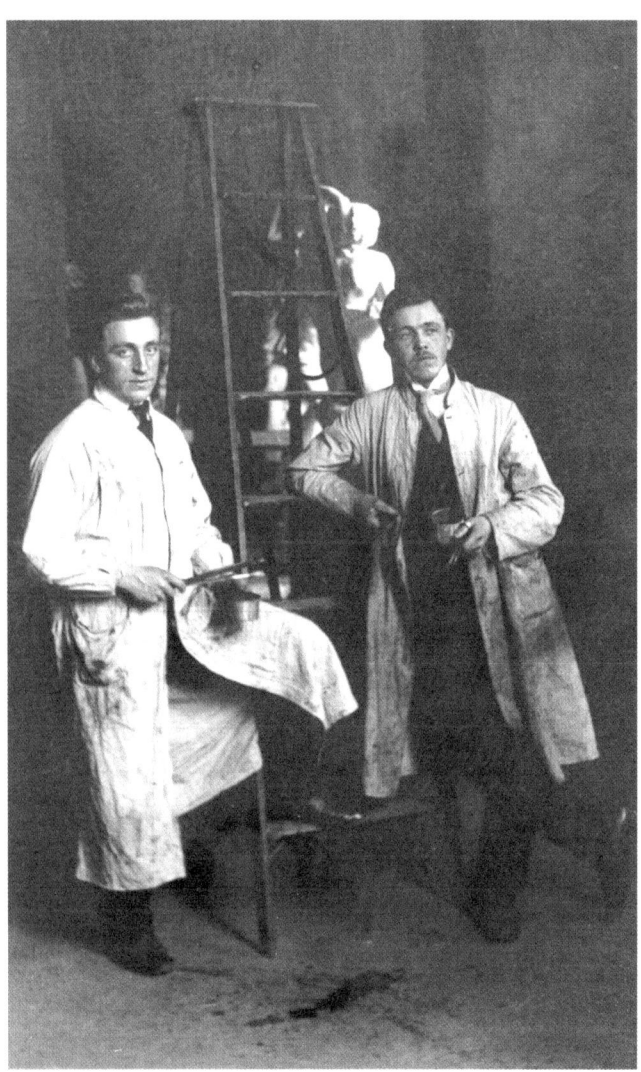

Restorer Harald Brun (right), 1913.
Photo: Nasjonalmuseet

paintings.[11] Varnishing consisted of the application of a traditional protective coat to the paint surface using mastic resin dissolved in a solvent.[12] This also had the effect of altering the gloss and saturation of the oil colours, which may have dulled over time. The two paintings *Night in Nice* and *Winter in the Woods* (cat. 37) still show evidence of a first layer of varnish applied by the museum while still framed.[13] As with the varnishing of Impressionist paintings, a series of public debates and criticisms challenged the museum's varnishing practice, especially regarding originally unvarnished works.[14] Munch's own intentions concerning surface finish were questioned. In June 1909, the art critic Jappe Nilssen accused the museum's conservator-restorer Harald Brun of "vandalism".[15] This allegation was in response to the recent varnishing of three newly acquired paintings, *Puberty* (cat. 26), *The Day After* (cat. 27), and *Ashes* (cat. 30). Some months earlier, Harald Brun had, however, written to Munch, describing the poor condition of the painting *The Day After*.[16] In fact, he had asked Munch both for permission and for advice concerning the painting's much-needed restoration prior to the re-opening of the newly decorated galleries. He described the canvas as having several holes, which had been badly filled and poorly retouched, without a proper colour match to the surrounding area. In addition, he recommended cleaning and varnishing. For his part, Munch remained silent about the proposed restorations and did not contribute to the public debate about varnishing, leaving the poor and fragile condition of his paintings as a headache for both the museum's director and Harald Brun. Paintings such as this required essential structural treatments to be displayed in the galleries. Harald Brun therefore took the decision both to reinforce the damaged canvas with a glue-paste lining[17] and to varnish its entire surface. The controversy concerning the museum's application of non-original varnishes to Munch's paintings has to do in large part with the artist's typically matt surfaces, which have an almost "fresco-like" finish. Furthermore, Munch's own attitude to varnishing remains unclear. This is due to ambiguities in the artist's correspondence and to the lack of contemporary critical sources.[18]

Authentic paint surfaces and cleaning

The painting *Self-Portrait with Cigarette* (cat. 32) is one of the few rare examples of an oil paint surface left untouched, as Munch intended it. The painting was acquired by the museum in the same year as it was painted, 1895, and according to conservation records it appears to have escaped any form of restoration.[19] In addition, recent examinations detected an original and locally applied glossy film (varnish?), which Munch has employed to saturate certain passages of colour in the composition.[20] In this light, it would appear that Harald

Brun did in fact have an understanding of and respect for Munch's paint technique. He was reluctant to carry out what he described as "the unnecessary periodic cleaning of the collection", which was strongly advocated by director Thiis.[21] A further three works were also left unvarnished during his watch, two tempera paintings, *Death in the Sickroom* (cat. 22) and *The Scream* (cat. 23), and the small oil study, *Moonlight by the Mediterranean* (cat. 18). The cleaning conflict between director Thiis and conservator Brun escalated in the years 1917-21, with both men vehemently accusing each other of ruining paintings. On one side, Brun attacked Thiis for allowing the caretaker to clean, or in his words, "destroy", the collections whilst he was on vacation. Thiis responded by accusing Brun of overcleaning and using secret restoration recipes which had removed original glazes and patinas. Although the dispute did not concern the Munch paintings, these strong differences of opinion may well be examples of early struggles just as restoration was gaining recognition as independent and respected discipline within the museum's organisation. Unfortunately for Brun, it cost him his position; he was dismissed from his duties in 1921.[22]

World War II evacuations

Jens Thiis quickly replaced Brun with the conservator-restorer Ole Dørje Haug (employed 1921-1952), who appeared to have had closer links to Munch. In 1916, Dørje Haug had assisted Munch with the installation of his monumental paintings for Oslo University's Aula assembly hall.[23] Dørje Haug's experience and exposure to Munch's experimental and challenging techniques possibly helped to foster a better relationship with the director. With the outbreak of World War II, Dørje Haug was given responsibility for the evacuation of all the museum's paintings to safety by road and rail. In 1938 the museum owned forty-three Munch paintings and the collection faced an uncertain future. Both war damage and destruction due to their categorisation by the Nazis as degenerate art were serious threats. The paintings were unframed and packed into thirty wooden crates, some mixed with other paintings according to their size, and sent to the silver mines at Kongsberg for storage.[24]

Post-war restorations

During the two decades after Munch's death (1944) and the end of World War II, Munch paintings in Norway were subjected to unprecedented restoration measures.[25] At Nasjonalgalleriet, the Munch collection underwent fairly extensive and structural treatments such as the consolidation of unstable paint layers by means of lining. Conservation treatment reports document five wax-linings, six

glue-paste linings, and one marouflage. In addition, 40% of the Munch paintings were cleaned and re-varnished. It is probable that these measures were prompted by a combination of damage incurred during their evacuation and subsequent storage. Although carefully packed and crated, the paintings were not as protected from the harsh Scandinavian winter and climatic fluctuations as they would have been if today's standards for climatically insulated crates had applied. The paintings also needed to be conserved for exhibitions, loans, and the much-awaited re-hanging of the Munch room. Despite the 1909 criticisms, varnishing appears to have continued as a preventive measure at the museum. Dørje Haug is documented as having restored and varnished at least nine of the Munch paintings, post war, while his apprentice, Jan Thurmann-Moe (1927-2018), varnished five.

By 1965, the conservation department had examined and documented most of the Munch paintings in the collection under the new leadership of conservator-restorer Leif Plahter (employed 1956-1999). During the 1970s and '80s, some structural work was also undertaken on the Mustad family's final donation of ten paintings. Criticisms of Nasjonalmuseet's varnishing practice continued throughout the 20th century, with the most ardent attacks stemming from the head of the newly established conservation department at the Munch Museum, Jan Thurmann-Moe (employed 1954-1997).[26] The varnish debate between Nasjonalgalleriet and the Munch Museum became entrenched during a period when the international conservation community was expressing concern about the impact of "overzealous restorations" and cleaning.[27] It was whipped up still further by Thurmann-Moe's promotion of the much debated idea that Munch had applied a "kill-or-cure" (hestekuren) technique.[28] The term was initially coined by the Norwegian art collector - and Munch's patron, friend, and biographer - Rolf Stenersen, who suggested that Munch deliberately exposed his paintings to the elements as part of his technique. However, recent research has provided a more nuanced interpretation of the so called "kill-or-cure" technique.[29] The last painting to be controversially varnished by Nasjonalgalleriet was *Self-Portrait with Spanish Flu* (cat. 55), in 1993.

The Scream theft

After the 1970s, the iconic status of Nasjonalmuseet's version of *The Scream* grew steadily. Between 1954 and 1993, the painting travelled to more than forty exhibition venues worldwide.[30] This represents approximately 124,000 km of travel (as the crow flies) in the space of thirty-nine years. But all that changed on 12 February 1994. While the nation's eyes were focused on the opening of the Winter Olympics in Lillehammer, the painting was stolen by

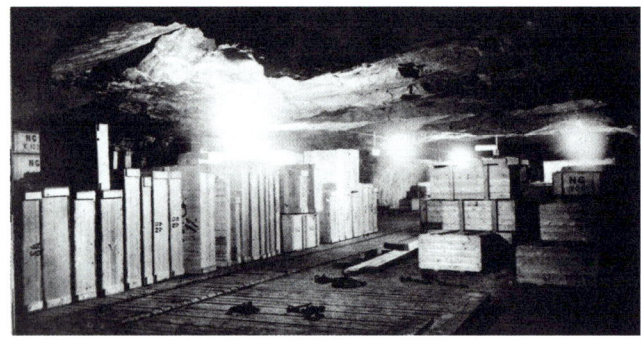

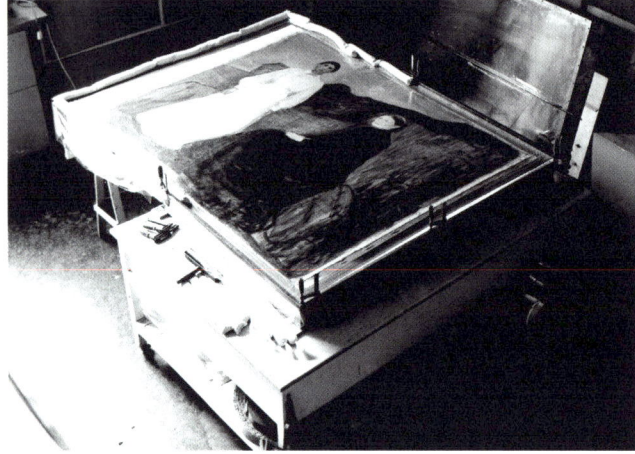

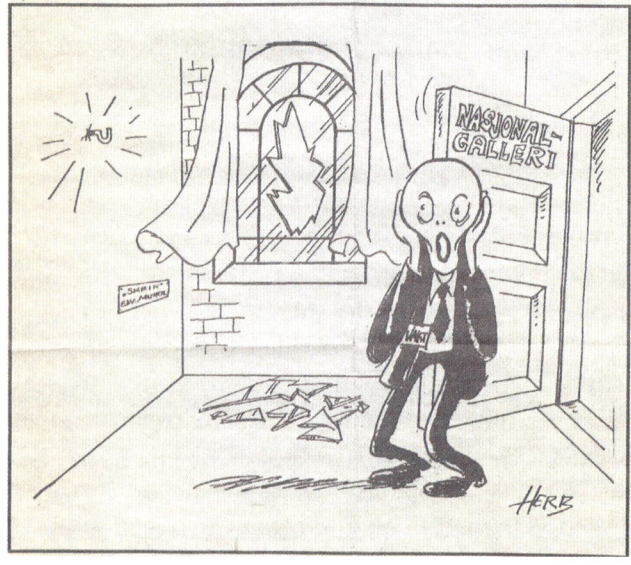

Crates evacuated during WWII in storage in the Kongsberg mines, 1943-46. Crate 11 contained *Ashes* (cat. 30),
Aase Nørregaard (cat. 38), and *Winter on the Fjord*
(cat. 50). Crate 94 contained *The Frenchman* (cat. 46).
Crate 95 contained *The Dance of Life* (cat. 40) (*Bilder*, no.
4, 1946, p. 20).

Lining of *Mother and Daughter* (cat. 35), 1966.
Photo: Nasjonalmuseet

Caricature of the *Scream* theft (Herb's Corner,
Dagningen, Lillehammer, 14 February 1994).

thieves who left a note that read "thanks for the poor security".[31] The painting was recovered within three months
in an undercover sting operation with help from Scotland
Yard and the head of conservation, Leif Plahter. Given
that the thin, cardboard support was brutally wrenched
from its frame and that the respective paint technique is
primarily matt tempera, it is remarkable that this most
fragile of the Munch paintings was returned unscathed.
In consequence, the year 1994 marked the end of travels
for *The Scream* and henceforth the painting remained in
the Nasjonalgalleriet building until its closure in 2019.[32]
Interestingly, almost half a year prior to the theft of *The
Scream*, a small portrait depicting Munch's model, *Betzy
Nilsen* (cat. 10) had also been stolen. Unfortunately, this
painting is still missing.

Framing

The framing of Nasjonalmuseet's Munch collection essentially stems from Jens Thiis' directorship. Munch's simple,
thin wooden frames were soon replaced with new, gilded,
ornate 19th century profiles with metal labels. These gave
the paintings a grander museum status and enabled Thiis
to integrate them according to the display traditions of
the national collection. In 1909, a total of 425 NOK was
spent on new frames, including for the five Munch paintings recently purchased from the Blomqvist exhibition.[33]
Throughout the second half of the 20th century, as
Munch's artistic status grew internationally, the museum
approved a steadily increasing number of requests for
exhibition loans. Accordingly, in the years just before
and after the millennium, conservation attitudes shifted
towards more preventive measures to facilitate this loan
activity and to improve security. Frame restoration and
research into original frames now play a significant role in
the conservation approach and have been accompanied
by the introduction of protective glazing and conservation
framing. Despite the museum's early tradition of changing
frames, the painting *Study of a Head* (cat. 4) is unique in
still having its original wooden frame, thus illustrating the
type of frame preferred by Munch.[34]

Scientific investigations

Nasjonalmuseet's conservation department, which has
also been central to the establishment of a conservation
profession in Norway, was the first institution worldwide
to undertake a series of in-depth examinations of Munch
paintings.[35] This was facilitated by access to a new and
better equipped conservation studio and a research initiative led by conservator-restorer Leif Plahter and conservation scientist Unn Plahter during the 1970s. The two
specialists used various imaging techniques (ultraviolet

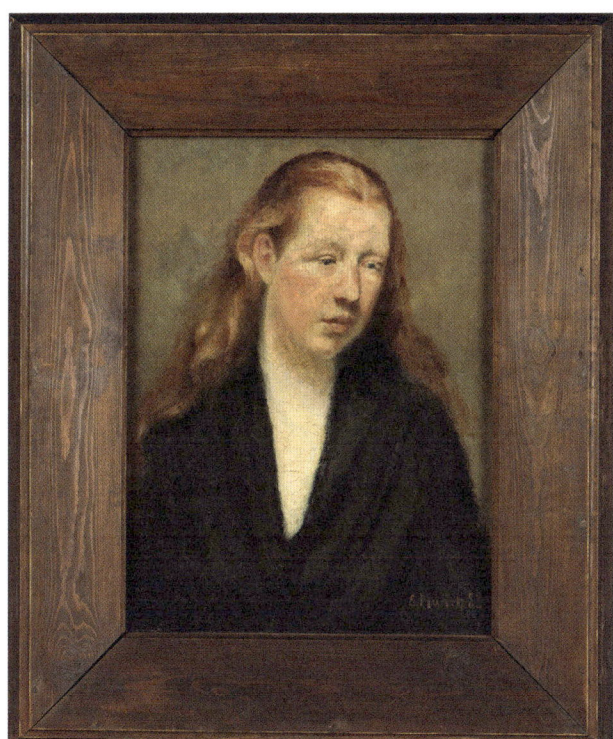

light, infrared reflectography (IRR) and X-radiography) to help them interpret Munch's compositional process in the case of a handful of the paintings: *Death in the Sickroom*, *Spring*, *The Sick Child* (cat. 8), *Betzy Nilsen*, and *Hans Jæger* (cat. 13).[36] These examinations were supplemented by the introduction of scientific analysis of Munch's painting materials. In 1974, Unn Plahter's pioneering work on the chemical identification of different types of cadmium yellow pigments helped to establish the difference in dates between the Nasjonalmuseet and the Munch Museum versions of the *The Scream*.[37] This research paved the way for future collaborative and scientific studies conducted by the conservator-restorer Trond Aslaksby (employed 1999-2014) on *The Sick Child* and *The Scream*.[38] Since 1974, *The Scream* has been the subject of continued extensive investigations and is currently the most documented painting in Nasjonalmuseet's painting collection. In 2016 it was also the first painting in Norway to be fully scanned using the novel in-situ Macro X-Ray Fluorescence technique[39] for the identification and mapping of pigments. Both Munch's initial sketch on the reverse and the front, were analysed in depth. Microscopic samples were also extracted from the white deposits, which were previously thought to be bird excrement, a consequence of Munch's "kill-or-cure" technique. However, analysis of the samples has since found them to consist solely of beeswax.[40] The white spots are in fact accidental splatters of molten wax from a candle in Munch's studio rather than the result of exposure to nature. Nevertheless, these obscuring surface deposits may well reflect Munch's relative indifference to the condition of his paint surfaces, in contrast to his aesthetic concern for the final motif, as witnessed by the example of the painting *Spring*.

Munch painted five versions of *Madonna* between 1894 and 1897, and, like *The Scream*, their chronology has been difficult to ascertain. However, dark underdrawings from the IRR examination revealed evidence of pentimenti in the form of alterations to the subject's right arm. This helps to confirm earlier theories that place Nasjonalmuseet's version as the first (cat. 29).[41] Recent IRR has also detected Munch's use of preliminary sketching prior to the final painted juxtaposition of the figures in *The Dance of Life* (cat. 40).[42]

Future perspectives

Since 1909, the Munch collection has acted as an important benchmark when tracing the history and development of conservation at Nasjonalmuseet and the changing attitudes and practices of its conservation department. Given its national and international art historical significance, it will continue to play this role in the context of new research initiatives and multidisciplinary collaborative projects. Today, the paintings have been relocated

Original wooden frame, *Study of a Head* (cat. 4).
Photo: Nasjonalmuseet/Børre Høstland, 2018

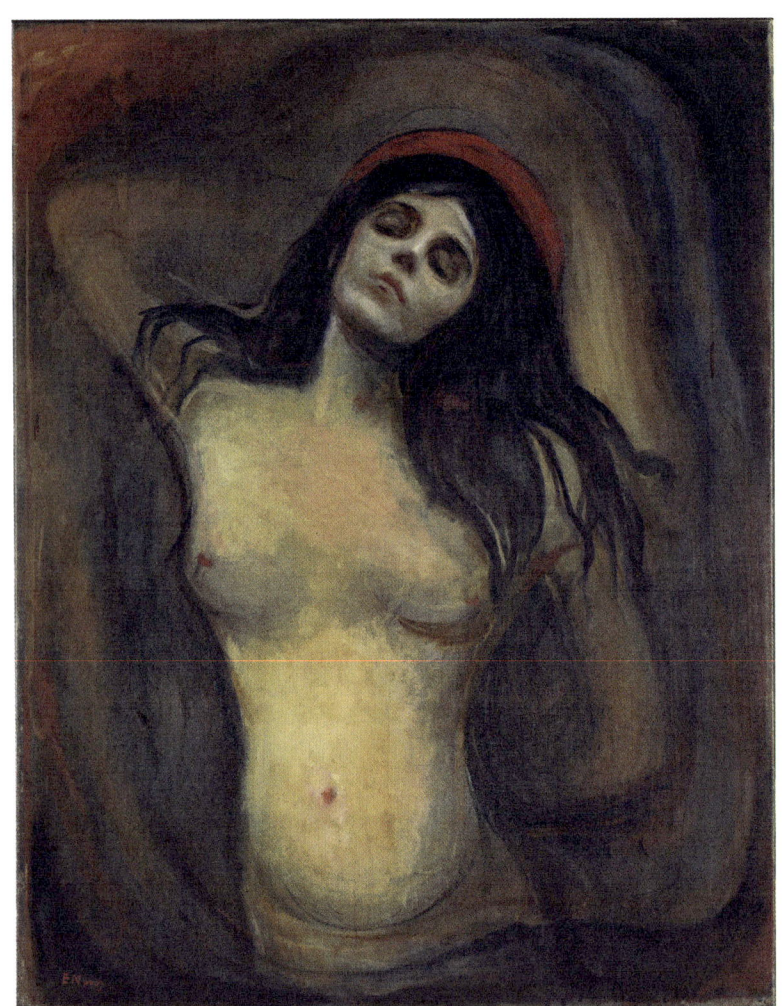

a

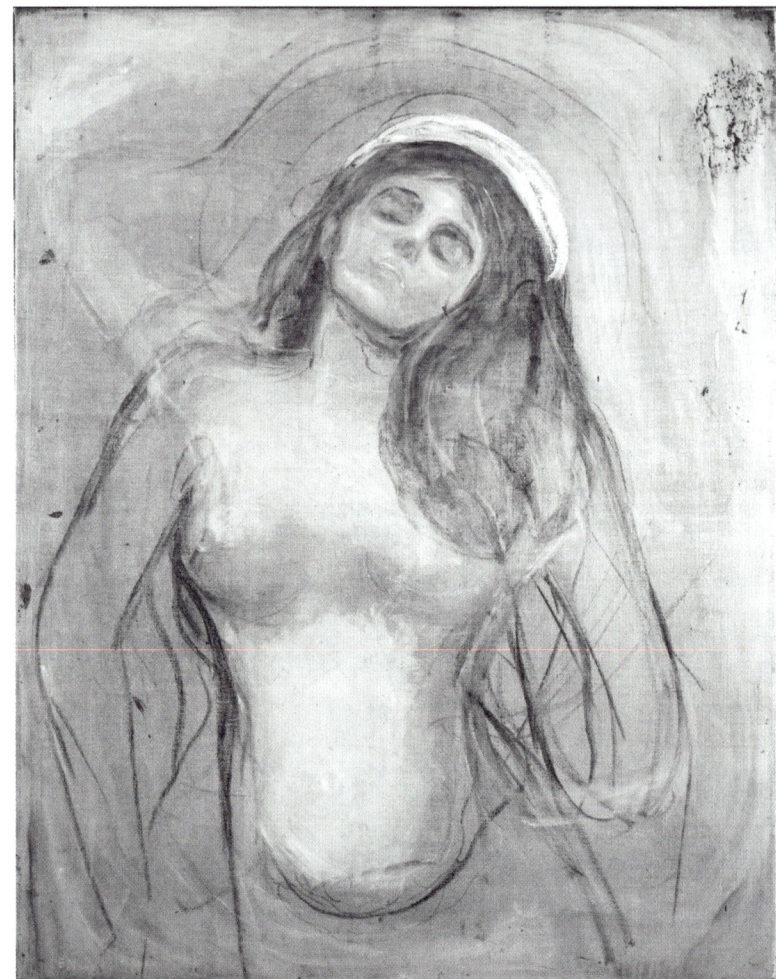

b

Madonna (cat. 29) (a) normal light, (b) IRR photograph
showing artist's underdrawings/contours.
Photo: Nasjonalmuseet/Børre Høstland, 2020

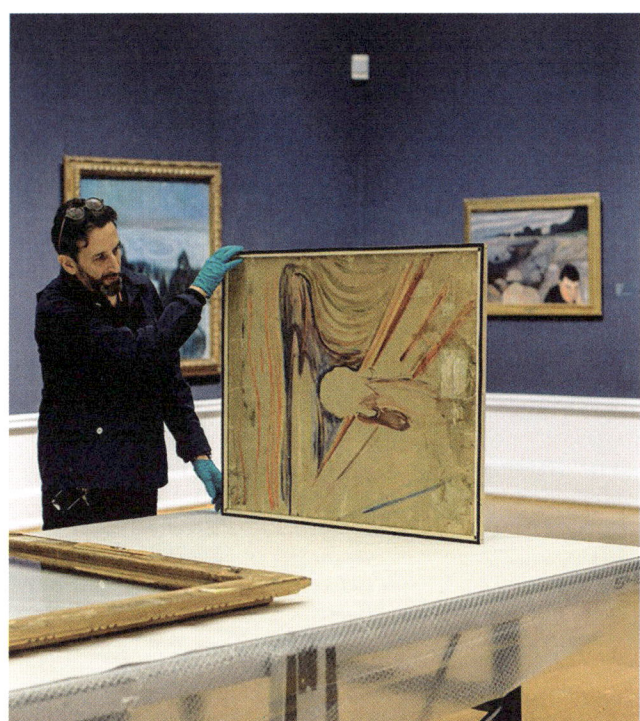

to a recreation of the original (Nasjonalgalleriet) Munch room in the new Nasjonalmuseet building. The conservation department's prime concern is the preservation and accessibility of the collection for both the public and for research. Given the collection's specific display legacy, the former Munch room, the goal is to address the paintings as a specific group in relation to conservation issues. The application of new technology that uses non-invasive methods of investigation will be favoured to analyse the various painting materials and degradation phenomena. Ongoing international and collaborative research projects are currently investigating the pigments and varnish layers. These will contribute both to long-term care strategies and to the increasing wealth of knowledge and scholarship concerning Munch's oeuvre.

The Scream (cat. 23), reverse side.
Unframing and inspection.
Photo: Nasjonalmuseet/Børre Høstland, 2020

Notes

1 According to ICOM Statutes (Vienna, 24 August 2007): "A museum is a non-profit, permanent institution in the service of society and its development, open to the public, which acquires, conserves, researches, communicates and exhibits the tangible and intangible heritage of humanity and its environment for the purpose of education, study and enjoyment." https://icom.museum/en/resources/standards-guidelines/museum-definition/
2 Mille Stein, "Edvard Munch og «hestekuren». En revurdering", *Kunst og Kultur* 100, nos. 01-02 (2017 A), 49-76.
3 For an overview of Munch's painting techniques see Biljana Topalova-Casadiego, "Tekniske aspekter ved Edvard Munchs malerier", in Gerd Woll, *Edvard Munch. Samlede malerier. Catalogue raisonné*, Vol. 2, 1898-1908 (Oslo: Cappelen Damm, 2008 B), 425-58; Brian Singer et al., "Investigation of Materials Used by Edvard Munch", *Studies in Conservation* 55, no. 4 (2013), 274-292; Tine Frøysaker (ed.), *Public Paintings by Edvard Munch and His Contemporaries: Change and Conservation Challenges* (London: Archetype, 2015); Jacapo La Nasa et al., "An Integrated Analytical Study of Crayons from the Original Art Materials Collection of the Munch Museum in Oslo", *Sci Rep* 11, 7152 (2021).
4 In 1837, the former National Gallery (Nasjonalgalleriet) collections were known as the National Museum of Art and subsequently renamed for a short period as the State Museum of Art. In 2003, Nasjonalgalleriet's collections became part of the new National Museum (Nasjonalmuseet), a fusion of four museum institutions. Both terms are used throughout the text depending on the historic context. See also Sigurd Willoch, *Nasjonalgalleriet gjennom hundre år* (Oslo: Gyldendal, 1937).
5 From 1837 to 1870 the care of the collections was entrusted to artists who essentially practised basic restoration (see Willoch 1937). After 1870, conservator-restorers were required to have a basic level of professional training. Over the past 150 years, the qualifications expected of a conservator-restorer have risen to the level of an academic (university) training involving both theory and practice. The term "conservator-restorer" is used as a compromise throughout the text, since the same professional can be called either a "conservator" or "restorer", depending on the type of training they have undergone abroad. The umbrella definition of conservation used here is according to ICOM's terminology and encompasses preventive conservation, remedial conservation, and restoration. https://www.icom-cc.org/en/definition-of-the-profession-1984
6 Oscar Thue, "Tidligere upubliserte brev fra Erik Werenskiold", *Kunst og kultur* 72, no. 4 (1989), 232-243.

7 Leif E. Plahter, "Beneath the surface of Edvard Munch: Technical examinations of four paintings by Edvard Munch", in Erling Skaug et al. (eds.), *Conservare necesse est: Festskrift til Leif Einar Plahter på hans 70-årsdag = For Leif Einar Plahter on his 70th birthday* (Oslo, Nordisk Konservatorforbund, Den norske seksjon, IIC-Nordic Group, 1999), 111-127.
8 Johannes Rød, "Cleaning of Paintings at the National Gallery in Oslo - An Historical Overview". *Congress preprints: Surface Treatments: Cleaning, Stabilization and Coatings* (Lyngby: Nordisk konservatorforbund, 1994), 15-25; Johannes Rød, "Harald Brun; Konservator ved Nasjonalgalleriet 1905-21", *Kunst og Kultur* 76, no. 2 (1993), 89-107.
9 Willoch, *Nasjonalgalleriet gjennom hundre år*; Nils Messel, "Den Smakfuldeste Dekoratør i Norden; Jens Thiis i Nasjonalgalleriet", *Kunst og Kultur* 95, no. 4 (2012), 200-17.
10 Willoch, *Nasjonalgalleriet gjennom hundre år*.
11 Mille Stein and Johannes Rød, "A Contribution to the Varnish History of the Paintings by Edvard Munch at the National Museum and Munch Museum, Oslo", in Tine Frøysaker (ed.), *Public Paintings by Edvard Munch and His Contemporaries. Change and Conservation Challenges* (London: Archetype, 2015), 257-270.
12 A mastic-turpentine picture varnish solution is noted on page 13 of Harald Brun's handwritten studio notebook (1906-7?): Johannes Rød, forskerarkiv, NMFK/NG-0007/E/L0002, The National Museum's documentation archive.
13 Thierry Ford, Adriana Rizzo, Ella Hendriks, Tine Frøysaker, and Francesco Caruso, "A Non-Invasive Screening Study of Varnishes Applied to Three Paintings by Edvard Munch Using Portable Diffuse Reflectance Infrared Fourier Transform Spectroscopy (Drifts)", *Heritage Science* 7, art. no. 84, 13th IRUG Conference (22 October 2019); Thierry Ford, "An Integrated Conservation Approach to a Historic Collection: The Controversial Varnishing of Munch's Paintings", in *Transcending Boundaries: Integrated Approaches to Conservation* (Beijing: ICOM-CC 19th Triennial Conference Preprints, 17.-21. May 2021).
14 Anthea Callen, "The Unvarnished Truth: Mattness, 'Primitivism' and Modernity in French Painting, c.1870-1907", *Burlington Magazine* 136, no. 1100 (1994), 738-746; Stein and Rød, "A Contribution to the Varnish History".
15 Jappe Nilssen, "Hærverk", *Dagens Nyt*, 14 June 1909.
16 Harald Brun, letter to Edvard Munch, dated 16 March 1909, Johannes Rød, forskerarkiv, NMFK/NG-0007/E/L0002, The National Museum's documentation archive.

17 This involved the adhesion of an additional canvas to the reverse to give the original canvas extra structural support. A restoration technique which Brun had learnt during his apprenticeships abroad in Copenhagen and Berlin in the years 1906-07. See Rød "Harald Brun; Konservator ved Nasjonalgalleriet 1905-21", 96. The lining technique is also mentioned on p. 1-5 of Brun's handwritten studio notebook (1906-7?): Johannes Rød, forskerarkiv, NMFK/NG-0007/E/L0002, The National Museum's documentation archive.
18 See Topalova-Casadiego, "Tekniske aspekter ved Edvard Munchs malerier", and Stein and Rød, "A Contribution to the Varnish History".
19 See NMFK/NG-1000/H/Hc/L0001 (Prepared by conservator Leif Einar Plather).
20 Ford et al., "A Non-Invasive Screening Study of Varnishes Applied to Three Paintings by Edvard Munch".
21 Rød, "Harald Brun; Konservator ved Nasjonalgalleriet 1905-21".
22 Johannes Rød, "The Cleaning Controversy and the Keeping of Secrets at the National Gallery in Oslo 1917-1921" (London: James, 1996).
23 Tine Frøysaker, "Bevaring av Edvard Munchs Aula-malerier før og nå", *Kunst og kultur* 91, no. 1 (2008), 2-17.
24 The Munch paintings are documented as being evacuated in six different groups to Bagn Bygdesamling and Hadeland Folkmuseum in the period 1940-43. After that, all but two (*Spring* and *Death in the Sickroom*) were stored together in the silver mines at Kongsberg until the end of the war. NMFK/NG-1000/D/Da/L0023 (1942), NMFK/NG-1000/D/Da/L0024 (1943-44) and NMFK/NG-1000/D/Da/L0026 (1945-1946).
25 Ford, "An Integrated Conservation Approach to a Historic Collection: The Controversial Varnishing of Munch's Paintings".
26 Stein and Rød, "A Contribution to the Varnish History".
27 See John Richardson, "Crimes against the Cubists", *The New York Review of Books*, 1983, accessed 23.10.2019, https://www.nybooks.com/articles/1983/06/16/crimes-against-the-cubists/; J.R.H. Weaver, George Stout and Paul Coremans, "The Weaver report on the cleaning of pictures in the National Gallery", *Museum International*, 3(2), (1950), 113-176.
28 Jan Thurmann-Moe, Sidsel De Jong, Svein Andersen, and Ruth Waaler, *Edvard Munchs «Hestekur» : Eksperimenter med teknikk og materialer* (Oslo: Munchmuseet, 1995).
29 Stein, "Edvard Munch og «hestekuren». En revurdering".
30 Gerd Woll, *Edvard Munch. Samlede malerier. Catalogue raisonné*, Vol. 1, 1880-1897, (Oslo: Cappelen Damm, 2008 B), 316.

31 Edward Dolnick, *The Rescue Artist: A True Story of Art, Thieves, and the Hunt for a Missing Masterpiece* (New York: Harper Collins, 2006).
32 *The Scream* was moved from Nasjonalgalleriet to the new Nasjonalmuseet building on 24 August 2021.
33 See NMFK/NG-1000/D/Da/L0009 (1909-1912).
34 The original wooden frame had initially been replaced with a new gilded frame at the time of purchase. It was re-discovered in the museum stores by Thierry Ford in 2015.
35 See Erling Skaug et al. (eds.), *Conservare necesse est: Festskrift til Leif Einar Plahter på hans 70-årsdag = For Leif Einar Plahter on his 70th Birthday* (Oslo: Nordisk Konservatorforbund, Den norske seksjon, IIC-Nordic Group, 1999).
36 Unn Plahter and Leif E. Plahter, "Munch's Paintings: Scientific Research Both Recent and in Retrospect", in Tine Frøysaker (ed.), *Public Paintings by Edvard Munch and His Contemporaries. Change and Conservation Challenges* (London: Archetype, 2015), 3-35.
37 Plahter and Plahter, "Munch's Paintings: Scientific Research Both Recent and in Retrospect".
38 Øystein Ustvedt and Trond Aslaksby (eds.), *Edvard Munch: Det Syke Barn: Historien om et mesterverk = The Sick Child: The Story of a Masterpiece* (Oslo: Nasjonalmuseet, 2009); Trond Aslaksby, "Edvard Munch's painting, 'the Scream' (1893): Notes on technique, materials, and condition", in Tine Frøysaker (ed.), *Public paintings by Edvard Munch and his contemporaries. Change and conservation challenges.* (London: Archetype, 2015), 52-71.
39 The MA-XRF scanning of *The Scream* was carried out in 2016 by Professor Geert van der Snickt, AXES group, University of Antwerp. See https://www.uantwerpen.be/en/projects/the-scream-munch/
40 Samples from the white deposits were analysed at the DESY synchrotron facility in Hamburg (P06, PETRAIII) by the AXES group, University of Antwerp. See https://www.uantwerpen.be/en/projects/the-scream-munch/
41 See Reinhold Heller, *Munch: His Life and Work* (London: John Murray, 1984), 127; Woll, *Edvard Munch. Samlede malerier. Catalogue raisonné*, Vol. 1, 354; Thierry Ford, Magdalena Iwanicka, Elena Platania, Piotr Targowski and Ella Hendriks, "Munch and optical coherence tomography: unravelling historical and artist applied varnish layers in painting collections." *European Physical Journal Plus* 136, art. no. 899 (2021).
42 IRR investigations undertaken in June 2020 by Børre Høstland and Thierry Ford.

Paintings – user's guide

The catalogue of paintings records all paintings by Munch that have entered the National Museum's collection as of 2021. One painting (cat. 10) was stolen from the museum in 1993 and has not been recovered.

Dating and order

The works are ordered chronologically. Some were developed over a protracted period and are dated with a time span. In some cases, the dating is uncertain and the year is given as (prob.).

Dimensions

The dimensions of the paintings are given in centimetres, height × width.

Inscriptions

Inscriptions in Munch's hand are reproduced verbatim, together with details of where on the work the inscription is located. E.g.: Signed u.l. "E Munch 1884"

Abbreviations

prob. = probably

Signed l.r. = signed lower right (u.r. = upper right, u.l. = upper left etc.)

NG.M. = National Gallery / National Museum inventory number

NG cat. 1968-1259; 1992-2442 etc. = numbers in the National Gallery's earlier published catalogues of Norwegian paintings

Woll M = Gerd Woll's oeuvre catalogue of Munch's paintings: *Edvard Munch. Samlede malerier. Catalogue raisonné*, bind I–IV (Oslo: Cappelen Damm, 2008) / *Edvard Munch. Complete Paintings. Catalogue raisonné*, Vols. I–IV (New York: Thames & Hudson, 2009)

Woll G = Gerd Woll's oeuvre catalogue of Munch's graphic work: *Edvard Munch. Samlede grafiske verk* (Oslo: Orpheus, 2012), a revised edition of *Edvard Munch. The Complete Graphic Works* (London: Philip Wilson Publishers, 2001)

The Munch Museum's inventory numbers:

    MM.M. = paintings

    MM.G. = graphic works

    MM.T. = drawings

    MM N = correspondences

Tegneskolen = Den Kongelige Tegne- og Kunstskole (The Royal School of Design) in Christiania

Other titles

Some pictures have over the years been referred to by titles other than the present one. Previously used and alternative titles are listed. Titles in other languages are not included, except where they differ significantly from the Norwegian ones.

Provenance

Details concerning when and how the painting entered the museum's collection are given. Donations are noted with the benefactor's name. Where the work was purchased from an exhibition, the title of the exhibition or the name of the exhibiting institution is given. Where the work was purchased by a private person, the seller's name is not normally stated. Where known, past owners of the individual works are also listed.

Literature references

References to the literature include primarily publications in which the respective work is discussed, not those where the work is merely listed among others or featured as an illustration / reproduction. For some of Munch's best known paintings, which are mentioned in most of the general literature on Munch, the listed references are to be regarded as a selection.

References in the literature that continue over two or more pages are indicated by f. (following page) and ff. (following pages).

Where an author has published several texts in the same year, the surname and year are followed by A, B, C, etc. in the literature references.

Bibliography

A comprehensive bibliography of publications relevant to the entire catalogue is included in the back matter. The bibliography is ordered alphabetically by surname. It is general and includes Munch literature of broader scope than just the National Museum's collection.

The bibliography does not include MA and Majors dissertations, children's literature or highlights catalogues.

Items are listed primarily on the basis of author and article title, rather than editor and book title.

Where an author has published several texts in the same year, the surname and year are followed by A, B, C, etc. in the bibliography.

Exhibitions

The exhibition list includes only exhibitions in which the respective National Museum painting was shown.

The list is ordered chronologically in terms of the year when the exhibition opened. This also applies to touring exhibitions that were shown over a longer period (ordered by year, place, plus, where relevant, A, B, C, etc.).

Touring exhibitions that visited several venues are given single entries in which the respective destinations are collated.

Additional information

The catalogue uses continuous numbering, beginning with the paintings and followed by works on paper. These work numbers are also used in cross-references to other works by Munch in the National Museum's collection, e.g. (cat. 5). By and large, no reference is made to inventory numbers or page numbers.

From Vestre Aker, 1881

Fra Vestre Aker

Oil on double-layered cardboard
20.5 × 30.5 cm
Signed l.r. "E Munch 13/5-81"
NG.M.02442
Woll M 17
NG cat. 1968-1259; 1992-2442

Other titles: *Fra Maridalen*. **Provenance**: Inger Munch; Ragnar Moltzau (before 1951-1958); purchased from Kaare Berntsen AS with financial support from the Olaf Schou and J.H. Beers trust fund 1958. **Literature**: Lande 1992, 70; Czymmek 1998, 69. **Exhibitions**: 1951, Oslo, no. 16; 1982, Oslo A; 2008, Oslo, no. 7.

A sense of spring hangs over the landscape. The snow has melted, the ground has a blush of green, and the trees are coming into leaf. This little painting was done shortly after Munch resolved to become a painter. It was done during a study trip to the north-west outskirts of Kristiania, in the region of Vestre Aker, Nordmarka.

In the spring of 1881, Munch attended evening classes at the Royal School of Design (Tegneskolen), where he was accepted as a student the following autumn. In the spring and summer of 1881, he made several trips to the Nordmarka area, sometimes alone, sometimes with other young artists, such as Gustav Lærum, Henning Kloumann, and Jørgen Sørensen. A fair number of drawings from these excursions have survived, including several from a lengthier trip to Hakloa, which may have been the context for this work (MM.T.02869; MM.T.00093). The National Museum's collection also contains a drawing from Bygdøy from around the same time (cat. 230).

From Vestre Aker is one of the earliest paintings by Munch that we know of. The format of its dating (13/5-81) is unusual and possibly even unique in Munch's oeuvre. For most artists, it was, however, common practice to date smaller paintings executed in situ, as this one was.

In the 1880s, Kristiania's younger artists were exploring their local surroundings as a source of material more than their predecessors had done. It has not been possible to identify the location with greater precision. But the sober, lucidly depicted scene with its pale palette and precise dating indicate an interest in meticulous study of the world as perceived and naturalistic outdoor painting.

The year of the picture's creation and its connection to specific persons is recorded on the back: "Fra Vestre Aker Edv. Munch 1881 Inger Munch og Karen Biölstad" (From Vestre Aker Edv. Munch 1881 Inger Munch and Karen Bjølstad). The picture was acquired for the collection in 1958. øu

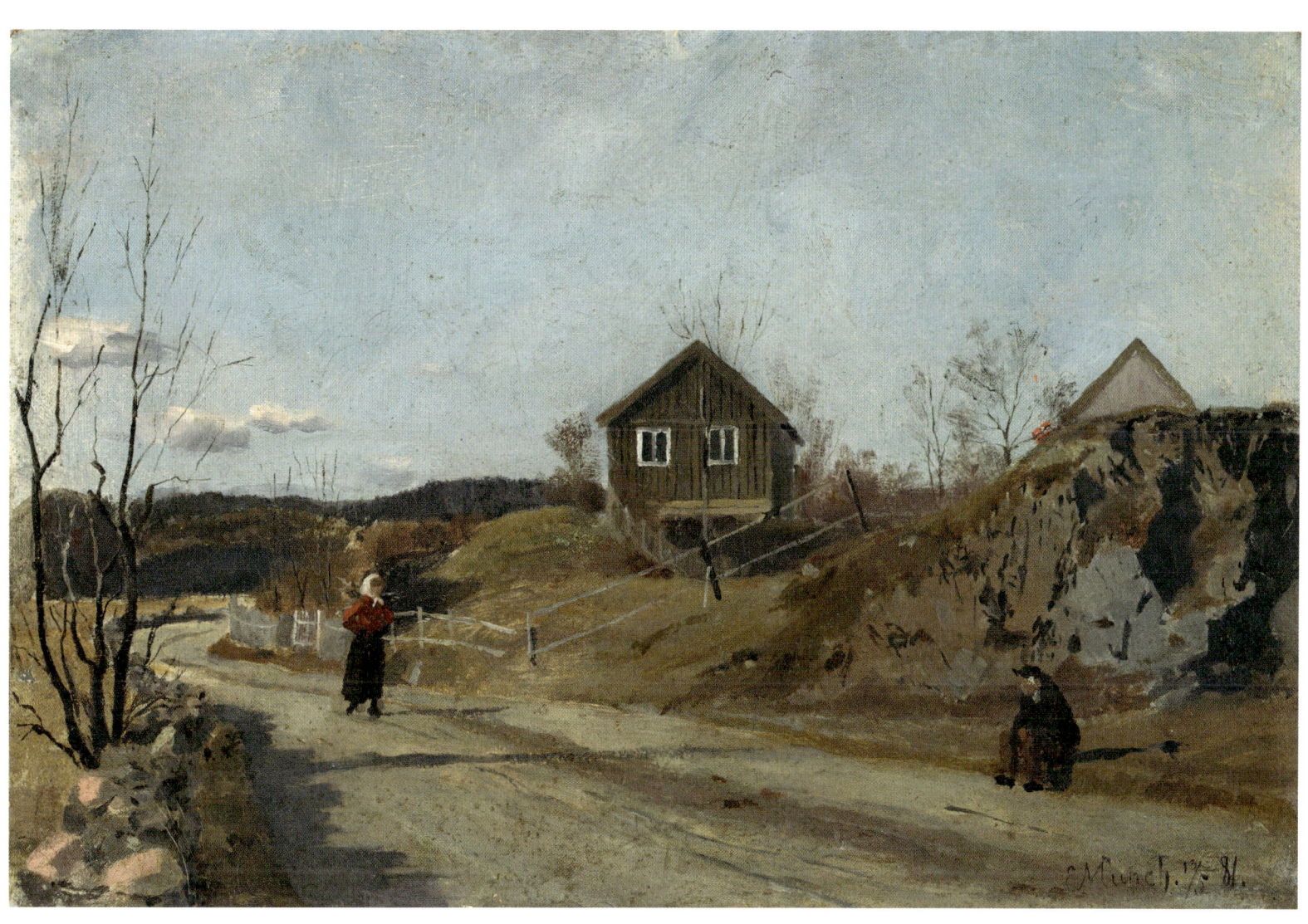

Oil on cardboard
35.5 × 28 cm
Signed u.r. "E Munch"
NG.M.01893
Woll M 75
NG cat. 1950-1044; 1968-1260; 1992-1893

Other titles: *Maleren Thorvald Torgersen.*
Provenance: W. Moebius, Trondheim
(before 1927); Harald Holst Halvorsen (–1938);
purchased from art dealer Harald Holst
Halvorsen 1938. **Literature**: Eggum 1994 A, 17f.,
38; Grøgaard 2013 A, 347f. **Exhibitions**: 1927,
Berlin, no. 2; 1927, Oslo, no. 2; 1932, Oslo B; 1982,
Oslo A; 1988, Oslo; 2008, Oslo, no. 31; 2013, Oslo,
no. 2.

Thorvald Torgersen (1862-1943) was a friend and colleague of Munch from student days. He is depicted frontally, against a neutral background, without dramatising elements, but with a sensitive expression. The painting is one of the first in a large number of small portraits and studies of heads that Munch produced as a student in the years 1882-1885, most of them of fellow students, friends and family members. The old-masterish lighting gives the face a well-articulated plasticity with highlights and areas of modelled shadows. The muted colour scheme, dominated by black, brown and grey, brings out the nuances of the skin and the features of the face. The rugged, pastose execution echoes the typical painterly realism of the period.

Torgersen and Munch belonged to a group of younger artists who banded together in the autumn of 1882 to rent a large top-lit studio in the so-called "Pultosten" (a building officially known as Centralgården) at Stortingsplass in Kristiania (Oslo). Here they took part in "correction sessions" held by Christian Krohg and others.

On the occasion of Munch's 1927 exhibition in Berlin and Oslo, the painting was dated to 1880-1881, while in the National Gallery's catalogue of works, this was later revised to "presumed 1882". Munch writes about the work in the draft for an undated letter to Jens Thiis: "The portrait of Torgersen [...] was painted before Krohg joined us" (1933, MM N 3110). This confirms the assumption that the work was executed in 1882. This dating is also accepted by Eggum (1994 A) and Woll (2008 B). The work was purchased in 1938.

As an artist, Torgersen was interested in modern *plein air* painting and realist figure drawing. He debuted at the National Annual Autumn Exhibition in 1883, the same year as Munch, with an exterior and a portrait study. Munch painted several portraits of Torgersen. We know of a similar, probably lost, study in three-quarter profile from around the same time (1882, Woll M 76). A few years later, in 1886, Munch painted a larger half-length portrait, one of several depictions of fellow artists from the 1880s (Woll M 140). ØU

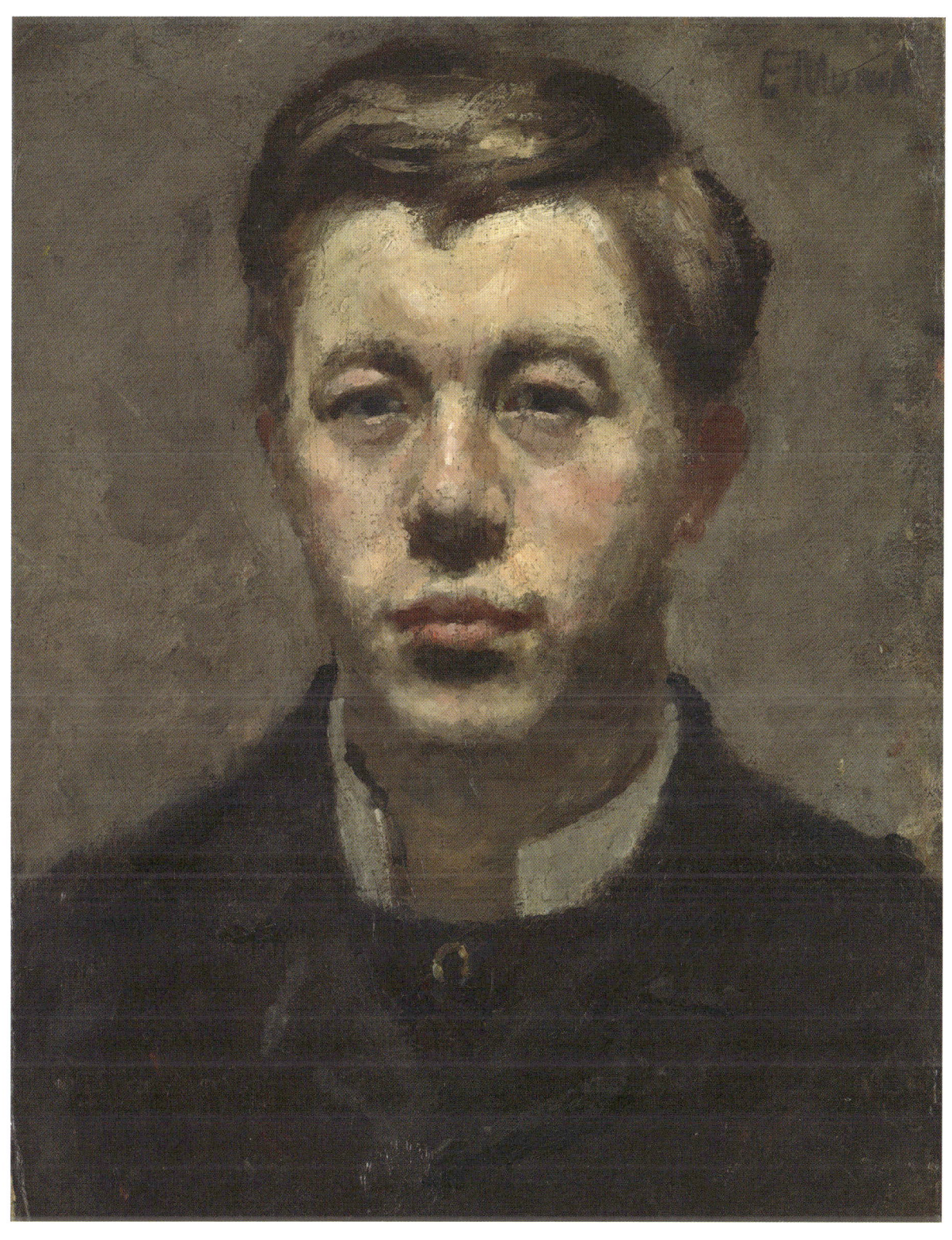

3

Andreas Reading, 1882–1883

Andreas leser

Oil on cardboard
51.5 × 35.5 cm
Signed u.r. "E. Munch"
NG.M.02810
Woll M 80
NG cat. 1992-2810

Other titles: *Kunstnerens bror i interiør*; *Broren foran bokhylden*. **Provenance**: Bequeathed by Charlotte and Christian Mustad to the National Gallery in 1959, received 1970. **Literature**: Thiis 1933, 54, 57; Romdahl 1946, 86; Fredlund (ed.) 2002, 34; Ustvedt 2009, 15; Volle 2012 A, 115. **Exhibitions**: 1982, Oslo A; 1999, Florence, no. 1; 2002, Gothenburg, no. 1; 2006, New York, no. 4; 2008, Oslo, no. 33; Oslo 2013, no. 3.

Munch's subject here is his younger brother Peter Andreas Munch (1865-1895). The small work is notable for its realism and meticulous detail. The picture gives the impression of a serious study of the observed situation, with particular attention paid to subtleties of colour. This is evident in the individual articulation of the books on the shelves and in other details, such as the highlights on the sitter's shoes and the legs of the chair. Having previously concentrated on landscape studies from the area around Kristiania, Munch has now turned his attention to interior scenes. Common to both categories is his use of locations and people he knew well.

From Munch's younger years, we know of a number of studies and smaller paintings set in the family home that variously feature his father, Aunt Karen, and siblings as models. Figures absorbed in reading are central to many of these works, and prominent among his sitters is the artist's two-year younger brother, who is shown either posing for the portrait or immersed in a book, often close to a window (Woll M 78; Woll M 79; Woll M 95; Woll M 96; Woll M 127; Woll M 134). *Andreas Reading* is one of Munch's early depictions of a contemplative figure, a popular theme of the period. The picture has much in common with, for example, Harriet Backer's interiors with women engaged in various pursuits.

Jens Thiis was the first to draw attention to Munch's early pictures. He accorded them a prominent place in the National Gallery's exhibition of 1927. "One should certainly not overlook the work Munch produced in his youth, 'in the bosom of the family'," wrote Thiis. For him, Munch's pictures from the various family homes were a key to understanding his art (Thiis 1933, 54).

In January 1882, the Munch family moved from Fossveien 7 to Olaf Ryes plass 4, both in the Grünerløkka district in the eastern part of Kristiania. In his diary, Munch described the new apartment: "A few days ago we moved into our new accommodation, Olaf Ryes plads 4, 3rd floor. We are now comfortable in every respect. The rooms are large and attractive, with dark-painted walls." (dated 28 January 1882, MM.T.2913). It was probably here that this work was painted. Gerd Woll relates this painting to another with the same title from the same year (Woll M 78), which includes a view through the window onto Olaf Ryes plass (Woll 2008 B, 96). Andreas Munch later trained to become a doctor, but died at the age of thirty in 1895. He was the only sibling to have children.

According to Thiis, the work was painted in 1883, a date that is retained in later National Gallery works catalogues (Thiis 1933, 57, 76). However, Woll places it in the context of two other paintings of the artist's brother Andreas (Woll M 78; Woll M 79), dating it to 1882-83. The painting was bequeathed to the museum by Charlotte and Christian Mustad and entered the collection in 1970. More recently, it has been included in a number of major exhibitions, both in Oslo (2008, 2013) and in New York (2006). wv

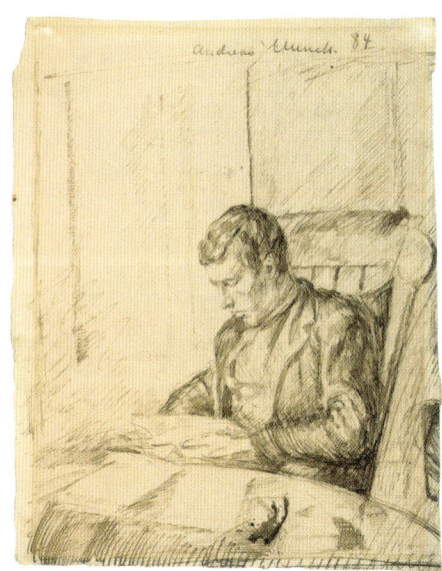

Edvard Munch: *Andreas Munch*, 1884
Pen, velin paper, 216 × 171 mm
Munchmuseet
MM.T.02283-recto
Photo: Munchmuseet / Tone Margrethe Gauden

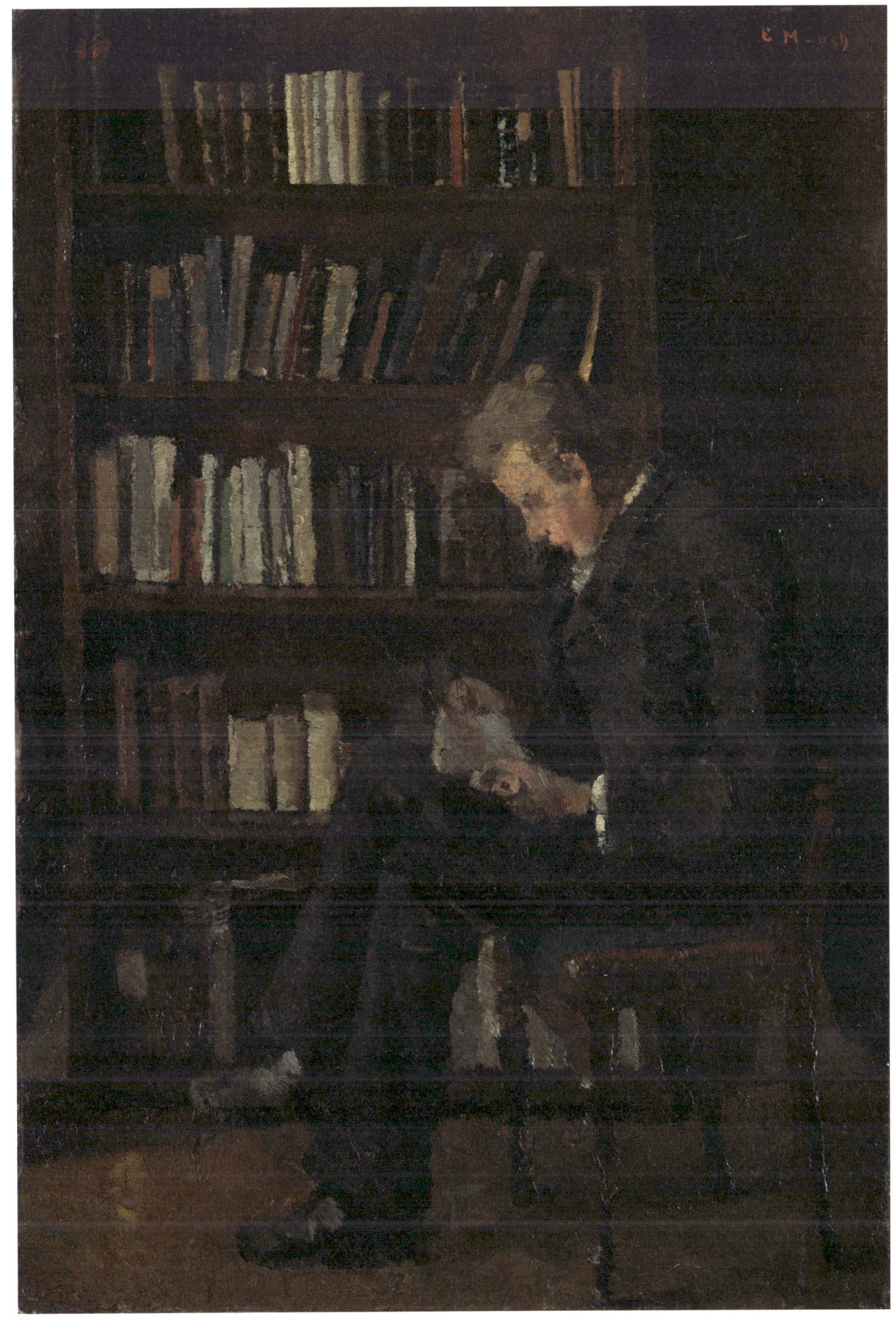

4

Study of a Head, 1883

Studiehode

Oil on canvas
60.5 × 46.5 cm
Signed l.r. "E Munch 83"
NG.M.02581
Woll M 98
NG cat. 1968-1261; 1992-2581

Other titles: *Studiehode av ung pike*. **Provenance**: Lucien Claudius Dedichen (before 1933-probably 1944); Sonja Dedichen (before 1951); purchased from Line Dedichen 1964. **Literature**: Thiis 1933, 87; I. Langaard 1960, 11, 13; Thue 1973, 243; Eggum 1983 A, 32; Næss 2004, 50; Bjerke 2008 B, 41; Malmanger 2013, 167, 182; Marcellàn 2015, 208; Nielsen 2015, 23; Mørstad 2016, 121. **Exhibitions**: 1883, Kristiania, no. 50; 1951, Oslo, no. 22; 1985, Moss; 1999, Florence, no. 2; 2008, Oslo, no. 48; 2013, Modum, no. 71.

The painting is Munch's first work to be accepted for an exhibition. It was shown at "Den norske Industri- og Kunstudstilling" (The Norwegian Industry and Art Exhibition) in Kristiania in 1883. Its subject puts it in a group of small portrait studies from the years 1882-85. This consists of nearly twenty pictures of identified and unidentified persons. It is unknown who the model is in this case. In a review of the exhibition in the newspaper *Dagbladet*, the correspondent wrote about the painting: "The very young Edv. Munch has contributed a Study of a Head. It is highly reminiscent of Hans Heyerdahl, but also shows a streak of independence. A young woman, red-haired, narrow-eyed and unattractive, yet distinctive and alive. The skin and the various lighting effects are the best aspects of the picture, indeed there is something truly excellent in the treatment of the skin." (*Dagbladet*, 12 July 1883). Many years later, in a letter to Jens Thiis from the 1930s, Munch mentions the picture and confirms that Heyerdahl was a source of inspiration: "The study of a women (Dedichen) was painted after I took corrections from Krohg. It is however quite unlike Krohg. More like Heyerdahl." (1933, MM N 3111).

The exhibition was also reviewed in *Bergens Tidende*, although without any specific mention of the painting. On the other hand, the critic expressed dismay at the number of young, immature artists who had been included: "Amateurishness - or examples, at least, of the novice-student stage - are spread across the walls; this is not to say that the young, or more precisely, the youngest, should be excluded from such company; but it is a sad sight when they dominate in an art exhibition of this kind." (*Bergens Tidende*, 30 July 1883). It is probable that the author is alluding here to Munch and his young "fellow painters", who were well represented in the exhibition.

It must have been motivating for a nineteen-year-old to be able to exhibit alongside established artists such as Frits Thaulow, Gerhard Munthe, Eilif Peterssen and Asta Nørregaard. This was the first official endorsement of Munch's talent - and in December of the same year he made his debut at the National Annual Autumn Exhibition.

Purchased in 1964, *Study of a Head* is the most recent addition of a Munch painting to the National Museum's collection. VWH

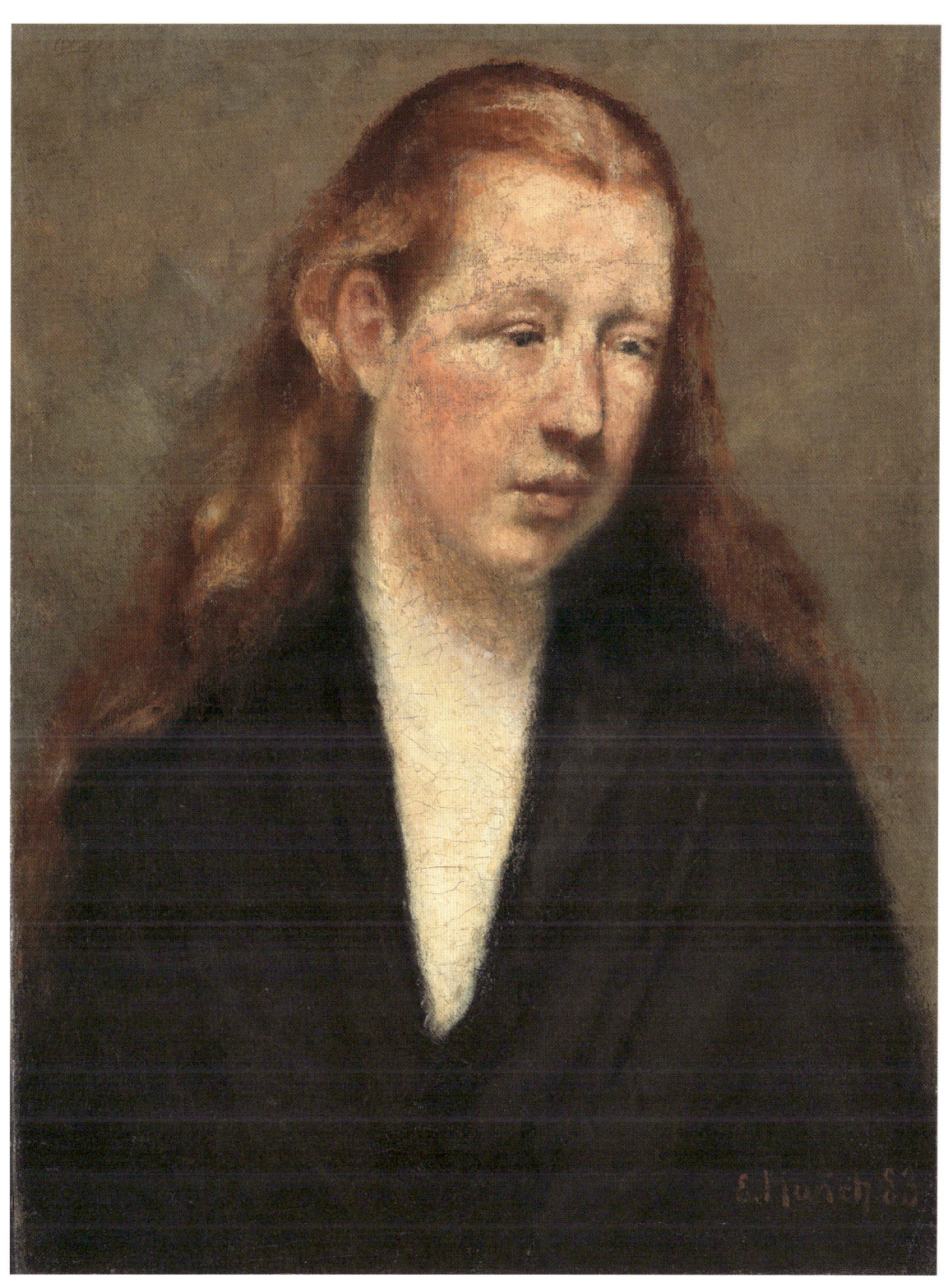

5

Around the Paraffin Lamp, 1883

Ved parafinlampen

Oil on wooden panel
27 × 39.5 cm
Signed l.r. "E Munch"
NG.M.02811
Woll M 104
NG cat. 1992-2811

Other titles: *Aften i hjemmet, Munchs far og søster i interiør; Familien omkring lampen; Munchs far og bror i interiør med lampelys; Kunstnerens far og søster i interiør*. **Provenance**: Ludvig Ravensberg; Charlotte and Christian Mustad (before 1933–1959/70); bequeathed by Charlotte and Christian Mustad 1959, received 1970. **Literature**: Thiis 1933, 54, 57, 63; Romdahl 1946, 84–86; Billeter 1998, 451; Bjerke 2008 B, 45; Ustvedt 2009, 15. **Exhibitions**: 1927, Oslo, no. 10; 1983, Dresden, no. 2; 1998, Munich, no. 256; 2001, Boston, no. 63; 2002, Oslo; 2008, Oslo, no. 52.

Around the Paraffin Lamp belongs to a group of works that feature Munch's family home as their subject matter. It is evening and people are reading at the living room table. The scene is captured as a diffuse, atmospheric sketch. The paraffin lamp on the table is the picture's light source. With thinning hair, a grey beard and puffing at a long pipe, the figure in the foreground with his back to the viewer can be identified as the artist's father. The figure on the left is more difficult to distinguish and is described in the literature as either the artist's brother or sister. The picture can be seen as a counterpart to the National Museum's *Andreas Reading* (cat. 3) from the same year. Both depict simple, private, everyday situations. *Around the Paraffin Lamp* is generally described as a sketch or study. The panel on which it is painted is unevenly cut at the bottom, and the back has been used as a palette.

The inclusion of the painting in the National Gallery's Munch exhibition of 1927 was probably its first showing. In the respective catalogue it is dated 1884–85. It was Jens Thiis who took charge of the exhibition, and he later revised the information about the picture's date: "cat. no. 10. Munch's father and brother indoors with lamplight was painted [18]83 at Olaf Ryes plass" (Thiis, 1933, 57). The picture is also reproduced in Thiis' book, this time with the title *Familien omkring lampen* (The Family around the Lamp). In this context, he mentions that it was previously owned by Ludvig Ravensberg, but had since been acquired by the Mustad family. Mustad must have purchased it sometime between 1927 and 1933, since it was still in the artist's possession at the time of the 1927 exhibition. In 1959, Charlotte and Christian Mustad bequeathed this and several other Munch paintings to the National Gallery. *Around the Paraffin Lamp* entered the collection following the death of Christian in 1970. VWH

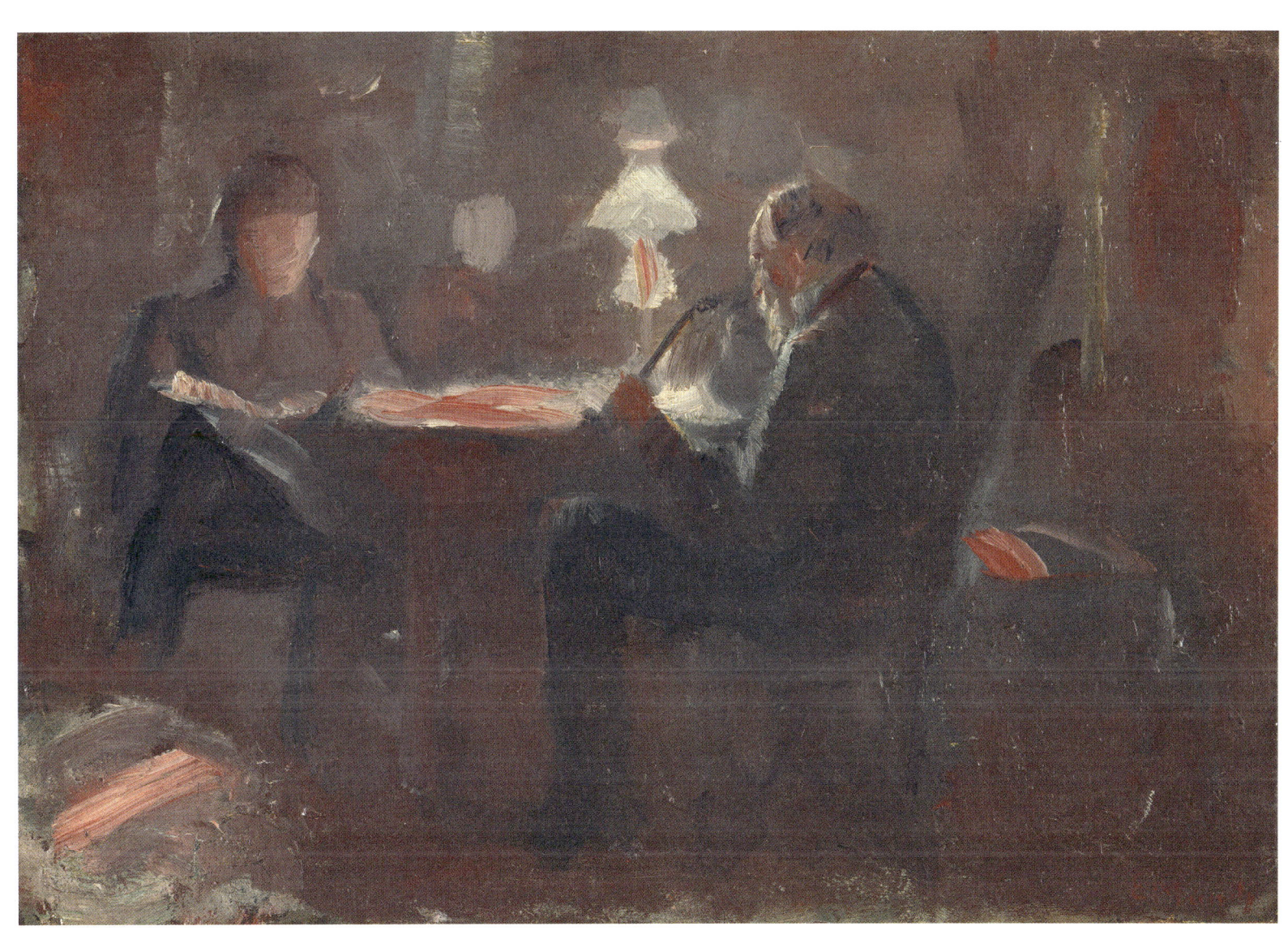

6

Inger Munch in Black, 1884

Inger Munch i svart

Oil on canvas
97 × 67 cm
Signed u.l. "E Munch 1884"
NG.M.01862
Woll M 113
NG cat. 1950-1045; 1968-1262; 1992-1862

Other titles: *Portrett*; *Munchs søster Inger*; *Knæbillede i sort*; *En pike (Munchs søster Inger)*; *Kunstnerens søster*; *Kunstnerens søster Inger*.
Provenance: Karl Vilhelm Hammer (before 1894–after 1919); Charlotte and Christian Mustad (1927–1937); gift from Charlotte and Christian Mustad 1937. **Literature**: Glaser 1917, 29; Thiis 1933, 132f.; Gauguin 1946 A, 52; Thue 1973, 245; Stang 1977, 36; Eggum 1983 A, 39; Heller 1984, 31; Eggum 1991, 43; Bischoff 1993, 12; Eggum 1994 A, 14, 18; Lange 2004, 128; Rutkowski 2008, 25; Pettersen 2008, 192; Guleng 2008, 213; Cathrine 2011, 20; Richard 2011, 12; Grøgaard 2013 A, 348; Ustvedt 2013 A, 234; Cox 2014, 170-183; Stein and Rød 2015, 262; Nielsen 2015, 24; Kongssund 2015, 89; Mørstad 2016, 112, 122, 145, 198; Knausgård 2017 A, 45f., 81f.; Ustvedt 2018, 35; Ford et al. 2021, [unpaginated]. **Exhibitions**: 1885, Antwerpen; 1886, Kristiania, no. 127; 1894, Stockholm, no. 10; 1910, Kristiania; 1927, Berlin, no. 4; 1927, Oslo, no. 12; 1932, Oslo A, no. 197; 1942, Oslo, no. 53; 1950, USA, touring exhibition, no. 3; 1951, Brighton–Glasgow–London–The Hague–Paris, no. 3; 1965, New York B, no. 1; 1987, Essen, no. 6; 1987, Zürich, no. 6; 1997, Tokyo, no. 4; 2008, Oslo, no. 58B; 2009, Oslo, no. 32; 2013, Oslo, no. 8.

The painting is one of Munch's first ambitious half-length portraits. The young woman portrayed in three-quarter profile is the artist's sister Inger Marie Munch (1868-1952). Five years younger than Edvard, Inger was confirmed in 1884, at the age of sixteen, and in the portrait she is wearing her confirmation dress, sewn by Aunt Karen. It was not uncommon to have a portrait painted in connection with such rites of passage. In this respect, the work anticipates a recurring theme in Munch's art: depictions of women at various milestones in life.

The work is distinctive for its blend of an old-masterly quality with carefully calibrated realism. In her dark dress, the figure is set against a black background so that attention focuses on the face and hands. Influences for the picture include Christian Krohg's picturesque realism, the portraits of Munch's somewhat older and highly acclaimed colleague Hans Heyerdahl, and an interest in the old masters.

Interior scenes and portraits of family members form a central group among Munch's early works. In these, no one features more prominently than the artist's sister Inger, the youngest member of the family. In addition to several portraits, she also features in a number of works with ensembles of figures. Of these many depictions, the most monumental are *Inger på stranden* (Inger on the Beach) (1889, Woll M 182) and the National Museum's *Inger in Black and Violet* (cat. 20). Inger was an important support to the artist throughout his life and the only one of his siblings to outlive him.

The painting was first shown at the World Exposition in Antwerp in 1885. This was also the first time Munch's work was presented outside Norway. Before he turned twenty-two, he was selected to represent Norway together with a number of older colleagues. The following year, the picture was shown at the National Annual Autumn Exhibition in Kristiania, where, together with *The Sick Child* (cat. 8), it attracted considerable attention. In 1937, it was among the many works bequeathed to the National Gallery by the couple Charlotte and Christian Mustad. The artist mentions the painting in an undated letter to his aunt, Karen Bjølstad: "Inger's first portrait – which Aftenposten scoffed at – was sold to Mustad for 20,000 kroner by Mrs Hammer, who bought it from me for 60 kroner" (MM N 1061). øu

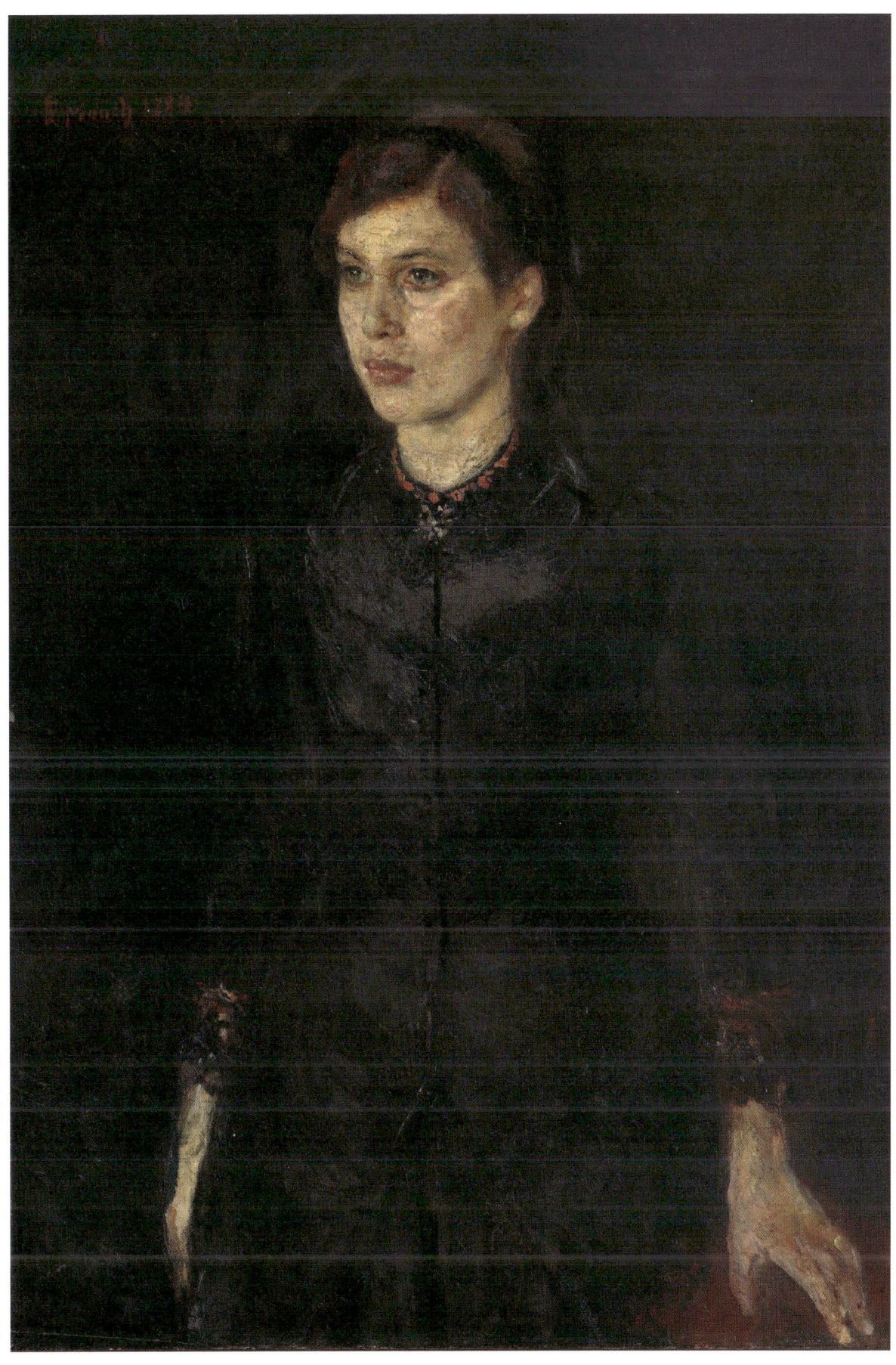

7

Jørgen Sørensen, 1885

Oil on canvas
36 × 31 cm
Signed l.r. "EM"
NG.M.00472b
Woll M 126
NG cat. 1933-938; 1950-1047; 1968-1264; 1992-472b

Other titles: *Maleren Jørgen Sørensen*; *Portrett-hode*. **Provenance**: Jørgen Sørensen; gift from Nikolai J. Sørensen 1895. **Literature**: Gauguin 1933, 44; Eggum 1994 A, 16f.; Grøgaard 2013 A, 348. **Exhibitions**: 1927, Berlin, no. 8; 1927, Oslo, no. 19; 1954, Venice, no. 3; 1954, Munich-Cologne, no. 6; 1955, Copenhagen-Odense, no. 6; 1983, Dresden, no. 4; 1997, Tokyo, no. 5; 2008, Oslo, no. 67; 2013, Oslo, no. 11.

Jørgen Sørensen (1861–1894) was a relative, colleague and friend of Munch from his youth. Their friendship dates back to 1881, when both were students at the Royal School of Design (Tegneskolen) in Kristiania. In 1883–1884 they joined forces with some other young artists to rent a shared studio at Lille Grensen 7 ("Pultosten"), close to Stortingsplass.

Munch made a number of such small-format portraits of friends, colleagues and models in the years around 1885. In its cropping, choice of colours and sketchiness, it has elements in common with the National Museum's *Self-Portrait* of 1886 (cat. 9).

There is some uncertainty about the dating of the picture. It was probably shown for the first time at the exhibitions in Berlin and Oslo in 1927, when it was dated to 1885. This is plausible in terms of genre, format and stylistic execution. The portrait was gifted to the National Gallery by State Auditor Nicolai Julius Sørensen, an older brother of the picture's subject. This was in 1895, shortly after Jørgen Sørensen's untimely death in 1894.

Sørensen made his debut at the National Annual Autumn Exhibition in 1883 and contributed regularly until his death. His prosaic landscapes and street scenes show the influence of Frits Thaulow's open-air realism. øu

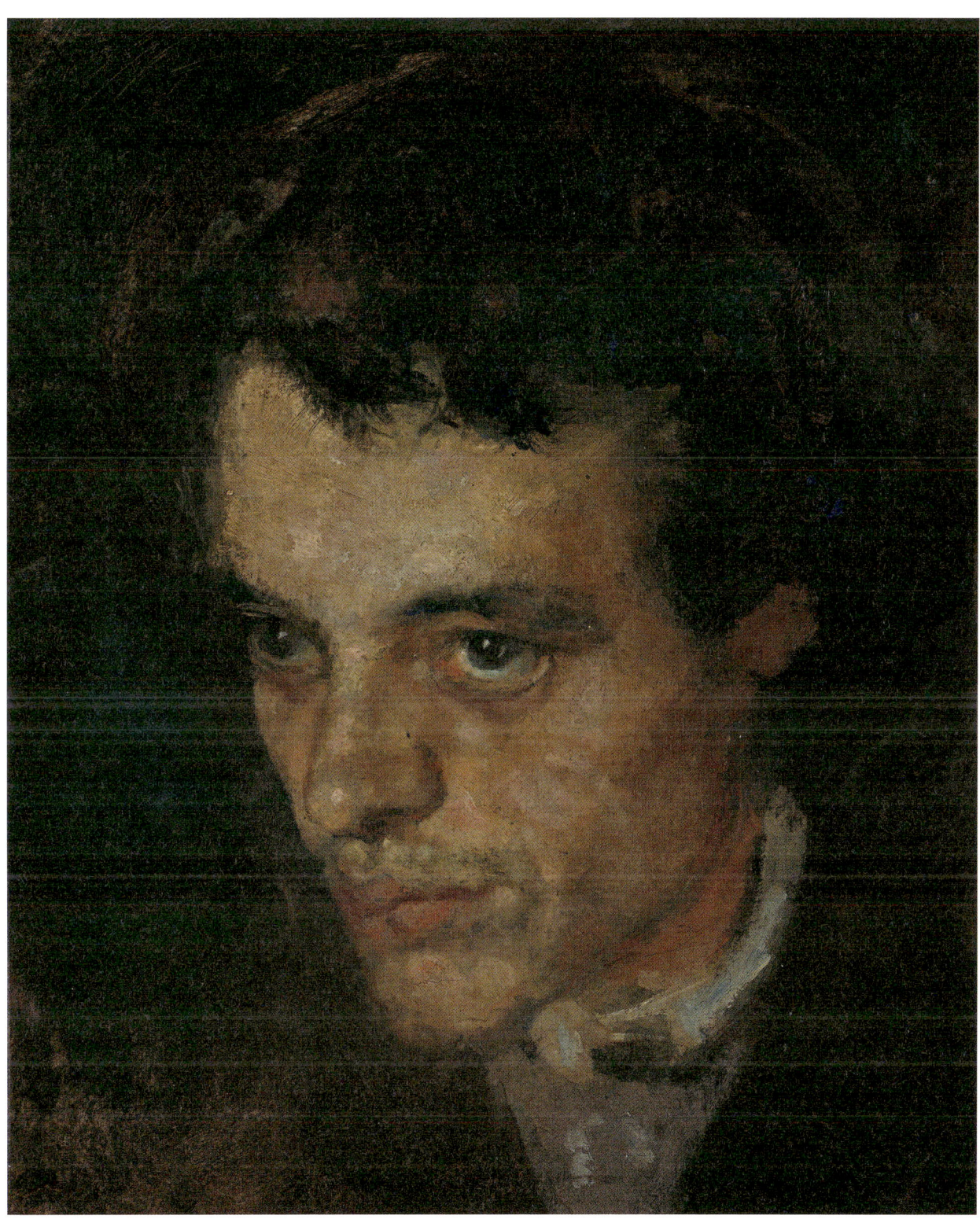

Oil on canvas
120 × 118.5 cm
Signed l.r. "E Munch"
NG.M.00839
Woll M 130
NG. Cat. 1933-939, 1950-1048, 1968-1265, 1992-00893

Other titles: *Studie*; *Den syke pike*; *Syk pike*; *Sykt barn*. **Provenance**: Christian Krohg (1886–1893); Olaf Schou (1893–1895); Harald Nørregaard/Christian and Oda Krohg (1903–1931/1895–1931, ownership rights disputed); acquired through exchange for a work by Oda Krohg 1931. **Literature**: One of Munch's best-known motifs, it is widely discussed in much of the general Munch literature. Nilssen 1913, 86f.; Thiis 1913, 69–70, 74; Munch 1928, 10; Thiis 1933, 132f.; Stenersen 1945, 16, 29–30, 153; Romdahl 1946, 88; Romdahl 1947, 168f.; Langaard 1960, 26f.; Svenæus 1968, 64, 67; Thue 1973, 245f.; Plahter 1974, 103f.; Buenger 1980, 43f.; Eggum 1978 B, 145f.; Skedsmo (ed.) 1981, 90–91; Eggum 1983 A, 44f.; Heller 1984, 31f.; Schneede 1984 A; Skedsmo 1985, 184f.; Thurmann-Moe 1985, 71; Bruno 1985, 29f.; Eggum 1987 A, 30f.; Skedsmo 1987 B, 100f.; Eggum 1991, 47f.; Plahter 1992, 85f.; Bischoff 1993, 10f.; Messel 1994, 222f.; Plahter 1994, 3–10; Aslaksby 1999, 139; Plahter 1999, 111f.; Schneede 2001, 11, 12, 16; Ebbestad 2002, 233f.; Vigtel 2002, 18f.; Schröder and Hoerschelmann (eds.) 2003, 249; Buchhart 2004, 29f.; Bjerke 2005, 22–23; Müller-Westermann 2005, 23; Bjerke 2006, 65f.; Clarke 2006, 45f.; Bjerke 2008 B, 54–57; Bruteig 2008 B, 63; Woll 2008 A, 86–87, 101; Messel 2008, 163, 168–169; Pettersen 2008, 178; Jacobsen 2008, 199–205; Guleng 2008, 227; Rutkowski 2008, 78; Templeton 2008, 13f.; Weinstein 2008, 317f.; Yvenes et al. (eds.) 2008, 7–8, 16, 18; Alessandrini 2009, 23f., 47; Aslaksby 2009, 57–76; Ustvedt 2009, 9–51; Junillon 2009, 239, 307; Buchhart 2010, [unpaginated]; Chang 2010, 181–183; Kuuva 2010, 192–193; Pettersen 2010, 103f.; Petruse-vičiūtė 2010, 59f.; Sjåstad 2010, 176; Bischoff 2011, 10; Helleland 2012, 23; Blegvad 2012, 67; Buchhart 2012 A, 24–25; Presler 2012, 65; Lampe 2012, 32; Ydstie 2012, 9f.; Eggum 2012, 138; Müller-Westermann 2012, 286; Volle 2012 A, 34, 259; Ness 2013, 7; Bjerke 2013, 15; Huber 2013, 21–28; Rognerud 2013, 45; Sørbø 2013, 93ff.; Grøgaard

A white pillow frames the main subject, a pale, red-haired girl in profile, her face turned towards a woman with her head bowed. The figures are depicted from close up, such that they fill much of the picture surface, thereby contracting the visible space. Details are sparse, although a few are included: a curtain, a half-empty glass and a bottle on a dresser. The painting is one of many contemporary depictions of a sickbed, which frequently signified tuberculosis, a bacterial infection that remained one of the most life-threatening human diseases in Europe until the 1950s.

The painting is often described as Munch's breakthrough work. It also meant a lot to the artist himself, who mentioned it in many of his letters and notebooks (Munch 1919; Munch 1928; MM N 76; MM N 77; MM N 415; MM N 570; MM.T.2748). The work is the result of a lengthy process, and with its scraped surface, flowing shapes and rugged execution it stands out from the artist's other paintings of the 1880s.

The Sick Child attracted considerable attention when first exhibited at the National Annual Autumn Exhibition in 1886, under the title *Studie* (Study). Many critics felt provoked by the sketchy, unfinished quality. Despite its large format and ambitious theme, the work seemed insufficiently developed and was a source of controversy. Some regarded its coarse, irregular style as symptomatic of the radical, dissolute bohemian culture of the day, others praised it for its boldness and emotive force. The picture was described, on the one hand, as a failure and "... an abomination", on the other, as a masterpiece. Since then, it has entered the literature as the artist's first major *succès de scandale*.

Depictions of sick children were a popular genre in the day, especially as a means to demonstrate the realist ideal of representing the world in unvarnished form. In the years before Munch produced his picture, several of his closest colleagues had tackled the same theme with considerable success, including Christian Krohg and Hans Heyerdahl. Munch's treatment stands out from those earlier versions, however, in its deliberate coarseness and obscuration. Like many in that era, both Krohg and Munch had lost siblings at a young age, an experience that informs their approach to the subject. But the unusual form of Munch's work, and his later emphasis on personal experience as a motivating factor in his art, have encouraged scholars to view that early loss as a more significant influence in the case of Munch's picture. The work is often associated with the death of the artist's one-year-older sister, Johanne Sophie, who died of tuberculosis in 1877, just fifteen years old. The models for the girl and the woman were probably Betzy Nilsen (cat. 10) and Munch's aunt, Karen Bjølstad.

We do not know of any preliminary sketches for the painting, although the small picture *Sykeværelset* (The Sickroom) from 1885–86 may have served as a study (Woll M 129). Several expert studies of materials and sources have shown that *The Sick Child* underwent a number of major revisions, both at the time of its creation and several years after it was first exhibited (Plahter 1974; Plahter 1994; Eggum 1978 B; Jakobsen, 2008; Aslaksby 1999; Aslaksby 2009). X-ray surveys have revealed changes in composition. In addition, an area to the right has been reworked at a later date, with the application of new paint. Stylistically, this section

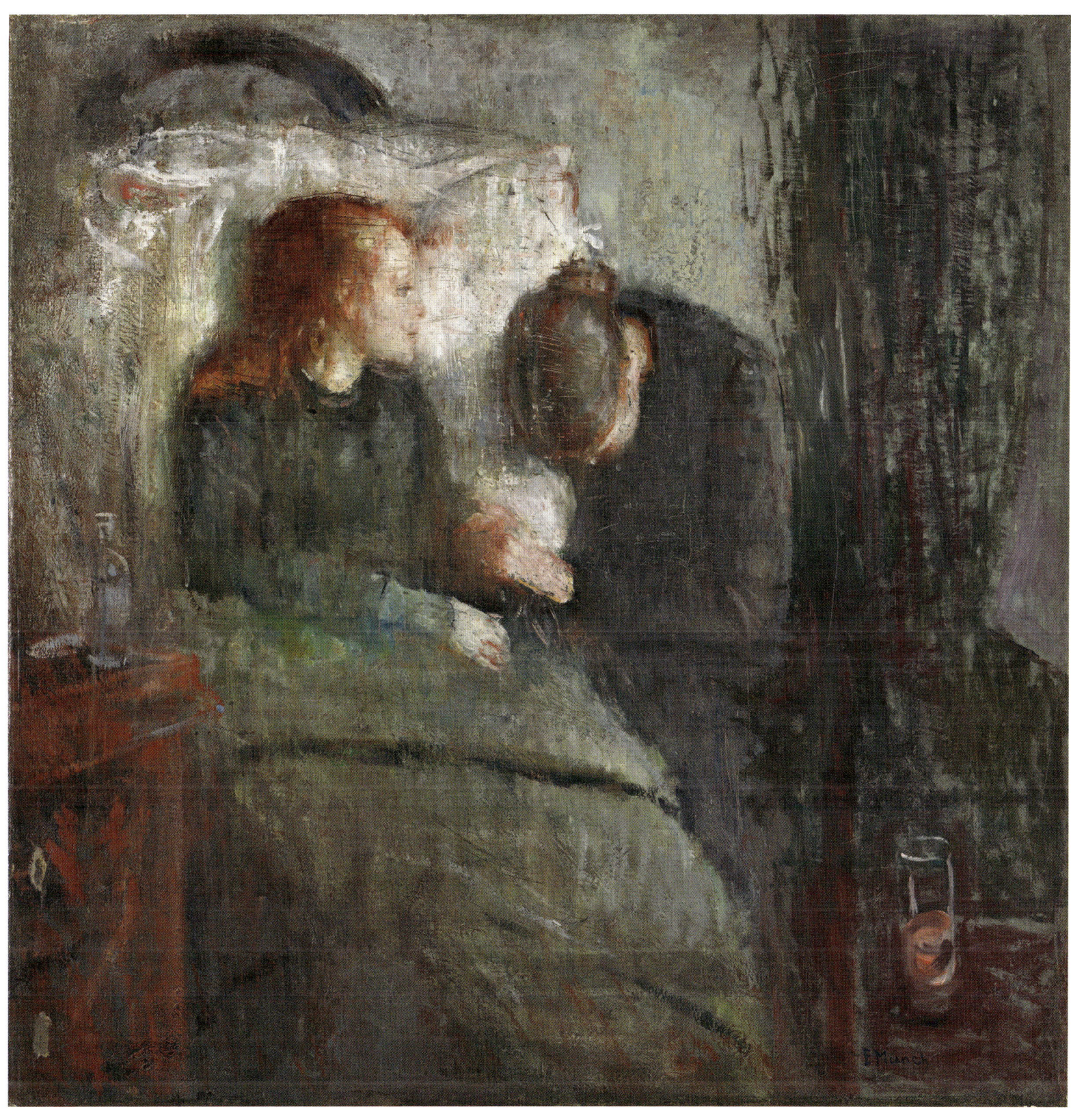

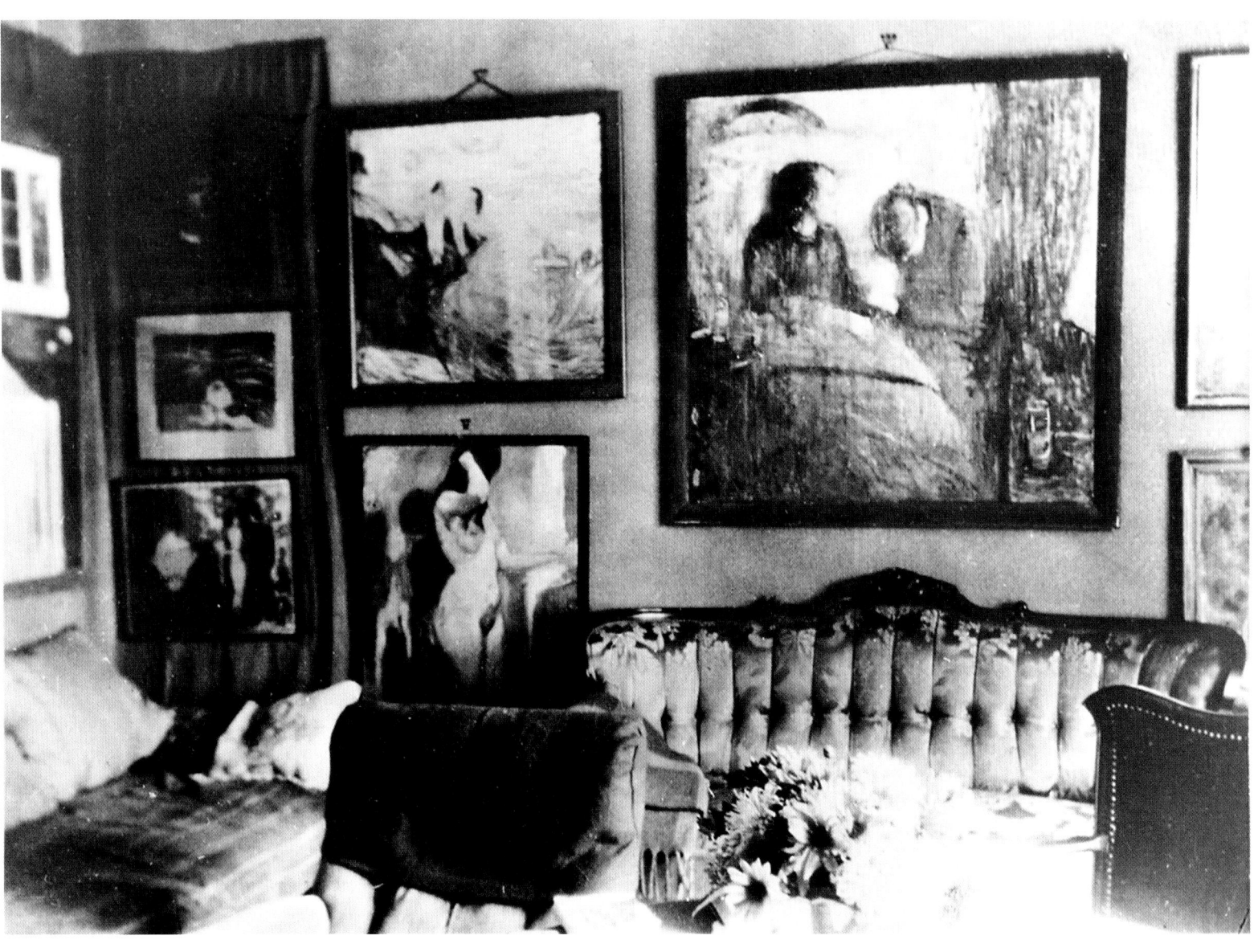

Interior from Aase and Harald Nørregaard's home in
Munkedamsveien 78, c. 1904–1907.
OB.Z12296
Photo: Oslo Museum / Unknown photographer

2013 A, 348; Grøgaard 2013 B, 74-79; Clarke 2013, 51-52; Guleng 2013, 135; Ohlsen 2013, 199; Flaatten 2014 B, 97; Guleng 2014, 357, 359-360; Cox 2014, 170-183; Clarke 2014, 53; Lomas 2015, 216; Pettersen 2015, 120, 123; Alarcó m.fl. 2015, 28; Zeiller 2015, 51; Gjessing 2016, 32; Ravenal 2016, 77; Mørstad 2016, 57, 115, 120, 171, 173; Jacob 2017, 168, 170, 174; Knausgård 2017 B, 13; Pedersen 2017, 5, 130-131, 139-150, 193-208, 231-235, 296-297; Ustvedt 2018, 12-13, 31, 52, 157; Bartrum 2019, 45, 47, 50; Coppel 2019, 126; Stein 2019, 39; Smith 2019, 62; Ford et al. 2021, [unpaginated]. **Exhibitions**: 1886, Kristiania, no. 128; 1889, Kristiania, no. 17; 1892, Berlin-Düsseldorf-Cologne-Berlin-Copenhagen-Breslau-Dresden-Munich, no. 15; 1894, Stockholm, no. 49; 1895, Kristiania-Bergen-Stavanger; 1896, Paris B, no. 3; 1897, Kristiania, no. 24; 1907, Berlin (probably); 1927, Oslo, no. 22; 1964, Oslo, no. 53; 1987, Oslo B, no. 57; 2009, Oslo, no. 30; 2013, Oslo, no. 12.

stands out from the rest of the picture. The alterations were probably carried out between 1896 and 1907, with the aim of repairing damage and surface weaknesses.

Munch went on to paint a further five versions of the same composition, in 1896, two in 1907, 1925 and 1927 (Woll M 392; Woll M 790; Woll M 791; Woll M 1561; Woll M 1631). Initially it was the second version, the one from 1896, that the National Gallery acquired, as part of Olaf Schou's substantial bequest of 1909. But in 1931, this painting was swapped with the first version from 1886, owned by Oda Krohg. Ever since, it has occupied a very central place in the museum's collection and in presentations of Munch's work. The 1896 version is now in the Gothenburg Museum of Art. In addition to the abovementioned paintings, Munch produced four print versions loosely based on the same subject and composition, plus many adaptations (1894, Woll G 7; 1896, Woll G 59; 1896, Woll G 72 and 73). In certain respects, the work *Spring* from 1889 (cat. 12) presents the same scene, although the painting is significantly different in size, form and composition. Other major works that address more or less the same subject include *Death in the Sickroom* (cat. 22).

The painting's long and complex provenance has been traced in detail by Tone Skedsmo (Skedsmo 1985). For many years, ownership was disputed, and the work became the subject of several lawsuits, leading to a Supreme Court ruling in 1914, which granted right of disposal, but not rights of ownership, to Harald Nørregaard. The painting was offered to the National Gallery as early as 1895, but at that point the museum chose *Self-Portrait with Cigarette* (cat. 32) in its place. The National Gallery acquired the painting as the result of an exchange proposed by Oda Krohg.

After its first showing in 1886, the painting featured in many of Munch's most important exhibitions throughout the 1890s. From the outset, it has occupied a prominent place in the academic literature and is now one of the most analysed and discussed of Munch's works. The picture's radical form signals an orientation that is already looking beyond the prevailing realism of the 1880s. It has been claimed that the work anticipates features that would set the tone in art around 1900, especially in relation to German expressionism (Schneede 2001). In 2009, the painting provided the central element for an exhibition at the National Museum – National Gallery, Oslo. Passages in Munch's own writings support the view that *The Sick Child* can be regarded as an experiment in psychologically charged realism. ØU

Self-Portrait, 1886

Selvportrett

Oil on canvas
33 × 24.5 cm
Signed l.r. "E. Munch"
NG.M.01915
Woll M 133
NG cat. 1950-1049; 1968-1266; 1992-1915

Provenance: Aase and Harald Nørregaard (before 1890-1938); purchased from Wangs Kunsthandel with financial support from the Olaf Schou trust fund 1938. **Literature**: Gauguin 1946 A, 60f.; Jedlicka 1958, 230; I. Langaard 1960, 23; Eggum 1978 B, 11f.; Eggum 1979 B, 14; Heller 1984, 39; Müller-Westermann 1989, 517; Müller-Westermann 1991, 6f.; Fredlund (ed.) 2002, 38; Buchhart 2003, 23; Buchhart 2004, 38f.; Lange 2004, 117; Müller-Westermann 2005, 20f.; Grøgaard 2013 A, 348; Steihaug 2013 A, 18-19; Bruteig m.fl. 2015, 29-30; Bal 2017, 47f.; Stein 2017 B, 34; Ford et al. 2021, [unpaginated]. **Exhibitions**: 1889, Kristiania, no. 1 (usikkert); 1927, Berlin, no. 11; 1927, Oslo, no. 23; 1938, Oslo, no. 22; 1954, Venice, no. 6; 1954, Munich-Cologne, no. 9; 1955, Copenhagen-Odense, no. 9; 1978, Washington, no. 3; 1979, New York; 1987, Essen, no. 12; 1987, Zürich, no. 12; 1988, Humlebæk, no. 1; 1989, Vienna; 1995, Venice; 1999, Modum, no. 4; 2002, Gothenburg, no. 3; 2005, Stockholm-Oslo-London, no. 3; 2006, New York, no. 6; 2007, Basel, no. 1; 2008, Oslo, Munchmuseet, no. 72 B; 2009, Oslo, no. 33; 2013, Oslo, no. 13; 2015, Oslo-Amsterdam, no. 23; 2017, San Francisco-New York-Oslo, no. 2.

Illuminated by a light source beyond the frame, the face emerges from surrounding darkness. The head is portrayed in three-quarter profile, relatively close to the picture plane and slightly offset to the left, leaving an open space in front of the face. The subtle variation in tones and the intensity of the subject's gaze, pointed slightly downwards, indicate a studious attitude. The young artist presents himself in an inquisitive yet ambitious pose. The work bears resemblances to self-portraits by famous artists, including some by Rembrandt, Francisco Goya, Gustav Courbet and Christian Krohg. Works by the latter two painters in particular may well have served as prototypes.

Munch painted self-portraits throughout his career. This is one of four in the National Museum's collection (cat. 9, cat. 32, cat. 47, cat. 55). In its colour scheme and painterly execution, the work strives to be true to nature, but there is also an emphasis on distinctive qualities and a clear subjectivity of approach. The diffuseness of form suggests an orientation that is reaching beyond the realism of the 1880s.

This work is Munch's only signed self-portrait from the 1880s. There is no date marking, but in the literature it has consistently been ascribed to 1886. In terms of technique, it has similarities with several paintings from the period 1885-86, e.g. its use of multiple layers of paint, in some places thickly applied with the palette knife, in others heavily diluted. Scratching and other surface abrasions produce an impression of coarse materiality that links the portrait to *The Sick Child* (cat. 8). The work was probably gifted to Aasta Carlsen (1869-1908), later to Aase Nørregaard, a close friend from the 1880s (cat. 38, cat. 39). It was in the possession of the Nørregaard family until 1938, when it was bought for the National Gallery with financial help from the Olaf Schou endowment fund. ØU

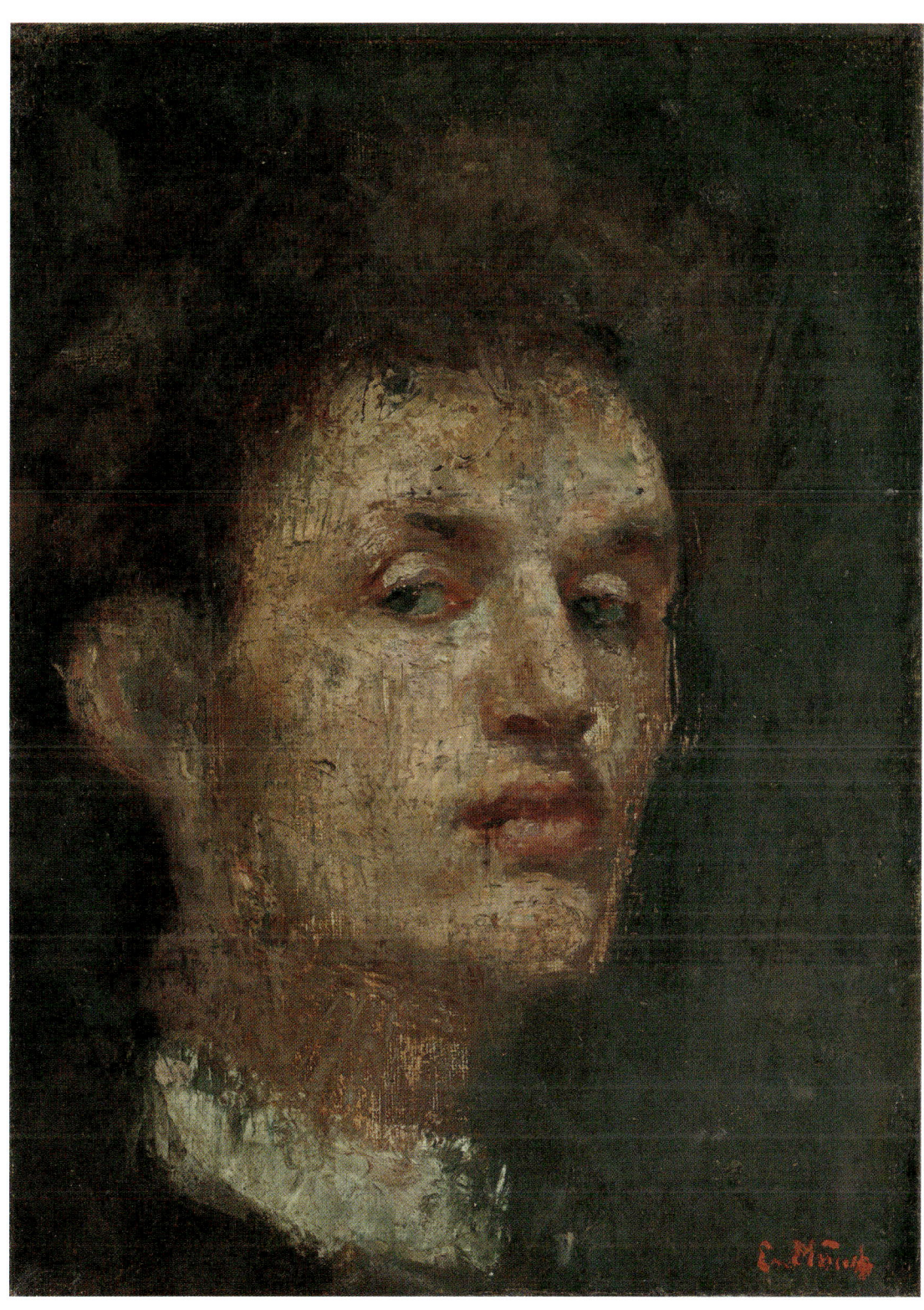

Oil on canvas
25.5 × 29 cm
Signed l.r. "E M 87" (painted over)
NG.M.03054 (stolen 1993)
Woll M 144
NG cat. 1933-937; 1950-1046; 1968-1263; 1992-3054

Other titles: *Studiehode*; *Pikebarn med rødt hår. Forarbeide til «Det syke barn», samme modell*; *Portrett av Betzy Nilsen*; *Portrettstudie (Betzy Nilsen)*. **Provenance**: Stolen 1993; gift from Olaf Schou 1909. **Literature**: Thiis 1933, 133–4; Gauguin 1933, 44; Plahter 1974, 115 (note 3); Eggum 1983 A, 45; Skedsmo 1987 B, 128. **Exhibitions**: 1927, Oslo, no. 20.

The painting depicts Betzy Nilsen, a young woman who was a model for several of Munch's works in the years around 1886, including for the paintings *Rødhåret pike med hvit rotte* (Red-Haired Girl with White Rat) (1886, Woll M 131), *The Sick Child* (cat. 8) and *Spring* (cat. 12). The muted colour scheme and the emphasis on the girl's bright face are typical of Munch's early portraits, although the execution is freer. The pale, pastose treatment of the face and the red hair contrast with the greyish-green of the wall-like background. Stylistically, the work has something in common with paintings such as *The Sick Child* and *Self-Portrait* (cat. 8 and cat. 9), both from 1886.

Munch produced a number of similar small portraits and study heads in the years around 1886. There are reasons to regard the painting as an independent portrait, but the combination of the girl's loose hair, remote expression and pale skin also attract comparison with his depictions of ailing girls. Munch became acquainted with Betzy Nilsen via his father's work as a visiting doctor. For a time she also worked as a maid in the Munch household (*Dagbladet,* 30 December 1950). The facial features are similar to those of the young girl in *Spring* and *The Sick Child*.

The work was stolen from the National Gallery on 23 August 1993 and has not been recovered. Exhibited for the first time in 1927, it was long assumed to be a preliminary study for *The Sick Child*. Accordingly, it was dated to 1885. But subsequent X-ray analysis revealed a signature that had been puttied and painted over and which indicates 1887 to be the earliest possible year of production (Plahter 1974). The painting was among the works that Olaf Schou gifted to the National Gallery in 1909. ØU

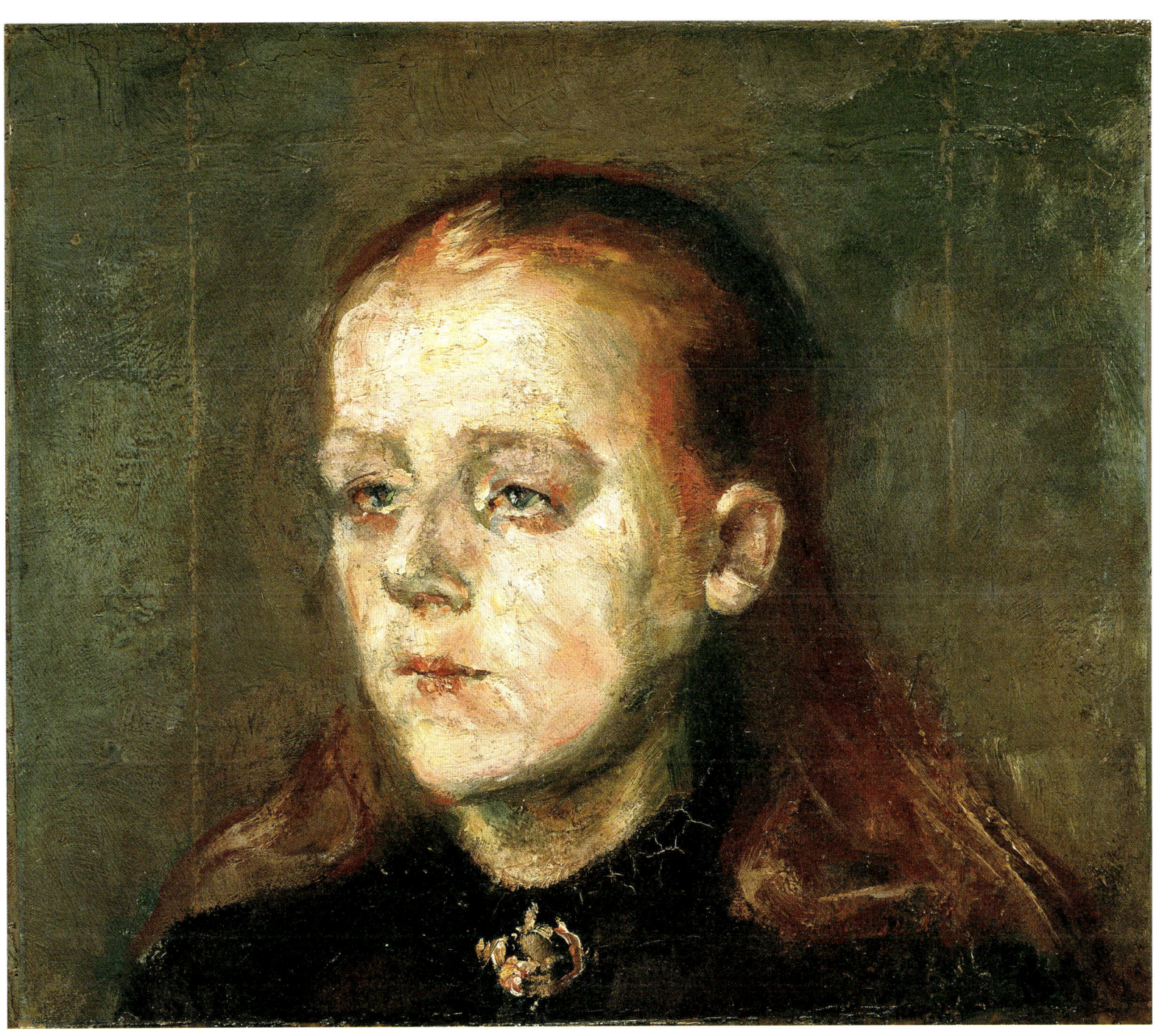

Flowery Meadow at Veierland, 1887

Blomstereng på Veierland

Oil on canvas pasted onto cardboard
66.5 × 44 cm
Unsigned
NG.M.01235b
Woll M 148
NG cat. 1933-940; 1950-1050; 1968-1267; 1992-1235b

Other titles: *Sommeraften på Veirland* (sic); *Blomstereng fra Veideland*; *Blomstereng, Veierland ved Tønsberg*. **Provenance**: Gift from Jacob Woxen 1921. **Literature**: Thiis 1933, 56; Heller 1984, 39; Lippincott 1988, 20; Eggum 1991, 52–53; Bøe 1992, 17; Eggum 1999 A, 14; catalouge Göteborg 2002–2003, 40; Kuuva 2010, 64; Flaatten 2010 A, 82; Flaatten 2010 B, 325; Flaatten 2013 A, 40; Mørstad 2016, 153, 187, 19; Ford et al. 2019, [unpaginated]; Ford et al. 2021, [unpaginated]. **Exhibitions**: 1889, Kristiania, no. 61; 1927, Oslo, nr. 27; 1980, Oslo, nr. 17; 1983, Dresden, nr. 5; 1987, Zürich, nr. 14; 1990, Cologne, no. 128; 1999, Modum, no. 6; 1999, Florence, no. 3; 2002, Gothenburg, no. 4; 2008, Oslo, no. 80; 2010, Codroipo, no. 93; 2013, Oslo, no. 14.

Munch found this scene during one of the family's many summer trips to the western shore of Kristianiafjord in the 1880s. In the summer of 1887, they rented a house on the island of Veierland. The picture has been described as "a small masterpiece, a richly coloured nocturnal landscape" from Munch's early years (Eggum 1991). The composition is formed around a high horizon that gives spatial depth. Technically, it shows that Munch was experimenting with new approaches to painting. The use of the upright format is rare in his landscapes, although the moon and moonlight would become a recurrent theme in the decades that followed, albeit in much larger formats.

The depiction of moonlight and the mellow twilight of midsummer nights aligns this work with other contemporary Nordic landscapes. At the National Annual Autumn Exhibition in 1886, the year before Munch painted his *Flowery Meadow at Veierland*, established artists including Kitty Kielland, Eilif Peterssen and Christian Skredsvig exhibited paintings inspired by their summer sojourn at Fleskum Farm in Bærum. The Fleskum paintings represented something new that encouraged a greater emphasis on atmosphere in Norwegian landscape art. Munch's picture can be seen in conjunction with this kind of neo-romantic shift.

The painting is neither signed nor dated, but the place name in the title corroborates the date attribution. X-ray photography has revealed one or more earlier compositions beneath the visible work. The picture was shown at Munch's first solo exhibition at the Studentersamfundet (Students' Association) in 1889, under the title *Sommeraften på Veirland* (Summer Evening at Veirland). When it appeared in the Munch exhibition at the National Gallery in 1927, it bore the title *Blomstereng på Veideland* (Flowery Meadow at Veideland). The painting was gifted to the National Gallery by Customs Inspector Jacob Woxen in 1921, and in the museum's supplementary record it is listed as *Blomstereng* (Flower Meadow). VWH

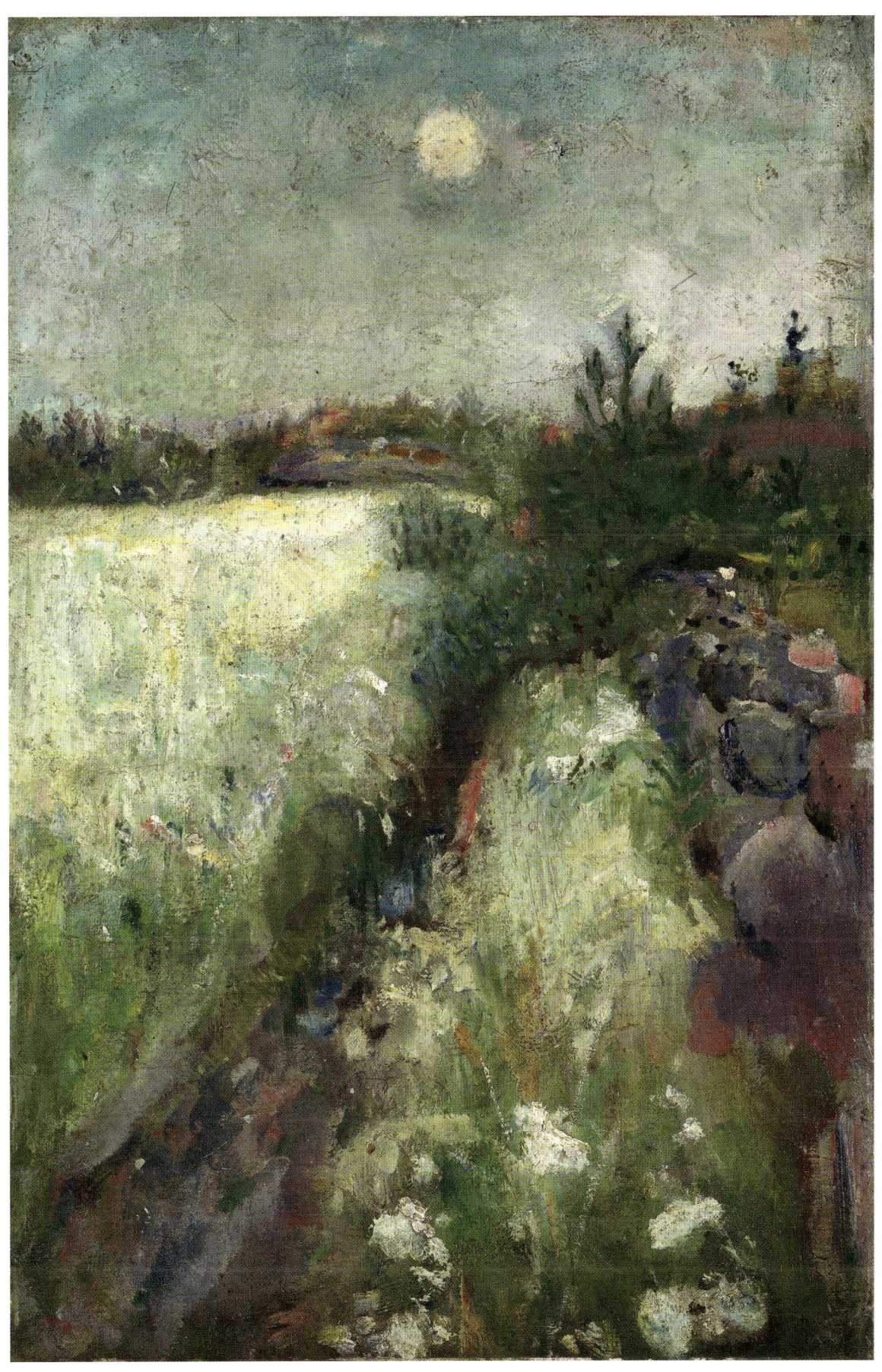

Spring, 1889
Vår

Oil on canvas
169.5 × 263.5 cm
Signed l.r. "E Munch 1889"
NG.M.00498
Woll M 173
NG cat. 1933-942, 1950-1052, 1968-1269, 1992-00498

Provenance: Purchased from the artist 1899.
Literature: Thiis 1904, 415; Nilssen 1913, 88;
Thiis 1913, 69f.; Vidalenc 1920, 142; Thiis 1933,
157f., 324f.; Stenersen 1945, 16; Romdahl 1946,
88; Romdahl 1947, 170f.; Gierløff 1953, 56; I.
Langaard 1960, 40; Stang 1977, 67f.; Plahter 1974,
108f.; Heller 1984, 44; Eggum 1987 A, 37; Eggum
1991, 49f.; Bischoff 1993, 16; Messel 1994, 223f.;
Aslaksby 1999, 139f.; Plahter 1999, 114f.; Vigtel
2002, 20; Lange 2005, 247; Bjerke 2006, 74f.;
Titus-Carmel 2007, 19f.; Bjerke 2008 B, 57; Guleng
2008, 216; Jacobsen 2008, 199, 202, 204, 208;
Messel 2008, 168; Pettersen 2008, 194; Rutkowski
2008, 80; Templeton 2008, 9; Aslaksby 2009,
69; Junillon 2009, 74, 98, 258, 275; Ustvedt 2009,
11f.; Pettersen 2010, 104f.; Bischoff 2011, 14; Volle
2012 A, 195; Guleng 2013, 135; Grøgaard 2013 A,
348; Ness 2013, 7; Ohlsen 2013, 199-200; Stokkan
2013, 79f.; Flaatten 2014 B, 97; Kongssund 2015,
80; Stein and Rød 2015, 260, 262; Gjessing 2016,
32; Mørstad 2016, 59, 118, 173, 180, 233, 244, 257;
Stein 2017 A, 68; Ustvedt 2018, 51. **Exhibitions**:
1889, Kristiania, no. 63; 1892, Berlin-Düsseldorf-
Cologne-Berlin-Copenhagen-Breslau-Dresden-
Munich, no. 14; 1894, Stockholm, no. 48; 1895,
Kristiania-Bergen-Stavanger; 1906, Copenhagen,
no. 183; 1927, Oslo, no. 37; 1942, Oslo, no. 54; 2008,
Oslo, no. 99; 2009, Oslo, no. 31; 2013, Oslo, no. 16.

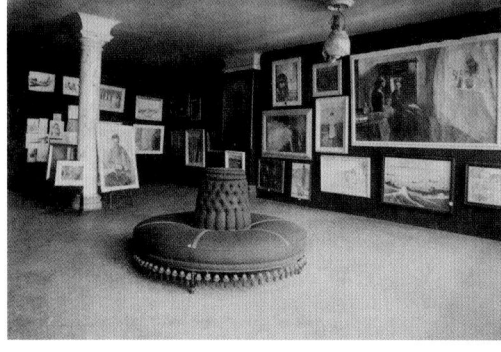

Photo from the Equitable Palast in Berlin 1892-1893.
MM.D.01029
Photo: Munchmuseet / Unknown photographer

Spring is Munch's largest and most realistic painting of the 1880s. With its sickbed and its emphasis on the contrasts between indoors and outdoors, deadly disease and life-giving light, it is similar to *The Sick Child* (cat. 8). The two works differ, however, in format, execution and composition. In *Spring*, the sickbed is located in a typical, late 19th century middle-class home. The figures sit deep within the pictorial space, and the picture owes much of its character to its true-to-life treatment of the setting. There is greater emphasis on realistic perspective, the play of light, volumes and details. The execution is more in line with the open-air realism of the 1880s.

For many years, this was one of Munch's most discussed and highly valued works. Jens Thiis described it as the artist's "... most accomplished painting" (Thiis 1907 A, 426) and gave it a central place in the so-called Hall of Honour for Recent Art in the National Gallery (MM K 5103). Unlike so many of his other major works, however, the artist did not explore the composition further in later versions, and neither did he render it as a print. We know of no specific preliminary studies for the painting. Munch himself mentions the work in a number of letters, notes and literary remarks. In one context, he mentions it as his "... farewell to impressionism and realism" (1928-1929, MM N 76).

The model for the girl in the chair was probably Betzy Nilsen, who may have been employed as a domestic servant in the Munch household at the time (*Dagbladet*, 30.12.1950). The older woman resembles the artist's aunt, Karen Bjølstad. The work was shown for the first time at Munch's first solo exhibition in Kristiania in spring 1889. A few years later, in 1895, it was proposed that the National Gallery should purchase the work, although it wasn't until 1899 that the museum finally decided to buy it.

Technical and X-ray studies have revealed that Munch made significant changes when developing the work, as well as early damage towards the right of the picture (Plahter 1974; Plahter 1994; Aslaksby 2009). The damage was discussed in connection with the purchase of the picture in 1899, and was probably repaired immediately. It is one of several matters mentioned in a letter from Munch to Jens Thiis (MM N 2146, undated), and in another from Erik Werenskiold (then a member of the purchasing committee) to Henrik Sørensen (reproduced in *Kunst og Kultur*, no. 4, 1989, 234).

Munch's use of the realistic idiom in this work is striking in light of his other paintings from the late 1880s. Ragna Stang has described *Spring* as an "academic bravura work" (Stang, 1977, 67). The painting was positively received when exhibited in 1889, and it probably contributed to the decision to grant the artist a state travel grant that year. During the 1890s, the work served as a centrepiece in numerous exhibitions. In a photograph that survives from the artist's exhibition at Equitable Palast in Berlin in 1892-93, it is undoubtedly the most dominant painting in the room. In recent times, however, it has been relegated to a more modest place in Munch's oeuvre. ØU

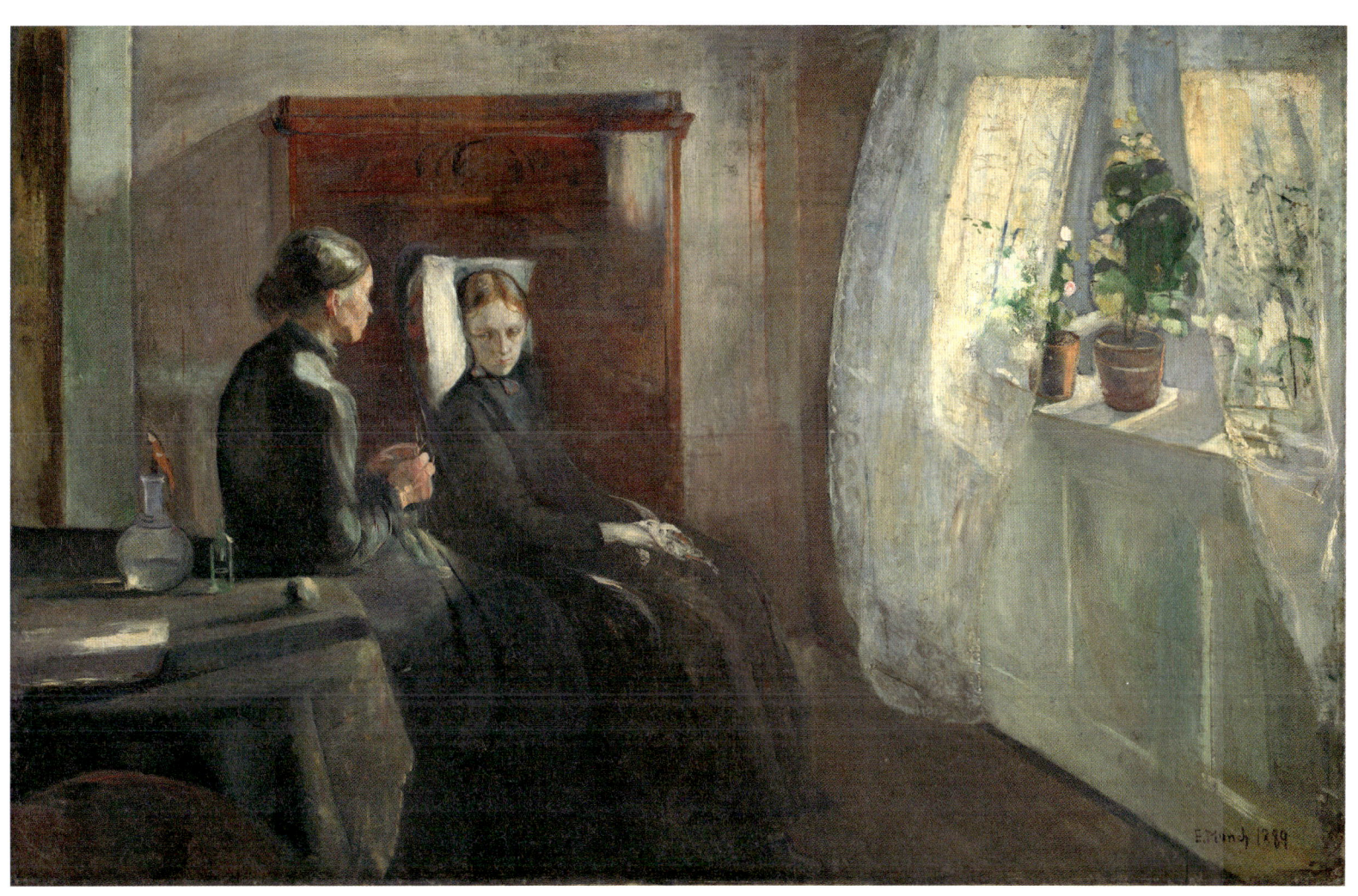

Oil on canvas
109 × 84 cm
Signed l.l. "E Munch 1889"
NG.M.00485
Woll M 174
NG cat. 1933-941; 1950-1051; 1968-1268; 1992-485

Other titles: *Portræt af Hans Jæger; Forfatteren Hans Jæger.* **Provenance:** Purchased from the artist 1897. **Literature:** Nilssen 1913, 88; Vidalenc 1920, 131f.; Glaser 1917, 14, 28; Thiis 1933, 172; Gauguin 1933, 64-65; I. Langaard 1960, 37f.; Brenna 1976, 196; Stang 1977, 45; Heller 1984, 44; Eggum 1994 A, 23f.; Fosli 1994, 519; Plahter 1994, 17f.; Messel 1993, 15, 106-109; Plahter 1999, 118f.; Jacobsen 2008, 202; Guleng 2008, 227; Grøgaard 2013 A, 348; Huber 2013, 32f.; Ustvedt 2013 A, 233; Flaatten 2016, 73; Woll 2017, 13; Ustvedt 2018, 40-42; Ford et al. 2019, [unpaginated]; Ford et al. 2021, [unpaginated]. **Exhibitions:** 1889, Kristiania, no. 42; 1892, Kristiania, no. 40; 1892, Berlin-Düsseldorf-Cologne-Berlin-Copenhagen-Breslau-Dresden-Munich, no. 47/46; 1894, Stockholm, no. 11; 1897, Kristiania, no. 26; 1927, Berlin, no. 19; 1927, Oslo, no. 35; 1985, Oslo-Stockholm-Helsinki-Copenhagen, no. 81; 1987, Essen, no. 18; 1987, Zürich, no. 18; 1993, Oslo, no. 37; 2006, New York, no. 16; 2008, Oslo, no. 100; 2013, Oslo, no. 17.

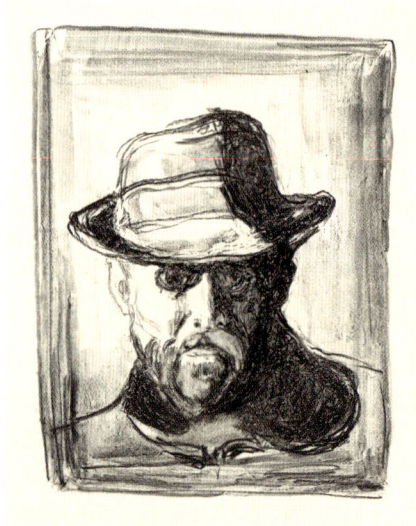

Edvard Munch: *Hans Jæger*, 1943-1944,
Litograph, 420 × 335 mm
Munchmuseet
MM.G.00548-17, Woll G 747
Photo: Munchmuseet / Halvor Bjørngard

The situation is casual, the subject seemingly captured in a fleeting moment. Still in his outdoor clothes, it is as if he has just flopped down on the sofa with a glass in front of him. The portrait is painted using a rich, pastose technique that emphasises brushstroke, materiality and nuances of colour. In its composition and style, it shows Munch's preoccupation with 1880s realism.

In 1889, Hans Jæger (1854-1910) was one of Munch's closest friends. The two had been following each other's activities since 1886. Munch admired the author's radical attitude and message. Nearly ten years older than Munch, Jæger advocated the ideals of naturalism. This involved a conscientious commitment to reality, diligent self-examination and thorough honesty about one's private life. Munch was one of those who would rigorously adopt the tenet of Jæger and the Kristiania Bohemians to "write your life".

Here the subject is first and foremost the front figure of those Bohemians, Jæger himself. One of Munch's best known and most widely discussed portraits, it is generally regarded as a defining work of the 1880s. It belongs to the genre of the informal artist portrait, which became popular in this period. Otherwise, in terms of style and the treatment of the cool light flooding in through the window, it has similarities with *Spring* (cat. 12), painted the same year.

Until 1887 Hans Jæger was employed as a stenographer at the Storting, the Norwegian parliament. But he was better known as a writer, social critic and anarchist, and as the leading light of the so-called Kristiania Bohemians. He attracted attention and controversy for his opinions, actions and personality. The portrait was painted shortly after his second period of imprisonment for his novel *Fra Kristianiabohemen* (From the Christiania Bohemians), which was confiscated by the authorities immediately after publication in December 1885. Jæger received a sixty-day prison sentence as penalty for the book's pornographic and blasphemous content, followed by a second sentence for attempting to smuggle the novel to Sweden. The punishment was also a reaction to the book's socially critical stance and its disregard for established morality.

The painting was shown in Munch's first solo exhibition in the small hall of Studentersamfundet (the Students' Association) in Kristiania in spring 1889. It was purchased from the artist by the National Gallery's purchasing committee in autumn 1897. X-ray analysis has revealed changes in the course of work, especially in the lower right corner (Plahter 1994). The table and glass were added at a late stage, possibly after the painting had been exhibited in spring 1889. This is the only portrait of Jæger by Munch that we know of. Later, however, he produced a lithograph of the head section (1896, Woll G 84). And finally, towards the end of his life, he prepared two further lithographs based on the full tableau. These are among his last works (1943-1944, Woll G 747; Woll G 748).

Munch's relationship to Jæger was ambivalent, but in his late correspondence he mentions him several times with great affection and respect. In connection with Jæger's terminal illness and death in January 1910, Munch wrote to his friend Jappe Nilssen: "- Poor Hans Jæger - He was one of the few I would have liked to see again - He was one of the most likeable of the Bohemians - and he wrote the best Kristiania novel as well." (21 January 1910, National Library, correspondence collection, 604, PN 732). Jæger's death may have been the starting point for several later compositions on the theme of "The Death of Bohemia" (1915-1920, Woll M 1166-1169). Clearly, Jæger was a major influence on Munch's development in his early years. ØU

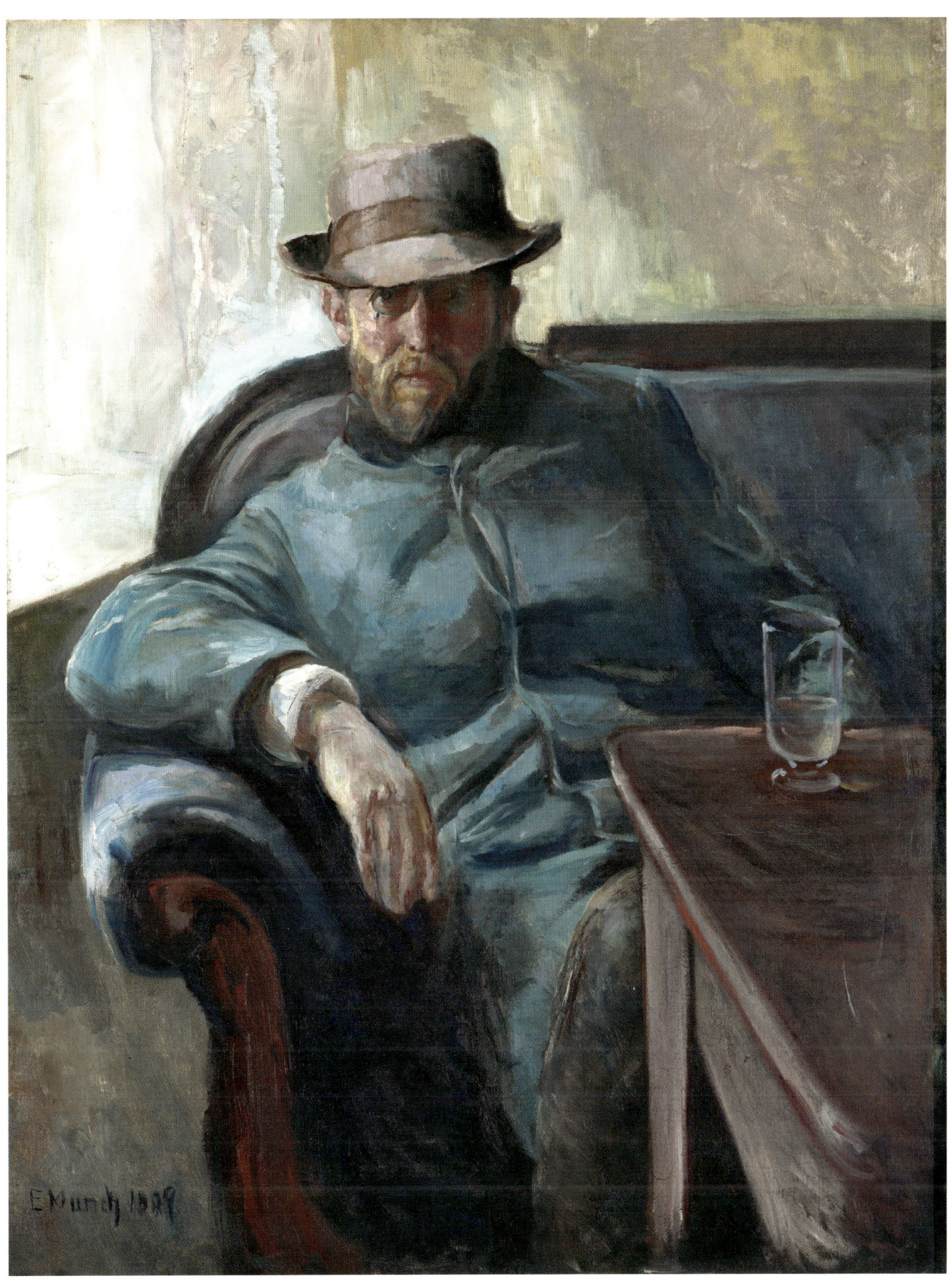

14

Night in Saint-Cloud, 1890

Natt i Saint-Cloud

Oil on canvas
64.5 × 54 cm
Signed l.r. "E Munch"
NG.M.01111
Woll M 192
NG cat. 1933-943; 1950-1053; 1968-1270; 1992-1111

Other titles: *Natt*; *Natt. Meudon ved Paris*. **Provenance**: Fredrik Arentz (1890-1914); the heirs of F. Arentz (1914-1917); purchased from the heirs of Fredrik Arentz 1917. **Literature**: Thiis 1933, 176; Romdahl 1947, 175f.; I. Langaard 1960, 106f.; Heller 1978 A, 80f.; Nergaard 1978, 118; Rosenblum 1978, 2; Varnedoe 1982, 186; Heller 1984, 58, 65f.; Eggum 1991, 108; Rapetti 1991 A, 90f.; Bischoff 1993, 18; Pietsch 1993, 29; Bjerke 1995, 30f.; Billeter 1998, 120; Lange 2003, 79f.; Næss 2004, 104–109; Guleng 2008, 216, 226f.; Woll 2008 A, 94, 98; López 2008, 26; Junillon 2009, 74; Alessandrini 2009, 93; Buchhart 2009, 13; Clarke 2009, 12, 37, 40, 50, 62; Kuuva 2010, 66; Pettersen 2010, 106; Arnaud 2011, 22–23; Bischoff 2011, 18; Hansen et al. 2011, 72, 74, 18; Volle 2012 A, 115, 196f.; Helleland 2012, 24; Grøgaard 2013 A, 349; Mørstad 2013, 209f.; Huber 2013, 40f.; Ohlsen 2013, 200; Lloyd 2015, 126; Van Dijk 2015 B, 118; Stein and Rød 2015, 262, 118; Mørstad 2016, 44, 191, 196, 229, 241, 244, 259; Krämer 2016, 118f.; Ustvedt 2018, 62; Kaaring 2019, 27. **Exhibitions**: 1890, Kristiania, no. 95; 1891, Munich; 1892, Kristiania, no. 6; 1892, Berlin-Düsseldorf-Cologne-Berlin-Copenhagen-Breslau-Dresden-Munich, no. 5; 1915, Copenhagen, no. 282a; 1927, Oslo, no. 40; 1954, Venice, no. 9; 1954, Munich-Cologne, no. 15; 1955, Copenhagen-Odense, no. 14; 1959, Vienna, no. 4; 1959, Warsaw, no. 6; 1965, New York B, no. 9; 1970, Japan, touring exhibition, no. 7; 1972, Kristiansand, no. 48; 1978, Washington, no. 26; 1979, New York; 1981, Tokyo-Sapporo-Nara-Nagoya-Leningrad-Moscow, no. 9; 1982, Washington-New York-Minneapolis, no. 63; 1987, Essen, no. 24; 1987, Zürich, no. 24; 1991, Paris-Oslo-Frankfurt, no. 7; 1995, New York, no. 4; 1999, Florence; 2003, Vienna, no. 81; 2005, Rome, no. 5; 2006, New York, no. 20; 2007, Basel, no. 16; 2008, Oslo, no. 107; 2013, Oslo, no. 19; 2015, Oslo-Amsterdam, no. 89.

The picture was painted in Saint-Cloud, on the outskirts of Paris. Having received his first state travel grant, Munch spent the winter of 1889-90 in the Paris area. It is night and the room is shrouded in hazy gloom. A dim light seeps in from outside, creating a cruciform shadow of the window frame on the expanse of open floor. The forms are generalised and flat, the paint applied with bold brushstrokes. The room and the figure stand in sharp contrast to the world beyond the window, producing a mood of melancholy. With reference to Munch's written notes from the time, the work has been interpreted as reflecting the loss of his father, who died a month before Munch moved to Saint-Cloud.

This is one of the ten paintings by Munch that were accepted for the National Annual Autumn Exhibition in 1890. There it was listed under the title *Nat* (Night). Apparently, Munch also referred to it as "Symphony in Blue", suggesting he might have drawn inspiration from James McNeill Whistler's blue-toned "Nocturnes" (Varnedoe 1982, 186). On the occasion of the exhibition, the art historian Andreas Aubert wrote a lengthy review of Munch's art in *Dagbladet*. In this, he describes the painting as "the finest work he has done in years". Aubert adds: "I have also noticed its potential to captivate people from well beyond the painter's own circle." For Aubert, the young artist displayed an unusual sensitivity that aligned his work with the new European decadent aesthetic, which placed the focus on the cultivation of the artist's personality (*Dagbladet*, 5 November 1890). The picture was praised by many at the time, including the writers Sigbjørn Obstfelder and Vilhelm Krag. Krag even took the painting as inspiration for his poem *Nat*. Many years later, Jens Thiis highlighted the work as "extremely important for Munch's new and highly individual direction" (Thiis 1933, 176). In his view, the evocative "blue painting" marked a new phase in the artist's development at the turn of the 1890s.

The doctor, geologist and outdoor enthusiast Fredrik Arentz bought the picture from the 1890 National Annual Autumn Exhibition. The picture featured in most of Munch's exhibitions in the 1890s, and the fact that the artist was willing to fetch it for each event indicates that he himself regarded it as important and successful. In 1891 Munch was planning an exhibition in Berlin, and in a letter to his Aunt Karen back in Norway, he asked for help with some of the pictures he wanted to include, one of which was the "moonlight picture that Dr Arentz bought" (MM N 76).

Munch often adapted his compositions in later works. *Night in Saint-Cloud* is one of the earliest examples of this practice. It was a popular picture, and he received orders for four copies. The second version, in oils on canvas, was probably done in Berlin in 1893 (Woll M 302). At that point he had access to the first version, which he had loaned from the owner for the exhibition at the Verein Berliner Künstler. He also made two versions in pastels (Woll M 285; Woll M 286) and one in oils on paper (Woll M 287). Further, he produced the image as an etching, which was included in a portfolio of prints published by Julius Meier-Graefe in 1895. In the latter, the cruciform shadow of the window frame on the floor is emphasised.

The National Gallery purchased *Night in Saint-Cloud* from Arentz's heirs in 1917. At that point it was entered into the museum's supplementary record under the title *Natt* (Night). The picture was known by this title up until the 1970s, since when the name of Saint-Cloud has been added. VWH

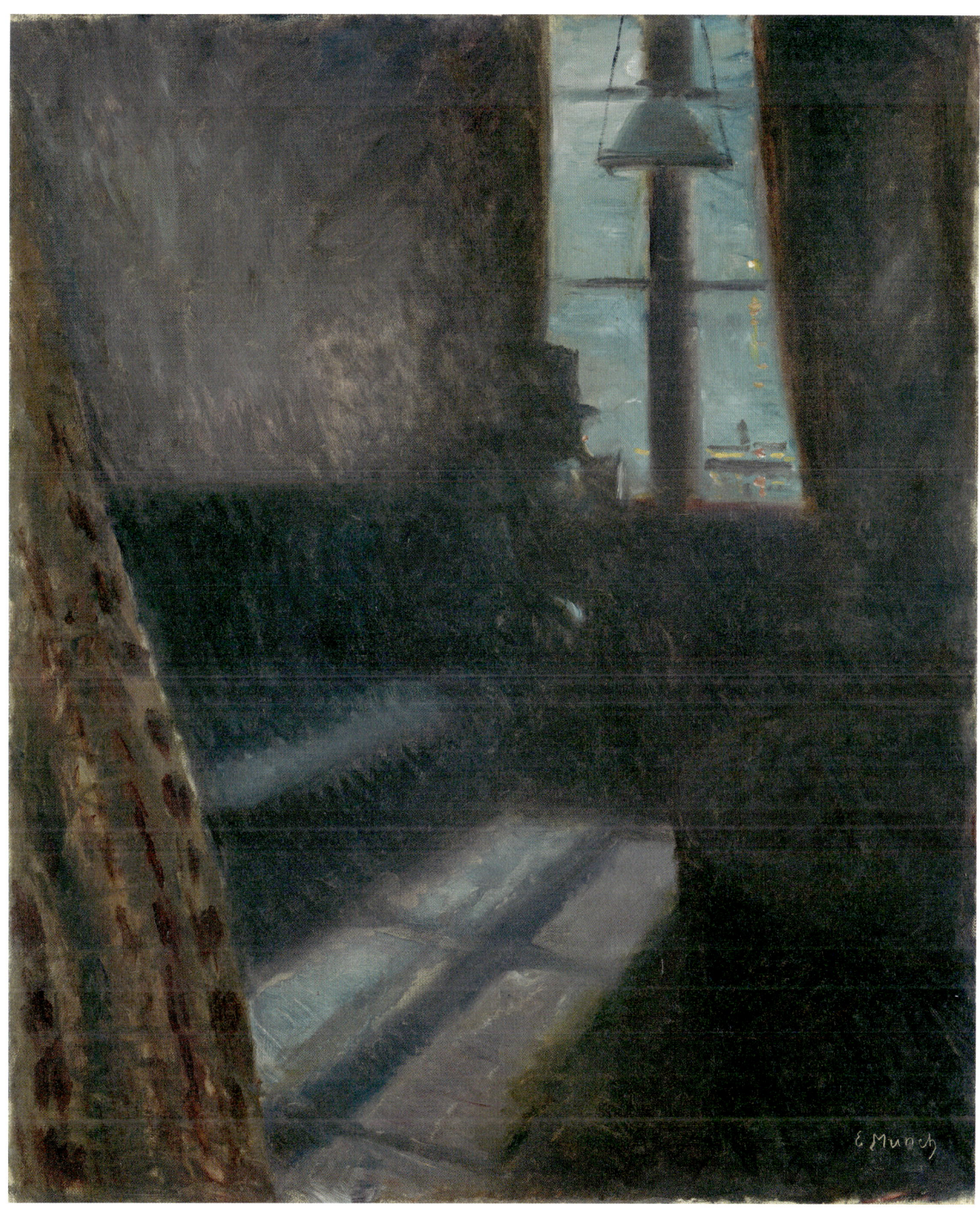

15

Night in Nice, 1891
Natt i Nice

Oil on canvas
48 × 54 cm
Unsigned
NG.M.00394
Woll M 224
NG cat. 1933-944; 1950-1055; 1968-1272; 1992-394

Other titles: *Natt i Nizza*. **Provenance**: Purchased from the National Annual Autumn Exhibition 1891. **Literature**: Skredsvig 1908, 113; Thiis 1933, 182; I. Langaard 1960, 118f., 135; Eggum 1991, 112; Fredlund (ed.) 2002, 50; Pettersen 2003, 189f.; Berman 2008 B, 146-147; Pettersen 2008, 192, 194; Grøgaard 2013 A, 349; Bruteig m.fl. 2015, 12; Marcellán 2015, 210; Stein and Rød 2015, 261; Mørstad 2016, 115, 163, 247; Ford et al. 2019, [unpaginated]; Ford et al. 2021, [unpaginated]. **Exhibitions**: 1891, Kristiania, no. 118; 1927, Oslo, no. 44; 1954, Venice, no. 10; 1954, Munich-Cologne, no. 17; 1955, Copenhagen -Odense, no. 16; 1983, Dresden, no. 7; 1987, Oslo A, no. 47; 1991, Paris-Oslo-Frankfurt, no. 9; 1999, Modum, no. 16; 1999, Florence, no. 5; 2002, Gothenburg, no. 9; 2003, Treviso; 2005, Dortmund-Høvikodden; 2008, Oslo, no. 126; 2009, Copenhagen-Oslo, no. 5; 2013, Oslo, no. 21.

The picture was painted during Munch's first stay in Nice in 1891. Having arrived in early January, he stayed there throughout the spring. He was able to make the trip thanks to a state travel grant, which he received for the second time. In a travelogue with the title "The Queen of the Mediterranean", printed in *Verdens Gang* on 11 February 1891, Munch described Nice as "a city of joy, health and beauty" (MM UT 3). This was one of just a few texts by Munch to be published during his lifetime.

While en route to Nice, Munch fell ill and was admitted to hospital in Le Havre. As soon as he had recovered sufficiently, he continued his journey via Paris. In Nice and the surrounding area, he found subject matter for a number of paintings. He painted the Promenade des Anglais, palm trees, the beach, a boy fishing and, as in *Night in Nice*, rooftops.

From an elevated vantage point, we look out across the roofs towards other buildings and a blue night sky. The architecture produces a horizontal and vertical structure beneath the undulating horizon of distant mountains. The city is asleep, but in a few windows, lights still burn. The dominant blue tones give the picture its atmospheric character, prompting Jens Thiis to describe it as the "blue painting in moonlight" (Thiis 1933, 182). A recurrent feature of Munch's pictures from the 1890s, this blue-tone approach follows on from *Night in Saint-Cloud* (cat. 14). One contemporary source of inspiration was James McNeill Whistler.

Munch had already experimented with a high vantage point in several of the works he had painted back home in Kristiania, for example the view of Olaf Ryes plass (Woll M 90). Was he inspired in this by Kalle Løchen, a friend and fellow artist? One painting by Løchen of a view across the roofs as seen from his studio at Vika had attracted much attention. Such depictions of vistas from high windows are a good example of how artists found subject matter in their local surroundings. Munch adopts the same perspective of looking down on the city in some of his Paris pictures, such as *Rue Lafayette* (cat. 16) and *Rue Rivoli* (Woll M 233). As a way to capture life in the modern metropolis, this approach puts Munch in the company of French painters such as Claude Monet, Gustave Caillebotte and Camille Pissarro.

In exploring the play of moonlight on the roofs and house façades, Munch experiments with a variety of light sources. The picture can be seen in relation to contemporary mood painting and neo-romantic currents. As such, it anticipates Munch's landscapes of the 1890s. The dominant, harmonic palette of blue tones, with hints of pink, purple, and contrasting orange, is typical in this respect. The loose, almost impressionistic treatment contrasts with the structure of more rigid vertical, horizontal and diagonal lines.

This was the first painting by Munch to be acquired for the National Gallery, which also thereby became the first public collection to incorporate an example of the artist's work. *Nat i Nizza* (Night in Nizza), as it was originally called, was purchased at the National Annual Autumn Exhibition in 1891. The price was set at 300 kroner, but Erik Werenskiold informed Munch that the museum had paid 200 kroner for the picture (MM K 1224). wv

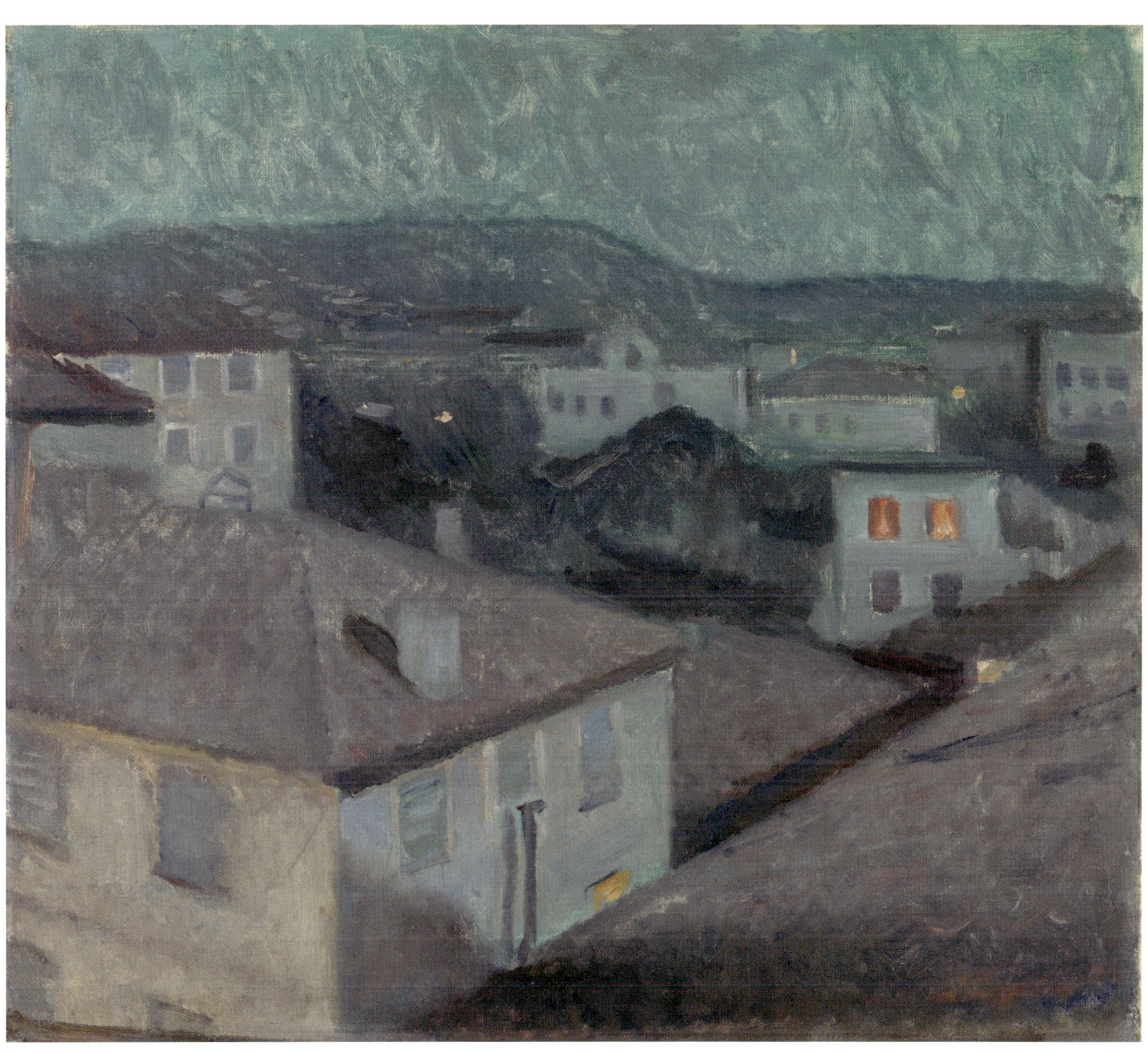

16

Rue Lafayette, 1891

Oil on canvas
92 × 73 cm
Signed l.r. "E. Munch 91"
NG.M.01725
Woll M 232
NG cat. 1950-1054; 1968-1271; 1992-1725

Other titles: *Udsigt over en gade i Paris*; *En gade i Paris*. **Provenance**: Johannes Lynneberg (–1924); Thora Lynneberg (before 1927); purchased with funds from Olaf Schou's donation 1933.
Literature: Romdahl 1946, 96; I. Langaard 1960, 123f.; Svenæus 1968, 39; Rosenblum 1978, 1; Eggum 1983 A, 72f.; Heller 1984, 72f.; Forssman 1985, 58; Rapetti 1991, 102f.; Eggum 1991, 114; Bischoff 1993, 20f.; Czymmek 1998, 72f.; Bjerke 2002, 126; Berman 2008 B, 139f.; Pettersen 2008, 194; López 2008, 10; Clarke 2009, 44, 50; Chang 2010, 45; Bischoff 2011, 11f.; Arnaud 2011, 22; Volle 2012 A, 174–176, 196; Chéroux 2012, 84; Blegvad 2012, 67; Guleng 2013, 131; Grøgaard 2013 A, 349; Heller 2015, 63; Lloyd 2015, 143; van Dijk 2015 A, 49; van Dijk 2015 B, 114; Mørstad 2016, 51, 162, 257; van Dijk 2017, 128; Ustvedt 2018, 57–58. **Exhibitions**: 1892, Kristiania, no. 13; 1892, Berlin–Düsseldorf–Cologne–Berlin–Copenhagen–Breslau–Dresden–Munich, no. 54/53/51; 1894, Stockholm, no. 1; 1927, Oslo, no. 48; 1954, Munich-Cologne, no. 16; 1955, Copenhagen-Odense, no. 15; 1958, Bern, no. 6; 1959, Vienna, no. 6; 1965, New York B, no. 10; 1968, Schaffhausen, no. 12; 1973, Munich–London–Paris, no. 8; 1974, Høvikodden, no. 24; 1983, Dresden, no. 6; 1987, Zürich, no. 23; 1991, Paris–Oslo–Frankfurt, no. 10; 1996, Tokyo; 2002, Turin; 2002, Stockholm–Copenhagen, no. 157; 2006, New York, no. 21; 2008, Oslo, no. 131; 2009, Chicago, no. 8; 2013, Oslo, no. 22; 2015, Oslo–Amsterdam, no. 28.

Munch painted this picture during the months he spent in Paris in spring 1891. In April he wrote to his aunt Karen: "I live in a lovely room with a balcony – Address: Rue Lafayette 49" (MM N 771). Several of his pictures from the years 1890-91 are street views from Paris, Nice and Kristiania. *Rue Lafayette* gives an immediate impression of modern metropolitan life. Here he depicts a long, wide street bustling with people and horse-drawn vehicles seen from a high balcony. The colours are muted, with much grey and dashes of clearer tones. Short, parallel brushstrokes give the illusion of shimmering activity. The choice of subject, the diffuse forms and conspicuous brushwork show that Munch has been studying the French impressionists. In a note from 1933, he recalled his early encounters with Paris and the impressionistic experiments he conducted at the time: "During my first stay in Paris I conducted a few experiments with pure Pointillism – simply spots of colour – *Karl Johan* (Bergen's gallery). It was a brief resumption of my Impressionism – The Picture from rue La Fayette was really only a subject for French painters but I was in Paris after all – The short strokes in the same direction I had long used in Norway." (1927–1933, MM N 122)

Munch had already visited Paris the previous year. On that occasion, he had painted *Night in Saint-Cloud* (cat. 14), a picture that was considered at the time as a transitional work, in its emphasis on the evocation of an emotional mood rather than the reproduction of an observed reality. However, Munch was highly receptive to new influences, and in subsequent years he painted several impressionistic sunlit scenes, such as *Rue Lafayette*. Even so, this work does have several features in common with *Night in Saint-Cloud*, such as the use of perspective lines, the emphasis on spatial depth and the application of the paint in small, parallel, diagonal brushstrokes that create a sense of rhythm. In *Rue Lafayette*, Munch borrowed compositional structures and themes that were common among French artists of the time, such as Claude Monet, Gustave Caillebotte and Camille Pissarro (Eggum 1991, Rappetti 1991 A, Berman 2008). Munch soon abandoned the neo-impressionist styles he had experimented with in the years 1889–91, while continuing to employ some of the striking perspective effects. He returns to the vertiginous vantage point of *Rue Lafayette* a few years later in *Scream* (cat. 23).

The picture was exhibited for the first time at Munch's solo exhibition at Tostrupgården in Kristiania in 1892, under the title *Udsigt over en gade i Paris* (View of a Street in Paris). Initially in private ownership, it was purchased for the collection with funds donated to the National Gallery by Olaf Schou in 1933. VWH

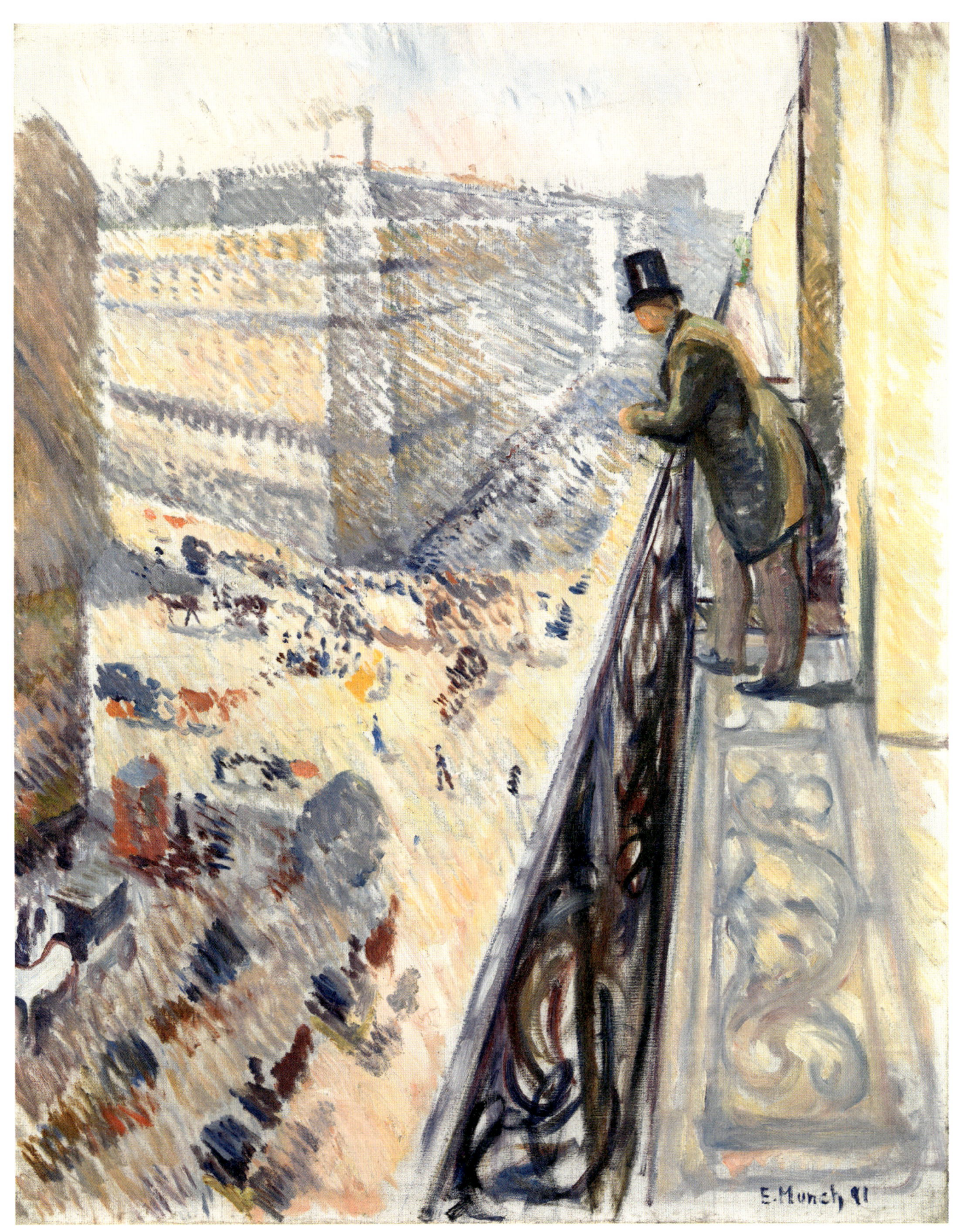

17

The Kiss, 1892

Kyss

Oil on canvas
73 × 92 cm
Signed l.l. "E. Munch 1892"
NG.M.02812
Woll M 266
NG cat. 1992-2812

Other titles: *Kyss ved vinduet*. **Provenance**: Charlotte and Christian Mustad (before 1933–1959/70); bequeathed by Charlotte and Christian Mustad to the National Gallery in 1959, received 1970.
Literature: I. Langaard 1960, 145; Svenæus 1968, 104; Heller 1984, 124; Eggum 1991, 124f.; Fredlund (red.) 2002, 52; Pettersen 2003, 196; Pettersen 2008, 194; Woll 2008 A, 92; Clarke 2009, 50–51, 65, 99, 124; Kuuva 2010, 61, 67; Hansen m.fl. 2011, 50; Volle 2012 A, 199; Clarke 2013, 53; Nordkvelle 2013, 271; Nyaas (red.) 2013, 84; Clarke 2014, 54; Alarcó 2015, 44; Lloyd 2015, 126; Schneede 2015, 161; Stein and Rød 2015, 266; Gjessing 2016, 36; Bartum 2019, 53; Vassenden 2019, 26.
Exhibitions: 1892, Kristiania, no. 6; 1892, Berlin–Düsseldorf–Cologne–Berlin–Copenhagen, no. 6; 1893, Berlin, no. 4b (version uncertain); 1894, Stockholm, no. 59 (version uncertain); 1927, Oslo, no. 63; 1950, USA, touring exhibition, no. 8; 1951, Brighton–Glasgow–London–The Hague–Paris, no. 7/8; 1971, Oslo, no. 33; 1978, Washington, no. 71; 1979, New York; 1983, Dresden, no. 8; 1986, West Palm Beach, no. 16; 1991, Paris–Oslo, no. 21; 1992, London, no. 17; 1993, Tokyo–Osaka, no. 15; 1995, Madrid–Barcelona–Reykjavik–Stockholm, no. 53; 2002, Gothenburg, no. 10; 2003, Vienna, no. 43; 2005, Rome, no. 13; 2006, New York, no. 49; 2007, Basel, no. 24; 2008, Oslo, no. 150; 2009, Chicago, no. 11; 2013, Oslo, no. 27; 2015, Oslo–Amsterdam, no. 97.

An interior with a couple in a tight embrace, kissing. They are standing in a darkened room, behind a white lace curtain. The view through the window shows the city at night, with lights in the windows of the buildings opposite, a few people on the pavement, and a cypress tree to the left. With many short brushstrokes, Munch has created a dynamic surface that gives the impression that the pair are in motion. The picture's blue tones echo the mood of *Night in Saint-Cloud*, 1890 (cat. 14).

The Kiss was painted during Munch's second stay in Nice. He had painted an earlier version during his first stay in the city in southern France the previous year (Woll M 257). In the National Museum's painting, he has shifted the kissing couple from the left to the right of the picture. Half turned away from the viewer, the man's face can be seen in oblique profile, while the woman's is hidden behind the kiss. The figures seem to merge into a single form. Ingrid Langaard has remarked that the picture suggests "a theatrical scene, with the protagonists locked in a close embrace" (I. Langaard 1960, 147).

The Kiss belongs to a series of works on the love theme that Munch developed in the 1890s. Kissing couples also figure in works by contemporary artists such as Gustav Klimt, Auguste Rodin, Stephan Sinding, and Gustav Vigeland.

Munch painted several versions of *The Kiss*, a theme he returned to repeatedly throughout his career. In his drawings and prints we can trace its evolution from the early, realistic drawing *Adjø (Kyss)* (Adieu (The Kiss)), 1889–1890 (MM.T.2356), through to the late woodcut *Kyss på marken II* (Kiss in the Field II) from 1943 (Woll G 746). *The Kiss* is a good example of Munch's use of repetition as an artistic method. The various versions illustrate how he experimented with spatial arrangements, colour schemes, narrative, simplification, and abstraction.

Trygve Nergaard discusses the work in relation to the window as a classical device anchored in romantic art. The window enhances the tensions between inside and out, between bounded and unbounded spaces, and between darkness and light, contrasts that Munch had also explored in works such as *The Sick Child* (cat. 8) and *Spring* (cat. 12) (Nergaard 2002, 118). The treatment of the window contributes to the painting's formal play of lines, with the vertical and horizontal lines of the window sill and glazing bars contrasting with the diagonal curve of the curtain and the irregular contours of the couple.

In 1902, *The Kiss* was shown in Berlin as one of the earliest works in the epic Frieze of Life series. It was included in the first section, which had the heading "The Seed of Love". As a depiction of an embrace, it anticipates the couples in *The Dance of Life* (cat. 40). Munch's so-called "Saint-Cloud Manifesto" of 1889 also contains a drawing of a couple embracing, which has similarities to *The Kiss* (I. Langaard 1960, 146; MM N 289, 5).

The Kiss is an early expression of Munch's ambivalence towards amorous relationships. The Polish poet Stanisław Przybyszewski was the first to write about the subject. He notes Munch's emphasis on the all-consuming power of desire:

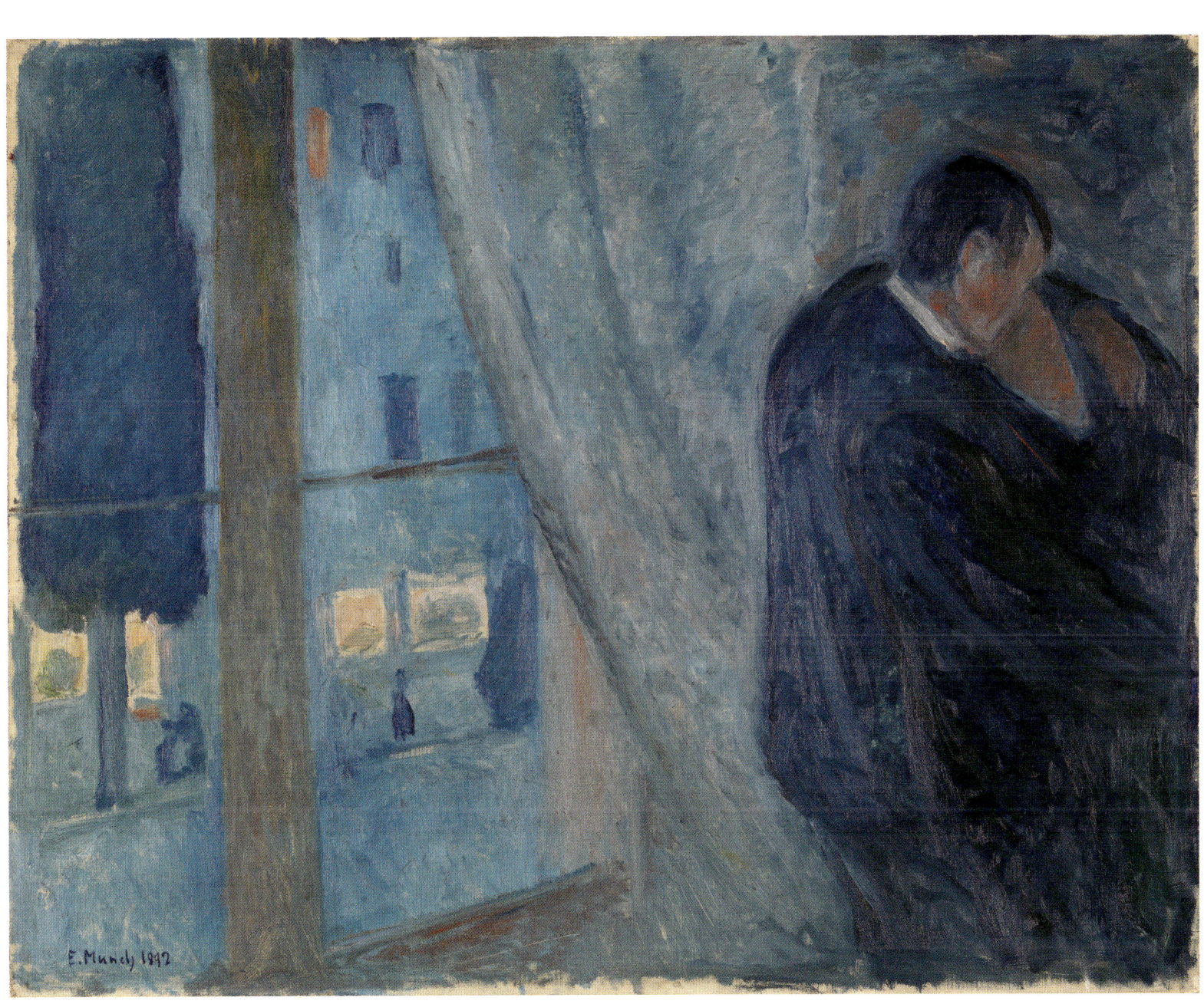

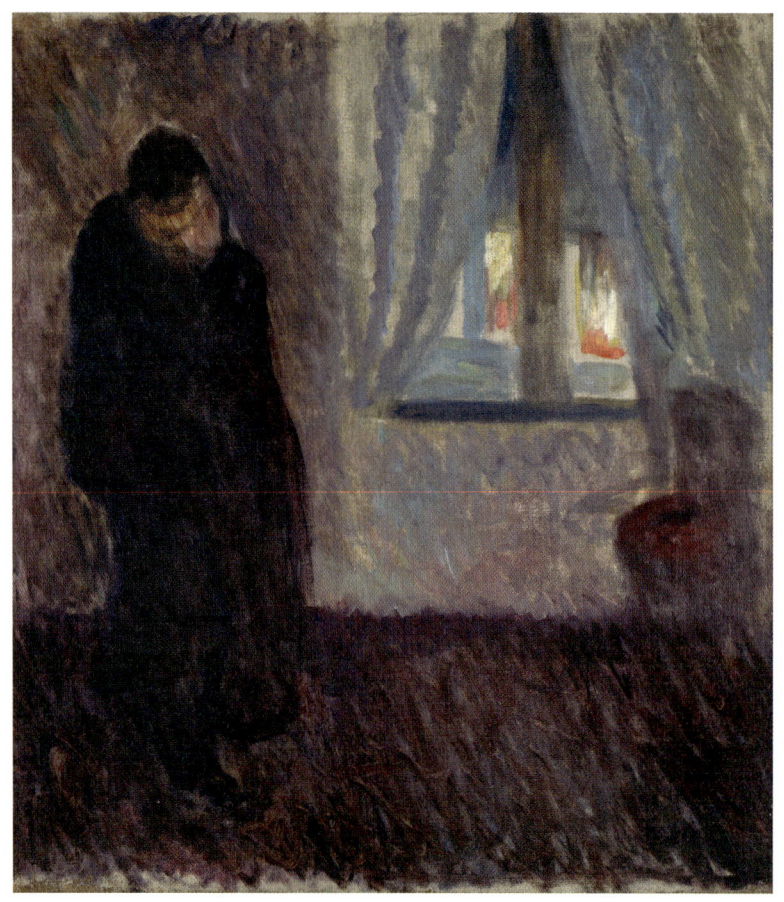

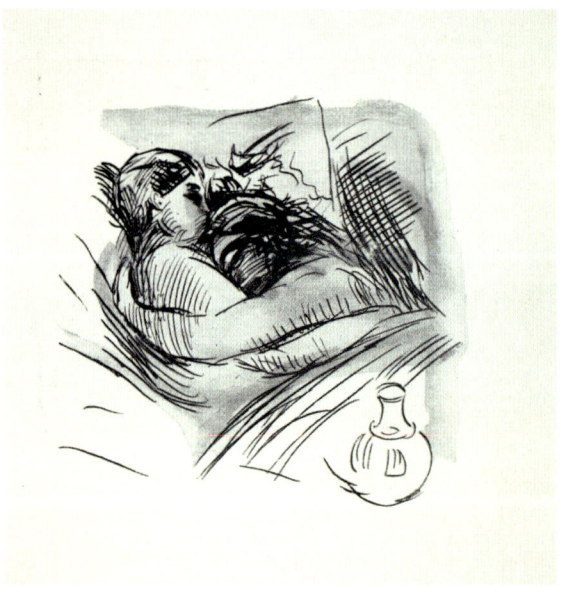

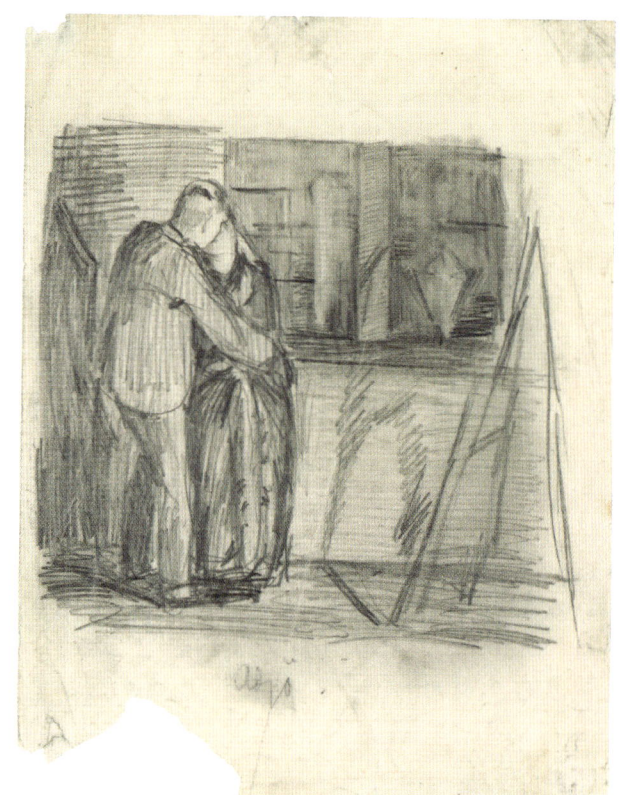

Edvard Munch: *Kiss by the Window*, 1891
Oil on canvas, 72 × 64,5 cm
Munchmuseet
MM.M.00622, Woll M 257
Photo: Munchmuseet/Ove Kvavik

From *Livsfrisens tilblivelse*, p. 5
Printed booklet with inscription by Munch, [undated]
Munchmuseet
MM.N.570-05

Edvard Munch: *Adieu (Kiss) 1*, 1889-1890 (probably)
Pencil, 271 × 207 mm
Munchmuseet
MM.T.02356
Photo: Munchmuseet/Tone Margrethe Gauden

... all the ardour of the kiss, the terrible power of the painfully lustful
sexual yearning, the disappearance of the awareness of self, the merging
of two naked individualities, all is so honestly felt that one rises above the
repellent and the unusual.

(Przybyszewski 1894 A, translation in *Vigeland + Munch* 2015, 85).

The painting entered the museum in 1970 as part of the Charlotte and Christian
Mustad bequest. Munch painted five versions of *The Kiss*, of which the National
Museum's is the second (Woll M 257; Woll M 266; Woll M 267; Woll M 400; Woll M
401). In addition, there is a variation in which the pair is depicted naked (Woll M
397). He also made four woodcuts on the theme (Woll G 114; Woll G 115; Woll G 124
and Woll G 204; cat. 103) and an etching in which the couple is naked (cat. 19, Woll
G 23). Further, he explored the device of the kissing couple in a number of other
contexts (Woll M 731; Woll M 1096; Woll M 1405; Woll 2008 B, 243; MM.T.2356).
In a list produced by the prestigious Hamburg gallery Commeter in 1906, the
painting is registered as no. 7. Although it has been known by the title *Kyss* (The
Kiss) since it was first shown at Munch's exhibition at Tostrupgården in autumn
1892, Gerd Woll has chosen to call it *Kiss by the Window*. WV

18

Moonlight by the Mediterranean, 1892

Månenatt ved Middelhavet

Oil on canvas
46 × 55 cm
Signed l.r. "E Munch"
NG.M.00842
Woll M 274
NG cat. 1933-945; 1950-1056; 1968-1273; 1992-338

Other titles: *Månenatt i Nizza*. **Provenance**: Gift from Olaf Schou 1909. **Literature**: Skredsvig 1908, 116; Thomsen 1999, 176; Pettersen 2008, 192; Kuuva 2010, 65-66; Hansen et al. 2011, 48; Ahtola-Moorhouse 2014, 32. **Exhibitions**: 1892, Berlin–Düsseldorf– Cologne–Berlin–Copenhagen–Breslau–Dresden–Munich, no. 43; 1927, Oslo, no. 45; 1958, Bern, no. 7; 1987, Oslo B, no. 59; 2001, Ferrara, no. 61; 2003, Treviso; 2008, Oslo, no. 155; 2014, Helsinki.

The picture was painted during Munch's second stay in Nice. In November 1891 he travelled to southern France with the artist Christian Skredsvig and his wife Maggie Plathe. Skredsvig described the journey and the stay in *Dage og Nætter blant Kunstnere* (Days and Nights among Artists) (1908), in a chapter entitled "Edvard Munch in Monte Carlo". Shortly before Christmas, the Skredsvig couple rented a house in Saint-Jean-Cap-Ferrat, between Nice and Monte Carlo. In February, Munch moved in with the married couple. In a letter to Aunt Karen, he writes: "Skredsvig lives in a beautiful villa near Nice – just beside a small bay –" (MM N 780).

At Saint-Jean-Cap-Ferrat, Munch developed an interest in the landscape of the coastline and the Mediterranean sea. In *Moonlight by the Mediterranean*, he paints the curve of the beach, the mountains in the distance and the silhouettes of the vegetation in the foreground. Skredsvig describes how Munch put "a candle stump in the garden wall and painted the moonlight" (Skredsvig 1908, 152). The picture anticipates Munch's later depictions of moonlight on meandering shorelines. Like many of the works he painted during his stays in Nice, this one also shows a unifying use of blue tones.

The painting was gifted to the National Gallery by Olaf Schou in 1909. In the past, the dating of the work was disputed. In the National Gallery's catalogue from 1992, it is attributed to 1891, together with *Night in Nice* (cat. 15; NG cat. 1992-394). However, according to Gerd Woll, it is more likely that Munch painted the picture after moving in with the Skredsvigs at Saint-Jean-Cap-Ferrat in late February 1892 (Woll 2008 B, 259). After its first showing at Munch's exhibition at Tostrupgården in the autumn of 1892, the painting was included in the so-called "scandal exhibition" at the Verein Berliner Künstler later in the same year and in the ensuing exhibition tour. Drawing consequences from the revised dating, in 2012 the title was changed from *Månenatt i Nizza* (Moonlight in Nice) to *Månenatt ved Middelhavet* (Moonlight by the Mediterranean). wv

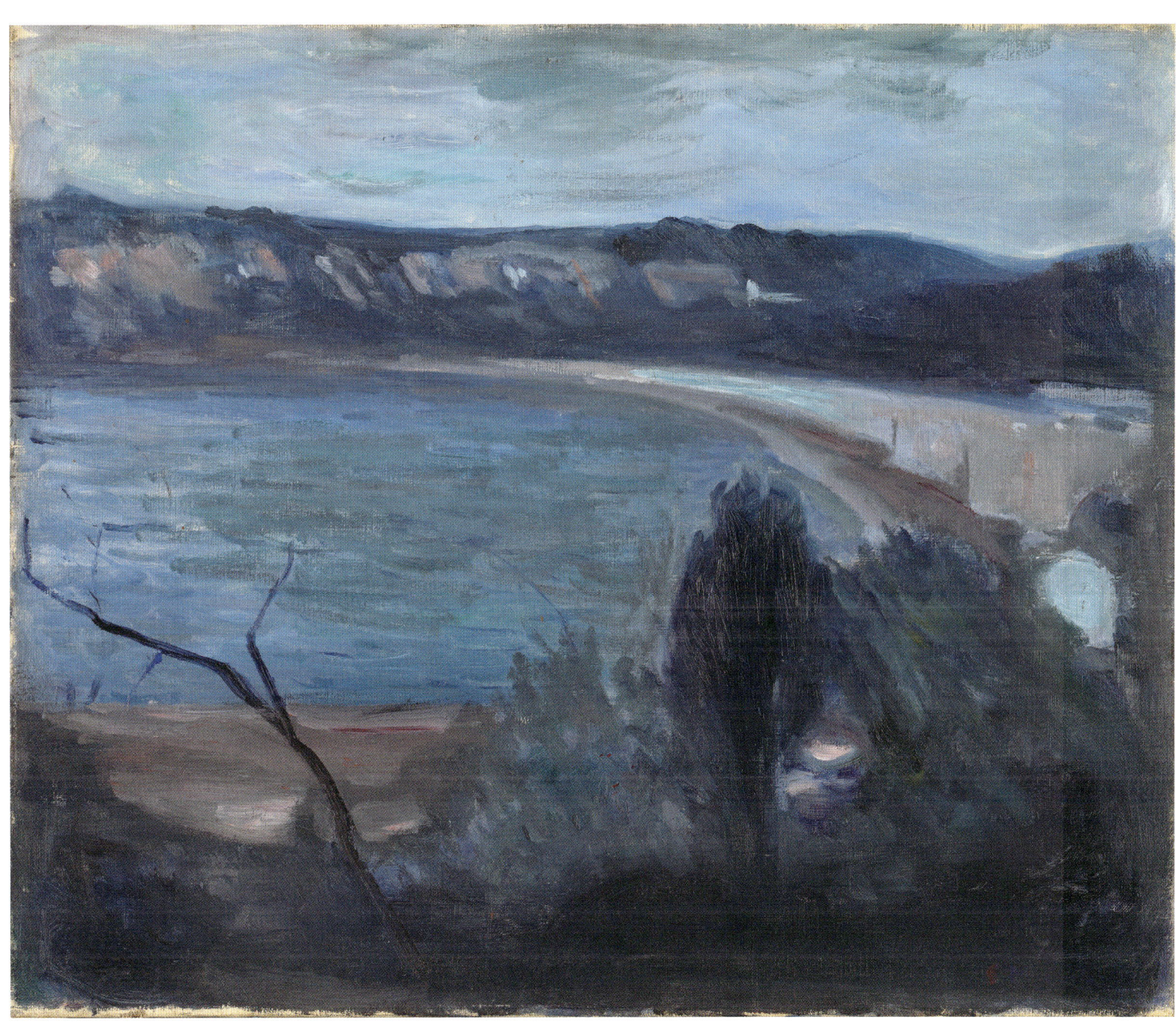

19

Melancholy, 1892

Melankoli

Oil on canvas
64 × 96 cm
Signed l.l. "E.M."
NG.M.02813
Woll M 284
NG cat. 1992-2813

Other titles: *Trist Aften*; *Sorgen*; *Jalousi*. **Provenance**: Conrad Pineus; Charlotte and Christian Mustad (before 1927–1959/1970); bequeathed by Charlotte and Christian Mustad to the National Gallery in 1959, received 1970. **Literature:** One of Munch's best-known motifs, it is widely discussed in much of the general Munch literature. Przybyszewski 1894 A, 86–87; Obstfelder 1896, 21; Ritter 1906, 49; Thiis 1933, 182f.; Langaard 1960, 136f.; Svenæus 1968, 150; Nergaard 1978, 124f.; Rosenblum 1978, 2f.; Eggum 1979 B, 20; Heller 1984, 79f.; Skedsmo 1987 A, 218–220; Eggum 1991, 135; Bøe 1992, 21; Berg 1993, 213, 222; Czymmek 1998, 74; Zarobell 2005, 12; Guleng 2008, 213; Pettersen 2008, 182; Woll 2008 A, 91–92, 100; Buchhart 2009, 19; Ditteney 2009, 111, 124, 140; Kuuva 2010, 61; Shiff 2010, [unpaginated]; Ydstie 2010, 39, 46; Volle 2012 A, 331, 333; Endresen 2013, 220; Flaatten 2013 A, 11, 75–77, 81; Guleng 2013, 131; Grøgaard 2013 A, 349; Nyaas (ed.) 2013, 178; Rognerud 2013, 48; Guleng 2014, 367, 370; Henningsen (ed.) 2014, 23; Alarcó 2015, 25; Berman 2015, 93; Hansen 2015, 164; Stafne-Pfisterer 2015, 91; Steihaug 2015, 155; Mørstad 2016, 23, 168, 191, 264–265, 268–269; Brandtzæg (ed.) 2017, 39; Ustvedt 2018, 65–67; Bartrum 2019, 53; Kaaring 2019, 30f.; Vassenden 2019, 26. **Exhibitions**: 1892, Kristiania, no. 10; 1892, Berlin–Düsseldorf–Cologne–Berlin–Copenhagen–Breslau–Dresden–Munich, no. 7; 1894, Stockholm, no. 66 (uncertain); 1895, Berlin, no. 11; 1922, Zürich, no. 4; 1922, Bern–Basel, no. 4; 1927, Berlin, no. 51; 1927, Oslo, no. 81; 1950, USA, touring exhibition, no. 7; 1951, Brighton–Glasgow–London–The Hague–Paris, no. 6; 1954, Venice, no. 18; 1954, Munich–Cologne, no. 29; 1955, Copenhagen–Odense, no. 28; 1968, Schaffhausen, no. 16; 1973, Oslo; 1973, Munich–London–Paris, no. 10; 1977, Warsaw, no. 5; 1977, Stockholm, no. 12; 1978, Washington, no. 27; 1979, New York; 1981, Tokyo–Sapporo–Nara–Nagoya–Leningrad–Moscow, no. 82/67; 1984, Toronto–Cincinnati, no. 2; 1986, London–Düsseldorf–Paris–Oslo, no. 57/67; 1993, Tokyo–Osaka, no. 43; 1994, Munich–Hamburg–Berlin, no. 1; 1998, Cologne, no. 56; 1999, Florence, no. 6; 2003, Vienna, no. 85; 2005, Rome, no. 14; 2005, Philadelphia; 2007, Ferrara–Rome, no. 62; 2008, Oslo, no. 158; 2009, Copenhagen–Oslo, no. 16; 2013, Stockholm; 2013, Oslo, no. 30; 2015, Oslo–Helsinki, no. 25; 2015, Madrid, no. 4.

The shoreline of a sweeping bay, a jetty in the distance with three figures and a boat. In the foreground sits a man in melancholy pose with his head resting on his hand. The painting has been described as "the defining image of *jealousy*" (Thiis 1933, 182).

The simplified, stylised form links the work to syntheticism, a movement whose leading figure was Paul Gauguin. In the period 1889–92, Munch had several stays in Paris, where he became acquainted with the latest trends in French art.

In this depiction of a sorrowful figure, the boulder-strewn shoreline of Åsgårdstrand plays a central role. The undulating contours of the sea, sky and landscape create a dynamic of flowing lines. A friend of the artist, the poet Sigbjørn Obstfelder, once wrote of Munch: "… he sees in wavy lines, for him the shoreline wends its way along the sea …" (Obstfelder 1896, 18). Jens Thiis also emphasises "the line of Aasgaardstrand, the gentle, sweeping, expressive and colourful shoreline, which occurs again and again in his pictures and etchings as a common denominator of his style" (Thiis 1933, 58). The painting was included in what later became known as The Frieze of Life, in which the shoreline seems almost to serve as an element that binds the series together. The depictions of melancholy and the kiss were among the first works Munch painted for his epic series about the course of love and life. Both are early examples of the way Munch repeated certain themes. Developing series with variations on a theme became an important aspect of his artistic practice.

Melancholy has been linked to the amorous encounter between Munch's friend, Jappe Nilssen, and Oda Krohg, the wife of Christian Krohg, which played out at Åsgårdstrand in the summer of 1891. Munch was a witness to the affair, in which the unfortunate Nilssen drew the shortest straw. As someone who was exploring the tribulations of love relationships in both texts and pictures (MM.T.2760), Munch found the situation interesting. Around this time, he enjoyed close contacts with literary circles, and writing would remain important to him as a tool for developing his pictures throughout the 1890s.

Munch painted five versions of the *Melancholy* motif (Woll M 241; Woll M 284; Woll M 316; Woll M 359; Woll M 360). There is uncertainty regarding their dating and order of production, and which exhibitions they appeared in (I. Langaard 1960, 135; Eggum 1991, 135; Eggum 1993, 213-223; Berg 1993, 213-223; Woll 2008 B, 267). The National Museum's *Melancholy* is assumed to be the second in the series and differs significantly from the others in its manner of execution and the placing of the main figure in the lower right corner facing out of the frame.

The Munch Museum's *Evening. Melancholy* (Woll M 241) is considered the earliest version (Berg 1993, 213-223; Woll 2008 B, 267). Dated 1891, it was shown at the National Annual Autumn Exhibition in that year under the title *Aften* (Evening). In the catalogue it is listed in the section "Hand Drawings, Pastels and Watercolours" (catalogue of the National Annual Autumn Exhibition 1891, no. 321). It uses oils, pencil and crayon on canvas, and its idiom is sketchier than that of the other pictures in the group.

After the National Annual Autumn Exhibition, Christian Krohg wrote an enthusiastic review of Munch's *Evening*, which he believed the critics had overlooked during the exhibition. An important contribution to the reception of the Melancholy theme, Krohg's article has also created confusion. Is it *Evening. Melancholy* he is writing about? "Munch should be thanked, because that boat is yellow – had it not been, he would not have painted the picture," Krohg wrote (*Verdens Gang* and *Dagbladet,* 27 November 1891).

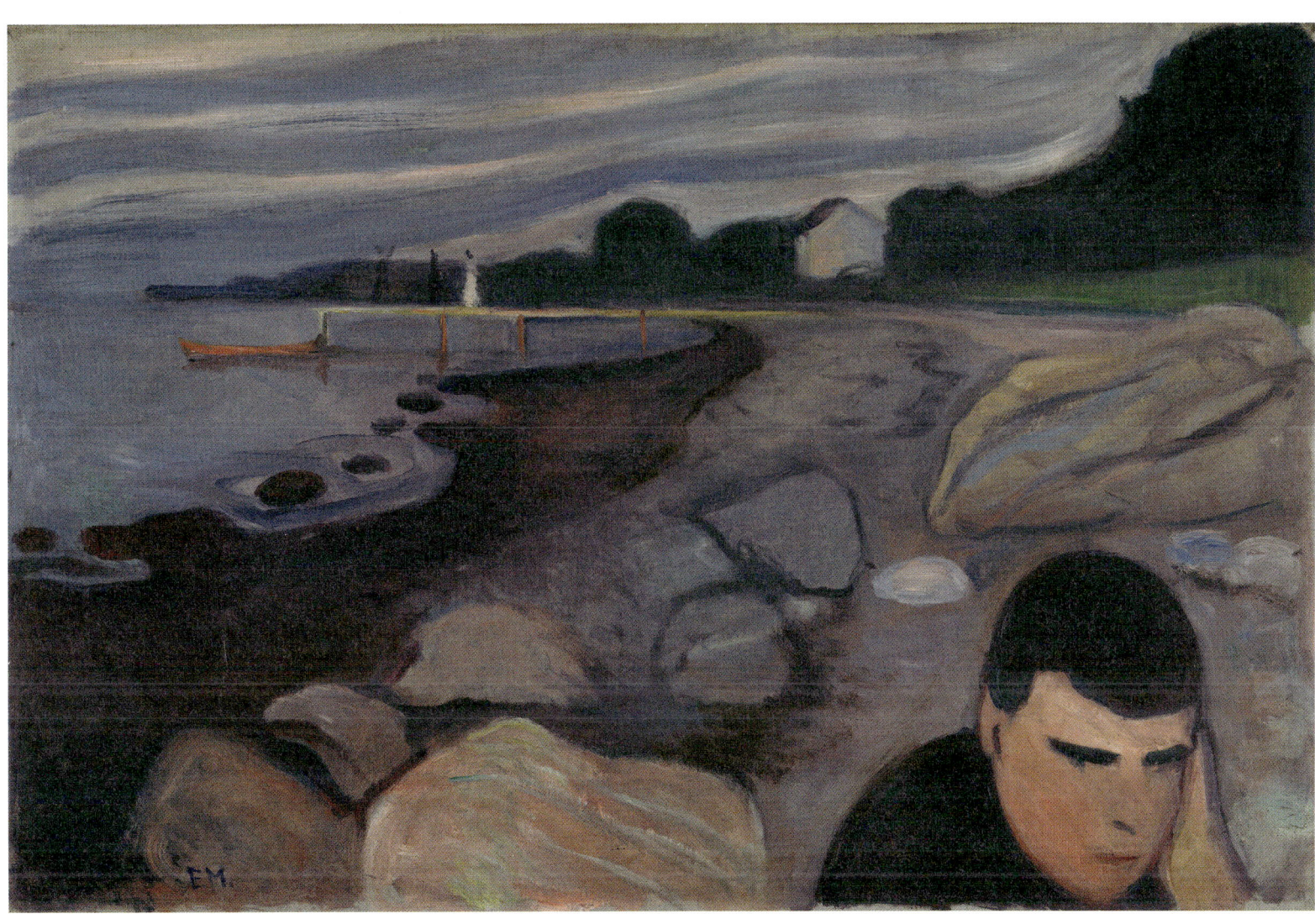

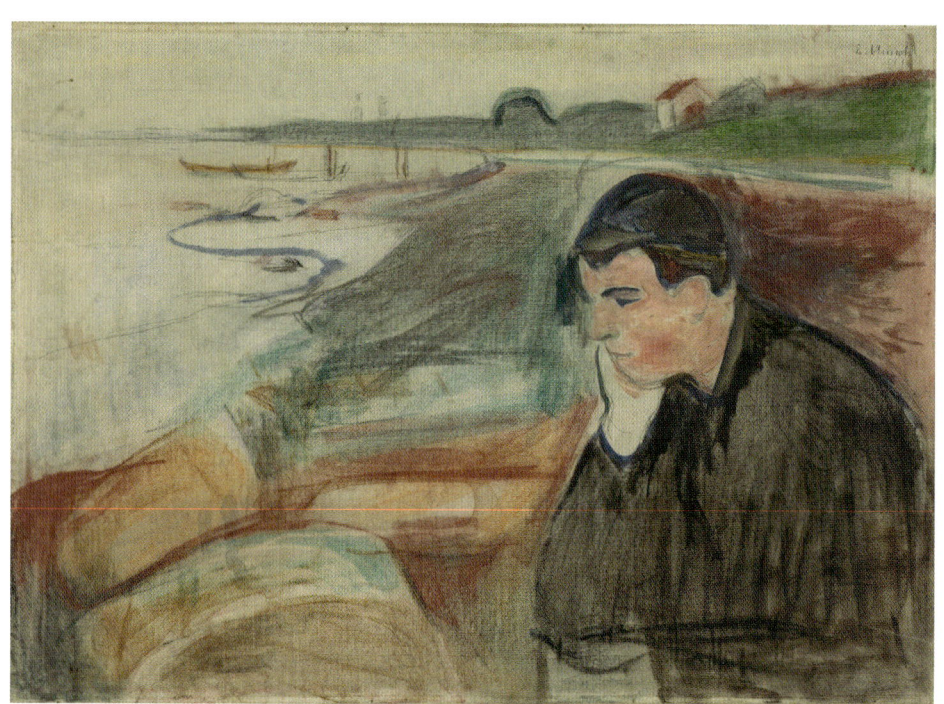

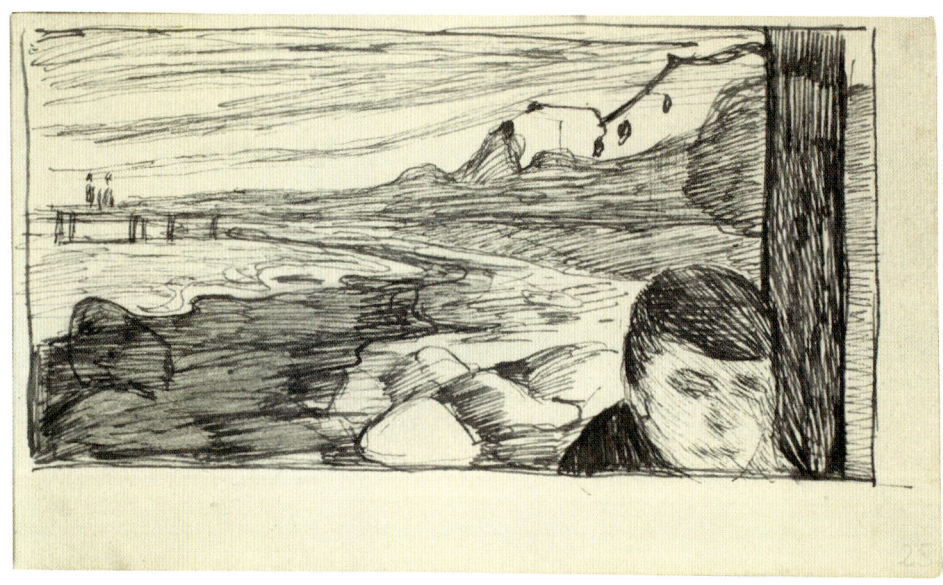

Edvard Munch: *Evening. Melancholy*, 1891
Oil, pencil and crayon on canvas, 73,5 × 100,5 cm
Munchmuseet
MM.M.00058, Woll M 241
Photo: Munchmuseet / Halvor Bjørngård

Edvard Munch: *Melancholy*, 1892
Pen, pencil on paper, 99 × 168 mm
Munchmuseet
MM.T.00128-25-recto
Photo: Munchmuseet / Halvor Bjørngård

Krohg considers the picture in the context of symbolism: "... the latest direction in French art. The latest catchword today is the 'timbre' of a colour. Has anyone ever heard such a timbre of colour as in this picture." He notes a shift in Munch's art that echoes the trends of contemporary French art. According to Krohg, Munch is the first Norwegian artist "who dares to bend nature, the model, etc. in response to the mood, and to alter them to achieve more" (*Verdens Gang* and *Dagbladet,* 27 November 1891).

One work that is often mentioned in conjunction with the National Museum's *Melancholy* is a vignette Munch did for an anthology of poetry by his friend Emanuel Goldstein, which had originally been published as *Alruner* (1892). For a new edition of the collection with the title *Vekselspillet. Psykologiske Digte* (Alternation. Psychological Poems) (1886), Goldstein asked Munch for a drawing. He added one stipulation: "It should be something symbolic" (letter 12 December 1891, MM K 1497). A few weeks later he agreed that the painting Munch had shown at the National Annual Autumn Exhibition would be relevant as a theme for the vignette (MM K 1545). In a letter sent from Nice, Munch complained about the difficulty of executing the assignment without having the painting in front of him. "If I were at home in Norway it would be easy, because then I could simply copy the painting - now we will be lucky if it turns out well" (MM N 3036). During his stay in southern France, Munch made a series of sketches of the subject from memory. In his sketchbooks from the period, we find drafts that are close to the National Museum's *Melancholy* (MM.T.00128; MM.T.00129). Like the painting, these drawings differ from the other versions of *Melancholy* in that the figure is placed in the bottom right corner with his face turned towards the viewer, rather than in profile. He is not shown looking "out over the same still water," as Krohg put it in his article about the first painting (*Verdens Gang* and *Dagbladet,* 27 November 1891).

The National Museum's painting was shown for the first time in Munch's exhibition at Tostrupgården in the autumn of 1892, where it had the title *Trist Aften* (Sad Evening). It also featured in the so-called scandal exhibition at Unter den Linden in Berlin the following year. Here it was included in the group with the heading "Study for a series: 'Love'". In his 1894 monograph about Munch, Przybyszewski writes of the work: "In the foreground you see, as in Chinese pictures, a male head gazing out of the picture frame, with an eye that looks like a triangle: a symbol of the eternal persistence of one of the most banal and painful emotions" (Przybyszewski 1894 A, translated in *Vigeland + Munch*, 2015, 86). Commenting on the latter, Thiis noted how the composition is "boldly truncated in the Japanese manner by the edge of the frame" (Thiis 1933, 182).

In this work, the figure is represented in the classic posture of melancholy, with his head resting on one hand. With its allusions both to dejection and artistic genius, this pathos-laden formula is firmly rooted in art history, and can be compared to works such as Albrecht Dürer's *Melencholia I* (1514) and Auguste Rodin's *The Thinker* from *The Gates of Hell*, begun in 1880. Munch had already used the melancholy pose in his earlier *Night in Saint-Cloud* (cat. 14).

The painting entered the museum's collection in 1970 as part of the Charlotte and Christian Mustad bequest. A series of sketches allows us to trace Munch's work on the theme (cat. 120; cat. 159; MM.T.2760; MM.T.2355; MM.T.00128-25 and sketchbook MM.T.00129). He also produced a number of prints based on the same design: the woodcut *Evening. Melancholy I* (1896, cat. 63; Woll G 91) and *Melancholy III* (1902, cat. 102; Woll G 203). In *Melancholy (The Reinhardt Frieze)*, from 1906-07 (Woll M 736), the male figure is replaced by a woman in a red dress. wv

20

Inger in Black and Violet, 1892

Inger i svart og fiolett

Oil on canvas
172.5 × 122.5 cm
Signed l.l. "E Munch 1892"
NG.M.00499
Woll M 294
NG cat. 1933-946; 1950-1057; 1968-1274; 1992-499

Other titles: *Harmoni i sort og violet*; *Farvest-emning i sort og violet*; *Sort og Violet*; *Portræt av kunstnerens søster, Inger Munch*; *Kunstnerens søster Inger*. **Provenance**: Purchased from the artist 1899. **Literature**: Glaser 1917, 49f.; Thiis 1933, 131; Romdahl 1946, 98-99; I. Langaard 1960, 163f.; Stang 1977, 54; Skedsmo (ed.) 1981, 92–93; Heller 1984, 81; London 1986, 188; Skedsmo 1987, 222; Messel 1989, 127; Eggum 1994 A, 52; Lange 2004, 133; Yvenes et al. (eds.) 2008, 28; Pettersen 2008, 194; Grøgaard 2013 A, 349; Ustvedt 2013 A, 235; Ustvedt 2018, 50. **Exhibitions**: 1892, Kristiania, no. 13; 1892, Berlin–Düsseldorf–Cologne–Berlin–Copenhagen–Breslau–Dresden–Munich, no. 12; 1911, Rome, no. 43; 1927, Berlin, no. 29; 1927, Oslo, no. 55; 1950, USA, touring exhibition, no. 9; 1951, Brighton–Glasgow–London–The Hague–Paris, no. 9; 1954, Venice, no. 11; 1954, Munich–Cologne, no. 21; 1955, Copenhagen–Odense, no. 20; 1960, Recklinghausen–Vienna–Berlin–Oslo–Helsinki, no. 7; 1968, Stockholm, no. 234; 1970, Japan, touring exhibition, no. 9; 1973, Munich–London–Paris, no. 11; 1975, Århus–Humlebæk, no. 148/2; 1980, Washington; 1983, Dresden, no. 9; 1986, London–Düsseldorf–Paris–Oslo, no. 58; 1991, Paris–Oslo–Frankfurt, no. 22; 2006, New York, no. 11; 2008, Oslo, no. 164 B; 2013, Oslo, no. 33; 2015, Amsterdam, no. 65.

The subject here is Munch's five-year younger sister Inger (1868-1952). As in the portrait of 1884 (cat. 6), Inger is wearing a dress with a buttoned bodice. In the new picture, however, the realism and the details are toned down in favour of a simpler, decorative idiom that emphasises colours, tones and an overall, monumental unity. With its floor-length skirt, high collar, long sleeves and muted colours, the dress is a characteristic example of contemporary bourgeois fashion. The figure is displaced slightly to one side, and the two-part background fills much of the canvas. The composition is dominated by repeated ovals; from the neck brooch and the clasped hands, to the head and the body contours. The meditative aura, produced by the reliance on simple, repeated forms and the dominant bluish tone, links the work to the romantic mood painting of the 1890s in the Nordic countries.

Portraits of family members, friends and colleagues were an important aspect of Munch's early activity as an artist, and Inger was one of his most frequent portrait subjects. The works that feature her include *Inger Munch in Black* (cat. 6) and *Inger på stranden* (Inger on the Beach) (1889, KODE Art Museums and Composer Homes, Bergen). She also served as a model in other compositions, for example as the frontal figure in the National Museum's *Death in the Sickroom* (cat. 22), probably painted the year after this portrait, and as the younger of the two women in *Mother and Daughter* (cat. 35). The frontal pose with the hands modestly clasped became a standard for his portraits of young women.

Munch turned to full-figure portraiture early in his career and continued with it until the end. It is a genre with strong links to historical representations of prominent public figures. One of the foremost practitioners in Norwegian art was Christian Krohg. The use of the blue palette and the sometimes hazy, translucent allow us to compare *Inger in Black and Violet* with the portraits of James A.M. Whistler, which were attracting considerable attention at the time Munch painted this work. The painting's original title, *Harmoni i svart og violet* (Harmony in Black and Violet), also indicates an interest in Whistler.

This is one of Munch's most important portraits and a seminal work from the 1890s. It was shown in the Kristiania exhibition of 1892 and the "scandal" presentation that followed later that year in Berlin. The work was purchased from the artist together with *Spring* in 1899 (cat. 12). ØU

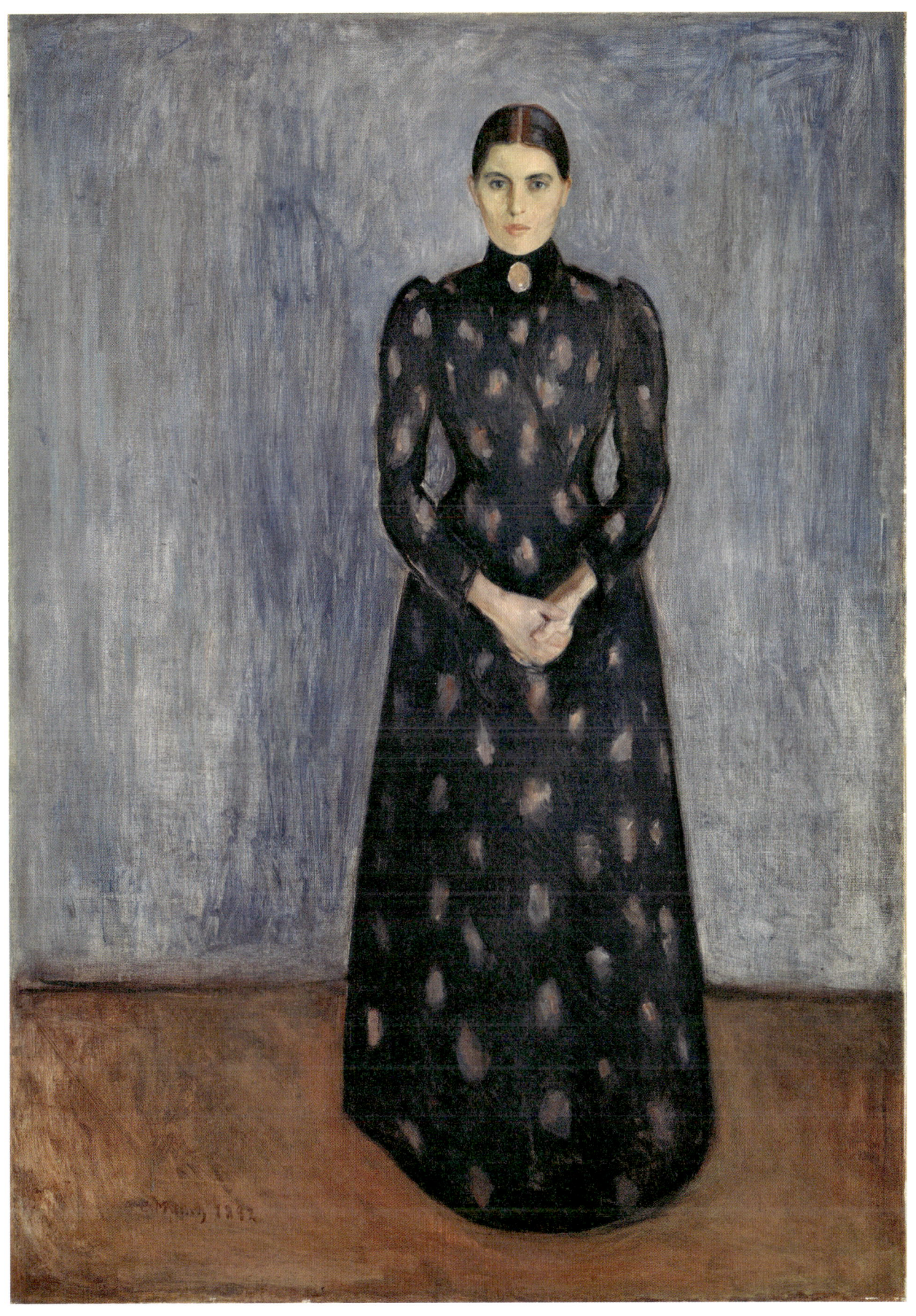

21

Moonlight, 1893

Måneskinn

Oil on canvas
140.5 × 135 cm
Signed l.r. "E Munch"
NG.M.01914
Woll M 322
NG cat. 1950-1060; 1968-1276; 1992-1914

Other titles: *Måneskinn. Dame foran gjærdet. Aasgaardstrand.* **Provenance**: Harald Nørregaard (before 1915-1938); purchased from Wangs Kunsthandel with financial support from Olaf Schou's donation 1938. **Literature**: I. Langaard 1960, 194f.; Skedsmo (ed.) 1981, 93-94; Varnedoe 1982, 190; Eggum 1983 A, 98; Bischoff 1993, 36f.; Skedsmo 1987 A, 222; Billeter 1998, 125; Eggum 1990, 41f.; Mørstad 2003 B, 77, 85f.; Schröder and Hoerschelmann (eds.) 2003, 124f.; Rutkowski 2008, 12; Sjåstad 2010, 177; Kuuva 2010, 76; Bischoff 2011, 37; Flaatten 2013 A, 89f.; Nyaas 2013, 146f.; Bal 2017, 172. **Exhibitions**: 1893, Berlin, no. 18; 1894, Stockholm, no. 43; 1895, Kristiania-Bergen-Stavanger; 1897, Kristiania (somewhat uncertain); 1898, Dresden, no. EM2-2; 1901, Kristiania, no. 17; 1906, Copenhagen, no. 182; 1915, Copenhagen, no. 284; 1927, Berlin, no. 35; 1927, Oslo, no. 64; 1938, Kristiania, no. 27; 1954, Venice, no. 15; 1954, Munich-Cologne, no. 25; 1955, Copenhagen-Odense, no. 25; 1958, Rotterdam, no. 2; 1960, Paris, no. 485; 1964, Oslo, no. 54; 1964, Kiel, no. 55; 1965, New York B, no. 18; 1968, Stockholm, no. 236; 1973, Munich-London-Paris, no. 19; 1975, Rotterdam-Brussels-Baden-Baden-Paris, no. 148; 1978, Madison-Minneapolis-Seattle, no. 184; 1982, Washington-New York-Minneapolis, no. 65; 1986, London-Düsseldorf-Paris-Oslo, no. 59/69; 1987, Essen, no. 35; 1987, Zürich, no. 35; 1992, London, no. 4; 1993, Tokyo-Osaka, no. 2; 1994, Oslo, no. 36; 1998 Paris, no. 98; 2003, Vienna, no. 8; 2006, New York, no. 40; 2013, Oslo, no. 42; 2015, Helsinki, no. 98; 2017, San Francisco-New York-Oslo, no. 6; 2019, Bergen, no. 27.

A woman in a dark dress and hat stands in front of a yellow weatherboard house with a white picket fence. The landscape beyond lies in darkness, while the wall of the house, the fence and the woman's face are lit by bright moonlight. The features of the face are somewhat blurred. Although the title refers to moonlight, it is the female figure who catches the eye. The white-painted fence and window frame stand out prominently. So too does the moon reflected in the window pane. The dark green shadow of the woman on the wall of the house has an undulating contour that contrasts with the picture's more rigorous vertical and horizontal elements. By means of these formal devices, Munch imbues a simple, everyday situation with a mood of mystery. The stylisation of details and a shallow pictorial depth create the impression of a stage set. The woman stands close to us, reducing the distance between the space of the picture and that of the viewer. *Moonlight* was probably painted in Åsgårdstrand in summer 1893. Two drawings of similar composition suggest that Munch was developing this theme while staying there, and that he used a model (sketchbook MM.T.00129).

Although the woman's frontal pose is typical of Munch's paintings during this period, the approach to colour distinguishes this work from most of the others that date from 1893. There are, however, a few from that summer that explore the same dark palette. It has been suggested that these reflect Munch's interest in the symbolist paintings of Arnold Böcklin. He was familiar with the Swiss artist's works, many of which he had seen during a visit to the Hamburger Kunsthalle in autumn 1891 (Eggum 1983 A, 98).

Thematically, the painting can be understood in a variety of ways. One approach stresses the biographical perspective. The female figure has been interpreted as a recollection and representation of the young Munch's first love, whom he refers to in his private notes as "Mrs Heiberg" (Billeter 1998, 125). The picture has also been compared to *Sommernattsdrøm. Stemmen* (Summer Night's Dream. The Voice) (Woll M 319), which was painted the same year. Both works have been interpreted as portrayals of female desire and of the desirous male gaze for the woman (Mørstad 2003 B, 86). The face, the reflection of the full moon in the window, and the white and red flowers have been seen as metaphors for the cycles of nature, the moon and the female body (Varnedoe 1982, 190).

The painting was first exhibited in Berlin in December 1893. Other related works include the *Hus i måneskinn* (House in Moonlight) (Woll M 323), owned by KODE Art Museums and Composer Homes, Bergen, and two pencil drawings in a sketchbook owned by the Munch Museum. Munch also made two colour woodcuts based on the same subject, in 1896 and 1901. For these he chose just a section of the figure, such that the woman's face dominates the picture (Woll G 90; Woll G 202). The painting was purchased for the collection in 1938 with financial support from the Olaf Schou endowment. VWH

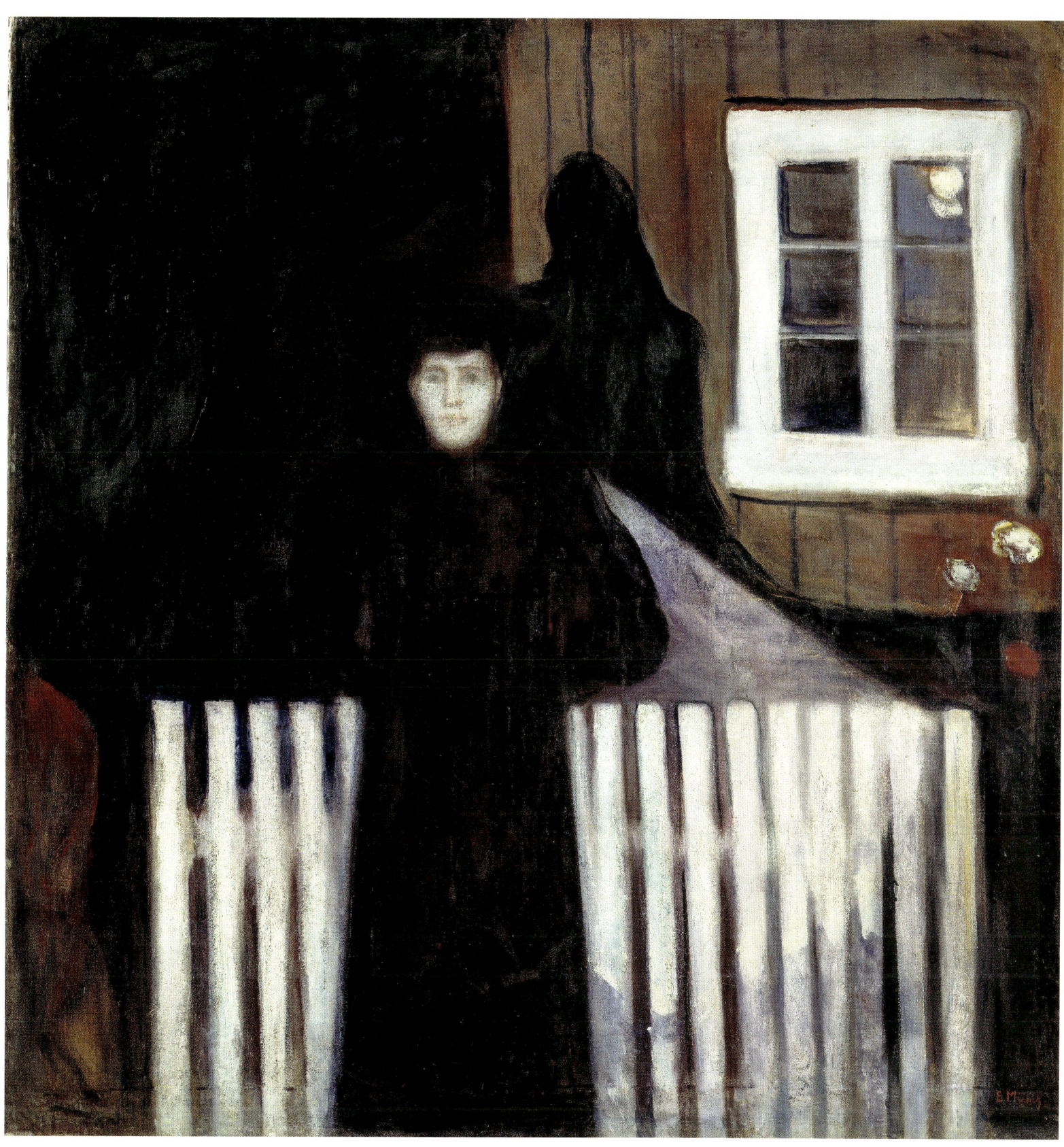

22

Death in the Sickroom, 1893

Døden i sykeværelset

Tempera and wax crayon on canvas
152.5 × 169.5 cm
Signed l.l. "E Munch"
NG.M.00940
Woll M 329
NG cat. 1933-952; 1950-1058; 1968-1277; 1992-329

Other titles: *En Død*; *Døden*; *Døende*; *Den døende*; *I Dødsværelset*. **Provenance**: Gift from Olaf Schou 1910. **Literature**: Thiis 1933, 218; Svenæus 1953, 72; I. Langaard 1960, 148f.; Svenæus 1968, 75; Eggum 1978 B, 52f.; Eggum 1983 A, 107–109; Heller 1984, 114f.; Aitken 1991 A, 226f.; Bischoff 1993, 56; Plahter 1994, 23–32; Plahter 1999, 121f.; Vigtel 2002, 27; Lange 2005, 247f.; Ustvedt 2009, 39; Kuuva 2010, 88, 95, 123, 168; Shiff 2010, [unpaginated]; Bischoff 2011, 56; Lampe 2012, 116, 132; Volle 2012 A, 195, 199–200, 234, 241; Guleng 2013, 134; Ohlsen 2013, 200–201; Endresen 2013, 229; Grøgaard 2013 A, 350; Stokkan 2013, 60–61; Clarke 2014, 54; Lomas 2015, 216; Alarcó 2015, 17, 30; Steihaug 2015, 157; van Dijk 2015 A, 46; Endresen 2015, 23; Gjessing 2016, 36; Ohlsen 2016, 58; Mørstad 2016, 151–152; van Dijk 2017, 123; Vassenden 2019, 26; Coppel 2019, 124, 126. **Exhibitions**: 1893, Berlin, no. 2; 1894, Stockholm, no. 51; 1895, Kristiania–Bergen–Stavanger; 1897, Paris, no. 832; 1897, Kristiania, no. 14; 1900, Dresden, no. 11; 1901, Kristiania, no. 53; 1902, Kristiania; 1902, Berlin, no. 205; 1903, Leipzig; 1904, Kristiania, no. 14; 1905, Prague, no. 37; 1910, Kristiania, no. 6; 1911, Helsinki, no. 82; 1927, Oslo, no. 86; 1971, Oslo, no. 37; 1978, Washington, no. 41; 1979, New York; 1987, Oslo B, no. 61; 2009, Oslo; 2013, Oslo, no. 44.

The painting can be interpreted both as the depiction of a personal memory and as a symbolic representation of death. Biographically, the scene is viewed in connection with the loss of the artist's sister Sofie, who died of tuberculosis in 1877 at the age of just fifteen. In his biographical writings, Munch recalls the moment his sister passed away: "Should she really die - in the last half hour she felt almost lighter - She tried to raise herself - pointed to the armchair that stood beside her - I would like to sit up she whispered ..." (1890, MM N 3670). In the picture, the dying person is sitting in a chair far back in the depicted space. The chair is turned with its back to the viewer, almost entirely obscuring its occupant. The focus is on the family members. Close to the invalid's chair stands an elderly man and a woman. The man has his hands clasped in prayer. In the foreground sits a young girl with bowed head, her folded hands resting in her lap. Just beyond her are two standing figures, a woman and a man. In the background to the left, another male figure stands with his back to the scene. The figures can be linked to Munch's own family. His sister Inger is identifiable from her similarity to the figure in the portrait *Inger in Black and Violet* (cat. 20), painted the previous year. But in *Death in the Sickroom*, Munch has transformed his personal memory into a scene that deals with death and grief on a general level. The identity of the dying person is hidden from us. The emphasis is on the reactions of the individuals in their encounter with death. Although they are together, each has to grapple with his or her grief alone. The colours intensify the picture's profound symbolic impact. The expanses of uniform colour indicate stylistic links to symbolism and synthetism.

Death in the Sickroom is constructed like a narrative or a scene from a theatre play. The theatrical analogy was also noted by contemporary commentators, who pointed out similarities between the situation described in the picture and the play *L'Intruse* by the symbolist playwright Maurice Maeterlinck. A sensation when first performed in Paris in 1891, this drama was a source of inspiration to several visual artists (I. Langaard 1960, 153). When Munch's painting was shown for the first time in Berlin in 1893, it had the title *Ein Tod* (A Death), and death in the family home is the theme of both Munch's painting and Maeterlinck's play. Munch knew of Maeterlinck, and shortly after producing the first sketches for *Death in the Sickroom*, common acquaintances conveyed to him an invitation from Maeterlinck to illustrate his play *Pelléas et Mélisande* (Eggum 1983 A, 109). The project was not pursued.

There are two main versions of *Death in the Sickroom*, and there has been some disagreement about which came first, the one now owned by the National Museum or the one in the collection of the Munch Museum (Woll M 330). It is known that a work with this composition was shown at Unter den Linden in Berlin in 1893, when it was listed as *Ein Tod*. The painting was known as *Døden* (Death) throughout the 1890s. According to Woll, however, it is uncertain which of the two versions was exhibited prior to 1902. According to the National Gallery's catalogues, the picture was most probably painted in 1893. Later research has supported this dating, in part through the discovery of many changes and considerable overpainting done during the production of this version (Heller 1984; Plahter 1999). Others have questioned the claim, but in Woll's catalogue of Munch's paintings both versions are dated 1893 (Woll 2008 B, 311). In addition to the two paintings, there exist two drawings, one in pastels (Woll M 328), the other in charcoal (MM.T.02380), with similar compositions and the same title, also dated 1893, and a lithograph from the year 1896 (cat. 100). A number of sketches relating to the theme have also survived. Olaf Schou purchased the painting from Munch's 1910 exhibition at the Diorama venue in Kristiania, gifting it immediately to the National Gallery. VWH

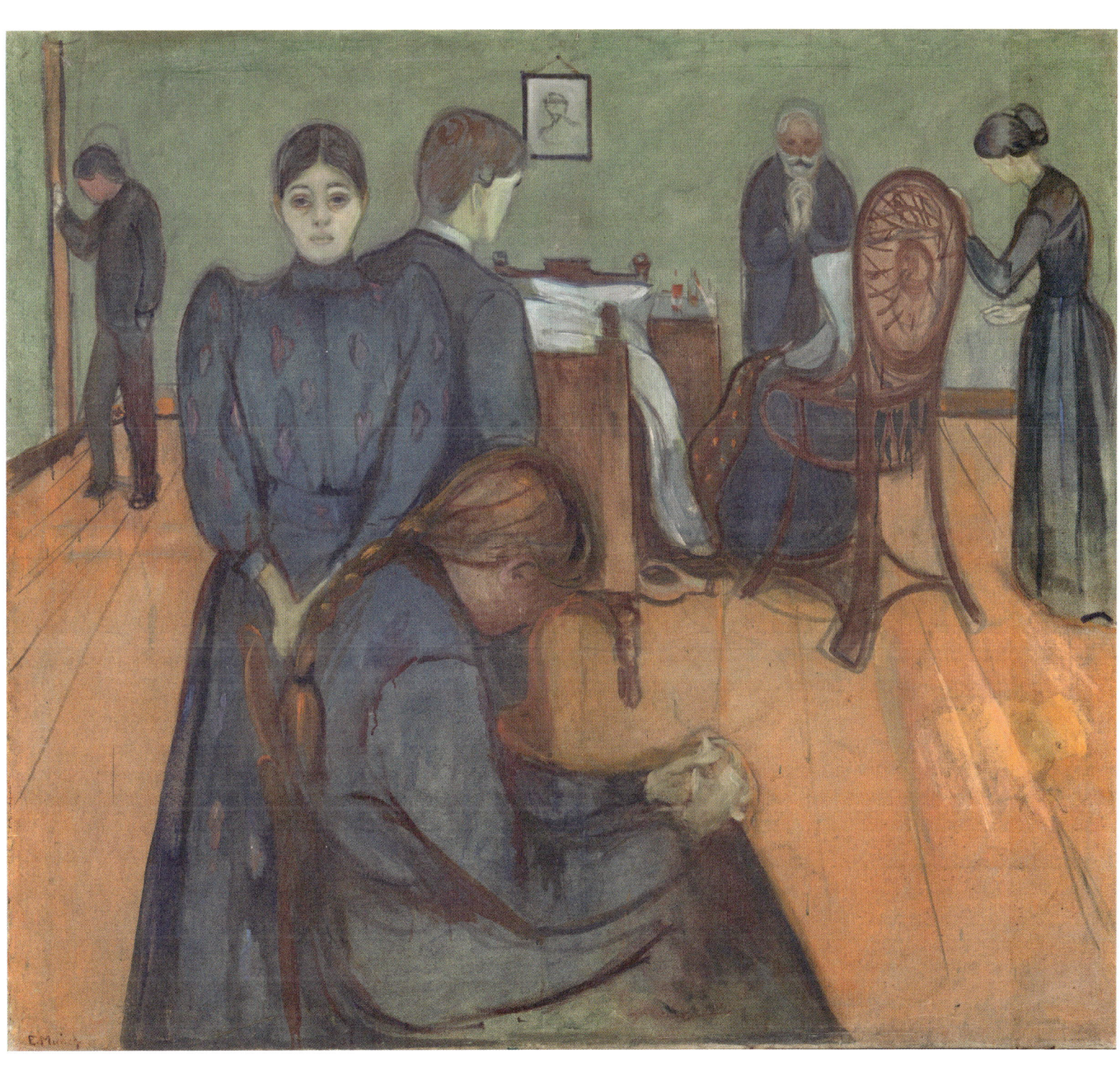

23

The Scream, 1893

Skrik

Tempera and crayon on unprimed cardboard
91 × 73.5 cm
Signed l.l. "E Munch 1893"
NG.M.0939
Woll M 333
NG cat. 1933-947; 1950-1059; 1968-1275; 1992-939

Other titles: *Verzweiflung (Fortvilelse).* **Provenance:** Gift from Olaf Schou 1910. **Literature:** One of Munch's best-known motifs, it is widely discussed in much of the general Munch literature. Przybyszewski 1894 A, 22f.; Ritter 1906, 15; Thiis 1913, 7f.; Stenersen 1945, 81; Hodin 1948, 47, 55; I. Langaard 1960, 201f., 213, 240; Svenæus 1968, 55; Heller 1973 B, 56f.; Rosenblum 1978, 2, 7f.; Eggum 1978 B, 38f., 162f.; Heller 1984, 130f.; Skedsmo 1989, 8; Eggum 1990, 221f.; Eggum 1991, 145f.; Bischoff 1993, 53f.; Woll 1993, 32f.; Bjerke 1995, 30f.; Lind 1997, 98f.; Kristoffersen 2000, 50f.; Prelinger 2000, 209f.; Lund 2001, 20f.; Flaatten 2002, 67f.; Næss 2004, 141, 142, 145; Olson 2004, 29f.; Lange 2005, 241f.; Heller 2006, 16f.; Morehead 2007, 434f.; Flaatten 2008, 105–106; Bjerke 2008 A,13–155; Ydstie 2008, 77–85; Topalova-Casadiego 2008, 87–99; Clarke 2009, 36, 44, 68, 70, 78, 88f., 98f., 102, 104, 136, 180f., 184, 196; Enoksen et al. (eds.) 2009, 55f.; Wennerberg 2010, 10, 20f.; Shiff 2010, [unpaginated]; Gohr 2010, 32f.; Topalova-Casadiego 2011, 192; Bischoff 2011, 54f.; Hedin 2011 A, 134–143; Nierhoff-Wielk 2011, 38f.; Blegvad 2012, 68; Temkin 2012, 3, 5, 14, 15; Guleng 2013, 131, 134; Flaatten 2013 B, 90–91; Ustvedt 2013 A, 239; Owesen 2013, 301; Tøjner and Gundersen 2013, 179–180; Nyaas 2013, 36–43; Berman 2013, 34f.; Lund 2012, 114f.; Mørstad 2013, 211f.; Endresen 2013, 222; Sørbø 2013, 59–61; Rognerud 2013, 11, 15; Bjerke 2013, 16–17; Grøgaard 2013 A, 167, 350; Lahelma 2014, 131, 138, 216, 220, 221; Dahlan 2014, 362; Guleng 2014, 362; Clarke 2014, 54, 64; Marcellàn 2015, 212; Alarcó 2015, 31; Toft-Eriksen 2015, 210–211; Zeiller 2015, 49; Heller 2015; 67f., 70; Presler 2015, 16–17; Lloyd 2015, 140; Endresen 2015, 23; Van Dijk 2015 B, 200; Aslaksby 2015, 52–71; Hardeberg et al. 2015, 72–83; Steihaug 2015, 151; Schneede 2015, 161; Ziemendorff 2015, 198f.; Eggum 2015, 192–199; Stein and Rød 2015, 262; Nielsen 2015, 28; Gjessing 2016, 36; Heller 2016, 37–38; Ravenal 2016, 21–22; Stene-Johansen 2016, 84; Morehead 2017 A, 22, 24, 29; Shiff 2017, 61, 64; Knausgård 2017 A, 55f.; Ustvedt 2018, 68–73; Woll 2018, 136f; Ford et al.

The Scream is a further development of the picture *Syk stemning ved solnedgang. Fortvilelse* (Sick Mood at Sunset. Despair) from 1892 (Woll M 264), and the stages that led to the final result can be traced in a number of sketches (see e.g. Eggum 1990). The two paintings coincide closely in terms of colours, format and composition. The simplified landscape is recognisable as a representation of the Kristianiafjord as seen from Ekeberg. Two men can be seen strolling in the background to the left. In his private notes about the picture, Munch describes them as two friends. The main difference between *The Scream* and the earlier *Despair* is the transformation of the main protagonist, from a clearly defined male figure to a schematic human face that is hard to categorise. A further significant change is that Munch has turned the figure to face the viewer front on. The effect of this modification is striking, in that it makes the image confrontational and immediately communicative. No less groundbreaking was the intimate linkage between content and form. Here Munch shows himself to be a pioneering experimental artist pushing for the dissolution of the artistic conventions and the aesthetic of the day. This unity between form and content makes *The Scream* a pivotal work in the evolution from symbolism to the expressionist art of the 20th century.

Before painting *The Scream*, Munch articulated the picture's theme in a prose poem in one of his notebooks:

> I was walking along the road with two friends – the sun was setting – suddenly the sky turned blood red – I paused and leaned on the fence in utter exhaustion – there was blood and tongues of fire above the blue-black fjord and the city – my friends walked on, and I stood there trembling with anxiety – and I sensed an infinite scream passing through nature. (1892, MM.T.2367)

The Scream exists in two painted versions. Over the years there has been considerable debate about which was painted first, but it is now widely agreed that the National Museum's version was painted in 1893, and that of the Munch Museum no earlier than 1910 (Woll M 896). The National Museum's version has been signed twice, with one signature superimposed on the other, and there is a rudimentary sketch version on the back. In addition to the two paintings and this sketch, two further versions exist in pastels. One of these lacks a signature and year, but has also been dated to 1893 (Woll M 332). The other is signed and dated 1895 (Woll M 327). The latter has a small panel on the lower part of the frame inscribed with a variation on the above-quoted prose poem. Munch also produced a lithographic version in black and white in 1895 (cat. 85).

The National Museum's *Scream* was shown for the first time at Galerie Unter den Linden in Berlin in the year it was painted, at that point with the title *Verzweiflung* (Despair). The first book about Munch's art, with contributions from four art critics and edited by Stanisław Przybyszewski, was published in 1894. Here the picture is mentioned for the first time in a scholarly text. Przybyszewski discusses *The Scream* (Die Verzweiflung) as part of the early "Love Series", describing it as "... the final tableau from a terrible battle between the brain and sex, from which the latter has emerged victorious" (Przybyszewski 1894 A). While this interpretation

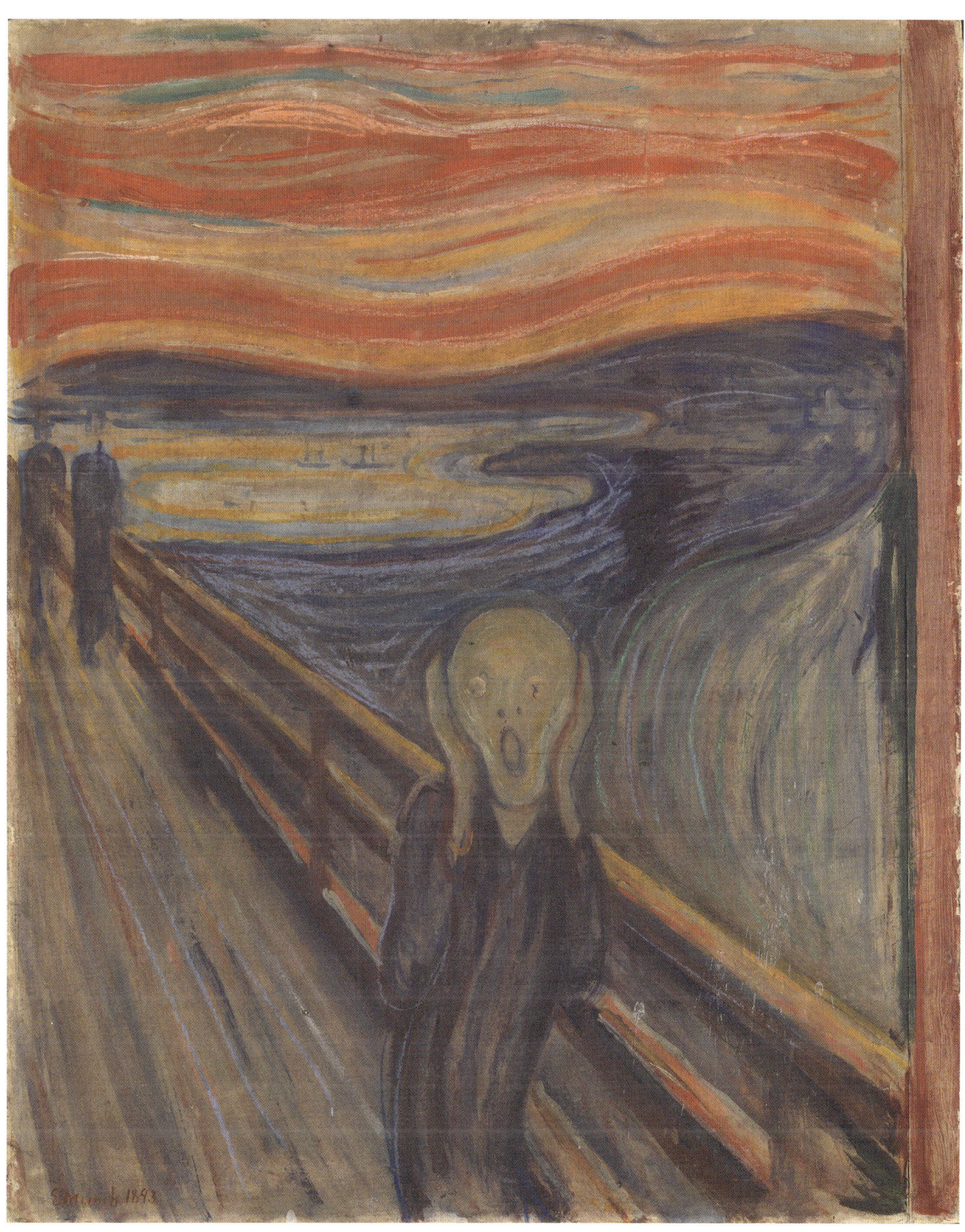

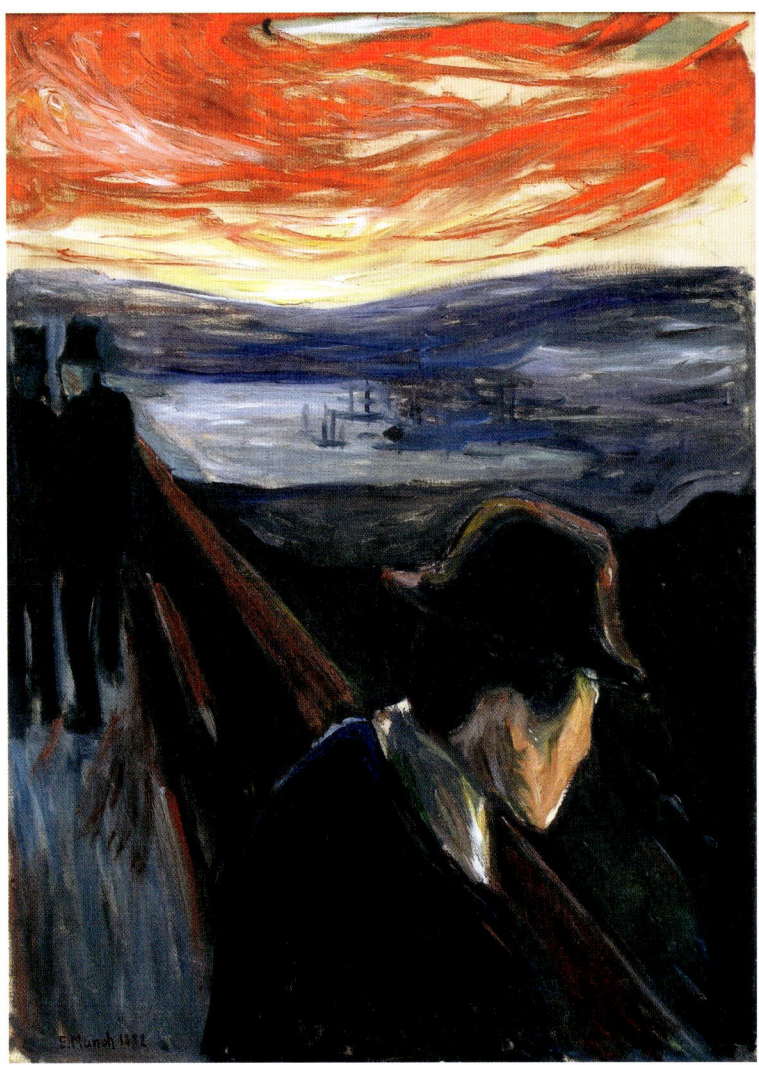

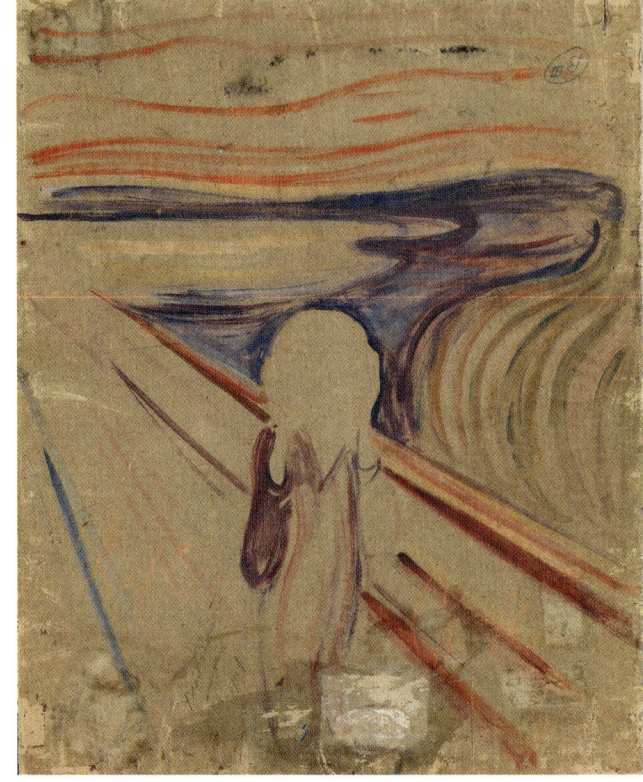

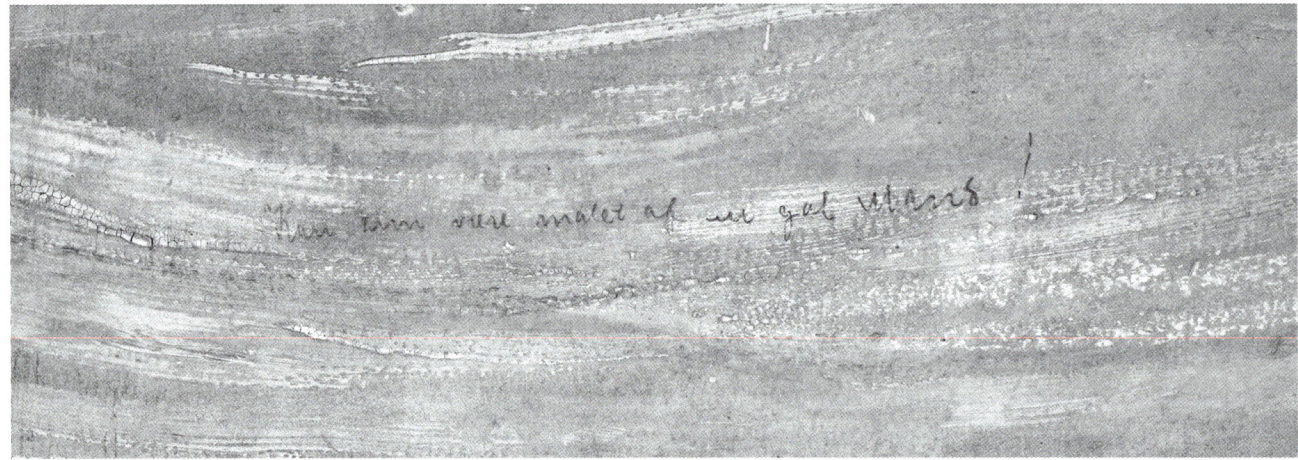

Edvard Munch: *Despair*, 1892
Oil on canvas, 92 × 67 cm
Thielska galleriet, Stockholm
Photo: Thielska galleriet / Tord Lund

Close-up of the text written with
pencil at the top of *The Scream*.

Edvard Munch: *The Scream*, 1893
Backside
Sketch (tempera) on cardboard, 91 × 73,5 cm
NG.M.00939 verso
Nasjonalmuseet
Photo: Nasjonalmuseet / Børre Høstland

2021, [unpaginated]. **Exhibitions:** 1893, Berlin, no. 4f; 1894, Stockholm, no. 68; 1895, Berlin, no. 14; 1895, Kristiania-Bergen-Stavanger; 1896, Paris B, no. 12; 1897, Kristiania, no. 7; 1898, Dresden, no. EM 5-1; 1900, Kristiania; 1900, Dresden, no. 26; 1901, Kristiania, no. 26; 1902, Berlin, no. 203; 1903, Leipzig; 1904, Copenhagen; 1904, Kristiania, no. 10; 1905, Prague, no. 34; 1909, Kristiania; 1909, Bergen; 1910, Kristiania, no. 8; 1927, Oslo, no. 74; 1954, Venice, no. 14; 1954, Munich-Cologne, no. 23; 1955, Copenhagen -Odense, no. 23; 1960, New York-Pittsburgh-Los Angeles-Baltimore, no. 208; 1962, Frankfurt, no. 17; 1963, Humlebæk, no. 50; 1963, Darmstadt, no. 2; 1965, Recklinghausen, no. 4; 1965, New York B, no. 20; 1968, Stockholm, no. 2, 235; 1970, Japan, touring exhibition, no. 11; 1971, Oslo, no. 34; 1973, Oslo; 1973, Munich-London-Paris, no. 20; 1977, Warsaw, no. 6; 1978, Washington, no. 29; 1979, New York; 1981, Tokyo-Sapporo-Nara-Nagoya-Leningrad-Moscow, no. 117/102; 1983, Dresden, no. 11; 1984, Paris; 1987, Essen, no. 30; 1987, Zürich, no. 30; 1987, Oslo B, no. 60; 1991, Paris, no. 25; 1992, London, no. 52; 1993, Tokyo-Osaka, no. 50; 2013, Oslo, no. 46.

does not accord with the way the picture is generally understood today, it has to be seen in terms of the context in which the work was presented in its early years. In time, *The Scream* came to be seen as a universal expression of anxiety and alienation. The first thorough academic study of the work in its own right was that of Reinhold Heller (Heller 1973 A). Since then, the picture has been written about on countless occasions. Notable publications in recent years include the Munch Museum's 2008 theme-based analysis of the various versions, and the exhaustive book with the title *Skrik. Historien om et bilde* (The Scream. The Story of a Picture) (Tøjner and Gundersen 2013).

The picture's iconic status has grown steadily from the 1970s to the present. In the academic literature about Munch from the first half of the 20th century, *The Scream* is reproduced only relatively rarely, but analysis of the painting's exhibition history clearly shows that both Munch himself, and later the National Gallery, regarded the work as central to the artist's development. *The Scream* featured in most of Munch's solo exhibitions through until 1910, the year Olaf Schou purchased and immediately gifted the work to the museum. There was an early understanding among Norwegian art experts that the picture represented something unique and that it was important to secure Norwegian ownership. With the exception of periods when it was on loan to other museums, *The Scream* remained on display in the National Gallery from the time it entered the collection. The painting was loaned out frequently during the 1960s and 1970s, but as its fame grew, the museum chose to be more restrictive in this regard, out of consideration both for its own visitors and for the picture itself. The last time it was loaned out was for an exhibition in Japan in 1993. In 1994 it was stolen but returned to the museum the same year.

At the top left of the painting is a barely legible inscription in pencil that reads: "Kan kun være malet af en gal Mand!" ("Can only be painted by a madman!"). It has been claimed that this was written by Munch himself (Heller 1973 B; Næss 2004; Stenseth 2004). By 2008, most Munch researchers were ready to accept that it was probably added by someone else. This conjecture was based on a contemporary review of Munch's 1904 exhibition in Copenhagen in which the reviewer wrote: "It is on the bright red clouds of this picture that a tactless hand has written in pencil: 'Can only be painted by a madman'" (Woll 2008 B, 316). However, a recent study using an infrared camera and graphological analysis (National Museum and Munch Museum 2020) confirms the earlier hypothesis, that the inscription was added by the artist himself.

The painting was proposed for purchase at the National Gallery as early as 1901 (NG minutes of committee meeting, 18.10.1901), but didn't enter the collection before it was gifted to the museum by Olaf Schou in 1910. It is clear that the purchasing committee was interested in acquiring several Munch pictures at the earlier point in time, and *The Scream* was high on the wish list. The artist Gerhard Munthe, then a member of the committee, wrote to Munch in 1901: "Finally, we wish to hear from you what you would want for the picture 'The Scream' or the other one you call 'Anxiety'" (14 October 1901, MM K 720). In the minutes from a committee meeting later that month, it is noted that Munch has "... agreed not to take 'The Scream' abroad and also to grant right of first refusal for a sale of the picture to either the National Gallery or Mr Olaf Schou" (NG minutes of committee meeting, 29.10.1901). In other words, at that point in time the artist was either unwilling to sell the picture or asking too high a price. Despite the promise, mentioned in the minutes, not to take the picture abroad, Munch included the work in exhibitions in Berlin, Leipzig, Copenhagen, and Prague during the period 1901–1910. VWH

Pastel on canvas
87 × 70 cm
Signed l.r. "E Munch"
NG.M.02814
Woll M 340
NG cat. 1992-2814

Other titles: *Fru Bäckström, født Juell*; *Fru Ragnhild Bäckström*. **Provenance**: Karl Vilhelm Hammer (1896? -1927); Charlotte and Christian Mustad (1927-1970); bequeathed by Charlotte and Christian Mustad to the National Gallery in 1959, received 1970. **Literature**: Thiis 1933, 213; Eggum 1994 A, 59f.; Pessler and Trummer 2000, 173; Lange 2004, 133f.; Woll 2013, 21. **Exhibitions**: 1895, Kristiania–Bergen; 1896, Paris B, no. 800 (somewhat uncertain); 1927, Oslo, no. 72; 1985, Milan–Rome, no. 26; 1987, Kongsvinger; 1999, Florence, no. 8; 2000, Vienna; 2004, Melbourne, no. 26; 2005, Rome, no. 21; 2013, Oslo, no. 49.

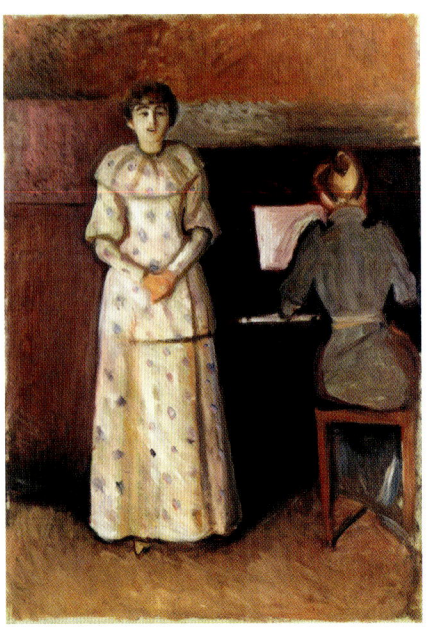

Ragnhild and Dagny Juel, 1892-1893
Oil on canvas, 95,5 × 66 cm
Woll M 300

The painting is one of several depictions of the sisters Dagny and Ragnhild Juell (Juel) that Munch produced in the years 1892-94. The simple, frontal pose with the hands folded in the lap is typical of Munch's portraits of young, contemporary women. The use of line and the colour of the dark dress contrast with the pale, undefined background. Attention is focused on the narrow eyes of the slender figure, her oval face, neck ornament and hands. She appears to be wearing a city dress with puff sleeves and a fur stole. The work is done in pastels on coarse canvas. This produces a characteristic matt surface that gives the work the appearance of something halfway between a painting and a drawing.

The portrait was done shortly after Ragnhild (1871-1908) married the Swedish geologist and politician Helge Bäckström in 1893. According to letters that passed between Ragnhild and Munch, the portrait was the idea of her husband, and was executed in Berlin in January 1894 (letter dated 3 January 1989, MM K 1620). The previous year, Munch had painted a similarly sized portrait of Helge Bäckström, which is now in the Thiel Gallery, Stockholm (Woll M 338). The portrait of Ragnhild was bequeathed to the National Gallery on the death of Christian Mustad in 1970.

The painting featured in several exhibitions around 1895, and it was probably during one of these that it was purchased by Karl Vilhelm Hammer, editor of the *Verdens Gang* newspaper. The signature was added later, probably at the request of the work's subsequent owners, Charlotte and Christian Mustad.

The Juell sisters came from the family of a doctor in Kongsvinger. Both were described as beautiful and gifted. Dagny made a name for herself as a pianist, Ragnhild as a singer. It is in these roles that they are depicted in the double-portrait *Musiserende søstre* (Music-making Sisters) (1892, Woll M 300). In addition, Dagny became a playwright and, together with her husband Stanisław Przybyszewski, a leading light in the Bohemian circles to which Munch belonged in the 1890s. The Bäckström couple settled in Stockholm, where they were an important contact for Munch.

It is interesting to note that when the work was exhibited at Blomqvist in 1895, Munch received a letter from Ragnhild's father, Dr Hans Lemmich Juell, asking the artist to remove the painting of his daughter from the exhibition (letter, 10 October 1895, MM K 1936). The doctor's reason for the request was a general scepticism towards the exhibition as a whole and towards the way Ragnhild was portrayed in particular: "For me it was downright embarrassing to see my daughter's face depicted in this manner." However, it is unclear whether he is referring to the portrait of Ragnhild or a painted version of *Madonna* (cat. 29), for which she may have also served as model. Munch complied with the request, but when the exhibition was later shown in Bergen, the portrait of Ragnhild Bäckström was back on the wall (Eggum 1994 A; Høifødt 2008). øu

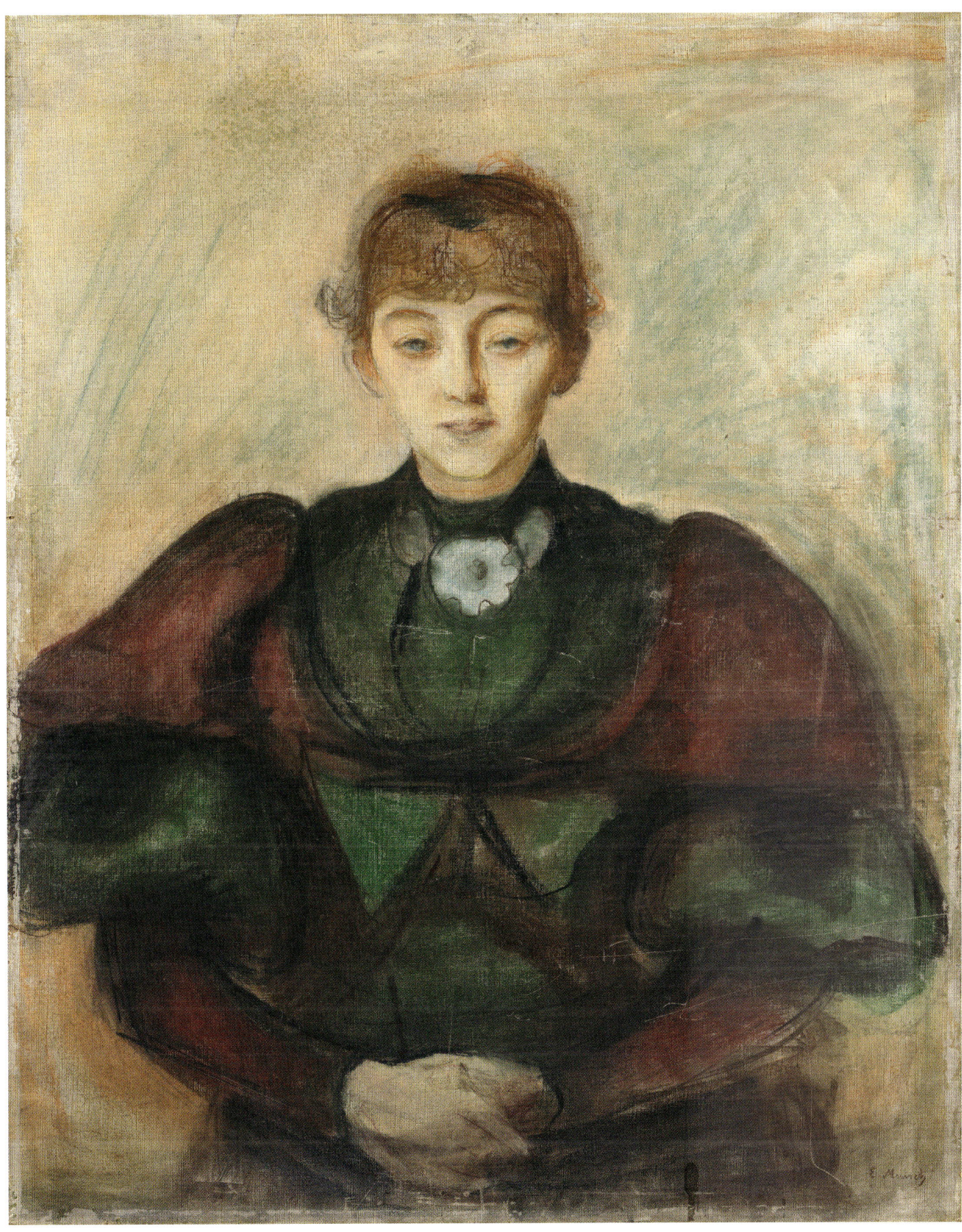

Oil on canvas
100 × 75 cm
Unsigned
NG.M.00995
Woll M 343
NG cat. 1933-955; 1950-1066; 1968-1283; 1992-995

Other titles: *Kunsthistorikeren Meier-Graefe.*
Provenance: Gift from Julius Meier-Graefe 1912.
Literature: Vidalenc 1920, 131-35; I. Langaard
1960, 246; Eggum 1994 A, 58; Skedsmo 1987 B,
[unpaginated]; Geskó (ed.) 2012, 474; Morehead
2017 B, 9f. **Exhibitions**: 1895, Berlin, no. 24; 1927,
Berlin, no. 44; 1927, Oslo, no. 95; 1983, Dresden,
no. 17; 1984, Berlin, no. 938; 1987, Essen, no. 44;
1987, Zürich, no. 44; 1994, Munich–Hamburg–
Berlin, no. 17; 1996, Berlin–Munich; 2006,
New York, no. 29; 2012, Budapest, no. 150; 2015,
Münster, no. 51.

The portrait was painted during Munch's stay in Berlin in 1894–95. The contrast between the plasticity of the face and the rough background is typical of Munch's portraits of this period. The distinctive top hat, beard and moustache indicate a modern lifestyle and urban fashion. This is one of several half-length portraits of friends and colleagues that Munch painted in the mid-1890s. His interest in the genre can be traced back to the art circles he frequented in Kristiania in the 1880s.

Around the time the picture was painted, Meier-Graefe (1867–1935) was active as a writer who was deeply immersed in Berlin's radical art scene. He had recently helped to launch the journal *PAN*, for which he also occasionally worked as editor. He came in contact with Munch via a broader community of intellectuals, artists and writers that included August Strindberg, Stanisław Przybyszewski and Dagny Juel. Meier-Graefe eventually forged a reputation as a major critic and connoisseur of modern art. His first writings were about Munch's work, and he contributed to the first monograph: *Das Werk des Edvard Munch* (1894). He also initiated the first portfolio of prints by the artist.

Meier-Graefe had a keen interest in contemporary French art. In 1895 he moved to Paris, where, as director of the gallery La Maison Moderne, and later as editor of the journal *Dekorative Kunst*, he spread the ideas of the art nouveau movement and its associated crafts. He was an important contact for Munch in Paris during these years, introducing the artist to gallery owners and others in the art community, such as Siegfried Bing, the man behind the Maison de l'Art Nouveau gallery. Later, Meier-Graefe moved back to Berlin, where in 1904 he published the three-volume *Die Entwicklungsgeschichte der modernen Kunst*, the first comprehensive presentation of modern, controversial art in Europe around 1900. In the first edition, Munch was discussed in a lengthy chapter together with Vincent van Gogh.

Although the portrait has been dated to 1895, it is mentioned in *Morgenbladet* as early as 1 May 1894. It was owned by Meier-Graefe until 1912, when he donated it to the National Gallery. øu

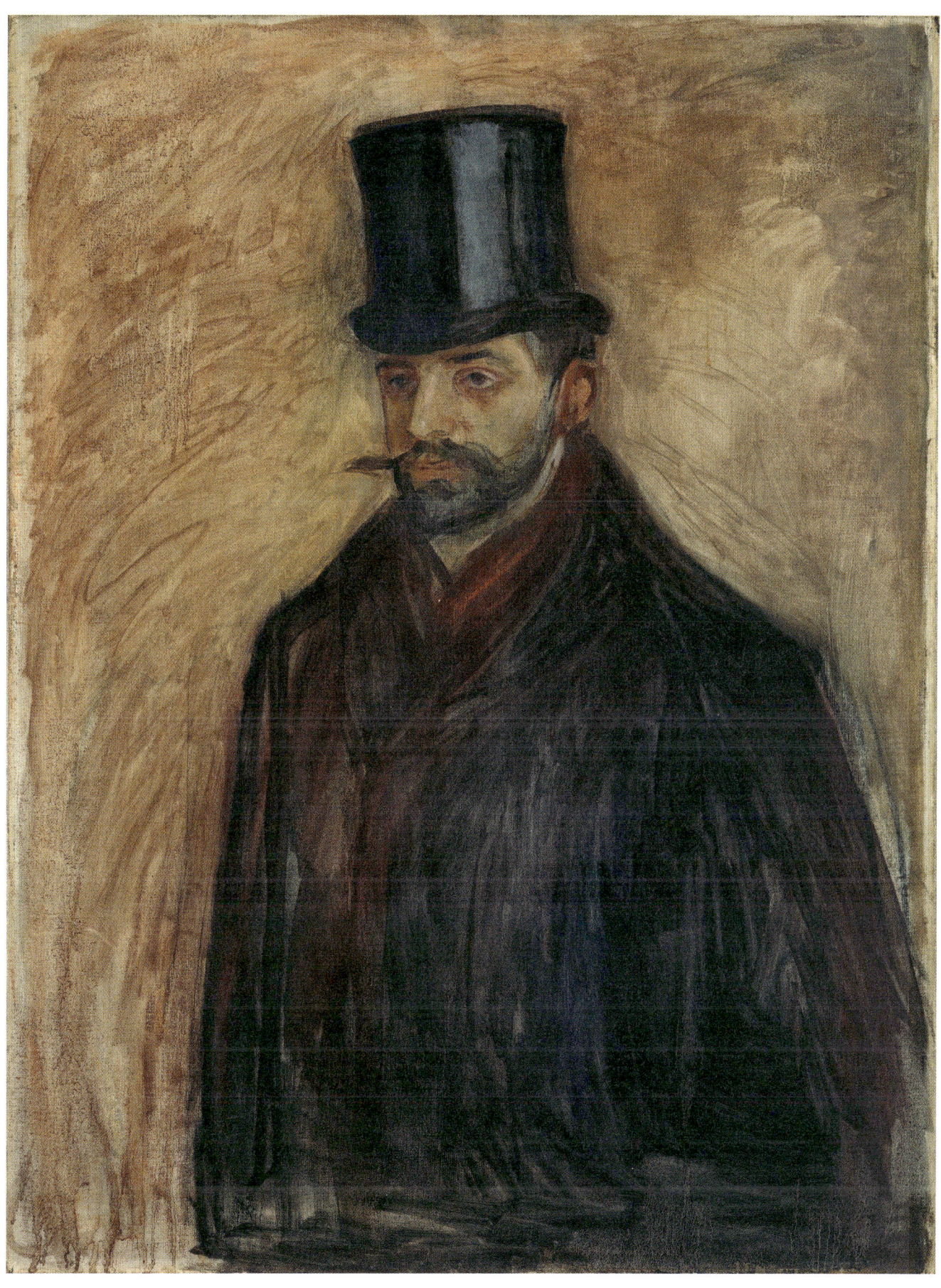

26

Puberty, 1894

Pubertet

Oil on canvas
151.5 × 110 cm
Signed l.r. "E Munch"
NG.M.00807
Woll M 347
NG cat. 1933-948; 1950-1064; 1968-1281; 1992-807

Other titles: *Ung Pike*; *In Nacht*; *Nacktes Mädchen*; *Nógen pige paa sengekanten (Puberte)*; *«Nat», ung pike på sengekanten*. **Provenance**: Purchased with financial support from the A.C. Houen's trust fund on the occasion of the artist's 1909 exhibition at Blomqvist Kunsthandel. **Literature**: Ritter 1906, 23; Nilssen 1913, 95; Glaser 1917, 18-19; Thiis 1933, 218f.; Romdahl 1946, 92; Romdahl 1947, 174f.; Gordon 1966, 335f.; Svenæus 1968, 55; Sherman 1976, 243; Eggum 1978 A, 50, 172; Eggum 1978 B, 50; Rosenblum 1978, 4; Skedsmo (ed.) 1981, 91-92; Bischoff 1993, 34f.; Schulze (ed.) 1995, 230; Berman 1997 A, 22f.; Schröder and Hoerschelmann (eds.) 2003, 133f.; Mørstad 2003 B, 86f.; Ormhaug 2004; Høifødt 2006, 24; Ydstie 2012, 9-29; Clarke 2012, 32-54; Topalova-Casadiego 2012, 66-84; Clarke 2013, 56; Owesen, 2013, 302, 304; Stein and Rød 2015, 257, 260, 262-263; Berman 2015, 90; Lahelma 2015, 19; Huusko 2015, 181, 183; Stafne-Pfisterer 2015, 91; Flaatten 2019, 70; Ford et al. 2021, [unpaginated]. **Exhibitions**: It is unclear which versions of *Puberty* were shown at exhibitions prior to 1904. For a comprehensive list of exhibitions earlier than 1904 in which a version of *Puberty* was shown, see Woll M 346. 1904, Vienna, no. 38; 1904, Kristiania, no. 45; 1905, Prague, no. 112; 1906, Hagen, no. 66; 1907, Bielefeld, no. 18; 1908, Breslau, no. 14; 1909, Bremen, no. 1128; 1909, Kristiania; 1914, Kragerø; 1950, USA, touring exhibition, no. 15; 1951, Brighton-Glasgow-London-The Hague-Paris, no. 14/15; 1952, Zürich, no. 12; 1952, Brussels, no. 3; 1954, Venice, no. 20; 1954, Munich-Cologne, no. 34; 1955, Copenhagen-Odense, no. 32; 1958, Rotterdam, no. 9; 1959, Vienna, no. 12; 1959, Warszaw, no. 12; 1960, Recklinghausen-Vienna-Berlin-Oslo-Helsinki, no. 11; 1970, Japan, touring exhibition, no. 12; 1971, Oslo, no. 112; 1978, Washington, no. 38; 1979, New York; 1979, London, no. 265; 1980, Berlin, no. 18; 1981, Tokyo-Sapporo-Nara-Nagoya-Leningrad-Moscow, no. 38; 1992, London, no. 59; 1997, Tokyo, no. 65; 1998, Paris, no. 106; 2003, Vienna, no. 16; 2006, New York, no. 44; 2007, Basel, no. 41; 2009, Chicago, no. 27; 2011, Paris, no. 3; 2013, Oslo, no. 50; 2015, Oslo-Helsinki, no. 9; 2019, Bergen, no. 24.

A young girl sits naked on the edge of a bed. With her arms crossed in front of her, as if attempting to hide her nakedness, she appears awkward and insecure. The striking dark shadow she casts on the wall behind her reinforces the impression of something disturbing. Ingrid Langaard provides an insightful description of *Puberty* in her monograph on Munch:

> With her legs pressed together, her gaze transfixed in fear and horror of the unknown that will overcome her body, she adopts an instinctive posture in an effort to halt the process that will turn her at a stroke from a child into a woman (...) The picture shows a deep psychological understanding of emotional reactions that we imagine would be alien to a man - a young girl's dawning awareness of the mystery of her sex. (I. Langaard 1960, 28)

Munch painted four versions of *Puberty*. The first (Woll M 141), from as early as 1886, was destroyed in a fire at the house of its owner, Axel Thoresen. Munch returned to the subject in Berlin in the 1890s, producing two relatively similar paintings in 1894, which now belong to the National Museum and the Munch Museum respectively. The Munch Museum's version (Woll M 346) dates from early 1894, the one in the National Museum from a little later that year. The former has visible underdrawing, is on unprimed canvas, and is somewhat sketchy compared with the National Museum's version, which appears more developed (Woll 2008 B; Topalova-Casadiego 2012). A fourth, more colourful and significantly smaller version that Munch produced some twenty years later is also in the collection of the Munch Museum (Woll M 1097). In addition to the paintings, Munch created a lithographic version in 1894 and an etching in 1902 (Woll G 14; Woll G 186).

The similarities to an etching by the Belgian symbolist artist Félicien Rops, *The Greatest Love of Don Juan*, were remarked by Munch's contemporaries. Munch claimed, however, that he had painted the first version of *Puberty* before becoming aware of Rops's picture. "No doubt you remember 'The Girl on the Edge of the Bed', which you owned and which burnt with your house," Munch writes to *Puberty*'s former owner, the doctor Axel Thoresen, in 1929.

> I would like a written description of the picture - You know that I painted it again and it is now hanging in the gallery - I know it to be an accurate reproduction of your picture. You surely remember it - the girl sitting just as she is in the one in the gallery, with a large dark shadow on the wall - Her hands between her knees in chasteness. She is sitting in the middle of a bed (...) I would like to have this description because the strange coincidence is that Felicien Rops has done a small etching that is closer to my picture than I would have thought possible, if it were by anyone else, I would swear it was blatant theft. The picture in the gallery was painted in 1894. (Letter dated 14 January 1929, PN 897)

The letter confirms that the National Museum's picture was painted in 1894, and that it reproduces the one from 1886 that was lost in the fire. The National Gallery bought the painting from an exhibition at Blomqvist in 1909. Determined to make a substantial purchase from the exhibition, the National Gallery's director, Jens Thiis, wrote to the Ministry of Culture requesting financial support: "I would not hesitate to describe the impending Munch exhibition as a major (...) event in Norwegian cultural life (...) His pictures are sought after by public and private

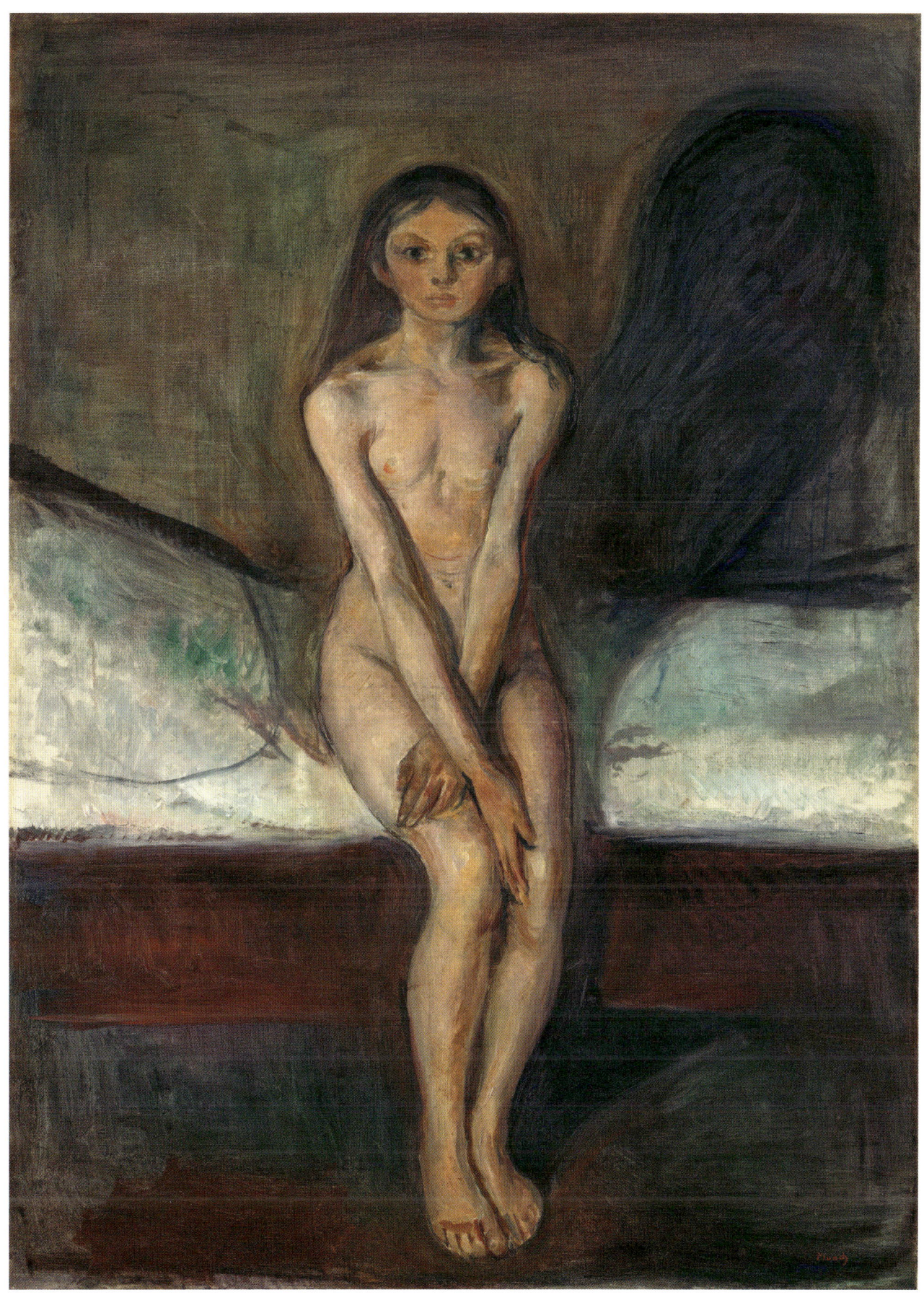

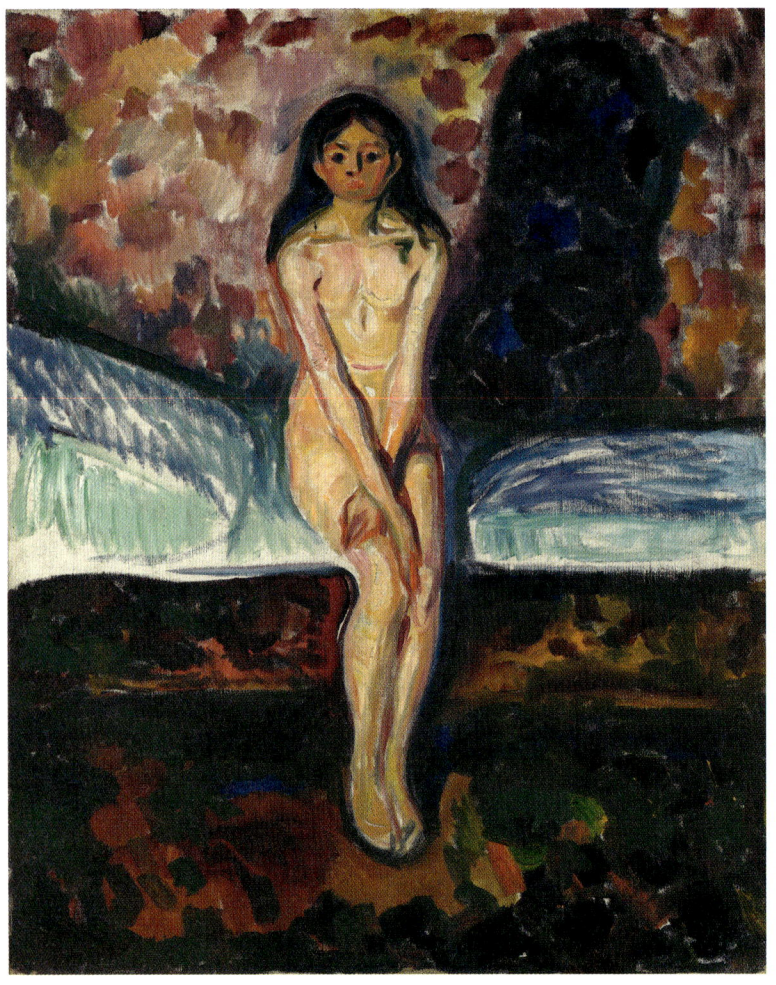

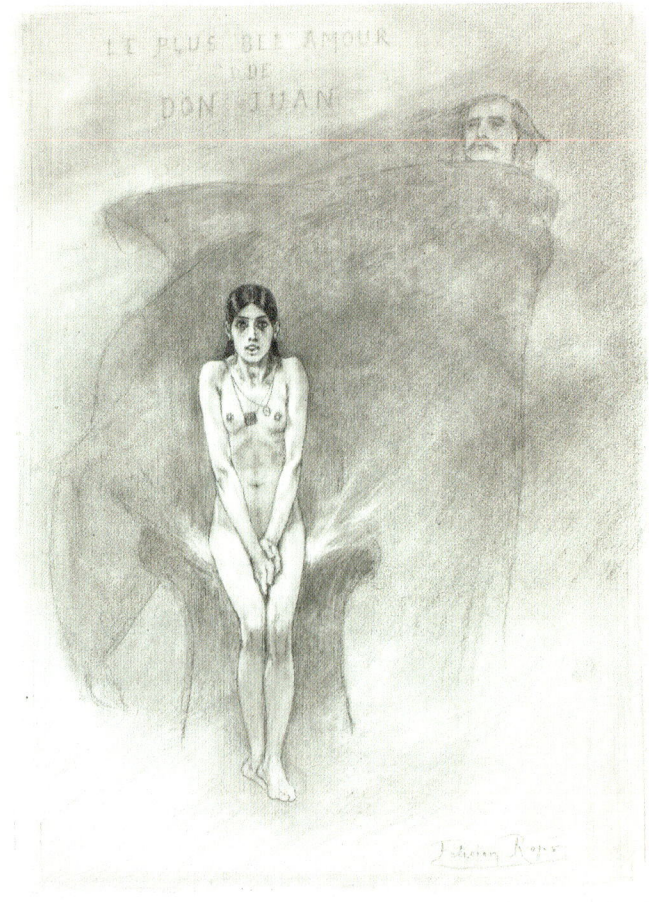

Edvard Munch: *Puberty*, 1914–1916
Oil on canvas, 97 × 77 cm
M.M.M.00450, Woll M 1097
Photo: Munchmuseet / Halvor Bjørngård

Félicien Rops: *The Greatest Love of Don Juan*, 1879
Graphite with stumping, scratching and erasing on
off-white wove paper, prepared with a white gouache
ground, 253 × 180 mm
Margaret Day Blake Collection
Photo: The Art Institute of Chicago

collectors and his prices have risen enormously" (letter from Thiis to the Ministry, 11 March 1909). Four days later, he wrote again, this time to say that, in consultation with various artists, he had drawn up a list of five pictures that were worthy of purchase, one of which was *Puberty* (letter from Thiis to the Ministry, 15 March 1909, 505 in correspondence log). When it entered the collection, the picture had the title *Nat, ung pike paa sengekanten* (Night, Young Girl on the Edge of the Bed). At different times, the lithographic version has gone by three different titles in addition to *Puberty*, namely: *Om natten* (At Night), *Den unge modellen* (The Young Model), and *Ung pike* (Young Girl) (inscription on one print) (Clarke 2012, 34). The first, lost, version of the painting from 1886 was included in Munch's exhibition at the Studentersamfundet (Students' Association) in 1889, probably as catalogue number 39, with the title *Modell for første gang* (Model for the First Time).

Puberty and *The Day After* (cat. 27) were purchased for the National Gallery's collection at the same time. Although the latter was also developed in the mid-1880s, two early versions were lost in the years that followed. Certain aspects of the 1894 versions of *Puberty* and *The Day After* relate them to 1880s realism. In terms of content, however, *Puberty* can also be linked to the symbolism of the 1890s, with its central interest in depictions of the various stages of life, from birth and self-awareness to old age and death. Today, *Puberty* is one of Munch's best known works. It has been shown in many exhibitions and is widely discussed in the Munch literature. In 2012, the Munch Museum devoted an exhibition and publication to its various themes and aspects (Ydstie (ed.) 2012). vwh

27

The Day After, 1894

Dagen derpå

Oil on canvas
115 × 152 cm
Signed l.l. "E Munch"
NG.M.00808
Woll M 348
NG cat. 1933-951; 1950-1063; 1968-1280; 1992-808

Other titles: *Dagen derpaa*; *Morgenstimmung*; *Dagen Efter*. **Provenance**: Purchased with financial support from the A.C. Houen's trust fund on the occasion of the artist's 1909 exhibition at Blomqvist Kunsthandel. **Literature**: Thiis 1907 A, 415; Marten 1905, 12-14; Ritter 1906 23f.; Nilssen 1913, 86; Glaser 1917, 42; Thiis 1933, 160, 164; Stenersen 1945, 29; Romdahl 1946, 92; Romdahl 1947, 173f.; I. Langaard 1960, 28f.; Torjusen 1971 A, 62; Eggum 1983 A, 114f.; Bischoff 1993, 43f.; Rutkowski 2008, 9f., 34, 38; Sjåstad 2010, 176; Bischoff 2011, 42f.; Arnaud 2011, 23; Ydstie 2012, 21; Kaspers 2012, 254; Schneede 2012, 67, 70; Clarke 2013, 53; Owesen 2013, 302-304; Nyaas (ed.) 2013, 36; Alarcó 2015, 37; Berman 2015, 93; Stein and Rød 2015, 257f.; Schroll 2016, 178; Brandtzæg 2017, 41-51; Ustvedt 2018, 35-39; Dam 2019, 177; Flaatten 2019, 69-70; Ford et al. 2021, [unpaginated]. **Exhibitions**: 1894, Stockholm, no. 32; 1895, Berlin, no. 28; 1895, Kristiania-Bergen-Stavanger; 1897, Kristiania, no. 8; 1898, Dresden; 1901, Kristiania, no. 46; 1903, Berlin, no. 125; 1904, Copenhagen; 1904, Hamburg; 1904, Kristiania, no. 28; 1905, Prague, no. 66; 1906, Berlin; 1906, Hagen, no. 42; 1906, Weimar, no. 10; 1906, Hamburg; 1907, Bielefeld, no. 11; 1908, Copenhagen, no. 8; 1909, Kristiania; 1909, Helsinki, no. 7; 1927, Berlin, no. 41; 1927, Oslo, no. 69; 1950, USA, touring exhibition, no. 14; 1951, Brighton-Glasgow-London-The Hague-Paris, no. 13; 1952, Zürich, no. 11; 1952, Brussels, no. 2; 1958, Rotterdam, no. 7; 1959, Warszaw, no. 8; 1960, Recklinghausen-Vienna-Berlin-Oslo-Helsinki, no. 10; 1963, Humlebæk, no. 52; 1971, Oslo, no. 66; 1973, Munich-London-Paris, no. 24; 1978, Madison-Minneapolis-Seattle, no. 185; 1986, Hamburg, no. 78; 1987, Berlin, no. H 35; 1987, Zürich, no. 11; 2001, Berlin; 2004, London; 2005, London-Torino; 2006, New York, no. 14; 2012, Essen; 2013, Oslo, no. 51; 2019, Bergen, no. 23.

Lying on the bed is a woman with an open blouse, her hair hanging loose and her eyes closed. The title of the picture and the empty bottles on the table indicate something has happened. Might she be sleeping off a hangover? Munch painted three versions of *The Day After*. The one in the National Museum was the last of the three and the only one we know of that still survives. The first version, dated to the period 1886-89, was destroyed in a fire at Christiania Forgyldermagazin in 1890 (Woll M 142). The second was probably painted shortly afterwards, but is now also lost (Woll M 258). It is documented in a photograph taken during Munch's exhibition at the Equitable-Palast, Berlin, in 1892 or 1893. In addition to the painting from 1894, there is a pen-and-wash drawing from some point in the period 1892-94 (MM.T.02348) and a print version from 1894 (cat. 67; Woll G 10).

A photograph dated 1894 shows the painting standing unfinished on the floor of Munch's studio in Berlin (Eggum 1983 A, 114). The glasses and bottles that stand in the foreground in the latest version are absent. On 1 May 1894, *Morgenbladet* printed an account of a visit to Munch's Berlin studio, which mentions some of his more recent paintings. This article, together with the aforementioned photograph, corroborate the dating of the painting:

> 'Puberty' and 'The Morning After' are the titles of two studies, two large pictures. The former shows a young, skilfully painted naked female figure, the latter a half-dressed woman who has thrown herself down on her modest bed, beside which stands a wooden chair with a glass and an empty wine bottle. The subject is not exactly appealing, but the drawing is well done and without the bizarre, outlandish colours. It really does seem as if, in the works currently in progress, Munch has taken a step back from his earlier aberrant penchant for harsh, peculiar colour effects and baffling subjects.

Madonna (cat. 29), *The Day After* and *Puberty* (cat. 26) were all painted in 1894. It would appear that Munch used the same model for the first two. All three works are central to Munch's conceptualisation of the woman, and in the scholarly literature they are often discussed as a group. Late in life, Munch reflected on the significance of the female gender during his own life time: "Kierkegaard lived in the time of Faust - Don Juan - Mozart - Don Juan. It was the man who seduces the innocent girl. I have lived in the period of transition in the midst of women's emancipation. Here it is the woman who seduces and lures and deceives the man - the time of Carmen" (22 February 1929, MM.T.2744). Many of Munch's pictures and texts demonstrate a lively awareness and deep fascination for this defining topic, which was one of the most widely debated of the era. Depictions of women figure prominently in his work. They deal with different themes and perceptions of women and are collectively open to a variety of conflicting interpretations. Although Munch's personal relationships with women were ambivalent, his attitudes to women in general seem modern (Owesen 2013).

The Bohemian circle in which Munch moved favoured gender equality, and his views on women were shaped by his connections with this community of intellectuals and artists. In his book on Munch, Jens Thiis discusses *The Day After* under

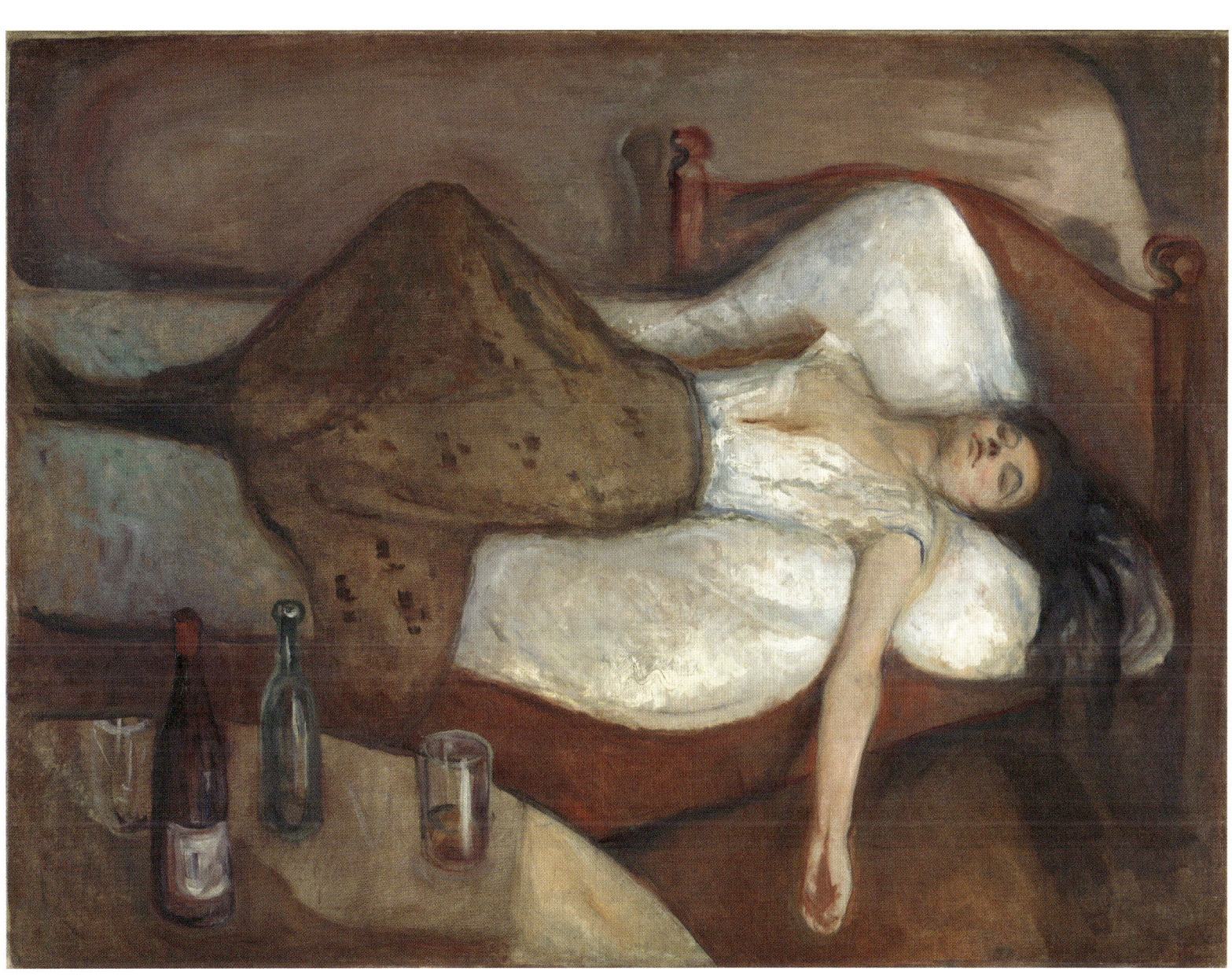

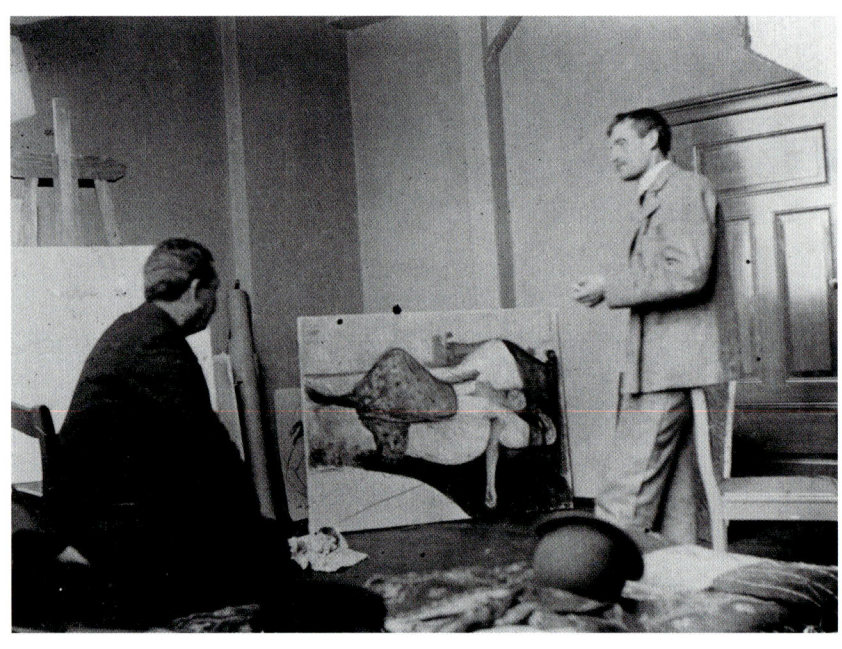

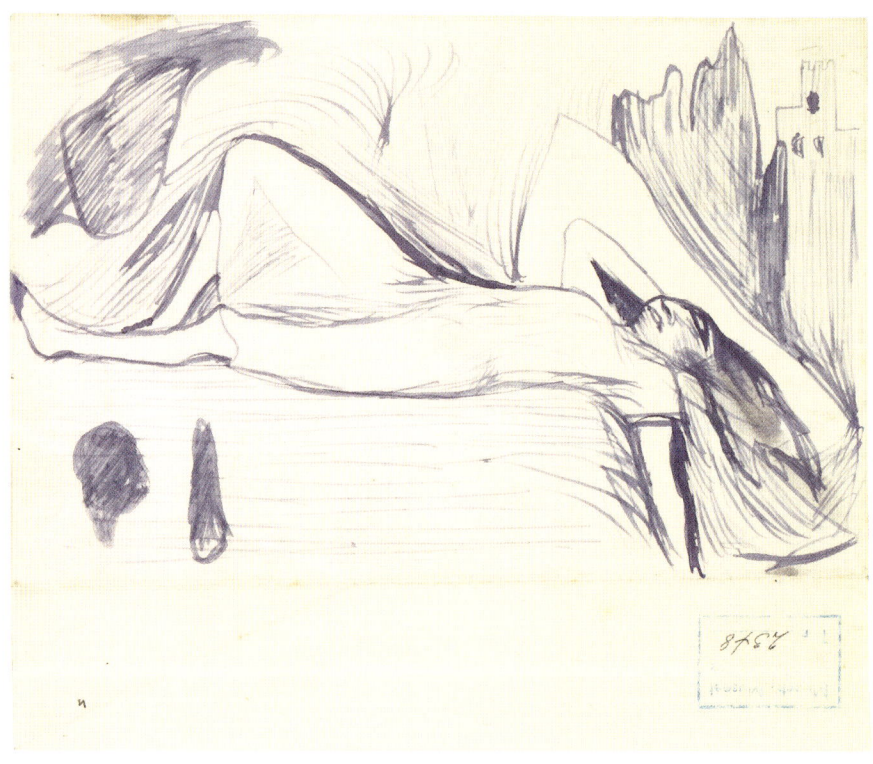

Edvard Munch and Adolf Paul in Munch's studio in
Berlin, c. 1894
Munchmuseet
MM.D.02713
Photo: Munchmuseet

Edvard Munch: *The Day After*, 1892–1894 (plausible)
Ink
MM.T.02348
Photo: Munchmuseet / Tone Margrethe Gauden

the heading "Munch and the Bohemians". He writes that some are likely to view the work as a "social" painting that reflects the lifestyle of this group, a view Thiis himself disputes (Thiis 1933). In terms of theme and execution, the picture does, however, have some features in common with the realism of the 1880s. Although it was painted in 1894, *The Day After* differs significantly from Munch's typically symbolist paintings of the 1890s. It was a controversial work in its day. The fact that the first version was painted in 1886 puts it in an interesting relation to Christian Krohg's works on the *Albertine* theme, which tackle the problem of socially vulnerable women. When *The Day After* appeared in a large Munch exhibition in Prague in 1905, the Czech writer Milos Martens also alluded to the realist context:

> And Munch painted these people ... scenes of Bohemian life and the *demi-monde*. 'The Day After' is his seminal work from this period ... The semi-naked body on the bed has stiffened in a posture of exhaustion and despair; the scene is permeated by the mundane aftertaste that indulgence leaves on the lips, for indulgence is what this is all about ... Degas would surely praise the picture's trenchant realism, its forthright idiom ... (Torjusen 1971 A, 62)

The Day After was one of five paintings the National Gallery acquired from a Munch exhibition at Blomqvist in 1909. VWH

28

Bathing Boys, 1894

Badende gutter

Oil on canvas
92 × 150 cm
Unsigned
NG.M.01866
Woll M 358
NG cat. 1950-1067; 1968-1284; 1992-1866

Other titles: *Aasgaardstrand*. **Provenance**: Gift from Charlotte and Christian Mustad 1937. **Literature**: Gether 2000, 15; Clarke 2009, 168f., 172; Sørbø 2011, 94f.; Flaatten 2013 A, 110, 206. **Exhibitions**: 1894, Stockholm, no. 21 (uncertain); 1914, Kristiania, no. 11; 1927, Oslo, no. 99; 1952, Zürich, no. 14; 1952, Brussels, no. 5; 2009, Chicago, no. 21; 2013, Oslo, no. 52.

Bathing Boys is one of Munch's first depictions of naked bodies in a natural outdoor setting. The boys are swimming and playing in the water, and the artist has emphasised how the sunlight refracts their submerged limbs, creating shifts in colour and strange distortions.

Bathers became a prominent theme in Munch's art in the latter part of the 1890s, both in his paintings and in his drawings and prints. Where these pictures feature men, such as the National Museum's *Bathing Man* (cat. 54), the emphasis is generally on the muscular male body in motion. These works are suggestive of classical sculpture, nude painting and anatomical studies. Women, men and children do not appear together in pictures of bathers. This is probably because he based these works on direct observation. Munch spent almost every summer by the coast, and both at Åsgårdstrand and at Hvitsten he used the seasonal holiday-makers as inspiration and models.

Bathers were a popular subject around the turn of the last century, especially in Nordic and German art. This can be attributed to the success in that period of the vitalist movement. *Bathing Boys* is an early example of this interest. Yet the theme was also addressed by some of Munch's older colleagues who worked in a more realistic vein. One notable example is Hans Heyerdahl's *Bathing Boys* from 1887. Like Munch, Heyerdahl was a regular summer visitor to Åsgårdstrand, and it was there he produced this painting.

Munch's *Bathing Boys* was gifted to the National Gallery by Charlotte and Christian Mustad in 1937. In the past it was dated ca. 1895, but we now know that it was probably shown at an exhibition in Stockholm in autumn 1894. Catalogue number 21 in the list of works for this exhibition has the title *Badende barn (utkast)* (Bathing Children (sketch)). Admittedly, the fact that the work is described as a sketch leaves room for doubt, since *Bathing Boys* is a large and well developed work. It is possible that the work shown in Stockholm was the less finished *Badende* (Bathers) (1894, Woll M 357). But one reason to suppose otherwise is a review of the Stockholm exhibition in a Swedish newspaper which describes the figures in the painting as "bathing frog-like boys" (*Aftonbladet*, 6 October 1894).

Throughout his career, Munch was inclined to transfer elements from one composition to another. Figures configured like some of the bathing children reoccur in different contexts in later pictures. A drawing in a sketchbook, assumed to be from 1895 (MM.T.00131-18 verso), bears similarities to the painting. A larger watercolour (MM.T.02374), probably also from 1895, has figures that resemble those in *Bathing Boys*. It cannot be concluded, however, that these sketches were preparatory material for the National Museum's painting; they may be of later date, since the theme was something Munch worked on regularly over the ensuing years. The Munch Museum's collection contains, for example, a painting with the same title and a similar composition that can be dated to either 1897 or 1898 (Woll M 409). There are two further paintings entitled *Bathing Boys*, both from roughly the same period (Woll M 410; Woll M 413), but although these also feature young boys and children swimming, in terms of composition they differ significantly from the National Museum's painting. VWH

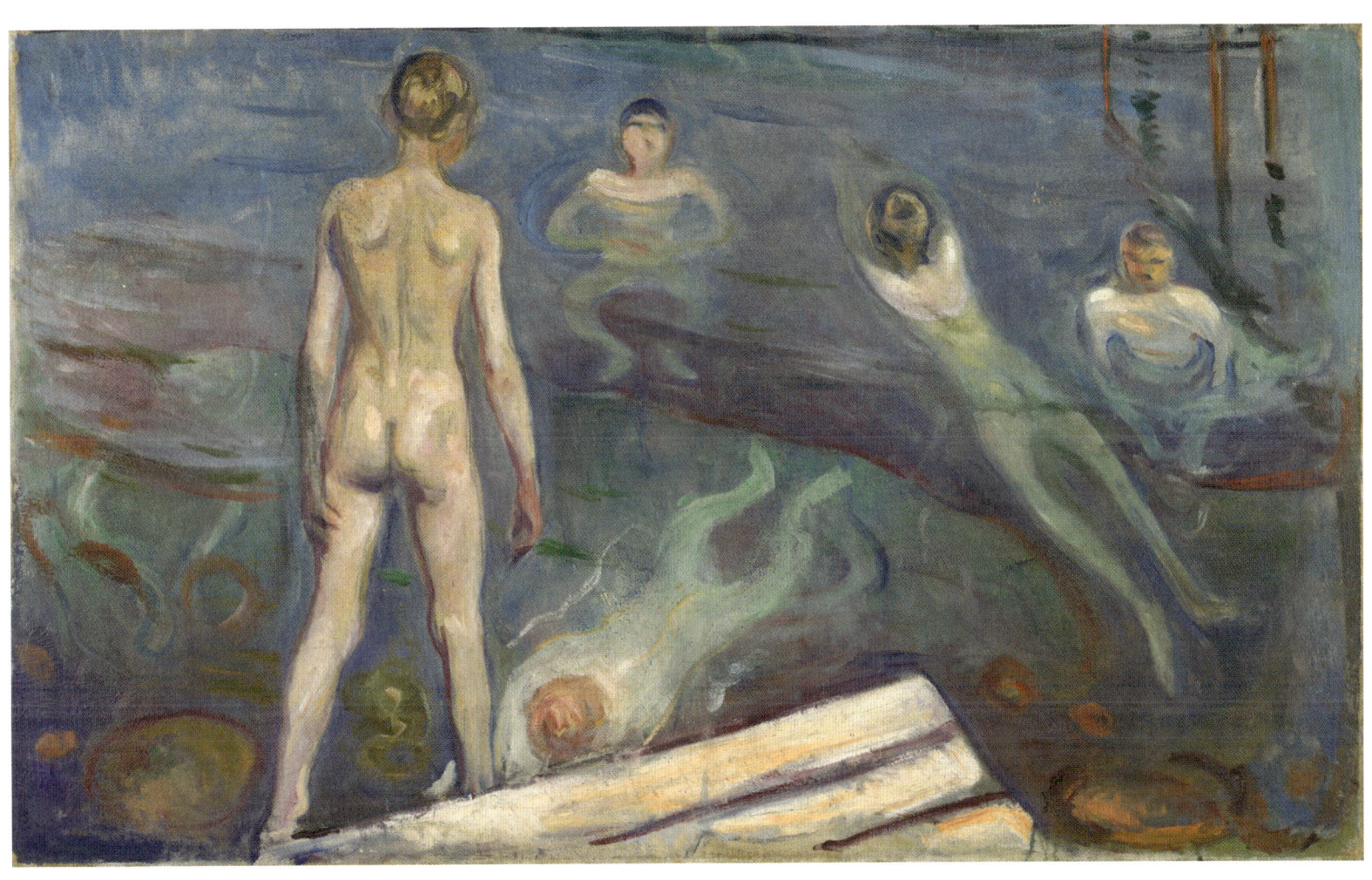

29

Madonna, 1894

Madonna

Oil on canvas
90.5 × 70.5 cm
Signed l.l. "E Munch"
NG.M.00841
Woll M 366
NG cat. 1933-950; 1950-1062; 1968-1279; 1992-841

Other titles: *Elskende kvinde*; *Monna*; *Kvinnan som älskar*. **Provenance**: Olaf Schou (1900–1909), gift from Olaf Schou 1909. **Literature**: One of Munch's best known motifs, it is widely discussed in much of the general Munch literature. Thiis 1933, 216f.; Stenersen 1945, 109, 147; Heller 1984, 127f.; Gerner 1993, 21; Thurmann-Moe 1995, 38; Buchhart 2004, 118; Høifødt 2008, 13, 46; Rutkowski 2008, 38f., 46; Woll 2008 A, 100; Ydstie (ed.) 2008; Alessandrini 2009, 100; Sjåstad 2010, 176; Sjåstad 2011, 36; Berman 2013, 30; Bjerke 2013, 16–18; Guleng 2013, 133; Mørstad 2013, 213; Owesen 2013, 302; Clarke 2014, 54; Steihaug 2014, 32; Alarcó 2015, 38, 91f.; Berman 2015, 91–92; Eggum 2015, 195, 197; Ustvedt 2018, 73–78; Vassenden 2019, 26; Ford et al. 2021, [unpaginated]. **Exhibitions**: It is uncertain which versions of *Madonna* was shown at several of the exhibitions prior to 1940. Only those that are certain are listed here. For a comprehensive list of exhibitions earlier than 1940 in which a version of *Madonna* was shown, see Woll M 365. 1894, Stockholm, no. 60 or 61; 1895, Berlin, no. 6; 1895, Berlin, no. 7; 1895 Kristiania, (three versions exhibited); 1896, Bergen, (as at Blomqvist); 1896, Stavanger, (as at Blomqvist); 1897, Kristiania, no. 40; 1900, Kristiania; 1902, Berlin, no. 192; 1903, Leipzig; 1904, Copenhagen; 1912, Gothenburg; Kristiania, no. 18; 1918, Kristiania, (uncertain); 1927, Oslo, no. 78; 1954, Venice, no. 19; 1954, Munich–Cologne, no. 32; 1955, Copenhagen–Odense, no. 30; 1958, Bern, no. 20; 1958, Rotterdam, no. 8; 1959, Warszawa, no. 9; 1960, Paris, no. 487; 1962, Frankfurt am Main, no. 18; 1964, Kiel, no. 57; 1968, Schaffhausen, no. 19; 1968, Stockholm, no. 237; 1970, Japan, touring exhibition, no. 13; 1973, Munich–London–Paris, no. 26/25; 1987, Oslo B, no. 62; 1992, London, no. 26; 1993, Tokyo-Osaka, no. 25; 1994, Oslo, no. 37; 2013, Oslo, no. 57; 2019, Bergen, no. 4.

A woman shown half-length arches her back, one arm behind her head, the other behind her back. Against a background of undulating, quivering lines, she is depicted with closed eyes and seems almost to be floating. The title *Madonna*, a common designation for the mother of Jesus, contrasts with both the figure and the alternative title, *Elskende kvinde* (Amorous Woman). The female figure has a halo, but it is red rather than gold, as it would be in a religious image.

The picture combines erotic and religious associations. Here the woman is simultaneously a lover and an exalted, holy figure. One of Munch's most popular and widely discussed paintings, the work has been analysed in depth in a monograph (Ydstie (ed.) 2008). Between 1894 and 1897, Munch painted five versions of *Madonna* (Woll M 365; Woll M 366; Woll M 367; Woll M 368; Woll M 369). During this period, he was part of the circle that regularly met at the café-restaurant "Zum Schwarzen Ferkel" in Berlin. This was a group of artists, writers and musicians that included August Strindberg, Stanisław Przybyszewski and Dagny Juel. In addition to art and the role of the artist, the group's discussions frequently revolved around the themes of the woman, love, sexuality and the complex relationship between the sexes.

The woman is a major and recurrent theme in Munch's art, and his depictions of women are predominantly ambiguous and full of contradictions. This attitude finds expression in a text Munch wrote in connection with the *Madonna* painting:

> Picture No. - The woman in a state of abandon
> - acquires the painful
> beauty of a Madonna -
> The mystique is from an entire development
> contracted into one
> - For the man, woman's equivocalness
> is a mystery
> The woman is all at once saint
> - whore and unhappy devotee
> (Note 1894–1895, MM N 30)

In his pictures and writings, Munch challenged preconceptions about male and female, the masculine and the feminine. He portrayed women of different types, ranging from the young and innocent to the seductive *femme fatale*, the mortal woman who ensnares men and leads them to their doom. This was a popular archetype of the day that encapsulated notions of sexuality, perdition, death and artistic creativity. The *femme fatale* has roots in both the literature of antiquity and the Bible.

In 1894, Przybyszewski initiated the publication *Das Werk des Edvard Munch*. In his own contribution to the volume, Przybyszewski wrote about the six paintings that had been exhibited the previous year at Unter den Linden 19 under the title "Study for a series: 'Love'". One of these was *Madonna ansiktet (Madonna-Gesicht)* (The Face of Madonna):

> The third picture presents a Madonna. ... a Madonna in a chemise on crumpled sheets with the halo of her impending martyrdom to childbirth, a Madonna captured at the moment when the arcane mystery of procreation's eternal rapture illuminates the woman's face with oceanic beauty ... (Przybyszewski 1894 A, translation in *Vigeland + Munch* 2015, 86)

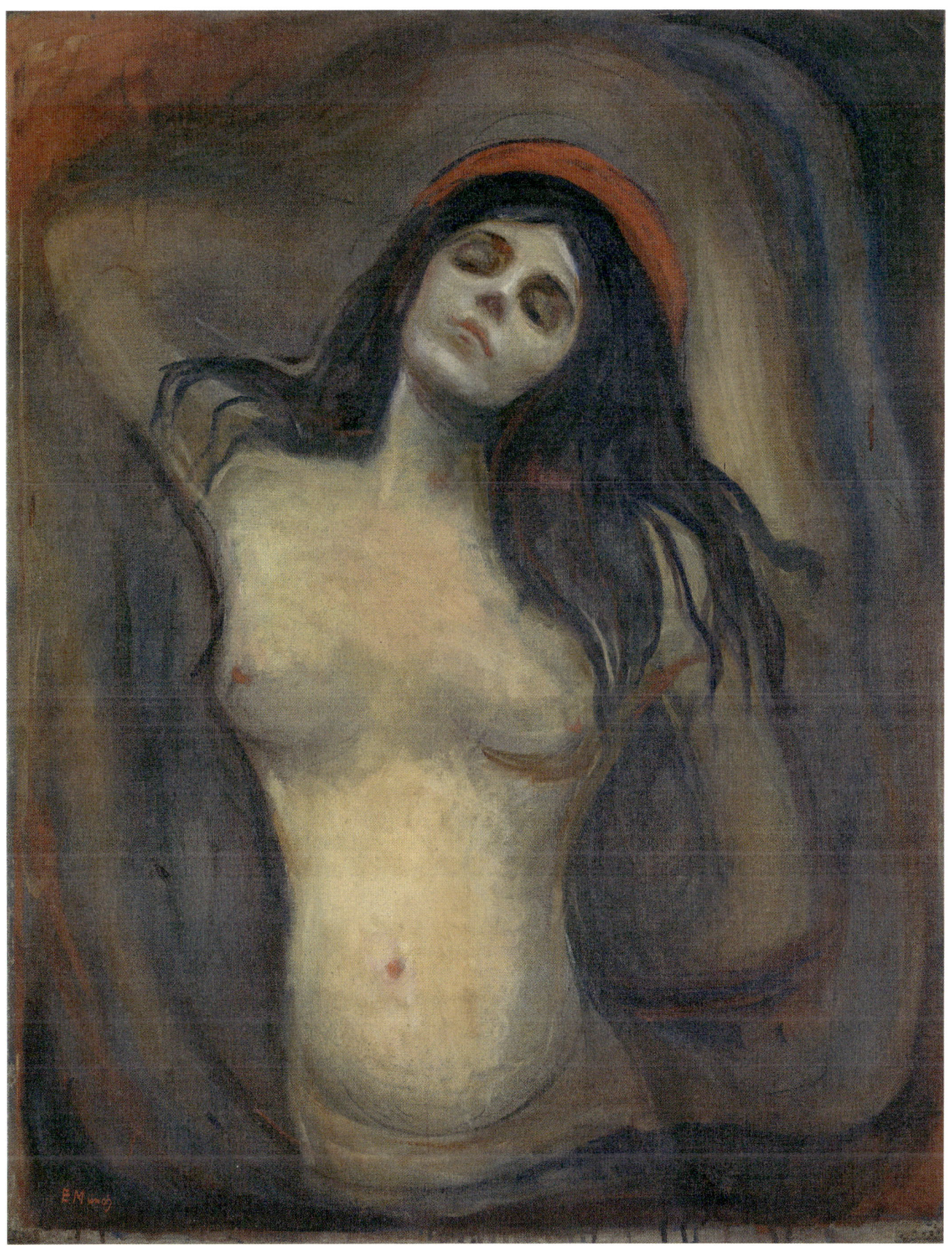

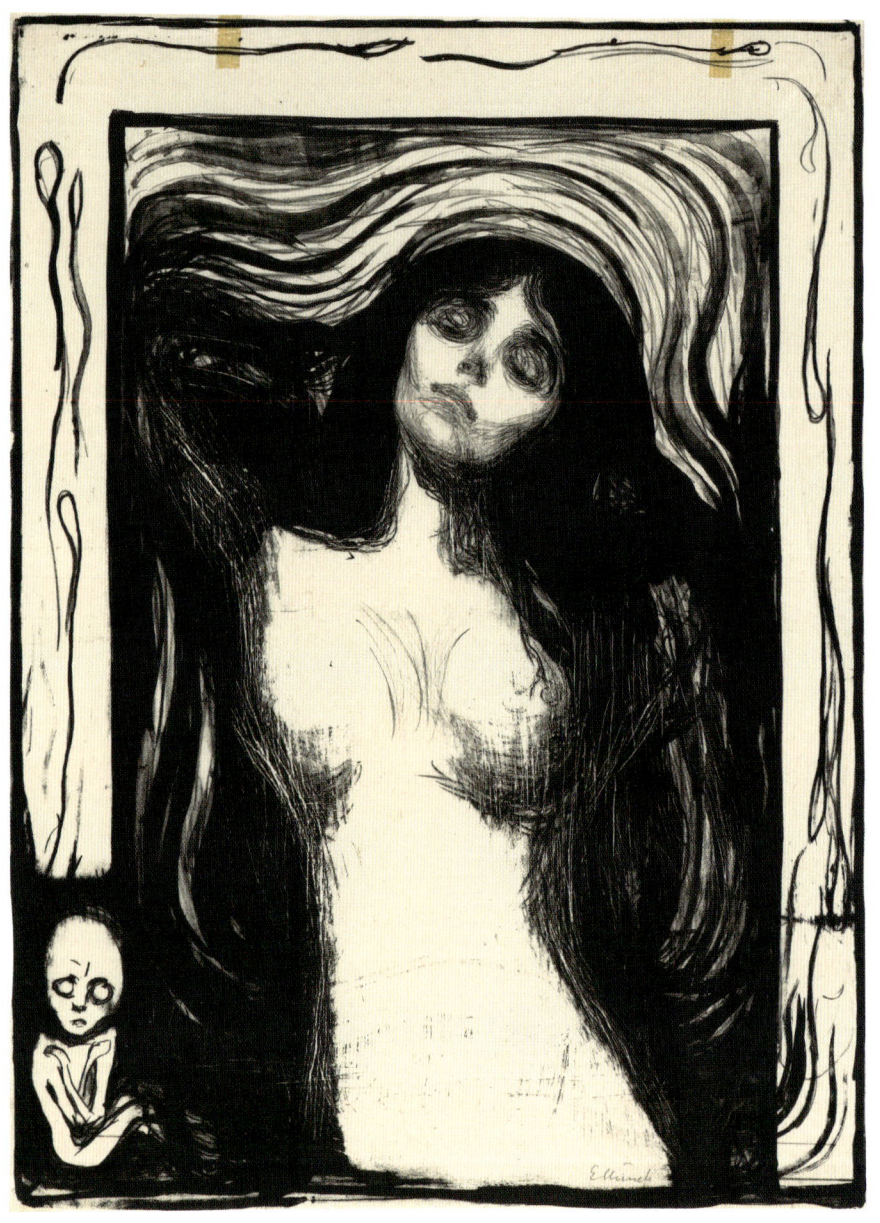

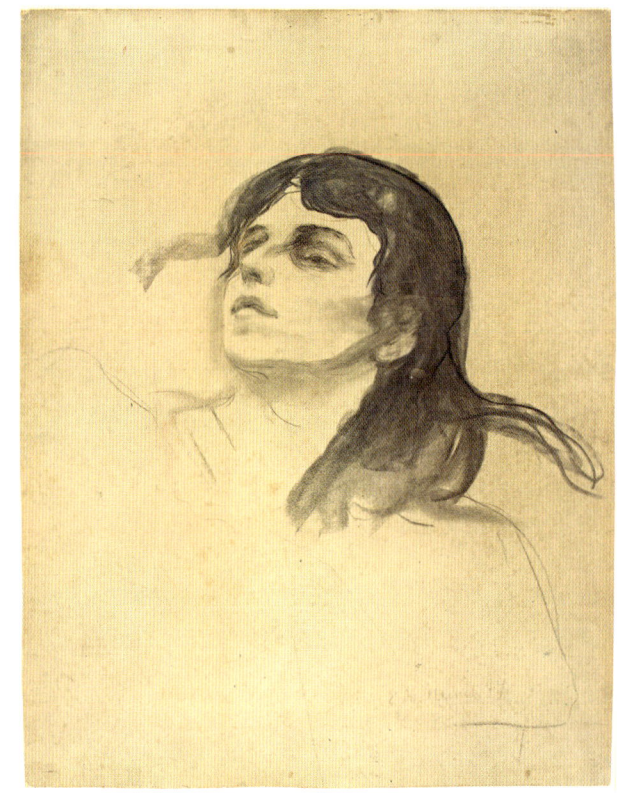

Edvard Munch: *Madonna*, 1895
Litograph, 600 × 440 mm
Munchmuseet
MM.G.00194-58, Woll G 39
Photo: Munchmuseet / Halvor Bjørngård

Printed booklet with inscriptions by Munch, [undated]
Munchmuseet
MM.N.570-05
Photo: Munchmuseet

This is evidently a description not of the *Madonna* we know, but of a forerunner that has since been lost. Even so, this passage may have influenced the way Munch developed the subject and his conception of it (Høifødt 2008, 16-17). Munch asserts the picture's concern with the relationship between life and death in his own writings, for example:

> Moonlight glides over your face
> full of the beauty and pain of the worldly realm
> For it is now death holds out a hand to life
> and a link is forged between the thousands of generations now dead
> and the thousands still to come
> (1896, MM.T.2907)

The notion of conception and human reproduction as something sacred and powerful is also echoed in the picture's reception, for example, in the remarks of Munch's friend, the poet Sigbjørn Obstfelder:

> To me, his Madonna picture is the epitome of his art. She is the Madonna of the Earth, the woman who gives birth in pain. I believe, one must turn to Russian literature to find a similarly religious view of woman, a comparable glorification of the beauty of pain (...) It is just such a woman, one who carries in her womb the greatest miracle of the earth, who Munch visualises. (Obstfelder 1896, 21)

One of the *Madonna* pictures included in the Ugo Barroccio exhibition in Berlin in March 1895 was apparently mounted in a frame that was symbolistically embellished with sperm cells and a foetus (Thiis 1933, 218). In a lithographic version (1895–1902, Woll G 39), the female figure is contained in just such a frame, with sperm cells and a foetus in the lower left corner.

All five versions of the Madonna motif are fairly similar in terms of presentation and format. This makes it difficult to determine which were shown in Munch's earliest exhibitions. The first showing of a version of the work was at the art dealership Blanch in Stockholm in 1894 (Woll 2008 B, 352). There it featured in a sequence entitled "Studies for a mood series: Love". In the catalogue there are two items with the title *Kvinnan som älskar* (The Amorous Woman). Munch exhibited two versions of the Madonna theme simultaneously in a number of exhibitions, for example at Barroccio in March 1895. There they were included in the sequence "Die Liebe". In this case, one painting had the title *Madonna*, the other *Das liebende Weib* (The Amorous Woman).

The picture was gifted to the National Gallery in 1909 by Olaf Schou. None of the five existing versions of *Madonna* carries a date, making it difficult to determine their chronological order. They have traditionally been dated between 1894 and 1897. Gerd Woll adopts the order proposed by Cornelia Gerner, in which the National Gallery's version comes second (Gerner 1993, 21, 1990 in the bibliography, PhD thesis). Recent research has confirmed that the National Museum's *Madonna* is the first in the series (see T. Ford's essay in this catalogue). There exist two graphic versions of *Madonna*, the etching from 1894 (Woll G 11) that was included in the portfolio edition of Munch prints published in that year by the German critic and writer Julius Meier-Graefe, and a lithograph (1895/1902) (cat. 86, cat. 87, Woll G 39). Several drawings indicate how Munch developed the subject (MM.T.0291; MM.T.2430).

Madonna was shown at Munch's exhibition in Leipzig at P.H. Beyer & Sohn in 1903. There he presented what would later become known as the Frieze of Life as a coherent series. Documentary photographs from the exhibition show that *Madonna* was hung to the left of *Ashes* (cat. 30) in the second section, which dealt with the flowering and fall of love (Woll M 400). wv

30

Ashes, 1895

Aske

Oil on canvas
120.5 × 141 cm
Signed u.r. "E Munch"
NG.M.00809
Woll M 378
NG cat. 1933-949; 1950-1061; 1968-1278; 1992-809

Other titles: *Adam und Eva nach dem Sündenfall*; *Nach dem Sündenfall*. **Provenance**: Purchased with financial support from the A.C. Houen's trust fund on the occasion of the artist's 1909 exhibition at Blomqvist Kunsthandel. **Literature**: Ritter 1906, 48; Thiis 1933, 218, 231; I. Langaard 1960, 87, 226; Eggum 1978 B, 59; Skedsmo (ed.) 1981, 94–95; Eggum 1983 A, 135; Skedsmo 1987 A, 226; Eggum 1990, 137; Bischoff 1993, 43f.; Kneher 1994, 397, note 171; Billeter 1998, 124; Mørstad 2004 B, 40f.; Berman 2006 A, 121; Rutkowski 2008, 64; Templeton 2008, 80; Clarke 2009, 98, 168, 176; Kuuva 2010, 61, 111; Høifødt 2010 A, 37; Høifødt 2010 B, 117; Clarke 2012, 47; Lampe 2012, 37; Guleng 2013, 133; Owesen 2013, 300; Nyaas (ed.) 2013, 160, 178; Gaillard 2013, 97f; Endresen 2013, 220f; Steihaug 2014, 32; Stein and Rød 2015, 257, 262–263; Berman 2015, 95f; Steihaug 2015, 159; Steihaug 2016, 53; Knausgård 2017 A, 77f, 196.
Exhibitions: 1895, Kristiania-Bergen-Stavanger; 1897, Kristiania, no. 41; 1898, Dresden; 1901, Kristiania, no. 49; 1902, Berlin, no. 193; 1903, Leipzig; 1904, Copenhagen; 1904, Kristiania, no. 5; 1905, Prague, no. 35; 1906, Hagen, no. 38; 1906, Weimar, no. 9; 1907, Bielefeld, no. 10; 1909, Kristiania; 1927, Berlin, no. 39; 1927, Oslo, no. 82; 1950, USA, touring exhibition, no. 16; 1951, Brighton-Glasgow-London-The Hague–Paris, no. 15; 1952, Zürich, no. 7; 1952, Brussels, no. 1; 1954, Munich-Cologne, no. 31; 1955, Copenhagen-Odense, no. 29; 1959, Warszaw; 1960, Recklinghausen–Vienna–Berlin–Oslo-Helsinki, no. 8; 1964; Munich, no. 389; 1964, Kiel, no. 56; 1964, Dublin, no. 190; 1970, Munich-Paris, no. 13; 1971, Oslo, no. 35; 1978, Washington, no. 47; 1979, New York; 1979, London, no. 264; 1986, London–Düsseldorf–Paris, no. 61; 1987, Berlin, no. H 36; 1987, Zürich, no. 40; 1994, Oslo, no. 38; 1998, Paris, no. 130; 1999, Florence, no. 7; 2006, New York, no. 64; 2009, Chicago, no. 29; 2012, London, no. 10; 2013, Oslo, no. 61; 2019, Bergen, no. 6.

In *Ashes*, a deep, dark forest forms the backdrop for an emotional drama between man and woman. With ashen face, the man huddles in the corner, holding his head in despair. Behind him stands the woman, half-dressed, her hair flowing loose and dishevelled. She turns to face the viewer, her hands raised to her head. The picture is mentioned in a letter from September 1895, under the title *Adam og Eva etter syndefallet* (Adam and Eve after the Fall) (MM K 2229), while in the big Frieze of Life Exhibition in Berlin in 1902, it was referred to as *Etter syndefallet* (After the Fall). Despite these allusions to the biblical story of the relationship between man and woman, the picture is also rooted in the 1890s debate about gender roles. A lithographic version of the picture has the inscription: "I felt our love lying on the ground like a heap of ashes." This explains the ultimate title and the stylised tree trunk in the foreground that frames the subject. In the lithograph, the tree trunk has been reduced to a pile of ash.

Forests and trees play a crucial role in Munch's symbolist repertoire. There are also many references to forests in the artist's writings. The fact that the scene is set in a forest is significant, and probably the human drama was conceptualised as taking place in such an environment from the start. *Skogsinteriør* (Forest interior) from 1893 (Woll M 279) is regarded as a preliminary study for *Ashes*. The two paintings were exhibited together at Blomqvist in autumn 1895. On that occasion, a former owner referred to *Skogsinteriør* as "… the wonderfully beautiful painted sketch for Ashes" (MM K 1637).

Ashes was accorded a central place in the 1902 Berlin exhibition. During the artist's lifetime, the Frieze was displayed with varying configurations of paintings, which also went by different names from one event to the next. The 22 paintings shown in Berlin in 1902 were grouped according to different themes for each of the gallery's four walls. The first wall was entitled "The Seed of Love", the main wall "Love's Flowering and Fall". *Ashes* was the first painting in this set.

In 1909, the National Gallery added a further five Munch paintings to its collection. One of them was *Ashes*. In connection with the purchase, Munch sent a telegram to museum director Jens Thiis with the following terms: "The pictures for 10,000 kroner in hand within 4 days. 'Vampire' and 'Ashes' conditional on short loan for 'copying'. Munch" (Telegram, 18 March 1909. NMFK / NG-1000 / B-0003 (copyist register)). The message may indicate that he was intending to make a new version of the picture, something he got round to only many years later. In January 1925, he signed into the National Gallery's copyist register to copy *Ashes* and *The Dance of Life* (cat. 40). Although the 1925 version is similar in composition and has the same title, some details differ; the colours are more intense and the execution more concise (Woll M 1562).

In the past, there has been some uncertainty about when the picture was painted. For a long time, 1894 was by far the most commonly cited date, but recent research suggests it was more probably finished in 1895. The evidence for this is a letter from A. von Franquet, in which he mentions a new painting by Munch, which he refers to as *Adam und Eva nach dem Sündenfall* (MM K 2229) (Kneher 1994; Eggum 1983 A; Eggum 1990: Woll 2008 B). Sketches for the picture are also found in one of the artist's sketchbooks which otherwise contains material, both texts and drawings, from 1895 (MM.T.000131). As mentioned, Munch produced lithographic versions of *Ashes* in 1896 and 1899 (Woll G 79; Woll G 146). The National Museum owns a copy of the 1899 version (cat. 136). Several other drawings relating to the subject have also survived (MM.T.00348: MM.T.0343). These were probably done in 1896 in connection with preparations for the first lithograph. VWH

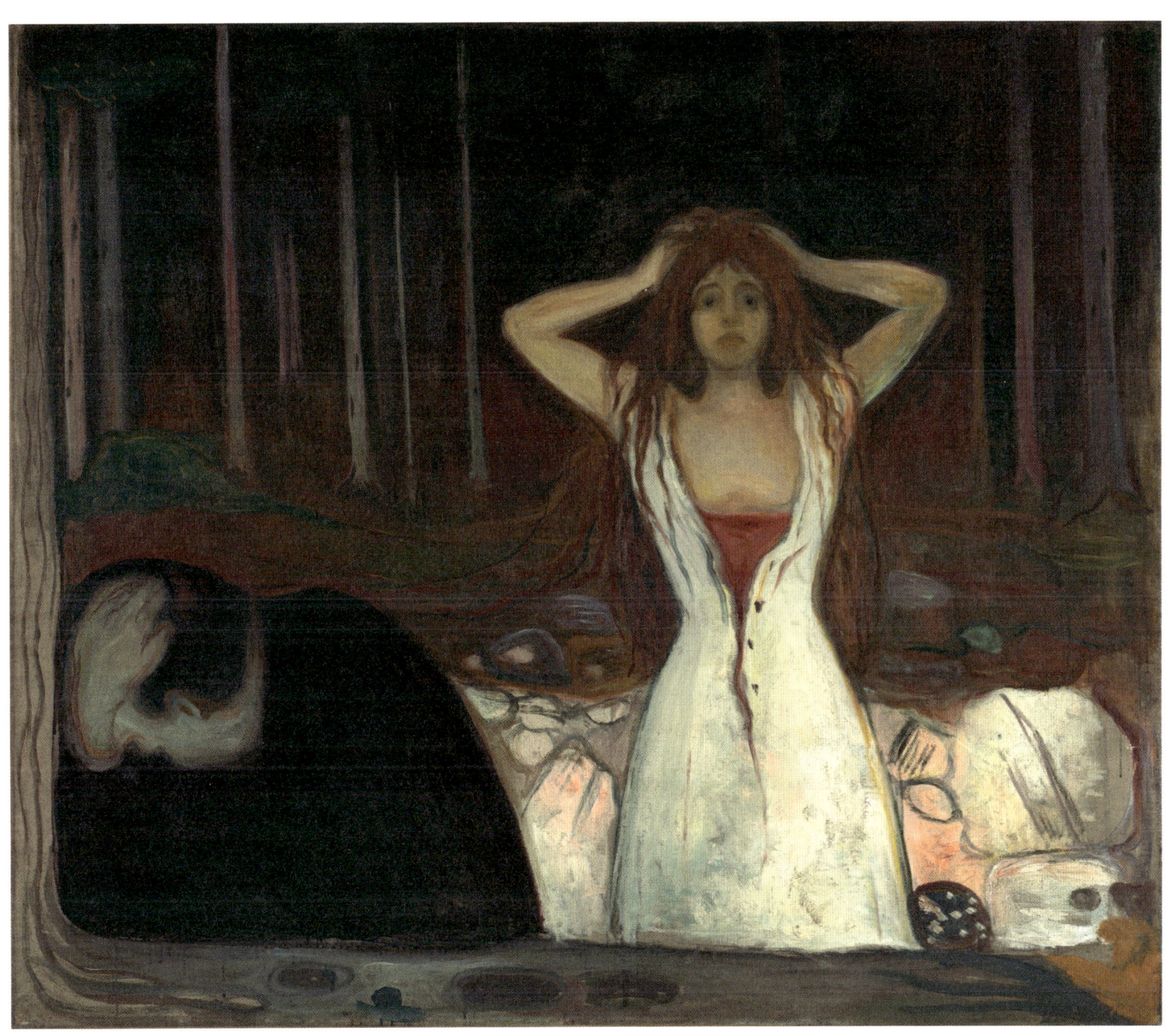

31

Moonlight, 1895

Måneskinn

Oil on canvas
93 × 110 cm
Signed l.l. "E Munch 95"
NG.M.02815
Woll M 381
NG cat. 1992-2815

Other titles: *Nuit claire*; *Maaneskin*; *Måneskinn. Aasgaardstrand 1895*. **Provenance**: Charlotte and Christian Mustad (1910–1959/1970); bequeathed by Charlotte and Christian Mustad to the National Gallery in 1959, received 1970. **Literature**: I. Langaard 1960, 228f.; Bischoff 1993, 32f.; Zarobell 2005, 18; Clarke 2009, 32, 66, 70, 96; Flaatten 2010 B, 48, 332–333; Kuuva 2010, 73–74; Pettersen 2010, 111; Bischoff 2011, 32f.; Flaatten 2013 A, 95–97; Nyaas (ed.) 2013, 146; Lahelma 2014, 220; Ustvedt 2016, 73. **Exhibitions**: 1897, Paris, no. 826; 1897, Kristiania (somewhat uncertain); 1910, Kristiania, no. 86; 1926, Mannheim, no. 5; 1927, Oslo, no. 92; 1937, Paris; 1975, Rotterdam–Brussels– Baden-Baden–Paris, no. 149; 1976, Darmstadt; 1979, Milan, no. 199; 1980, Washington; 1983, Dresden, no. 16; 1985, Milan–Rome, no. 33; 1987, Barcelona, no. 8; 1987, Tokyo, no. 16; 1989, Høvikodden; 1992, London, no. 12; 1993, Tokyo–Osaka, no. 1; 1994, Oslo, no. 39; 1995, Montreal, no. 300; 1998, Cologne, no. 57; 1998, Lugano, no. 31; 1999, Florence, no. 10; 2001, Ferrara, no. 62; 2003, Vienna; 2004, Melbourne, no. 24; 2005, Rome, no. 23; 2005, Philadelphia; 2006, Helsinki–Stockholm–Oslo–Copenhagen–Minneapolis, no. 100; 2009, Chicago, nr. 35; 2010, Codroipo, no. 104; 2012, Essen, no. 103; 2013, Oslo, no. 63; 2015, Oslo–Helsinki, no. 78; 2018, Oslo.

The forest fringe, the curving shoreline, the stylised tree trunks, the moon and the pillar of moonlight. These are elements that reoccur in many of Munch's pictures. Frequently he uses this landscape as a setting for various human activities, but here it assumes the main role alone. There are no figures present.

As a central genre throughout his career, landscape painting played an important part in Munch's art. He became attached to specific places and liked to paint landscapes he knew well. His early landscapes depict locations on the outskirts of Kristiania (Oslo). He painted the scenery of Åsgårdstrand, along the coast of the Kristianiafjord, in the south of France, and in the vicinity of Kragerø, Hvitsten, Moss, and Ekely.

The location in *Moonlight* is Åsgårdstrand, where Munch found many of his themes. This coastal landscape provides the setting for a number of pictures, including *Melancholy* (cat. 19) and *The Dance of Life* (cat. 40). Here we see it distilled and stylised. The horizontal and vertical dimensions are rendered palpable by the accentuation of the upright tree trunks that transect the shoreline and the horizon. The lines bind the painting together, justifying Sigbjørn Obsfelder's observation that Munch saw a "certain architecture" in nature (Obstfelder 1896, 19).

The painting is particularly rich in shades of blue, ranging from the pastel blue of the sea to the violet of the horizon. Obstfelder praised Munch's use of colour early his career: "Above all else, he is a poet of colour. He feels colours, and feels in colours. He doesn't merely see them" (Obstfelder 1896, 17).

Moonlight stands as an example of romantic landscape painting. In a neo-romantic mood, Munch captures the characteristic luminosity of a Nordic summer night. The landscape is abstracted and presented in monumental form. For the American art historian Robert Rosenblum, Munch's landscape painting extends the legacy of Caspar David Friedrich and J.C. Dahl (Rosenblum 1975, 118). Munch uses landscapes to convey human emotions and yearnings.

The moonlight theme is recurrent in his art. During his early stay in the south of France he explored its effects in works such as *Moonlight by the Mediterranean* (cat. 18). Disregarding the lack of a female figure and boat(s) on the fjord, *Moonlight* compares closely with *Sommernattsdrøm. Stemmen* (Summer Night's Dream. The Voice), 1893 (Woll M 319) and *Sommernatt. Stemmen* (Summer Night. The Voice), 1896 (Woll M 394).

Moonlight came into the museum's possession in 1970 as a bequest from Charlotte and Christian Mustad. The painting was first exhibited at the Salon des Artistes Indépendants in Paris in 1897. It was probably also included in Munch's exhibition in the Dioramalokalet in Kristiania the same year (Woll 2008 B, 371). The picture has similarities with *Strandbredd i Åsgårdstrand* (Beach in Åsgårdstrand) (Woll M 380). Munch's sketchbook of 1895 contains a number of sketches of the shoreline that correspond with these paintings (MM.T.131–26 verso). At the large retrospective at the National Gallery in 1927, the painting was shown for the first time with a place name in the title: *Måneskinn. Aasgaardstrand 1895* (Moonlight. Åsgårdstrand 1895). The precise location is probably Fjugstadskogen just north of Åsgårdstrand (Flaatten 2013 A, 95). wv

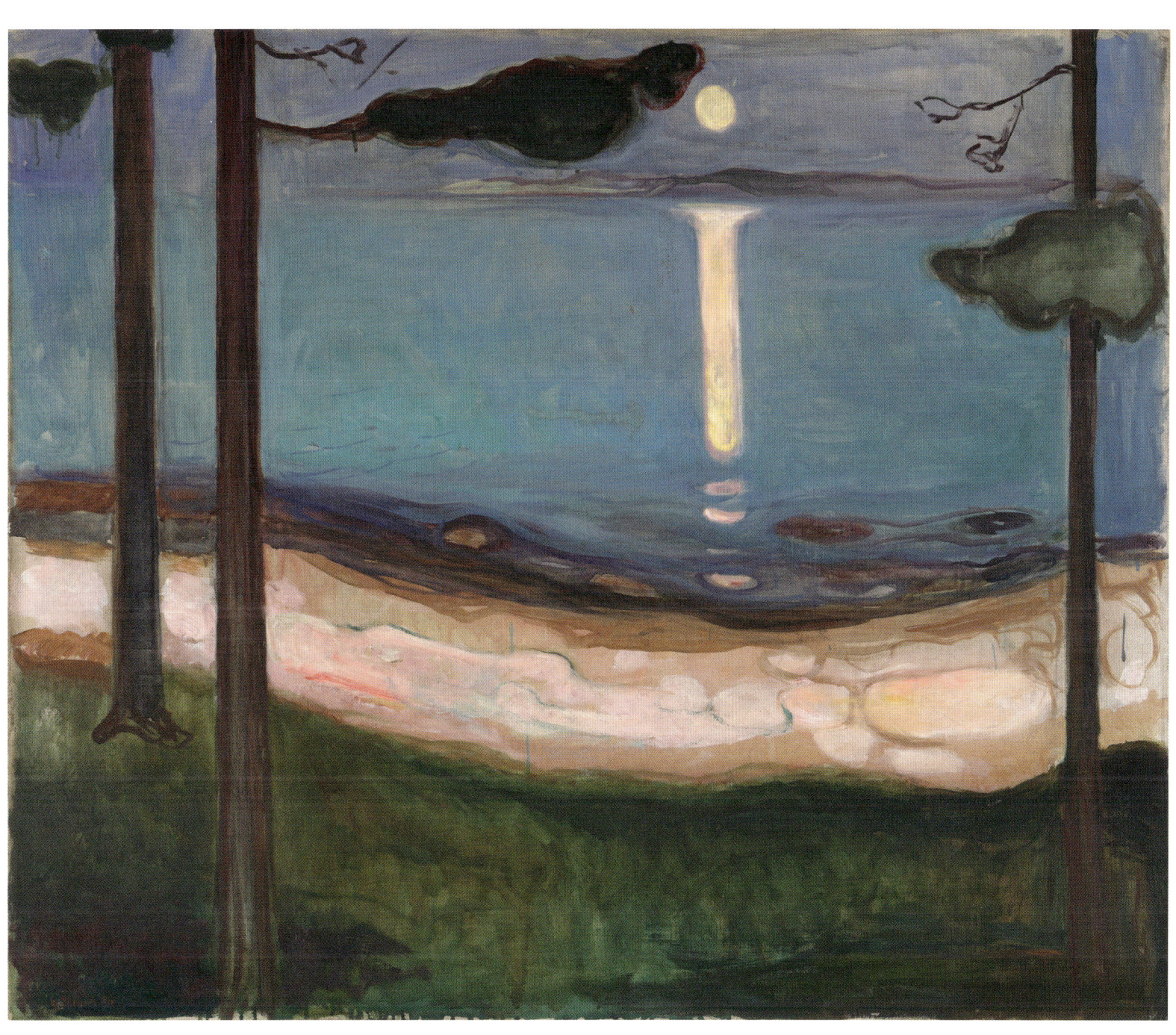

32

Self-Portrait with Cigarette, 1895

Selvportrett med sigarett

Oil on canvas
110.5 × 85.5 cm
Signed l.l. "E. Munch 1895"
NG.M.00470
Woll M 382
NG cat. 1933-953; 1950-1065; 1968-1282; 1992-470

Other titles: *Selvportræt.* **Provenance:** Purchased from the artist 1895. **Literature:** Obstfelder 1896, 18; Vidalenc 1920, 135-136; I. Langaard 1960, 232; Jedlicka 1958, 230f.; Svenæus 1968, 97; Eggum 1978 B, 21f.; Schneede 1984 B, 65f.; Arnold 1986, 73f.; Eggum 1987 A, 60; Eggum 1988 B, 24; Berman 1993 B, 627-646; Bischoff 1993, 7f.; Müller-Westermann 1994, 39f.; Berman 1997 A, 35; Tøjner 1997, 137f.; Billeter 1998, 122; Mørstad 2003 B, 91f.; Lange 2004, 118; Woll 2004 B, 4f.; Müller-Westermann 2005, 47f.; Xani 2005, 45; Mørstad 2006 B, 88-117; López 2008, 44; Clarke 2009, 61, 108, 122, 128; Hansen 2011 B, 214; Borgmann 2011, 48; Bischoff 2011, 7f.; Goldberg 2011, 45; Temkin 2012, 21; Buchhart 2012 B, 76; Huber 2013, 87; Woll 2013, 17; Grøgaard 2013 A, 350; Steihaug 2013 A, 17f.; Buchhart 2013, 23; Nyaas (ed.) 2013, 84f., 155; Steihaug 2014, 29, 34; Steihaug 2015, 153; Lloyd 2015, 126; Gjessing 2016, 32; Krämer 2016, 120; Ravenal 2016, 88; Ohlsen 2016, 58, 63; Berman 2016, 83, 90; Stein 2017 B, 36-37; Berman 2017, 45-47; Carey 2019, 131; Ford et al. 2019, [unpaginated]; Ford et al. 2021, [unpaginated]. **Exhibitions:** 1895, Berlin, no. 26; 1895, Kristiania–Bergen–Stavanger; 1897, Stockholm; 1897, St. Petersburg; 1927, Berlin, no. 46; 1927, Oslo, no. 97; 1950, USA, touring exhibition, no. 22; 1951-1952, Brighton–Glasgow–London–The Hague–Paris, no. 21/22; 1952, Zürich, no. 13; 1952, Brussels, no. 4; 1954, Munich–Cologne, no. 33; 1955, Copenhagen–Odense, no. 31; 1958, Rotterdam, no. 10; 1978, Washington, no. 4; 1979, New York; 1982, Washington–New York–Minneapolis, no. 67; 1987, Essen, no. 43; 1987, Zürich, no. 43; 1988, Humlebæk, no. 5; 1992, London, no. 1; 1994, Munich–Hamburg–Berlin, no. 16; 1998, Paris, no. 110; 1999, Florence, no. 9; 2004, Melbourne, no. 32; 2005, Stockholm–Oslo–London, no. 21; 2006, New York, no. 37; 2009, Chicago, no. 38; 2012, Norway, touring exhibition; 2013, Oslo, no. 64; 2015, Helsinki, no. 36; 2015, Oslo–Amsterdam, no. 95; 2017, San Francisco–New York, no. 16; 2019, Bergen, no. 20.

In this painting, Munch celebrates himself as an artist. The picture is large, with a format that itself signals ambition. He had good reason to be happy with the way his career was developing. He was thirty-two years old, living in Berlin and part of a circle that included several prominent artists and intellectuals. Despite his relatively young age, he could already look back on many exhibitions that had been positively reviewed and from which he had sold many pictures. His work was controversial, but first and foremost he was a young man enjoying success. Although the setting is indistinct, the figure appears to be standing in a smoky room. It is dark except for the light from a low source that creates a dramatic effect. The face and the right hand holding the cigarette, the painting hand, stand out clearly against the otherwise sombre surface.

Self-promotion was something Munch worked on throughout his sixty-year career. His self-portraits number almost sixty. *Self-Portrait with Cigarette* is central to this genre. Since the 1950s, the work has featured in many exhibitions, and over the years it has assumed an increasingly important place in the Munch literature. It has been argued that with this portrait he consciously identifies himself as a Bohemian. For one thing, it has been pointed out that the cigarette was associated with Bohemian culture, modernity and a decadent lifestyle (Berman 1993 B, 17). The work has been compared to Christian Krohg's *Portrait of Gerhard Munthe*, painted ten years earlier. In both cases the subject is rendered half-length holding a cigarette in a smoky room. The difference lies in the respective settings. In Krohg's portrait of Munthe it is immediately obvious that the subject is in a café. In his self-portrait, Munch uses the colours and diffuse brushwork to evoke a mysterious atmosphere and to demonstrate his allegiance to the new symbolist direction (Müller-Westermann 1997, 47).

The picture was shown for the first time in Berlin the year it was painted. In autumn 1895 it was exhibited at Blomqvist in Kristiania (Oslo). Several of the paintings in the latter solo exhibition, including the self-portrait, became the subject of heated debate in the Norwegian press. The poet Sigbjørn Obstfelder, a friend of Munch, held a lecture at the Studentersamfundet (the Students' Association) on 9 November 1895, in which he defended Munch and countered the harsh criticism levelled at the exhibition. In the discussion that followed the lecture, the medical student Johan Scharffenberg publically questioned Munch's mental state, making specific reference to *Self-Portrait with Cigarette* (Mørstad 2006 B, 108). In response, Obstfelder wrote the article "Edvard Munch. Et forsøk" (Edvard Munch. An Essay), which appeared in *Samtiden* the following year (1896). In this he discusses the self-portrait as new and different: "... his self-portrait represents a painting of the soul rather than of facial traits, a work of wondrously profound beauty rather than observational truth." Obstfelder also noted a parallel to Rembrandt's self-portraits: "... because they also reveal the inner state through the use of the artist's proper medium ..." (Obstfelder 1896, 18).

The painting was purchased on the occasion of the exhibition at Blomqvist in 1895. It was the artist himself who approached the National Gallery, with an offer to sell several pictures. The other paintings in that offer were *Spring* (cat. 12), *The Sick Child* (cat. 8) and *Soloppgang* (Sunrise). The fact that the artist wanted to be represented in the National Gallery in terms of this self-portrait suggests he considered the work important. The painting is unusual among Munch's major works in that he never produced another version of it, either in paint or as a print. We also know of no preliminary studies or sketches for this work. VWH

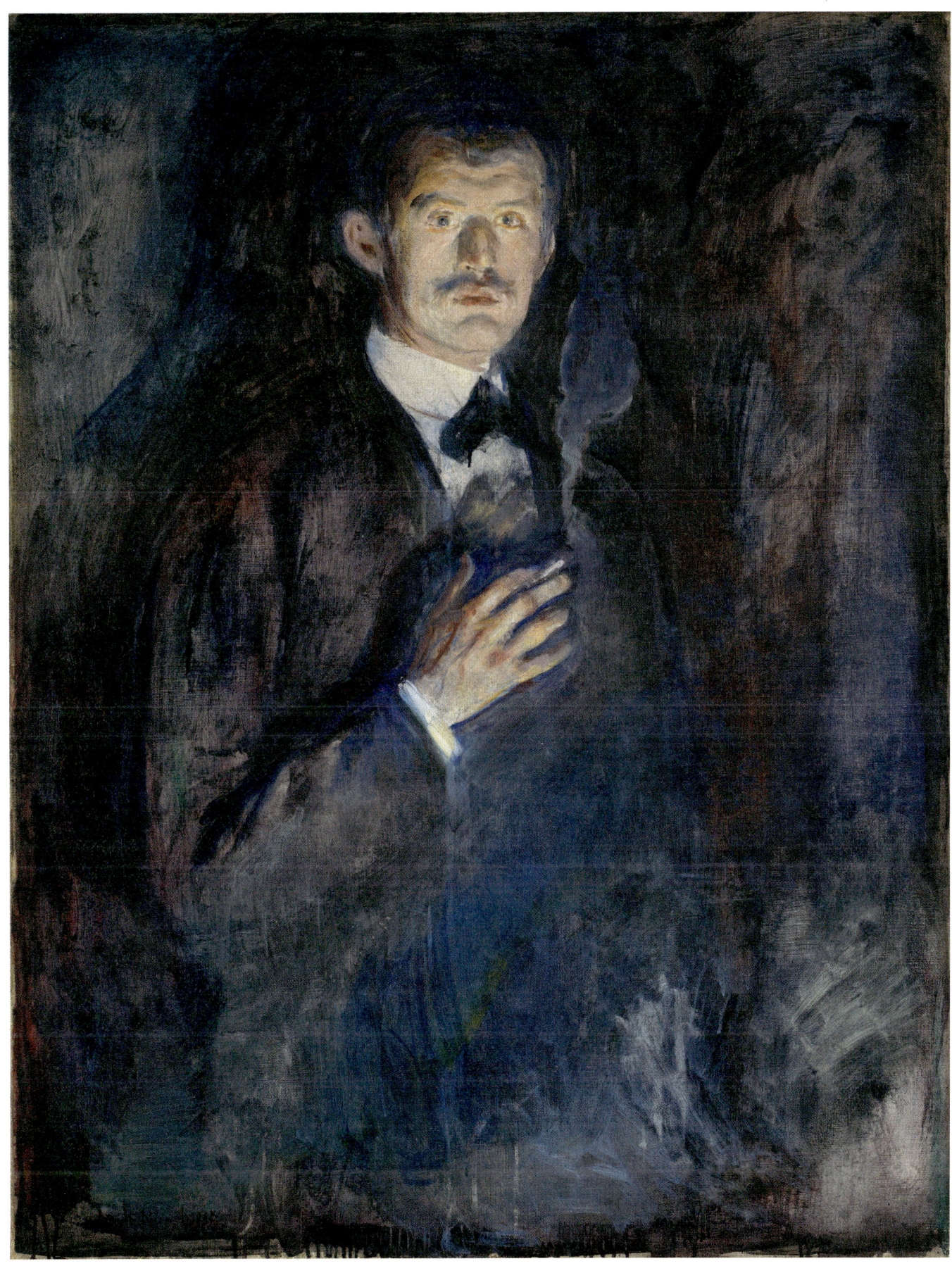

Oil on wood panel
74.5 × 59 cm
Unsigned
NG.M.00843
Woll M 387
NG Cat. 1933-954, 1950-1068, 1968-1285, 1992-843
NG.M.00843

Other titles: *Pike som vasker seg*. **Provenance**:
Gift from Olaf Schou 1909. **Literature**: I. Langaard 1960, 392; Skedsmo 1989, 10. **Exhibitions**:
1927, Berlin, no. 61; 1927, Oslo, no. 102; 1987,
Oslo B, no. 63.

In the years around 1896, Munch painted several female nudes and studies of models, including this one. Here he may have used the same model as in another painting in the National Museum's collection, *Parisian Model* (cat. 34). *Young Woman Washing* is somewhat different from the other works in this group in terms of the emphasis placed on the interior and other details of the location. The window and the sink with running water suggest a modern urban setting around the turn of the last century.

Light from the window illuminates the room and the female figure, who stands with her back half turned to the viewer. The palette is restrained, with dominant hues of cool grey-green blue and warm skin tones with hints of red. The work is striking in terms of technical execution. The colours are applied in thin, diluted washes that contrast with isolated pastose strokes. The texture and grain of the underlying wood shimmer through the layers of paint in a way that gives unity and coherence. Munch's use of the panel's inherent structure to enhance the idiom echoes his handling of the wood matrix in his woodcuts, a medium he began to explore in the year he painted this picture.

In the latter half of the 19th century, indoor scenes depicting women in the process of dressing or undressing, washing or bathing, naked or semi-naked, were very popular. Sometimes they carry erotic overtones. This was especially true among the trendsetting artists of Paris, such as Edgar Degas, Henri de Toulouse-Lautrec and Pierre Bonnard, who forged a genre from such situations.

The painting was probably done during Munch's 1896 stay in Paris. It is not marked with a date, but was ascribed to the year 1896 at the major exhibitions in Berlin and Oslo in 1927. The work is painted on a wooden panel consisting of five sections, made from poplar and birch. The painting was part of Olaf Schou's sizeable donation to the National Gallery in 1909. It has been little discussed in the literature. ØU

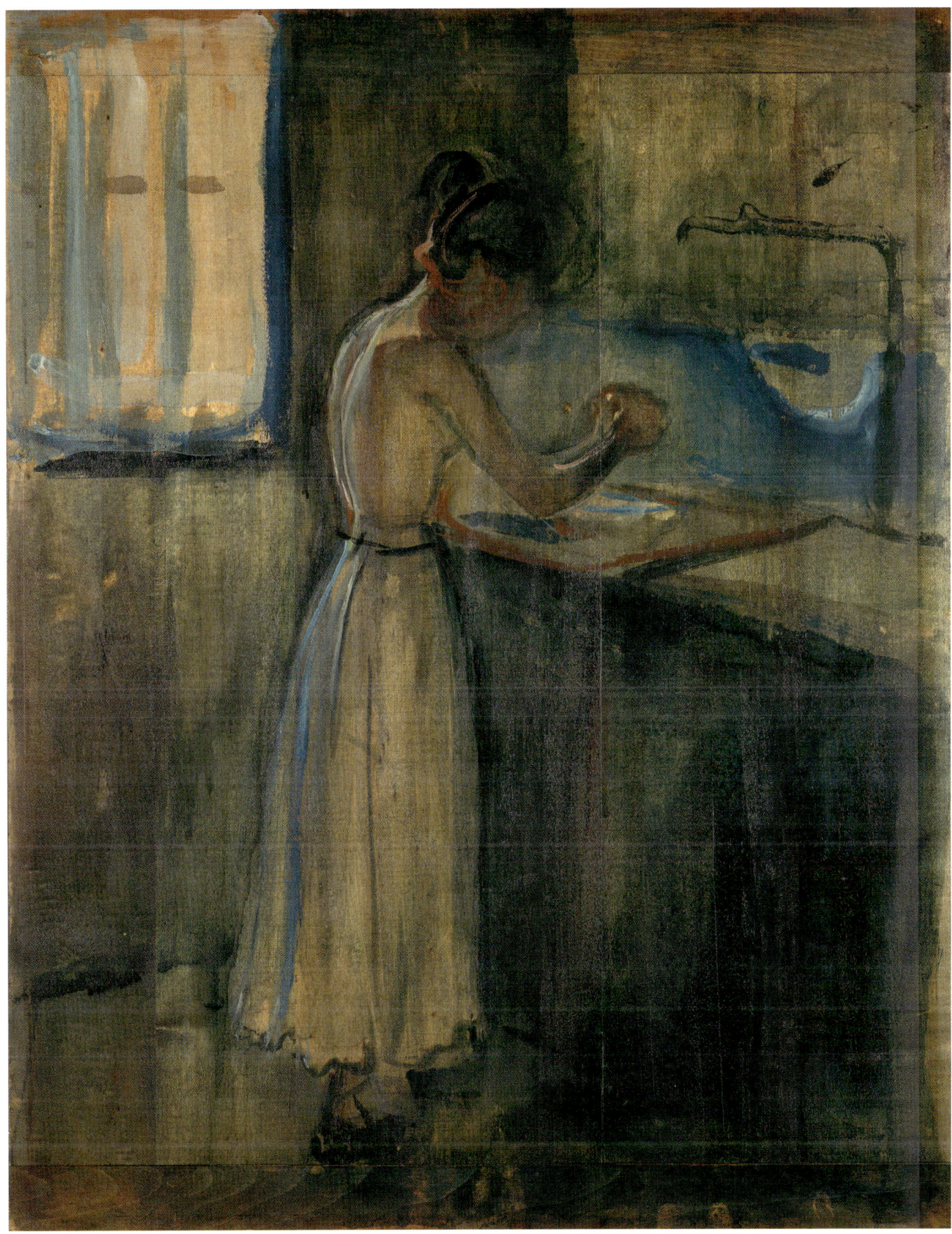

34

Parisian Model, 1896

Parisermodell

Oil on canvas
80 × 60 cm
Signed u.l. "E Munch"; l.l. "E.M"
NG.M.02816
Woll M 388
NG kat. 1992-2816

Other titles: *Parisermodell, sittende akt mot rød bakgrunn*; *Påkledningen*; *Kvinlig akt.*
Provenance: Charlotte and Christian Mustad (before 1946-1959/1970); bequeathed by Charlotte and Christian Mustad to the National Gallery in 1959, received 1970. **Literature**: I. Langaard 1960, 392; Eggum 1991, 195f.; Hansen et al. 2011, 88; Hansen 2011 A, 212. **Exhibitions**: 1908, Breslau, no. 1; 1909, Bremen; 1912, Munich, no. 33; 1913, Stockholm A, no. 4; 1927, Oslo, no. 101; 1950, USA, touring exhibition, no. 23; 1951, Brighton–Glasgow–London–The Hague–Paris, no. 22/23; 1975, Århus–Humlebæk, no. 94/20; 1978, Madison–Minneapolis–Seattle, no. 186; 1985, Milan–Rome, no. 36; 1987, Barcelona, no. 10; 1991, Paris–Oslo–Frankfurt, no. 32; 1999, Florence, no. 11; 2001, Boston, no. 48; 2002, Venice, no. 105; 2003, Vienna, no. 171; 2005, Rome, no. 24.

The woman's naked body is depicted against a background of intense red. The contrasting elements and the shallow pictorial space give prominence to the body and skin. The white dress the woman is holding reflects light onto her face, creating subtle paler tones. Pictures like this form a prelude to a major theme in Munch's later work, based on his depictions of the female body and the relationship between the artist and his model. Later, he generally preferred to work with individual female models over a longer period, in some cases many years. The model here may be the same as in *Young Woman Washing* (cat. 33).

Munch painted the picture during his 1896 stay in Paris. No date is marked on the work, but in the list issued by the Hamburg gallery Commeter in 1906, it was ascribed to 1896. In the collection of the Munch Museum, there is a smaller drawing of the scene dated to the same year (MM.T.00384-verso). Around this time, Munch produced a number of smaller female nudes and studies of models, most as drawings (MM.T.01081; MM.T.00805; MM.T.00807; MM.T.00852) and one as a painting (cat. 33). *Parisian Model* entered the National Gallery's collection in 1970, as part of Charlotte and Christian Mustad bequest. ØU

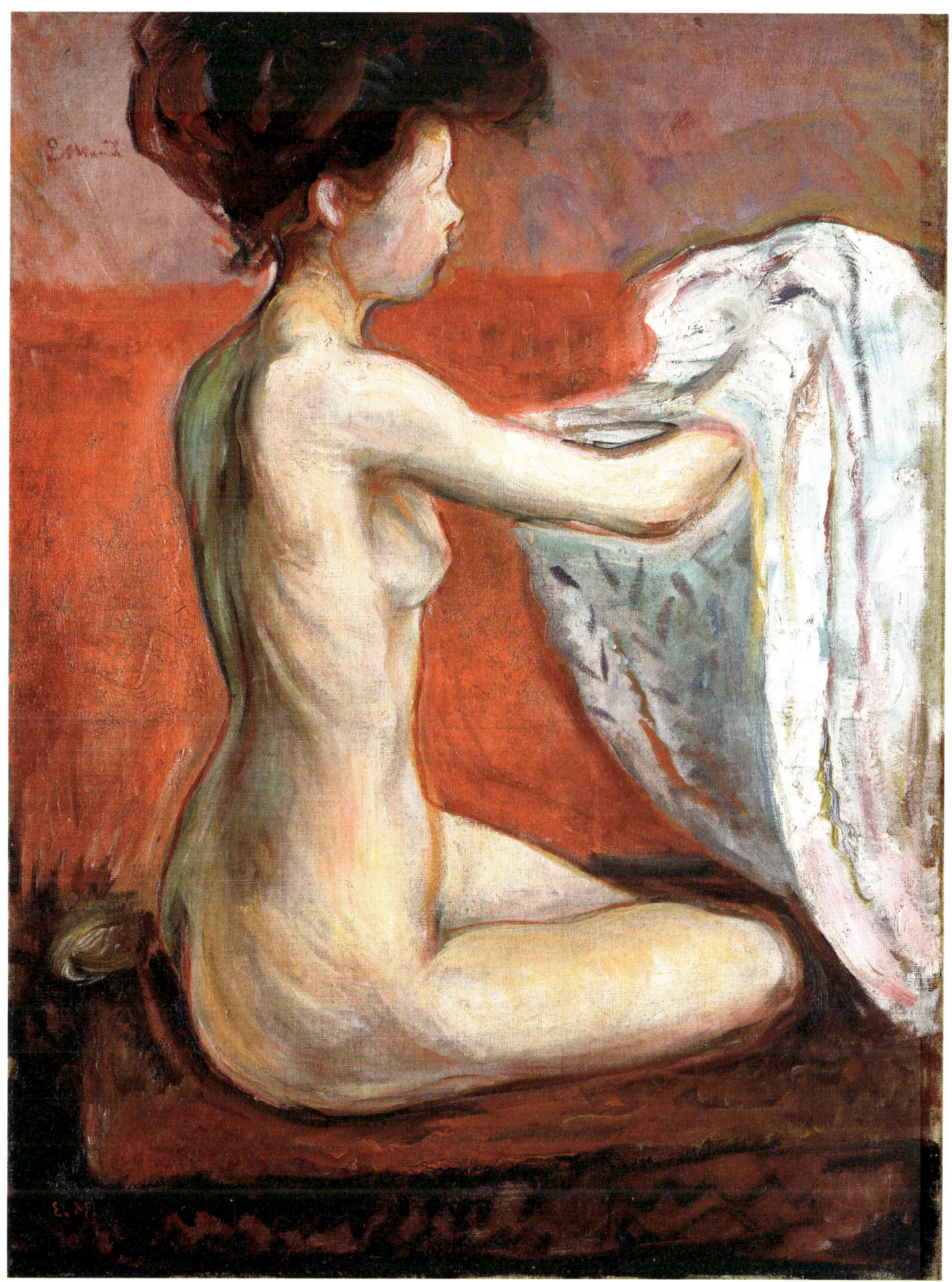

35

Mother and Daughter, prob. 1897

Mor og datter

Oil on canvas
135 × 163 cm
Unsigned
NG.M.00840
Woll M 404
NG cat. 1933-956; 1950-1070; 1968-1287; 1992-840

Other titles: *Sommernatt.* **Provenance:** Olaf Schou (before 1898–1909); gift from Olaf Schou 1909. **Literature:** Thiis 1907 A, 431; Thiis 1933, 230; I. Langaard 1960, 396; Bischoff 1993, 68; Høifødt 2003, 58; Ustvedt 2009, 44; Junillon 2009, 246, 293; Høifødt 2010 A, 81ff.; Bischoff 2011, 68; Rognerud 2013, 48; Flaatten 2013 A, 112, 157; Stokkan 2013, 137; Alarcó 2015, 25; Coppel 2019, 109. **Exhibitions:** 1898, Copenhagen, no. 126; 1927, Oslo, no. 109; 1954, Munich–Cologne, no. 38; 1955, Copenhagen-Odense, no. 36; 1958, Bern, no. 28; 1965, New York B, no. 27; 1983, Dresden, no. 18; 1987, Essen, no. 47; 1987, Oslo B, no. 64; 1998, Lugano, no. 35; 2010, Codroipo, no. 112; 2013, Oslo, no. 69; 2013, Stockholm; 2015, Madrid, no. 6.

It is summer and two women are outdoors in an open landscape. The colour contrasts, the differences in the women's postures, directions of gaze, and disposition, and the atmospheric setting all invite symbolic interpretation. The picture can be read as a representation of different stages of life. Munch's pictorial universe contains many examples of different female archetypes in juxtaposition. Together, they constitute a kind of typology of women. Good examples include *Kvinnen i tre stadier* (The Woman in Three Stages) (1894, Woll M 362) and *The Dance of Life* (cat. 40). In terms of its monumentality, treatment of figures in a simplified landscape, and melancholy mood, *Mother and Daughter* is also comparable to works such as *Inger på stranden* (Inger on the Beach) (1889, Woll M 182), *Sommeraften* (Summer Evening) (1889, Woll M 183), *Moonlight* (1893, cat. 21), and *Separation* (1896, Woll M 393). But with regard to theme, it is one of Munch's woodcuts, *Two Women on the Shore* from 1898 (cat. 133), that bears the closest resemblance to the painting, which probably also served as model for the graphic work. By and large, Munch based his print works on earlier paintings, rather than the other way around. The woodcut exaggerates the difference in age between the older and the younger woman (Flaatten 2013 A, 112), using an idiom that is notable for its stylisation. In the painting, the passage to the right is sketchy, with just a few shapes indicated in brown. One of these appears to be the outline of a rock on which the older woman is sitting. In the woodcut, the rock is clearly defined.

Mother and Daughter is often discussed in relation to melancholy, most recently in the exhibition "Edvard Munch. Archetypes" at the Museo Thyssen-Bornemisza in Madrid (2015). In the accompanying catalogue, the picture is compared with *Aftenstund* (Evening) (1888, Woll M 163), which is regarded as the starting point for the melancholy theme in Munch's art. X-ray analysis has shown that in its original form, *Aftenstund* included a standing, front-facing female figure, in a composition that clearly links it to that of *Mother and Daughter* (Alcaró 2015, 23).

The somewhat stylised treatment of figures and landscape in *Mother and Daughter* enhances the impression of the women's individual solitude and isolation. The monumentality of the work is striking. In his major book about Munch from 1933, Jens Thiis alludes to the classical quality of the picture's composition. Although he criticises the figures as schematic and rigid, it is precisely this formality that he finds interesting. For him there is something "thoroughly classical, almost Egyptian" about the picture (Thiis 1933, 230).

In the National Gallery's 1927 Munch exhibition, the painting was listed with the date "1897?", an attribution that has been accepted ever since. It is assumed that the picture was shown at Den Frie Udstilling in Copenhagen in 1898, where it was listed as cat. 126 and went by the title of *Sommernatt* (Summer Night). By that point it already belonged to Olaf Schou (Skedsmo 1987 C, 113). Later commentators have noted similarities to Munch's monumental works from 1899, and the fact that in 1897 he concentrated largely on printmaking, leading to speculation that it might have been some other picture with the title *Sommernatt* that was shown in Copenhagen in 1898 (Høifødt 2003).

Mother and Daughter was probably painted at Åsgårdstrand. Both this inference and the dating of 1897 are backed up by a letter Munch wrote to Aunt Karen on 19 March 1898. In this he refers to a painting he intends to show in Copenhagen in the spring: "I have been invited to exhibit a few things at Den Frie Udstilling in Copenhagen (...) I will probably include, among other things, you and Inger from the summer and the big picture of Inger – thus Inger will be on show in two versions –" (MM N 828). The painting was gifted to the National Gallery by Olaf Schou in 1909. vwh

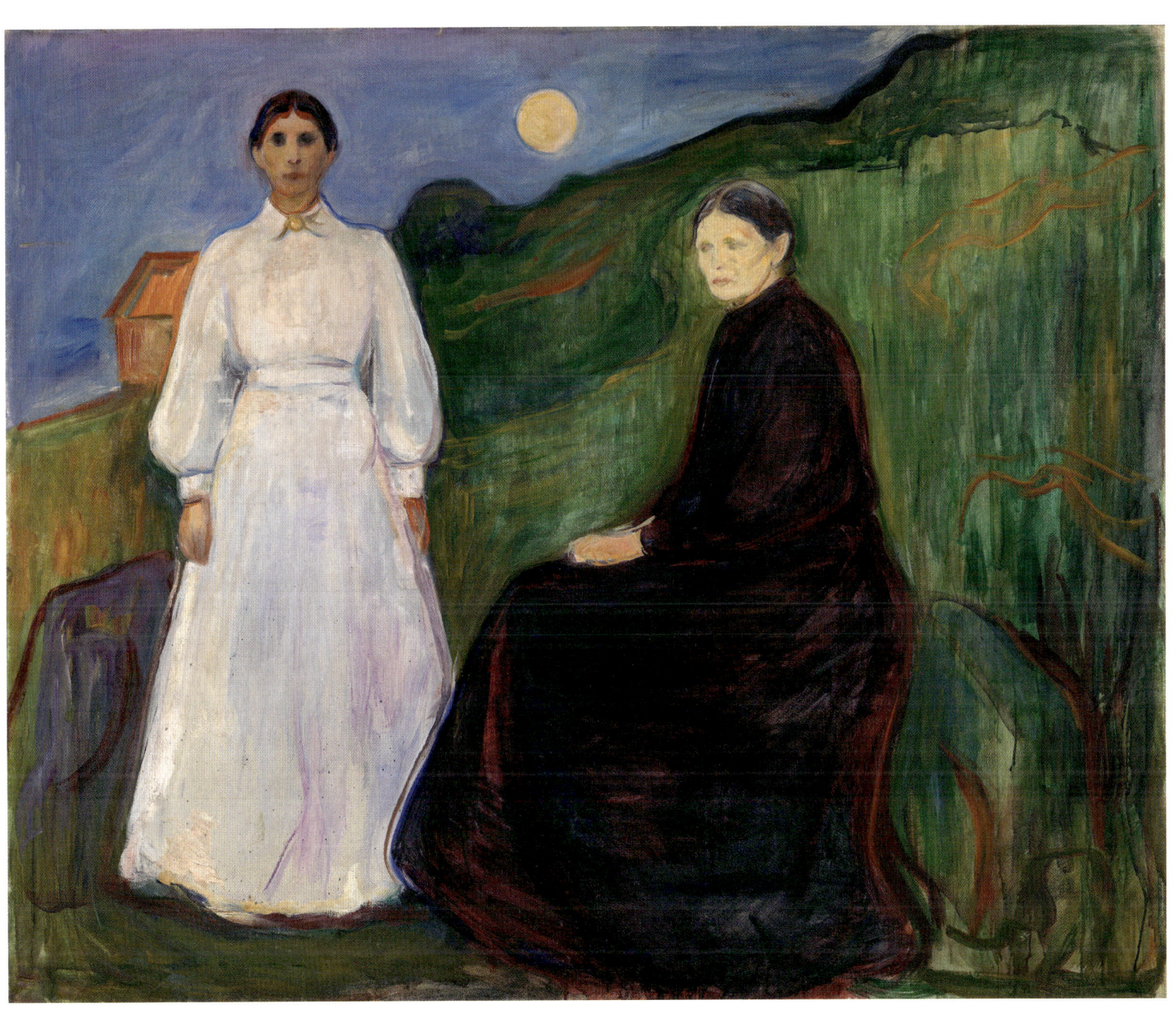

36

House with Red Virginia Creeper, 1898–1899

Hus med rød villvin

Oil on unprimed wood
32.5 × 48 cm
Signed l.r. "E M"
NG.M.01894
NG cat. 1950-1075; 1968-1291; 1992-1894
Woll M 439

Other titles: *Rød villvin, Åsgårdstrand.* **Provenance:** Purchased from the art dealer Harald Holst Halvorsen 1938. **Literature:** Høifødt 1995 A, 141; Kivelitz ans Selter 2005, 17. **Exhibitions:** 1995, New York, no. 20; 2001, Boston, no. 74; 2005, Dortmund-Høvikodden; 2007, Basel, no. 102.

House with Red Virginia Creeper is often regarded as a preliminary study for the Munch Museum's *Red Virginia Creeper* (1898–1900, Woll M 440), as is also a larger version of the same subject (1898–1899, Woll M 438). In the National Museum's version, the creeper is almost entirely an unadulterated red, while in the other preliminary study, it has deeper tones shading into brown. The pure colour is repeated in *Red Virginia Creeper*. The main difference between the Munch Museum's version and the two preliminary studies is the male figure in the foreground. *Red Virginia Creeper* was exhibited in Berlin in 1902 as part of the Frieze of Life as the central item in a series of five works on the angst theme, culminating in *The Scream* (cat. 23).

It is probable that the three versions were executed around the same time. When the National Gallery purchased the painting in 1938, its date was recorded as ca. 1900. Recent research has shown, however, that in all probability the works were painted in late summer 1899 (Høifødt 1995 A). In both of the preliminary versions, the trees are still green. This supports the idea that they were painted in the early autumn, some time before the final version, in which the trees have shed their leaves and the landscape as a whole is tending towards winter. In all three versions, the red creeper to which the title refers covers most of the façade of the house. The house is Kiøsterudgården in Åsgårdstrand, which also features in the background of *Girls on the Bridge* (cat. 42), although in the latter it lacks the creeper. Munch did not stay at Åsgårdstrand in the summer or autumn of 1900. He was there in autumn 1898 and may have painted the picture then (Woll 2008 B, 481). Stylistic features suggest, however, that all three versions were executed in 1899. VWH

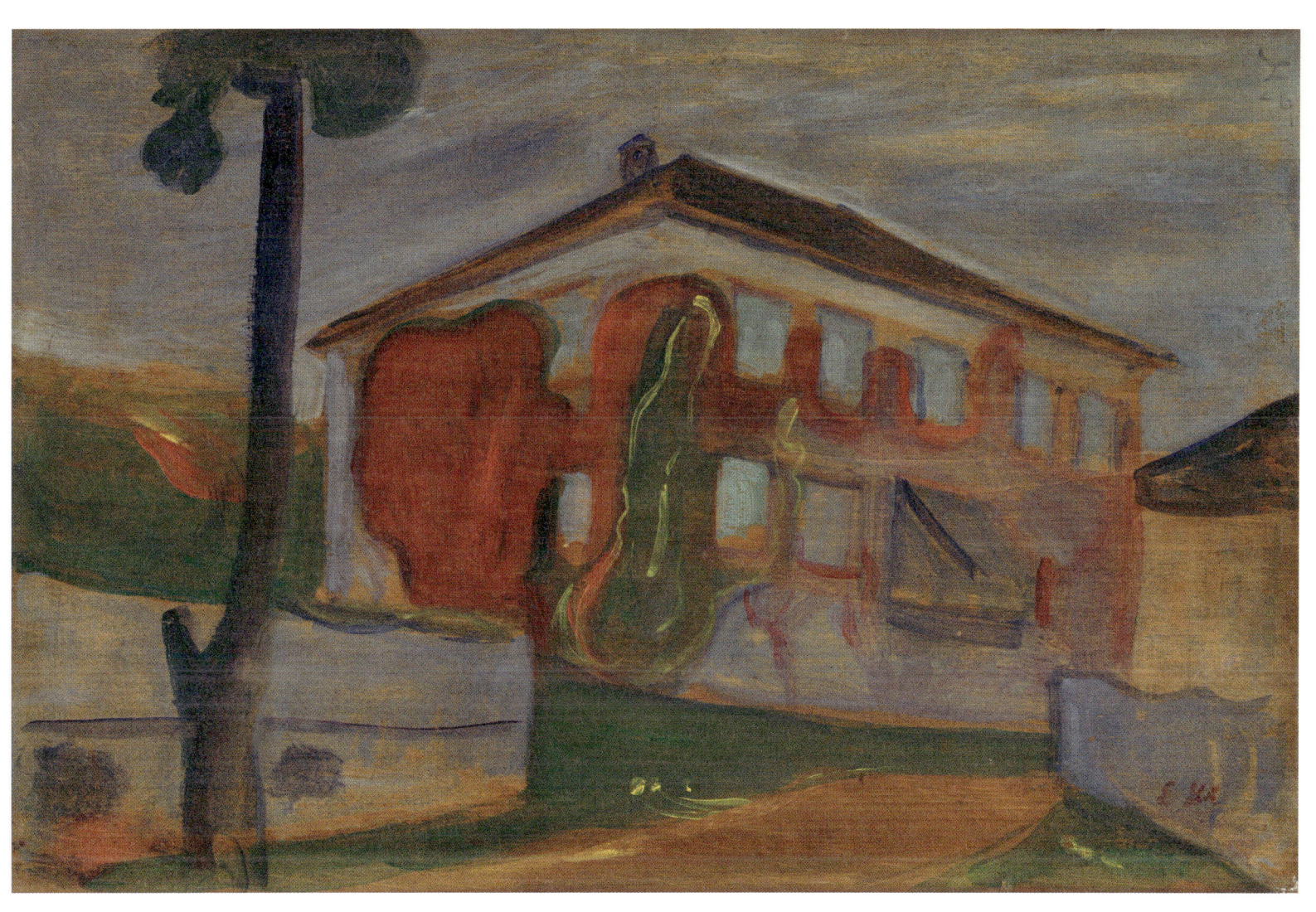

37

Winter in the Woods, 1899

Vinter i skogen

Oil on unprimed cardboard
60.5 × 90 cm
Unsigned
NG.M.00570
Woll M 445
NG cat. 1933-957; 1950-1072; 1968-1289; 1992-570

Other titles: *Vinterbillede*; *Vinter i skogen, Nord-strand*. **Provenance**: Purchased from the artist 1901. **Literature**: Thiis 1933, 274; I. Langaard 1960, 400; Monrad (ed.) 1995, 168; Bjerke 1995, 42; Larsen (ed.) 2000, 289; Fredlund (ed.) 2002, 72; Pettersen 2010, 111; Huusko 2015, 79; Ford et al. 2021, [unpaginated]. **Exhibitions**: 1927, Oslo, no. 106; 1954, Venice, no. 22; 1954, Munich–Cologne, no. 40; 1955, Copenhagen–Odense, no. 38; 1964, Kiel, no. 59; 1984, Tromsø; 1995, Madrid–Barce-lona, no. 55; 1995, New York–Høvikodden, no. 16; 1998, Paris, no. 114; 1999, Florence, no. 12; 2000, Copenhagen, no. 48; 2001, Ferrara, no. 63; 2002, Gothenburg, no. 20; 2004, Melbourne, no. 44; 2010, Codroipo, no. 114; 2012, Groningen–Munich; 2015, Helsinki, no. 90.

The painting shows an unusual section of forest landscape in winter. The picture is surprisingly colourful, given that fir trees in themselves can seem rather dull and that winter is a season of low light. The snow-covered trees in the foreground have blue contours, as do the tracks in the snow that lead into the forest. At first glance, the branches on the tree in the middle give an impression of green, but on closer inspection they reveal hints of red and yellow.

"Nature is not only that which is visible to the eye – it is also the inner Picture of the Soul – on the Back side of the Eye –" (MM.T.2785), Munch wrote in his note-book in 1908. In general, nature is a foundation for his art, and in many of his best known and most central works from the 1890s, it plays a significant role, often as a means to convey the emotional content. Where people interact with the landscape, they produce in a symbolic unity. In the late 1890s, there occurs a shift in thematic emphasis, with landscapes assuming greater importance as subjects in their own right, as *Winter in the Woods* exemplifies. Here, nature is present but silent rather than menacing; if anything, it is secretive. Although we confront it close up, it conveys a sense of something grander and more infinite. Munch's landscapes usually feature places close to civilisation and generally contain traces of human activity.

Paintings of snow-covered landscapes were popular in the period. Snow and winter were considered as exotic and defining aspects of the Nordic countries. Reflecting the desire for themes that captured something characteristically national, winter landscapes began to feature prominently in Nordic art during the 1880s. A number of artists also cultivated the idea that contact with, and observations of, nature could enhance one's sensitivity and ability to capture impressions. The simplified painting style and the unusual view in *Winter in the Woods* are features that we also find in snowscapes by some of Munch's Nordic colleagues, such as the Finns Pekka Halonen and Akseli Gallen-Kallela, and the Swedish artists Gustav Fjæstad and Bruno Liljefors.

For many years, the painting was dated to 1897. But in preparation for his book about Munch (1933), Jens Thiis wrote to the artist to ensure his information was right: "The Gallery's small winter picture, beneath the trees, was painted at Nordstrand in 1899. This is correct – is it not?" (1933, MM K 1181). Munch's reply is affirmative: "The winter picture was painted in March 1899 at Nordstrand as, after my illness in hospital, I stayed for 14 days with my family at Nordstrand" (1933, MM N 3105).

The picture was purchased in 1901. At that point, the National Gallery owned six Munch paintings, including a self-portrait (cat. 32), three portraits of others (cat. 6, cat. 7 and cat. 13), *Spring* (cat. 12) and *Night in Nice* (cat. 15). As a member of the museum's purchasing committee, Andreas Aubert proposed the acquisition of two landscapes, but the committee opted for just the one (minutes from a meeting on 28 May 1901, item 8, NG 1893-1905). *White Night* (cat. 41) was also purchased later that same year.

The Munch Museum's collection contains a sketch that relates to the picture, a pencil drawing dated 1899 (MM.T.02873 verso). The painting is done on card pasted onto a plywood board. This was an unusual material for Munch, although he also used it in some few of his later works (Woll M 473; Woll M 479; Woll M 481, Woll M 482). VWH

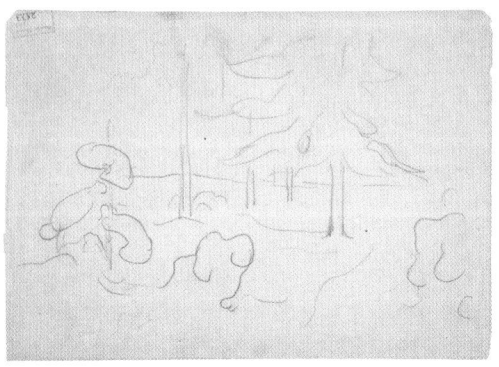

Edvard Munch: *Winter in the Forest*, 1899
Pencil, wove paper, 345 × 241 mm
MM.T.02873 verso
Photo: Munchmuseet/Tone Margrethe Gulden

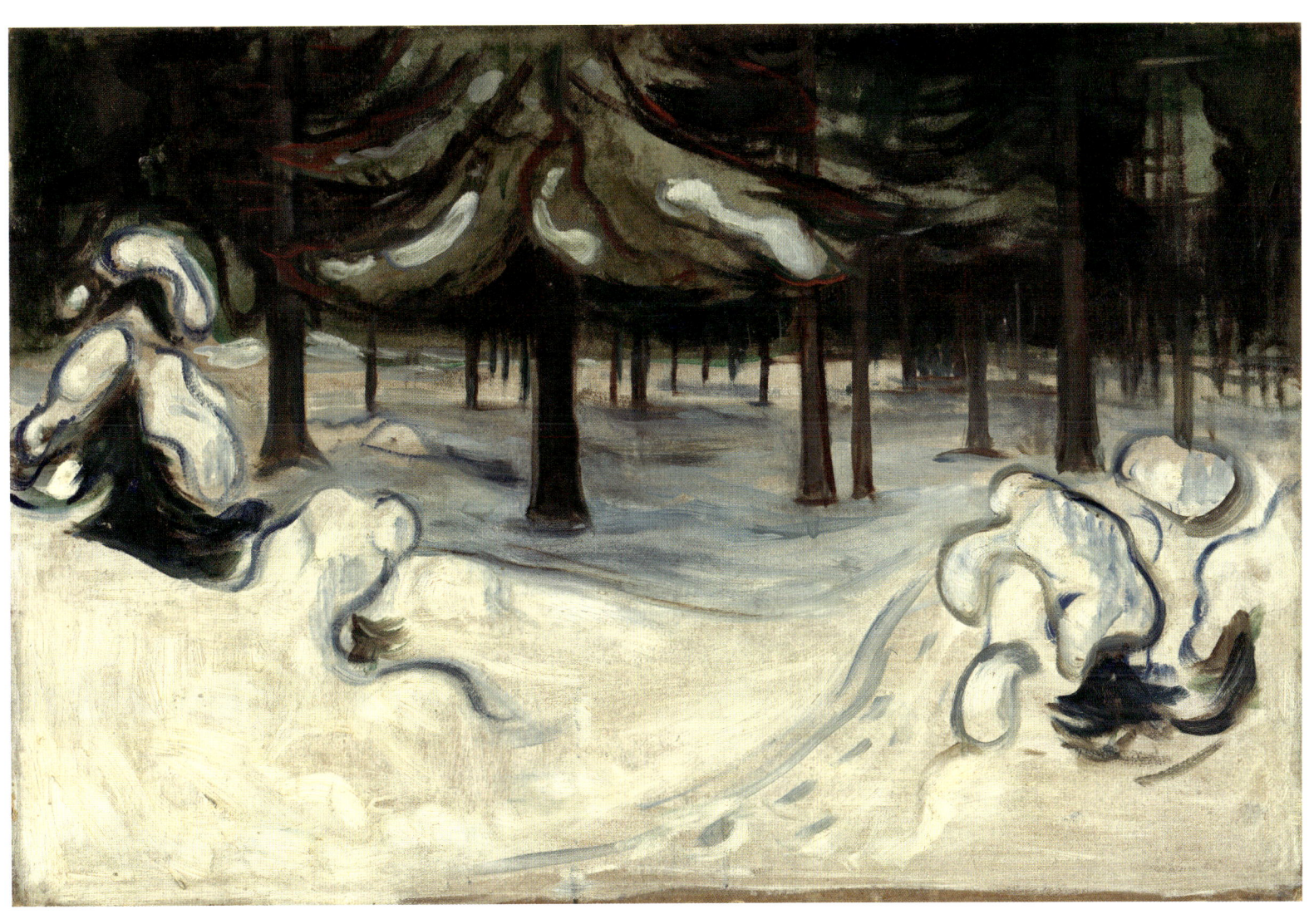

Oil on canvas
131 × 109 cm
Signed l.r. "E. Munch"
NG.M.01793
Woll M 457
NG kat. 1950-1069; 1968-1286; 1992-1793

Other titles: *Portræt af fru N.*; *Fru Aase Nørre-gaard*; *Fru Aase Nørregaard, født Carlsen*; *Maler-innen Aase Nørregaard*; *Portrett av kunstneren Aase Nørregaard*. **Provenance:** Gift from Harald Nørregaard 1935. **Literature:** Glaser 1917, 80; Thiis 1933, 279; Eggum 1994 A, 9, 89; Lange 2004, 136f. **Exhibitions:** 1906, Copenhagen, no. 180; 1912, Gothenburg; 1913, Kristiania, no. 42; 1915, Copenhagen, no. 283; 1922, Zürich, no. 10; 1922, Bern–Basel, no. 11/10; 1927, Berlin, no. 63; 1927, Oslo, no. 110; 1968, Schaffhausen, no. 23; 1984, Tromsø; 2001, Boston, no. 61; 2004, Melbourne, no. 29; 2014, Wiesbaden-Emden, no. 147.

The subdued palette and frontal depiction of the figure against a crude background are typical of Munch's portraits around 1900. This is a variation on the approach he used in portraits such as *Inger in Black and Violet* (1892, cat. 20) and *Ragnhild Bäckstrøm* (1894, cat. 24). As with the former, *Aase Nørregaard* is painted with thin layers of colour to create subtle effects of light and haze that contrast with the greater plasticity of the face. Nørregaard is wearing a stylish dress with puff sleeves, a wide neckline with sections of sheer fabric, typical of the bourgeois fashions of the day. Beyond this, there are few details that betray the period or the setting.

Aase Nørregaard (b. Aasta Carlsen, 1869-1908) was a close friend of Munch from the late 1880s onwards. She too was a painter with a training from the Royal School of Design (Tegneskolen). In 1888, she made her debut at the National Annual Autumn Exhibition, an event she participated in several times until 1902. She later studied under both Gerhard Munthe and Harriet Backer. In her own work, Nørre-gaard focused in particular on modern, urban exteriors, in an idiom that reflected contemporary realism and mood painting. This can be seen, for example, in her 1898 painting *Kristianiagårder* (View from Kristiania) in the National Museum's collection (NG.M.00960b).

Munch painted several portraits of Nørregaard (1888-1889, Woll M 167; 1902, Woll M 542). She also served as model for several figures in larger compositions such as *Damene på bryggen* (The Women on the Bridge) (1902, Woll M 541). Various letters and draft letters indicate that they developed a close relationship in the late 1880s. In 1889, however, she married the lawyer Harald Nørregaard. Since her married name was then identical to that of the more famous Aasta Nørregaard (1853-1933), also a painter, she changed her first name to Aase. Her friendship with Munch endured even after she married.

Nørregaard's significance for Munch is evident from a letter he wrote to her bereaved husband after Aase's death in 1908: "You know that I know what you have lost - You think You have lost all Spring and Summer - And there are no words of comfort - You also know how great my own loss, the best of my women friends." (letter, 1908, MM N 3671).

The date of the portrait has been a subject of debate. It may have been exhibited in Paris in the spring of 1896, and it is assumed that it was painted the previous year. However, in the exhibition shown in Zurich, Bern and Basel in 1922, and later at the National Gallery in 1927, it was ascribed to 1899. The painting has simila-rities to the double portrait *Aase and Harald Nørregaard* from 1899 (cat. 39). It is reasonable to infer that these works were executed at around the same time (cf. Eggum, 1994 A and Woll B 2008). øu

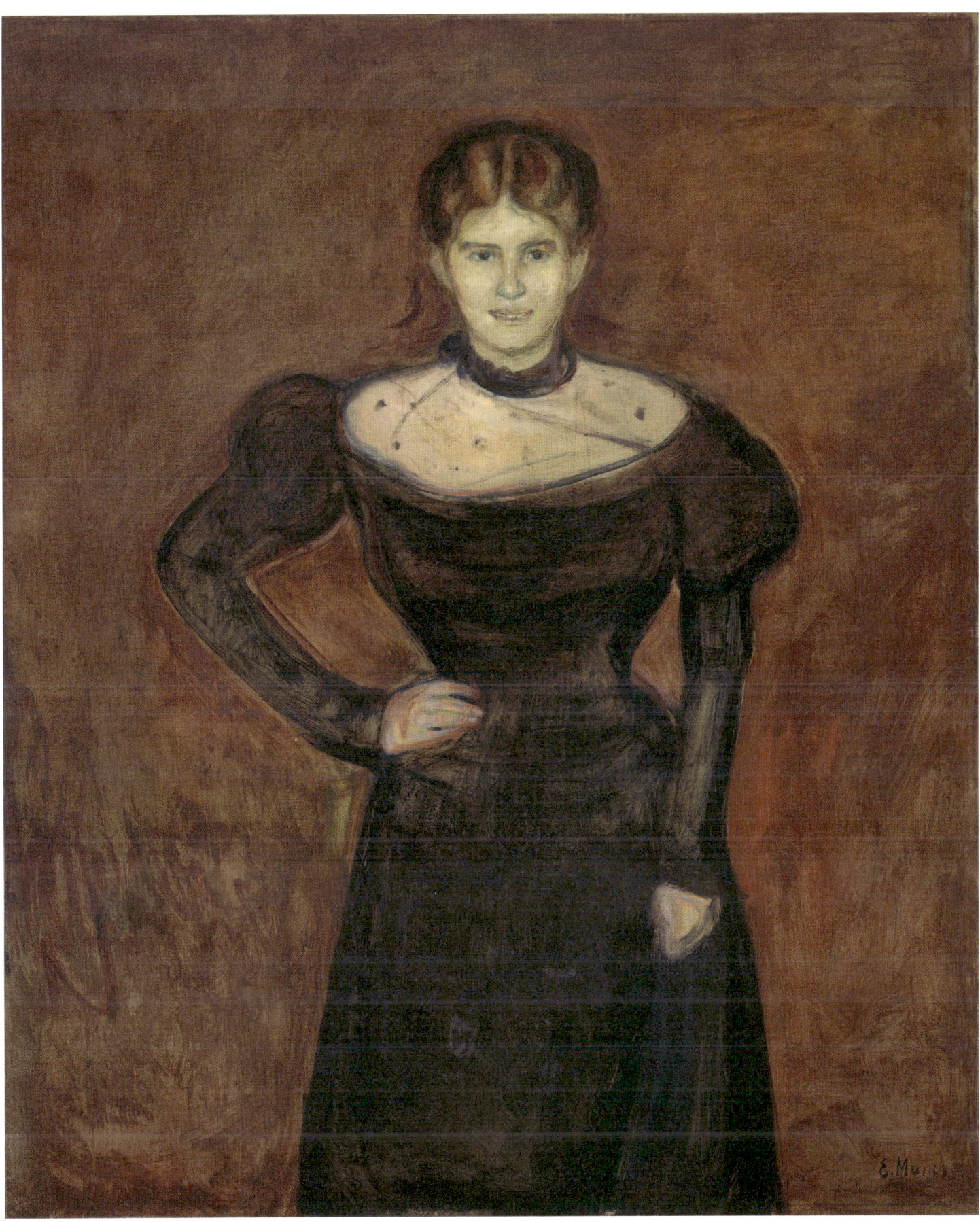

39

Aase and Harald Nørregaard, 1899

Aase og Harald Nørregaard

Oil and crayon on unprimed cardboard
49.5 × 75 cm
Signed l.l. "E Munch 1899"
NG.M.01794
Woll M 458
NG cat. 1950-1071; 1968-1288; 1992-1794

Other titles: *Portræt*; *Dobbeltportræt*; *Portræt af fru N. og hr. N.*; *Dobbeltportræt, Nørregaard og frue.* **Provenance:** Gift from Harald Nørregaard 1935. **Literature:** Thiis 1933, 232, 280; I. Langaard 1960, 394; Heller 1984, 167; Eggum 1994 A, 89; Rutkowski 2008, 55; Smith 2019, 65-66. **Exhibitions:** 1901, Kristiania, no. 56; 1904, Kristiania, no. 42; 1906, Copenhagen, no. 181; 1927, Oslo, no. 111; 1986, West Palm Beach, no. 43; 2000, London–New York, no. 109.

Munch produced several double portraits in the period around 1900, often of couples. In the painting of Aase and Harald Nørregaard, he highlights the relationship between the two by portraying the woman's face as active and frontal and that of the man in profile. They look beyond each other while also engaging in dialogue.

Aase (b. Aasta Carlsen, 1869-1908) and Harald Nørregaard (1864-1938) married in 1889. To avoid confusion with Aasta Nørregaard, an already well-established painter, the former changed her first name to Aase. Aase was a fellow painter who had been befriended with Munch since the 1880s. She and Harald maintained close contacts with Munch and several other artists. Over the years, they built up a significant art collection that contained several works by Munch, including this double portrait, the portrait of Aase alone (cat. 38), a self-portrait (cat. 9), and *The Sick Child* (cat. 8).

Harald Nørregaard studied law and became a Supreme Court lawyer. In 1894–95 he fought and won a case on Munch's behalf against the lawyer Ludvig Meyer, who wished to cancel a commission for a portrait of his children. Later, Nørregaard assisted Munch both financially and in other private matters on a number of occasions. In 1892, after several years in Stavanger, the couple moved to Kristiania, where Harald became a barrister and established a law firm.

In a letter dated 1 June 1935, Harald Nørregaard offered to donate a double portrait to the National Gallery, together with the portrait of Aase (cat. 38). The letter states that the gift was made at the request of Munch, who wanted both works to accrue to the National Gallery. It is mentioned that, on making the request, Munch had described the double portrait as an "anthem to [their] marriage" (National Museum's documentation archive, j.no. 3/135). ØU

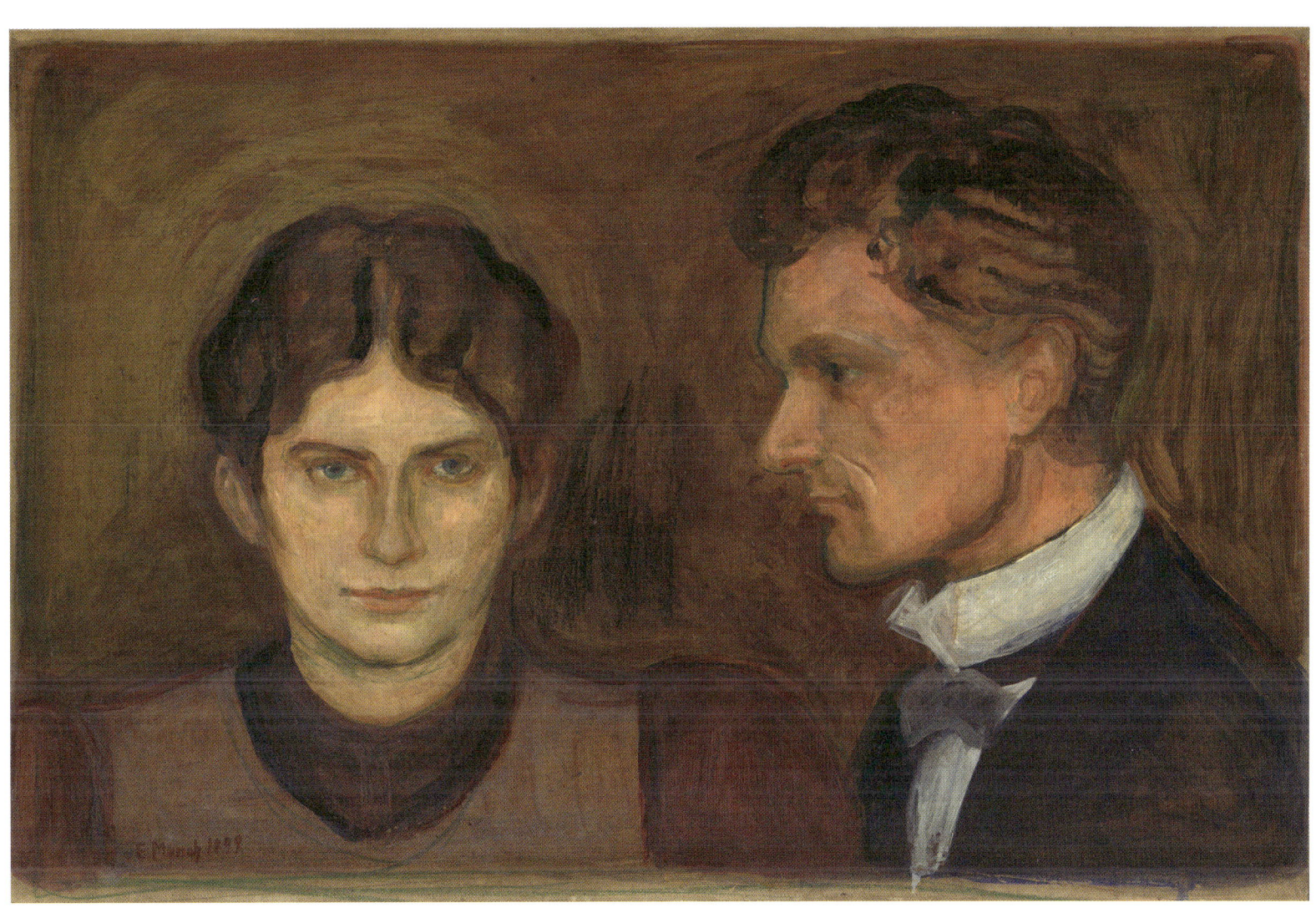

40

The Dance of Life, 1899–1900
Livets dans

Oil on canvas
125 × 191 cm
Signed l.l. "E Munch 99"; u.r. "E Munch 1900"
NG.M.00941
Woll M 464
NG cat. 1933-958; 1950-1074; 1968-1290; 1992-941

Other titles: *Johannisnacht*; *Midsommernat*,
Provenance: Gift from Olaf Schou 1910.
Literature: One of Munch's best-known motifs,
it is widely discussed in much of the general
Munch literature. Ritter 1906 (translation 2015),
47; Glaser 1917, 36; Thiis 1933, 274; Stenersen
1945, 41; Gauguin 1946 A, 166; I. Langaard 1960,
405; Svenæus 1968, 120; Hodin 1972, 88; Stang
1977, 120; Krieger 1978, 43; Hofstätter 1982, 11–20;
Eggum 1983 A, 168; Heller 1984, 172; Høifødt
1990, 166f.; Bischoff 1993, 47f.; Forssman 1993,
307f.; Eggum 1994 A, 88f.; Müller-Westermann
1994, 38; Høifødt 1995 A, 155f.; Larsson 1998, 24f.;
Høifødt 2003, 56f.; Lange 2005, 246f.; López
2008, 50f.; Rutkowski 2008, 72; Templeton 2008,
80f.; Woll 2008 A, 101; Alessandrini 2009, 111, 113;
Clarke 2009, 157; Chang 2010, 128, 171, 174–176;
Diana 2010, 13f.; Høifødt 2010 A, 71–75; Kuuva
2010, 40-41, 50, 56, 127, 136-137, 187-188, 194-196;
Petruševičiūtė 2010, 73; Autin-Grenier 2011, 74;
Bischoff 2011, 50; Lampe 2012, 36; Volle 2012 A,
239–242, 340–341, 358; Volle 2012 B, 24; Endresen
2013, 221; Grøgaard 2013 A, 351; Guleng 2013,
133; Flaatten 2013 A, 126–128; Owesen 2013, 300;
Ahtola-Moorhouse 2014, 53f.; Steihaug 2014, 32;
Stein and Rød 2015, 262; Zeiller 2015, 50; Stein
2017 B, 40-41; Ustvedt 2018, 87; Coppel 2019,
105; Stein 2019, 39; Vassenden 2019, 25; Ford
et al. 2021, [unpaginated]. **Exhibitions:** 1900,
Dresden, no. 4; 1901, Kristiania, no. 54; 1902,
Berlin, no. 195; 1903, Leipzig; 1904, Copenhagen;
1904, Kristiania, no. 11; 1905, Prague, no. 28; 1910,
Kristiania, no. 51; 1927, Berlin, no. 58; 1927, Oslo,
no. 89; 1950, USA, touring exhibition, no. 25; 1951,
Brighton–Glasgow–London–The Hague–Paris,
no. 24/25; 1952, Zürich, no. 18; 1952, Brussels, no.
9; 1958, Brussels, no. 240; 1959, Vienna, no. 16;
1965, New York B, no. 31; 1967, Montreal, no. 71;
1968, Schaffhausen, no. 26; 1970, Japan, touring
exhibition, no. 16; 1971, Oslo, no. 28; 1973, Munich–
London–Paris, no. 34/33; 1980, Washington; 1982,
Washington–New York–Minneapolis, no. 69; 1987,
Oslo B, no. 65; 1992, London, no. 31; 1994, Oslo,
no. 40; 1998, Lugano, no. 41; 2006, New York, no.
84; 2009, Chicago, no. 73; 2013, Oslo, no. 81; 2019,
Bergen, no. 9.

On a summer night, people have come together to dance on a meadow beside the
fjord. The couple in the foreground are pressed together, she in a long red dress
with one arm around the shoulder of the man, who is dressed in black. They are
flanked by a young woman in a white dress and an older woman in black. Behind
them, other couples dance, succinctly captured in sweeping brushstrokes. They
convey a sense of speed and rhythm that contrasts with the static poses of the
foreground figures. The shoreline, the horizon and the moon reflected in the sea
combine to form an atmospheric background.

The Dance of Life was the last of the paintings that Munch added to his Frieze
of Life With its depiction of love and the passage of human life, it brings together
many of the themes of the Frieze. The relationship between man and woman,
loneliness, grief and death were all themes that Munch addressed in both his
writings and his pictures during the 1890s. In *The Dance of Life*, the woman is
portrayed at different stages in life and in different moods, from young and hopeful
to elderly and careworn. Locked in an embrace, the woman of the central couple
is dressed in red, the colour of love. Munch described the painting and its place
in the cycle of love in a lyrical text:

> The large Frieze the Frieze of Life
> that he had begun
> many Years ago – which would
> depict the Cycle of Life –
> the awakening of Love – The Dance
> of Life – Love
> at its Peak and its Decline
> and then Death –
> (1908, MM.T.2800).

The Dance of Life was accorded a central place in the Frieze of Life and featured
in the major exhibitions where the frieze was presented: in Berlin in 1902, Leipzig
in 1903, Kristiania in 1904, and Prague in 1905. In Berlin the picture was included
in the second group, under the heading "Love's Flowering and Fall". It featured in
all of Munch's friezes, whether realised or merely planned.

Munch painted *The Dance of Life* after a trip to Florence, where he studied
Italian Renaissance painting. Friezes were in vogue at the time, and Renaissance
paintings were a frequent source of inspiration. The intense colours in the picture
and its use of well-defined colour fields also indicate the influence of Paul Gauguin
and syntheticism. *The Dance of Life* can be seen as the culmination of Munch's
symbolist period.

Concerning the picture, Munch wrote to Jens Thiis: "Do You not find a similarity between 'The Dance of Life' and the rhythm and movement in the dance of the
past 20 years? In the Frieze of Life on the Whole?" (MM N 43, Munch Museum.
Dated 1933-1940. Draft letter to Jens Thiis.) Like Manet, Degas, and Seurat, Munch
represented dance around the turn of the century as a cultural phenomenon. Pio-
neers in modern dance were performing on the stages of Paris and Berlin. In literature, dance occurs as a theme in Henrik Ibsen, Knut Hamsun, and the works of
Munch's poet friends Helge Rode, Sigbjørn Obstfelder, and Vilhelm Krag. Munch's
first depiction of dance was the painting *Ball* (1885, Woll M 115). Concerning his
personal relationship to dance, he wrote to the writer Barbra Ring: "... In my pious
home, I never learnt to dance and suffered from an unrequited love for dance –"
(National Library of Norway, correspondence collection 782, PN 762).

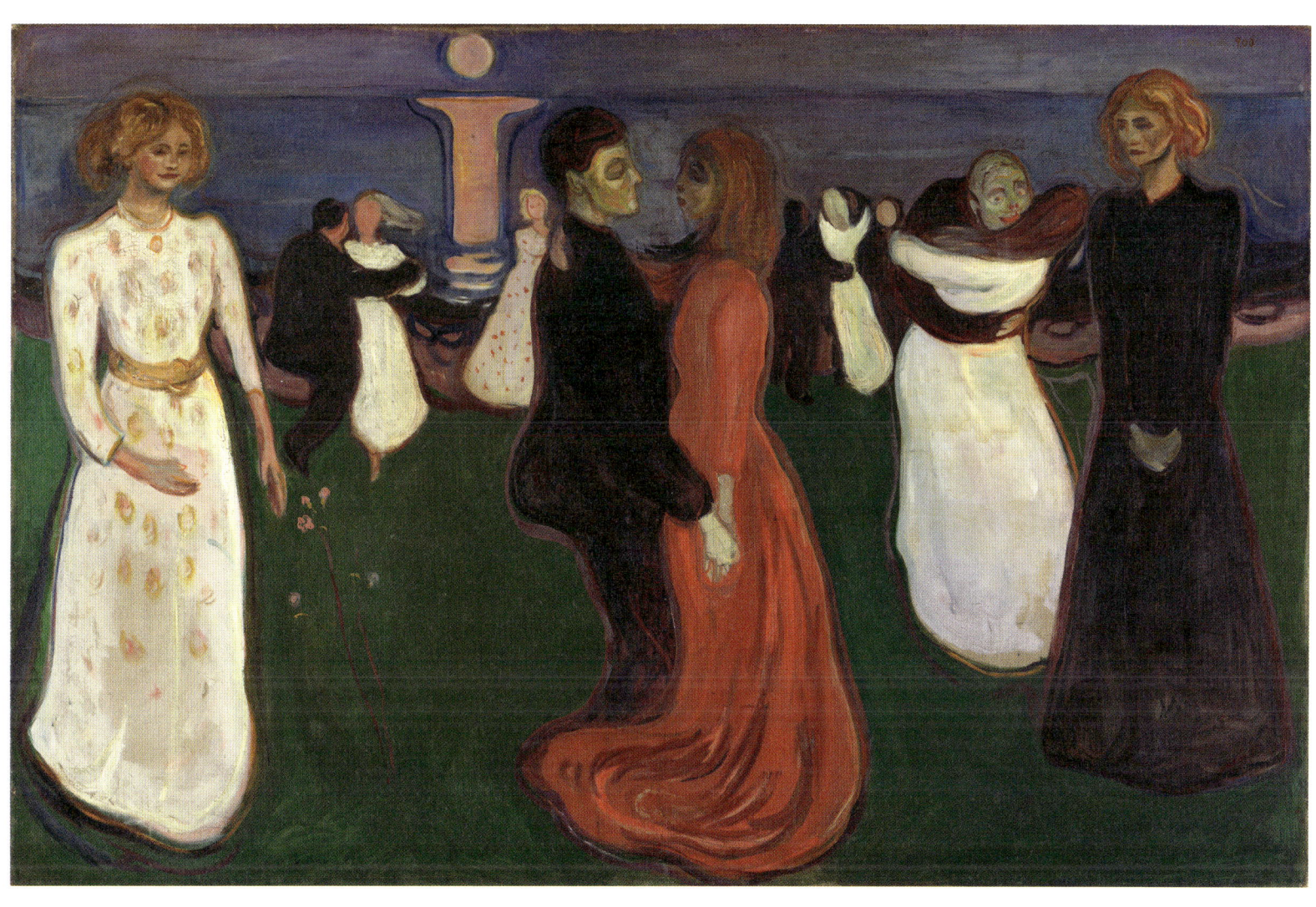

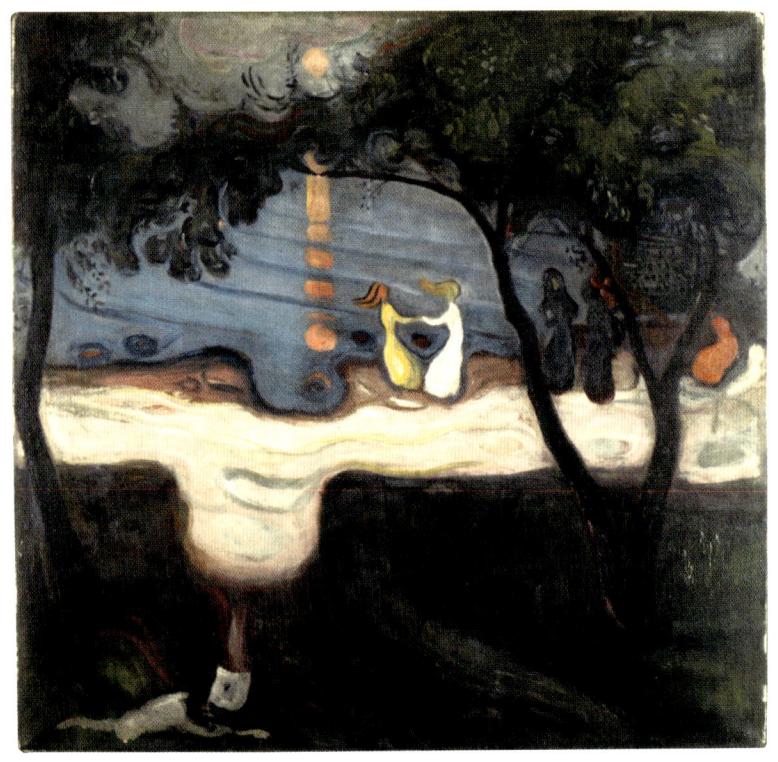

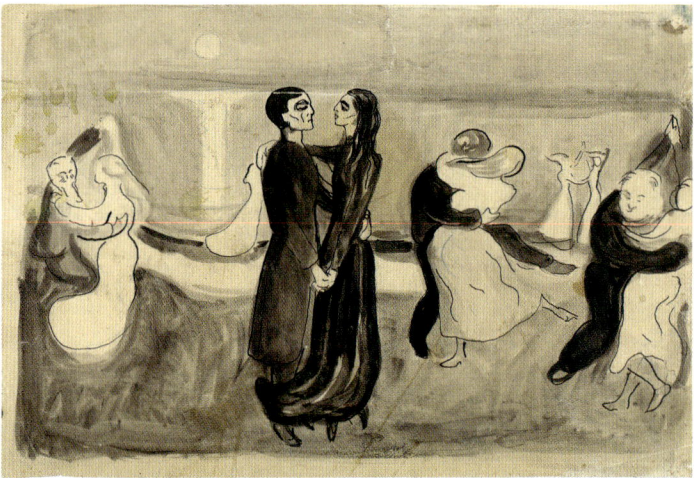

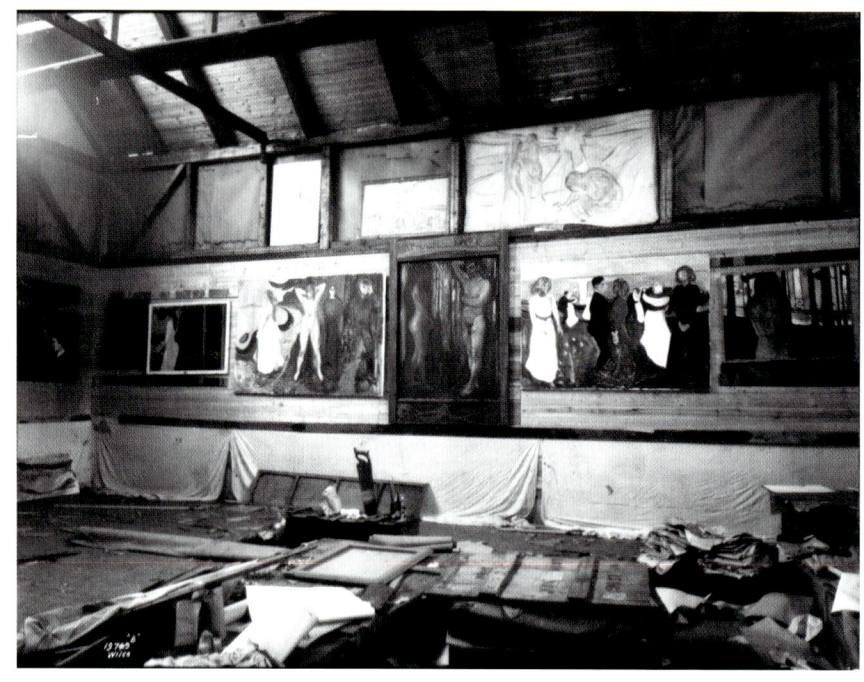

Edvard Munch: *Dans pa stranden*, 1899–1900
Oil on canvas, 99 × 96 cm
Narodni Galerie, Praha
Woll M 460
Photo: Munchmuseet

From Edvard Munch's studio at Ekely, 1925
NF.WB19769
Photo: Norsk Folkemuseum / Anders Beer Wilse

Edvard Munch: *Dance of Life*, 1898–1899
Wash, 323 × 478 mm
Munchmuseet
MM.T.02392
Photo: Munchmuseet / Halvor Bjørngård

The Dance of Life was donated to the museum by Olaf Schou in 1910. Schou had purchased the painting at Munch's exhibition at the Dioramalokalet that same year and donated it directly to the museum. The picture has two signatures, indicating that Munch began work on it in 1899 and finished it in 1900. Its first appearance in an exhibition was in Dresden in 1900, where it had the title *Johannisnacht*, the German name for Saint John's Eve, or Midsummer Eve. When shown at the Dioramalokalet in Kristiania in 1904, it had the title *Livets dans* (The Dance of Life). In the list prepared by the Commeter'sche Kunsthandlung in 1906, the painting appears as No. 44 with the title *Tanz des Lebens*. Munch later produced several variations on the same composition. Dancing couples feature in the Linde Frieze (1904, Woll M 614), the Reinhardt Frieze (1906-1907, Woll M 730), and the Freia Frieze (1922, Woll M 1414). The Frieze of Life also included *Dans på stranden* (Dance on the Beach) (1899-1900, Woll M 460), which Munch painted shortly before *The Dance of Life*. In January 1925, he signed the National Gallery's copyist register in order to copy his own pictures *Ashes* (cat. 30) and *The Dance of Life*. The later version of *The Dance of Life* is richer in its colours (1925, Woll M 1563). Two drawings from 1898–99 (MM.T.02392; PE T 00505) relate to the composition. WV

41

White Night, 1900–1901
Hvit natt

Oil on canvas
115.5 × 111 cm
Unsigned
NG.M.00581
Woll M 477
NG cat. 1933-959; 1950-1076; 1968-1292; 1992-581

Other titles: *Hvit natt. Nordstrand*; *Hvid nat*.
Provenance: Purchased from the artist 1901.
Literature: Glaser 1917, 38; Thiis 1933, 274; Østby 1966,151-158; Stang 1978, 81; Eggum 1978 B, 63; Marx 1988, 120; Eggum 1991, 218; Høifødt 2010 A, 174; Huber 2013, 103; Rognerud 2013, 48; Huusko 2015, 78; Kongssund 2015, 80; Heller 2016, 40.
Exhibitions: 1901, Kristiania, no. 48; 1927, Oslo, no. 105; 1929, Kiel, no. 178; 1942, Oslo, no. 59; 1950, USA, touring exhibition, no. 32; 1951, Brighton-Glasgow-London-The Hague-Paris, no. 31/32/29; 1952, Zürich, no. 23; 1952, Brussels, no. 10; 1958, Bern, no. 33; 1958, Rotterdam, no. 14a; 1959, Vienna, no. 20; 1959, Warsaw, no. 1076; 1960, Paris, no. 490; 1978, Washington, no. 51; 1979, New York; 1981, Tokyo-Sapporo-Nara-Nagoya-Leningrad-Moscow, no. 192/181; 1984, Toronto-Cincinnati, no. 58; 1988, Mannheim, no. 17; 1993, Atlanta-Tokyo-Barcelona-Munich-Lillehammer, no. 34; 1994, Oslo, no. 41; 1995, Madrid-Barcelona, no. 57; 1998, Cologne, no. 60; 2001, Ferrara, no. 64; 2003, Basel; 2004, Turin; 2006, Helsinki-Stockholm-Oslo-Copenhagen-Minneapolis, no. 101; 2013, Stockholm; 2013, Oslo, no. 86; 2015, Oslo-Helsinki, no. 24; 2016, New York, no. 10.

In the winter of 1899, Munch spent several weeks at his parental home at Nordstrand just outside Kristiania. The following winter he decided to stay in the same area again. In planning his stay, he wrote to his Aunt Karen, asking for help in finding accommodation: "... Could you look into it - it should be up on the hill and in the woods." (MM N 837). Munch took a room in Birgitte Hammer's guest house, which he already knew, and during his stay there he produced a number of winter pictures (Høifødt 2010 A). In *White Night* we see both the elevation of the hill and the woods he had asked for. The work is composed according to the classic principle of a foreground, middle ground and background, giving the impression of a broad vista. The foreground is dominated by large, decoratively rendered pine trees. A slanting line leads the gaze down towards a yellow house, while towards the horizon we see the fjord covered with ice. Above the landscape hangs a starry sky. Although it is night, a dim light pervades the scene. The sun has set, and the colours and contrasts of nature have faded in the encroaching darkness. It is as if Munch's aim here were to capture the characteristic light of a nocturnal landscape blanketed in snow. The pervasive bluish tones allow us to compare this work with the many mood paintings he produced in the 1890s where blue is also the dominant colour, such as *Night in Saint-Cloud* (cat. 14), *Night in Nice* (cat. 15) and *The Kiss* (cat. 17).

During his stay at Nordstrand in 1899, he had painted *Winter in the Woods* (cat. 37), a picture that could be described as signalling a new interest in the landscape genre. Woods and trees now become a focus of attention, and in the months between his first and second stays at Nordstrand, he painted several forest interiors. These were probably done at Åsgårdstrand in the summer of 1899 (Woll M 452-456).

In September 1901, Munch held a large solo exhibition at Hollændergaarden in Kristiania, where *White Night* was shown for the first time. Earlier that year, the National Gallery had purchased *Winter in the Woods* (cat. 37), but the purchasing committee wanted to enlarge its collection of Munch paintings still further. Several works were mentioned for consideration. These included *Girls on the Bridge* (cat. 42), *The Scream* (cat. 23) and *The Day After* (cat. 27), all of which later found their way into the collection, but ultimately the committee opted for *White Night*. Thus the collection acquired another winter landscape in the same year.

No date is marked on the painting, but in 1933, Munch wrote to Jens Thiis: "White Night, Birch in Snow, Island and Melancholy were painted in the winter of 1900-01" (MM N 3105). He painted an entire group of landscapes based on the woodlands and views in the area of Bunnefjord. *Vinternatt* (Winter Night), now in the Kunsthaus Zurich (1900-1901, Woll M 475), is an alternative version of the same view, but in a wider format, in contrast to the almost square format of *White Night*. The Munch Museum's somewhat simpler *Vinternatt* (Winter Night) (1900-1901, Woll M 476) shows almost the same prospect, although here we also see some details of the balcony at Hammer's guest house. It is *White Night* that is now seen as Munch's principal work of that winter. VWH

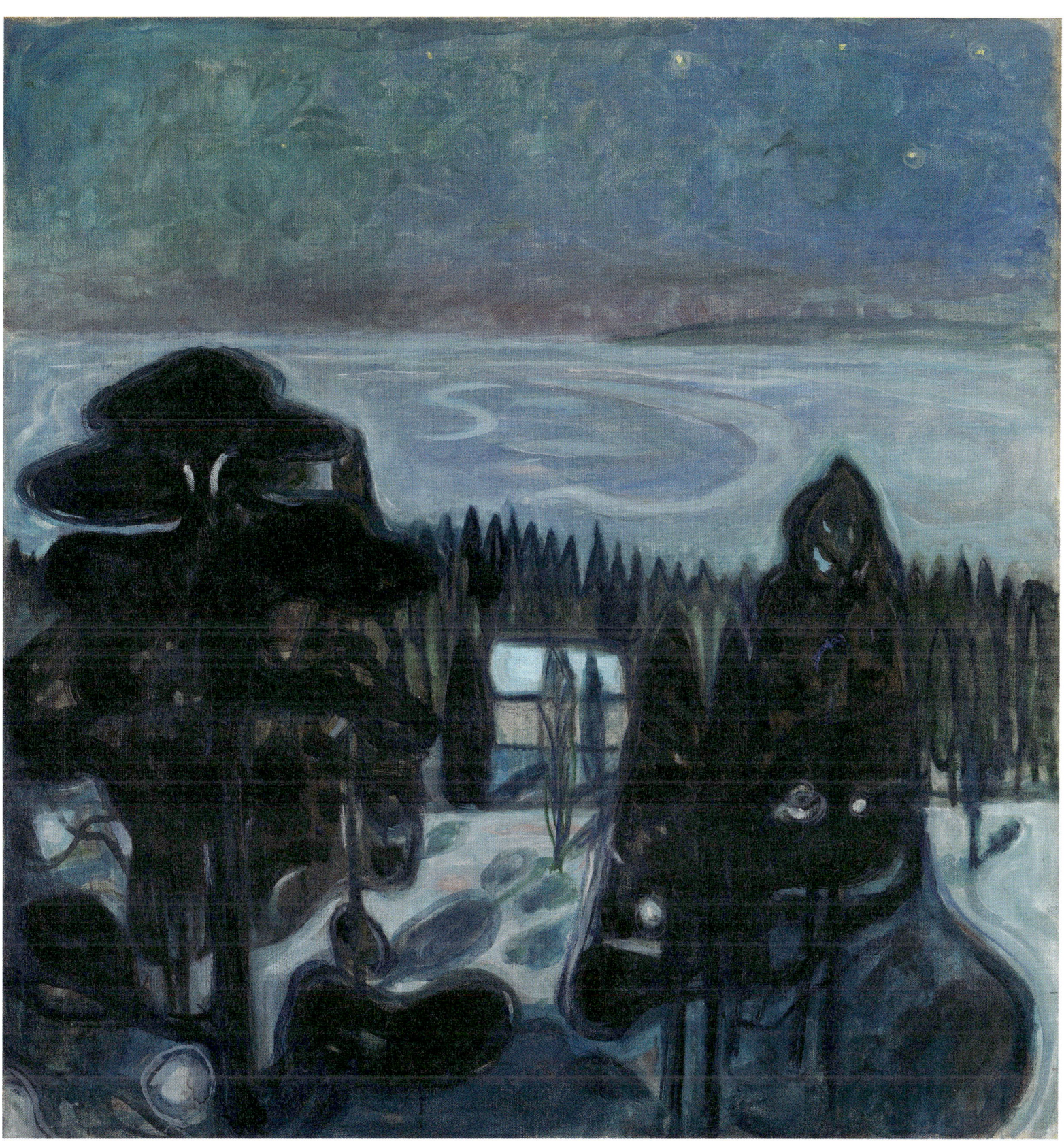

Oil on canvas
136 × 125 cm
Signed l.l. "E.M"
NG.M.00844
Woll M 483
NG cat. 1933-960; 1950-1073; 1968-1294, 1992-844

Other titles: *Sommeraften*; *Sommernatt, de tre pikene på broen*; *Pikene på bryggen*; *Smaapikerne paa broen*; *Pikene på broen. Aasgaardstrand 1900.* **Provenance**: Olaf Schou (1902-1909); gift from Olaf Schou 1909. **Literature**: One of Munch's best-known motifs, it is widely discussed in much of the general Munch literature. Glaser 1917, 43f.; Vidalenc 1920, 138; Thiis 1933, 267f., 277; Stenersen 1945, 80; Gauguin 1946 A, 167f.; Revold 1952, 42f.; I. Langaard 1960, 403f.; Svenæus 1968, 75; Stang 1977, 170f.; Rosenblum 1978, 5; Eggum 1978 B, 62; Skedsmo (ed.) 1981, 95-97; Eggum 1982 A, 6; Prelinger 2002, 142; Sommer 2004, 78; Trabuco 2009, 139; Johannesen 2010, [unpaginated]; Høifødt 2010 A, 185f.; Kristensen 2010, 57f.; Autin-Grenier 2011, 74f.; Hansen et al. 2011, 153; Flaatten 2013 A, 11, 142-143, 146, 149-150, 161, 214, 240; Flaatten 2013 B, 92; Huber 2013, 105; Grøgaard 2013 A, 351; Nyaas (ed.) 2013, 40; Henningsen (ed.) 2014, 20; Kongssund 2015, 80; Gjessing 2016, 32; Ustvedt 2018, 112. **Exhibitions**: 1901, Kristiania, no. 58; 1902, Berlin, no. 185; 1904, Düsseldorf, no. 1137; 1915, Copenhagen, no. 267; 1927, Oslo, no. 117; 1928, New York-San Francisco, no. 247 (see 1927, Pittsburgh); 1942, Oslo, no. 55; 1950, USA, touring exhibition, no. 30; 1951, Brighton-Glasgow-London-The Hague-Paris, no. 29/30/28; 1952, Zürich, no. 17; 1952, Brussels, no. 8; 1954, Venice, no. 23; 1954, Munich-Cologne, no. 39; 1955, Copenhagen-Odense, no. 37; 1958, Rotterdam, no. 12; 1960, Paris, no. 489; 1964, Oslo, no. 56; 1978, Washington, no. 49; 1979, New York; 1981, Tokyo-Sapporo-Nara-Nagoya-Leningrad-Moscow, no. 102/88; 1985, Milan-Rome, no. 46; 1987, Oslo B, no. 66; 1994, Oslo, no. 42; 1995, Madrid-Barcelona-Reykjavik-Stockholm, no. 56; 1998, Lugano, no. 48; 1999, Florence, no. 13; 2003, Vienna, no. 163; 2004, Melbourne, no. 13; 2005, Rome, no. 32; 2006, New York, no. 102; 2011, Paris, no. 11; 2013, Oslo, no. 88.

Three girls in white, red and green dresses stand on a bridge with their backs to the viewer. They are leaning against the railing and looking out to sea. The figures are depicted simply, in clean, clear colours. The view from the bridge is towards Åsgårdstrand, the coastal town on Kristianiafjord. Munch has included Kiøsterudgården, an imposing house that features in several of his paintings, the distinctive lime tree in the garden with its dome-shaped crown, and the white weather-board fences. The picture has a compelling perspective thanks to the railing that leads into the landscape. The girls are standing on the footbridge that leads out to the pier where the steamships dock. It is a bright summer night, laden with expectations of what life has to offer.

The picture marks something new in Munch's art. In terms of its monumental form, simplification, and palette, it has similarities to *The Dance of Life* (cat. 40). But whereas *The Dance of Life* concludes the symbolist love theme of the Frieze of Life, this picture is one of Munch's first depictions of children. The preoccupation with death, melancholy, eroticism, and hopeless love is replaced by an interest in childhood and the child's view of the world. Here, form and colour become important in themselves. "The picture is a marvel of composition and harmonious colour," writes Jens Thiis, who continues "... the balancing of volumes and contours, and the use of lines, straight, curved, even domed, together with the play of the horizontal and diagonal, all are masterfully welded together into a single whole" (Thiis 1933, 276).

In 1898, Munch had bought a little mariner's cottage in Åsgårdstrand, and in 1899 he travelled to Florence, where he studied the city's Renaissance paintings. Both events had an impact on his art. The purchase of the house allowed him to become involved with the local community and to forge stronger contacts with the permanent residents, some of whom served as models, as in *The Girls on the Bridge*. At the same time, the trip to Italy and the opportunity to update his knowledge of contemporary painted friezes prepared him to undertake some major public art commissions.

The Girls on the Bridge is one of Munch's most popular and best known works. Concerning life in the coastal town and its colours, the artist wrote: "Summer arrived - with its intense colours - Vivid green against vivid blue - vivid yellow against vivid Red. The Town's brightly dressed Women came and filled it - Backfisch filled the Streets" (MM.T.2759).

The picture was one of seven paintings by Munch that Olaf Schou donated to the National Gallery in 1909. Munch painted several versions of the composition (Woll M 483; Woll M 484; Woll M 539; Woll M 540; Woll M 639; Woll M 1632; Woll M 1715) as well as a variation with young women instead of girls (Woll M 541). The National Museum's painting is the first of the series. The dating of the picture has been debated (I. Langaard 1960, 403; Woll 2008 B, 522). It has been pointed out that Munch himself wrote that it was painted in Åsgårdstrand in the summer of 1901 (Høifødt 2010 A, 185; MM N 3105). It has had various titles. At its first showing, in the exhibition at Hollændergaarden, Kristiania in 1901, the title was *Sommeraften* (Summer Evening). It was also included in Munch's exhibition at the Berlin Secession in 1902, where the title was *Norwegische Sommernacht*. There also exist several print versions of the motif, for example, an intaglio from 1903 (Woll G 232), a woodcut from 1905 (Woll G 271), and a combined woodcut and lithograph from 1918 (Woll G 628; Woll G 629). wv

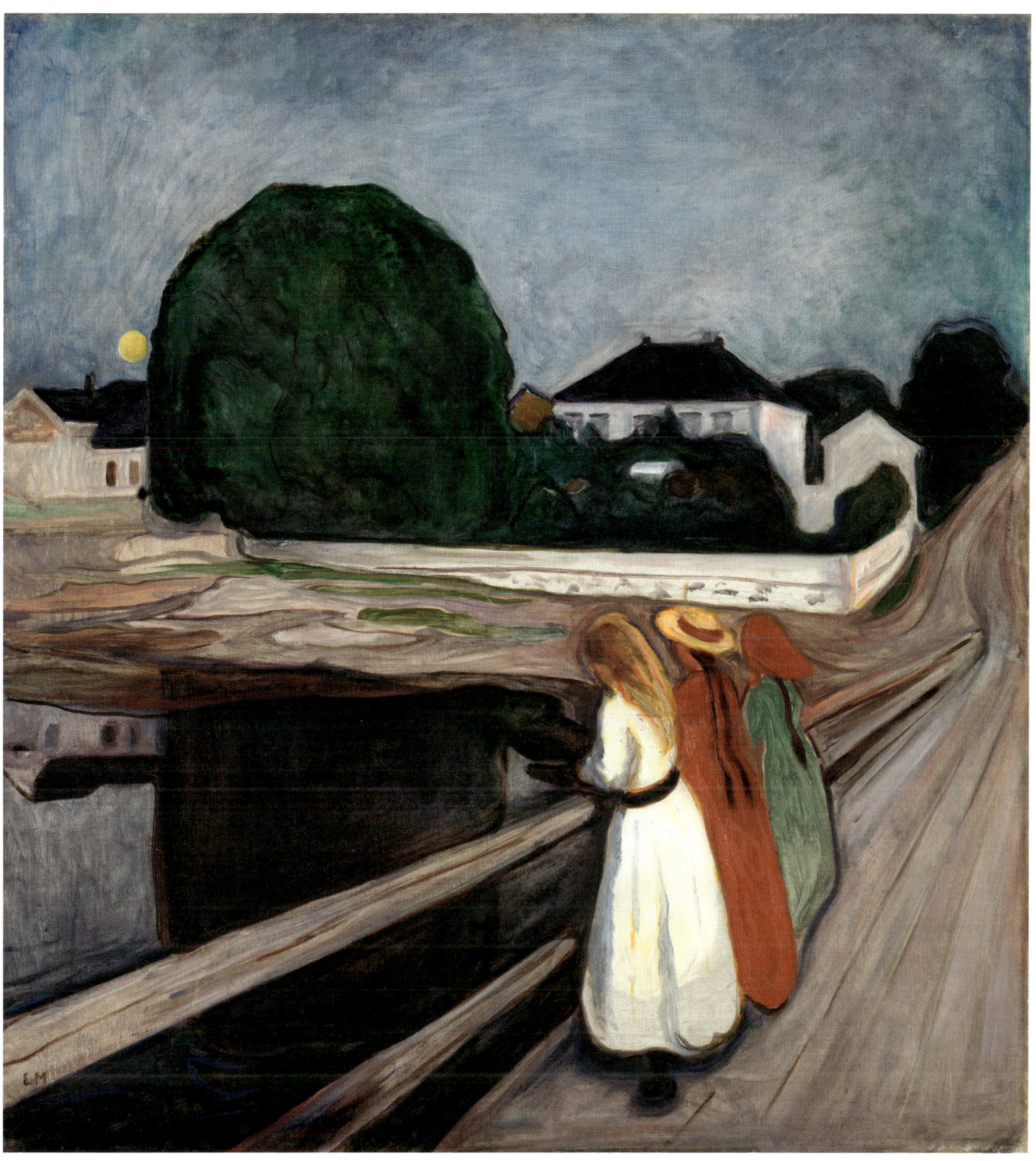

43

Enchanted Forest, 1901–1902

Eventyrskogen

Oil on canvas
79 × 106.5 cm
Signed l.r. "Edv Munch"
NG.M.02237
Woll M 495
NG cat. 1968-1296; 1992-2237

Other titles: *Barn i skogen*; *En skog*; *Gran- og furu-billeder*. **Provenance**: Alfred Larsen (before 1946–1950); bequeathed by Alfred Larsen 1950, received 1951. **Literature**: Eggum and Woll 1979, [unpaginated]; Eggum 1991, 288; Woll 2008 B, 534; Pettersen 2010, 111; Sørensen 2012, 189; Blegvad 2012, 176; Rognerud 2013, 48; Flaatten 2013 B, 124, 159; Huusko 2015, 79; Ustvedt 2018, 123–124. **Exhibitions**: 1902, Kristiania; 1903, Paris, no. 1829 (uncertain); 1927, Oslo, no. 108; 1979, Nyköbing–Copenhagen, no. 12; 1979, Oslo; 1982, Oslo B; 1997, Tokyo, no. 123; 1998, Cologne, no. 63; 2010, Codroipo, no. 115; 2012, Århus, no. 11; 2013, Oslo, no. 94; 2015, Oslo-Helsinki, no. 69.

In the years 1901 to 1904, Munch painted several pictures featuring children and adolescents, one of which was *Enchanted Forest*. Munch's interest in children finds expression in group portraits, depictions of children at play, and in more independent figure compositions. Most of these pictures were produced during the artist's summer sojourns at Åsgårdstrand. In *Enchanted Forest*, the childhood theme is underscored by the difference in size between the figures and the landscape, and by the fact that the children are holding hands. They stand hesitantly on a track that curves in towards the outer edge of a dark, looming forest. The children are on the threshold of something that seems both alluring and alarming.

Munch painted two other pictures with a similar design, *Barn i skogen* (Children in the Forest) (1901–1902, Woll M 492) and *To barn på vei til eventyrskogen* (Two Children on Their Way to the Enchanted Forest) (1901–1902, Woll M 494). In the latter, the section of landscape and the track leading into the forest resemble those of *Enchanted Forest*, but there are only two children. In *Barn i skogen*, the children are seen from a greater distance and appear small against the trees and the dense, dark forest. *Enchanted Forest* combines elements from these two pictures but differs in its use of colours that are paler and less saturated. *Enchanted Forest* is executed with a diluted binder so that much of the paint has been absorbed by the canvas. This creates an effect of transparency and dryness reminiscent of fresco painting.

The date of the painting has been a matter of debate, varying from 1897 to 1903. When it entered the museum's collection as a bequest from the wholesaler Alfred Larsen in 1951, its date was recorded as "ca. 1903". Since then, it has been established with reasonable certainty that the picture was exhibited at Blomqvist in the autumn of 1902. The painting can be associated with the Blomqvist exhibition based on the following humourous account in the satirical magazine *Tyrihans* (no. 42, 1902): "We stopped in front of 'Children Going to the Woods'. 'Superb!' says Hansen. 'Look at the fresh yellow forest and the colourful joy of the children!'" (Woll 2008 B, 536). Moreover, it is known that when the Munch Museum's *Barn i skogen* (Woll M 492) was shown at the Sonderbund exhibition in 1912, it was dated to 1901. And finally, either that or *Enchanted Forest* was exhibited in Paris in February 1903, further suggesting a dating of 1902 or earlier (Woll 2008 B, 534). VWH

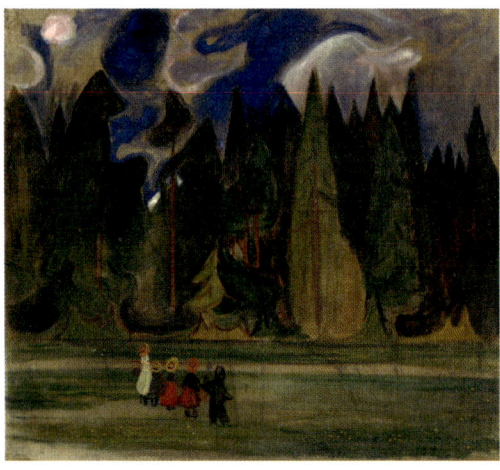

Edvard Munch: *Children in the Forest*, 1901–1902
Oil and casein on canvas, 90 × 100 cm
Munchmuseet
MM.M.00317, Woll M 492
Photo: Munchmuseet / Sidsel de Jong

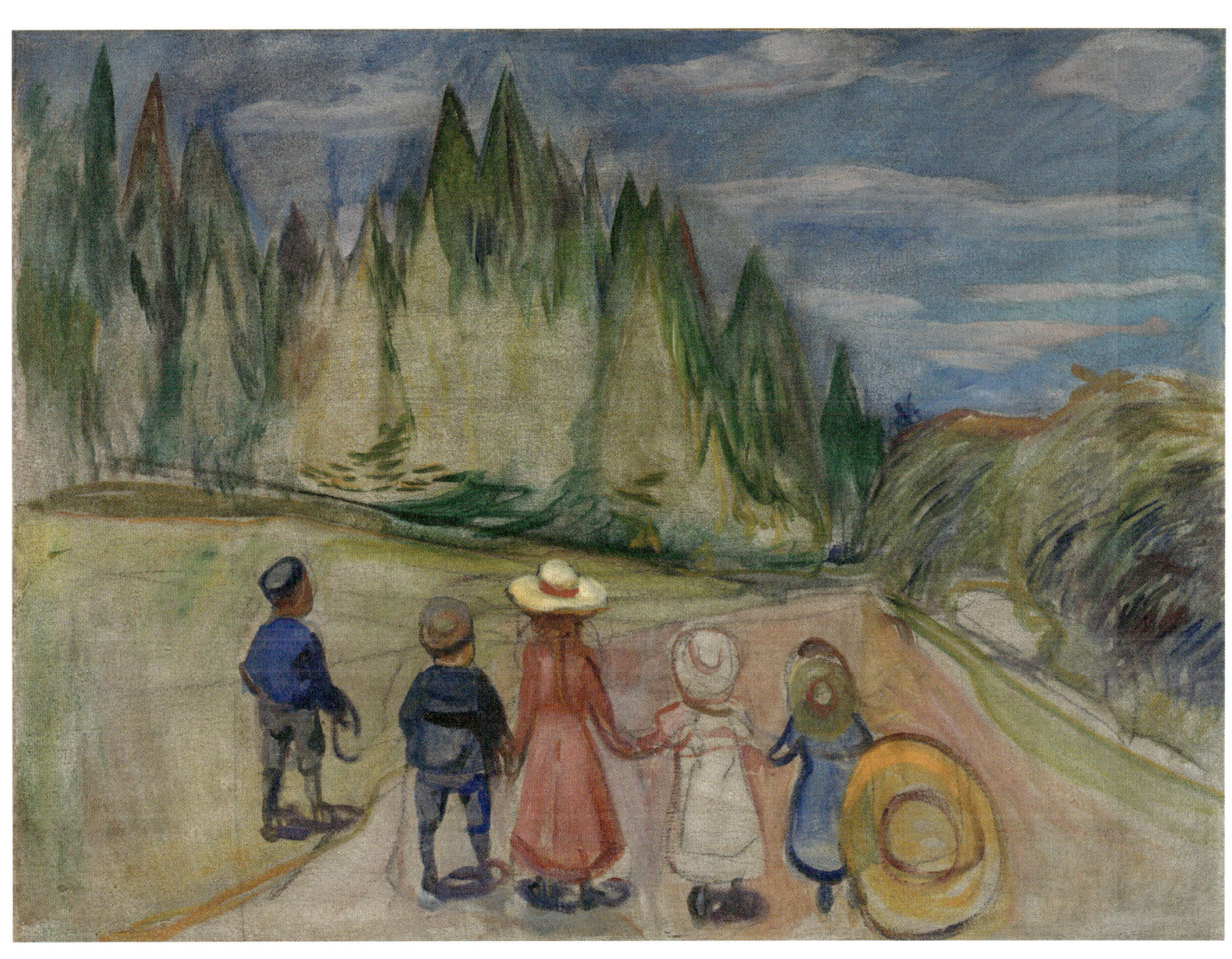

44

Two Nudes, 1902–1903
Dobbeltakt

Oil on canvas
110 × 161 cm
Signed u.r. "E Munch"
NG.M.01868
Woll M 514
NG cat. 1950-1080; 1968-1298; 1992-1868

Other titles: *Kvinne. Akt*; *Aktstudie*; *Dobbelakt*.
Provenance: Charlotte and Christian Mustad (1919–1937); gift from Charlotte and Christian Mustad 1937. **Literature**: Chang 2010, 54. **Exhibitions**: 1904, Hamburg; 1908, Copenhagen; 1909, Helsinki, no. 6; 1919, Kristiania A.

Two Nudes was painted in a period when Munch worked frequently with nude female models. He portrayed women in various poses, sitting, standing and reclining (Woll M, 504-518). Several of the works in this group include clear interiors, others focus almost exclusively on the figure(s). Munch painted nudes throughout his career, and several of his models are discussed in the Munch literature. The National Museum's drawing *Kvinneakt* (Female Nude) from 1887 is an example of the artist's approach to this genre from early in his career (cat. 237).

A popular theme at the time, female nudes played a central role in modernist painting. *Two Nudes* has a sensitive, cautious quality. One woman is sitting modestly on a chair, the other is reclining, her head tilted slightly forward. Neither is looking directly at the painter and the viewer. The depiction of the two women differs from his other nudes of the period in terms of its pale palette. The sensitivity is reinforced by a treatment suggestive of watercolour.

Two Nudes was one of seven paintings gifted to the museum by Charlotte and Christian Mustad in 1937. In the National Gallery's catalogues, it has previously been dated to around 1905. Gerd Woll, however, relates it to a number of other nudes that Munch painted in the period 1902–03 (Woll 2008 B, 543-553). She believes it was included in an exhibition at Cassirer in Hamburg in 1904 (Woll 2008 B, 551). Woll draws attention to Gustav Schiefler's description of the picture: "die beiden nackten Mädchen (das eine liegend, das andere sitzend)" (Schiefler, 1987–1990, 91). The same two women feature in the painting *Blond og mørk aktmodell* (Blond and Dark-Haired Nude) (Woll M 512). wv

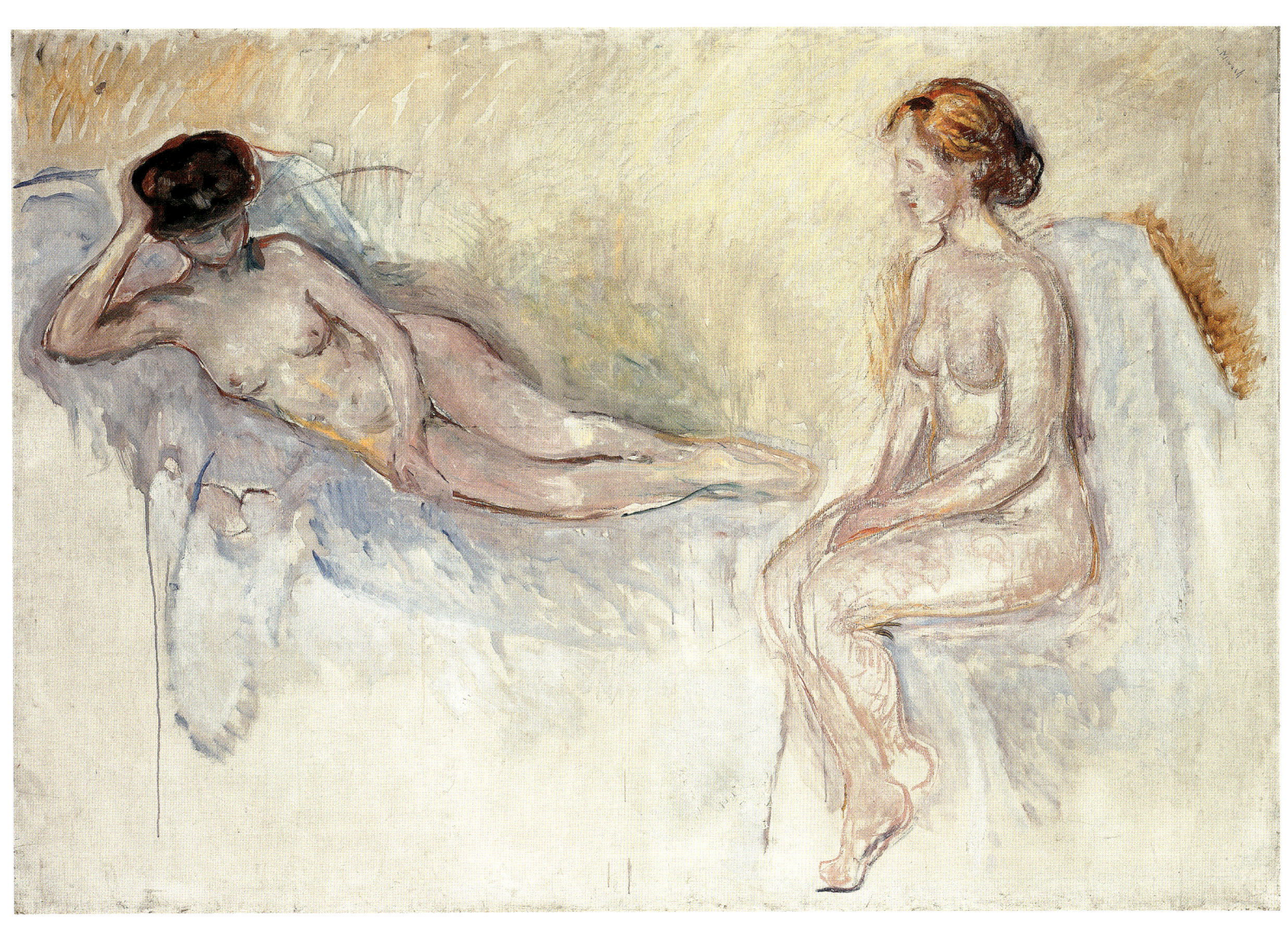

45

On the Veranda, 1902

På verandaen

Oil on canvas
86.5 × 115.5 cm
Unsigned
NG.M.00810
Woll M 549
NG cat. 1933-962; 1950-1078; 1968-1295; 1992-810

Other titles: *La pluie (Rain)*; *Høst*; *På terrassen*; *Paa verandaen*; *På verandaen. Høst. Aasgaard-strand 1902*; *Paa verandaen, regnveir*. **Provenance**: Purchased with financial support from the A.C. Houen's trust fund on the occasion of the artist's 1909 exhibition at Blomqvist Kunsthandel. **Literature**: Flaatten 2010 B, 339–340; Henningsen 2010, 95; Flaatten 2013 A, 181–182; Ahtola-Moorhouse 2014, 56; Dagen 2016, 37. **Exhibitions**: 1903, Paris, no. 1831; 1904, Copenhagen; 1904, Kristiania, no. 90; 1905, Prague, no. 224; 1909, Kristiania; 1912, Gothenburg; 1913, Kristiania, no. 14; 1927, Oslo, no. 127; 1959, Warsaw, no. 17; 1964, Florence, no. 17; 1965, New York A; 1968, Schaffhausen, no. 34; 1971, Oslo, no. 114; 1978, Madison-Minneapolis-Seattle, no. 187; 1981, Tokyo-Sapporo-Nara-Nagoya-Leningrad-Moscow, no. 193/182; 1983, Dresden, no. 22; 1984, Tromsø; 1991, Paris-Oslo-Frankfurt, no. 38; 1995, New York, no. 22; 1999, Modum, no. 25; 2010, Codroipo, no. 118; 2013, Oslo, no. 101; 2014, Helsinki; 2016, Paris–Martigny, no. 7.

On the Veranda is an example of Munch's use of vivid colour after the turn of the century. It shows the view from the artist's veranda in Åsgårdstrand. Two young girls look out over the landscape and the fjord. An earlier title *På verandaen. Høst. Aasgaardstrand* (On the Veranda. Autumn. Aasgaardstrand) identified both the place and the season.

Vertical streaks against the sky indicate that it is raining, as do the reflections in the water that has settled on the veranda. Munch has painted the scene in autumnal colours, rusty reds and yellows against the green of the grass. This is one of Munch's many representations of children and young people at Åsgårdstrand, which began with *The Girls on the Bridge* (cat. 42), painted the previous year. In a number of pictures painted during the summers of 1901 and 1902 he used local residents as models. The two girls have been identified as Henriette Marthe Gjermundsen and a friend. Henriette and her sister were neighbours of Munch in Åsgårdstrand (Flaatten 2013 A, 181).

The painting was shown for the first time at the Salon des Artistes Indépendants in Paris in 1903, where it had the title *La Pluie* (Rainy Weather). Many years later, when Henri Matisse sent greetings to Munch on the occasion of his 70th birthday, he praised him for his sense of colour: "I salute the great Norwegian artist (...) He was one of the first at the Salon des Indépendants in Paris to give colour a new expression in canvases of rare harmony" (*Tidens Tegn*, 12 December 1933).

On the Veranda was purchased for the National Gallery with financial support from the A.C. Houen fund in 1909 from that year's exhibition at Blomqvist. The painting is unsigned and has no date marking, but has been dated to autumn 1902. Other paintings by Munch featuring the same girls working in the garden in Åsgårdstrand appear to support the attribution (Woll M 546; Woll M 548; Woll 2008 B, 580). This is the last picture Munch painted at Åsgårdstrand that year and the last before the drama with Tulla Larsen on 11 September, which ended with him shooting himself in the finger. wv

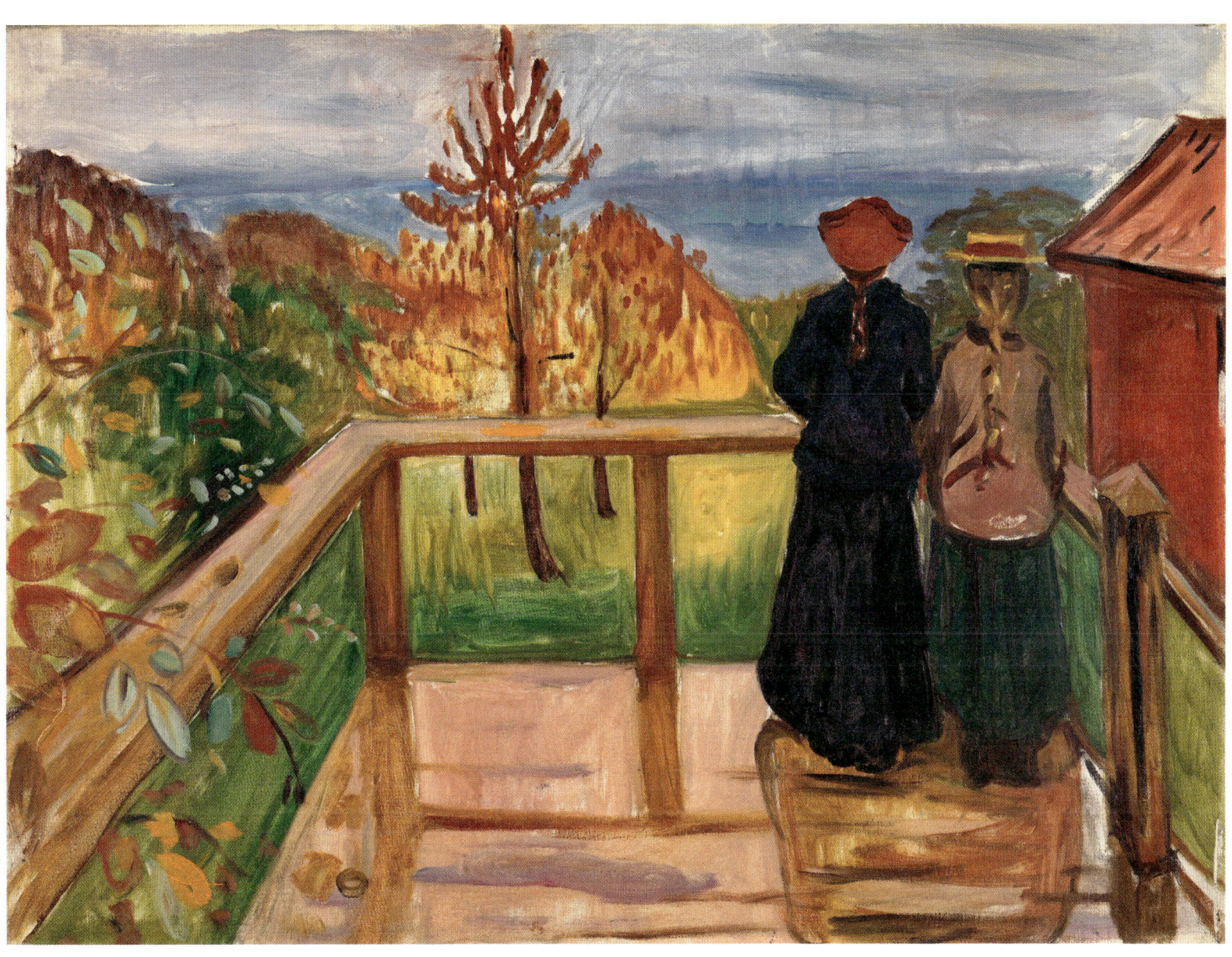

46

The Frenchman. Marcel Archinard, 1904

Franskmannen. Marcel Archinard

Oil on canvas
185 × 70 cm
Unsigned
NG.M.00811
Woll M 578
NG cat. 1933-961; 1950-1077; 1968-1293; 1992-811

Other titles: *Fransk type*; *Portrett av herr A*. **Provenance**: Purchased with financial support from the A.C. Houen's trust fund on the occasion of the artist's 1909 exhibition at Blomqvist Kunsthandel. **Literature**: Heilbut 1904, 489–492; Vidalenc 1920, 131–135; Thiis 1933, 232, 282; Eggum 1994 A, 94–96; Lange 2004, 131; Llorens and Llorens 2011, 226; Hansen 2011 A, 210; Ustvedt 2013 A, 236; Stein and Rød 2015, 260, 262; Lloyd 2016, 22–23; Ustvedt 2016, 77; Berman 2016, 85. **Exhibitions**: 1904, Copenhagen; 1904, Kristiania, no. 40; 1904, Berlin, no. 33; 1905, Prague, no. 52; 1906, Dresden, no. 13; 1906, Chemnitz, no. 13; 1906, Hagen, no. XV; 1906, Weimar, no. 23; 1907, Bielefeld, no. 28; 1907, Hamburg; 1908, Breslau, no. 3; 1909, Kristiania; 1927, Berlin, no. 71; 1927, Oslo, no. 120; 1931, Budapest-Vienna, no. 69; 1959, Warsaw, no. 16; 1971, Oslo, no. 52; 1983, Dresden, no. 21; 1987, Barcelona, no. 15; 2004, Melbourne, no. 12; 2005, Rome, no. 35; 2009, Copenhagen-Oslo, no. 39; 2011, Valencia-Barcelona, no. 74; 2013, Oslo, no. 106; 2016, New York, no. 2.

The painting is typical of Munch's many full-length portraits, a genre he worked with extensively in the years 1902–1909, a period when he established himself as a modern portrait painter in Germany. The figure stands facing us frontally in a shallow pictorial space with a minimum of elements that define the setting. The viewer is placed in direct dialogue with the subject. Even so, little is known about the depicted man, other than that he was a French-Swiss *littérateur* by the name of Archinard, with whom Munch was acquainted during his time in Berlin (Thiis 1933, 282). Here we see him dressed in a three-piece suit, with a red necktie strategically placed to provide a dash of colour. The moustache, well-groomed beard and the elegant, pointed shoes reinforce the impression of an urbane, fashion-conscious figure. His pose with a cigarette in one hand attracts comparison with *Self-Portrait with Cigarette* (cat. 32). Munch also painted a smaller portrait of the same man (Woll M 577).

Many of Munch's portraits from this period were commissions, but some were the outcome of the artist's own initiative, as may be the case here. Evidently the work was considered significant, because it featured in a major exhibition of portraits at the Kunstsalon Cassirer in Berlin in the winter of 1904-1905, together with Munch's portraits of Henrik Ibsen, Max Linde and August Strindberg.

The work was purchased for the National Gallery from a solo exhibition at Blomqvist (Kristiania) in 1909, along with four other pictures. The dating has been debated. In several exhibitions that showed the work during Munch's lifetime, it was attributed to 1901. According to a number of more recent scholars, however, a more likely date is 1904 (Eggum 1994 A; Lange 2004; Woll 2008 B). The work was probably exhibited for the first time in 1904 (Heilbut 1904), a claim corroborated by a passage in Hermann Schlittgen's book *Erinnerungen* (Schlittgen 1926, 244). Munch painted a portrait of Schlittgen, which in this book is dated to 1904 (Woll M 579). Schlittgen's text suggests that the portrait of Archinard was produced at roughly the same time. In later years, the two portraits have often been compared as contrasting character portraits, the *Frenchman* and the *German* respectively (Eggum 1994 A). Munch himself mentions the painting in a note dated 1904-1905 (MM N 31). Several other surviving letters suggest that the artist and his subject were in regular contact in the years 1903-1905 (MM K 1866; MM K 1867; MM K 1868; MM K 1895: MM K 1897). øu

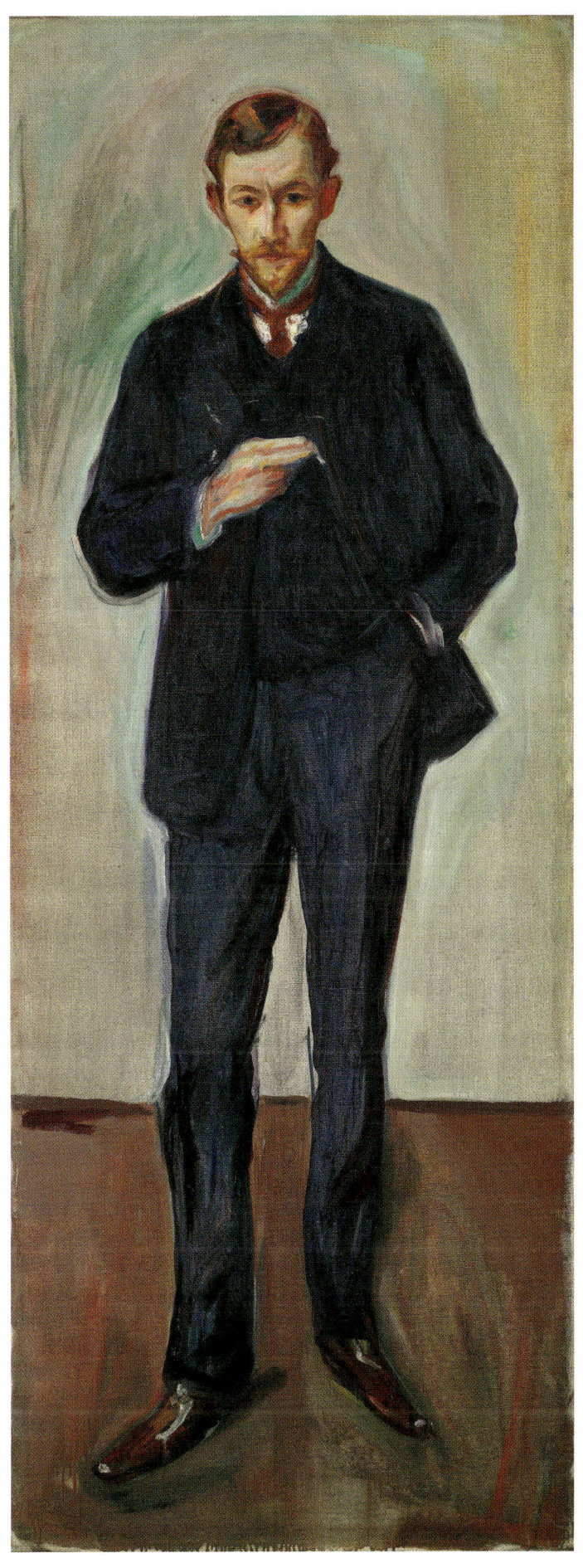

47

Self-Portrait, 1905

Selvportrett

Watercolour, gouache, pastel and coloured pencil
over pencil on cardboard
44 × 41.5 cm
Signed u.r. "E Munch 1905"
NG.M.01229
Woll M 649
NG cat. 1933-963; 1950-1079; 1968-1297; 1992-1229

Other titles: *Selvportræt. Hode*; *Selvportrett med bart og høy snipp*. **Provenance**: Commeter, Hamburg (1906); privately owned (1906-); Purchased 1921. **Literature**: Jedlicka 1958, 235f.; Müller-Westermann 1997, 107. **Exhibitions**: 1906, Hamburg; 1927, Oslo, no. 148; 1981, Tokyo-Sapporo-Nara-Nagoya-Leningrad-Moscow, no. 2; 1999, Modum, no. 30; 2013, Oslo, no. 111.

Munch made self-portraiture an important aspect of his art. He painted his first self-portrait in 1882, the last in 1943 (Woll M 47; Woll M 1789). This example is from a period when Munch painted many portraits. Exhibitions and commissions, not least for portraits, made Germany an important place to be in the years after 1900. Munch's acquaintances included a number of prominent art collectors and cultural figures. He painted portraits of, among others, the art collectors Max Linde and Hanni and Herbert Esche, and he was part of the circle of artists, writers, and architects associated with the art collector Harry Graf Kessler. These were wealthy, influential people with international contacts.

"Here I associate with, e.g. Counts and Barons - and I constantly have to wear tails and a frock coat," Munch wrote to his Aunt Karen (1904, MM N 870). His appearance in *Self-Portrait* may indicate that he wanted to make a good impression in this company. The white starched collar stands out as a highlight in the picture. The artist has pictured himself against a yellowish-orange background that exploits the colour of the cardboard. The use of watercolours contributes to the picture's fluid, translucent quality. The portrait shows an earnest and sophisticated man.

The painting was first exhibited at the Commeter'sche Kunsthandlung in Hamburg in 1906 and later in the major 1927 exhibition at the National Gallery. At the former it was listed as no. 122, with the title *Selbstporträt (Klein)*. It was sold in March 1906, probably to a friend of Munch's (MM K 3840). It would appear that the National Gallery bought the painting in Germany in 1921, but it is not known where or from whom. In recent years, the image has acquired an alternative title, *Self-Portrait with Moustache and Starched Collar* (Woll M 649). wv

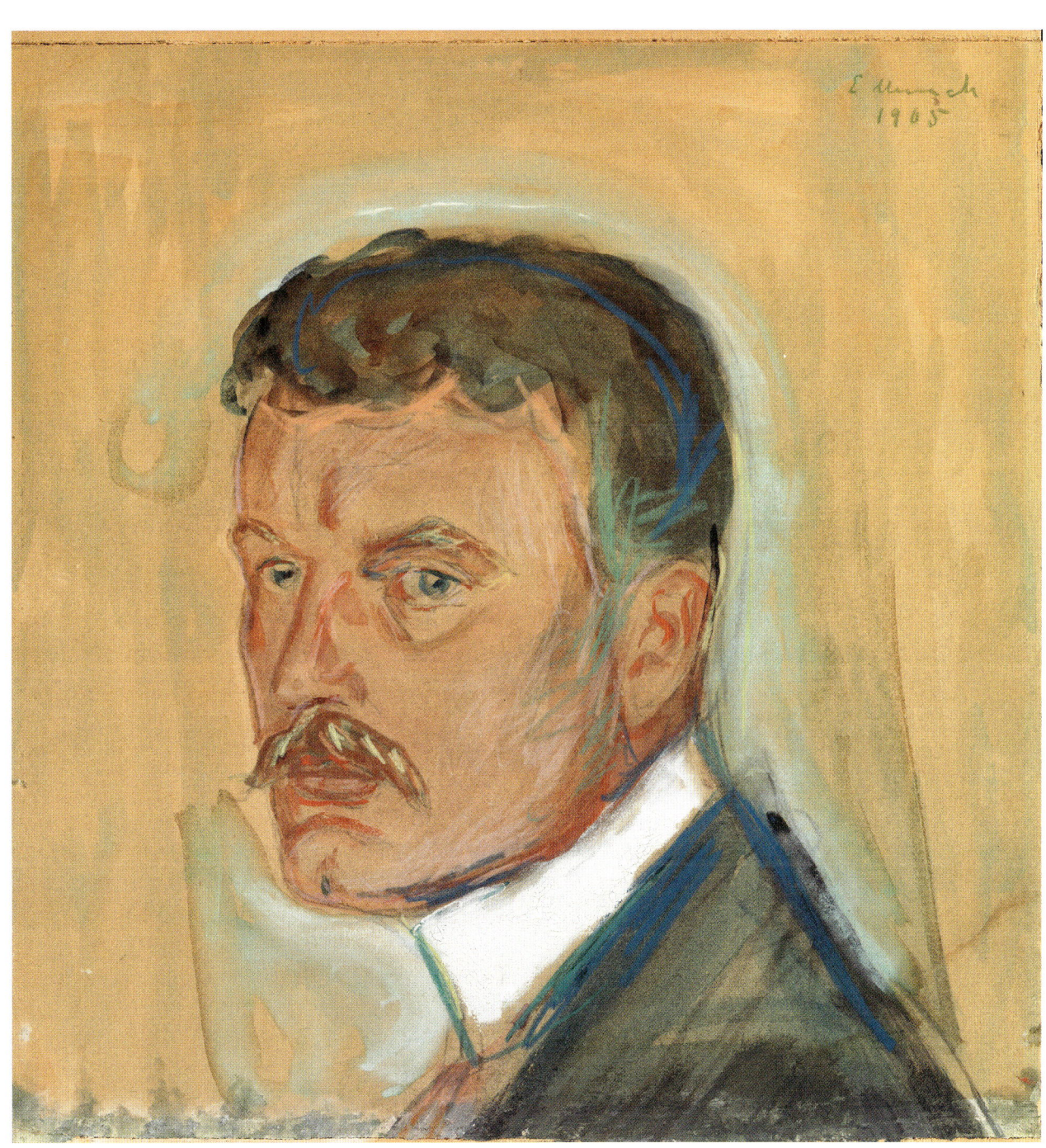

48

Mrs Schwarz, 1906

Fru Schwarz

Oil on canvas
99.5 × 60.5 cm
Signed u.r. "E Munch"
NG.M.02817
Woll M 698
NG cat. 1992-2817

Other titles: *Portrett av kvinne i grønn bluse*. **Provenance**: Charlotte and Christian Mustad (1927-1959/1970); bequeathed by Charlotte and Christian Mustad 1959, received 1970. **Literature**: Eggum 1994 A, 130; Fredlund (ed.) 2002, 78; Johannesen 1999, 60; Lange 2004, 137; Ustvedt 2013 B, 218-229. **Exhibitions**: 1909, Kristiania; 1909, Trondheim; 1909, Bergen; 1913, Stockholm B, no. 1; 1914, Berlin, no. 51; 1922, Zürich, no. 28; 1922, Bern-Basel, no. 25/24; 1923, Gothenburg, no. 179; 1926, Mannheim, no. 23; 1927, Berlin, no. 91; 1927, Oslo, no. 141; 1927, Pittsburgh–New York–San Francisco, no. 325/286/254; 1999, Florence, no. 14; 2001, Boston, no. 66; 2002, Gothenburg, no. 23; 2004, Melbourne, no. 27; 2010, Tromsø. Nordnorsk kunstmuseum (long-term loan).

The painting was made during a period when Munch produced several portraits of wealthy patrons, collectors and connoisseurs in German cultural circles, many of them on commission. The frontal pose with the hands at rest or gathered in front of the body is characteristic of his depictions of young women; comparable works include his portraits of Inger Munch, Ragnhild Bäckström and Aase Nørregaard (cat. 6; cat. 20; cat. 24; cat. 38). The loose painting style, on the other hand, with its broad, sweeping brushstrokes, clear colour contrasts and distinctive touches of green, is typical of his paintings around 1906. The rendering of the blouse is particularly eye-catching, and seems to influence the idiom as a whole. Both the overall form and the woman's costume are indicative of the period's defining interest in elegance.

Munch also produced a lithographic portrait of the same woman (1906, Woll G 282) and two prints of her son Andreas Schwarz (1906, Woll G 280; Woll G 281). In addition, he depicted the woman seated in another painting from the same period (1906, Woll M 697).

The identity of Mrs Schwarz has been debated. It was once believed that she was married to the German art historian Karl Israel Schwarz (Eggum 1994 A), but this has since been refuted (Johannesen 1999, Lange 2004, Ustvedt 2013 B). In a letter addressed to the National Gallery (20 February 1992), Marlene de Man-Flechtheim claimed that the portrait was of her mother, Maria-Helene Flechtheim, née Kohlsted (1882-1971). Maria-Helene's first marriage was to Georg Schwarz (1861-1936?), with whom she had two children: Andreas, born 1906, and Nickel, born 1908. The couple divorced in 1911, and Maria-Helene later married Julius Flechtheim (1882-1978). The identification seems plausible, since Georg Schwarz was a partner in Paul Cassirer's art dealership in the period 1901-1911. Munch had close contacts with the Paul and Bruno Cassirer brothers during these years and exhibited several times at the Kunstsalon Cassirer in Berlin. The date is also confirmed in a letter from Munch, in which he writes: "Ich male Frau Schwarz" (MM N 2334). The letter is undated, but written on the headed notepaper of Hotel Beyer in Berlin, a hotel where Munch stayed frequently in the years 1905-1906.

The painting was gifted to the National Gallery as part of the Charlotte and Christian Mustad bequest that was agreed in 1959, although it was only incorporated into the collection on the latter's demise in 1970. ØU

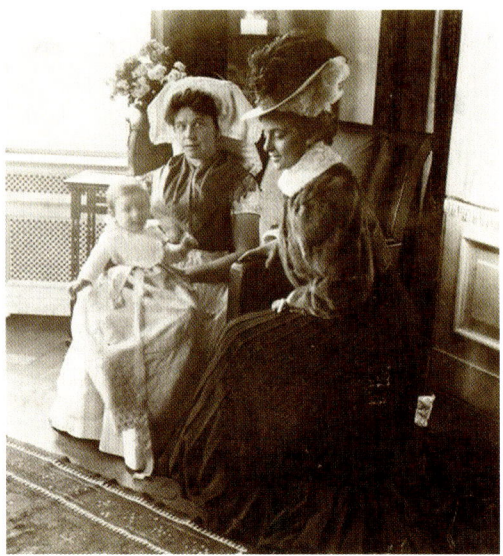

Mrs. Schwarz (on the right) with her son Andreas and probably a nursemaid, Berlin ca. 1906.
Photo: Private collection, Antwerp

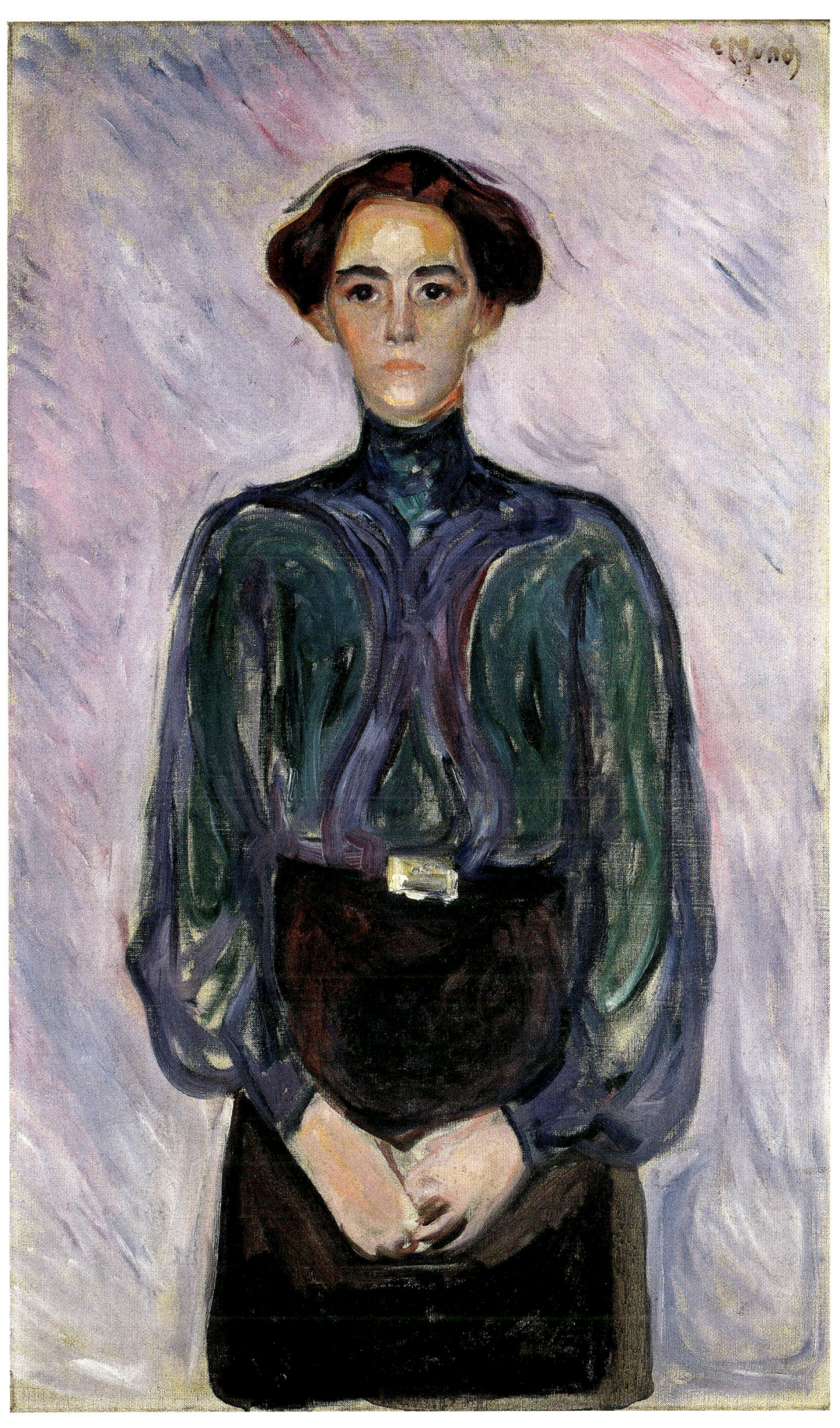

49

Seated Nude, 1913

Sittende akt

Oil on canvas
103 × 72.5 cm
Signed l.r. "E. Munch"
NG.M.02818
Woll M 1083
NG cat. 1992-2818

Other titles: *Knælende kvinde på rødt leie*; *Akt*; *Knelende akt*; *Knelende kvinne*.
Provenance: Charlotte and Christian Mustad (before 1939-1959/1970); bequeathed by Charlotte and Christian Mustad 1959, received 1970. **Exhibitions**: 1915, Kristiania, no. 46; 1927, Berlin, no. 153; 1927, Oslo, no. 203; 1934, Copenhagen, no. 69; 1983, Dresden, no. 28; 1986, West Palm Beach, no. 34; 1999, Florence, no. 15; 2001, Boston, no. 50.

Nudes and studies of female models in everyday situations were a theme Munch worked with extensively. Treated as anonymous (semi-)naked figures or as individuals engaged in mundane tasks, such depictions were popular in Paris in the mid-1890s.

The model for this picture was probably Ingeborg Kaurin (1894–1972), a young woman who worked as both a maid and a model for Munch in the years 1911–1915. In the literature she is often referred to as the "Moss girl", since she spent long periods at the Grimsrød farm in Moss, a property Munch used frequently up until 1916. Their working relationship was evidently good, for it endured for many years. It would also appear to have been platonic (Eggum, 1988 A, 20). Several paintings and watercolours, and a large number of drawings from the years 1911–1915, in which Kaurin served as model, have been preserved. In terms of idiom, some are similar to this painting, such as *Kvinnelig akt, sittende på kne* (Female Nude, Kneeling) (1912–1914, MM.T.01032). In many cases, the woman's hair is as an eye-catching feature, either loose and flowing, arranged, or, as here, hanging in heavy vertical plaits that partly obscure, partly accentuate, her bodily curves.

The nude was a favoured genre among many of the leading artists of the day. The rugged technique and the bold, toxic yellow palette with hints of pink, green and violet make it reasonable to compare this painting with the work of the German expressionists, who were just emerging at the time.

There is no date on the painting, but in the National Gallery's 1927 exhibition, it was dated to 1913. It was among the works that Charlotte and Christian Mustad bequeathed to the National Gallery in 1959, entering the museum's collection following the latter's demise in 1970. ØU

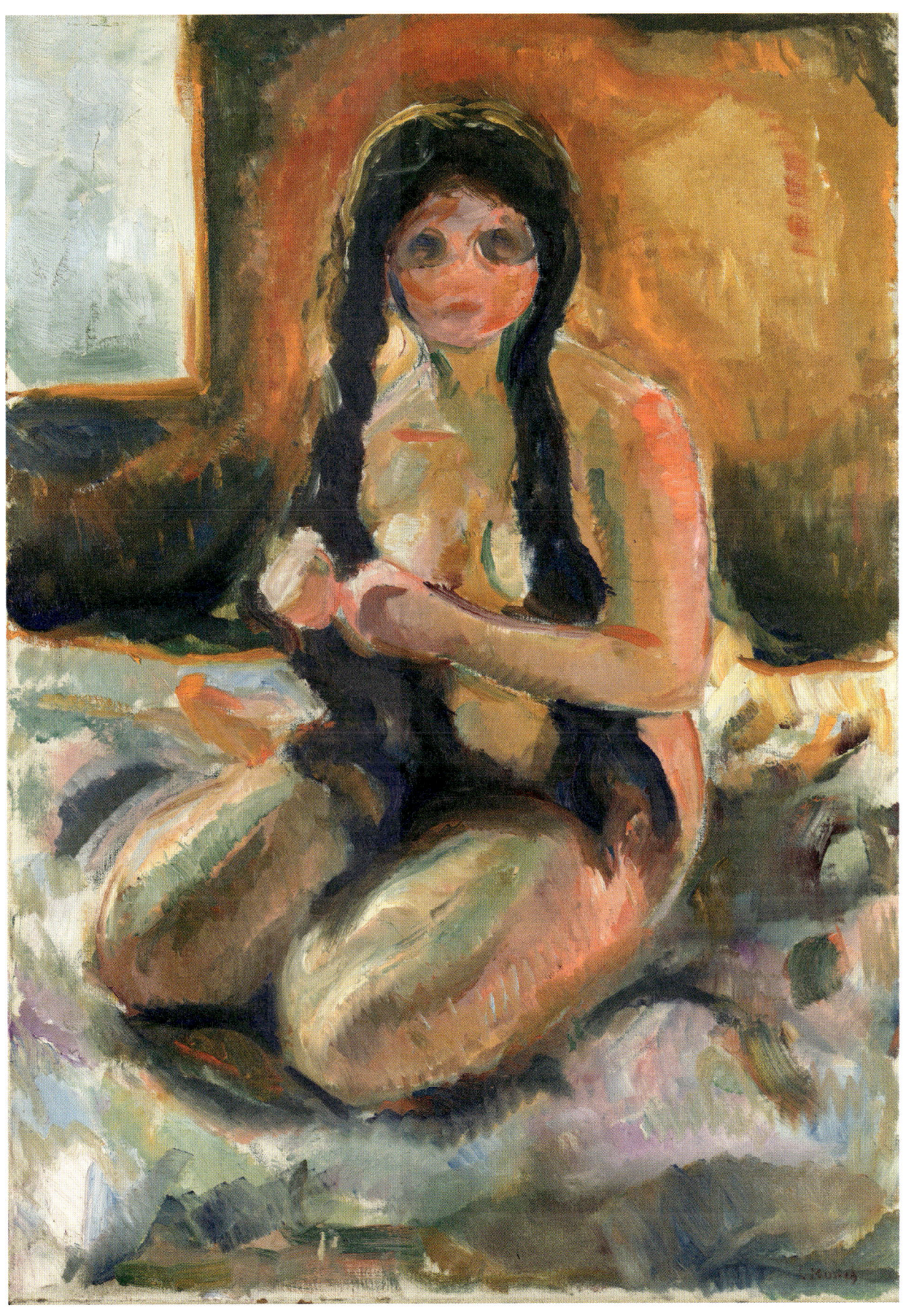

50

Winter on the Fjord, 1915

Vinter ved fjorden

Oil on canvas
103 × 128 cm
Signed l.r. "E Munch 1915"
NG.M.01864
Woll M 1126
NG cat. 1950-1082; 1968-1301; 1992-1864

Other titles: *Snelandskap i Kragerø; Vinter ved kysten; Vinterlandskap fra Kragerø*. **Provenance**: Gift from Charlotte and Christian Mustad 1937. **Literature**: Thiis 1933, 297; Stang 1977, 220; Fredlund (ed.) 2002, 108–109; Prelinger 2002, 49; Ohlsen 2004, 19; Flaatten 2009, 121; Hamran 2009, 131; Flaatten 2010 B, 341; Grøgaard 2013 A, 352. **Exhibitions**: 1916, Kristiania; 1927, Berlin, no. 170; 1927, Oslo, no. 217; 1954, Venice, no. 33; 1954, Munich–Cologne, no. 84; 1955, Rome, no. 4075; 1959, Vienna, no. 54; 1984, Toronto–Cincinnati, no. 65; 1987, Essen, no. 95; 1987, Zürich, no. 95; 1988, Mannheim, no. 26; 1991, Kristiansand; 2001, Ferrara, no. 65; 2002, Gothenburg no. 38; 2003, Rovereto; 2005, Dortmund–Høvikodden; 2010, Codroipo, no. 121; 2019, Düsseldorf, no. 26.

Munch often painted outdoors, and many of his landscapes are direct responses to the places they depict. Here, it was the hills and rock formations near Kragerø with a view of the fjord that provided the subject matter. The combination of site-specific nature study with a relatively free, expressive idiom is characteristic of many of the landscapes he produced at Kragerø. The stark contrast between the patches of black rock and the white snow produces a graphic effect, which is softened by rich nuances of colour in the snow and the unifying bluish-violet key tone. The vivid light and the use of coarse, heavy brushstrokes signal dynamism and energy, a quality we find in many of Munch's paintings from this period.

Following his convalescence at Dr. Jacobson's private clinic in Denmark from autumn 1908 to spring 1909, Munch returned to Norway. Initially, he set up home at Kragerø, where he rented the Skrubben property. The months he spent there were artistically rewarding. He produced works of renewed vitality and cultivated a growing network of collectors and clients. The period culminates in the decorative paintings for the central hall, the Aula, at the university in Kristiania (Oslo), which he completed in 1916. Both thematically and stylistically, *Winter on the Fjord* can be read in conjunction with that major commission. The contours and shapes of the landscape are echoed in several of the Aula paintings, including *Solen* (The Sun).

During the period 1909–1916, Munch produced a number of comparable winter landscapes while staying either at Kragerø or at Hvitsten deeper into the fjord on the opposite shore. This painting is one of several such pictures from 1915, the last year he stayed at Kragerø. Two works from the same year can be related to this one (Woll M 1125; Woll M 1127).

This is the only landscape painting from Kragerø in the National Museum's collection. It was gifted to the National Gallery by Charlotte and Christian Mustad in 1937. ØU

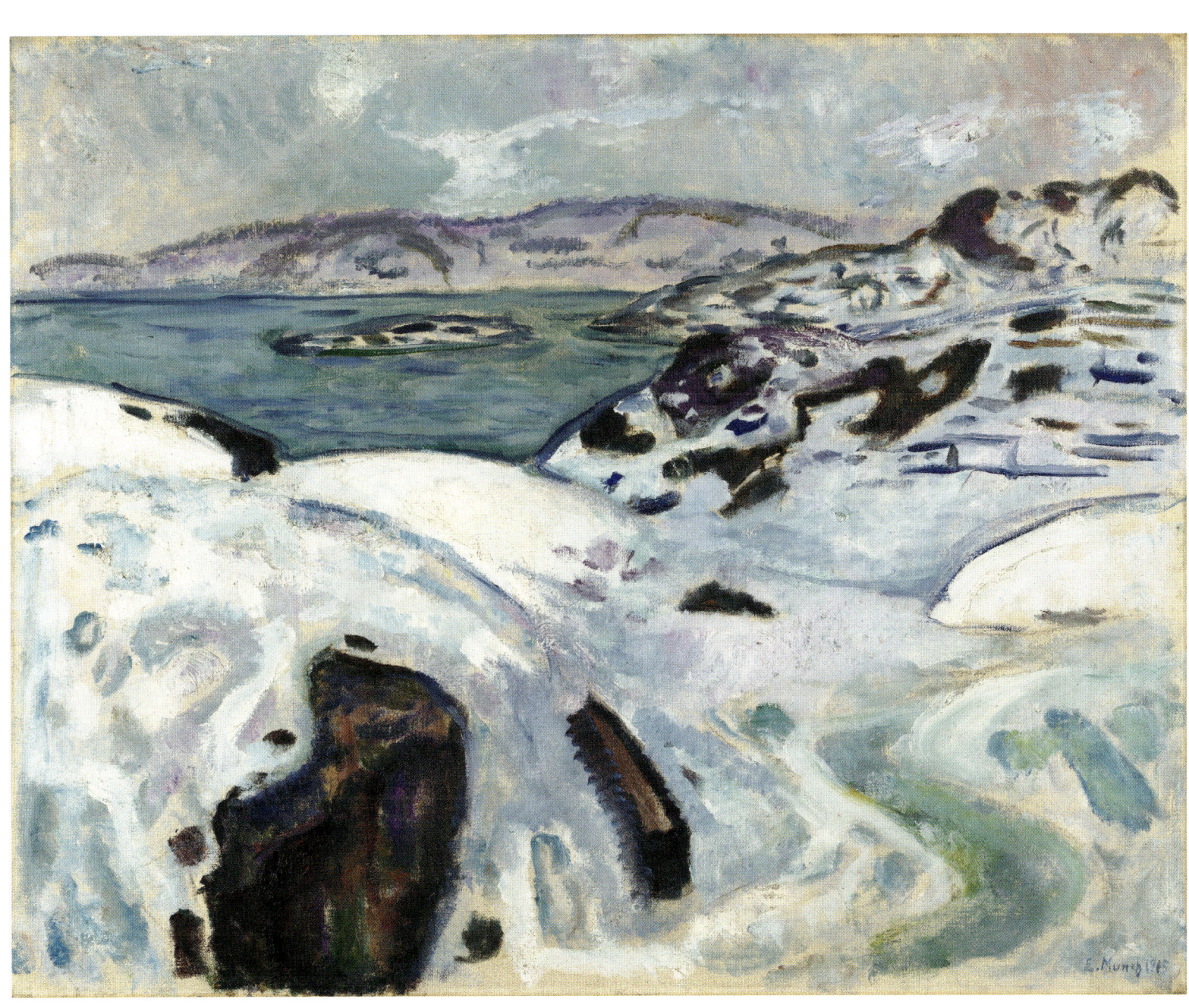

51

Midsummer, 1915

Høysommer

Oil on canvas
150.5 × 151 cm
Signed l.r. "E Munch 1915"
NG.M.01159
Woll M 1158
NG cat. 1933-965; 1950-1081; 1968-1300; 1992-1159

Other titles: *Sommer*; *Badende kvinner*; *Høisommer, badende kvinner*. **Provenance**: Gift from Olaf Schou 1915. **Literature**: Glaser 1917, 194; Thiis 1933, 311; Gauguin 1933, 241-242; Eggum 1988, 34-37; Buchholz (ed.) 2001, bd. 2, 223; Flaatten 2013 B, 95; Flaatten 2016, 8, 9, 134f., 215. **Exhibitions**: 1915, Kristiania, no. 2; 1915, Copenhagen, no. 272; 1927, Oslo, no. 219; 1972, Kristiansand, no. 49; 1981, Tokyo–Sapporo–Nara–Nagoya–Leningrad–Moscow, no. 205/193; 1983, Dresden, no. 29; 1985, Milan–Rome, no. 64; 1987, Barcelona, no. 42; 1987, Oslo B, no. 67; 2001, Darmstadt, no. 4.14; 2005, Oslo; 2013, Oslo, no. 178.

Munch's interest in the theme of bathers can be traced back to the 1890s and paintings such as *Bathing Boys* (cat. 28). But it was in the early years of the new century that naked people bathing and soaking up the summer sun in outdoor settings became a focal concern generating many variations. Several works that Munch produced at Warnemünde on the Baltic Sea in north Germany during the summers of 1907 and 1908 seem to have encouraged this interest. Pictures such as *Midsummer* and *Bathing Man* (1918, cat. 54) illustrate how Munch developed the theme, although they also represent a continuation of his enduring preoccupation with the nude as such.

In *Midsummer* it is the female body that predominates. Six naked figures are spread out seemingly at random on the rocks beside the sea – sitting, lying, standing. The bodies interact with the warm rocks, or seem to grow from them. The work is loosely composed around a triangular structure, which converges on one figure standing vertically on the central axis. A lush green area in the foreground contrasts with the warmer tones of the middle ground and the sparkling blue of the sea beyond, and the green-tinged hills on the far side of the fjord.

The work was painted at Hvitsten in 1915. In November 1910, Munch bought Nedre Ramme, a property in this village on the eastern shore of the Oslo Fjord. The location in the painting has been identified as a section of rocky shoreline just below the main house, while the models were probably Ingeborg Kaurin and her sister Solveig (Thiis 1933; Gauguin 1933; Flaatten 2016). The former worked frequently as a model around this time and is the subject of many nude paintings. Munch often came to Nedre Ramme to work and stay, not just during the summers, but also in the winter months. It was here that he produced several of the large canvases for the central hall, or Aula, at the university in Kristiania (Oslo). The property was sold after Munch's death in 1944.

The picture is a good example of Munch's artistic renewal in the early decades of the 20th century. The theme and idiom reflect the popularity in that period of vitalistic ideas, which celebrated outdoor activity, sports, health and body culture as expressions of a life-affirming attitude. Sunbathing was perceived as especially beneficial for health and well-being.

The painting was acquired by Olaf Schou from Munch's 1915 exhibition in Kristiania (Oslo) and immediately donated to the National Gallery. Munch produced another slightly smaller version of the same scene, probably around the same time (Woll M 1157). There are also several related, colour woodcuts with people sunbathing on the rocks from the same year (*Solbad I* (Sunbathing I) and *Solbad II* (Sunbathing II), 1915, Woll G 536; Woll G 537). øu

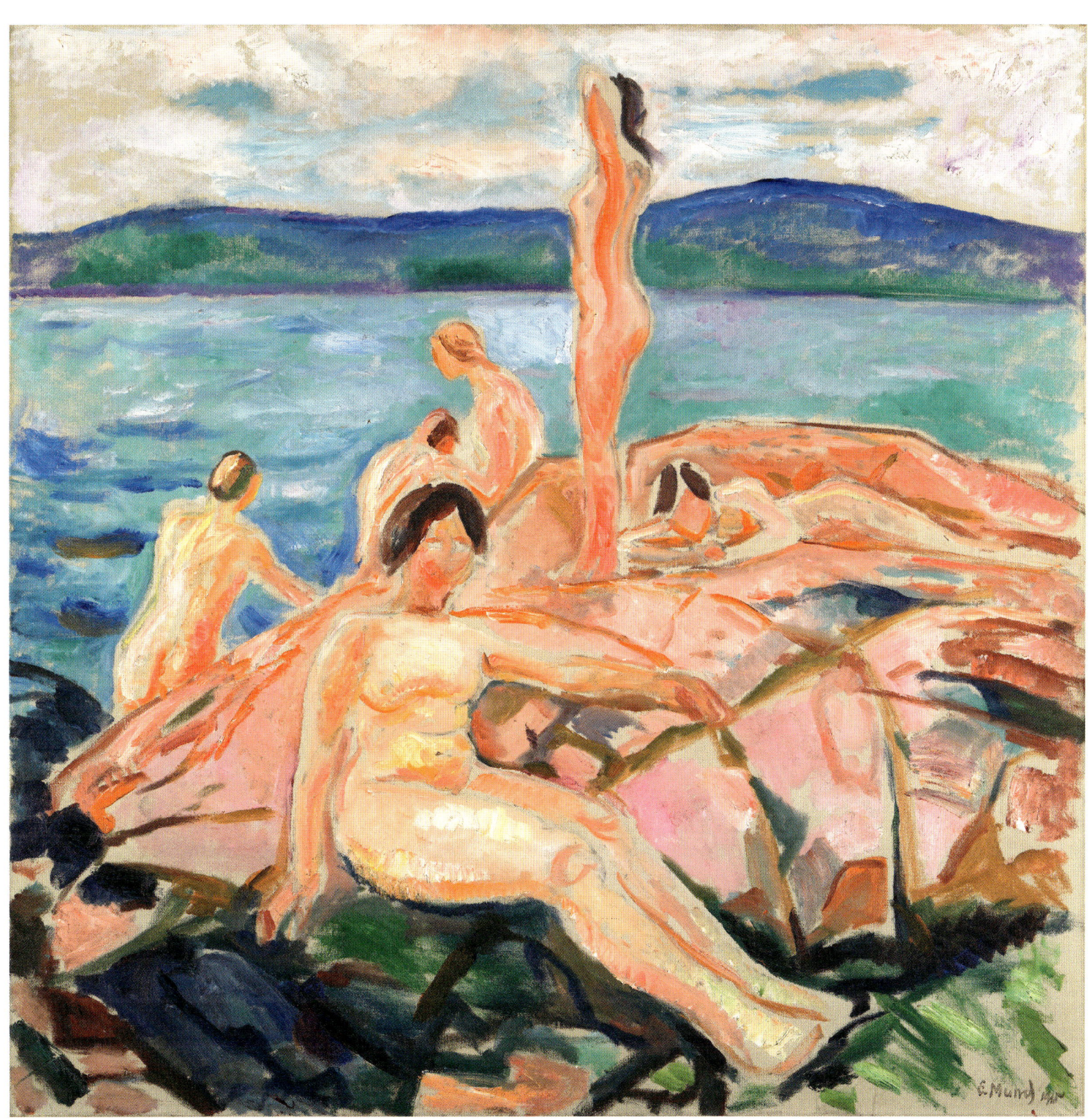

52

Man in the Cabbage Field, 1916

Mannen i kålåkeren

Oil on canvas
136 × 180 cm
Signed l.l. "E Munch 1916"
NG.M.01865
Woll M 1195
NG cat. 1950-1083; 1968-1302; 1992-1865

Provenance: Charlotte and Christian Mustad (before 1919-1937); gift from Charlotte and Christian Mustad 1937. **Literature**: Thiis 1933, 313-314; Gauguin 1933, 249-250; Stang 1977, 258-259; Skedsmo (ed.) 1981, 96-98; Bøe 1992, 54; Woll 1993, 76; Eggum 1998 B, 13, 61; Pettersen 1998, 126; Prelinger 2002, 53, 63; Körber 2006 A, 169; Clarke 2013, 58; Flaatten 2013 B, 97; Clarke 2014, 61; Flaatten 2014 A, 266; Stein and Rød 2015, 269 (note 41); Gjessing 2016, 38, 42; Ustvedt 2018, 159-160. **Exhibitions**: 1917, Copenhagen, no. 23; 1918, Kristiania, no. 31; 1919, Kristiania A; 1922, Zürich, no. 52; 1922, Bern-Basel, no. 47/45; 1923, Gothenburg, no. 193; 1927, Berlin, no. 172; 1927, Oslo, no. 222; 1931, Budapest-Vienna, no. 67/56; 1952, Zürich, no. 59; 1952, Brussels, no. 17; 1965, New York B, no. 59; 1970, Japan, touring exhibition, no. 27; 1993, Lillehammer, no. 45; 1998, Paris, no. 123; 1998, Oslo, no. 80; 1999, Florence, no. 16; 2013, Oslo, no. 182; 2016, Oslo, no. 86.

The painting of the farmer standing upright against an open agricultural landscape, his arms laden with the produce of the field, is one of the best known and most widely discussed of Munch's later works, created after he moved back to Norway in 1909. It was painted in the same year as he completed the major commission to decorate the Aula, or central hall, of the university in Kristiania (Oslo). In its simple, monumental composition, its use of bright colours and occasional pastose brushwork, the painting has much in common with the large Aula paintings.

The picture was probably one of the first Munch created after moving to Ekely, the property on the outskirts of Kristiania that he bought in the spring of 1916 (Thiis 1933; Gauguin 1933). Depictions of ordinary people at work or in everyday situations had long been a central item in his repertoire of themes. It was a focus that became more pronounced during the period he spent in Warnemünde, but it was only after his return to Norway that he began to paint straightforward scenes of farming life. Munch had begun exploring the subject matter during his stays at Hvitsten, Kragerø and Moss. But it was during the early months at Ekely that the genre became central to his art.

In essence, the picture is a monumental triangular composition. The lines of the landscape meet in the man's embrace, while his undefined face stands out in silhouette against the paler sky. The lush green tones of the foreground with its patches of blue and the predominantly red and orange tones of the middle ground indicate Munch's shift towards more vivid colours in the early 1900s. The figure and the landscape are rendered with a similar use of the brush, their forms merging with one another in a way that suggests a close connection between the farmer and the landscape. The blue clothes make the figure stand out, reinforcing the farmer's status as an everyday hero. In older traditions of European painting, blue was often used to signal holy or heroic qualities.

The work reflects the vitalist philosophy of the early 20th century, with its emphasis on the generative, life-affirming aspects of life. Fertility, germination and growth, sun, health and outdoor activities were dominant themes in much of the pioneering literature, philosophy and visual arts of the day, as well as in contemporary lifestyles. The painting has often been viewed in connection with Knut Hamsun's Nobel Prize-winning novel *Growth of the Soil*, which was published in 1917, the year after Munch painted the picture. In relation to Munch's earlier work, this turn towards agricultural themes can be understood as a reaction to the industrialisation, urbanisation and increased alienation that were all part of the modernisation process.

In the decades after it was painted, the work featured in most of Munch's major exhibitions around Europe. In 1943, he produced a slightly smaller version (Woll M 1788). The National Museum's version was part of the donation that Charlotte and Christian Mustad made to the National Gallery in 1937. ØU

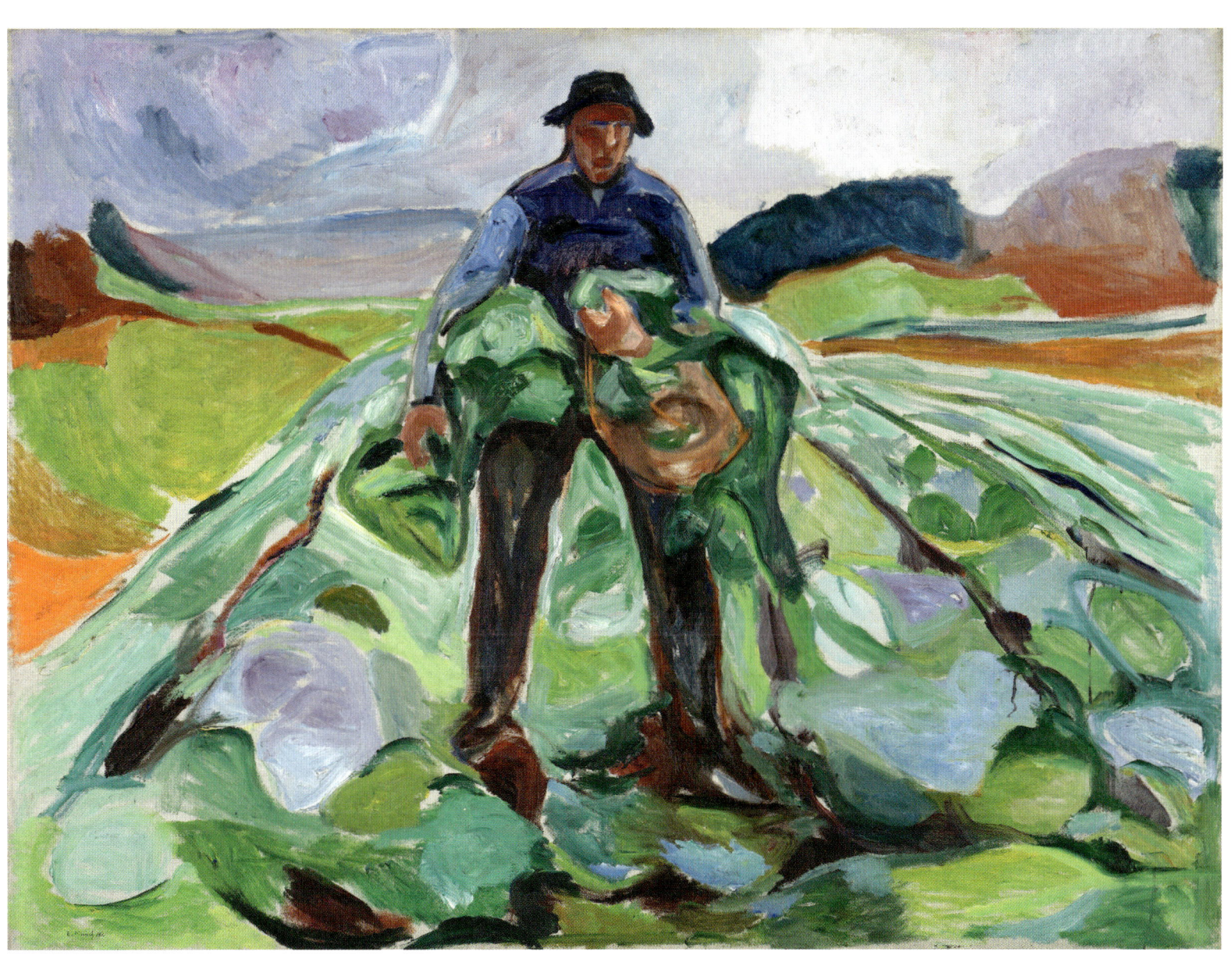

Oil on canvas
200 × 120 cm
Signed u.r. "E Munch 1918"
NG.M.02080
Woll M 1256
NG cat. 1950-1085; 1968-1304; 1992-2080

Other titles: *Portræt av Amtmann L (1)*; *Amt-mand Løchen*; *Fylkesmann Torvald Løchen*.
Provenance: Ingeborg and Thorvald Løchen (1917-1946); bequeathed by Ingeborg and Thorvald Løchen 1946. **Literature**: Løchen 1946, 64; Eggum 1994 A, 193f. **Exhibitions**: 1918, Kristiania, no. 11.

While the composition, colour scheme and painterly execution of this work are all typical of Munch's later full-length portraits, the treatment of space and the posture are unusual. The tilting of the floor creates a dramatic effect that is reinforced by the picture's vertical divisions. This and the suggestion in the figure of active movement indicate a willingness to try out new solutions within an established form. The hand holding the cigarette seems to allude to Munch's earlier *Self-Portrait with Cigarette* and the portrait *The Frenchman* (cat. 32 and cat. 46). It suggests sympathy for the bohemian lifestyle.

Munch worked with the full-length portrait throughout his career. The painting of Løchen belongs to a phase when Munch was receiving an increasing number of commissions from well-situated Norwegians: politicians, lawyers, doctors and people in the public sphere. This work was commissioned by Thorvald Løchen, who at that point was governor of the county of Nordre Trondhjem (from 1902). Løchen's wife, Ingeborg Motzfeldt Løchen, later wrote an account of her contacts with Munch, in which she states that it was she who initiated the commission (Løchen 1946). The order was confirmed by Løchen in a letter from 1917 (MM K 671). On this basis, the painting is dated to 1917 (Woll M 1256), although the signature says 1918. In this case, however, there is no reason to reassess the signature. One of Munch's friends, the doctor and politician Karl Wefring, mentions the work in a letter dated 1918: "Have been down to Hamar to look at your picture of Thorvald Løchen. He made the right choice in my opinion, and they are very pleased with the picture. They also have the satisfaction that the art connoisseurs do not snort at it" (1918, letter, MM K 1214).

Thorvald Løchen (1861–1943) had studied law and could already look back on a long career in the civil service when the painting was done. In 1916 he became county governor in Hedmark. He became acquainted with Munch in the 1880s via his brother, the painter and actor Kalle Løchen (1865–1893), a close colleague and friend of Munch from his student years in Kristiania. An unsigned version of the painting is now in the Munch Museum, as is another portrait of the same person (1917, Woll M 1254; Woll M 1255).

The work was bequeathed to the museum by Thorvald Løchen and his wife in 1946, together with a painting by Kalle Løchen, *The Studio at Modum* (1883, NG.M.02081). ØU

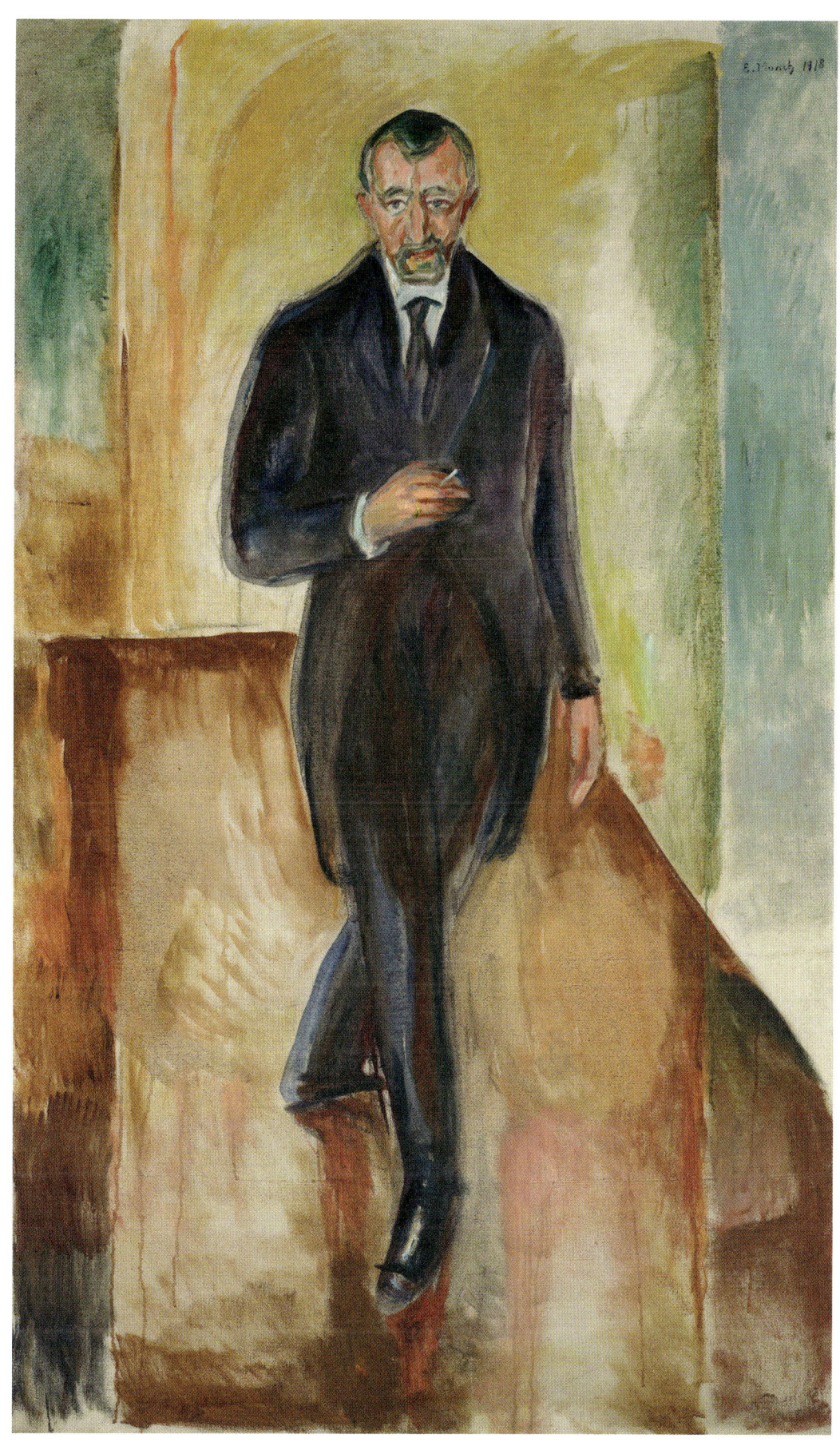

54

Bathing Man, 1918

Badende mann

Oil on canvas
160 × 110 cm
Unsigned
NG.M.01699
Woll M 1284
NG cat. 1933-966; 1950-1084; 1968-1303; 1992-1699

Other titles: *Badende mand; Badende mand. Høidebilledet.* **Provenance:** Gift from the artist, received 1927. **Literature:** Fredlund (ed.) 2002, 114-115; Stein and Rød 2015, 265; Flaatten 2016, 160, 185, 215; Ustvedt 2016, 77. **Exhibitions:** 1921, Kristiania, no. 31; 1922, Zürich, no. 65; 1922, Bern-Basel, no. 62/60; 1926, Mannheim, nr. 52; 1927, Berlin, no. 178; 1927, Oslo, no. 231; 1954, Venice, no. 35; 1954, Munich-Cologne, no. 87; 1955, Rome (not in catalogue); 1998, Paris, no. 124; 2002, Venice, no. 106; 2002, Gothenburg, no. 41; 2004, Melbourne, no. 5; 2013, Oslo, no. 184; 2016, New York, no. 22; 2016, Oslo, no. 88.

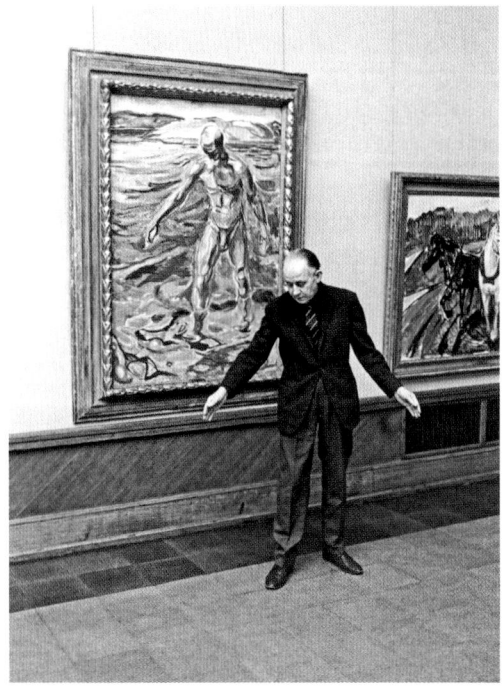

Claude de Beriot modelled for numerous artists in Norway over a period of more than fifty years. He posed for Gustav Vigeland, Edvard Munch, and life classes at the National Academy of Fine Art. Photographed here in 1968 in front of Munch's painting *Bathing Man*.
Photo: Ivar Aaserud/Aktuell/SCANPIX, 1968

The figure stands with arms held out to the sides, head bent forward, and legs slightly apart. The paint is applied in bold, sweeping curves, in a manner that suggests spontaneity. Colouristically, the yellow-green tones of the body form an effective contrast to the blue-green hues of the water. The depiction of a naked, muscular man in the open air set against the clear, rippling surface of the sea reflects the vitalist current in the art and culture of the day.

Bathing Man was probably painted at Hvitsten. The probable location has been identified as a large bay facing the fjord, not far from the artist's house (Flaatten 2016, 160). In the late autumn of 1910, Munch purchased Nedre Ramme, a property at Hvitsten on the Oslo Fjord. Around 1900, Hvitsten began to gain popularity as a seaside resort, with bathing huts and other sea bathing facilities added to its attractive beaches and rocky shoreline. In a letter to Aunt Karen (Karen Bjølstad), Munch describes the place as "... almost the most beautiful along the entire coast" (MM N 964). The model for *Bathing Man* was Claude Beriot, who had previously modelled for Gustav Vigeland. Beriot was also a dancer, hence his well-trained physique (Flaatten 2016, 160).

Munch's interest in bathers can be traced back to the mid-1890s, as exemplified by the National Museum's *Bathing Boys* from 1894-1895 (cat. 28). Munch's earliest works on this theme show women sunbathing and children playing by the sea. In 1907-1908, during his stay at Warnemünde on the Baltic Sea in north Germany, his approach to the subject changed, becoming more intense. There he produced a number of paintings of tall, naked men on the sunny beach and/or out in the water.

The painting is unsigned and has no date marking, but has been dated on the basis of its similarities to another a work in wider format with the same figure and background, signed 1918 (Woll M 1283). The work was first shown at Munch's 1921 exhibition at Blomqvist in Kristiania. In the late 1920s, Munch painted a further version, this time as one section of a larger, three-part composition with a number of figures (Woll M 1577). He produced a smaller version with the same motif (Woll M 1578). In addition, there is a large, undated drawing of similar composition in the Munch Museum (MM.T.01545). Munch gifted the painting to the National Gallery on the occasion of its major retrospective of his work in 1927 (see Nils Messel's text in this catalogue). The generous gift may have been an attempt to remedy the museum's lack of representative works from Munch's later phase. *Bathing Man* is one of few works by Munch in the National Museum that still has its original frame. With its distinctive gold and blue colouration, which reflect the hues of the body and the sea, it is clear that the frame was conceived together with the painting. wv

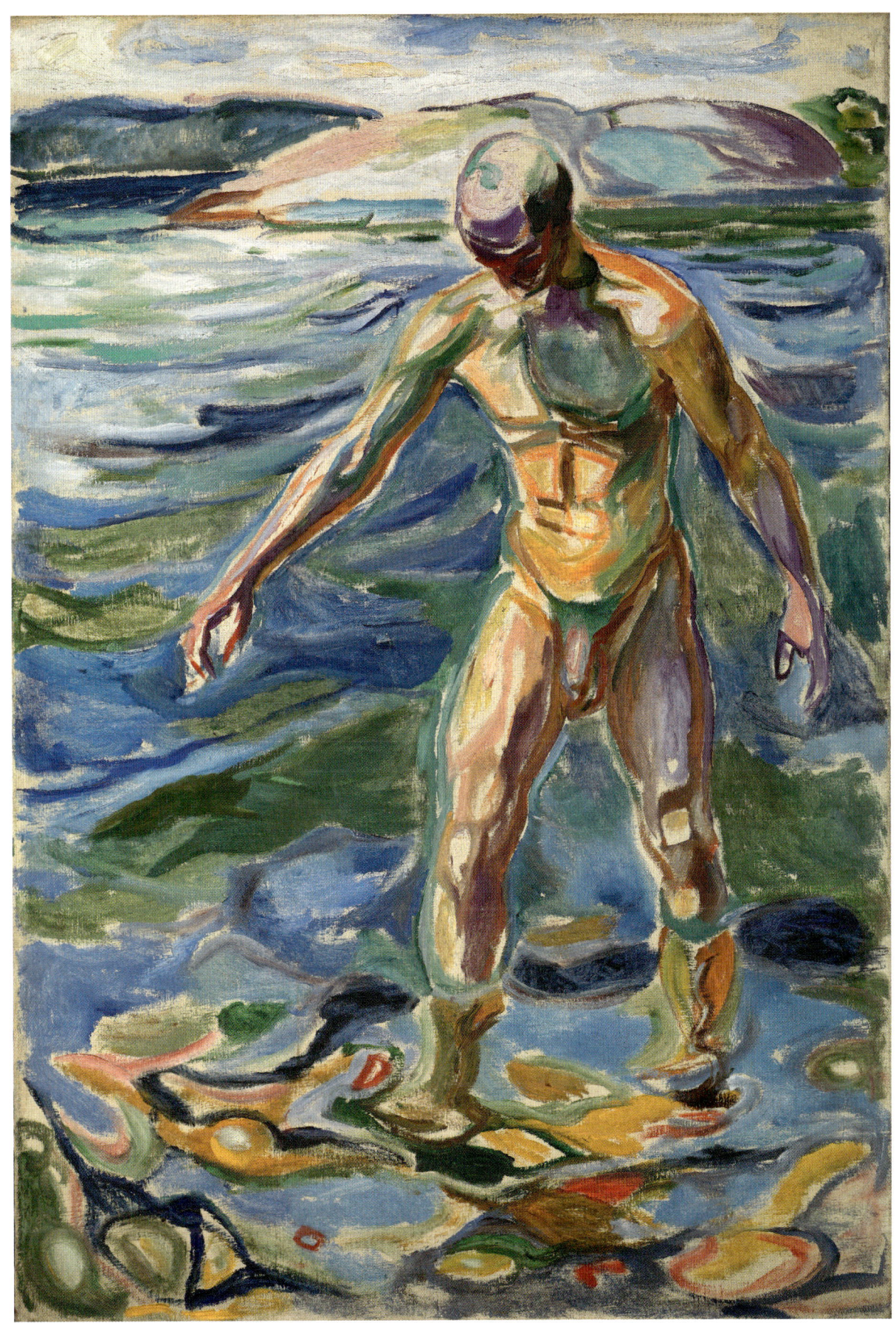

55

Self-Portrait with the Spanish Flu, 1919

Selvportrett i spanskesyken

Oil on canvas
150 × 131 cm
Signed u.l. "Edv. Munch 1919"
NG.M.01867
Woll M 1296
NG cat. 1950-1087; 1968-1306; 1992-1867

Other titles: *Spansk syke*; *Selvportræt i slåbrokk
- Influenza*; *Influensa*. **Provenance**: Charlotte
and Christian Mustad (before1922–1937); gift
from Charlotte and Christian Mustad 1937.
Literature: Thiis 1933, 316; Gauguin 1946 A, 272;
Deknatel 1950, 59; Jedlicka 1958, 244f.; Bruno
1985, 4; Lange 2002, 14–15; Prelinger 2002, 68f.;
Müller-Westermann 2005, 136–140; Junillon
2009, 99; Chang 2010, 150, 204–205; Bischoff
2011, 88; Goldberg 2011, 47; Müller-Westermann
2012, 285f., 290; Grøgaard 2013 A, 352; Steihaug
2013 A, 19–20, 22; Endresen 2015, 28; Berman
2016, 92; Ravenal 2016, 80; Steihaug 2016, 19;
Jacob 2017, 171; Ustvedt 2018, 166; Johannesen
2019, 47. **Exhibitions**: 1919, Kristiania B, no.
34; 1922, Zürich, no. 62; 1922, Bern-Basel, no.
57/55; 1923, Gothenburg, no. 196; 1927, Berlin, no.
179; 1927, Oslo, no. 234; 1934, Copenhagen, no.
70; 1950, USA, touring exhibition, no. 53; 1951,
Brighton-Glasgow-London-The Hague-Paris, no.
51/53; 1952, Zürich, no. 65; 1952, Brussels, no. 19;
1954, Venice, no. 37; 1954, Munich-Cologne, no.
89; 1955, Rome, (not in catalogue); 1998, Paris, no.
126; 1999, Florence, no. 17; 2003, Basel; 2005, Oslo
B; 2005, Rome, no. 46; 2011, Paris-London-Frank-
furt-Oslo, no. 135; 2013, Oslo, no. 185; 2017, San
Francisco-New York-Oslo, no. 35.

The artist who faces us here is clearly worn out, yet the manner in which he is painted suggests vitality and energy. The figure, the chair and the sickbed are rendered with bold colour fields and large, sweeping lines. The dominant tones are yellow, green and brown, with interpolations of red and blue. The details are toned down, but the shape and position of the head and its open mouth seem to allude to the face in the artist's own painting *The Scream* from 1893 (cat. 23).

Around the turn of the year 1918-1919, Munch fell ill, possibly with the Spanish flu, a pandemic that killed many millions of people across Europe in the years 1917-1920. In a series of studies, sketches and paintings, Munch documented the impact the illness had on him in its various stages. With its focus on sickness and convalescence, the painting evokes human vulnerability and mortality, themes that preoccupied Munch throughout his career. The chair is a recurrent prop in several of his best known depictions of sickness and death, such as *Spring* and *Death in the Sickroom* (cat. 12 and cat. 22).

Ageing and change are aspects of life Munch addresses in many of his late self-portraits. The reference in the title to the Spanish flu reinforces the idea of disease as existentially life-threatening. Close contact with serious illness and death had been a feature of Munch's younger years, forming a theme he explored in works such as *The Sick Child* and *Spring* (cat. 8 and cat. 12). In many of his surviving letters, Munch often expresses a fear of illness and worries about his own health. In recent years, however, it has been questioned whether Munch did in fact catch the Spanish flu in 1919, or whether the painting should rather be viewed as a deliberate dramatisation (Steihaug 2013 A).

The work is the latest of four painted self-portraits by Munch in the National Museum's collection (cat. 9; cat. 32; cat. 47; cat. 55). It belongs to a late phase in his production and was painted a few years after he settled at Ekely, on the western outskirts of Kristiania (today within Oslo). The large format of the work, its broad painterly register and powerfully expressive quality are typical of his portrait art in the first decades of the new century. Also characteristic is the concise style with bold colours, a shallow pictorial space and the sweeping brushstrokes.

This is one of Munch's largest and most monumentally conceived self-portraits. An undated sketch in red crayon probably served as a preliminary study (MM.T.00218-11 verso). There also exist several loosely related drawings and two smaller works, but in these the subject is differently framed (Woll M 1295; Woll M 1297).

Together with works such as *Man in the Cabbage Field* and *Autumn Ploughing* (cat. 52 and cat. 56), the painting has assumed a prominent place in the museum's presentation of the later phase of Munch's production. It was gifted to the National Gallery by Charlotte and Christian Mustad in connection with the museum's 100th anniversary in 1937. ØU

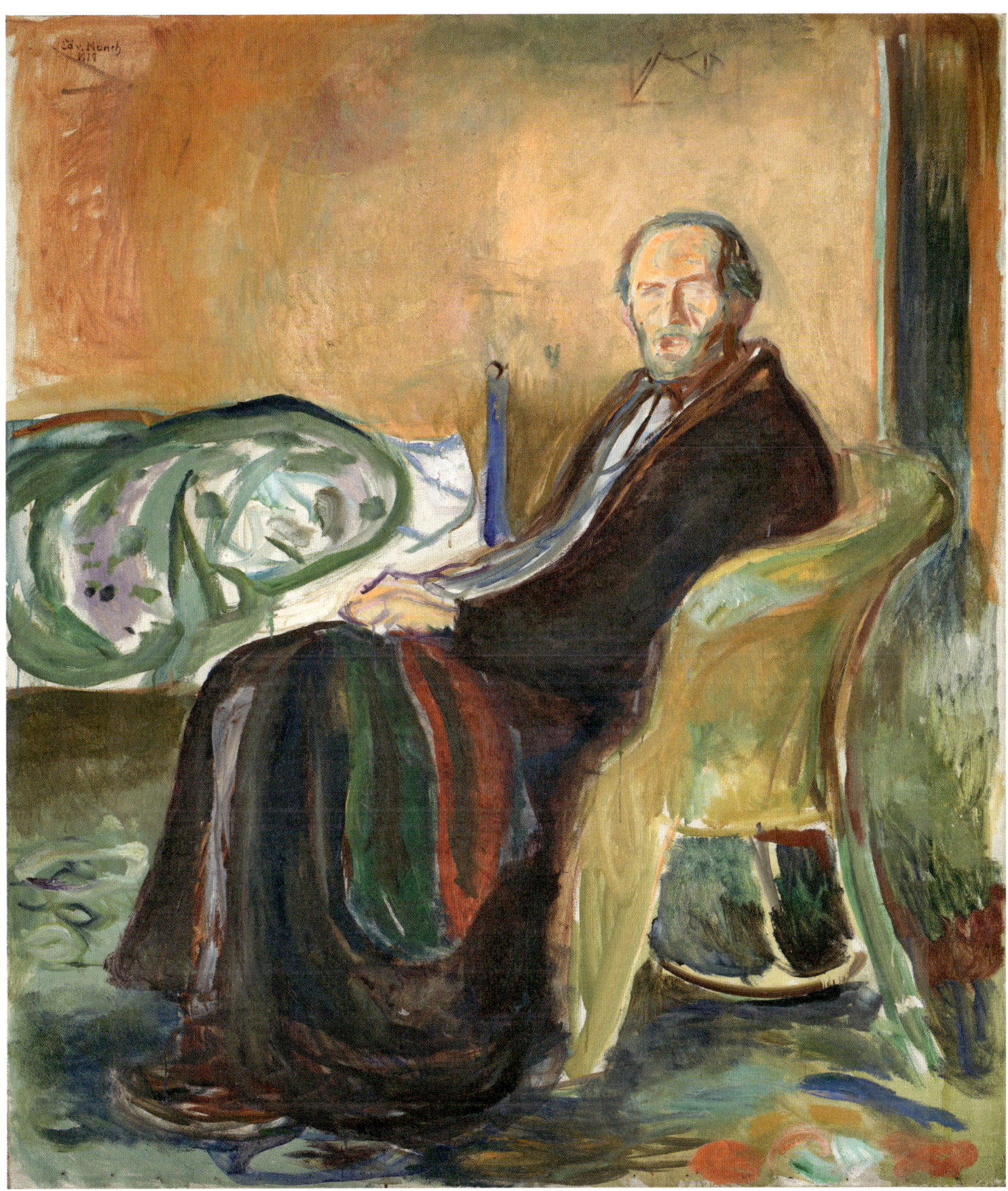

56

Autumn Ploughing, 1919

Høstpløying

Oil on canvas
110.5 × 145.5 cm
Signed l.r. "E Munch 1919"
NG.M.01863
Woll M 1341
NG cat. 1950-1086; 1968-1305; 1992-1863

Other titles: *Hestene*; *Hestespann*; *Pløyende hester*. **Provenance:** Charlotte and Christian Mustad (before 1923-1937); gift from Charlotte and Christian Mustad 1937. **Literature:** Stang 1977, 259-260. **Exhibitions:** 1919, Kristiania B, no. 12; 1923, Gothenburg, no. 194; 1952, Brussels, no. 18; 1958, Bern, no. 77; 1964, Kiel, no. 65; 1983, Dresden, no. 31.

In the spring of 1909, after an eight-month period of convalescence at Dr. Jacobson's clinic in Copenhagen, Munch returned to Norway. Over the following years, he moved between several homes - at Kragerø, Hvitsten, Jeløy - all of them in rural surroundings. Landscapes and farms with labourers and animals established themselves as a new theme in his paintings. In 1916, he bought Ekely, a property on the outskirts of Kristiania with a vegetable garden, orchard and fields. It was here he would live and work for the rest of his life. Munch was fond of animals and eventually kept chickens, cows, pigs, horses, and dogs at Ekely. Horses became particularly important as subject matter. *Autumn Ploughing* is one of the more imposing works in this thematic group and, like the better known *Man in the Cabbage Field* (cat. 52), effuses qualities of vitality and physical strength. Common to both pictures is the combination of a spontaneous moment with a monumentally conceived composition. The difference in size between the horses and the farmer following the plough creates an impression of significant depth. Broad curving brushstrokes converge on a point somewhere behind the horses and the farmer. The landscape is built up from clear, distinct colour fields, forming an overall scene that is notable for its rich and varied palette. At a time when many of Munch's continental artist colleagues were interested in representing the dynamism of modern life, the industry of the machine age, and the bustle of the metropolis, Munch chose to concentrate on the forces of nature. Here it is the sturdy strength and energy of the horses that dominates. But far from being a nostalgic depiction of some rural idyll, *Autumn Ploughing* has all the markings of a directly observed scene from everyday life.

It is said that Munch loved his horses, and that some of his last articulated thoughts were concerned with the care of his horse Rousseau, who had been his model for many years (Stang 1977). Horses were working animals not just for the farmer, but also for the artist. Among the notes in Munch's literary estate, we find a draft letter addressed to the Norwegian tax authorities, in which he argues for tax deductions to compensate his expenses in maintaining a horse as a model:

> Expenses for my white horse [...] 600 kr. This horse I keep exclusively for use as a model since it can be used for little else. It is very important for my painting, and pictures of it can be found in large collections such as e.g. the Münchener Statsgalleri, and it has brought in a lot of money to the tax authority and will continue to do so - (undated note, MM N 3597)

The painting was gifted to the museum by Charlotte and Christian Mustad in 1937. For many years it was known by the title *Hestespann* (Horse Team), but this has since been revised to *Autumn Ploughing* (Woll 2008 B), which was also the title it had when first exhibited at Blomqvist in 1919. Produced at Ekely, there exist three closely related paintings from the same year (Woll M 1342; Woll M 1343; Woll M 1344). VWH

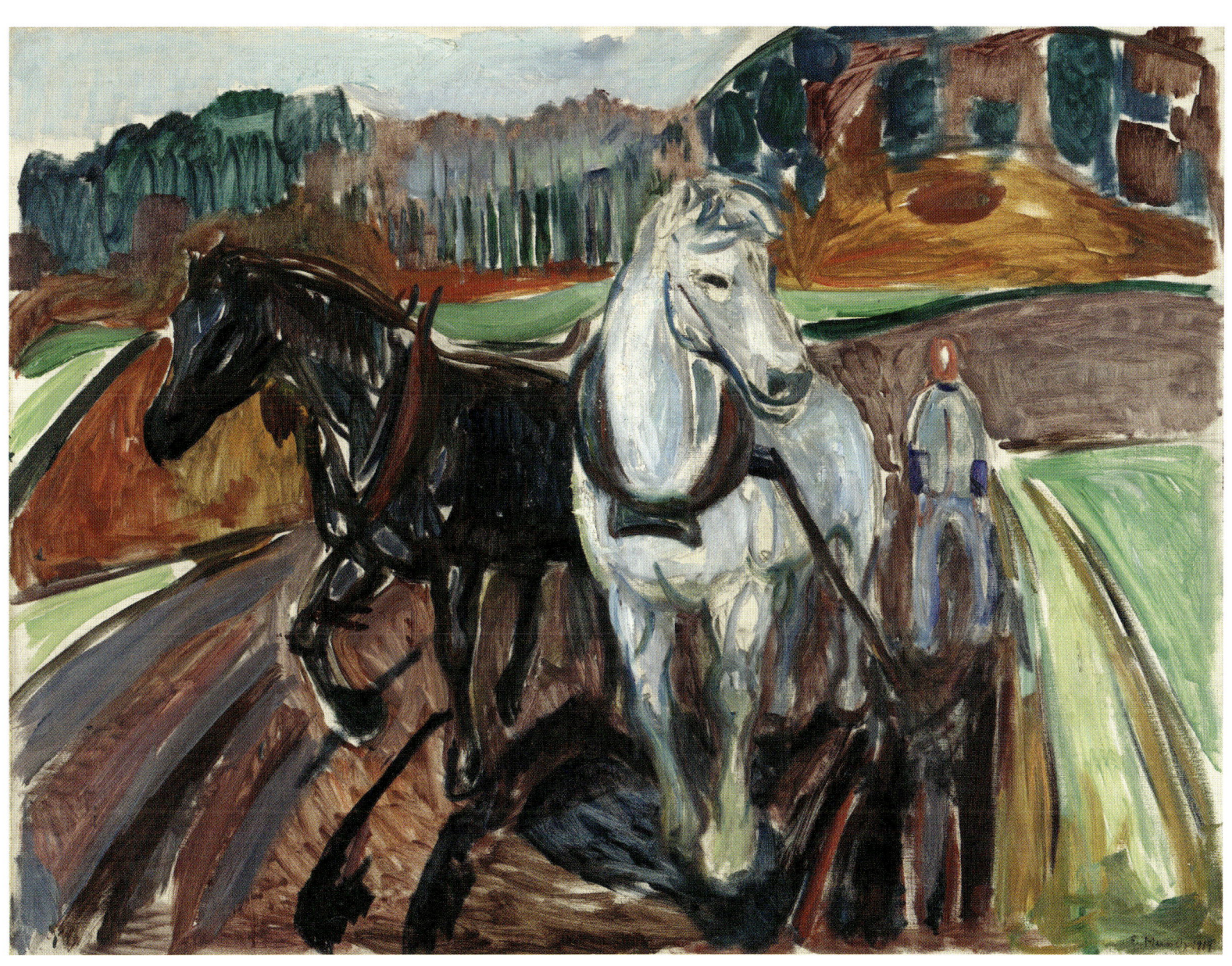

57

Workers Returning Home, 1920

Arbeidere på hjemvei

Oil on canvas
79.5 × 138.5 cm
Signed l.r. "E Munch 1920"
NG.M.02819
Woll M 1361
NG cat. 1992-2819

Other titles: *Arbeidere*; *Arbeidere fra fabrikken*; *Hjemvendende arbeidere*. **Provenance**: Charlotte and Christian Mustad (before 1927-1959/1970); bequeathed by Charlotte and Christian Mustad 1959, received 1970. **Literature**: Woll 1993, 81; Woll 1998 A, 99; Woll 2012, 231. **Exhibitions**: 1921, Kristiania, no. 15; 1926, Munich, no. 2244; 1926, Mannheim, no. 53; 1927, Berlin, no. 183; 1927, Oslo, no. 241; 1929, Kiel, no. 179; 1977, Stockholm, no. 161; 1977, Oslo; 1978, Hamburg-Stuttgart-Berlin-Frankfurt, no. 58; 1980, Liège; 1983, Dresden, no. 32; 1984, Newcastle-London-Edinburgh-Belfast-Liverpool-Dublin, no. 58; 1988, Humlebæk, no. 45; 1989, Dal; 1993, Lillehammer, no. 34; 2007, Tokyo–Kobe, no. 98.

The picture probably shows a view of the Eureka Mekaniske Verksted, a factory at Skøyen, near Munch's home at Ekely (Woll 2008 B, 1232). Manual labourers became a central theme of Munch's art from around 1910. He depicted workers from shipping, forestry, agriculture and manufacturing industries, and even those who helped to build his studio at Ekely. He developed plans for a monumental frieze on the theme of manual labour for Oslo City Hall, also called the Oslo Frieze (Woll 1993, 99). Although the work was never realised, his sketches and studies reveal his vision, and the theme is thoroughly discussed by Gerd Woll (Woll 1993). Munch first addressed this theme in 1909, having just moved to Kragerø after many years abroad (Woll M 873; Woll M 874; Woll M 876; Woll M 877). It was an interest he pursued during the period he lived at Jeløy near Moss, where he frequently encountered local factory workers.

After moving to the property he had bought at Ekely in 1916, Munch found new material for his series on labourers, including the scene depicted here. A mass of people trudges forward towards the viewer, some in black, others in paler clothes. In the background stands the factory with its tall chimney stack, which is balanced in the picture by an electrical pylon to the left. Munch has chosen to set the workers in a snow-covered winter landscape. With rapid brushstrokes, he evokes the dynamic of the flowing crowd, the speed and motion of the workers as they head home at the end of their working day. With this work, Munch created an image of modern society at the phase of industrialisation, expansion, and growing solidarity among the working class. In his pictures, he alternates between the themes of actual physical labour and groups of workers on their way home at the end of their shifts. His pictures of smaller towns or forestry work differ from the representations of factories in modern urban centres. One of the art historical precedents for these labourer scenes is the work of Belgian artist Constantin Meunier (1831-1905) and his depictions of miners.

The picture was first shown at an exhibition at Blomqvist in Kristiania in 1921. It also featured in the major 1927 retrospective in Berlin and Oslo. In addition, Munch painted a large watercolour of the same scene (MM.T.01855), and in connection with the commission for Freia Chocolate Factory, it served as the basis for a small preparatory sketch in coloured pencil (MM.T.2025; Woll 2008 B, 1232). The painting entered the museum's collection in 1970 as part of the Charlotte and Christian Mustad bequest. WV

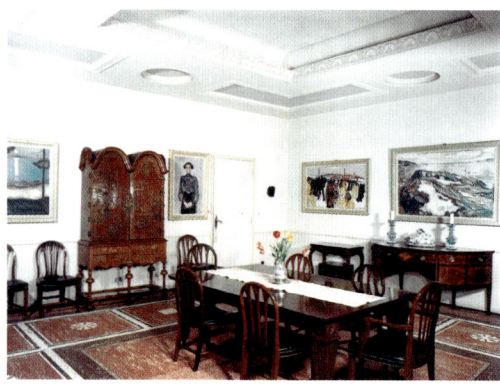

From the home of Charlotte and Christian Mustad in Oslo. Edvard Munch's painting *Workers Returning Home* is seen on the right-hand wall. Photo from the museum's archive.

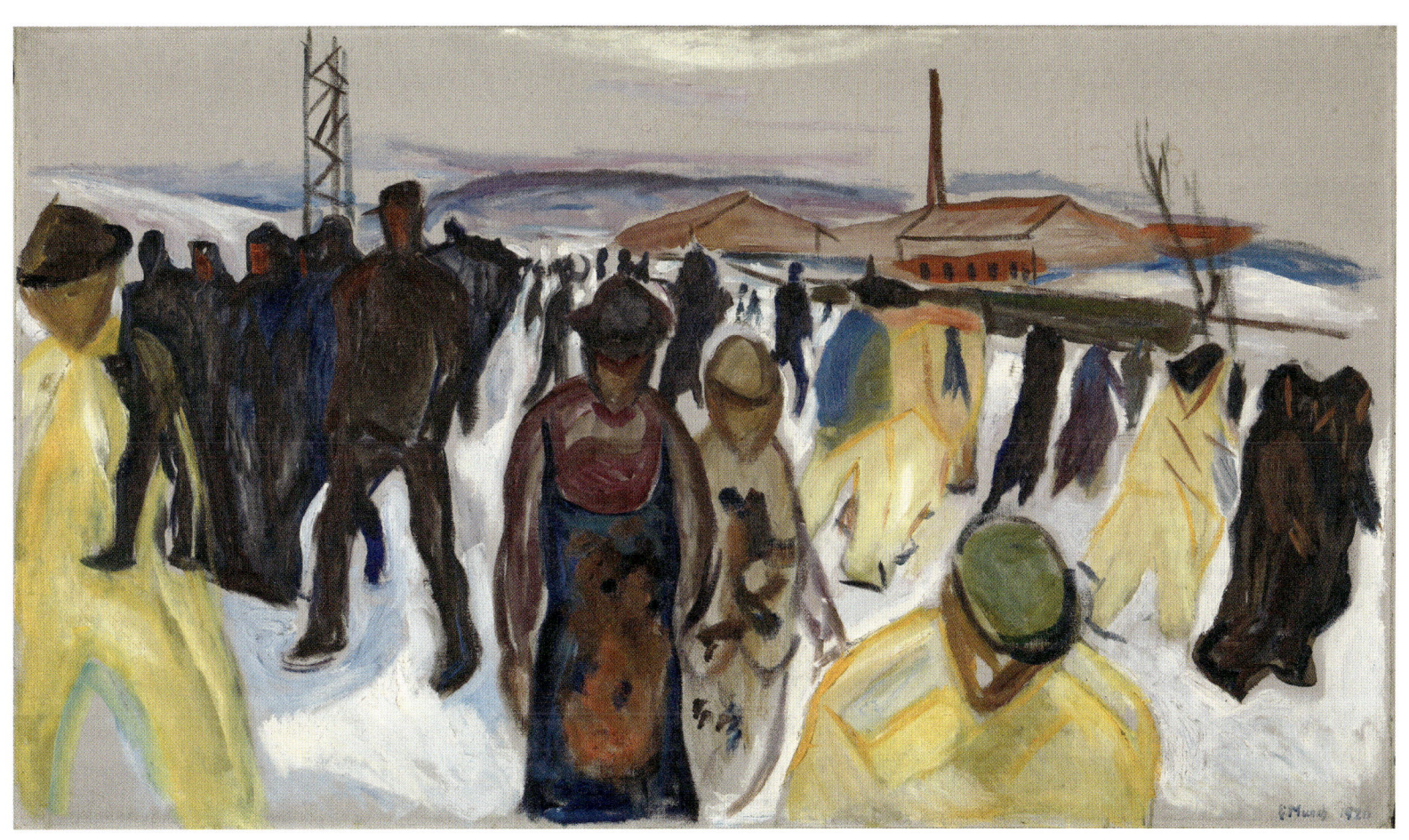

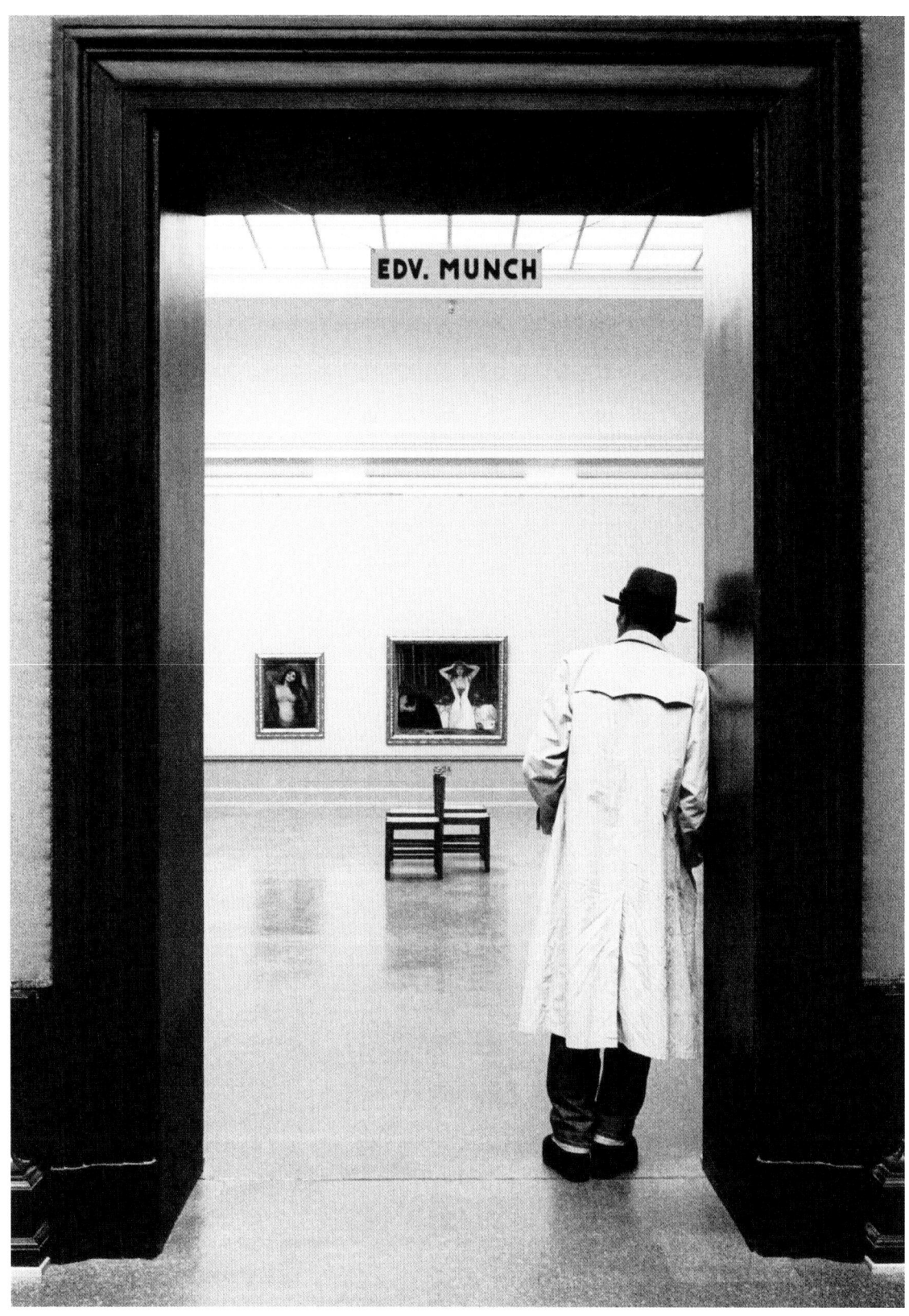

Jamie Parslow: *Joseph Beuys Meets Edvard Munch*, 1982
Photography, 32 × 22 cm
NMK.2018.0391

Prints and drawings

The catalogue is intended primarily as a reference work. Consequently, some information may reoccur in various catalogue entries, since it is intended that each entry should be readable independently of the others.

By and large, the catalogue follows Gerd Woll's 2012 oeuvre catalogue of Munch's graphic works: *Edvard Munch. The Complete Graphic Works*, London: Philip Wilson Publishers 2012 (revised edition of *Edvard Munch. The Complete Graphic Works*, London: Philip Wilson Publishers, 2001), referred to as Woll 2001/2012 or, in the entries, as Woll G. When we diverge from Woll 2012, this is stated. Woll 2012 is in turn based on Gustav Schiefler: *Verzeichnis des graphischen Werks Edvard Munchs bis 1906*, Berlin: Bruno Cassirer, 1907, and *Edvard Munch, Das graphische Werk 1906-1926*, Berlin: Euphorion Verlag, 1928 (Facsimile edition, Oslo: Cappelen, 1974). Divergences from Schiefler's information about printers, dating of matrices are noted, as are interesting differences with regard to titles.

Information on whether an impression is "registered" or "not registered" (alternatively "known" or "unknown") draws on Gerd Woll's study of impressions in connection with the preparation of Woll 2001/2012.

The catalogue's number sequence follows Woll's oeuvre catalogue.

Titles

Many of Munch's graphic works have had different titles at different times. Wherever possible, Woll 2012 adopts the title used by the artist or by his contemporaries (albeit with the addition of I, II etc. when the same title is applied to different works), although the artist himself occasionally used different titles for one and the same work. In the following, alternative titles are only mentioned where they are associated with different interpretations of the motif or are of particular relevance to the respective impression in the National Museum's collection.

Dating

Where we diverge from Schiefler's dating of Munch's treatment of the matrix, this is remarked. Schiefler had first-hand knowledge of Munch's production, and, especially when compiling the first volume (completed in October 1906), he worked closely with the artist. Even so, he was aware that his information about plates and prints was not always correct (cf. the preface to Volume 1, p. IV, and Volume 2, p. 4).

The dating of printing plates is one thing, the dating of the impressions another. Munch was rarely satisfied with restricting the actual printing to a period shortly after working the plate. On the contrary, he often arranged for prints to be pulled from a plate or stone in different sessions, sometimes at intervals of several years and by different printers. In a number of cases, he had in the meantime reworked the matrix, or even supplemented it with additional plates. For this reason, the dating of individual impressions is both important and interesting. But since Munch only rarely dated his impressions, and since the dates he did supply are not always reliable, and since we usually lack any other reliable information as to when different print-runs or versions were produced, the dating of impressions remains a challenging exercise. Reluctant, however, to settle for the usual practice of dating impressions to the same year as the matrix, we have commented on the probable dating of individual impressions, even though this often involves adopting a fairly generous time span from a *terminus ante quem* to a *terminus post quem*.

Dates inscribed on the impression by the artist or printer are listed without parentheses. Dates given by the artist are accepted, despite, as already mentioned, not always being reliable. Dates in parentheses are supplied by the authors, based on various evidence such as type of paper, the quality and condition of the print, and secondary documentation such as exhibition listings, early mentions (e.g. the publication of Schiefler's first volume provides a *terminus ante* or *post quem* for certain impressions; cf. cat. nos. 109, 120, 133, 134, 138, 139, 153 and 157), and just occasionally the impression's provenance.

Technique

Details of technique are based on Woll 2012, supplemented by an examination of the National Museum's impression. Indicated first is the main category of intaglio, lithograph, or woodcut, followed by more specific information such as the possible use of more than one plate and the type of tools used.

Graphic techniques used by Munch:

Intaglio - etching

Ink is transferred from depressions in the printing plate, while in principle the surface of the plate does not transfer any pigment. When the surface of the plate is less than entirely free of ink (intentionally or accidentally), some colour will be transferred to the impression. This is known as plate tone. For his intaglio prints, Munch used plates of copper or zinc. The plate also leaves a physical imprint on the paper, the edge of which is referred to as the plate edge. Intaglio printing requires high pressure and often involves the use of a special press with rollers (cylinder press).

Drypoint: Lines are incised directly into the plate using a hard-tipped needle. The process of incision creates a rough metal edge (burr) on either side of the line. As a result, when printed, the lines appear velvety.

Etching: Acid is used to produce recesses in the plate. The plate is covered with an acid-resistant material (an etching ground); any part of the ground that is removed exposes the underlying metal to the acid and will be etched.

Line etching: The exposed parts are "drawn" into the etching ground with a blunt needle (etching needle). The acid then etches the lines in the metal. The print appears as a line drawing.

Aquatint: An etching technique that uses powdered resin as an acid-resistant material. The acid etches into the metal around the powder grains. The print consists of surfaces with pale spots against a dark ground; gradations of tone can be achieved by regulating the size and dispersal of the grains.

Open bite: Direct etching of the plate's surface without the use of etching ground.

Mezzotint: The plate has a pitted surface, made with a special toothed metal tool or machine; the ink is held by the recesses in the surface. Parts that are subsequently burnished produce expanses that are free of ink (lighter) in the impression. Munch used ready-made (probably sandblasted) zinc plates.

Relief printing

The ink is transferred to the paper from the surface of the matrix, whereas depressions in the plate do not transfer ink. Woodcuts can be printed by hand, e.g. with a roller, or in a press.

Woodcut: Recesses are incised into a woodblock cut along the grain (plank or veneer) using a gouge or knife, or by scratching with a burin. Munch used a variety of wood types.

Lithography

A planographic printing technique that involves drawing or painting onto a lithographic stone (preferably limestone, although Munch also used zinc plates) with a greasy medium (e.g. tusche or crayon), after which the stone is moistened prior to the application of an oil-based ink. The printing ink adheres to the parts that are already greasy. Lithographs are printed on a special, powerful press.

Transfer lithography: The image is executed on a sheet of paper (often specially prepared) before being transferred to the stone. Whereas lithography, intaglio, and relief printing produce inverted images, those of transfer lithography have the same orientation as the original.

Colour printing

In principle, there is one matrix for each colour. Each matrix, carrying the corresponding part of the final image, is inked in its appropriate colour and printed successively on the sheet of paper. Further colours can be created by overprinting. The matrix can also be cut into sections that are then inked with different colours, reassembled, and printed in a single process. This "jigsaw puzzle" method is particularly suited to woodcuts, and Munch is known for his groundbreaking use of it. Munch also sometimes painted different colours directly onto the woodblock (a technique sometimes referred to as mono-printing). The method is not suitable for printing several identical impressions (editions). Munch produced a number of colour mezzotints where different parts of the image were inked using small wads of cloth (à la poupée). The method was often used by professional printers.

Paper

The type of paper influences the character of the print. Different qualities of paper are also sometimes used in connection with marketing strategy (e.g. for more or less exclusive editions of a work). For the printmaker, the choice of paper is therefore significant as both an artistic and a commercial variable. Availability is, of course, a further factor - what the artist or the printer is able to obtain, or already has in stock. This is also true for Munch, who used various types of paper. In some cases, the type of paper can help to determine where, when, and by whom a work was printed (see Woll 2001, p. 4). Identifying paper types can, however, be difficult, not least because we lack a standard terminology and system of categorisation. Nevertheless, and despite deficiencies in our knowledge of the kind of paper Munch used during different periods of production and the associated implications about where, when, and by whom an impression was printed, we have included general information about the type of paper used in each impression.[1]

The principal types that occur in the following are: wove paper, laid paper, Ingres paper, Japan paper, laid Japan paper, imitation Japan paper, China paper and cardboard. As general types, these are relatively easy to identify. The specific quality is harder to determine. Where the general type is given without further specification, the respective quality is "average", i.e. neither particularly heavy, light, nor stiff. For "non-average" qualities, we have used the following categories: for wove paper: lightweight, medium-weight, heavy, stiff, and smooth; for laid paper: medium-weight; for Japan paper: light-weight, medium-weight, and heavy; for laid Japan paper: light-weight and medium-weight; for imitation Japan paper: heavy and medium-weight.

The colour tone of the paper is only mentioned where notably significant.

Dimensions

Dimensions are in mm height × width. For intaglios, dimensions are given both for the plate and for the paper; for lithographs and woodcuts, dimensions are given for the vertical and horizontal axes of largest extent of the image and for the paper. For drawings, dimensions are given for the paper.

Inscriptions

A distinction is made between the artist's inscriptions (including signature and dating) and inscriptions applied by others.

Munch's signature is quoted without further commentary for each impression. It is consistently in pencil and placed to the lower right of the image. Munch's other inscriptions are also in pencil and usually placed together with the signature; where the placing differs, this is mentioned.

On a number of impressions, Munch has written *avant lettre*, an inscription that normally indicates that an impression is without the usual text on a standard edition. It is unclear how Munch intended this inscription.

Inscriptions by O. Felsing are quoted for each impression but not further commented. These are consistently in pencil and placed to the lower left, just below the image.

Secondary inscription on recto is not specified as such. Many impressions have secondary inscriptions in addition to those that are recorded. We have included only those that can be identified with reasonable confidence, are demonstrably informative about the history of the impression, and are not recognisable as the standard inscriptions of museum staff. All inscriptions are, however, registered in a National Museum database. Among those that are not included here are replications of Schiefler's titles, and various numbers and letters whose meaning we have been unable to establish. Several of these inscriptions have features in common that may be significant, despite our own lack of conclusions. We have assumed that in order to make progress in solving these puzzles - as we hope will be possible - mere transcriptions would be of little use and first-hand examination of the originals would be a necessity.

/denotes a new line; //denotes a new inscription

Stamps

Over the years, the National Gallery/the Department of Prints and Drawings has used a number of different collector's stamps. However, these are not reliable as indicators of when a work was acquired, in part because several were used in parallel during the same period, and in part because, in the past, the museum's holdings of graphics and drawings were not stamped and inventoried at the point of acquisition, but in batches later in time. Consequently, these stamps are neither described nor discussed. Other stamps are also ignored, insofar as they do not appear to provide any information relevant to the provenance of an impression or its time of acquisition.

Provenance

Year of acquisition and provenance are known for only a small number of Munch's graphic works (for a discussion of the inventorying and cataloguing of the collection, see p. 33-34). The current state of provenances, based on reliable sources and confident assumptions, is as follows:

In October 1895, the painter Thorolf Holmboe put forward an interesting proposal, unfortunately not pursued, to purchase all the intaglios from Munch's exhibition at Blomqvist (*Morgenbladet*, 16.10.1895), the first presentation of his prints in Norway.

In 1898/1899, 31 intaglios and lithographs were acquired. Sigurd Willoch mentions this in his *Nasjonalgalleriet gjennem hundre år* (The National Gallery through a hundred years) (Oslo: Gyldendal, 1937, p. 107), where he adds: "At that time they were being sold at ten kroner each!". The information has only recently been verified.[2] Apart from one probable identification (*Harpy*, cat. 61), it has not been possible to establish which works were involved. An undated letter from Munch to Fredrik Gundersen, in which *Harpy* is mentioned (copy in the Munch Museum, eMunch PN 787), indicates that the works were bought from the artist. A search in the National Museum's archives did not bring to light either the letter or any documentation of the payment. For some forty of the impressions in the collection, which with varying degrees of confidence can be dated to 1898 or earlier, the provenance is unknown. Since the impressions in the 1898/1899 acquisition were probably bought from Munch himself, in other words, they had not been in circulation, we looked for impressions without secondary inscriptions. Only 25 of the works in question dated prior to 1898, are without such inscriptions. The inscriptions have various features in common, but here - as in the material as a whole - we have not succeeded in establishing significant connections. Munch's exhibition at the Dioramalokalet in autumn 1897 included a number of prints, yet the catalogue does not contain any information that allows us to infer a direct link to the works acquired by the Department of Prints and Drawings in 1898/1899. Nevertheless, it is likely that the exhibition encouraged the acquisition.[3]

According to an announcement in *Social Demokraten* of 06.10.1902 concerning Munch's exhibition at Blomqvist, the Department of Prints and Drawings had purchased several "drawings", among them "a self-portrait and portraits of Gunnar Heiberg and Hans Jæger". This makes it probable that *Self-Portrait* (cat. 84), *Gunnar Heiberg* (cat. 114), and *Hans Jæger I* (cat. 115) were bought at this exhibition. (All three are lithographs. At that time it was not unusual to refer to lithographs, and indeed graphic works in general, as drawings.) In one photograph from the exhibition (MM.F.00012-01), a number of prints can be seen.[4] They include impressions of *The Scream* (cat. 85), *Death in the Sickroom* (cat. 100), *Funeral March* (cat. 126), and *Male Nude* (cat. 157), all of which are in the National Museum's collection and are believed to date from before 1902, meaning that they may well have been purchased from Blomqvist that year. Frederik Gundersen inventoried the portrait of Hans Jæger and two portraits of August Strindberg (cat. 101 and 102) in the supplementary record "A II". The handwriting and numbering sequence in that source indicate that the entries were made on the same occasion, probably in 1902 or shortly after. A surviving accounts ledger for the "Art Museum" (National Gallery) for the period (roughly) 16.04.1903-31.12.1922 contains an entry for 1902-03 concerning the Department of Prints and Drawings that reads "Edvard Munch Intaglios and Lithographs kr. 350.20" (p. 231). This too probably relates to the acquisition from Blomqvist. Further details are, however, not known. All things considered, the mystery remains unsolved. Why did Fredrik Gundersen (curator from 1883 to 1927), who gives every impression of having been conscientious and orderly, inventory only the three mentioned works by Munch, despite the fact that many more were acquired during his time as curator? And why precisely, or only, these three, if more prints were acquired at the Blomqvist exhibition? Here one can only speculate about excessive workloads and the like.

At Blomqvist's Munch exhibition in spring 1909, director Jens Thiis selected "for the Department of Prints and Drawings the best – in my opinion – of what we lack".[5] This purchase is confirmed by two entries in the above-mentioned accounts ledger, under the year 1909 (p. 47): on 14 April, "Blomqvist part-payment for Munch intaglios kr. 200", and on 31 July, "Blomqvist balance for Munch etchings". It has not been established which works this applies to.

In the same accounts ledger, under the year 1911 (p. 48), we find the entry "Erlandsen 8 etchings by Munch kr. 30". It has not been established either who Erlandsen was, nor which eight works were acquired for a mere 30 kroner.

In the National Gallery's "Report on Purchases and Donations 1916-1917", under the year 1917, we read that "Edvard Munch donated 25 intaglios, lithographs and woodcuts (some in several colours) to the Department of Prints and Drawings, works the collection did not previously own and which it now possesses as exquisite prints. The sales value of the gift is estimated at around 6,000 [kroner]."[6] No information has been found concerning the reason for the gift. Could it have been the National Gallery's 80th anniversary? (The 40th anniversary of the Department of Prints and Drawings passed virtually unnoticed.)

In 1927, *Gustav Schiefler* (cat. 171) and *Jens Thiis* (cat. 197) were bought for 132.75 kroner from an auction at Wangs Kunst- og Auktionsforretning.[7]

According to Sigurd Willoch (op. cit., p. 107), the Department of Prints and Drawings received a selection of Munch's more recent graphic works in connection with an exhibition shown on the occasion of the artist's seventieth birthday. The ten donated works and the exhibition are mentioned in an article in *Aftenposten* from 07.06.1934. Apparently the gift was not incorporated into the collection until 1936/1937.[8] The ten works are: *Arve Arvesen* (cat. 206), *Woman's Portrait* (cat. 208), *Woman with Her Hand by Her Mouth* (cat. 209), *Fire. Vaterland* (cat. 210), *Grenadierstrasse in Berlin after the War* (cat. 211), *Two People* (cat. 212), *Peasant Girl* (cat. 213), *Frankfurter Bahnhofplatz during Rahtenau's Funeral* (cat. 215), *Henrik Bull* (cat. 217), and *Kristian Schreiner* (cat. 218).

In the supplementary record "Norsk grafikk I", Eli Ingebretsen Greve (curator from 1927 to 1942 and from 1945 to 1949) noted that she bought *Seated Nude. The Flea* (cat. 191) and *The Storm* (cat. 183) at auction, but fails to state the year, the auction in question, or the price.[9] It may have been the auction held at Wangs Kunst- og Antikvitetshandels on 14-16 March 1936 (in the auction catologue, item 40 was "*Ung pike*, lito [Young Girl, lithograph] kr. 155", and item 49, "*Landskap*, tresnitt [Landscape, woodcut] kr. 130").

In the same record, Ingebretsen Greve has noted beside the next entry, *Hjørdis Gierløff* (cat. 195), "purchased from Swedish collector at EI in 35/36."[10] No further information on this acquisition has been found.

At City Auksjon held at Hotel Bristol on 12 and 13 September 1938, a total of 26 graphic works were purchased: *Tête-à-Tête* (cat. 66), *Stanislav Przybyszewski* (cat. 91), *Marcel Réja* (cat. 122), *Farewell after the Party* (cat. 130), *Nude* (cat. 131), *Woman's Head* (cat. 137), *Man and Woman* (cat. 139), *Two Human Beings. The Lonely Ones* (cat. 140), *Fertility* (cat. 141), *Encounter in Space* (cat. 143), *The Oak* (cat. 165), *Salome* (cat. 168), *Goldstein Three-Quarter Face* (cat. 180), *Tiger's Head I* (cat. 182), *Jappe Nilssen* (cat. 184), *Self-Portrait* (cat. 185), *Wolfgang Gurlitt* (cat. 189), *Street Musicians* (cat. 196), *Garden in Snow II* (cat. 200), *The Tree I* (cat. 203), *Richard Strauss* (cat.

204), *Self-Portrait with Beard* (cat. 205), *Frederick Delius* (cat. 207), *Inger Barth* (cat. 214), *Brothel Scene* (cat. 219), and *Self-Portrait with a Bottle of Wine* (cat. 220).[11] Printed on the front of the catalogue is the statement that "The collection is reputed to be Germany's largest and is sold on behalf of a bank". Based on an announcement in the evening edition of *Aftenposten* on 14.01.1939, Nils Messel has identified the former owner as Martin Flersheim, who died in Frankfurt in 1935.[12]

At City Auksjon held at Håndverkeren on 19 January 1939, two works were purchased: *Woman's Head* (cat. 149) and *Weeping Woman. Morning* (cat. 221).[13]

In 1947, the National Gallery received *The Brooch. Eva Mudocci* (cat. 167) as a bequest from Hans Aall.

In 1968, *Evening. Melancholy I* (cat. 120) was purchased from Karen Schieldrop, wife of the deceased Professor Edgar B. Schieldrop (financed in part by the sale of a duplicate of *The Brooch. Eva Mudocci*, see cat. 167).

In 1982, *Old Man Praying* (cat. 162) was purchased from the estate of Ingrid Lindbäck Langaard.

In 1997, *Mrs Schwarz* (cat. 174) was received as a bequest from Anna (Vesla) and Jean Heiberg.

References to oeuvre catalogues
Sch /(Schiefler 1907, 1928): Gustav Schiefler, *Verzeichnis des graphischen Werks Edvard Munchs bis 1906* (Berlin: Bruno Cassirer, 1907), and *Edvard Munch, Das graphische Werk 1906-1926* (Berlin: Euphorion Verlag, 1928) (Facsimile edition, Oslo: Cappelen, 1974).

W /(Willoch 1950): Sigurd Willoch, *Edvard Munchs raderinger* (Oslo: Johan Grundt Tanum, 1950).

Woll G /(Woll 2001/ 2012): Gerd Woll, *Edvard Munch. The Complete Graphic Works* (London: Philip Wilson Publishers, 2001)/*Edvard Munch. The Complete Graphic Works* (revised edition) (London: Philip Wilson Publishers, 2012).

Sch and W do not contain a determination of an impression's state. Details concerning state are based on Woll 2012, with some divergences.

Concerning the drawings discussed, see the Munch Museum's digital catalogue of Munch's drawings: www.munch.emuseum.com

References to the Munch Museum's inventory numbers
MM.G.: graphic work
MM.T.: drawing
MM P: printing plate

For further references, see Bibliography, p. 323ff.

Printers
Angerer and Sabo, Berlin: According to Schiefler, Munch initially used Angerer Kunstanstalt and Carl

Sabo. We have no information that allows us to distinguish between them. Sabo also printed intaglios after 1900.

Norges Geografiske Opmaaling, Kristiania: In autumn 1895, several trial proofs were pulled at Norges Geografiske Opmaaling (NGO). Further intaglios were printed here at later dates.

Liebmann and Lassally, Berlin: Munch's first lithographs were printed by A. Liebmann and M.W. Lassally. Lassally regularly printed lithographs and woodcuts up until 1914.

Clot, Paris: As of winter 1896, Munch regularly used August Clot in Paris as a printer for his lithographs and for his early woodcuts (concerning uncertainties about which printers Munch used in Paris, see p. 36 with note 27).

Lemercier, Paris: Apart from Clot, as of 1896 Munch also used Lemercier & Cie for both lithographs and woodcuts. He may also have had a number of intaglios printed by Lemercier, although his usual Paris printer for intaglios was Alfred Porcabeuf.[14]

Porcabeuf, Paris: Alfred Porcabeuf was master printer at the Atelier Alfred Salmon.

Felsing, Berlin: O. Felsing (proprietor, Wilhelm Felsing) was Germany's most renowned printer for intaglios. Munch used Felsing from 1902 to 1914.

Petersen and Waitz, Kristiania: Lithographs from 1899.

Weimarer Kunstschule: Some lithographs in 1906.

Dansk Reproduktionsanstalt, Copenhagen: Used by Munch while a patient at the clinic of Dr. Jacobson, 1908-09.

Nielsen, Kristiania: Anton Peder Nielsen (Kildeborg), Danish lithographer, an employee of Hagen & Kornmann and Halvorsen & Larssen, founded his own printshop in 1922. Munch worked closely with him from shortly after his return to Norway in 1909.

Remarks

In the remarks, the title of the work is used to refer to the work in general, as are also "this woodcut", "this intaglio", "this lithograph", while "impression" is used to refer to one particular imprint. The emphasis is on details relating to printmaking as a specialisation and the justification for datings, although in the case of certain works we allow ourselves to comment on notable pictorial qualities as well. Biographical information about identified persons is included; further, to a modest degree we discuss interpretations of the image. Reference is made to other works by Munch with the same or similar motif.

Notes

1 Gerd Woll, "Paper in Prints by Edvard Munch" in Klaus Albrecht Schröder and Antonia Hoerschelmann (eds.): *Edvard Munch - Theme and Variation*, exhibition catalogue (Vienna: Albertina, 2003), 41-53); Gry Landro and Magdalena Ufnalewska-Godzimirska, "Papiret historisk tilbakeblikk" and "Å ta vare på Munch - med papir i fokus" in Magne Bruteig and Ute Kuhlemann Falck (eds.), *Munch på papir. Tegning - grafikk - akvarell*, exhibition catalogue (Oslo/Brussels: Munchmuseet/Mercatorfonds, 2013), 282-288 and 289-294.

2 "1898/99 Munch, 31 Raderinger og Lithografier Kr. 310,-". "Regnskab vedkommende Christiania Kobberstik- og Haandtegningssamling fra dens Stiftelse i 1877 til og med Regnskabsaaret 1899/1900", unpaginated, The National Museum's documentation archive.

3 "Edvard Munch - Maleriudstilling", 15.09.-17.10.1897. Of the prints listed in the exhibition catalogue (nos. 86-144), it can be said with confidence that 21 were acquired by the Department of Prints and Drawings; several of the items have, however, not been identified.

4 Thanks to Trine Nordkvelle for bringing the announcement and the photograph to our attention.

5 Undated letter from Jens Thiis to Edvard Munch (incomplete) www.emunch.no MM K 1182. Thiis continues: "Together with the 70-odd sheets we already have, they will form an important representative collection of your art in this field. Fortunately, for the Collection of Prints and Drawings I was able to make the purchase alone without having to seek anyone's permission; when choosing, I only conferred with Gundersen and could pick what I wanted without hesitation." Of the items Thiis purchased at this exhibition, Sigurd Willoch discusses only the paintings, op. cit., p. 150.

6 See p. 3, and corroborating information on p. 11; journal no. 8/1917, The National Museum's documentation archive.

7 Supplementary record "Norsk grafikk I", nos. 106 and 107, and catalogue for the auction of 19 September, nos. 74 and 84, with prices (66 and 52 kroner respectively) added in pencil. The source of Munch's prints at this auction was an unidentified private seller.

8 Acquired "1936/37" and "Gift from the artist" noted in the supplementary record "B I", nos. 611 and 612.

9 "Norsk grafikk I", nos. 147 and 148.

10 "Norsk grafikk I", no. 149.

11 Supplementary record "B I", no. 613.

12 Thanks to Nils Messel for this reference.

13 "Norsk grafikk I", nos. 144 and 145.

14 Woll 2012, p. 14 and note 31.

Sidsel Helliesen and Gerd Woll

Catalogue: Prints and drawings

58
Richard Mengelberg

Plate 1894; impression 1895
Intaglio: drypoint; black ink; laid paper, ARCHES
Image: 138 × 99; paper: 445 × 311
Artist's inscription: E Munch 95
NG.K&H.A.19049
Provenance unknown
Sch 1; W 1; Woll G 1 I/I
Printer: Sabo or Angerer

Produced in Berlin in autumn 1894, this intaglio is regarded as Munch's first graphic work. Schiefler uses the title *Herrenporträt*, adding "(Herr M)" in the description. Richard Mengelberg (1853-1932) was a German businessman with an interest in art.

59
Portrait of a Young Woman
Portrett av en ung kvinne

Plate 1894; impression 1895
Intaglio: drypoint; black ink; laid paper, ARCHES
Image: 131 × 103; paper: 446 × 306
Artist's inscription: E Munch 95
NG.K&H.A.19050
Provenance unknown
Sch 2; W 2; Woll G 2 II/II
Printer: Sabo or Angerer

The intaglio is probably a portrait of the American Kate Crawley, or possibly her sister Nellie. Both were art students in Berlin in 1894-95 and close friends of Munch. The intaglio was reproduced with the title *Amerikanerin* in an article by Jens Thiis in *Zeitschrift für bildende Kunst*, 1908, vol. 6.

60
Death and the Woman
Døden og kvinnen

Plate 1894; impression (1894 or 1895)
Intaglio: drypoint; black ink; smooth wove paper
Image: 237 × 167; paper: 562 × 442
Artist's inscription: Edv. Munch. No 20
NG.K&H.A.19051
Provenance unknown
Sch 3; W 3; Woll G 3 B/B
Printer: Sabo or Angerer

The richness of the drypoint and the fact that Munch himself has numbered the impression suggest an early dating. One of Munch's first graphic works, the intaglio shows how quickly he mastered the pictorial potential of the drypoint technique. The central field is based (inverted) on a painting Munch had executed shortly before (Woll M 345). The theme of the woman in a close embrace with a skeleton can be traced back to medieval dance-of-death motifs, but the inclusion of sperm and foetuses in the surrounding border adds a strong erotic element. The allusion to conception and reproduction broadens the context of life and death. Munch used similar borders in his *Madonna* pictures (see cat. 86).

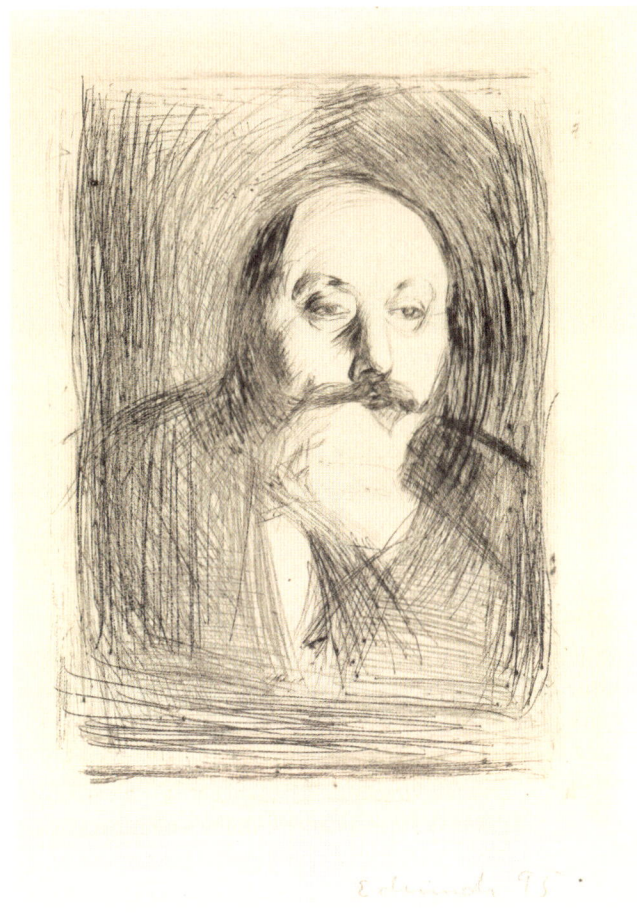

58

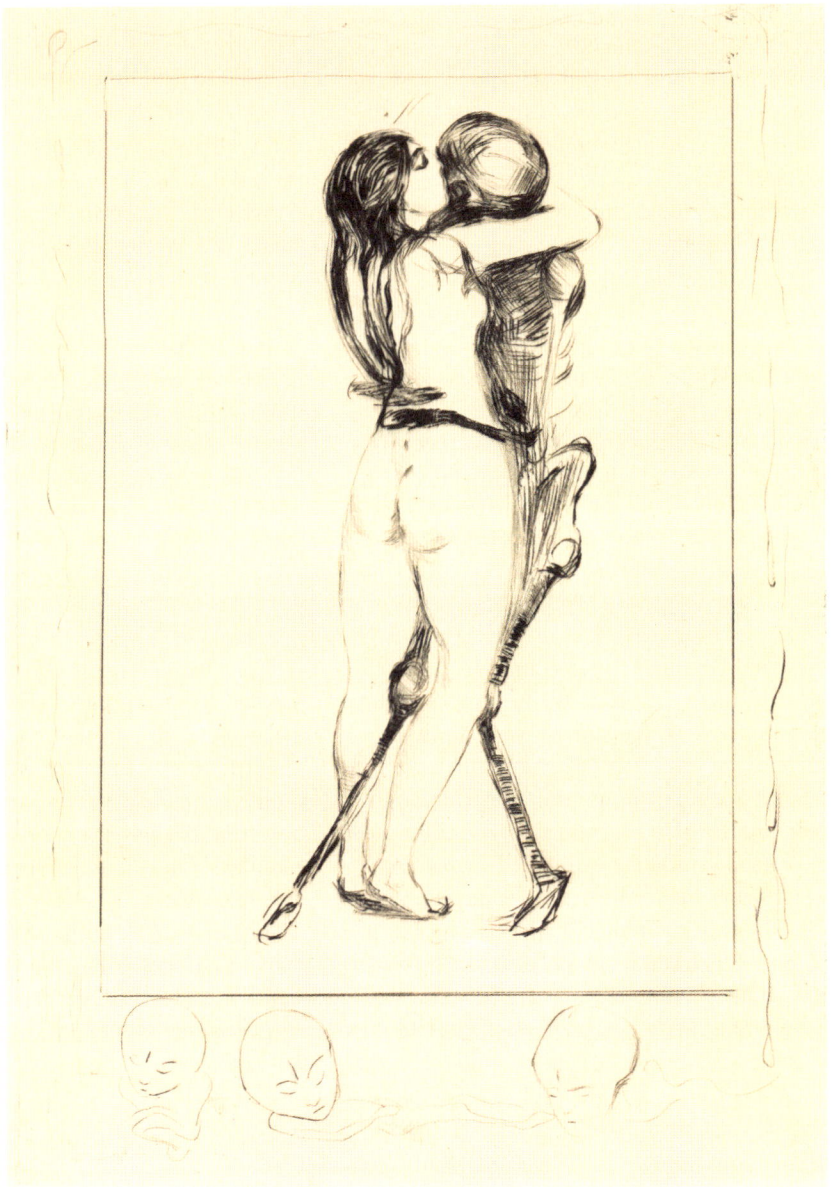

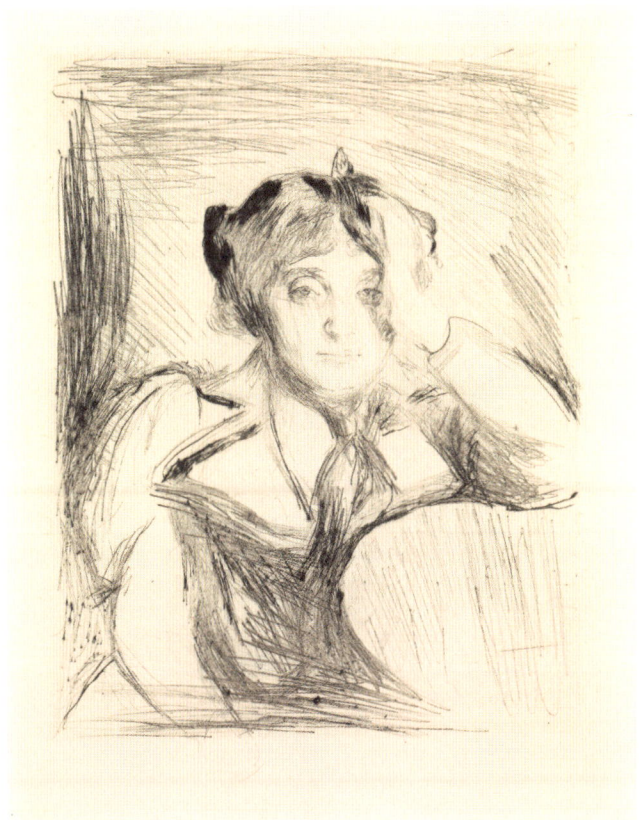

59

60

61
Harpy

Plate 1894; impression 1895
Intaglio: drypoint; black ink; laid secondary
paper, ARCHES
Image: 287 × 218; paper: 568 × 385
Artist's inscription: E Munch 1895
NG.K&H.A.19052
Probably acquired 1898
Sch 4; W 4; Woll G 4 III/IV
Printer: Sabo or Angerer

Schiefler and Willoch initially adopt Munch's
characterisation of the picture's mythical figure
by using the title *Vampire*. Schiefler, however,
uses *Harpy* for Munch's later lithograph with a
similar figure (Woll G 145), an interpretation that
is mythologically more appropriate (Nergaard
1978, 134 f.). In a letter (undated) to Fredrik Gundersen at the National Gallery's Department of
Prints and Drawings, Munch writes: "I thank you
for the 100 Frcs sent to me as an advance for the
purchase of my intaglios and lithographs. It came
in very handy. Among the intaglios I have sent
there is one, depicting a vampire sitting on corpse
–. Since one of the heads resembles a famous
man in Kristiania, I ask you to set this print aside,
as I intend to modify the plate [...]" (quoted from
a photocopy in the Munch Museum, eMunch
PN 787). The famous man in Kristiania (Oslo) to
whom Munch alludes in the letter was probably
the painter Christian Krohg, whose features are
recognisable in the head at the lower left. Munch
eventually modified the plate as announced, but
not until several years later. Felsing, who probably began printing for Munch in 1902, pulled
impressions from the plate both before and after
Munch had changed it. Munch's acknowledge-
ment in the letter of a payment in francs suggests
that he was in Paris at the time of writing. This
was not the case in 1902–03. He did, however,
have several stays in the city in 1898–99. Based
on this, *Harpy* is the only work that can be linked
with reasonable probability to the acquisition
made in 1898 (see p. 190).

62
The Girl at the Window
Piken ved vinduet

Plate 1894; date of impression unknown
Intaglio: drypoint, roulette and burnisher; ink
and paper unknown
Plate dimensions according to Woll G 5: 204–
208 × 144–148
Sch 5; W 5; Woll G 5
Other details unknown
Impression lost

In the Department of Prints and Drawings' supplementary record "Norwegian Graphics I", the
impression is listed as "No. 5 Girl in nightgown by
the window 1894. Drypoint intaglio [Schiefler] 5".
It is registered as missing in the collection audits
of 1955 and 1969-70, and is not included in Liv I.
Jones' catalogue *Norsk grafikk til 1970* (Norwegian
Graphics until 1970) (Oslo: Nasjonalgalleriet,
1971). The print was one of eight in a portfolio
published by Julius Meier-Graefe in June 1895.
The portfolio was produced in two editions, one
printed in ten impressions from non-steel-faced
plates on Japan paper, numbered and signed by
the artist, the other in 55 unsigned impressions
from steel-faced plates on wove paper. Since the
record of the missing impression in "Norwegian
Graphics I" mentions neither a signature nor any
other inscription, it is reasonable to assume that it
was neither signed nor printed by Felsing. While
it may have been part of the Meier-Graefe publication, it is also possible that the lost impression
of *The Girl at the Window* was printed earlier or
later than those for the portfolio.

63
Consolation
Trøst

Plate 1894; impression (1894 or 1895)
Intaglio: drypoint and open bite; black ink; laid
Japan paper
Image: 208 × 314; paper: 291 × 460
Artist's inscription: E. Munch avant lettre.
NG.K&H.A.19053
Provenance unknown
Sch 6; W 6; Woll G 6 III/VI
Printer: Sabo or Angerer

Munch made some minor modifications to the
plate, but the criteria for differentiating states are
not obvious. The National Museum's impression
is in state III/VI, suggesting a date of 1894 or 1895.
In the drypoint sections the smudge of the burr is
rich. Munch made several drawings with similar
compositions (MM.T.2264 verso, MM.T.2458,
MM.T.126-36).

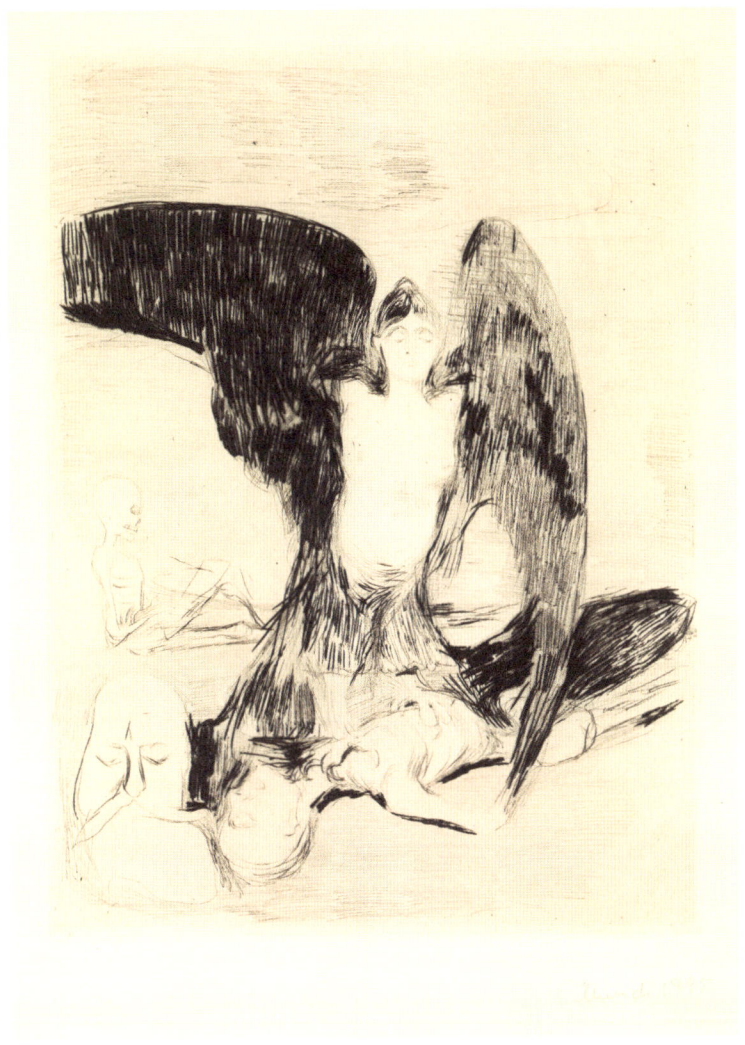

61

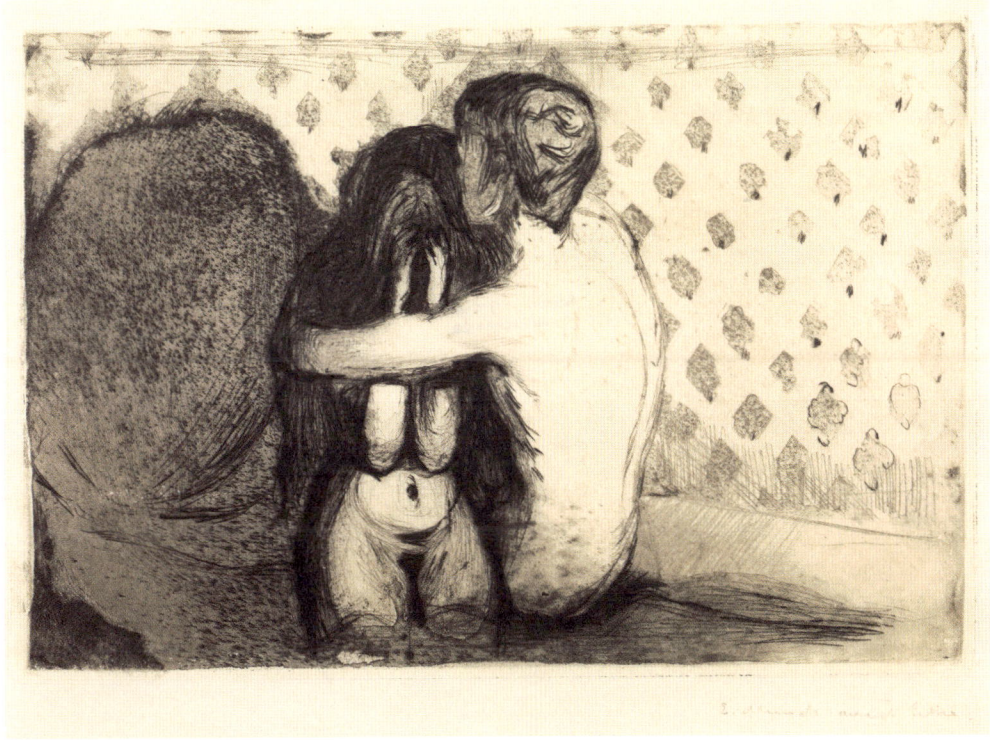

63

64
The Sick Child
Det syke barn

Plate 1894; impression (1894 or 1895)
Intaglio: drypoint, roulette and burnisher; black ink; medium-weight Japan paper
Image: 362 × 272; paper: 575 × 457
Artist's inscription: Edv Munch/avant lettre
NG.K&H.A.19054
Provenance unknown
Sch 7; W 7; Woll G 7 IV/VII
Printer: Sabo or Angerer

The image was one of eight intaglios by Munch in a portfolio published by Julius Meier-Graefe in June 1895 (see cat. 62). The inscription on the National Museum's impression of *The Sick Child* indicates that it is not from the portfolio. Several impressions in the same state as the one belonging to the National Museum are dated 1894 or 1895, suggesting a similar date can be assumed for the National Museums' impression. Further, the burr of the drypoint is prominent, indicating that the impression was pulled before the plate was steel faced. In that case, it predates the publication of the portfolio. In this intaglio, Munch first developed the portrayal of the sick girl and the woman as an inversion of the painting *The Sick Child* (which he had shown at the National Annual Autumn Exhibition in 1886, see cat. 8). He then added the landscape below. This lower section was later cut from the plate, probably after 1906. In 1896, Munch produced a lithograph (see cat. 107 and 108) and an intaglio (Woll G 59) that concentrate on the girl's head. The motif is central to Munch's production and is discussed in greater depth in connection with the National Museum's painting.

65
Study of a Model
Modellstudie

Plate 1894; impression (between 1902 and 1914)
Intaglio: drypoint; dark brown ink; wove paper
Image: 259 × 185; paper: 507 × 348
Artist's inscription: Edvard Munch/avant lettre
Secondary inscription: O Felsing Berlin gdr.
NG.K&H.A.19055
Provenance unknown
Sch 9; W 8; Woll G 8 III/III
Printer: Felsing

The impression cannot be dated more precisely than to the years when Felsing was printing for Munch.

66
Tête-à-Tête

Plate 1894; impression (1895)
Intaglio: line etching, drypoint and burnisher; black ink; heavy, stiff wove paper
Image: 203 × 309; paper: 343 × 477
Secondary inscription: E Munch [l.r.; pencil]
NG.K&H.A.19057 (formerly NG.K&H.B.00613)
Purchased at City Auksjon, Oslo, September 1938 (cat. 134 or 269)
Sch 12; W 11; Woll G 9 III/III
Printer: Angerer

The inscription "E Munch" is not an authentic signature. The picture was one of eight in a portfolio of Munch's intaglios that Julius Meier-Graefe published in June 1895. The type of paper and dimensions suggest that the National Museum's impression is from the standard edition of the portfolio (see cat. 62). The male figure has been identified as the painter Karl Jensen-Hjell (1861–88); the identity of the woman is unknown. The intaglio is an inversion of a painting from 1885 (Woll M 116).

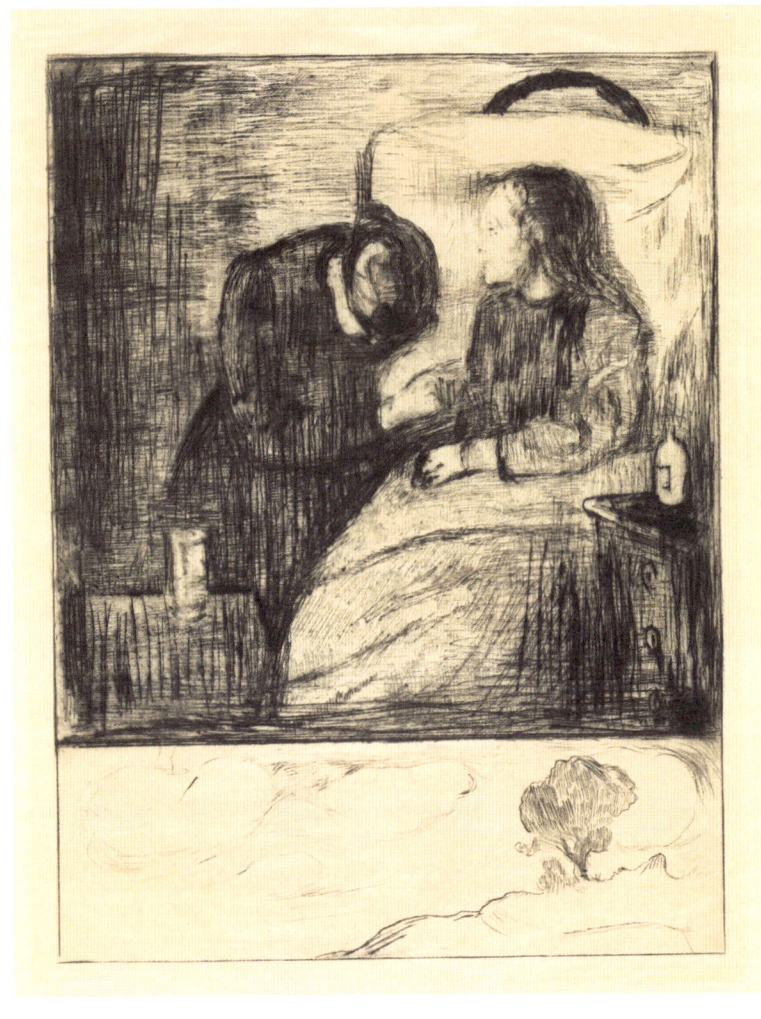

64

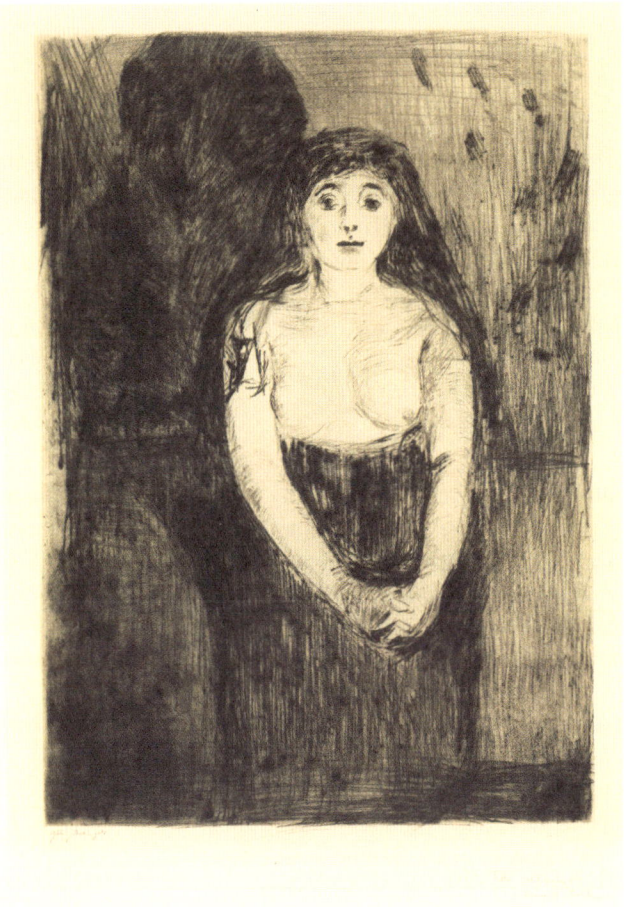

65

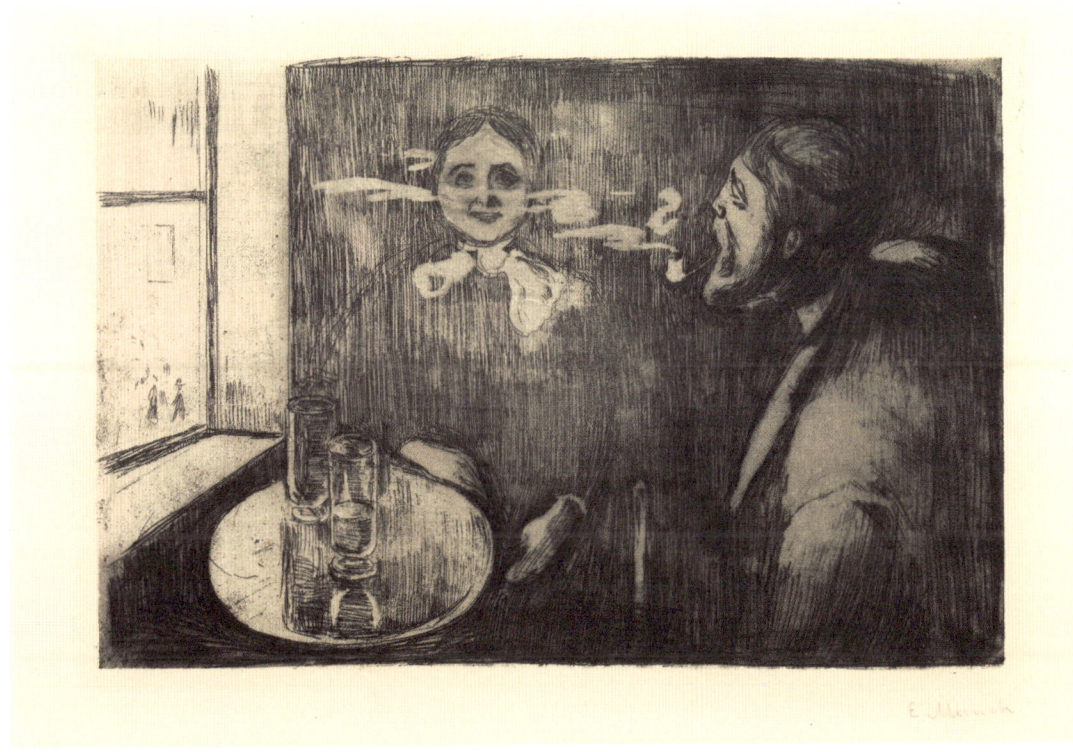

66

67
The Day After
Dagen derpå

Plate 1894; impression 1895
Intaglio: drypoint and aquatint with plate tone;
black ink; laid paper, ARCHES
Image: 192 × 275; paper: 385 × 567
Artist's inscription: E Munch 1895
NG.K&H.A.19060
Provenance unknown
Sch 15; W 14; Woll G 10 VII/VII
Printer: Angerer

The artist's inscription and the type of paper indicate that the National Museum's impression of
The Day After is not from the portfolio that Julius
Meier-Graefe published in June 1895, which contained eight of Munch's intaglios (see cat. 62). The
museum's impression is, however, dated to that
year by the artist. The burr of drypoint is richtly
printed, but it is difficult to discern whether the
plate was steel-faced or not, i.e. whether the
impression was pulled before or after the printing
of the portfolio. The intaglio is an inversion of
a painting (see cat. 27). The same motif is also
found in an early drawing (MM.T.2348). It is
discussed in greater depth in connection with the
National Museum's painting.

68
Summer Night. The Voice
Sommernatt. Stemmen

Plate 1894; impression 1895
Intaglio: drypoint, aquatint and open bite, with
plate tone; black ink; laid paper
Image: 238 × 314; paper: 387 × 565
Artist's inscription: E Munch 95
NG.K&H.A.19062
Provenance unknown
Sch 19; W 19; Woll G 12 II/III
Printer: Sabo or Angerer

Munch produced several versions of this
motif, as a painting (Woll M 319, 349), drawings
(MM.T.2373, MM.T.328, MM.T.329, MM.T.2547-
7), and prints (Woll G 92, 106, 129). The scene
probably relates to a meeting between the artist
and Milly Thaulow (often referred to in Munch's
written notes as "Fru Heiberg") in Åsgårdstrand
in 1885 (www.emunch.no).

69
Two Human Beings. The Lonely Ones
To mennesker. De ensomme

Plate 1894; impression 1896
Intaglio: drypoint; black ink; laid paper, ARCHES
Image: 150 × 215; paper: 312 × 446
Artist's inscription: E Munch 96
NG.K&H.A.19063
Provenance unknown
Sch 20; W 19; Woll G 13 VI/VI
Printer: Sabo or Angerer

Two Human Beings is a prosaic characterisation of
the subject, whereas *The Lonely Ones* captures the
picture's mood. Proposed by Schiefler, the double
title combines a title often used by Munch to refer
to this motif with the title given to the intaglio in
the portfolio that Julius Meier-Graefe published
in June 1895 (see cat. 62). The National Museum's
impression is dated by the artist for the year after
the publication of the portfolio. Munch's sensitive
use of the drypoint technique and halftones,
together with the intimate format and close focus
on the subject, highlights the strained calm of this
amorous moment. Although *Two Human Beings.
The Lonely Ones* is one of Munch's first intaglios,
the expressive force of this small print makes it
a graphic masterpiece. The intaglio reproduces
(inverted) the composition of a painting Munch
had done in the early 1890s (lost in 1901, but
known from a photograph, Woll M 283). He later
revisited the motif in a colour woodcut (1899, see
cat. 139) and in two new painted versions, dating
from 1905 (Woll M 640) and 1906-07 (Woll M
735), respectively. In a drawing (MM.T.275) and
a painting from the 1930s (Woll M 1719) the motif
has the same orientation as in the first painting.

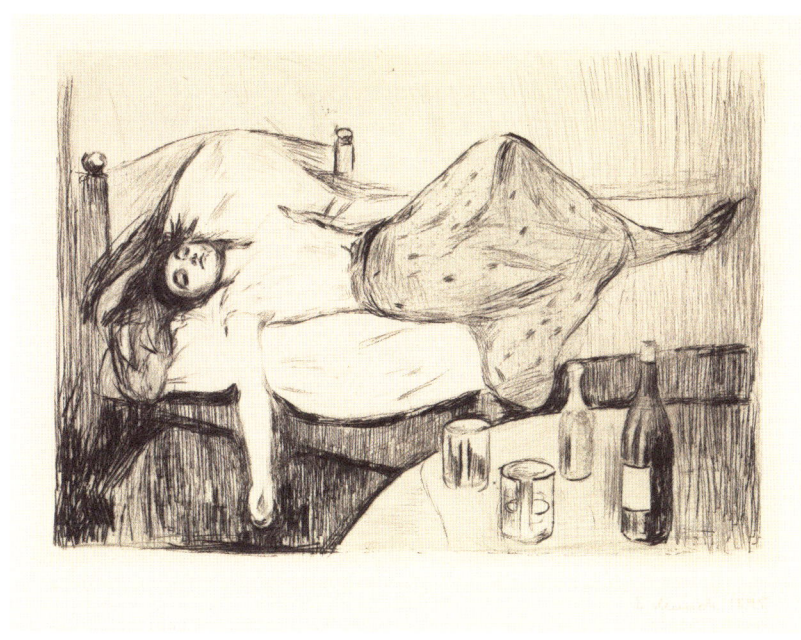

67

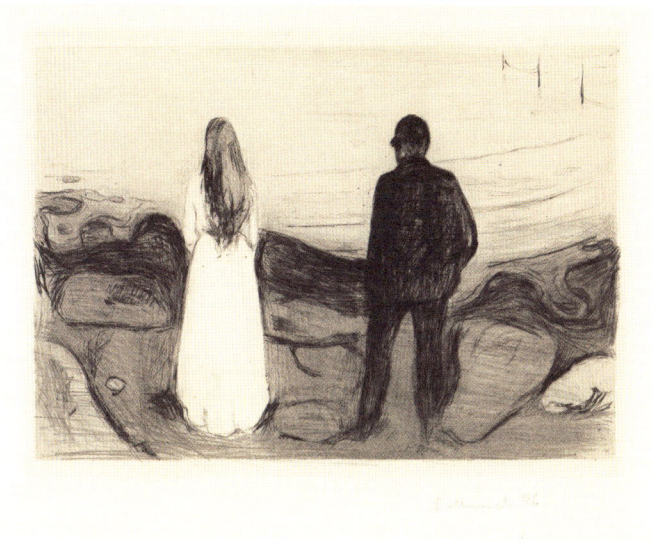

69

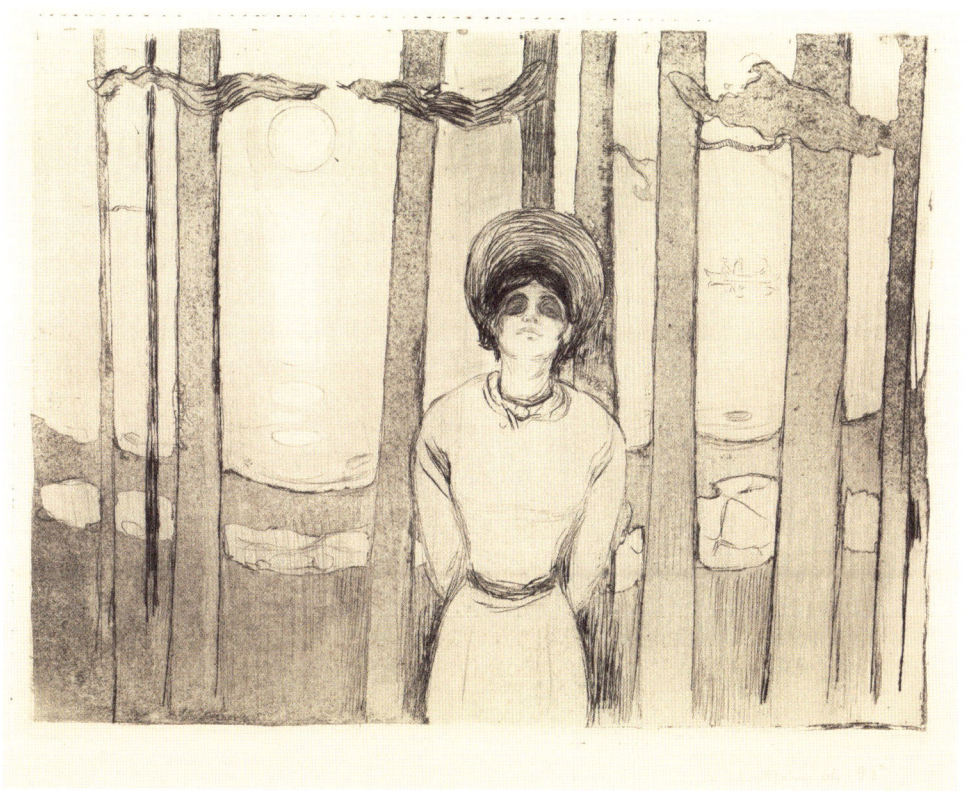

68

70
Puberty
Pubertet

Stone 1894; impression (1894 or 1895)
Lithograph: crayon; black ink; heavy, stiff wove paper
Image: 411 × 275; paper: 526 × 403
Artist's inscription: Edv Munch/No 20
Secondary inscription: Pris 10 Kr [verso u.r.; pencil]
NG.K&H.A.18993
Provenance unknown
Sch 8; Woll G 14 I/I
Printer: Liebmann

According to Schiefler, *Puberty* is Munch's first lithograph. Only early impressions of this work are known, as is reflected by Munch's numbering of the National Museum's impression. Schiefler uses the title *Das junge Modell*. The lithograph is based (with inversion) on paintings from the mid-1880s (lost in a fire; Woll M 141), 1894 (Woll M 346) and 1894–95 (Woll M 347). Munch also produced an intaglio version in 1902 (Woll G 186). The theme is discussed in greater depth in connection with the National Museum's painting, cat. 26.

71
Kristiania Bohemians I
Kristiania-Boheme I

Plate 1895; impression (between 1902 and 1914)
Intaglio: line etching, drypoint and burnisher, dark brown ink; stiff wove paper
Image: 206 × 286; paper: 330 × 507
Artist's inscription: Edv Munch
Secondary inscription: O Felsing Berlin gdr.
NG.K&H.A.19056
Provenance unknown
Sch 10; W 9; Woll G 15 III/III
Printer: Felsing

The National Museum's impression of *Kristiania Bohemians I* cannot be dated more precisely than to the years when Felsing was printing for Munch, i.e. several years after the picture was included in a portfolio of eight intaglios by Munch that Julius Meier-Graefe published in 1895 (see cat. 62). The title, borrowed from the book by Hans Jæger, *Fra Kristiania-Bohêmen* (1885), refers to a social circle to which Munch also belonged for a time. The group's defining characteristic was its commitment to a literary direction based on French naturalism. But its members were also interested in political and societal issues, sometimes showing clear socialist and anarchist sympathies, which in their time were considered a threat to broader social order and morality. What aroused the greatest indignation was their demand for free love. Three of the four men around the café table have been identified as the student Holmsen, the author Axel Maurer and Munch himself (on the left). The print is based on a painting by Munch from 1887 (now lost, Woll M 151; later version, Woll M 792).

72
Women Bathing
Badende kvinner

Plate 1895; impression 1895
Intaglio: drypoint and aquatint with some plate tone; laid paper, ARCHES
Image: 208 × 307; paper: 385 × 568
Artist's inscription: E Munch 95
NG.K&H.A.19058
Provenance unknown
Sch 14; W 13; Woll G 18 IV/XV
Printer: Sabo or Angerer

The National Museum has two impressions of *Women Bathing*, which show different stages of Munch's development of the plate (see cat 73). Munch had produced a pastel version of this motif the previous year (Woll M 356). The intaglio is inverted.

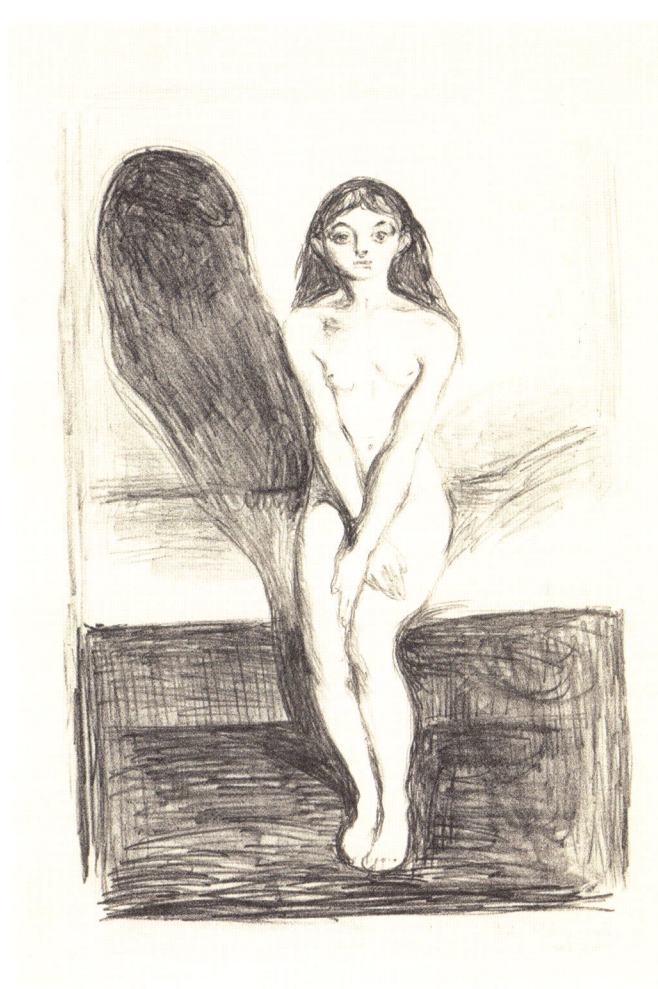

70

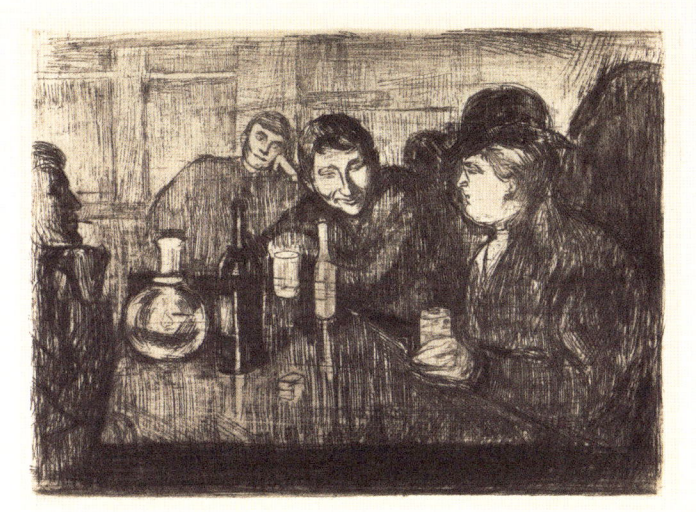

71

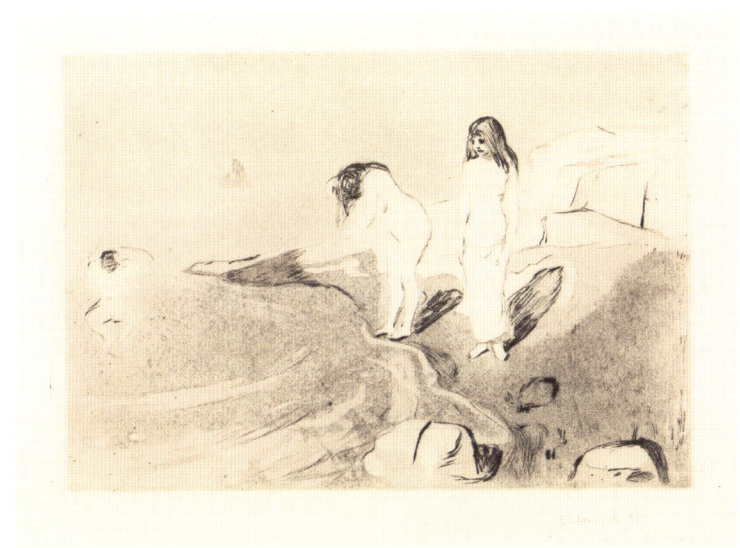

72

73
Women Bathing
Badende kvinner

Plate 1895; impression (between 1902 and 1914)
Intaglio: drypoint, aquatint and open bite; dark
brown ink; wove paper
Image: 212 × 311; paper: 438 × 600
Artist's inscription: E Munch [c.r.]//Edv.
Munch/avant lettre
Secondary inscription: O Felsing Berlin gdr.
NG.K&H.A.19059
Provenance unknown
Sch 14; W 13; Woll G 18 V/XV
Printer: Felsing

The impression cannot be dated more precisely
than to the years Felsing was printing for Munch.
The National Museum has two impressions
showing different states of this intaglio (see cat.
72). The difference between the two consists in
modifications to the etching in the lower part
of the picture and to the women's hair, making
these areas darker in the later state. Interestingly,
this intaglio exists in an unusually large number
of states. The additional signature in the right
margin can probably be explained by assuming
that the impression lay in a pile of other prints
that Munch has signed consecutively.

74
Attraction II
Tiltrekning II

Plate 1895; impression 1895
Intaglio: line etching, open bite, drypoint and
burnisher; black ink; laid paper
Image: 218 × 316; paper: 390 × 566
Artist's inscription: E Munch 95
NG.K&H.A.19061
Provenance unknown
Sch 18; W 17; Woll G 20 II/IV
Printer: Angerer

The setting in *Attraction II* can be identified as a
location at Åsgårdstrand. The intaglio seems to
be an adaptation of an earlier version that Munch
had probably rejected, which used an upright
format and gave greater prominence to the landscape (Woll G 19). In 1893, Munch had depicted
the same landscape in two paintings, *Starry Night*
(Woll M 320, 321). The intaglio's motif is also
found in a drawing from 1895 (MM.T.317). The
following year, Munch produced two lithographs
with designs similar to that of the two intaglios
(see cat. 109 and Woll G 76).

75
The Woman II
Kvinnen II

Plate 1895; impression 1895
Intaglio: drypoint, line etching and open bite;
black ink; laid paper, ARCHES
Image: 285 × 335; paper: 383 × 566
Artist's inscription: E Munch 95
NG.K&H.A.19064
Provenance unknown
Sch 21B; W 21; Woll G 22 V/VIII
Printer: Angerer

The Woman II corresponds largely to an intaglio
of which only one impression is known (Woll G
21). There are also essential similarities to two
paintings from 1894 (Woll M 361, 362), although
these latter also include a shadowy male figure towards the right-hand edge. Depicted as
archetypes, the three female figures reflect two
fundamental themes in Munch's art: the cycli-
cal passage of life from youth through maturity
to old age, and the characteristic qualities of
womanhood. The picture also suggests various
mythological references that echo prevailing
ideas of the period, such as the sphinx as an
alternative embodiment of the *femme fatale*.
Several drawings relate to the intaglio (see cat.
240). One impression with a wash (MM.G.20-6)
probably represents a step in the preparation of
the intaglio, which Munch reworked to a number
of states. In 1899 Munch made a lithograph on the
same motif (inverted; Woll G 147).

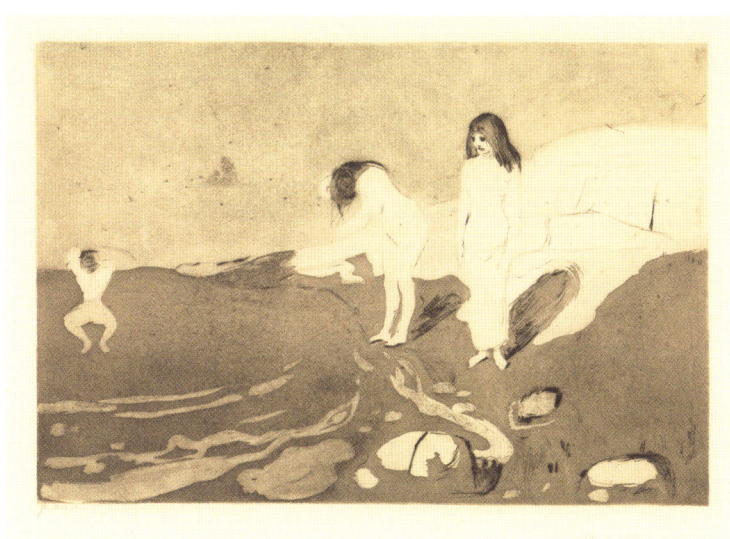

73

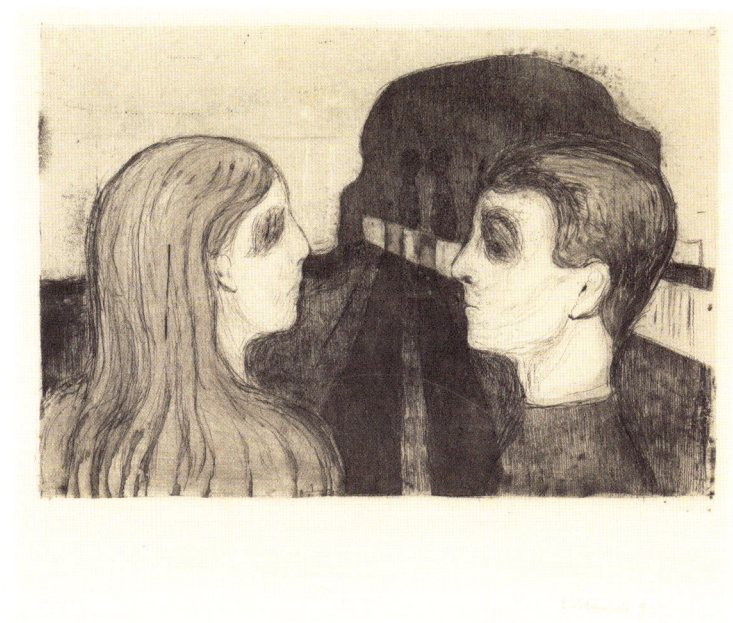

74

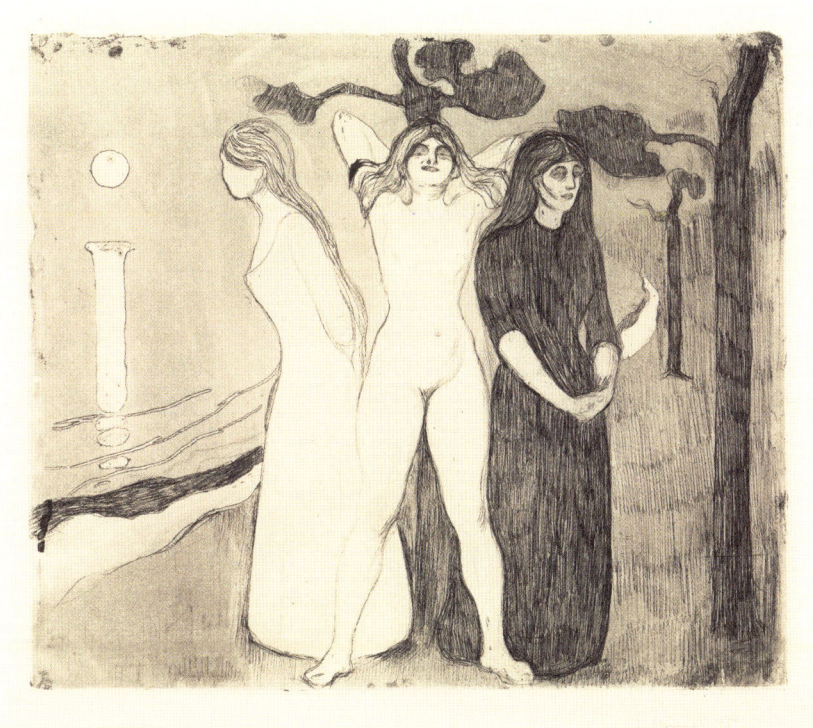

75

76
The Kiss
Kyss

Plate 1895; impression (1895)
Intaglio: line etching, open bite, drypoint and burnisher; black ink; laid paper, ARCHES
Image: 329 × 262; paper: 424 × 313
Artist's inscription: Edv. Munch avant lettre / No 5
NG.K&H.A.19065
Provenance unknown
Sch 22; W 22; Woll G 23 I / I
Printer: Sabo or Angerer

The black ink and type of paper used in the National Museum's impression suggest an early print, as is further indicated by the artist's numbering. A standing couple in a close embrace is the central element in a number of Munch's drawings, paintings and prints. In relevant paintings that predate the intaglio, the couple are dressed and placed either to the left or the right of the window (Woll M 257, 266 (see cat. 17), 267). The depiction in the intaglio of a naked couple standing in front of the window's central mullion is repeated in a painting executed in Paris in 1897 (Woll M 397). A drawing in the Munch Museum (MM.T.421) seems to be a preparatory sketch for the intaglio. For the woodcut versions of the *Kiss* motif, see cat. 160.

77
Dr. Max Asch

Plate 1895; impression (between 1902 and 1914)
Intaglio: drypoint with plate tone; dark brown ink; heavy, stiff wove paper
Image: 249 × 173; paper: 508 × 349
Artist's inscription: Edv. Munch
Secondary inscription: O Felsing Berlin gdr.
NG.K&H.A.19068
Provenance unknown
Sch 27; W 27; Woll G 25 III / III
Printer: Felsing

Schiefler uses the title *Porträt (Herr Dr. A)*. The National Museum's impression cannot be dated more precisely than to the years when Felsing was printing for Munch, i.e. several years after the picture was included in a portfolio of eight intaglios by Munch that Julius Meier-Graefe published in 1895 (see cat. 62). Max Asch (1856–1911) was a German doctor in Berlin and a friend since student days of Stanisław Przybyszewski (see cat. 91). According to a letter that Asch wrote to Munch on 14.03.1895, the plate was finished by the time of writing, although Asch had not yet received an imprint (original in the Munch Museum, MM K 2035).

78
Portrait of a Woman
Kvinneportrett

Plate 1895; impression 1895
Intaglio: drypoint, black ink; medium-weight laid paper, ARCHES
Image: 195 × 137; paper: 446 × 316
Artist's inscription: E Munch 95
NG.K&H.A.19066
Provenance unknown
Sch 24; W 24; Woll G 26 I / I
Printer: Sabo

There are few early prints of this intaglio. Although the plate was probably executed in only one state, the quality of the prints varies considerably. In the National Museum's impression, for example, some of the areas of drypoint work are relatively weak. The plate was later damaged with a scratch across the woman's face. The person portrayed is probably Emmy Seidel (Eggum 1994, cat. 177), the wife of Dr. Hermann Seidel (see cat. 79).

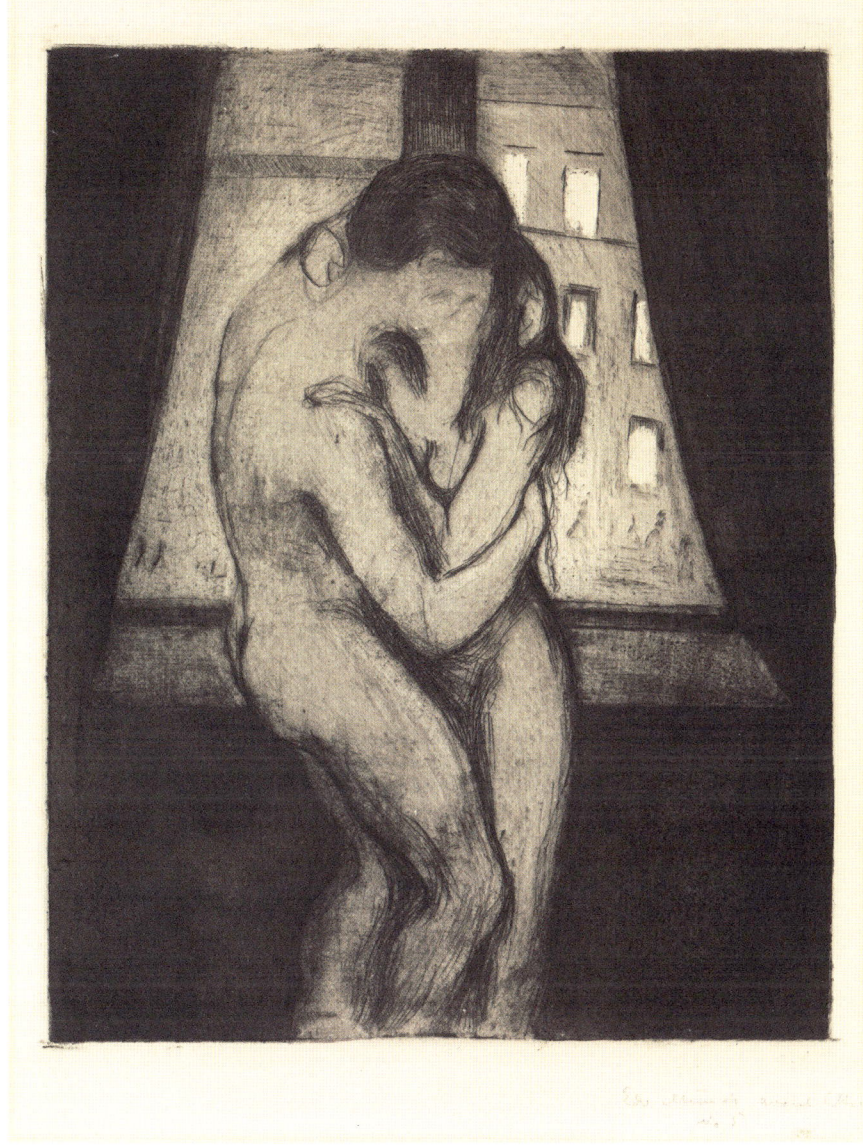

76

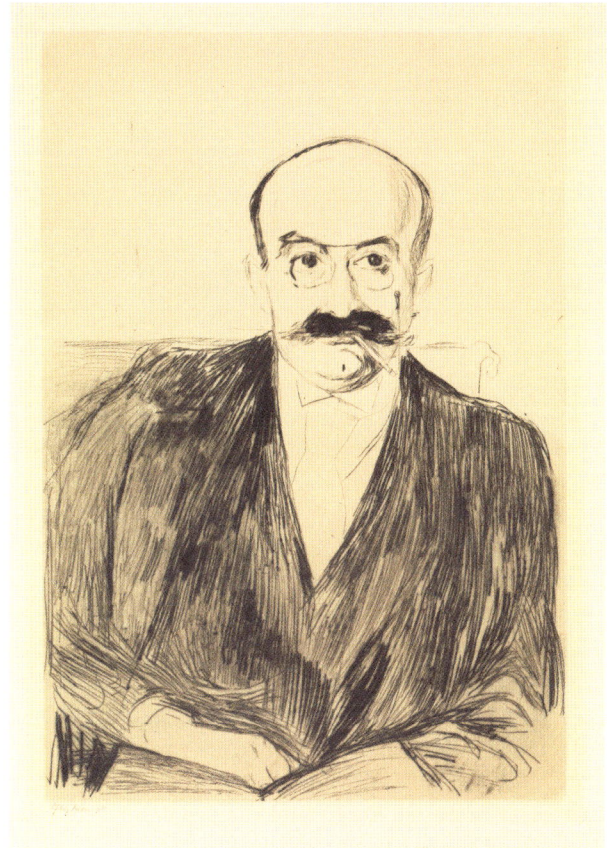

77

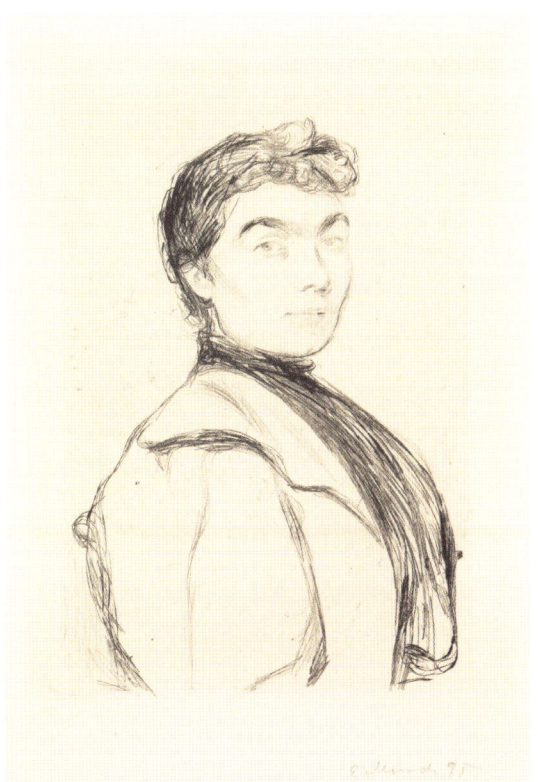

78

79
Dr. Hermann Seidel

Plate 1895; impression (between 1902 and 1914)
Intaglio: drypoint and roulette; dark brown ink;
stiff wove paper
Image: 322 × 221; paper: 508 × 349
Artist's inscription: Edv. Munch/avant lettre
Secondary inscription: O Felsing Berlin gdr.
NG.K&H.A.19067
Provenance unknown
Sch 26; W 26; Woll G 28 I/I
Printer: Felsing

The National Museum's impression cannot be
dated more precisely than to the years when
Felsing was printing for Munch. Lower left on
the printing plate (MM P 22) is a small sketch
of a head. There exist impressions both with
this sketch (Woll G 28 A) and without (Woll G
28 B). The National Museum's impression is
without. Shiefler used the title *Porträt (Herr Dr.
S)*. The person portrayed has been identified as
Hermann Seidel (1858–95), a surgeon living in
Braunschweig. He was the brother of Paul Seidel,
the director of the Hohenzollern Museum, who
owned a collection of Munch prints to which
Schiefler had access. *Portrait of a Woman* (cat. 78)
is possibly a depiction of Hermann Seidel's wife.

80
Tiergarten, Berlin

Plate 1895; impression 1895
Intaglio: open bite, drypoint and burnisher; black
ink; laid paper, ARCHES
Image: 119 × 151; paper: 311 × 447
Artist's inscription: E Munch 95
NG.K&H.A.19077
Provenance unknown
Sch 54; W 46; Woll G 30 I/II
Printer: Sabo or Angerer

Schiefler dates *Tiergarten, Berlin* to 1896. A comparable drawing (MM.T.131-3) in a sketchbook,
which can be dated to 1895 on the basis of its
subject and inscriptions, together with the artist's
dating on the National Museum's impression,
indicate that the plate is from 1895. In the intaglio,
the design is not inverted relative to the sketch.

81
Ingeborg Heiberg

Plate 1895; impression 1895
Intaglio: drypoint and roulette with plate tone;
black ink; wove paper
Image: 371 × 274; paper: 644 × 489
Artist's inscription: E Munch 1895
NG.K&H.A.19069
Provenance unknown
Sch 38; W 29; Woll G 31 II/II
Printer: Norges Geografiske Opmaaling

Ingeborg Heiberg (1884–1974) was the daughter of
Ragnhild and Axel Heiberg (see cat. 82). Munch
made a portrait in pastels of Ingeborg with her
brother Oscar, which he dated 1896 (Woll M 384),
although it was probably executed in 1895. (Letter
from Axel Heiberg to Edvard Munch 03.12.1896:
"you have captured little Ingeborg particularly
vividly, just as she was last year"; original in the
Munch Museum, MM K 0273.) Around the same
time, Munch also made an intaglio portrait of
Ingeborg's mother, Ragnhild (see cat. 82). Schiefler, who did not know the identity of the model,
uses the title *Kopf eines ganz jungen Mädchens*;
in the catalogue of Munch's 1922 exhibition in
Zurich, the title was *Fräulein Heiberg* (cat. 97).

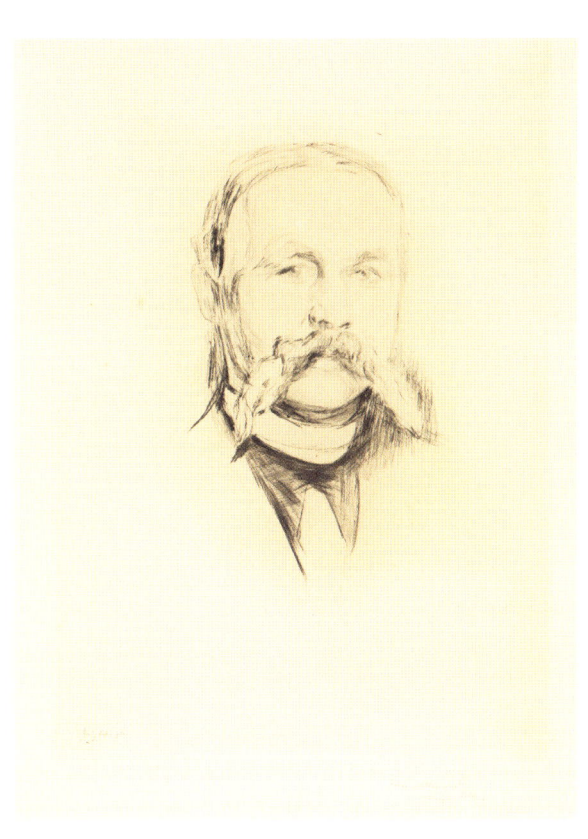

79

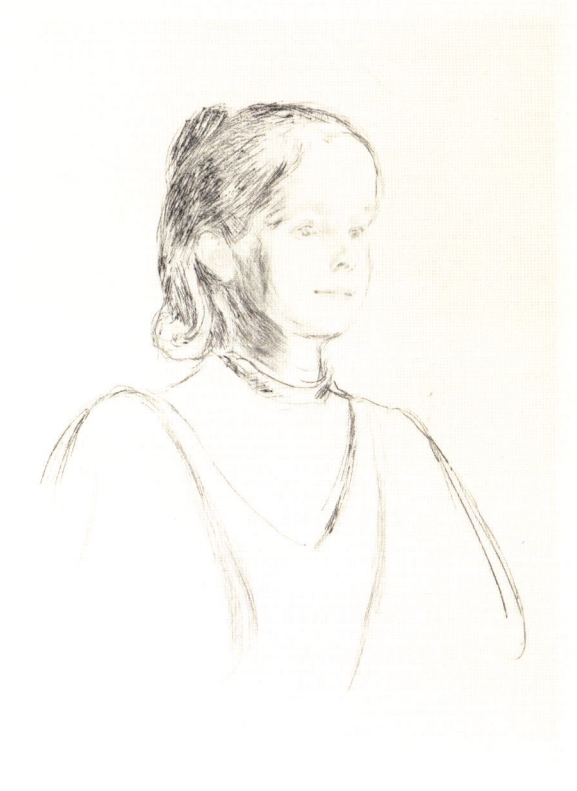

81

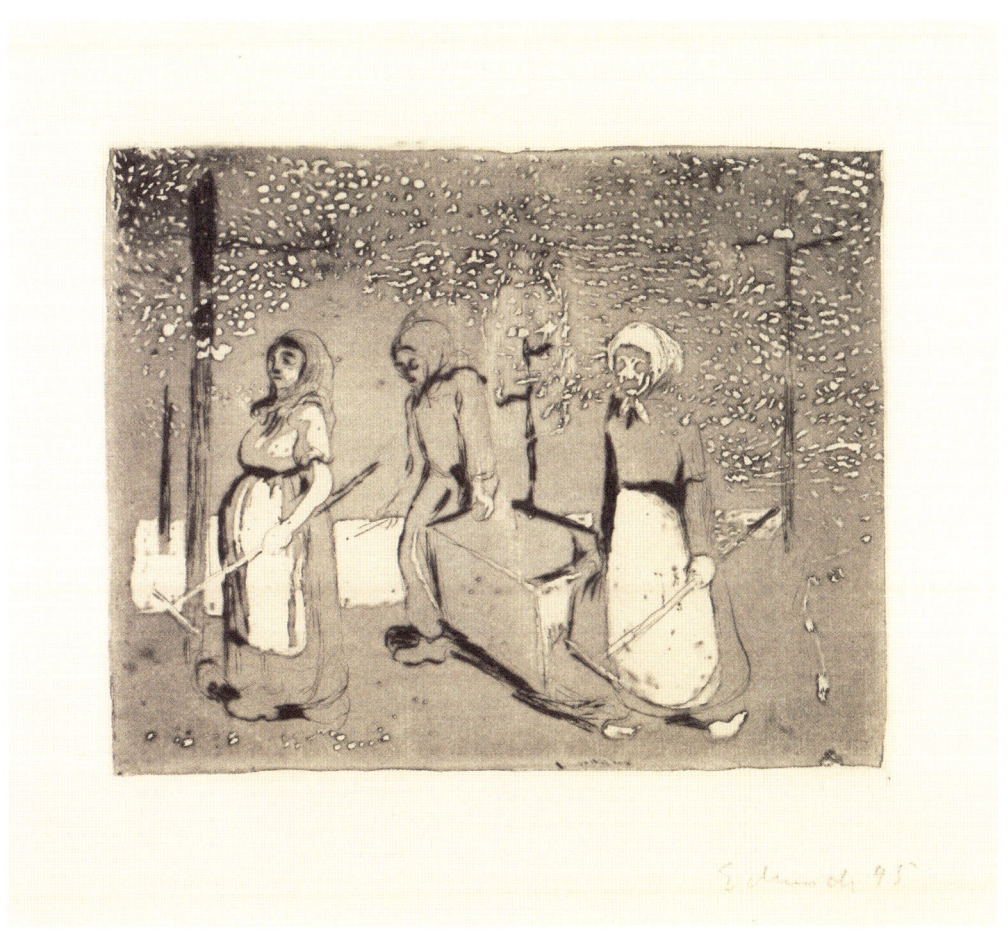

80

82
Ragnhild Heiberg

Plate 1895 or 1896; impression 1896
Intaglio: drypoint with plate tone; black ink;
medium-weight laid paper, ARCHES
Image: 284 × 223; paper: 567 × 384
Artist's inscription: E Munch 96 [the 6 overwrites
a 5]
NG.K&H.A.19076
Provenance unknown
Sch 53; W 45; Woll G 32 I/I
Printer: Angerer (?)

The artist's correction of the dating from 95 to 96
may indicate that the National Museum's impression was signed and dated some time after it was
printed. Since the depiction has the quality of a
private portrait, it is likely that Munch executed
the plate while in Kristiania (Oslo). The first
trial proofs were pulled at Norges Geografiske
Opmaaling (the Norwegian mapping authority).
However, the type of paper used for the National
Museum's impression indicates that it was
printed by Angerer. After New Year 1896, Munch
spent only a short time in Berlin on his way to
Paris. The National Museum's impression may
have been printed while in Berlin, or by Angerer
at a later time. Schiefler uses the title *Porträt einer
Dame*; in the catalogue of Munch's exhibition at
the Dioramalokalet, Kristiania (Oslo), in March
1910, the intaglio had the title *Portræt af fru Heiberg* (Portrait of Mrs Heiberg) (cat. 16). Ragnhild
Heiberg (1849–1939), daughter of Thorvald Meyer,
was married to the financier and arts patron Axel
Heiberg (1848–1932) and the mother of Ingeborg
(see cat. 81).

83
The Cat
Katten

Plate 1895; impression (1896)
Intaglio: drypoint and aquatint, with some plate
tone; black ink; laid paper
Image: 92 × 137; paper: 445 × 622
Artist's inscription: E Munch/avant lettre No. 4
NG.K&H.A.19082
Provenance unknown
Sch 89; W 54; Woll G 33 I/III
Printer: Probably Sabo or Angerer

Schiefler dates this intaglio to 1897, although it
was evidently executed before that. An impression was exhibited at Bing in Paris in May 1896,
and one in the National Library in Oslo (Plv.
2965-66) is dated 1895. There is also a drawing
dated to the same year (see below). The plate is
from Berlin (stamped verso "W Otto, Berlin", MM
P 44). It is therefore probable that Munch made
this intaglio while in Berlin in 1895. The type of
ink and paper used in the National Museum's
impression together with the artist's inscription
suggest that this is an early print; another impression is dated 1896 and inscribed "No 2" (Christie's
London, June 1984). Several drawings with comparable themes are known: MM.T.1375 (undated),
Epstein Collection (signed and dated 1895), and
a loose sheet with various sketches from around
1895 (MM.T.490).

84
Self-Portrait
Selvportrett

Stone 1895; impression (1895)
Lithograph: crayon, tusche and scraper; black
ink; heavy, stiff wove paper
Image: 461 × 325; paper: 625 × 465
Inscription on stone: EDVARD MUNCH [u.l.;
tusche]//1895 [u.r.; tusche]
Artist's inscription: E Munch
Secondary inscription: No 41 [l.r.; pencil]
NG.K&H.A.18994
Probably acquired at Munch's exhibition at
Blomqvist in 1902
Sch 31; Woll G 37 II/IV
Printer: Lassally

The inscription "No 41" is probably the printer's.
Other impressions dated 1895 and numbered in a
similar manner (Hamburger Kunsthalle, inv. no.
1954/234) indicate that the National Museum's
impression is from 1895. Given that *Self-Portrait*
is one of Munch's first lithographic works, the
graphic and expressive qualities of the depiction
are remarkable. The combination of tusche and
crayon together with the frugal scattering of
bright scratches in the rich dark surface is mas-
terful. The intensity of the image is attributable
in part to the contrast between the pale head and
the dark background, which makes the former
stand out against the latter and produces a spatial
interaction between the painted and the drawn
areas. The contemplative expression on the face
adds to the picture's lifelike quality. At the same
time, the juxtaposition of the frontal head against
a dark ground and a skeletal arm prompt associations to a grave monument.

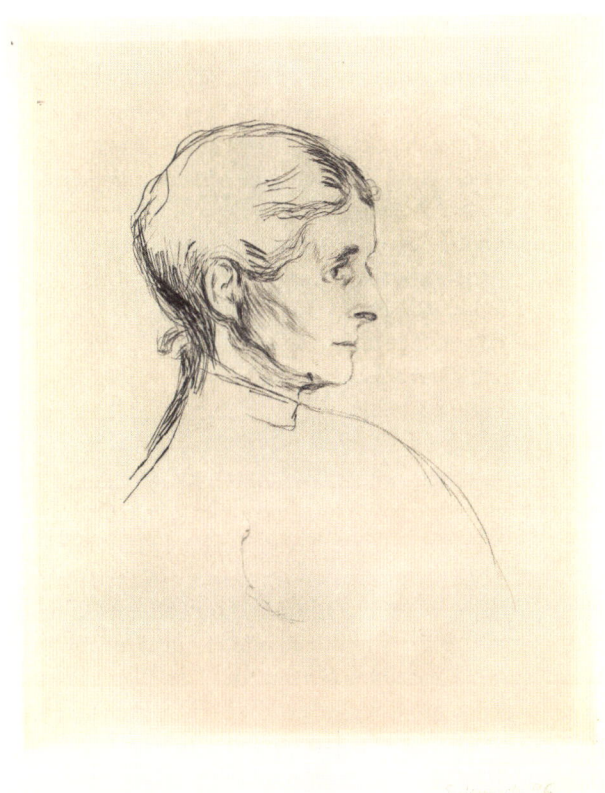

82

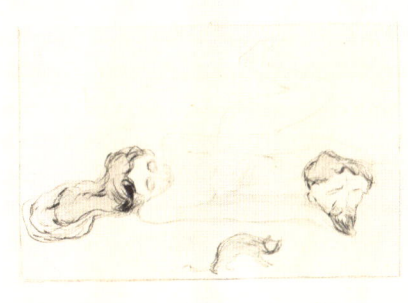

83

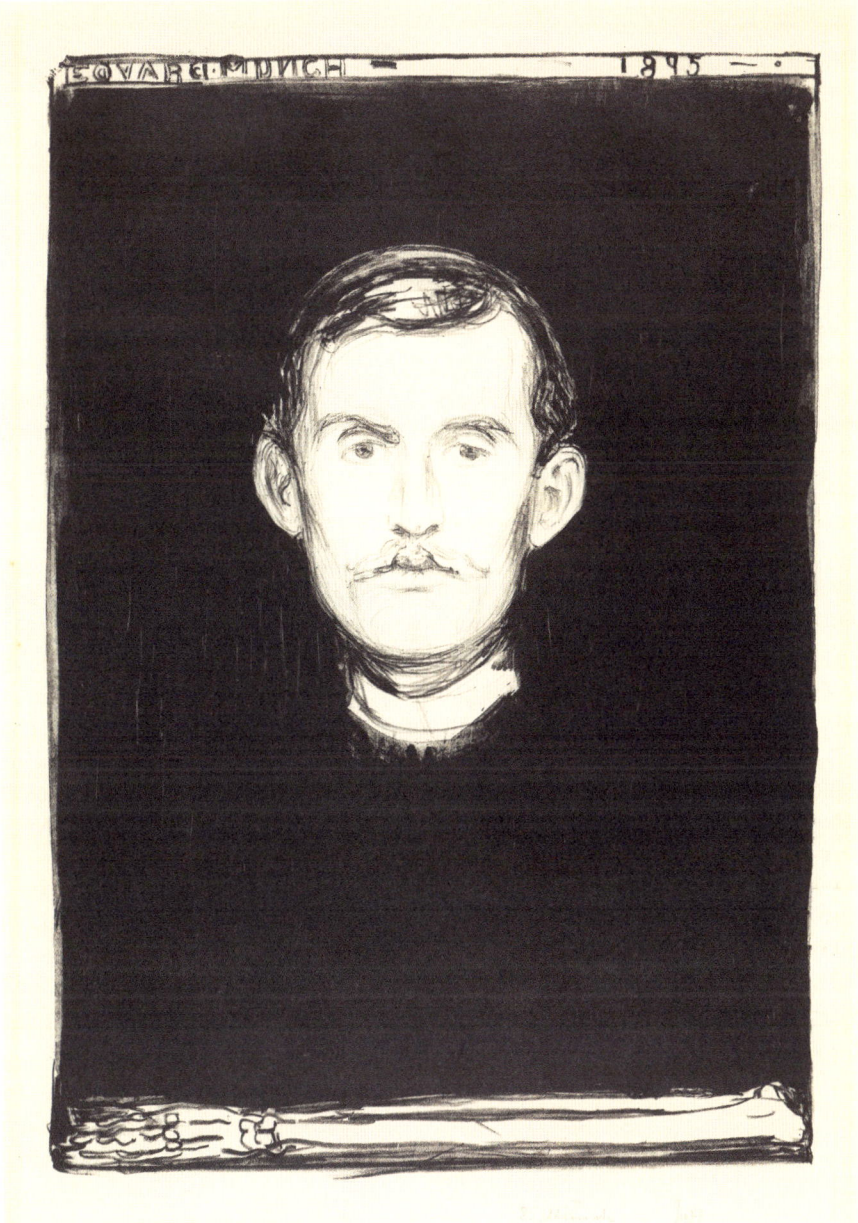

84

85
The Scream
Skrik

Stone 1895; impression (1895)
Lithograph: tusche and crayon; black ink; heavy, stiff wove paper
Image: 355 × 254; plate: 443 × 254; paper: 514 × 400
Inscription on stone: Geschrei [l.c.; tusche] // Ich fühlte das grosse Geschrei durch die Natur [l.r.; tusche]
Artist's inscription l.r.: Edv Munch No 22
NG.K&H.A.18995
Possibly acquired at Munch's exhibition at Blomqvist in 1902
Sch 32; Woll G 38 A/C
Printer: Liebmann

All the known impressions of this lithograph date from 1895. Some carry the full text, some only the word "Geschrei", and some have no text at all. The lithograph was reproduced in *La Revue Blanche* in December 1895. Alongside "Madonna" (see cat. 86, 87 and 23), "The Scream" is now one of Munch's best known images. It is discussed in greater depth in connection with the National Museum's painting, cat. 23. Munch produced two painted versions of the image and two in pastels (Woll M 332, 333, 372, 896).

86
Madonna

Stone 1895; impression 1895
Lithograph: crayon, tusche and scraper; black ink; grey cardboard
Image: 423 × 445; paper: 656 × 490
Artist's inscription: E Munch 95 [the 5 overwrites a 6]
NG.K&H.A.19515
Provenance unknown
Sch 33; Woll G 39 B I 1 / VII
Printer: Lassally

The artist's correction of the date from 96 to 95 might indicate that the National Museum's impression was signed and dated some time after it was printed. The impression is slightly light-damaged; the cardboard was originally a purer grey, as it still is on the verso. Munch modified the lithographic version of this motif many times. The most conspicuous change is in the cropping. The National Museum's impression does not include the lower part of the woman's torso and the foetus (masked during printing). The purpose may have been to render the image less provocative, although it has the appearance of being truncated. Munch also made a colour version of the lithograph (see cat. 87). The back of the stone (MM P 155) was used as the keystone for *Vampire II* (see cat. 88 and 89). In 1893–95, Munch produced several painted versions of *Madonna* (Woll M 365, 366, 367, 368, 369) and a drawing (MM.T.2430). Alongside "The Scream" (see cat. 85 and 23), "Madonna" is now one of Munch's best known motifs. It is discussed in greater depth in connection with the National Museum's painting (see cat. 29).

87
Madonna

Keystone 1895, colour stone/plate probably 1902; impression (between 1902 and 1913)
Colour lithograph: keystone: crayon, tusche and scraper; black ink; colour plates (zinc plates?): tusche; red, yellowish green and blue ink; light-weight Japan paper
Image: 559 × 351; paper: 642 × 451
Artist's inscription: E Munch
NG.K&H. A.19516
Provenance unknown
Sch 33; Woll G 39 C IV 2 / VII
Printer: Lassally

The first impressions of this print were monochrome (see cat. 86). According to Schiefler, Munch made the colour plates in 1902 (none of which are preserved). Clearly visible in the imprint of one of the colour plates (with blue ink) are traces of the annual rings from a woodblock. While it is unknown how this block was involved in the printing process, the likely explanation is that the motif was transferred from a woodblock to a stone or zinc plate, which was then used for the blue colour. The structure of the wood is barely visible in the National Museum's impression. The signature that Munch scratched into the keystone at the lower right is not visible in this impression. Munch modified the lithographic version of this image numerous times. The most conspicuous change is in the cropping (see cat. 86). In the museum's colour impression, the entire border around the woman was masked out during printing. At various times, Munch pulled large numbers of prints in the same state as the National Museum's impression, and we have no evidence for the production date other than Schiefler's dating of the colour plates (*post quem*) and Munch's later modification of the keystone, probably in 1913 (*ante quem*). For other versions of the motif and further discussion thereof, see cat. 86 and 29.

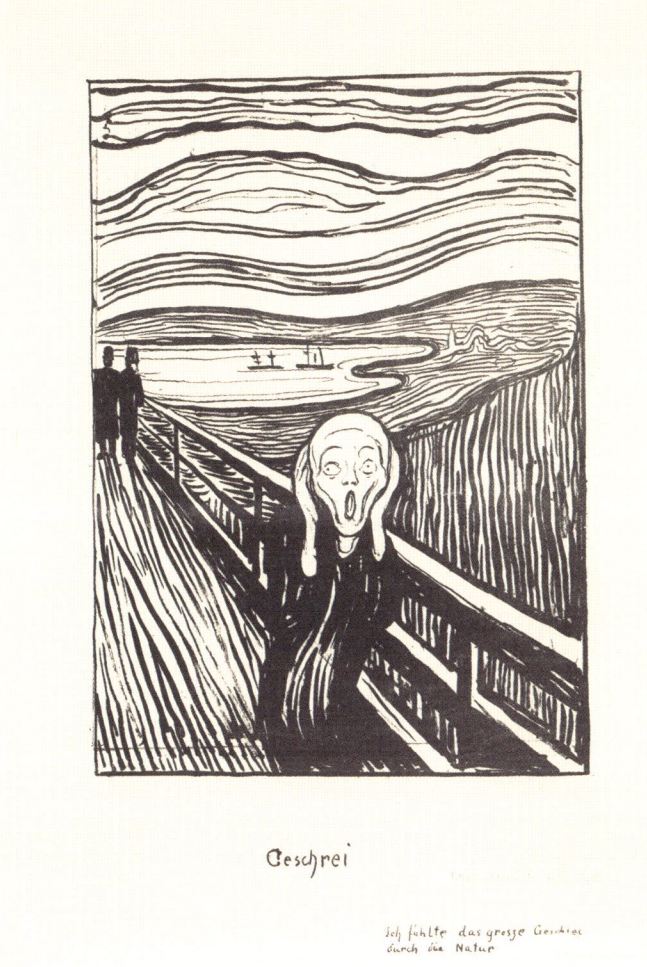

Geschrei

Ich fühlte das grosse Geschrei
durch die Natur

85

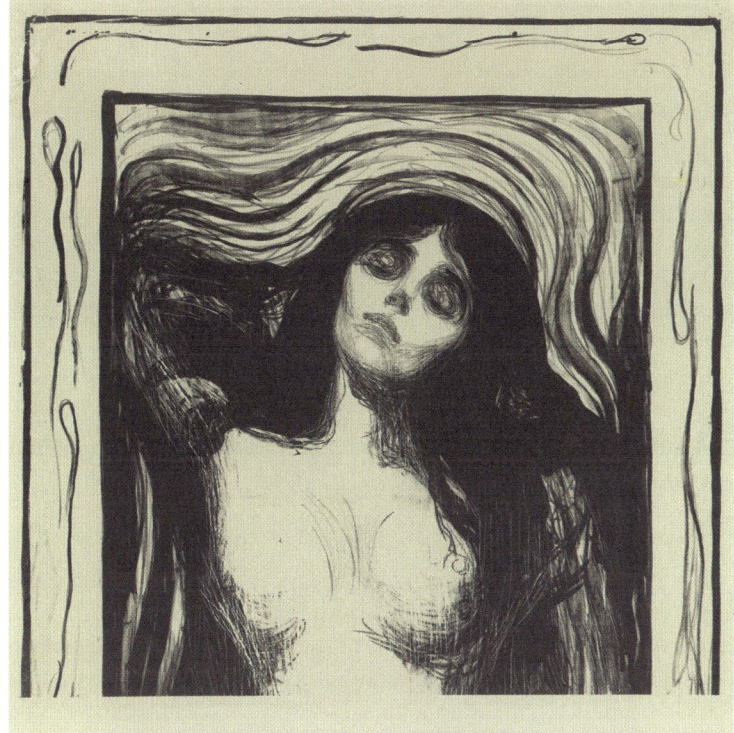

86

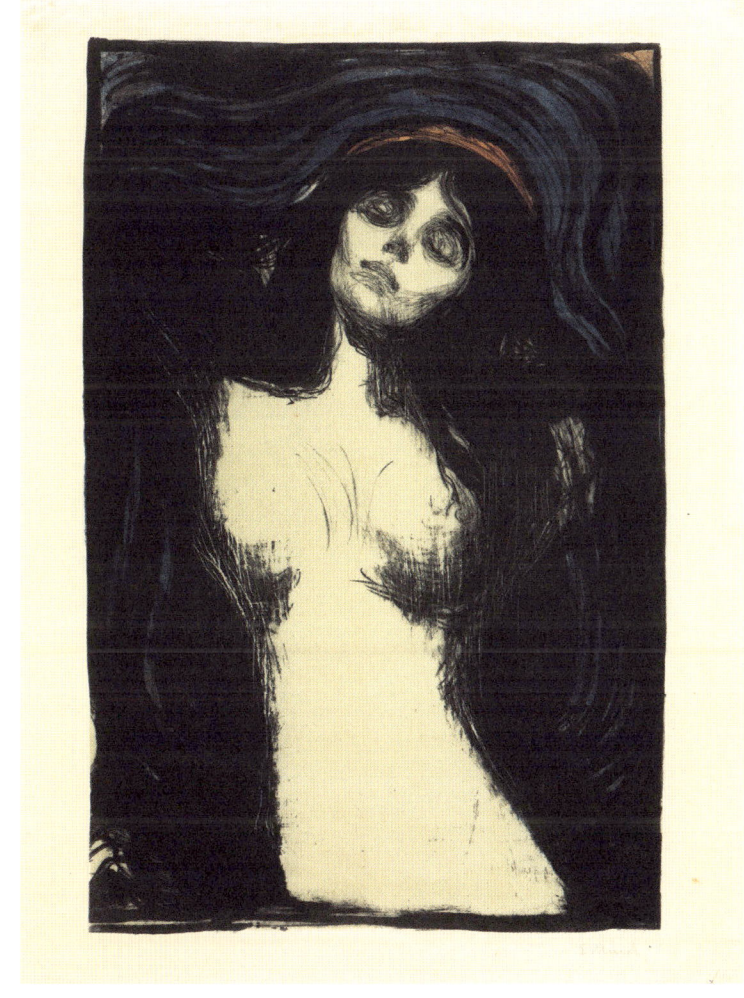

87

88
Vampire II
Vampyr II

Stone 1895; impression (1895)
Lithograph: crayon, tusche and scraper; black
ink; heavy, stiff wove paper
Image: 394 × 557; paper: 480 × 643
Artist's inscription: E Munch No 18
NG.K&H.B.00616
Provenance unknown
Sch 34; Woll G 41 I/X
Printer: Lassally

In the first version that Munch made of this motif,
a window is clearly visible in the background to
the right of the couple (Woll G 40). In the same
year, however, he also made this version, from
which the window is entirely absent. The inscription "No 17" and dating to 1995 of a comparable
impression in the Munch Museum (MM.G.567-
62) indicate that the National Museum's is from
the same time. The other side of the stone (MM
P 155) was used for *Madonna* (see cat. 86). There
are several hand-coloured impressions of this
lithograph, and in 1902 Munch produced a multicolour version using a combination of lithograph
and woodcut (see cat. 89). The prints reiterate
a painting from 1893 (Woll M 334), which was
exhibited that year in Berlin under the title *Liebe
und Schmerz*. Munch also painted two further
early versions of the image, and several more in
later years. The title *Vampire* - which was soon
adopted for both the paintings and the graphic
versions - probably stems from Stanisłav Przybyszewski (see cat. 91), who was one of the first to
write about Munch's art.

89
Vampire II
Vampyr II

Keystone 1895, colour stone and colour block
1902; impression (1902 or slightly later)
Combination of colour lithograph and colour
woodcut: keystone: crayon, tusche and scraper;
black ink; colour stone: tusche, red ink; colour
block: fretsaw (the plate is cut into four pieces);
green, blue and ochre ink; heavy wove paper
Image: 388 × 550; paper: 488 × 651
Artist's inscription: E Munch
NG.K&H.A.18996
Provenance unknown
Sch 34; Woll G 41 V/X
Printer: Lassally

Munch first executed the keystone for this print
in 1895 (see cat. 88). According to Schiefler, he
prepared the colour plates for the multicolour
version in 1902. In the National Museum's impression, the image is printed from the keystone in
black, while the red hair is printed from a second
lithographic stone. The other colours, green,
blue and ochre, are printed from a woodblock
that was cut into four pieces with a fretsaw (MM
P 314). The National Museum's impression is on
grey wove paper with a yellow striped pattern on
the recto side. Several impressions of different
pictures with a similar stripe pattern on paper of
the same quality are known, indicating that the
yellow colour originates from a substance (glue or
resin?) that was applied to the paper before it was
used for printing, and which has turned yellow
over time due to light exposure (three impressions
in the Munch Museum of the lithograph *Salome*,
MM.G.256-2 (dated in pencil 1902, MM.G.256-3,
MM.G.256-13); an impression of the lithograph
The Brooch in state I (private collection), registered
by the Munch Museum; the National Museum's
impression of the woodcut *Melancholy III* (see cat.
159), and a further impression of the same (on the
art market in 2014)). On the recorded prints, the
yellow colour of the stripe pattern varies from
prominent to almost invisible, a variation that
is probably due to the tendency of the applied
substance to discolour when exposed to light.
The works in question can be dated to 1902–03
and were printed by Lassally. (Paper conservators
Magdalena Godzimirska of the Munch Museum
and Kari Greve of the National Museum participated in a discussion about the cause of the yellow
stripe pattern in March 2014.) The state and type
of paper of the National Museum's impression
indicate that it is one of the earliest multicolour
prints of this motif. Munch later made several
colour plates that were combined with the keystone in various ways. A drawing with a similar
composition from 1895 is preserved (MM.T.379).
Munch also explored the theme in a number of
paintings (Woll M 331, 334, 335, 377, 1174, 1175, 1176).

90
The Hands
Hendene

Stone 1895; impression (1895)
Lithograph: crayon and tusche, black ink; heavy,
stiff wove paper
Image: 485 × 305; paper: 514 × 401
Artist's inscription: Edv. Munch No 20
NG.K&H.A.18997
Provenance unknown
Sch 35; Woll G 42 I/I
Printer: Liebmann

Only early impressions of this lithograph are
recorded. The fact that the National Museum's
impression is numbered by Munch also suggests an early date. Schiefler uses the title *Die
Begierde nach dem Weibe*. Originally conceived
as a painting in 1893-94 (Woll M 336), the theme
is also explored in several drawings (MM.T.2292,
MM.T.2442 and MM.T.1380). The image can
be read as a somewhat caricatured nude study
surrounded by the hands of male artists, which
serve as a potent symbol for the man's perpet-
ual craving for the woman. It is a theme that
runs through much of Munch's art, not least his
graphics.

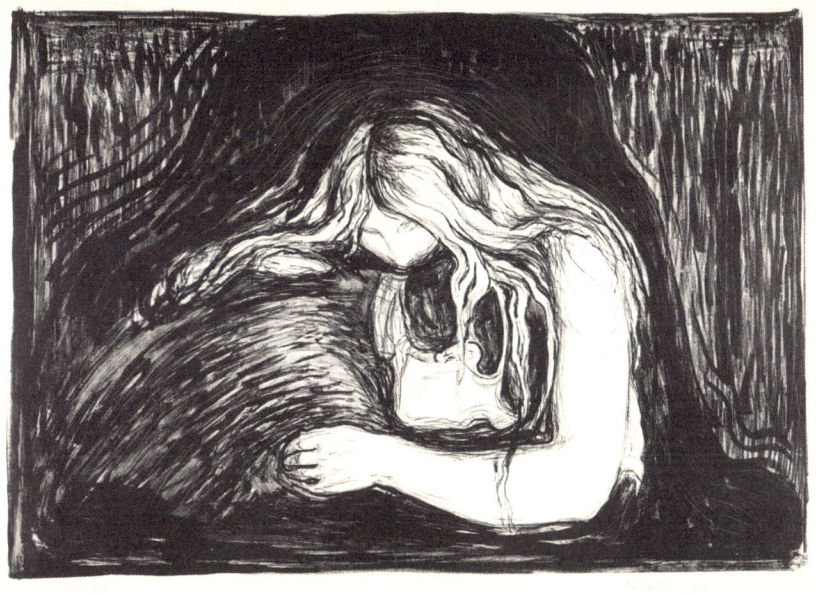

88

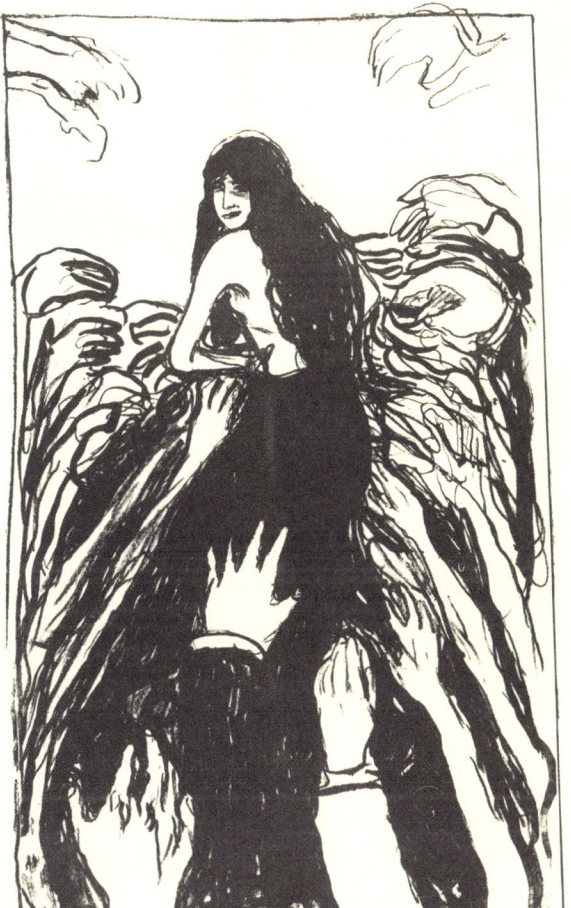

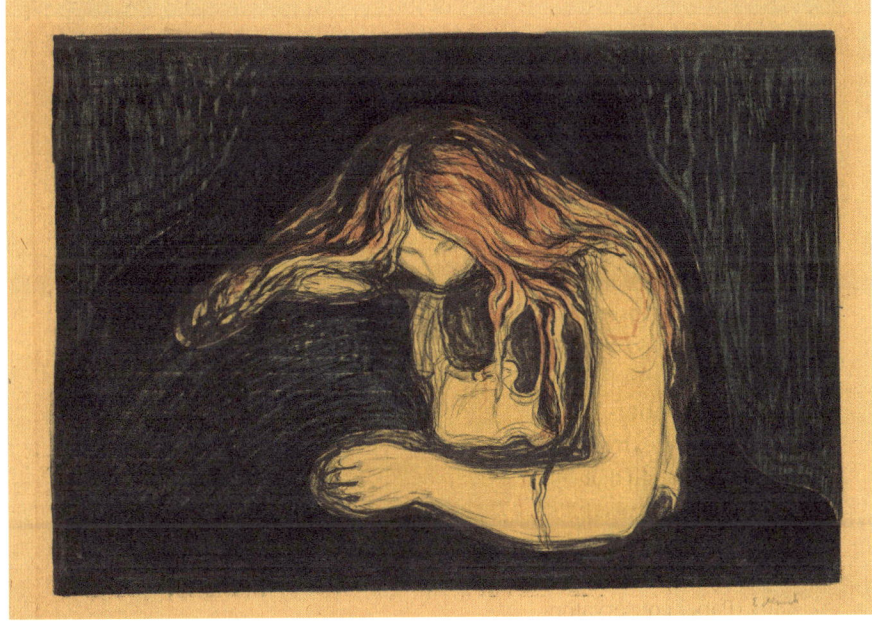

89

90

91
Stanislav Przybyszewski

Stone 1895 (probable) and 1916 or 1917; impression
(1916 or 1917)
Lithograph: crayon, tusche and scraper; stone
modified with crayon; black ink; Japan paper
Image: 543 × 447; paper: 705 × 546
Artist's inscription: Edv Munch // Portræt [l.r.]
NG.K&H. A.19034 (formerly NG.K&H.B.00613)
Purchased at City Auksjon, Oslo, September 1938
(cat. 279)
Sch 105; Woll G 45 II / III
Printer: Nielsen

The stone was first printed by Lassally in Berlin.
In 1916 or 1917, Nielsen probably transferred the
design from an imprint Munch had received from
Lassally to a duplicate stone, which was then
somewhat reworked. Stanisław Przybyszewski
(1868-1927) was a German-Polish writer who
belonged to the same social circle as Munch and
Strindberg in Berlin in the mid-1890s. He was
married to the Norwegian author Dagny Juel from
1893 until her death in 1901. Munch painted portraits of Przybyszewski in 1893–94 (Woll M 354)
and 1895 (Woll M 383).

92
The Women and the Skeleton
Kvinnene ved skjelettet

Plate 1896; impression (between 1902 and 1914)
Intaglio: drypoint with plate tone; black ink;
heavy, stiff wove paper
Image: 299 × 408; paper: 437 × 600
Artist's inscription: E Munch
Secondary inscription: O Felsing Berlin gdr.
NG.K&H.A.19070
Provenance unknown
Sch 44; W 36; Woll G 51 II 3 / III
Printer: Felsing

The impression cannot be dated more precisely
than to the years when Felsing was printing for
Munch. The National Museum has two impressions in the same state of *The Women and the
Skeleton*, both printed by Felsing. Neither is dated,
and both are of unknown provenance. Cat. 92 is,
however, a richer imprint than cat. 93.

93
The Women and the Skeleton
Kvinnene ved skjelettet

Plate 1896; impression (between 1902 and 1914)
Intaglio: drypoint with slight plate tone; black ink;
heavy, stiff wove paper
Image: 303 × 411; paper: 425 × 524
Artist's inscription: Edv Munch / avant lettre // Das
Gerippe und das [sic.] beide Madchen [sic.]
Secondary inscription: O Felsing Berlin gdr.
NG.K&H.A.19071
Provenance unknown
Sch 44; W 36; Woll G 51 II 3 / III
Printer: Felsing

The impression cannot be dated more precisely
than to the years when Felsing was printing for
Munch. The National Museum has two impressions in the same state of *The Women by the
Skeleton*, both printed by Felsing (compare cat.
92). Neither is dated, although as an imprint cat.
93 is not as rich as cat. 92.

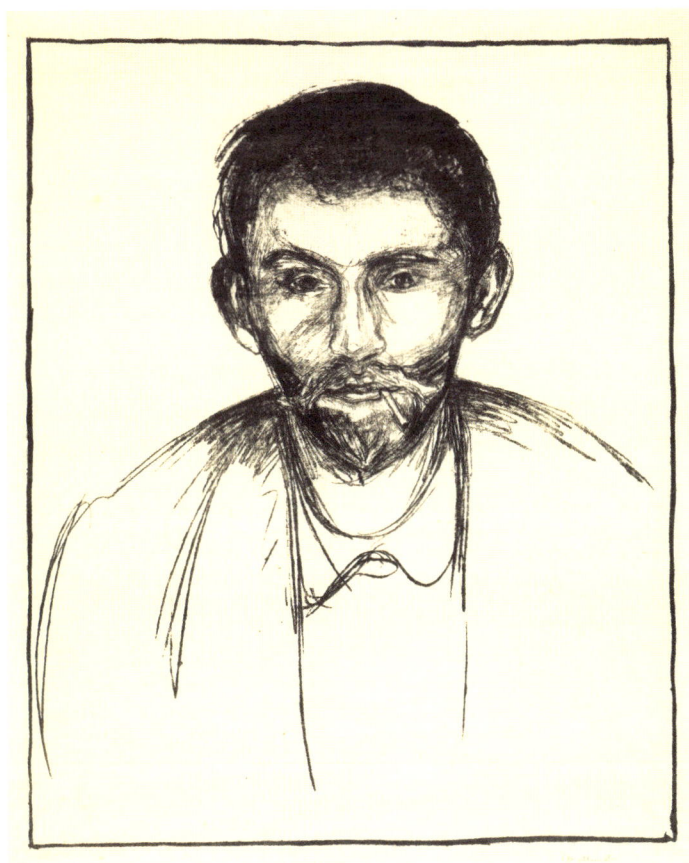

91

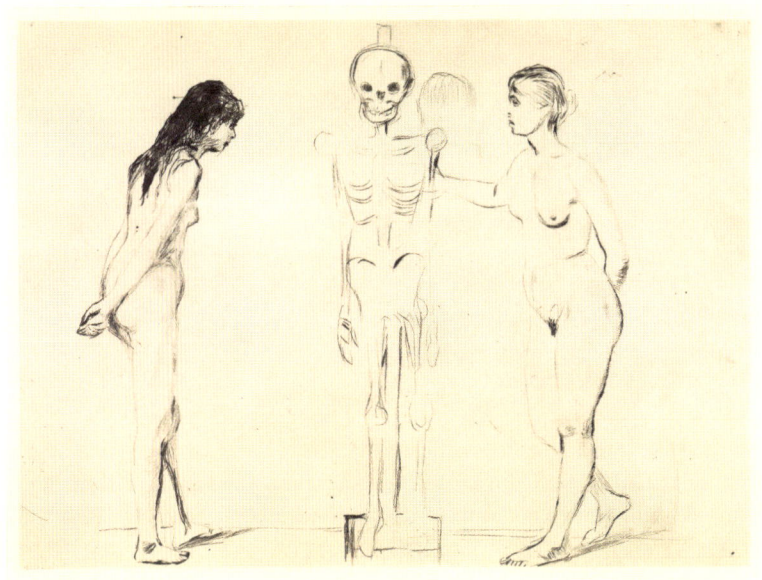

92

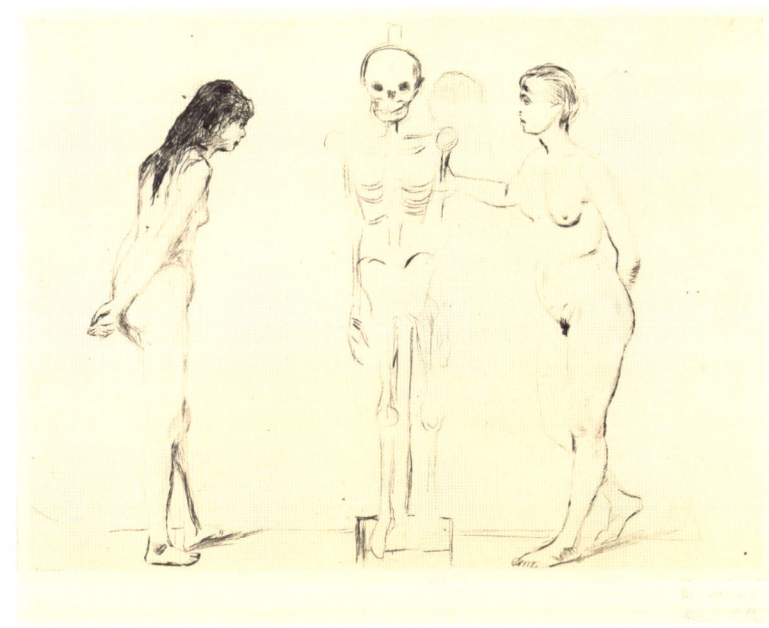

93

94
Woman Putting on her Nightgown
Kvinne som tar på seg linnetet

95
Model Warming Her Hands
Modell som varmer hendene

96
Woman with Long Hair
Kvinne med langt hår

Plate 1896; impression 1896
Intaglio: etching; black ink; laid paper, ARCHES
Image: 276 × 179; paper: 452 × 308
Artist's inscription: E Munch 96 [the 6 overwrites a 5]
NG.K&H. A.19072
Provenance: 1898?
Sch 45; W 37; Woll G 52 I/II
Printer: Lemercier or Porcabeuf

The artist's correction of the dating from 95 to 96 may indicate that the National Museum's impression was signed and dated some time after it was pulled. The plate is from Berlin (stamped verso "W Otto, Berlin", MM P 30). It is nevertheless probable that Munch made the intaglio in Paris, since the depiction closely resembles a painting shown in Munch's 1927 exhibition at the National Gallery, which had the title *Parisermodell, sittende akt på rød bakgrund* (Parisian Model. Seated Nude against a Red Background) and was dated 1896 (see cat. 34 and 95). Schiefler uses the title *Aktfigur*.

Plate 1896; impression (between 1902 and 1914)
Intaglio: line etching and roulette; dark brown ink; medium-weight, stiff wove paper
Image: 272 × 180; paper: 510 × 329
Artist's inscription: Edv Munch
Secondary inscription: O Felsing Berlin gdr.
NG.K&H. A.19073
Provenance unknown
Sch 46; W 38; Woll G 53 I/I
Printer: Felsing

The plate is from Berlin (stamped verso "W Otto, Berlin", MM P 31). It is nevertheless probable that Munch prepared the intaglio in Paris. The model here is possibly the same as he used for *Woman Putting on her Nightgown* (see cat. 94) and for the painting *Seated Nude* (see cat. 34). Schiefler uses the title *Aktstudie*. The National Museum's impression cannot be dated more precisely than to the years when Felsing was printing for Munch.

Plate 1896; impression (between 1902 and 1914)
Intaglio: line etching; dark brown ink; heavy, stiff wove paper
Image: 237 × 96; paper: 508 × 350
Artist's inscription: Edv. Munch/[...] lettre
Secondary inscription: O Felsing Berlin gdr.
NG.K&H. A.19074
Provenance unknown
Sch 47; W 39; Woll G 54 III/III
Printer: Felsing

The National Museum's impression cannot be dated more precisely than to the years when Felsing was printing for Munch. Munch began work on the plate in Paris in 1896. The image was originally on the same plate as *The Woman and the Heart* (see cat. 97), but the plate was later cut in two.

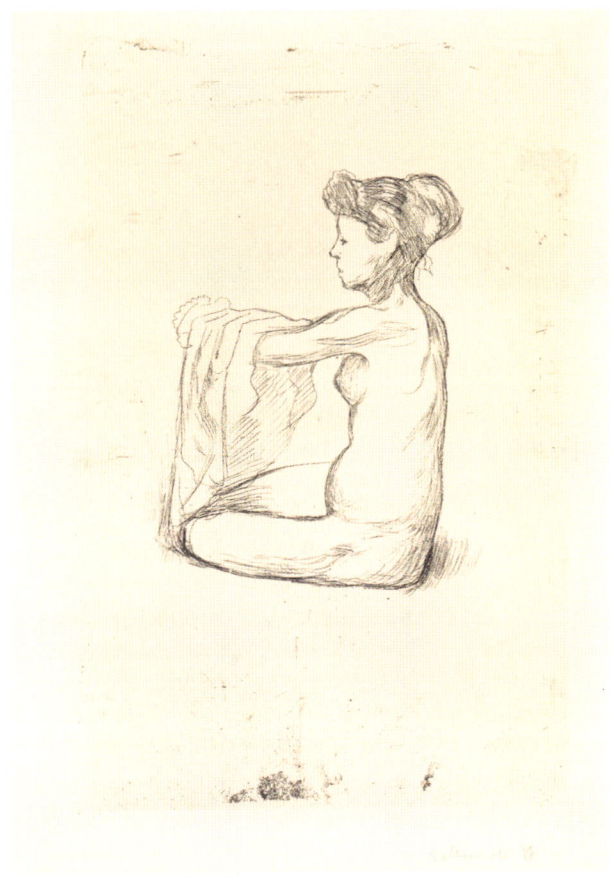

94

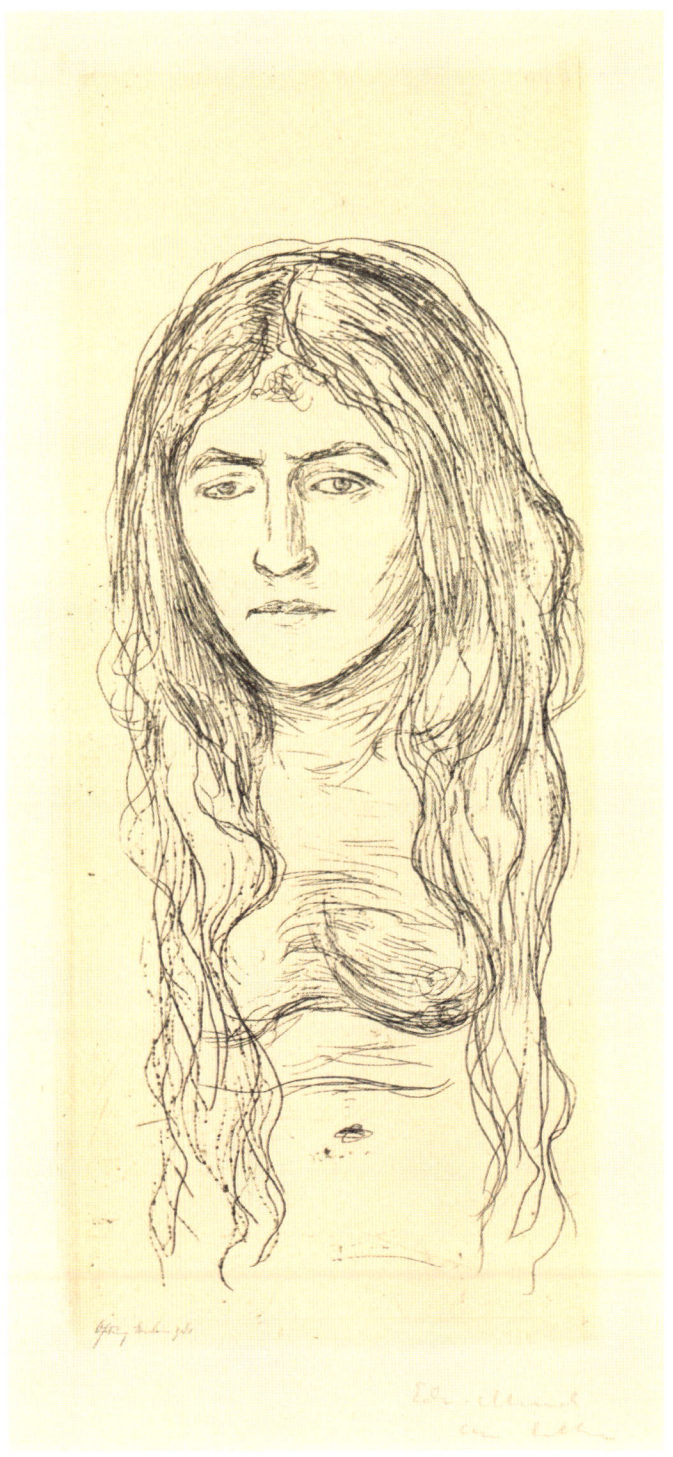

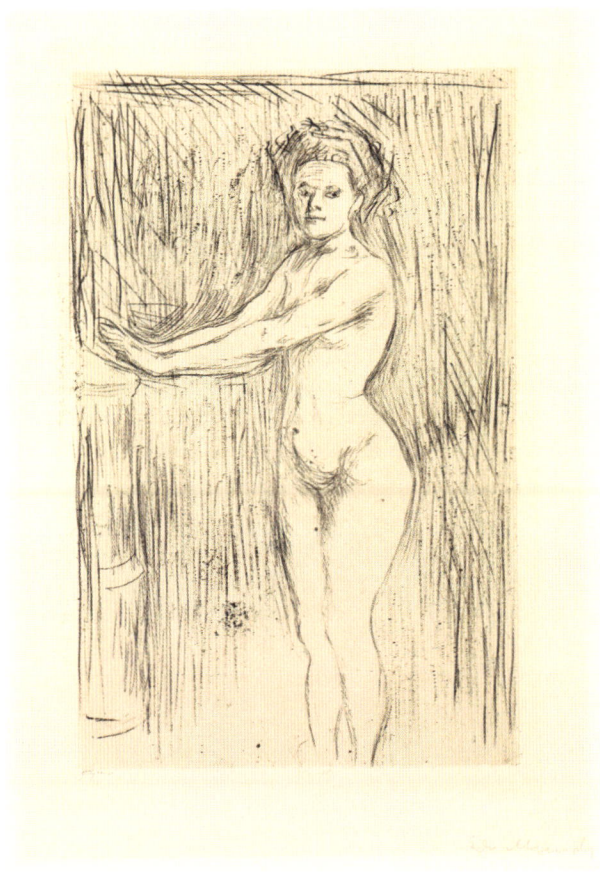

95

96

97

The Woman and the Heart

Piken og hjertet

Plate 1896; impression (between 1902 and 1914)
Intaglio: line etching and drypoint; dark brown
ink; heavy, stiff wove paper
Image: 238 × 233; paper: 603 × 439
Artist's inscription: Edv. Munch / avant lettre
Secondary inscription: O Felsing Berlin gdr.
NG.K&H. 19075
Provenance unknown
Sch 48; W 40; Woll G 55 IV / IV
Printer: Felsing

The National Museum's impression cannot be
dated more precisely than to the years when
Felsing was printing for Munch. Munch began
work on the plate in Paris in 1896. The image was
originally on the same plate as *Woman with Long
Hair* (see cat. 96). This print, together with several
others by Munch, appeared in the magazine
Quickborn (vol. 4 January 1899) alongside texts
by August Strindberg. Munch also explored the
theme in several drawings (MM.T.377, MM.T.374,
MM.T.2466, MM.T. 371) and as a woodcut (Woll
G 135).

98

Young Woman and Portrait of the Artist

Ung kvinne og kunstnerens portrett

Plate 1896; impression (between 1902 and 1914)
Intaglio: line etching with plate tone; dark brown
ink; heavy wove paper
Image: 229 × 148; paper: 412 × 308
Artist's inscription: E Munch / avant
lettre // Liggende Dame [n. v.]
Secondary inscription: O Felsing Berlin gdr.
NG.K&H. A.19079
Provenance unknown
Sch 87; W 52; Woll G 60 I / I
Printer: Felsing

Munch executed the plate in Paris in 1896. The
National Museum's impression cannot be dated
more precisely than to the years when Felsing
was printing for Munch. The upper part of the
intaglio shows Tupsy (Martha Caroline) Jebe
(1871-1959), later Clement (married name), who
studied in Paris and was a friend of Munch in
1896. The portrait of Munch on the lower half of
the plate is attributed to her. According to Schiefler, Felsing pulled some impressions without the
lower image. For a drawn portrait assumed to be
of Tupsy Jebe, see cat. 241.

99

Helge Rode

Plate 1896 (?); impression 1896 (?)
Intaglio: drypoint and burnisher; black ink; laid
paper, ARCHES
Image: 255 × 186; paper: 445 × 305
Artist's inscription: E Munch 96 [the 6 overwrites
an indistinct digit (5?)]
NG.K&H.A.1908
Provenance unknown
Sch 103; W 55; Woll G 62 IV / V
Printer: probably Sabo or Angerer

It is uncertain when Munch produced this
portrait, which was apparently done with Rode
sitting as model. Schiefler, who dates the plate to
1898, asserts that it was first printed by Norges
Geografiske Opmaaling (the Norwegian mapping
authority) and later by Felsing. The print was,
however, included in Munch's exhibition at the
Dioramalokalet, Kristiania (Oslo), in September-
October 1897 (cat. 142). The inscription on the
National Museum's impression indicates an even
earlier dating. On the other hand, the correction
to the date suggests that it was added some time
after the impression was pulled. From the information we have today, it is impossible to say with
any certainty whether the plate was executed in
1895, 1896 or 1897. The type of paper used in the
National Museum's impression indicates that it
was printed by either Sabo or Angerer (we know
of other, similar impressions, see Woll G 62 I–IV).
Helge Rode (1870-1937) was a Danish poet. After
his father's death, his mother (Margrethe née
Lehman, later married to Erik Vullum) moved to
Norway, where Helge spent his youth. Rode and
Munch had been friends since the early 1890s.
Munch made a lithographic portrait of Helge
Rode in 1908-09 (Woll G 310).

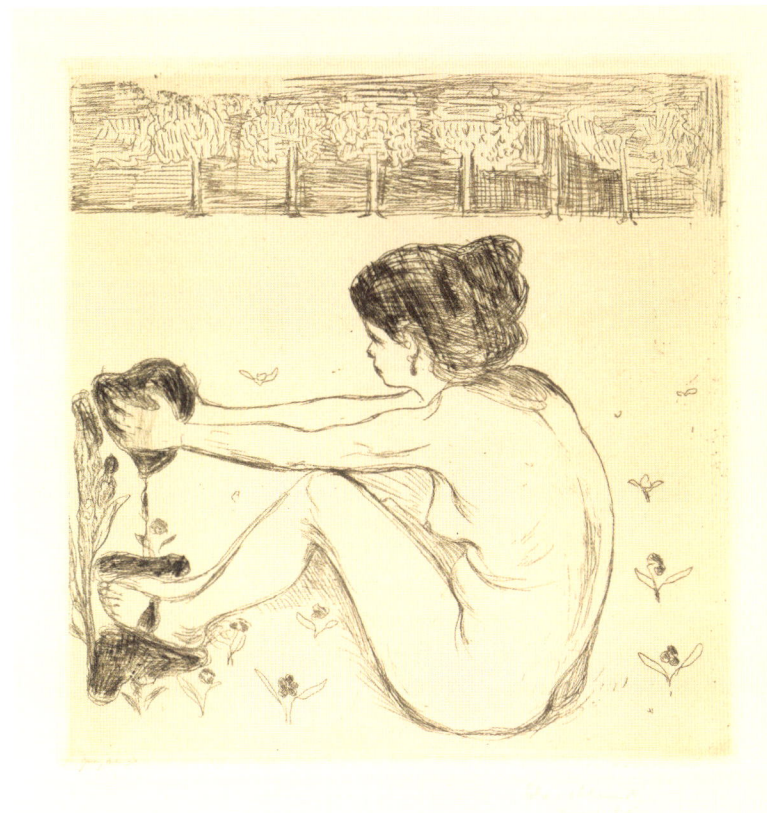

97

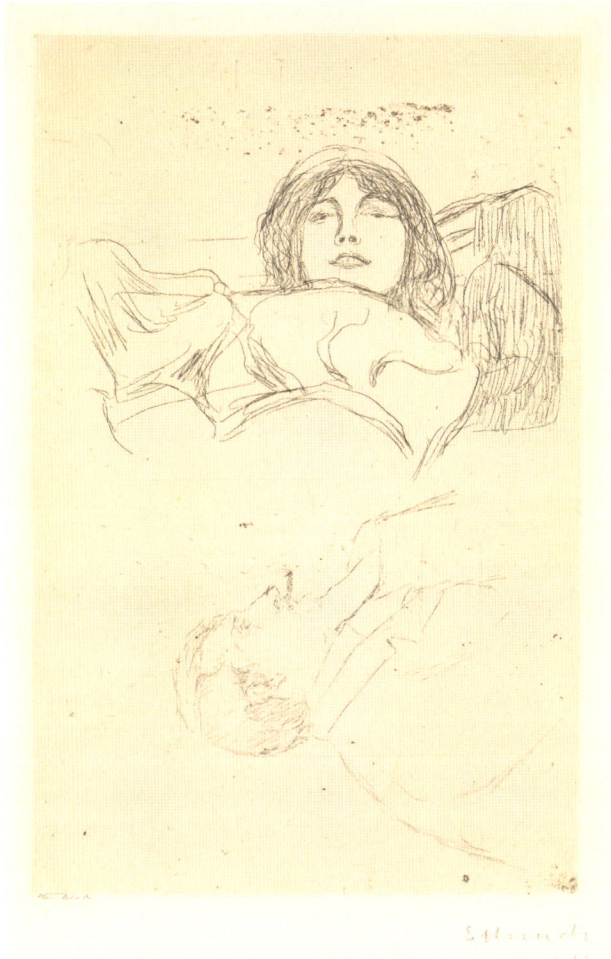

98

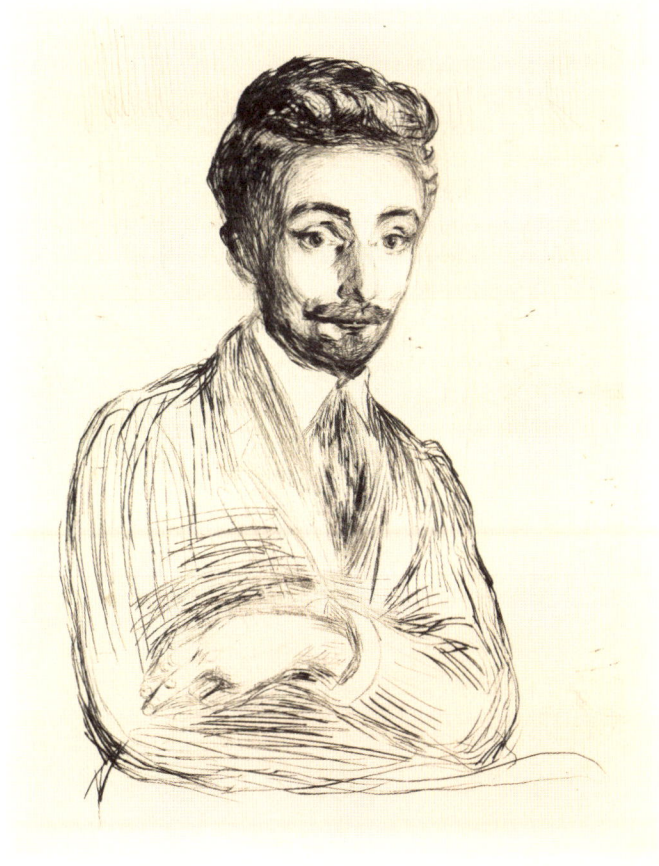

99

100
Death in the Sickroom
Døden i sykeværelset

Stone 1896; impression (1896)
Lithograph: crayon, tusche, scraper; black ink;
laid paper, MBM
Image: 389 × 558; paper: 477 × 627
Artist's inscription: E Munch
Secondary inscription: No 14/30 [l.r.; pencil]
NG.K&H.A.19032
Possibly acquired at Munch's exhibition at
Blomqvist in 1902
Sch 73; Woll G 65 I/I
Printer: Clot

The inscription "No 14/30" is probably by the
printer. Another impression, numbered 16/30,
is dated 1896 (MM.G.215-16). The image corresponds to three paintings from around 1893 (Woll
M 328, 329, 330) and is discussed in connection
with the National Museum's version (see cat. 22).

101
August Strindberg

Stone 1896; impression 1896
Lithograph: crayon, tusche and scraper; black
ink; chine collé, on heavy, stiff wove paper
Image: 444 × 317; paper: 444 × 317
Artist's inscription: E Munch/1896
Secondary inscription: 2 [l.r.; pencil]
NG.K&H. A.09239
Probably acquired at Munch's exhibition at
Blomqvist in 1902
Sch 77; Woll G 66 III B/V
Printer: Clot

The inscription "2" was added before the
National Gallery acquired the impression. Munch
executed the portrait of Strindberg in Paris. The
dating and type of paper indicate that it was
printed by Clot. The portrait exists in one version
with a border that contains a female figure to
the right and the subject's name, misspelt, to the
lower left. In another version, the female figure is
replaced by a continuation of the border's wave
pattern, and the name corrected (see cat. 102).
A third version lacks the border. In the latter,
either the border was masked for the printing, or
it was cropped after printing. Most of the early
impressions that lack the border were printed
from two stones (a black keystone and a brown
colour stone), whereas the National Museum's
impression is monochrome black. *The Urn* and
Jealousy I (see cat. 103, 104 and 105) were printed
from the other side of the same stone (MM P 156).
August Strindberg (1849-1912) was a Swedish
writer and close friend of Munch during his
early years in Berlin and in Paris in 1896. Munch
painted a portrait of him in 1892 (Woll M 301).

102
August Strindberg

Stone 1896; impression (1896 or 1897)
Colour lithograph: keystone: crayon, tusche
and scraper, black ink; colour stone: tusche and
scraper, blue ink; China paper (lined 1973)
Image: 643 × 485; paper: 710 × 549
Signature and text on stone: E Munch [l.l.;
scraper]//A. STRINDBERG [l.l.; tusche]
Artist's inscription: Edv Munch No 12
NG.K&H. A.09238
Probably acquired at Munch's exhibition at
Blomqvist in 1902
Sch 77; Woll G 66 III A/V
Printer: Clot

The various versions of the portrait of Strindberg are discussed in connection with cat. 101.
Other impressions in the same state as this one
and dated 1897 (MM.G.219-2) indicate that the
National Museum's impression is from that year
or possibly the year before.

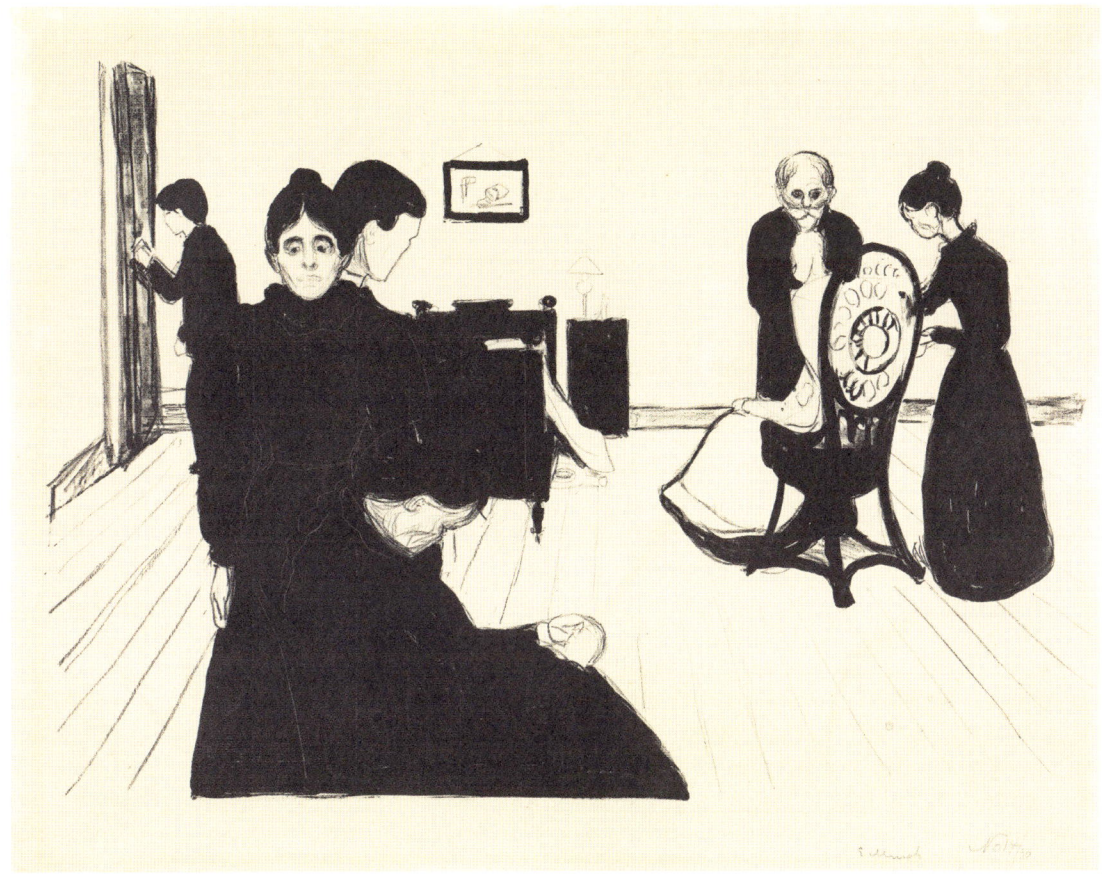

100

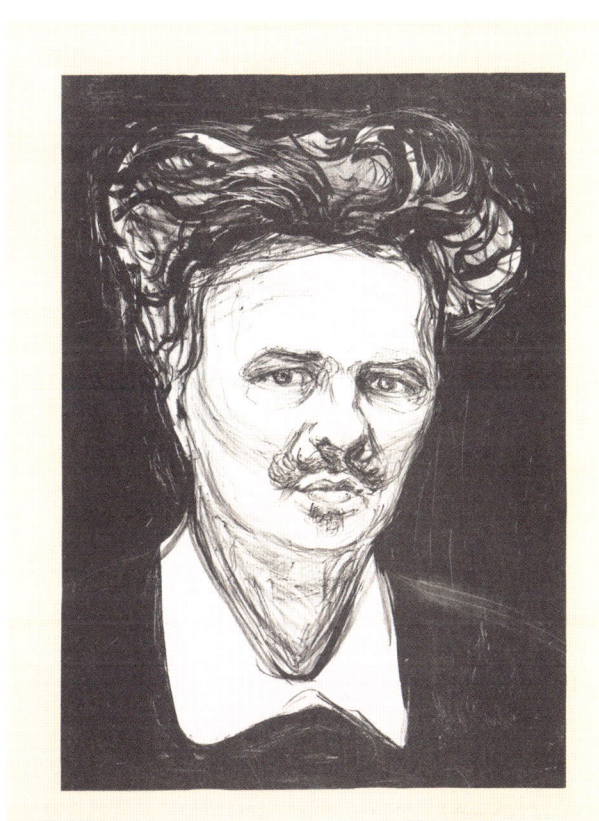

101

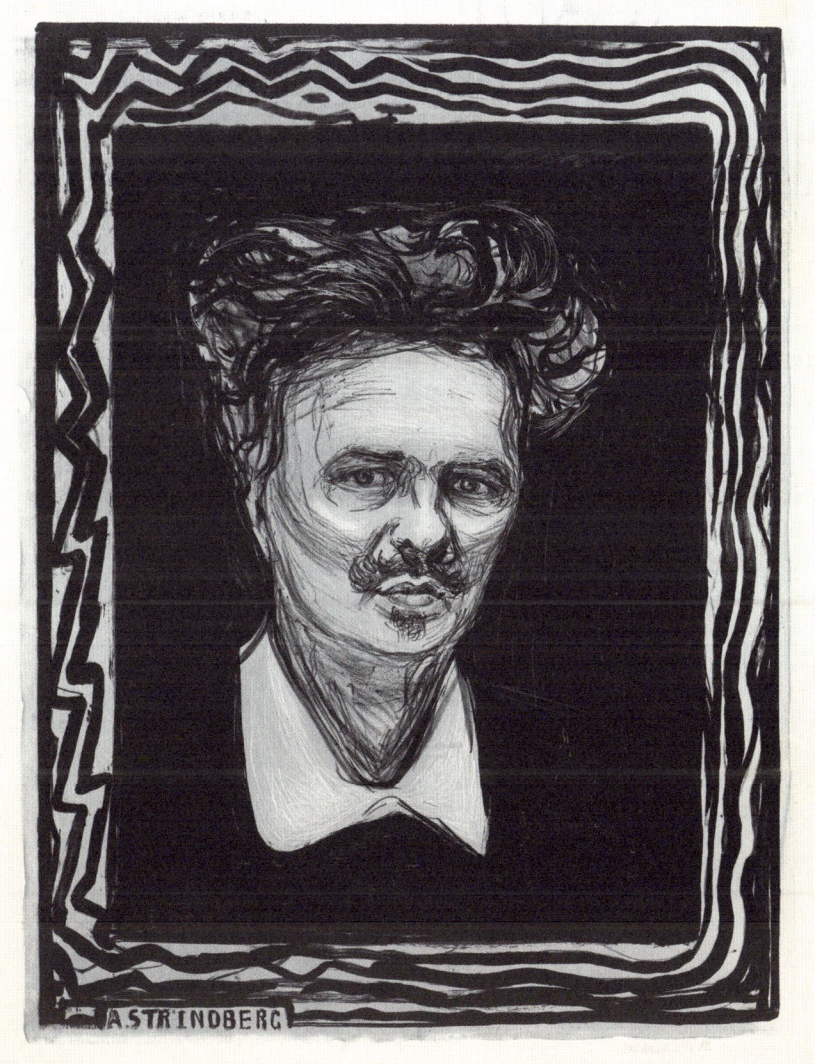

103
The Urn
Urnen

Stone 1896; impression (1896 or 1897)
Lithograph: tusche, crayon and scraper; black
ink; medium-weight wove paper
Image: 461 × 269; paper: 500 × 665
Artist's inscription: E Munch / No 10
NG.K&H. A.19037
Provenance unknown
Sch 63; Woll G 67 III / III
Printer: Clot

The Urn and *Jealousy I* (cat. 105) are executed on
the same stone (MM P 156), turned 90° relative
to each other. The National Museum once had
two impressions of *The Urn* (see cat. 104). Cat. 103
was printed on the same sheet as *Jealousy I*; both
are signed below the image. In this impression
of *The Urn*, the scratches in the stone are clear,
whereas in later impressions, the same scratches
are less distinct, indicating an early dating for this
impression. *August Strindberg* is executed on the
other side of the same stone (see cat. 101 and 102).
In many civilizations, urns are associated with
burial. Munch's intention in using this symbol, in
combination with naked female bodies around
the base of the vessel and a beautiful woman's
face hovering above, is far from clear. The first
state included a mask-like face on the urn itself,
but this was painted over on the stone, making
the urn solid black. The design can probably be
viewed as a symbol of metabolism and rebirth.
In the following years, Munch explored the same
theme in other compositions, both as drawings
and lithographs, including *Funeral March* (cat.
126), where the urn has been replaced by a
human column topped by a coffin. During World
War I, he produced a variation on the theme
as a commentary on the horrors of war and an
expression of hope for a better future in a united
Europe (Woll G 582, 583, 584).

104
The Urn
Urnen

Stone 1896; date of impression unknown
Lithograph: tusche, crayon and scraper; black
ink; paper unknown
Dimensions according to Woll 2012: 460 × 265
Other details unknown
Sch 63; Woll G 67
Impression lost

The National Gallery once had two impressions
of *The Urn* (see cat. 103 and 104). This one was
entered in the list of works by Munch in the
Department of Prints and Drawings' supplementary record "Norwegian Graphics I" as No. 44,
"Urnen Litografi 1896 // [Schiefler] 63 II". It is registered as missing in the collection audits of 1955
and 1969-70, and it receives no mention in Liv I.
Jones' catalogue *Norsk grafikk til 1970* (Norwegian
Graphics until 1970) (Oslo: Nasjonalgalleriet, 1971).
For a discussion of the image, see cat. 103.

105
Jealousy I
Sjalusi I

Stone 1896; impression (1896 or 1897)
Lithograph: tusche, crayon and scraper; black
ink; heavy wove paper
Image: 331 × 457; paper: 665 × 500
Artist's inscription: E Munch
NG.K&H.A.19037
Provenance unknown
Sch 57; Woll G 68 I / I
Printer: Clot

Jealousy I and *The Urn* (cat. 103 and 104) are
executed on the same stone (MM P 156), turned
90° relative to each other. The National Museum's
impression of *Jealousy I* is printed on the same
sheet as cat. 103; both are signed below the image.
In this impression, the scratches in the stone are
clear, whereas in later impressions, they are less
distinct, indicating an early dating for this impression. Munch executed the lithograph in Paris.
In parallel, he produced a second lithograph
with a similar design (see cat. 106). The man on
the left is often identified as the Polish author
Stanisław Przybyszewski (1868-1927), a central
figure in the bohemian circle to which Munch
belonged in Berlin in the 1890s and a friend of
the artist (see cat. 91). The treatment of the couple
on the right, whom we perceive as being in the
man's thoughts, references depictions of the
Fall of Man. On the personal level, it has been
suggested that Przybyszewski's gloomy mood can
be attributed to his wife, the Norwegian author
Dagny Juel (1867-1901). The image corresponds
(inverted) to a painting from 1895 (Woll M 379).

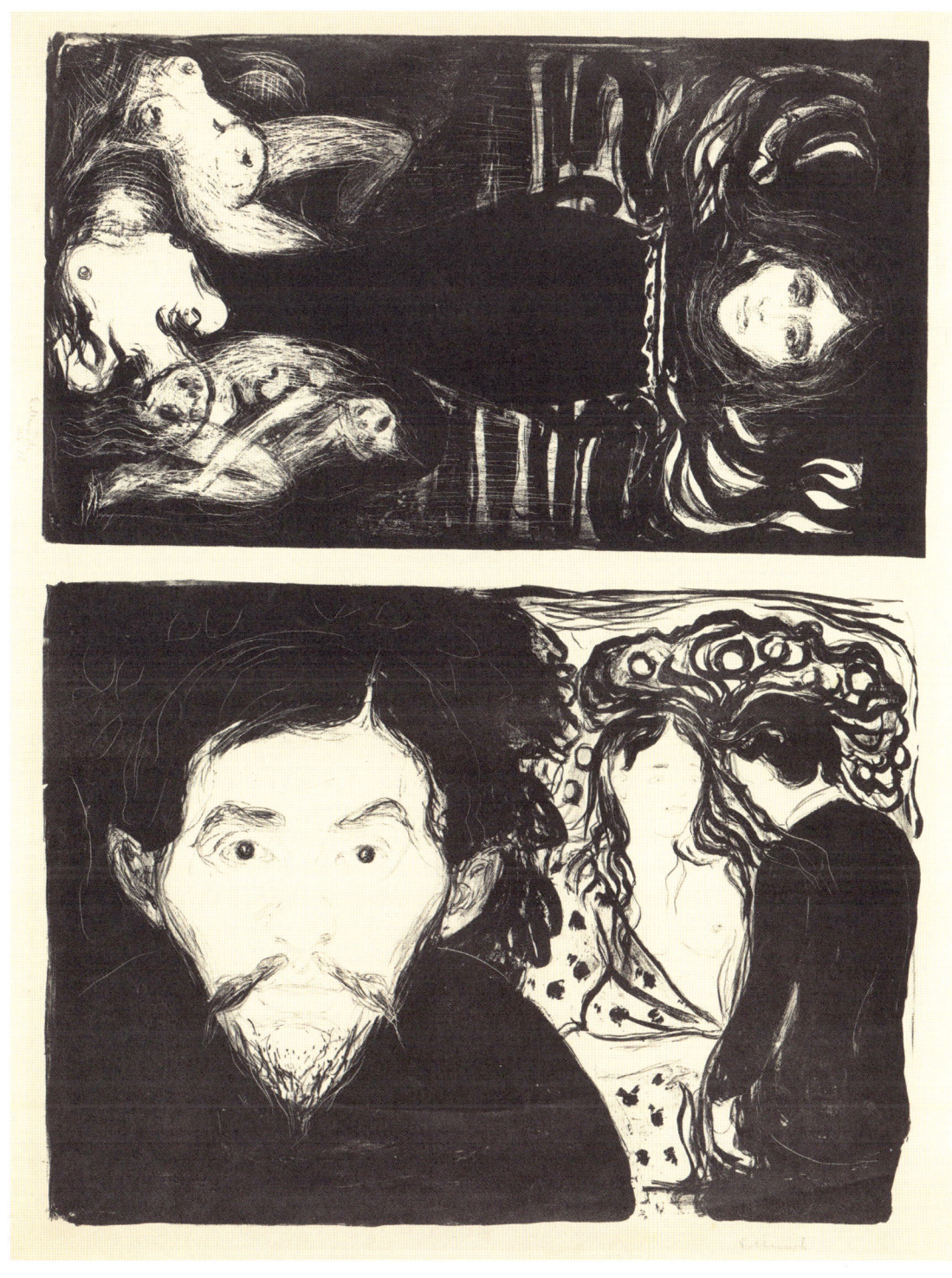

103, 105

106
Jealousy II
Sjalusi II

Stone 1896; impression (1896 or 1897)
Lithograph: tusche, crayon and scraper; black
ink; heavy wove paper
Image: 473 × 574; paper: 500 × 634
Artist's inscription: E Munch. No 8
NG.K&H.A.19027
Provenance unknown
Sch 58; Woll G 69 I/I
Printer: Clot

The National Museum's impression is numbered
by Munch, indicating that it is an early imprint.
Munch produced the lithograph in Paris. The
scene closely resembles that of the lithograph
Jealousy I (see cat. 105).

107
The Sick Child I
Det syke barn I

Stone 1896; impression 1896
Lithograph: keystone: transfer lithograph, crayon,
black ink; colour stone: crayon, tusche, scraper,
sandpaper and pumice, grey ink; medium-weight
wove paper
Image: 426 × 576; paper: 543 × 721
Signature on keystone: E Munch [l.r.; tusche]
Artist's inscription: E Munch 1896/No 3 af 50
NG.K&H. A.19028
Provenance unknown
Sch 59; Woll G 72 VIII/X
Printer: Clot

The National Museum has two impressions of
The Sick Child I, Munch's only truly multicolour
lithograph. It is a version of one of his most
important motifs. He must have prepared a total
of six stones for this lithograph, using as many
as five of them for the most complex prints.
Surprisingly, none of the stones has survived. It is
likely that all the impressions were printed before
1900. The keystone, onto which the drawing
was transferred from paper, exists in two states,
one with, the other without the signature "E.
Munch". Both of the National Museum's impressions are of the state with the signature. The
current impression was printed from two stones,
in black and grey, a variant of which only a few
examples exist. The National Museum's second
impression is printed with a colour combination
not previously described (see cat. 108). Munch
had already made an intaglio (inverted, see cat.
64) based on the painting from 1885 (see cat. 8).
In 1896, Olaf Schou commissioned a replica of
the painting (Woll M 392) while Munch was in
Paris, and it was probably in connection with this
work that Munch made the lithograph. In the
lithograph Munch concentrates on one section
of the painting, namely the head of the sick girl,
as he also did in an intaglio made the same year
(Woll G 59). That intaglio was inverted relative to
the painting, whereas the lithograph has the same
orientation, indicating that the image was drawn
on paper and then transferred to a lithographic
stone. In terms of details and size, the section in
the lithograph is very similar to the new painting
from 1896. Munch later painted several further
versions of *The Sick Child* (Woll M 790, 791, 1561,
1631).

108
The Sick Child I
Det syke barn I

Stone 1896; impression (1896 or 1897)
Colour lithograph: keystone: transfer lithograph:
crayon, red ink; colour stone: crayon, tusche,
scraper, sandpaper and pumice, grey ink; colour
stone: yellow ink; medium-weight wove paper
Image: 425 × 577; paper: 540 × 675
Signature on keystone: E Munch [l.r.; tusche]
Artist's inscription: Edv Munch
NG.K&H.A.19029
Provenance unknown
Sch 59: Woll G 72 IX / X
Printer: Clot

The keystone for this lithograph is in the same
state as it was for the National Museum's other
impression (see cat. 107). However, in this case
the impression is printed from three stones, in
a colour combination not previously described.
The keystone is printed in red, while the impressions described in Woll 2012, cat. 72, state IX, are
all printed in black. In addition, the colour stones
are printed in grey and pale yellow, rather than
blue and yellow. Munch printed *The Sick Child
I* in a large number of different colour combinations, and it cannot be ruled out that further
variations exist in addition to those described
so far. One frequently quoted story about how
Munch approached the printing of this lithograph is attributed to the graphic artist Paul
Herrmann, a close friend of Munch at the time:
"I went to Clot to ask him to print, but he said:
'Can't be done, Mr. Munch has already booked.'
The lithographic stones with the large head were
already lying there, side by side, in a row, ready
to be printed. Munch came in, stood in front of
the row, screwed up his eyes, and waved a finger
blindly through the air. 'Print ... grey, green, blue,
brown.' Then he opened his eyes and said to
me: 'Come on, let's have a schnapps." Then the
printer printed until Munch came back and again
commanded blindly: 'Yellow, pink, red ...' And
this was repeated several more times." (Quoted
from Erich Büttner, "Der leibhaftige Munch", in
Thiis 1934, p. 92).

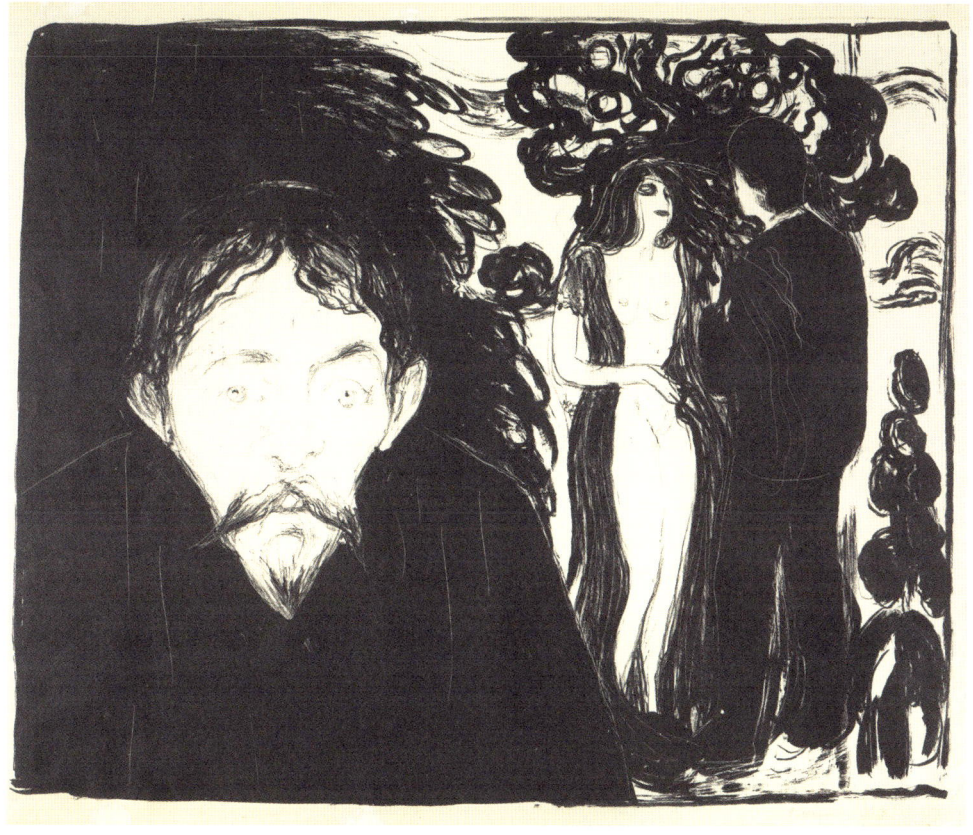

106

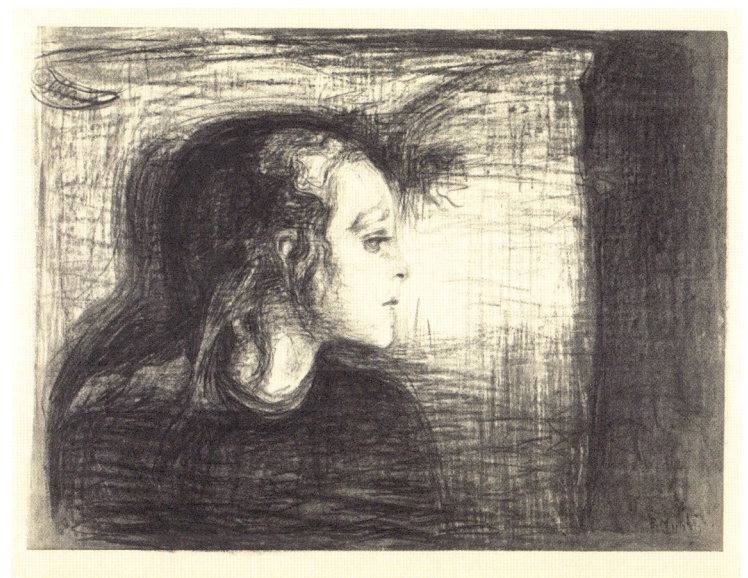

107

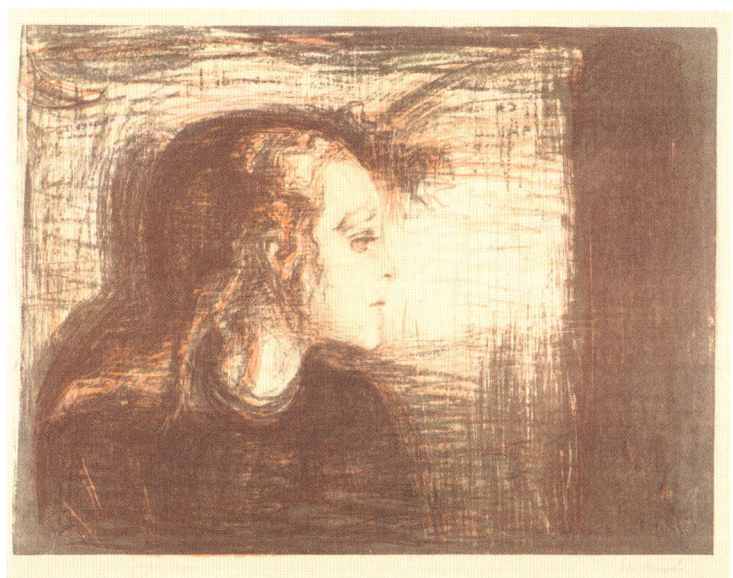

108

109
Attraction I
Tiltrekning I

110
Separation II
Løsrivelse II

111
The Flower of Love
Kjærlighetsblomsten

Stone 1896; impression (after 1906)
Lithograph: tusche, crayon and scraper; black
ink; light-weight Japan paper
Image: 479 × 361; paper: 514 × 391
Artist's inscription: E Munch
NG.K&H.A.18998
Provenance unknown
Sch 65; Woll G 75 I/I
Printer: Lassally

The type of paper indicates that the National
Museum's impression was printed by Lassally.
Since Schiefler does not mention prints pulled by
Lassally, it is probable that they date from after
1906. Munch executed the stone in Paris, and it
was first printed by Clot. Munch had produced an
intaglio with essentially the same design in 1895
(inverted, Woll G 19) and another, in which the
theme is reconceived (Woll G 20, see cat. 74). The
landscape closely resembles that of two paintings
with the title *Starry Night* from 1893 (Woll M 320,
321).

Stone 1896; impression (1896 or 1897)
Lithograph (transfer lithograph): crayon; blue
ink; China paper (lined 1973)
Image: 406 × 607; paper: 406 × 607
Signed on stone: E Munch 96 [partly cropped; l.r.;
tusche]
NG.K&H.A.19030
Provenance unknown
Sch 68; Woll G 78 I/II
Printer: Clot

Munch produced *Separation II* in Paris, printing
black, blue and multicolour versions of the image
at Clot. The blue and multicolour versions are
early examples of Munch's work with colour
using the lithographic technique. In *Separation
II*, there is evidence that he used a drawing folder
as a pad when drawing on the transfer paper.
In 1973, the National Museum's impression was
removed from the original cardboard to which
the China paper was glued and then glued on to
a new piece of paper. In terms of both design and
theme, *Separation II* is related to the "attraction"
motif, which Munch explored in several versions
(see cat. 74 and 109), although this image explores
the antithetical relationship. The motif of a man's
and a woman's head connected by the woman's
hair is also used in the lithograph *Man's Head in
Woman's Hair* (Woll G 88) and a woodcut with the
same title (see cat. 118).

Stone 1896; impression (1896 or 1897)
Lithograph (transfer lithograph): crayon; black
ink; China paper
Image: 633 × 304; paper: 705 × 454
Artist's inscription: Munch
Secondary inscription: 20 Kr [upside down; u.r.;
pencil]
NG.K&H. A.19031
Provenance unknown
Sch 70; Woll G 80 I/I
Printer: Clot

The theme of a naked couple in an embrace surrounded by foliage has also been used by other
artists, and can be read as a symbol for human
unity with nature and the recognition of desire
and reproduction as necessary preconditions for
the continuation of the species.

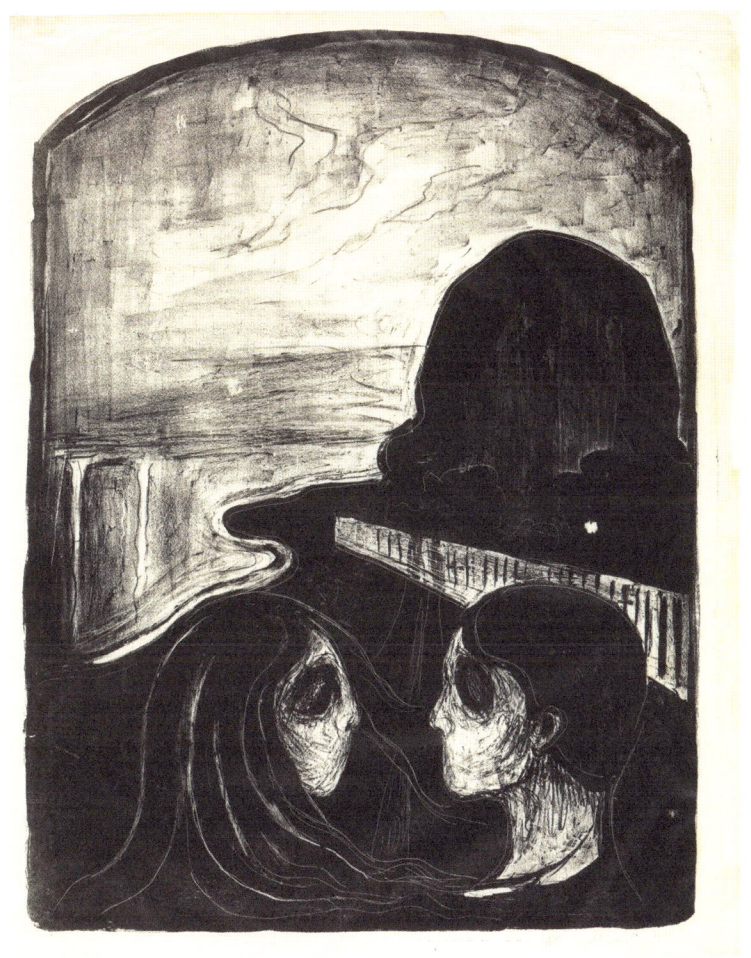

109

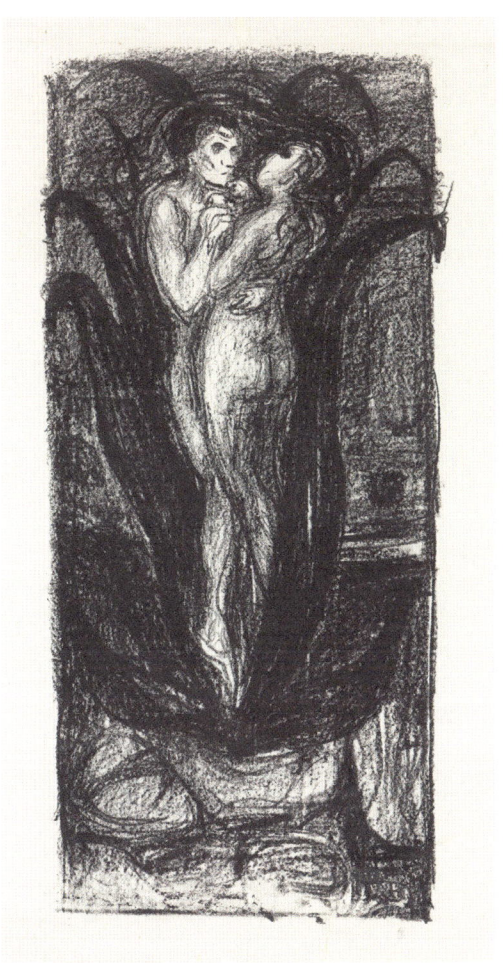

111

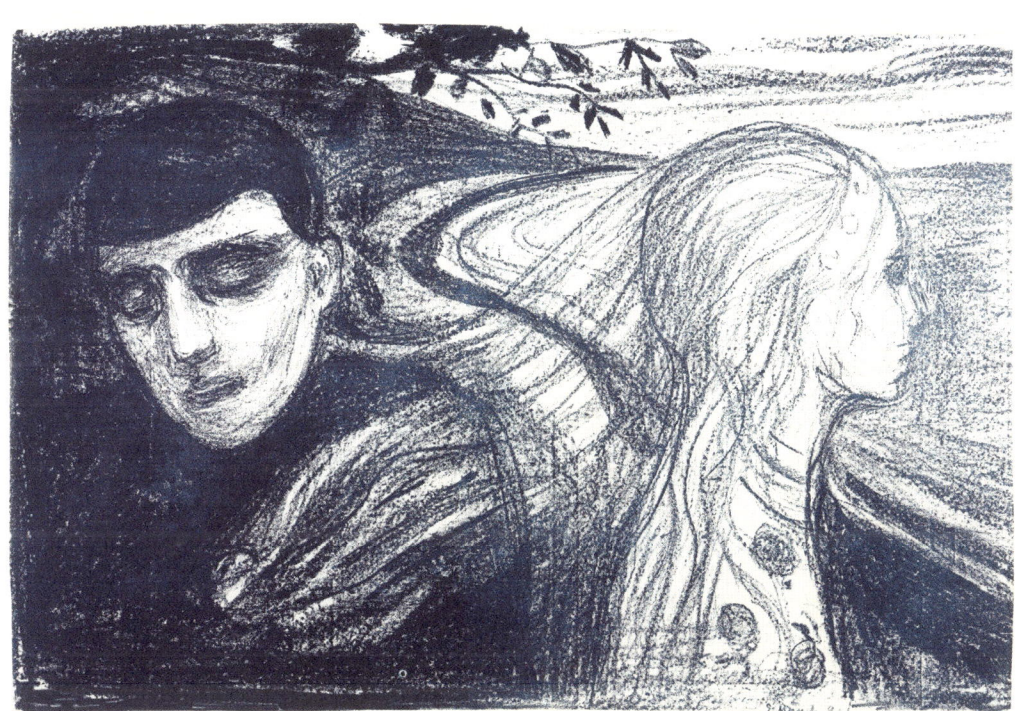

110

112
On the Waves of Love
På kjærlighetens bølger

Stone 1896; impression (1896 or 1897)
Lithograph: crayon, tusche and scraper; black
ink; wove paper
Image: 311 × 422; paper: 460 × 641
Artist's inscription: E. Munch No 8
NG.K&H.A.18999
Provenance unknown
Sch 71; Woll G 81 V / V
Printer: Clot

The National Museum's impression is on grey-
blue paper, which has discoloured slightly
towards green where exposed to light. The
quality of the paper and state of the impression
indicate that it was printed by Clot. Schiefler
uses the title *Liebespaar*. In early exhibitions,
the lithograph often had titles such as *Bølger*
(Waves), *Kjærlighetshavet* (The Sea of Love), or
På kjærlighetens bølger (On the Waves of Love). In
recent times, it has most commonly been referred
to as *Elskende par i bølger* (Lovers in Waves), yet
this title does not appear in the surviving exhibition catalogues from Munch's time. Munch produced an intaglio version of the image (mezzotint;
Woll G 50) the same year.

113
Theatre programme: Peer Gynt
Teaterprogram: Peer Gynt

Stone 1896; impression (1896)
Lithograph (transfer lithograph): crayon; black
ink; medium-weight wove paper
Image: 250 × 299; paper: 250 × 303
Signed on stone: E Munch [l.l.; tusche]
Artist's inscription: Edv Munch
NG.K&H. A.19000
Provenance unknown (acquired after 1904–07)
Sch 74; Woll G 82 I / I
Printer: print works of *La Critique*, Paris

The lithograph was made as a programme for
a production of Henrik Ibsen's *Peer Gynt* at the
Théâtre de l'Œuvre in Paris in November 1896.
Two editions were printed for the periodical *La
Critique*, one with and one without a programme
text. The National Museum's impression is from
the edition with text. In this case, the artist's
signature can safely be viewed as a mark of
approval for the edition. The number 134 on the
verso refers to a list that Bruno Cassirer compiled
between 1904 and 1907, recording the prints by
Munch that he had in commission (Woll 2012, p.
485). The programme informs us that Jane Avril,
known from many of Henri de Toulouse-Lautrec's posters, played Anitra, while the graphic
artist and writer Alfred Jarry played the part of a
troll. Interestingly, Jarry's own play *Ubu Roi* was
the theatre's next production. Some sources state
that Frits Thaulow and Edvard Munch contributed stage sets for the latter. It has, however,
not been possible to determine what form they
took. A pencil sketch for this design is found on
the same sheet as a couple of other drawings
(MM.T.257 recto). Munch further developed the
theme of two women, one young, one old, in the
woodcut *Two Women on the Shore* (see cat. 133).

114
Gunnar Heiberg

Stone 1896; impression 1897
Colour lithograph (transfer lithograph): keystone:
crayon; reddish brown ink; colour stone: crayon,
green ink; China paper
Image: 488 × 423; paper: 561 × 460
Artist's inscription: E Munch 97
NG.K&H.A.19033
Probably acquired at Munch's exhibition at
Blomqvist in 1902
Sch 75; Woll G 83 II / III
Printer: Clot

On 22.08.1897, Munch wrote to Clot telling him
not to destroy the colour stone with the green bor-
derline and the champagne glasses because he
now liked these details. (The letter is difficult to
decipher accurately. Original in the Bibliothèque
Nationale, Paris; copy in the Munch Museum, PN
45.) Gunnar Heiberg (1857–1929) was a Norwegian
author and a well-known figure in Kristiania's
bohemian circle in the 1880s.

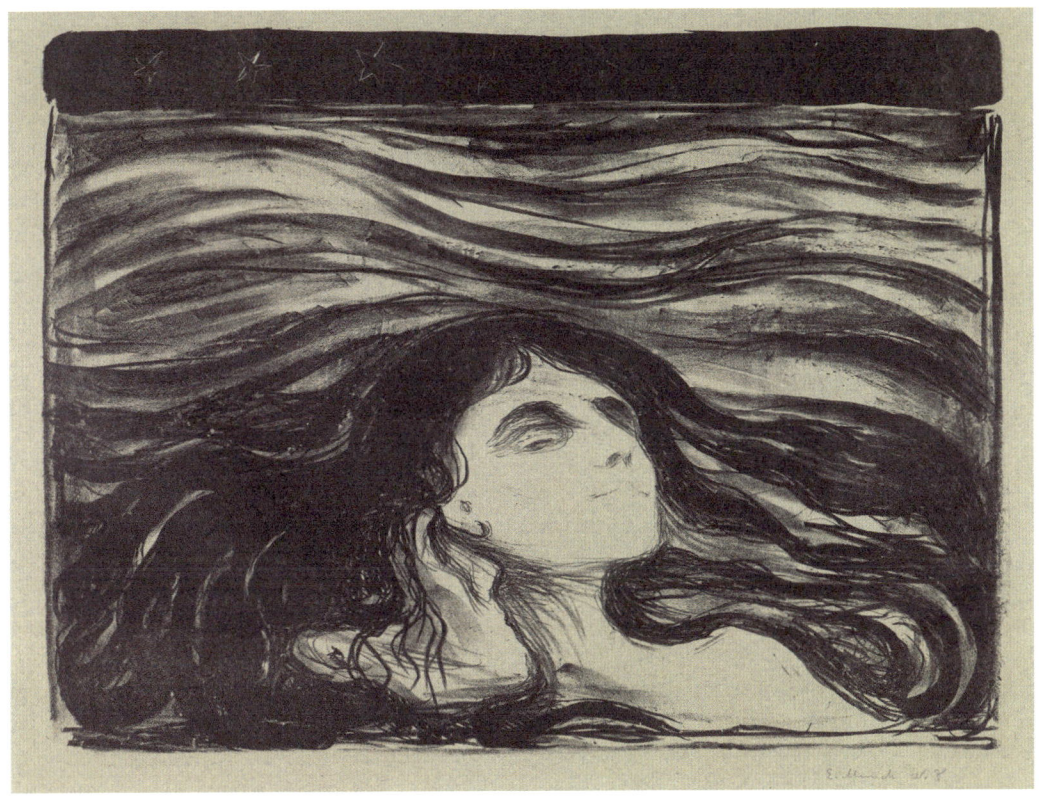

112

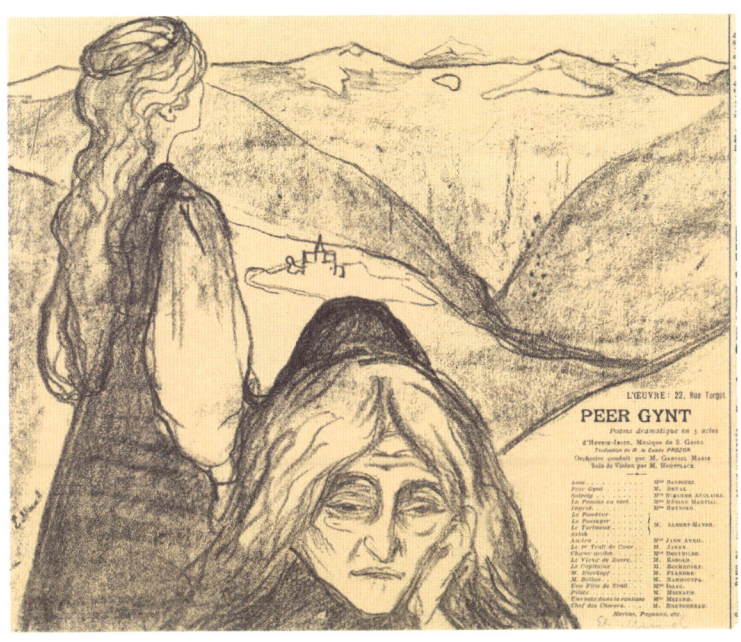

113

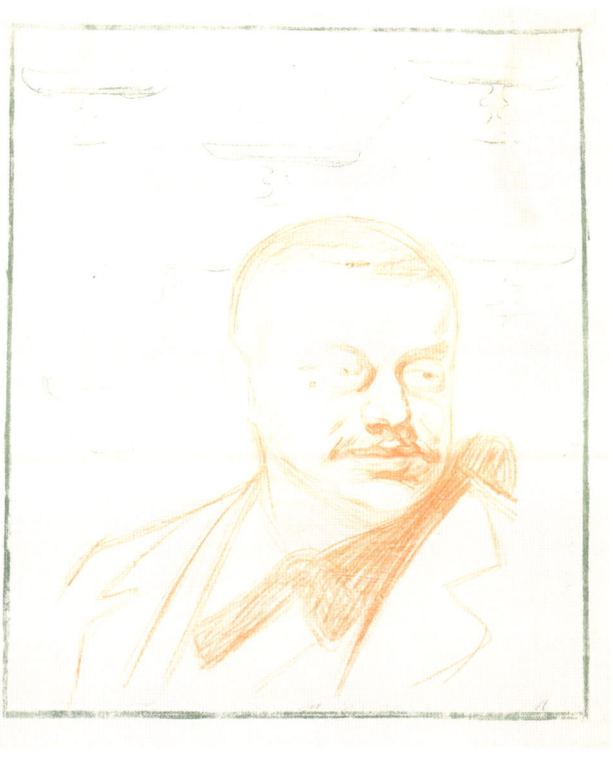

114

115
Hans Jæger I

Stone 1896; impression 1897
Lithograph (transfer lithograph): crayon; stone modified with crayon and tusche; black ink; medium-weight wove paper
Image: 468 × 343; paper: 539 × 393
Artist's inscription: E Munch 1897
NG.K&H.A.09240
Probably acquired at Munch's exhibition at Blomqvist in 1902
Sch 76; Woll G 84 III/III
Printer: Clot

The image concentrates on a section of Munch's 1889 painting of Jæger (see cat. 13). The head has the same dimensions in the lithograph as in the painting, indicating that the former is based directly on the latter. In 1943 or 1944, Munch produced two further lithographic versions of the portrait, his last graphic works (Woll G 747, 748). Hans Jæger (1854–1910) was a Norwegian writer and a central figure in Kristiania's bohemian circle in the 1880s. See commentary on cat. 71 and 13.

116
Sigbjørn Obstfelder I

Stone 1896; impression (1896)
Lithograph: crayon and scraper; black ink; medium-weight, stiff wove paper
Image: 372 × 285; paper: 640 × 465
Artist's inscription: Edvard Munch
Secondary inscription: No 5/30 [l.r.; pencil]
NG.K&H.A.19002
Provenance unknown
Sch 78; Woll G 85 I/I
Printer: Clot

The inscription "No 5/30" is the printer's. Most of the known impressions are numbered in an edition of 30, and one of them is dated 1896, indicating that the National Museum's impression is also from that year. Munch produced two other graphic portraits of Obstfelder (see cat. 117 and 127). Sigbjørn Obstfelder (1866–1900) was a Norwegian poet and a close friend of Munch for many years.

117
Sigbjørn Obstfelder II

Stone 1896; impression (1896)
Lithograph: crayon, tusche and scraper; black ink; medium-weight, stiff wove paper
Image: 413 × 288; paper: 459 × 323
NG.K&H.A.19001
Provenance unknown
Sch 78 A; Woll G 86 I/I
Printer: Clot

Only three impressions of this portrait of Obstfelder are recorded. None of them has any significant inscription. On the verso of the National Museum's impression, Munch has drawn a portrait of a woman (see cat. 241). He produced two other graphic portraits of Obstfelder (see cat. 116 and 124). This lithograph and the intaglio from 1897 (cat. 124) are similar in terms of composition and characterisation. Since so few impressions were pulled of the lithograph, it is tempting to assume that the intaglio is a further development of the lithographic version. In all three depictions, Munch emphasises the intensity of the writer's gaze. It is, however, in this lithographic portrait that the poet's visionary personality is most pronounced. Sigbjørn Obstfelder (1866–1900) was a Norwegian poet and a close friend of Munch for many years.

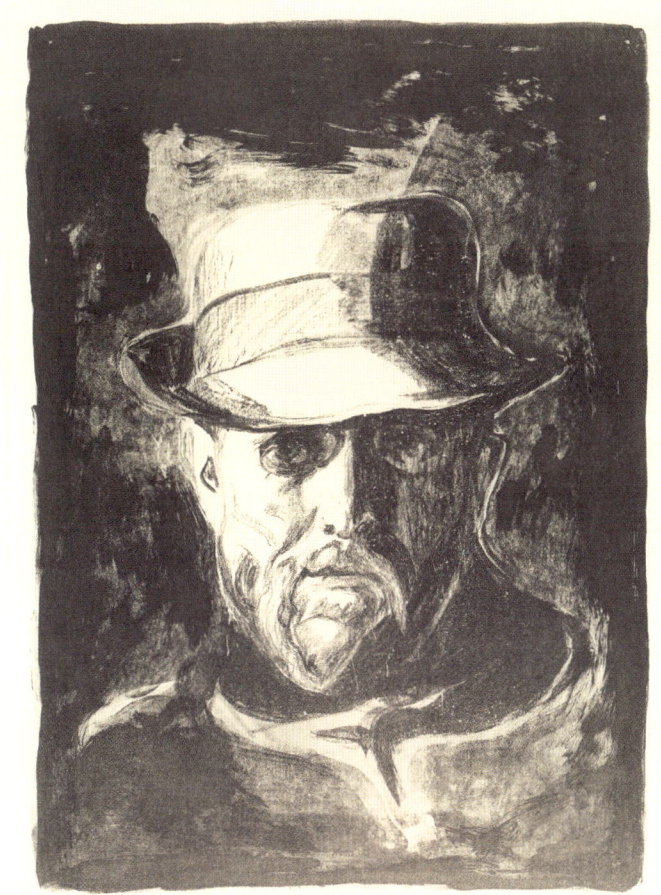

115

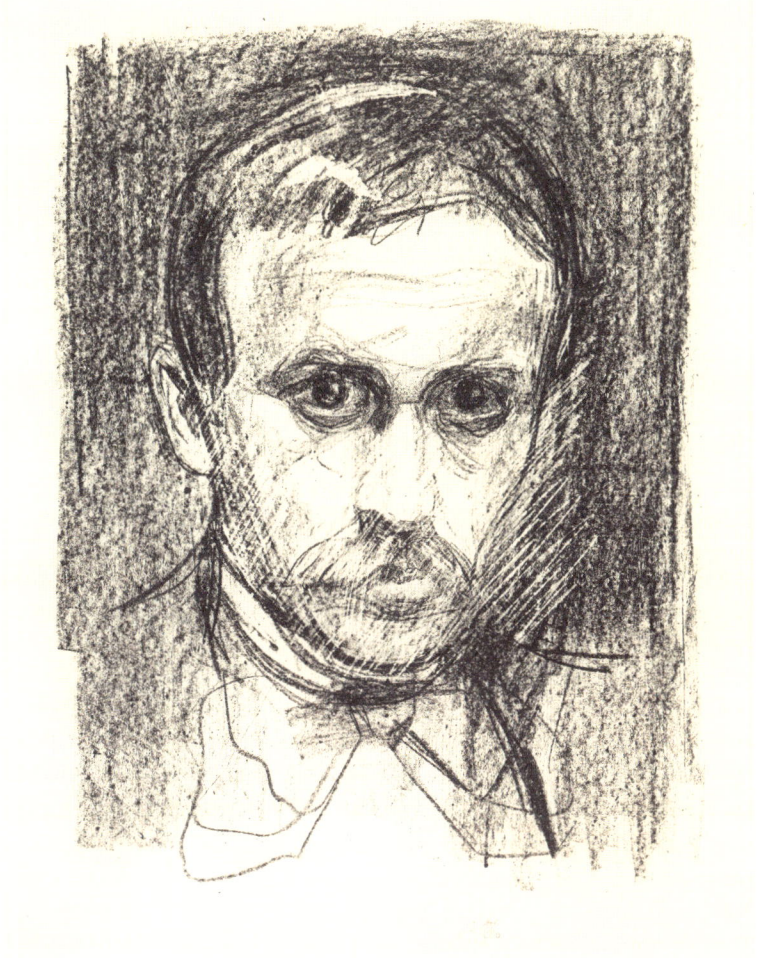

117

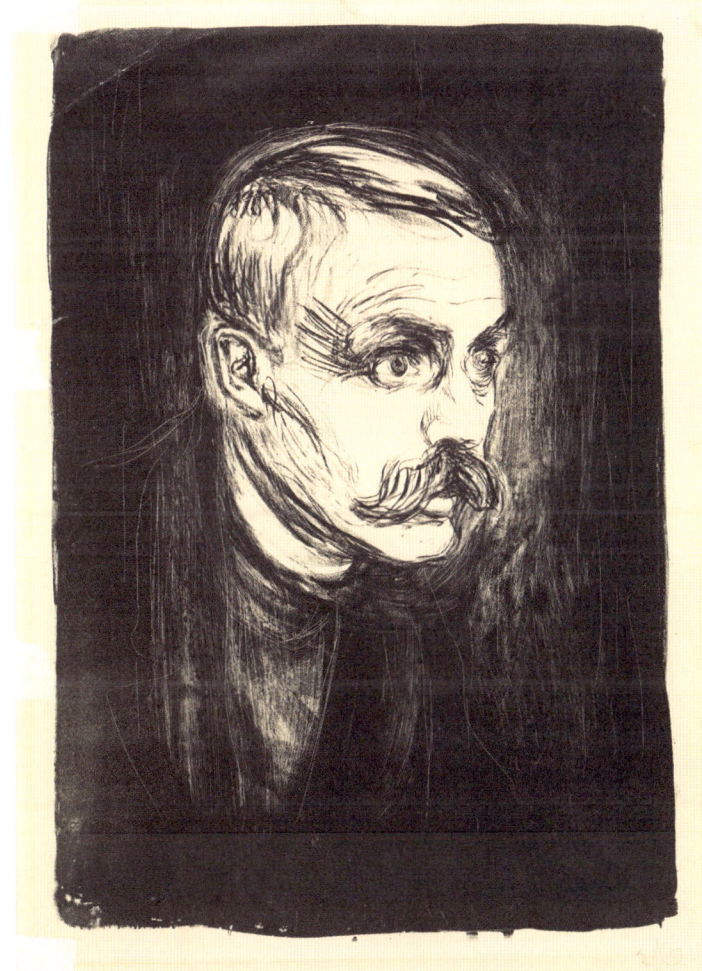

116

118
Man's Head in Woman's Hair
Mannshode i kvinnehår

Keyblock 1896 or 1897, colour block probably 1897;
impression (1897 or 1898)
Colour woodcut: keyblock: gouges; dark grey ink;
colour block: fretsaw (block cut into four pieces);
blue, red and green ink; China paper
Image: 551 × 384; paper: 668 × 521
NG.K&H.A.19096
Provenance unknown
Sch 80; Woll G 89 II/III
Printer: Clot or Lemercier

The National Museum's impression has no
significant inscriptions. The image is printed at
an angle on the sheet with a wide margin to the
right and below. The sheet has later been folded
in order to fit the passepartout. The keyblock for
Man's Head in Woman's Hair is one of Munch's
first woodcuts, which he made while in Paris (the
block is marked A. Mouraux, Paris, MM P 320).
Schiefler ascribes the woodcut to 1896, a dating
that Woll 2012 also adopts. There is, however,
no clear evidence for a date earlier than 1897,
when the image figured prominently in Munch's
exhibition at the Dioramalokalet, Kristiania
(Oslo), in September–October of that year (cat. 121,
"Speilet, haandfarget" (Mirror, hand-coloured)).
A frottage from the block was used as a basis for
the exhibition poster, printed lithographically
by Petersen & Waitz (Woll G 107). In the accompanying catalogue, Munch announced plans to
publish a separate portfolio of prints under the
title "Speilet" (The Mirror). Several of the prints
in the exhibition have been identified as belonging to such a portfolio (Torjusen 1978, pp. 185–227,
and 1980, pp. 377–386). For the cover of the portfolio, Munch cut the section with the two heads
from a monochrome woodcut and mounted it on
greyish-brown cardboard of the same type used
for the other prints intended for the portfolio. He
then painted the woman's hair red and gold and
added the text "SPEILET - ANDEN DEL 1897"
(THE MIRROR - SECOND PART 1897) above the
image (Harvard Art Museum, inv. no. M20285).
This may indicate that as late as the autumn of
1897, Munch had still not produced a multicolour
version of this print. The Munch Museum has
a monochrome impression in black, where the
woman's hair has been painted with red watercolour (MM.G.569-5). This may have been a
preparation for a multicolour print. In addition to
the keyblock, Munch prepared a new woodblock
and with a fretsaw cut out the heads in much the
same way as he had done for the portfolio cover.
He then inked he individual pieces separately,
reassembled them, and printed the divided block
as if it were one coherent piece. This may have
been one of the first cases of the jigsaw-puzzle
technique that was to become one of the most
innovative aspects of Munch's woodcuts. The
National Museum's impression is one of two
surviving prints that use four colours, with the
part of the block representing the man's face
printed in green. In this impression, the entire
colour plate is intact, and both the print quality
and the paper type indicate that this was one of
the earliest colour prints to be pulled. In all later
impressions, the man's face is without colour and
fragments of the colour plate have progressively
fallen off: a long section to the left along the line
of the woman's hair and a smaller piece from
beneath the man's chin. Although the envisaged
portfolio was never finished, the Munch Museum
holds several impressions of *Man's Head in Woman's Hair* printed on grey cardboard prepared as
double covers and with inscriptions that suggest
Munch stuck to the plan to produce such a portfolio for several years. The thematic elements of
the woman's head in profile and the man's face
viewed frontally are perceived as a single item,
giving the image a concise, symbolic character. In
terms of content, the image relates to a number of
other works, including the lithographs *Attraction
I* and *Separation II* (see cat. 109 and 110), which
Munch executed in Paris in 1896. In all these
images, the woman's hair forms a link between
the heads of the man and the woman, while in
the colour woodcut, her blood-red hair com-
pletely encloses the free-floating head of the man.
There is also a kinship with Munch's "vampire"
theme. The portrayal of woman as a *femme fatale*
was popular among the symbolists of the 1890s.
Myths about women who caused men's downfall
and death were common material in literature
and the visual arts, where the various narratives
were often mixed, making it sometimes difficult
to distinguish Judith from Salome, or the head
of Holofernes from that of John the Baptist. The
figurative element of this woodcut was used for
a lithographic poster for the exhibition at the
Dioramalokalet (see cat. 226).

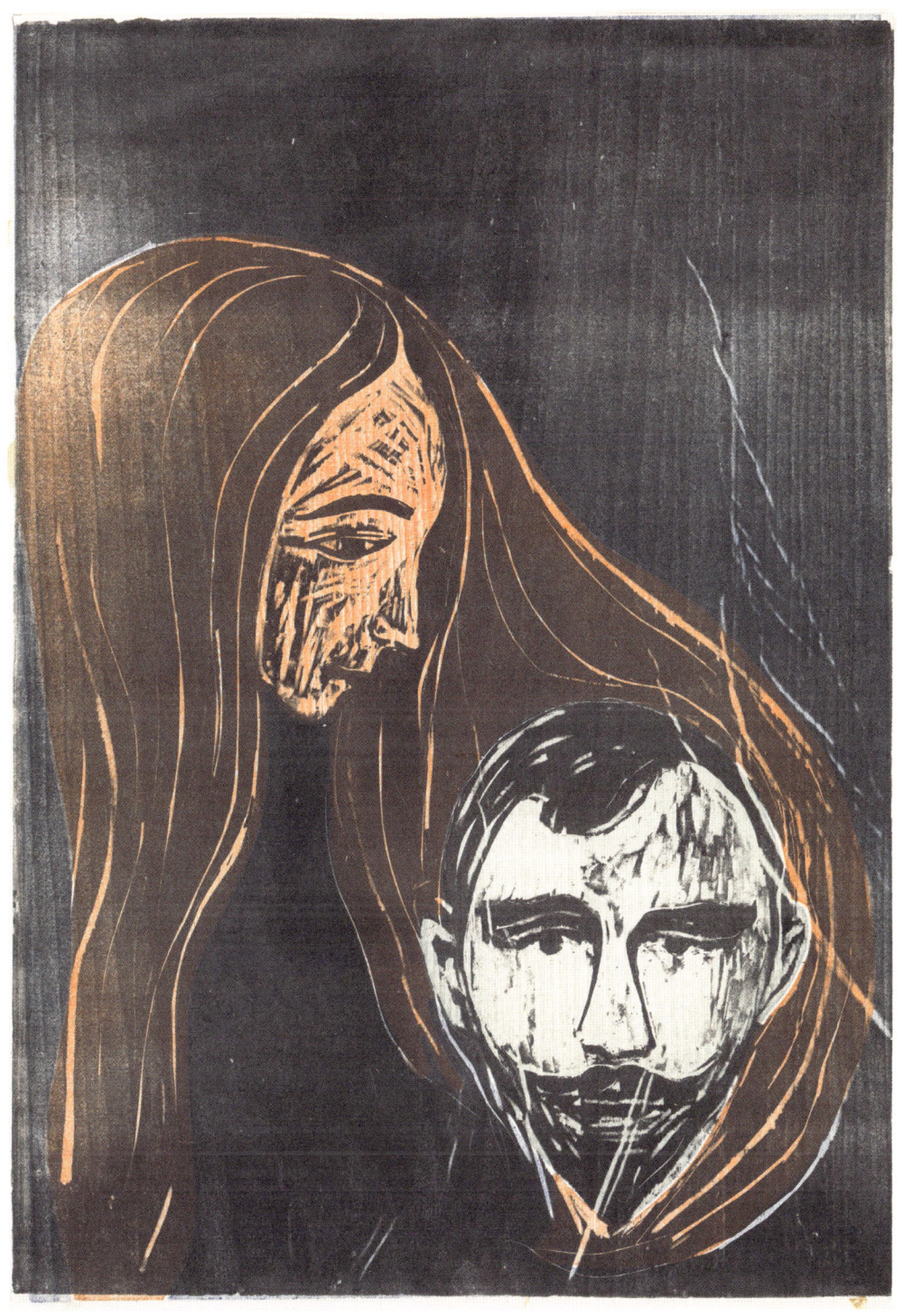

118

119
Moonlight I
Måneskinn I

Keyblock 1896 or 1897, colour block 1897 or 1898; impression (between 1897 and 1899)
Colour woodcut: keyblock recto, gouges; black ink, verso, gouges; pale grey ink; colour block: fretsaw (block cut into three pieces); brown, blue-grey and pale grey-green ink; China paper
Image: 414 × 467; paper: 443 × 569
Artist's inscription: E Munch
NG.K&H.B.00615
Provenance unknown
Sch 81A, Woll G 90 III / I7V
Printer: Clot or Lemercier

This print is among the first Munch made using the woodcut technique. He probably executed the keyblock (MM P 322) while in Paris. The block is carved both recto and verso, and a complete impression requires printing from both sides, for example black from recto and pale blue from verso (as in MM.G.570-18). This shows that the work was conceived as a colour print. Colour trial proofs indicate that, in these cases, Munch applied different colours to another plate, but without cutting it up. This colouring method is not suitable for the printing of numerous impressions (editions). Further, at some point Munch employed a separate colour block (MM P 323), which he cut into three pieces with a fretsaw, such that each piece could be inked with a different colour before being reassembled and printed as a single block. It is unknown exactly when he subdivided the colour plate. Munch varied the colour combinations in different prints. Hence the National Museum's impression

is one of several variants. It combines imprints from the recto and verso of the keyblock and from the subdivided colour plate. The imprint from the verso is very faint; it is most conspicuous in the window, but barely visible on the woman's face and elsewhere in the image. One area in the imprint from the middle section of the colour plate, which shows some damage, is in a shade of brown that differs from the other parts of the imprint from this section. The type of paper indicates that the museum's impression was printed in Paris. According to Schiefler, who knew of only four impressions of *Moonlight I*, this woodcut was printed not just by the artist himself, but also by either Clot or Lemercier. An undated letter from Tulla Larsen to Munch written in early June 1899 (original in the Munch Museum, MM K 0513) mentions that the artist had ordered prints from Lemercier in 1899. *Moonlight I* is probably one of Munch's first works using the so-called jigsaw-puzzle technique. Already in evidence here are the technical and artistic prowess that would make him a significant pioneer in modern woodcut art, and the print has remained a principal work among his woodcuts. The image is based on a painting from 1893 (see cat. 21). In the woodcut, the dominant element is the woman's head beside the almost square window frame. The special atmosphere of the summer night, of yearning and eroticism are, however, equally well evoked in the woodcut as in the painting. Believing the blocks to be lost, Munch made a new woodcut version in 1902 (Woll G 202).

120
Evening. Melancholy I
Aften. Melankoli I

Keyblock 1896, colour block 1897 or 1898; impression (between 1906 and 1914)
Colour woodcut: keyblock: gouges and fretsaw (block cut into two pieces); black ink, colour block: fretsaw (block cut into two pieces); bluish green and ochre ink; light-weight Japan paper (lined 1966 or 1967)
Image: 387 × 460; paper: 396 × 485
Artist's inscription: EMunch [partly cropped]
NG.K&H.1968.0167
Purchased from Professor Edgar B. Schieldrop's widow, Karen Schieldrop, Oslo, 1968. Formerly owned by Nobel Rode (1930s)
Sch 82; Woll G 91 IV / IV
Printer: Lassally

This is one of the first works Munch created using the woodcut technique. The keyblock was probably prepared primarily in Paris. However, the National Museum's impression is from a later stage of development, after Munch had cut the keyblock into two pieces and added the use of a separate colour block. According to Schiefler, only a few impressions of this woodcut were pulled, either by Clot or Lemercier. This, together with the type of paper used, indicate that the National Museum's impression was printed by Lassally, implying a date later than 1906. The blocks were among those that were sent to Norway in 1914, on Munch's request. Munch painted many versions of this image (Woll M 241, 284, 359, 360). The woodcut is inverted relative to the paintings. A new woodcut version that Munch made in 1902 has the same lateral orientation as the paintings (see cat. 159). The image is discussed in greater depth in connection with the National Museum's painting (see cat. 19).

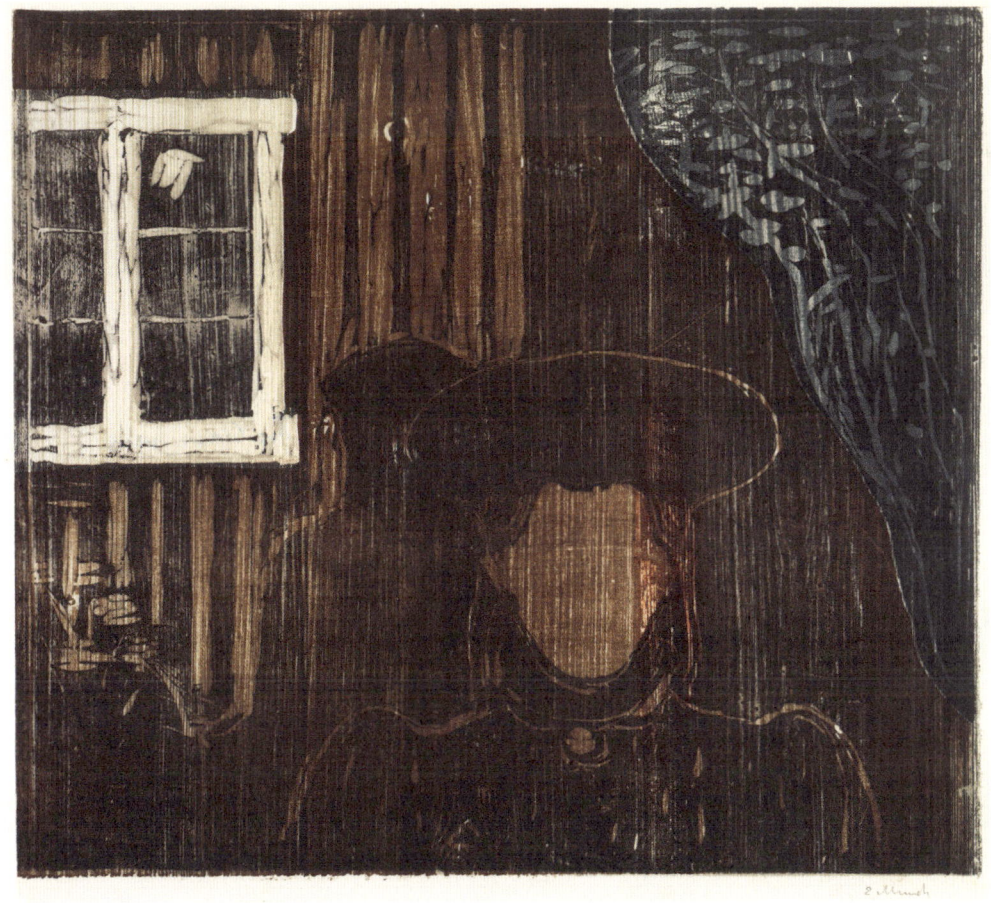

119

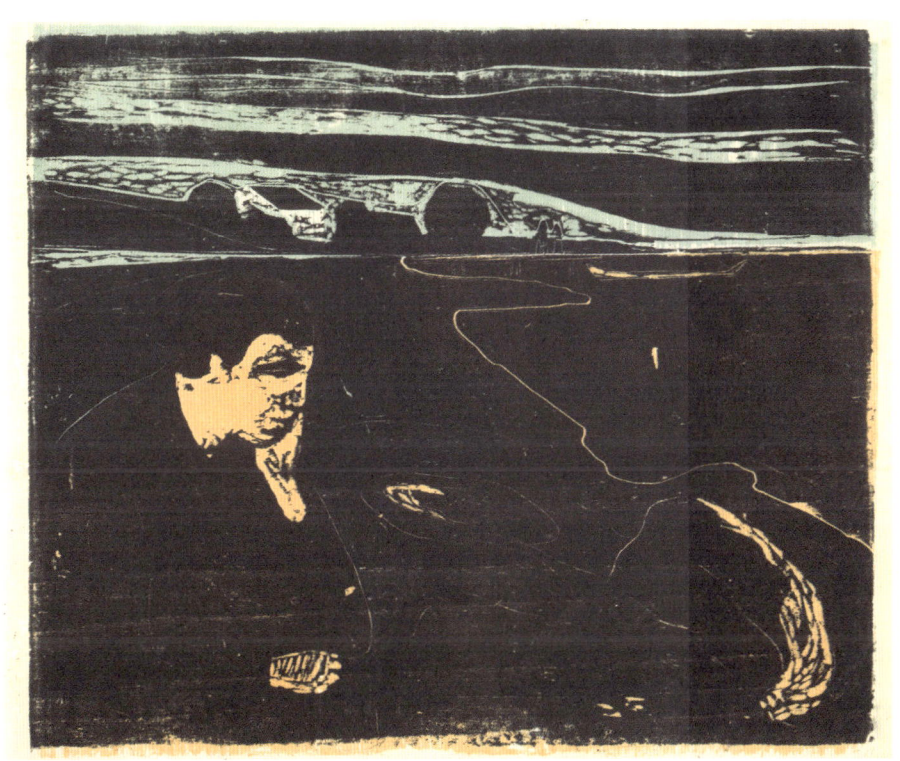

120

121
Angst

Woodblock 1896; impression (1896 or 1897)
Woodcut: gouges; black ink; heavy Japan paper
Image: 465 × 380; paper: 725 × 539
Unsigned
NG.K&H.A.19110
Provenance unknown
Sch 62; Woll G 93 I/I
Printer: Clot or Lemercier

This is one of the first works Munch created using the woodcut technique while in Paris. It was probably produced in 1896 (the block carries the trademark A. Moureaux, Paris, on the verso, MM P 319). There are monochrome prints, some black and some red, two-colour prints from the same block (where sections of the block have been inked separately, the upper part red, the lower part black, before printing in one process), and three-colour prints (where the verso of the block has been used as a colour plate), and a few early hand-coloured prints. The National Museum's impression is monochrome black and was pulled before the block developed a V-shaped crack (as it had by the time Lassally printed from it, after 1906). Schiefler claims that the early impressions were printed by Clot, but it is equally likely that they were printed by Lemercier. In the spring of 1896, Munch had made a lithograph with a similar design (Woll G 63) that was included in Ambroise Vollard's portfolio *Les peintres graveurs*. Both images are based on a painting from 1894 (Woll M 363). Whereas the lithograph is inverted relative to the painting, the woodcut has the same orientation, indicating that Munch probably used the lithograph as a model here.

122
Marcel Réja

Woodblock 1896 or 1897; impression (1896 or 1897)
Woodcut: gouges; dark grey ink; wove paper
Image: 397 × 331; paper: 613 × 472
Artist's inscription: Edv Munch
NG.K&H.A.19109 (formerly NG.K&H.B.00613)
Purchased at City Auksjon, Oslo, September 1938 (cat. 30)
Not in Sch; Woll G 94 I/I
Printer: Clot or Lemercier

Schiefler was unaware of this woodcut and only a few impressions have been recorded. Marcel Réja (the pseudonym of Paul Meunier, 1873–1957) was a French writer and psychiatrist who belonged to Munch's circle of friends in Paris during his 1896–97 sojourn.

123
Model with Hood and Collar
Modell med hette og krage

Zinc plate 1897; impression (between 1902 and 1914)
Intaglio: mezzotint, burnisher; black ink; heavy, stiff wove paper
Image: 396 × 298; paper: 600 × 440
Artist's inscription: E Munch
Secondary inscription: O Felsing Berlin gdr.
NG.K&H.A.19078
Provenance unknown
Sch 86; W 51; Woll G 96 I/I
Printer: Felsing

The National Museum's impression cannot be dated more precisely than to the years when Felsing was printing for Munch. *Model with Hood and Collar* belongs to a small group of mezzotint intaglios that Munch made while in Paris. For these he used zinc plates that had been prepared by sandblasting. They were probably printed by Porcabeuf. Most of Munch's mezzotint intaglios exist as both black-and-white and multicolour prints. They hold an unusual position in Munch's production. Despite a few highly successful prints, especially among the colour versions, he did not pursue the technique. There is also a colour version of *Model with Hood and Collar*. Felsing's monochrome prints lack the nuance of the early prints.

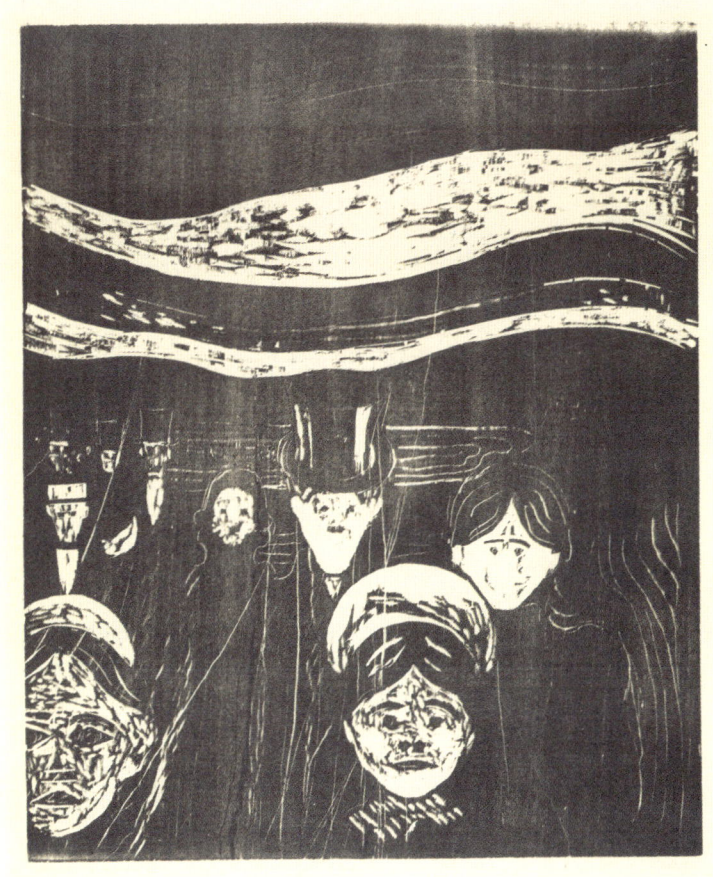

121

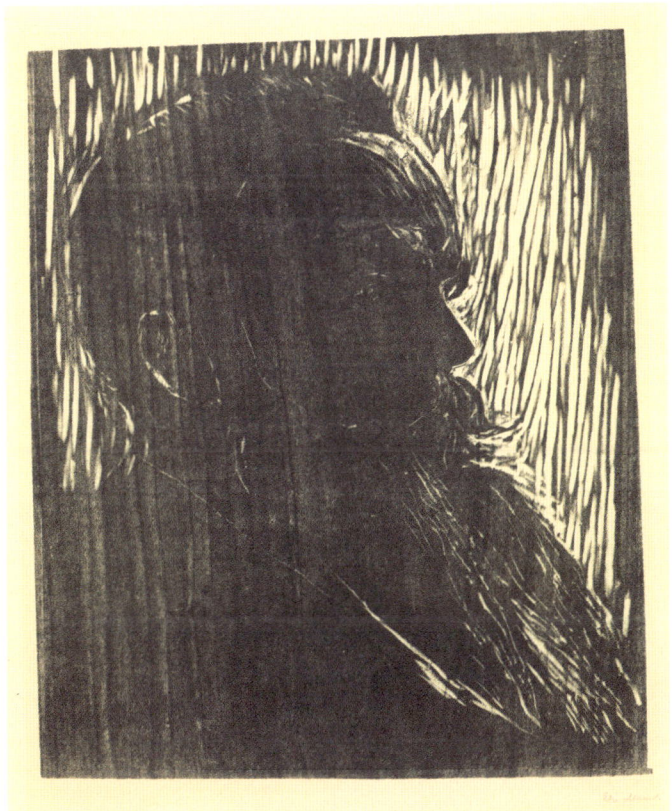

122

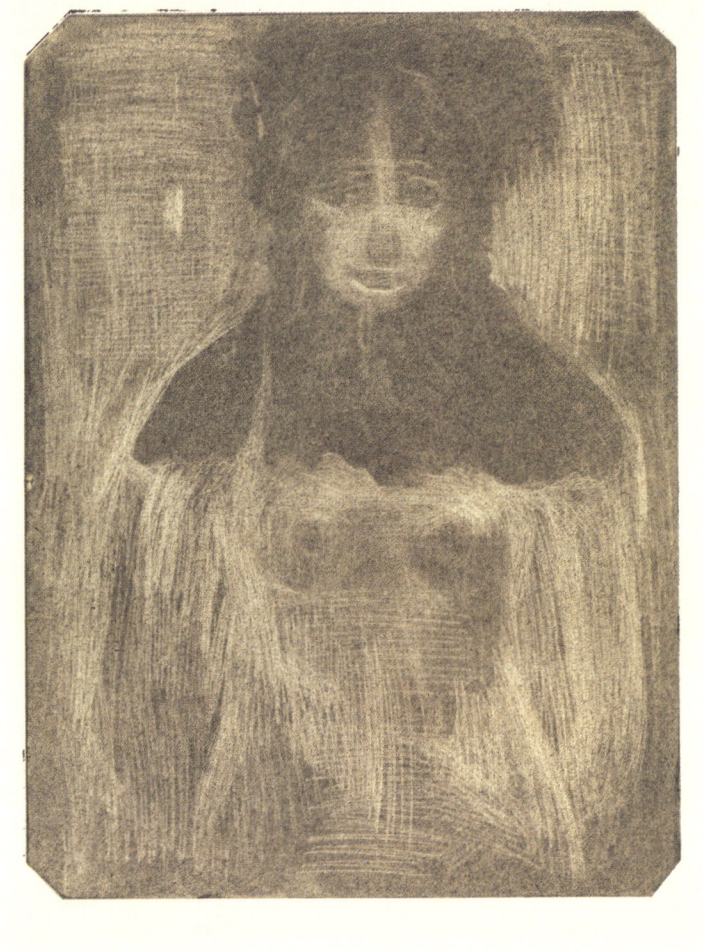

123

124
Sigbjørn Obstfelder

125
Stéphane Mallarmé

126
Funeral March
Sørgemarsj

Plate 1897; impression (between 1902 and 1914)
Intaglio: line etching and drypoint; dark brown ink; wove paper
Image: 168 × 130; paper: 480 × 327
Artist's inscription: Edv Munch
Secondary inscription: O Felsing Berlin gdr.
NG.K&H.A.19080
Provenance unknown
Sch 88; W 53; Woll G 97 I/I
Printer: Felsing

The National Museum's impression cannot be dated more precisely than to the years when Felsing was printing for Munch. In terms of composition and characterisation, the image closely resembles a lithographic portrait of Obstfelder that Munch made in 1896 (see cat. 117). Only a few impressions of the latter were printed. Another lithographic portrait of Obstfelder from the same year was printed as an edition (see cat. 116). Sigbjørn Obstfelder (1866-1900) was a Norwegian poet and a close friend of Munch for many years.

Stone 1897; impression (1897)
Lithograph (transfer lithograph): crayon; stone modified with crayon and scraper; green ink; heavy Japan paper
Image: 404 × 295; paper: 672 × 541
Artist's inscription: E Munch
NG.K&H.A.19003
Provenance unknown
Sch 79; Woll G 99 I/I
Printer: Clot

In early impressions of this lithograph (printed by Clot), the sitter's name on the stone below the image was masked during printing, whereas in later impressions (printed by Lassally) the name was often included. The National Museum's impression is without Mallarmé's name. Stephane Mallarmé (1842-1898) was a French symbolist poet. Munch also produced an intaglio portrait of him (inverted relative to the lithograph; Woll G 98). Although Munch met Mallarmé in Paris, the portraits are based on a photograph (Eggum 1987, p. 98).

Lithographic zinc plate 1897; impression (1897)
Lithograph: crayon, tusche and needle; black ink; heavy, stiff wove paper
Image: 554 × 371; paper: 631 × 454
Artist's inscription: E Munch. No 5
NG.K&H.A.19004
Possibly acquired at Munch's exhibition at Blomqvist in 1902
Sch 94; Woll G 103 I/I
Printer: Lemercier (?)

The image can be seen as a variation on, or further development of, the theme of metabolism and rebirth, which Munch addressed in *The Urn* (see cat. 103). Around the same time, he explored the same concepts in lithographs such as *In the Land of Crystals* (Woll G 102) and *Metabolism* (Woll G 104). In 1909, he used a variation on the design as his first draft for the central panel of the decorations for Oslo University's central hall, *The Human Mountain* (Woll M 863). Although that proposal was rejected by the jury, Munch continued to work on large, monumental drafts well into the 1920s.

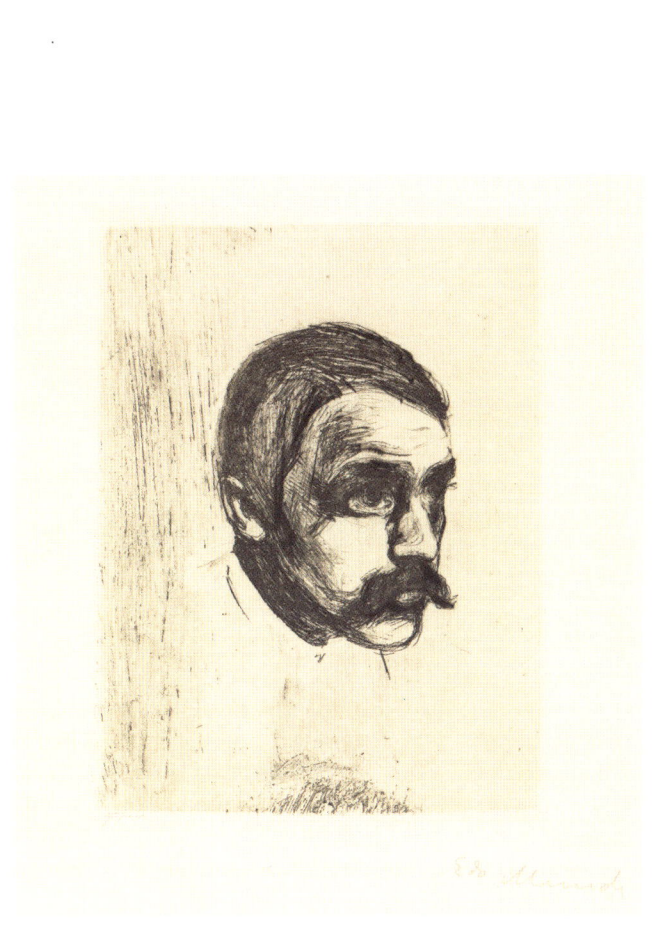

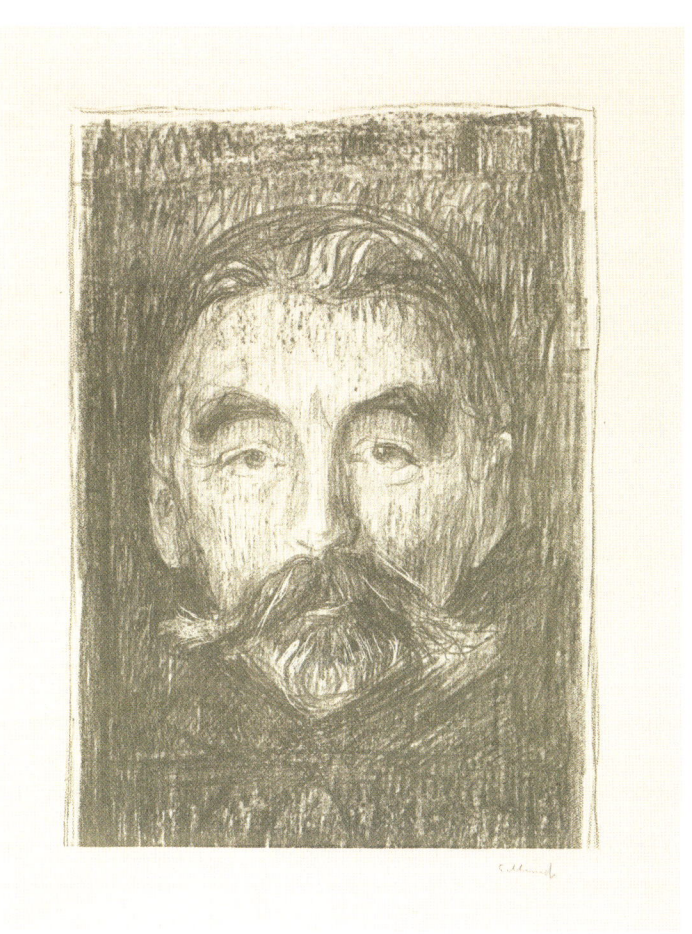

124

125

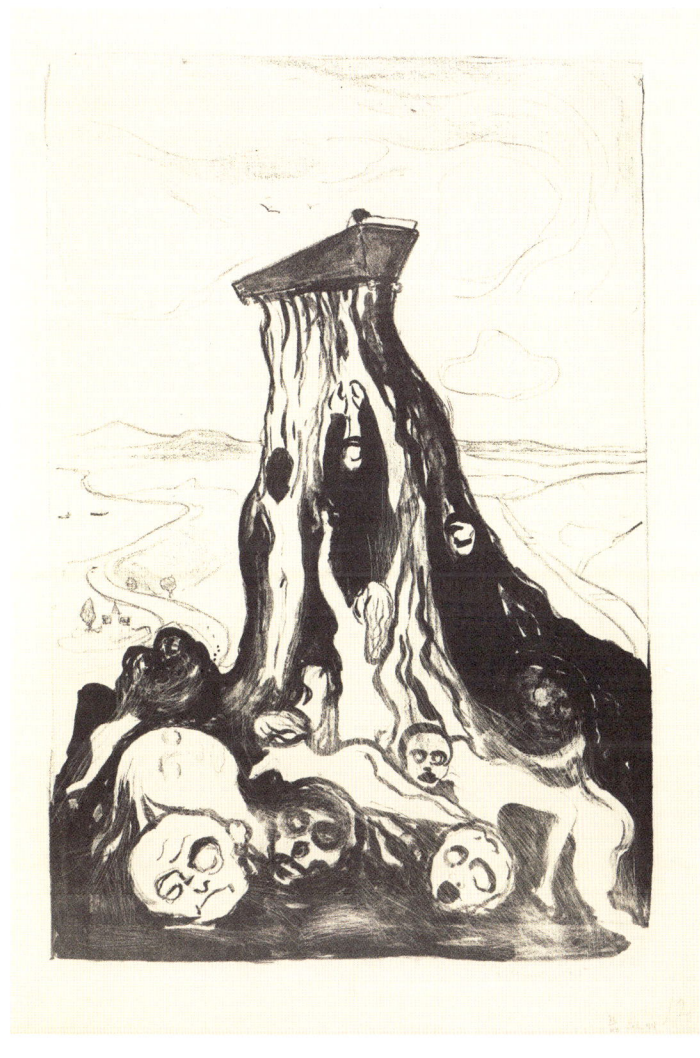

126

127
Towards the Forest I
Mot skogen I

Woodblock 1897; impression (between 1897 and 1899)
Colour woodcut: keyblock: gouges; dark grey ink, colour block: fretsaw (block cut into three pieces); blue, grey and reddish brown ink; probably China paper (lined 1973)
Image: 522 × 562; paper: 522 × 562
Artist's inscription: E Munch [on the cardboard on which the impression was originally mounted]
NG.K&H.A.19520
Provenance unknown
Sch 100; Woll G 112 II / III
Printer: Lemercier

The type of paper and the state indicate that the National Museum's impression was printed by Lemercier. The sheet is cropped on the right and left sides, cutting away sections of the image from the keyblock. The colour block is roughly 30 mm higher than the keyblock, corresponding to the strip of blue sky in the National Museum's impression. The work was originally pasted onto cardboard, with Munch's signature on the latter. During restoration in 1973, the cardboard was removed and the sheet was lined on Japan paper. Munch began work on *Towards the Forest I* in Paris. A few monochrome black impressions from the keyblock exist, printed by Munch or Lemercier. According to Schiefler, some early multicolour prints were made using a colour plate cut into three sections in addition to the keyblock. The National Museum's impression belongs to this group. Munch varied the colouring of the plates, in some cases inking the keyblock with several colours. He later reworked the colour block with gouges and cut it into several pieces, and finally, in 1915, promoted it to keyblock for a new version of the woodcut (Woll G 541), while relegating the former keyblock to the function of colour block. The existing impressions show a broad range of colour combinations and variants, with almost fluid transitions between individual impressions, making it very difficult to distinguish clear states for this woodcut. Although the motif has a central place in Munch's treatment of the relationship between man and woman, this woodcut is not based on an earlier painting – and neither did he produce a painted version later on. A drawing of similar composition from around 1895 did, however, figure in the series "De første mennesker" (The First Human Beings), which Munch exhibited in 1901 and reworked several years later as the lithographic series "Alpha and Omega". Unlike the woodcut versions, in these later cases, both the man and the woman are naked.

128
Old Fisherman
Gammel fisker

Woodblock 1897; impression (before 1914)
Woodcut: gouges and needle; black ink; medium-weight wove paper
Image: 444 × 354; paper: 506 × 386
Artist's inscription: E Munch // alter Mann [l.l.]
NG.K&H.A.19101
Provenance unknown
Sch 124; Woll G 116 I / I
Printer: probably Lasssaly

As title for this woodcut, Munch used both *Alter Mann* and *Fischer*. Schiefler dates it to 1899. An impression was, however, probably included in Munch's exhibition at the Dioramalokalet, Kristiania (Oslo), in September–October 1897 (*Gammel Mand*, cat. 125). A dating to 1897 is corroborated by an inscription on an impression in private ownership. At Munch's exhibition at the Dioramalokalet in March–April 1910, the woodcut apparently had the title *Hans Dalen* (cat. 1). Munch's sister Inger and his aunt Karen Bjølstad lived in the house of the fisherman Hans Dalen in Åsgårdstrand in the summer of 1897. This makes it likely that the block was prepared in 1897. The National Museum's impression was probably printed by Lassally, in which case it would predate the sending of the blocks to Norway in 1914. *Old Fisherman* is a characteristic example of Munch's woodcut style, which exploits the contrast between the deep grooves and the dark surfaces. Left as clear traces of a gouge applied to the wood, the grooves form a pattern of mottled white streaks in the picture plane. Munch's woodcut style became influential for a number of expressionist-oriented woodcut artists.

129
Mystical Shore
Strandmystikk

Woodblock 1897; impression (1897)
Colour woodcut: keyblock: gouges; black ink; colour block (verso of keyblock): gouges; blue-grey ink; China paper
Image: 378 × 573; paper: 454 × 702
Artist's inscription: Træsnit. / Edv Munch No 2 [the 2 overwrites a 6]
NG.K&H.A.19112
Provenance unknown
Sch 125; Woll G 117 III / V
Printer: Lemericer

Among the early impressions of *Mystical Shore*, which were probably printed by Lemercier, some are monochrome prints in black, some in two colours (imprints from the recto and verso of the same woodblock). The type of paper and the colours indicate that the National Museum's impression was printed by Lemercier. The artist's numbering on the sheet also indicates that it is an early impression. Although Schiefler dates *Mystical Shore* to 1899, two impressions, one hand coloured and one printed in two colours, were included in Munch's exhibition at the Dioramalokalet, Kristiania (Oslo), in September–October 1897 (under the title *Strand*, cat. 122 and 123). This would make it the only colour woodcut to be included in that exhibition. The other woodcuts were either black and white or hand-coloured. After 1906, Lassally pulled new two-colour prints. Having requested his plates to be sent to Norway in 1914, Munch later printed multicolour impressions of *Mystical Shore*. The image is an inverted version of two paintings from 1892 (Woll M 281, 282) and a watercolour (MM.T. 2387), probably from the same year.

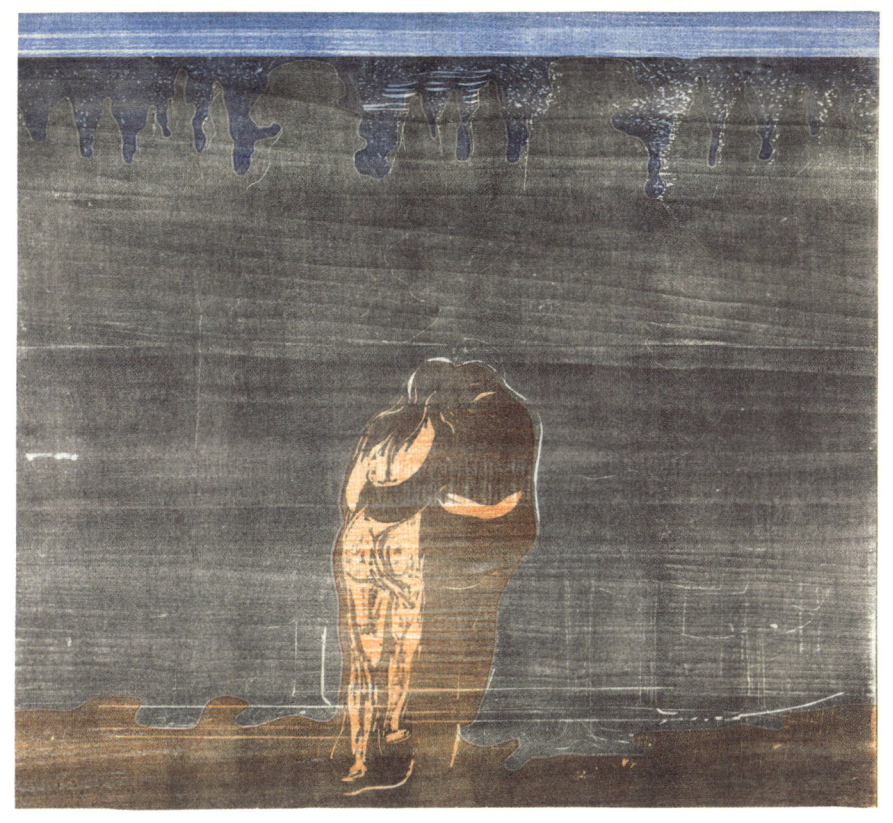

127

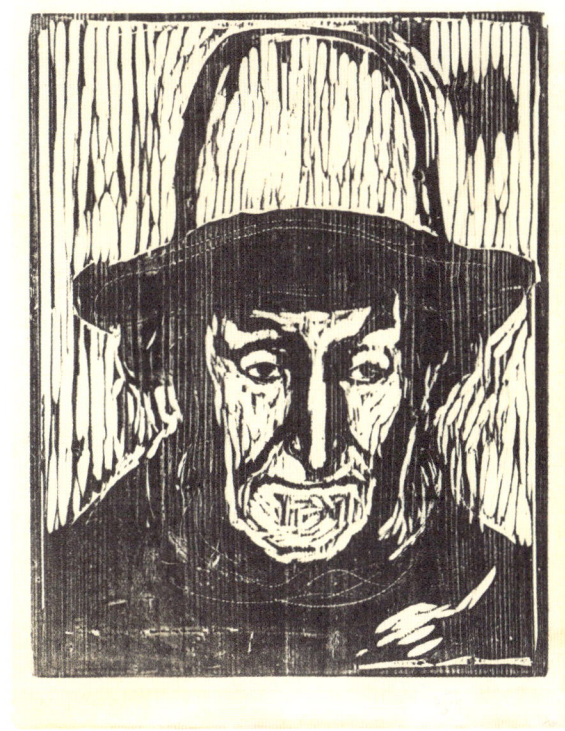

128

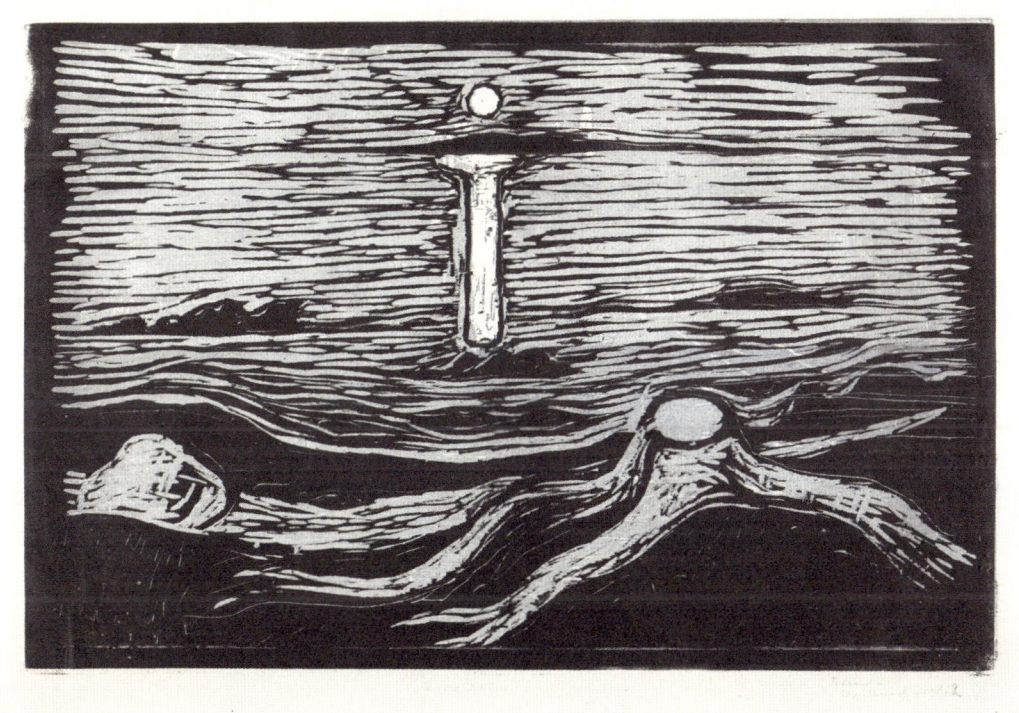

129

130
Farewell after the Party
Avskjed etter selskapet

131
Nude
Aktstudie

Stone 1898 or 1899; impression (between 1898 and 1902)
Lithograph: crayon and tusche; black ink; heavy, stiff wove paper
Image: 424 × 540; paper: 542 × 747
Artist's inscription: Edv Munch
NG.K&H.A.19035 (formerly NG.K&H.B.00613)
Purchased at City Auksjon, Oslo, September 1938 (cat. 189 or 232)
Sch 121; Woll G 123 2/3
Printer: Lassally

Schiefler dates the lithograph to 1899, but there are reasons to doubt this dating. On one impression, Munch has written "printed around 1898" (MM.G.237-23), and although clearly written at a later point, this may suggest a somewhat earlier dating. The lithograph is drawn directly on the stone and was printed by Lassally. Munch was only briefly in Berlin in 1899, following a longer stay the previous year. In a few early exhibition catalogues, the lithograph is dated to 1901, and it cannot be ruled out that it was only made after Munch had returned to Berlin late that year. The picture shows a group of guests still gossiping after leaving a party, in a style reminiscent of Honoré Daumier's caricatures. Thematically, it also has much in common with the acerbic depictions of small-town life in *Trangviksposten*, a satirical supplement issued with the Sunday edition of *Aftenposten* starting in 1899, with drawings by Theodor Kittelsen, Olaf Gulbransson, and others.

Woodblock 1897; impression (1913)
Woodcut: gouges; greyish colour, wove paper
Image: 435 × 380; paper: 506 × 450
Artist's inscription: E Munch
Secondary inscription: <Halbakt> [l.l.; pencil] // <180,-> [?; l.c., pencil]; verso: Handdruck 1913 [l.l.; pencil]
NG.K&H.A.19107 (formerly NG.K&H.B.00613)
Purchased at City Auksjon, Oslo, September 1938 (cat. 187)
Sch 112 (and 415); Woll G 128 I/I
Printer: probably Munch

The grey tone of the National Museum's impression is due to it having been pulled without the block being re-inked after the previous printing. Schiefler appears to have registered this woodcut twice, both as no. 112, with the title *Aktstudie*, dated 1898, and as no. 415, *Halbakt*, dated 1913. It is, however, probably a new impression from the same block. The woodblock bears the stamp of the firm A. Moureaux, Paris, on the verso (MM P 340) and was probably executed during Munch's stay in Paris in 1897. Two of the three impressions in the Munch Museum are marked "Tirage d'essai" (Trial proof) (MM.G.584-1-2), probably by the printer (Clot or Lemercier?). In Schiefler's catalogue, the 1913 edition is recorded as slightly smaller than the earlier one (425–430 × 330 as opposed to 460 × 380). On the National Museum's impression, the upper part of the block is masked, despite which the dimensions are still larger than those given for Sch 415. Differences in print quality compared to the Munch Museum's impressions also support the assumption that this is an impression pulled by the artist. Further, the inscriptions "Halbakt" and "Handdruck 1913" make it likely that it was this impression that Schiefler saw and registered as no. 415. Under both catalogue numbers, Schiefler notes that very few impressions exist, and so far only the three in the Munch Museum have been registered in addition to the one belonging to the National Museum. At the exhibition of Munch's woodcuts that Eli Ingebretsen Greve arranged at

the National Gallery in spring 1946 (Greve 1946), one of the impressions from the Munch Museum collection was shown as Sch 112 (no. 15 in Greve's catalogue) and that of the National Museum as Sch 415 (no. 64 in Greve's catalogue). Both were listed with the titles and dimensions from Schiefler's catalogue. The information for cat. 64, "*Halvakt fra 1913*", notes that this print does not occur in the Munch Museum's collection, while also remarking the similarity to Sch 112. On the other hand, the impression reproduced in Eli Ingebretsen Greve's book *Edvard Munch. Liv og verk i lys av tresnittene* (Edvard Munch. Life and Work in the Light of the Woodcuts) (Oslo: Cappelen, 1963, p. 79) is that of the National Museum's impression, where it has the title *Aktstudie* and is dated to 1898. (The book was published posthumously, and the captions were probably prepared by Arve Moen. The catalogue from 1946 is reproduced on pp. 161–192.)

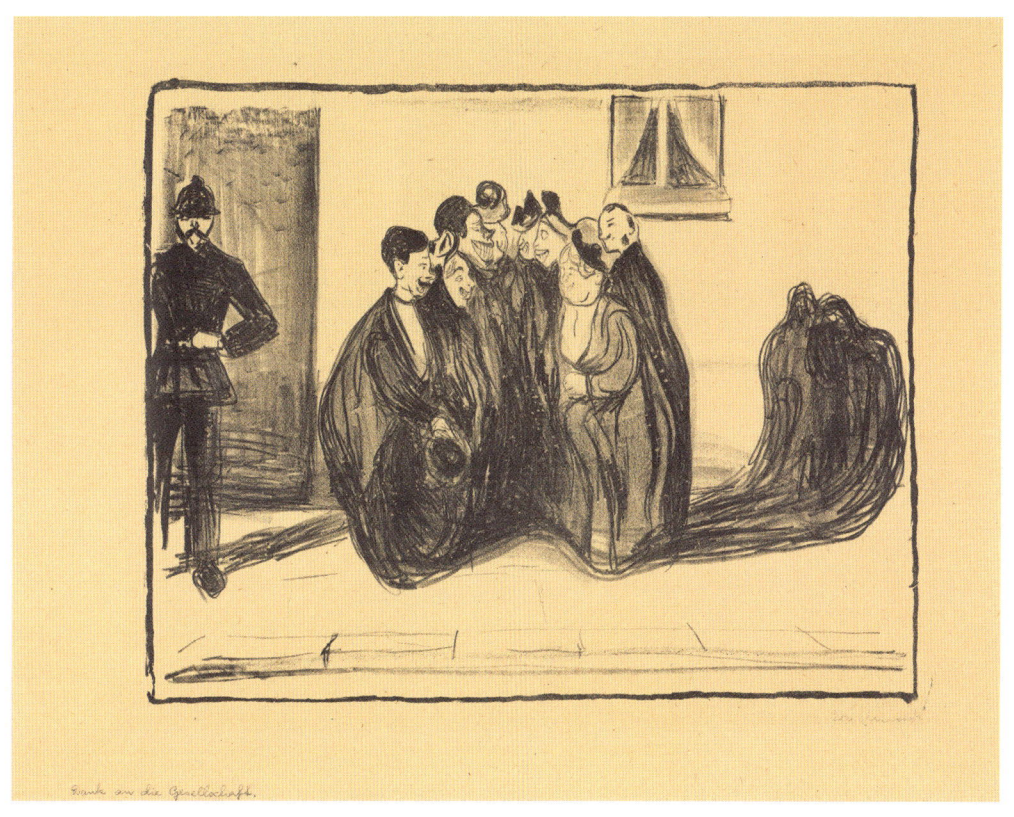

130

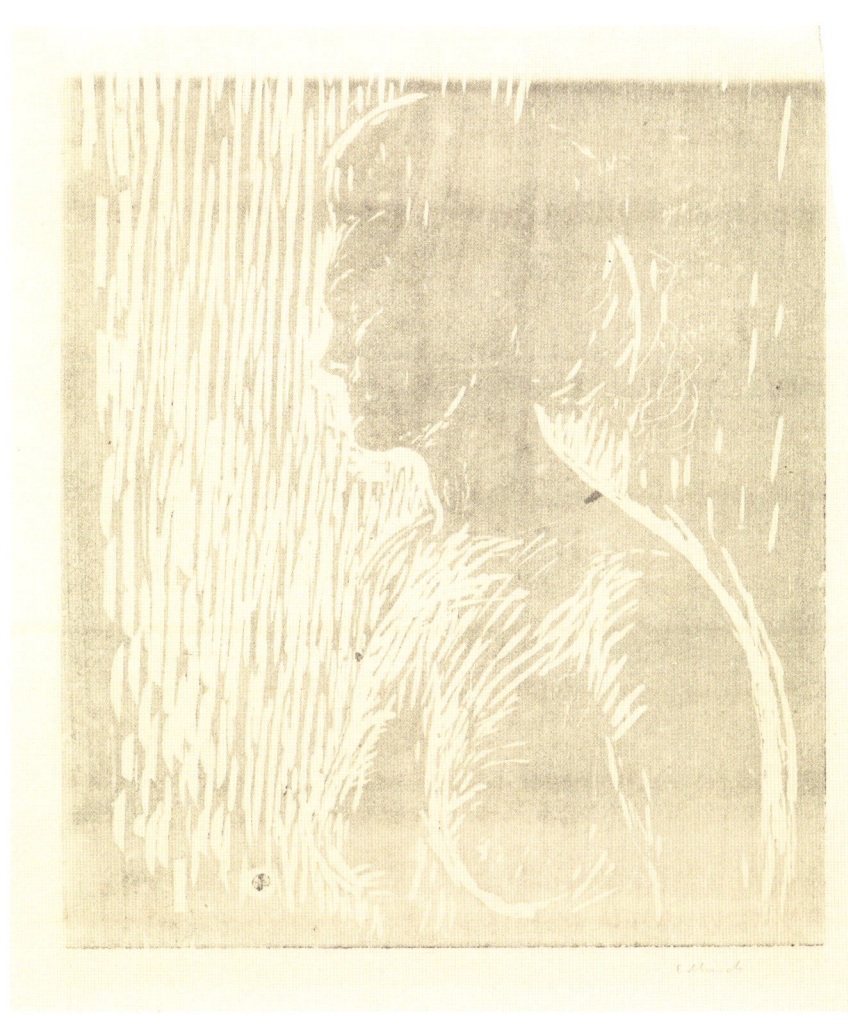

131

132
Blossom of Pain
Smertens blomst

Woodblock 1898; impression (between 1906 and 1914)
Woodcut: gouges; black ink; light-weight imitation (?) Japan paper
Image: 460 × 328; paper: 557 × 413
Artist's inscription: EMunch
NG.K&H.A.19097
Provenance unknown
Sch 114; Woll G 130 I/I
Printer: Lassally

The image was originally designed as a cover for the magazine *Quickborn* (vol. 4, January 1899) (see comments to cat. 97), and Schiefler referred to the woodcut simply as *Titelzeichnung*. Munch himself used titles such as *Blodblomster* (Blood Flowers) and *Mannen som bløder og blomsten* (The Man Who Bleeds and the Flower). The image is interpreted as an allegory of artistic creation. Munch used the bleeding heart as a symbol for the artist who creates art from his own pain and suffering.

133
Two Women on the Shore
To kvinner ved stranden

Woodblock 1898; impression (probably 1906)
Colour woodcut: gouges and fretsaw (block cut into three pieces); black, green and reddish brown ink; medium-weight wove paper
Image: 377 × 513; paper: 430 × 556
Artist's inscription: Edv Munch//Sortklædt <Kvinde> [o]g hvidklædt/kvinde ved en Strandbred
NG.K&H.A.19098
Provenance unknown
Sch 117; Woll G 133 II 1/IV
Printer: Lassally

This woodcut exists in a number of variants in different states and colours. It is essentially a good illustration of Munch's so-called jigsaw-puzzle technique: the two women are on one piece, the landscape on a second, the sea and sky on a third. Munch himself pulled several early impressions before a small part of the landscape piece, the promontory, broke off. In 1906, Schiefler described some recently registered prints in which the promontory is missing and the sea and sky appear white (the colour of the paper), as is the case in the National Museum's impression. In most of the registered impressions, the promontory is either retouched or printed from a replacement piece, while the sea and sky are printed in one colour. In some impressions, a stencil has been used to add the moon and its reflection. Munch had previously used the subject of a young woman standing beside a seated older woman in the programme for the 1896 production of Henrik Ibsen's *Peer Gynt* at the Théâtre de l'Œuvre in Paris (see cat. 113). In the more concise design of the woodcut, the juxtaposition of the tall, pale young woman looking out to sea, and the dark, hunched, elderly woman facing the spectator, captures a complex interplay of opposites: youth and old age, innocence and wisdom, expectation and resignation.

134
Winter Landscape
Snølandskap

Woodblock 1898; impression (after 1906)
Woodcut: gouges; black ink; light-weight imitation (?) Japan paper
Image: 322 × 458; paper: 482 × 640
Artist's inscription: E Munch
NG.K&H.A.19099
Provenance unknown
Sch 118; Woll G 134 II/III
Printer: Lassally

Schiefler mentions only few impressions printed by the artist. This makes it reasonable to assume that impressions by a professional printer were not pulled until after 1906. The latter were most probably printed by Lassally.

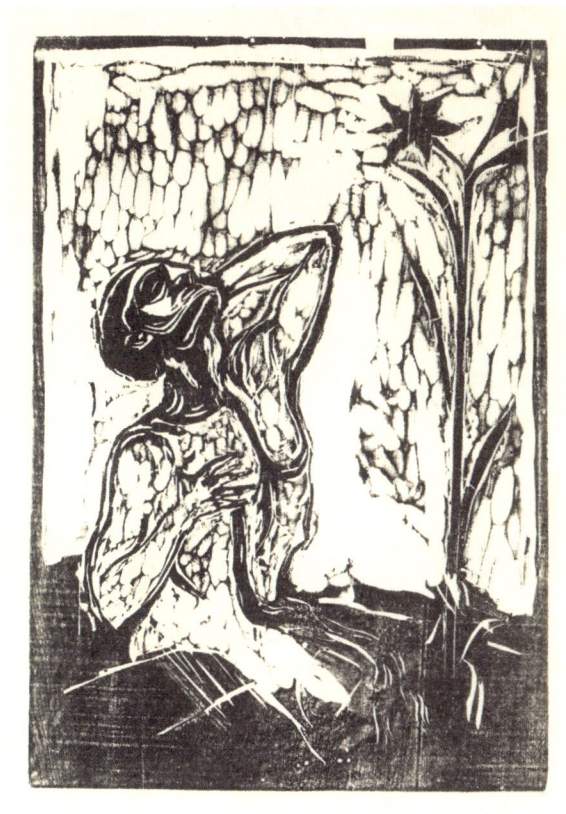

132

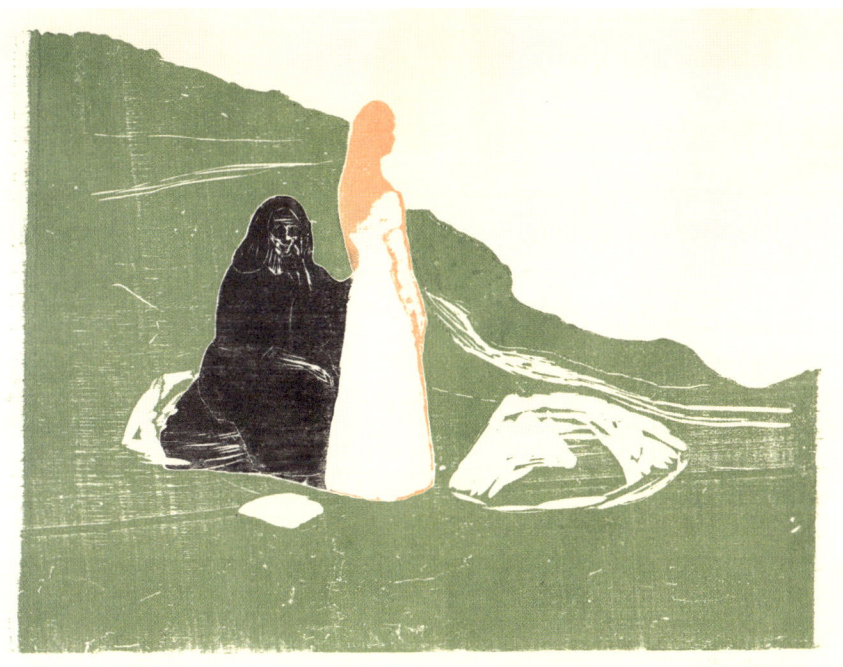

133

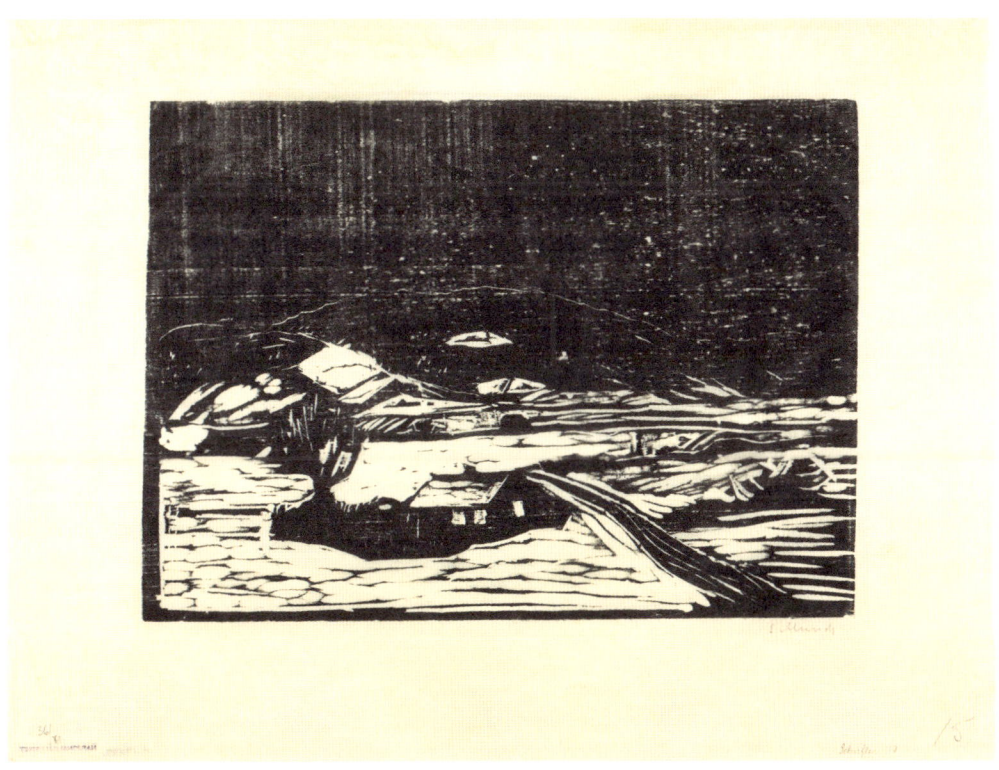

134

135
Encounter in Space
Møte i verdensrommet

Woodblock 1898 or 1899; impression (probably between 1902 and 1914)
Colour woodcut: gouges and fretsaw (block cut into three pieces); black, red and green ink; Japan paper
Image: 190 × 254; paper: 853 × 482
Artist's inscription: Edv Munch
NG.K&H.A.19103
Provenance unknown
Sch 135; Woll G 136 3/3
Printer: Lassally

Early impressions pulled by either Munch himself or Lemercier show slight cracks in the block at the tip of the woman's toe and the tip of the man's left foot, which later resulted in the loss of two pieces from the block. These are missing from the block as preserved (MM P 363). In later impressions, printed by Lassally, new pieces appear to have been substituted for those that are missing. The National Museum's impression belongs to this group. The depiction of the floating couple and the accompanying sperm carries powerful erotic overtones; at the same time, the configuration and movement of the figures suggests the complex relationship between man and woman. Munch himself commented on the picture's cosmic connotations. On one impression he wrote: "Human destinies are like the planets. They come from the unknown to meet and vanish again." (private collection). In 1902 Munch produced an intaglio version of the picture (see cat. 143); there also exists a drawing of the same (MM.T.389).

136
Ashes II
Aske II

Stone 1899; impression (probably 1899)
Lithograph: crayon, tusche and scraper; black ink; blue laid Ingres paper, pasted onto heavy, stiff wove paper
Image: 355 × 460; paper: 355 × 460
Artist's inscription: E Munch [on the wove paper]
NG.K&H.A.19005
Provenance unknown
Sch 120; Woll G 146 II 2/II 2
Printer: Petersen & Waitz

The National Museum's impression is clear with rich nuance in the printing, and the blueish colour of the Ingres paper is unusually well preserved. Munch produced an earlier lithograph of this motif in 1896 (Woll G 79). Both lithographs are based on a painting from 1894 (Woll M 378). For a discussion of the subject, see cat. 30.

137
Woman's Head
Kvinnehode

Woodblock 1899; impression (1905 or later)
Woodcut: gouges; black ink; medium-weight laid Japan paper
Image: 252 × 198; paper: 389 × 264
Artist's inscription: Edv Munch
NG.K&H.A.19100 (formerly NG.K&H.B.00613)
Purchased at City Auksjon, Oslo, September 1938 (cat. 125)
Sch 123 (and 234); Woll G 148 I/I
Printer: Lassally

Schiefler appears to have registered this wood-cut twice. Under cat. 123 he only notes a few trial proofs pulled by the artist. However, he also records an impression with a very similar description as cat. 234 among works from 1905, printed by either the artist or Lassally. This proba-bly indicates that Lassally printed an edition from the woodcut in 1905.

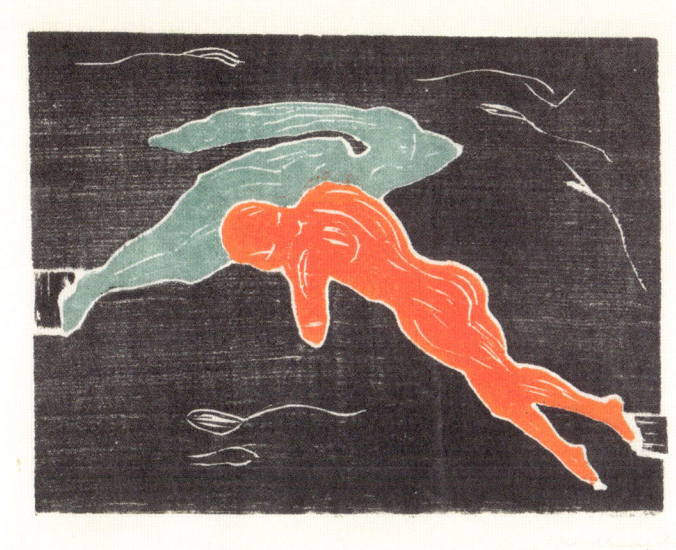

135

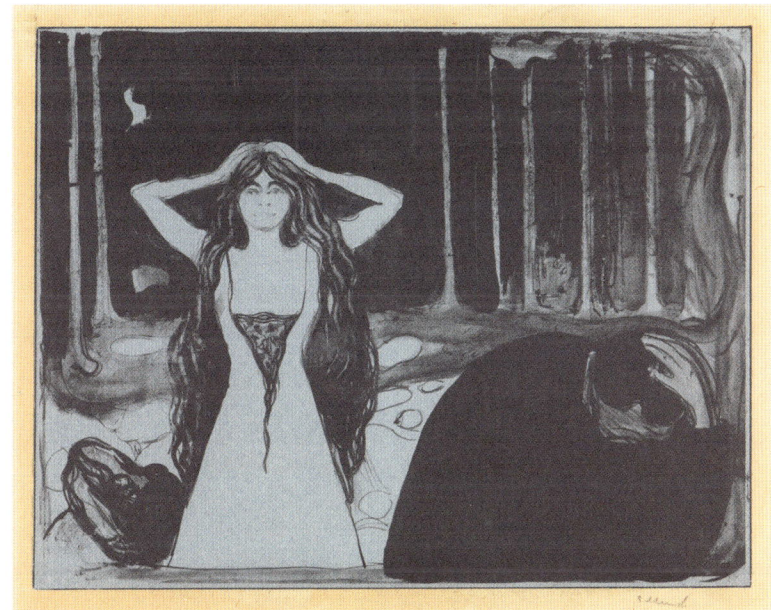

136

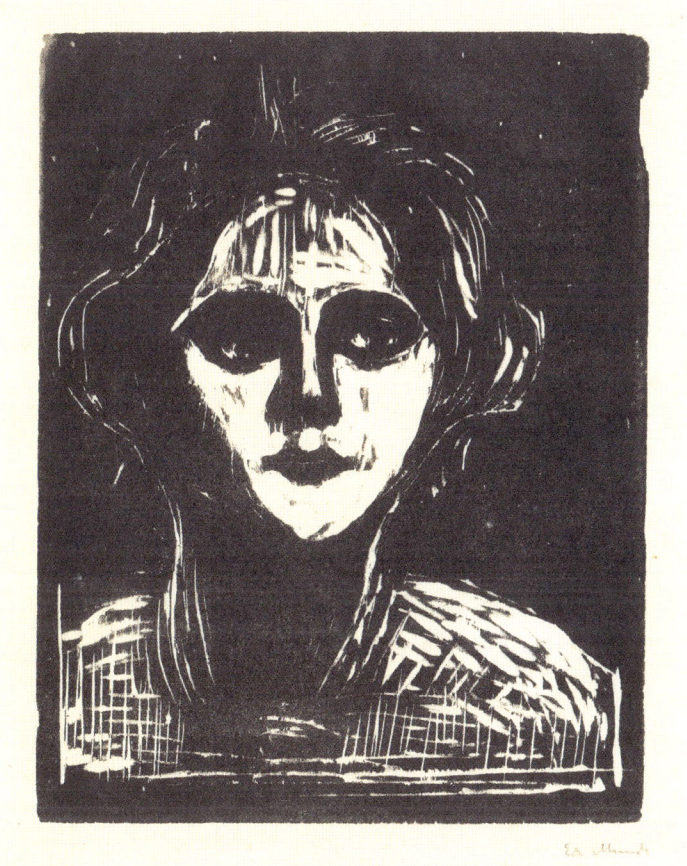

137

138
Woman's Head against the Shore
Kvinnehode mot stranden

139
Man and Woman
Mann og kvinne

140
Two Human Beings. The Lonely Ones
To mennesker. De ensomme

Woodblock 1899; impression (after 1906)
Colour woodcut: keyblock: gouges and fretsaw
(block cut into two pieces); green and red ink;
colour block: gouges and fretsaw (block cut into
two pieces); yellowish red and greyish yellow ink;
light-weight Japan paper
Image: 466 × 415; paper: 548 × 467
Artist's inscription: Edv Munch // Kvinnehoved i
Landskab / med rød Luft [l.l.]
NG.K&H.A.19111
Provenance unknown
Sch 129; Woll G 152 II 3/ II 4
Printer: probably Lassally

The National Museum's impression is printed
from two blocks, each cut into two pieces. In early
impressions, one piece of the keyblock forms
the beach with the woman's head and the cloud
formation above, while the other piece forms
the water and the sky. The other block (colour
block) is cut so that one piece forms the woman's
head and the beach in the foreground while the
other covers the rest of the picture surface. In
the National Museum's impression, the keyblock
is printed in red and green across the divided
sections, such that both the beach and the water
appear green and the sky red, while omitting
the cloud formation. This colouring produces a
more abstract composition with a high red sky
above a uniformly green landscape. Schiefler
only mentions the early proofs pulled by Munch
himself, while implying (in 1906) that there
also exist a number of "Maschinendrucke", i.e.
impressions pulled by a professional printer. The
National Museum's impression does not belong to
the group described by Schiefler and was printed
later, probably by Lassally. The slight haziness
heightens the mellow mood of the subject, creating the impression of a handmade print. This
effect is, however, not unique to this impression,
but also present in a number of others.

Woodblock 1899; impression (probably between
1906 and 1914)
Woodcut: gouges and fretsaw (part of block);
black ink; light-weight laid Japan paper
Image: 410 × 510; paper: 533 × 594
Artist's inscription: E Munch
NG.K&H.A.19113 (formerly NG.K&H.B.00613)
Purchased at City Auksjon, Oslo, September 1938
(cat. 156)
Sch 132; Woll G 156 I / II
Printer: Lassally

Schiefler mentions only a few hand-printed
impressions in black and dark red, indicating
that the prints by Lassally were not made until
after 1906. The woodblock was sent to Norway
following the outbreak of World War I, and in 1916
Nielsen pulled some impressions in which the
section with the figures is combined with a new
block with a prominent pattern of wood grain for
the background. Munch painted a similar subject
in 1898 (Woll M 426).

Woodblock 1899; impression (between 1906 and
1914)
Colour woodcut: gouges and fretsaw (block cut
into three pieces); black and blue-grey ink; light-
weight laid Japan paper
Image: 400 × 548; paper: 460 × 595
Artist's inscription: E Munch
NG.K&H.A.19102 (formerly NG.K&H.B.00613)
Purchased at City Auksjon, Oslo, September 1938
(cat. 91)
Sch 133; Woll G 157 I / VIII
Printer: Lassally

In the early 1890s, Munch developed the same
subject as a painting (lost in 1901, Woll M 283) and
as an intaglio in 1894 (Woll G 13, see cat. 69). The
first impressions of the woodcut were probably
pulled by Munch himself. The blocks were later
printed by Lassally (between 1906 and 1914)
and Nielsen (ca. 1917). There are versions in two
colours, black and blueish-grey (of which the
National Museum's impression is one) and multicolour versions in a variety of colour combinations. In both print versions, the image is inverted
relative to the lost painting, but between 1905 and
1907 Munch painted new versions with the same
orientation as the intaglio and woodcut (Woll
M 640, Woll M 735). In 1933–35 he painted yet
another version in which the image has the same
orientation as the original painting (Woll M 1719).

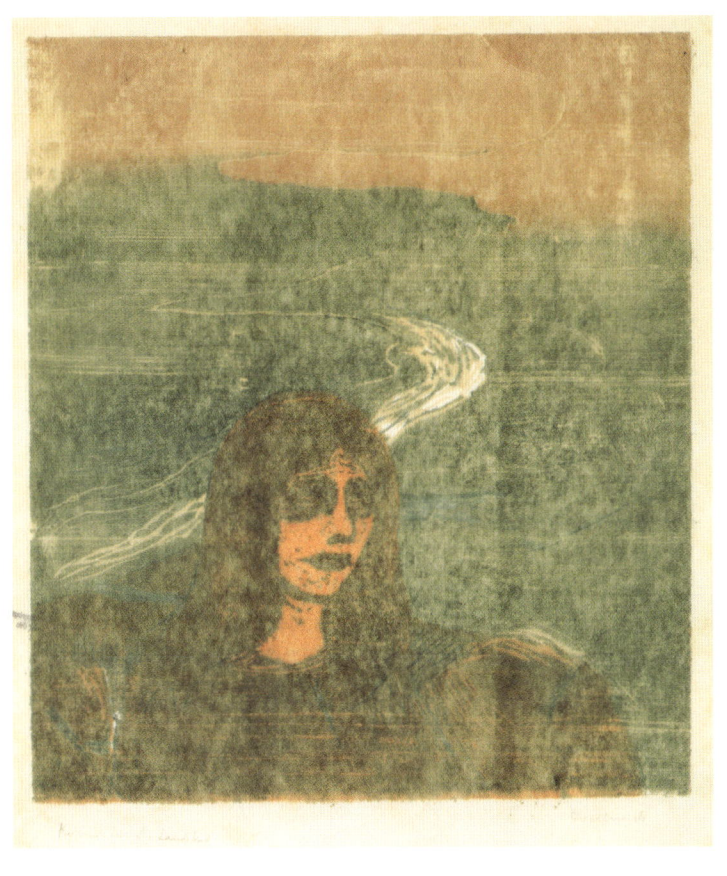

138

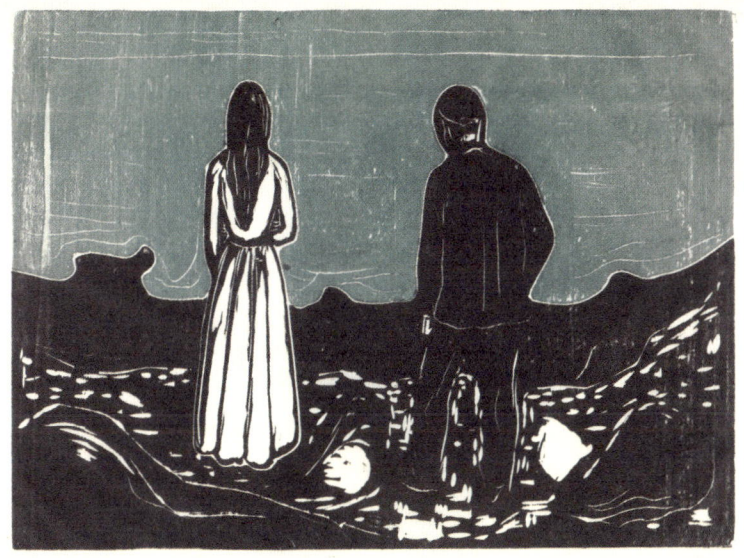

140

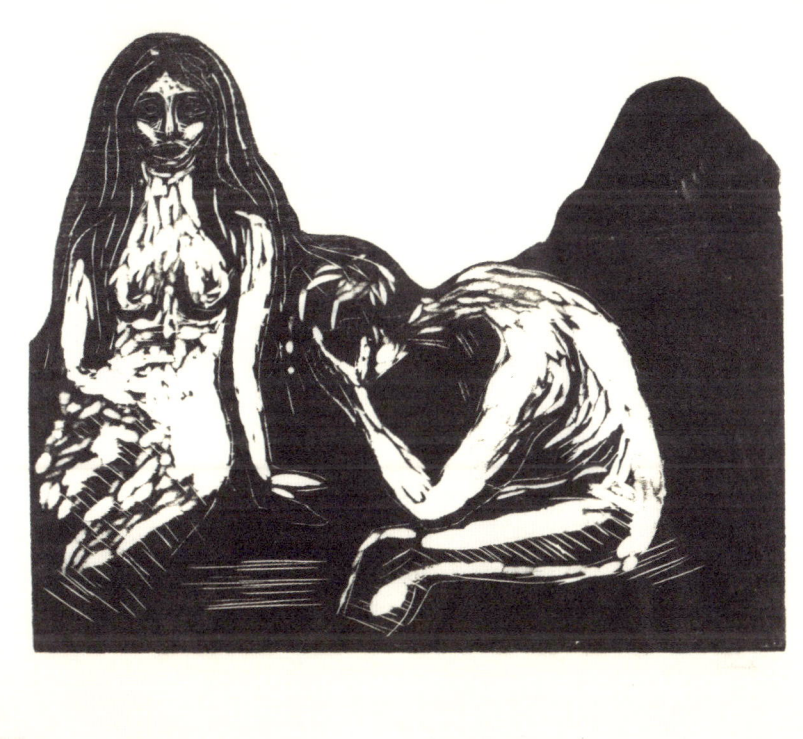

139

141
Fertility
Fruktbarhet

Woodblock 1900; impression 1921
Woodcut: gouges; black ink; stiff wove paper
Image: 421 × 523; paper: 603 × 698
Artist's inscription: Edv Munch
Secondary inscription: 18/4 1921//
<Geschlechtsbaum/Weib u. Mann> [l.l.; pencil]
NG.K&H.A.19521 (formerly NG.K&H.B.00613)
Purchased at City Auksjon, Oslo, 1938 (cat. 318)
Sch 110; Woll G 160 I/II
Printer: Nielsen

The inscription recto "18/4 1921" is the printer's
and shows the date of printing. The composition corresponds (inverted) to a painting from
1899-1900 (Woll M 426).

142
The Dead Mother and Her Child
Den døde mor og barnet

Zinc plate 1901; impression (between 1902 and
1914)
Intaglio: etching, open bite and drypoint; dark
brown ink; medium-weight, stiff wove paper
Image: 324 × 494; paper: 439 × 604
Artist's inscription: Edv. Munch/avant lettre
Secondary inscription: O Felsing Berlin gdr.
NG.K&H.A.19083
Provenance unknown
Sch 140; W 59; Woll G 163 II/II
Printer: Felsing

The impression cannot be dated more precisely
than to the years when Felsing was printing
for Munch. Munch also produced a drawing
(MM.T.301) and two paintings of the same subject
(inverted) (1899; Woll M 446, 447).

143
Encounter in Space
Møte i verdensrommet

Plate 1902; impression (between 1902 and 1914)
Intaglio: line etching and open bite; dark brown
ink; heavy, stiff wove paper
Image: 126 × 185; paper: 232 × 289
Artist's inscription: Edv Munch [l.r.]
Secondary inscription: O Felsing gdr.
NG.K&H.A.19085 (formerly NG.K&H.B.00613)
Purchased at City Auksjon, Oslo, September 1938
(cat. 83)
Sch 151; W 166; Woll G 168 II/II
Printer: Felsing

The impression cannot be dated more precisely
than to the years when Felsing was printing for
Munch. For a woodcut version of the same subject, see cat. 135.

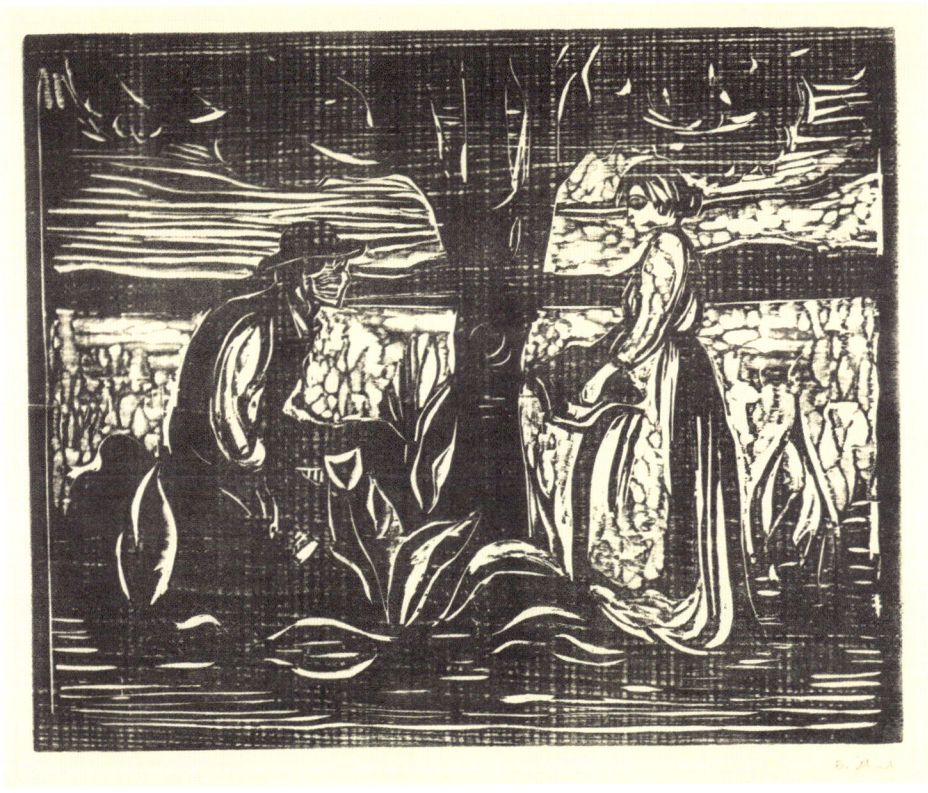

141

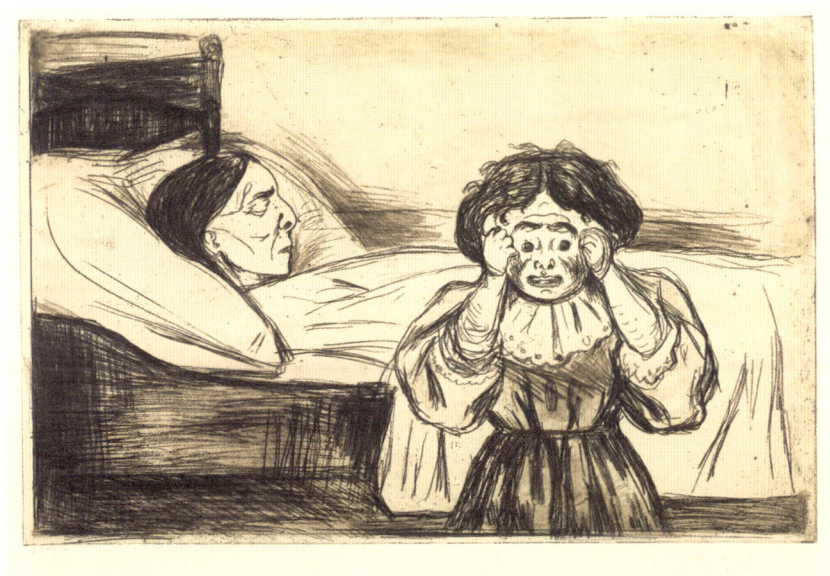

142

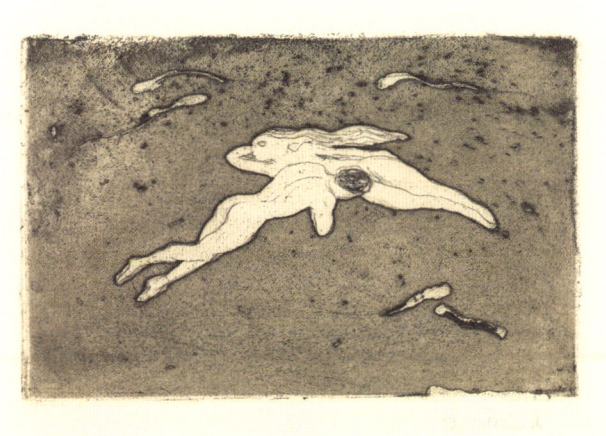

143

144
Square in Berlin. Potsdamer Platz
Plass i Berlin. Potsdamer Platz

Plate 1902; impression (between 1902 and 1914)
Intaglio: drypoint and open bite with plate tone;
dark brown ink; heavy, stiff wove paper
Image: 111 × 161; paper: 248 × 349
Artist's inscription: E Munch
Secondary inscription: O Felsing Berlin gdr.
NG.K&H.A.19086
Provenance unknown
Sch 155; W 70; Woll G 177 I/I
Printer: Felsing

The impression cannot be dated more precisely
than to the years when Felsing was printing for
Munch. Munch also produced two paintings of
the same subject (the intaglio is partly inverted) in
1902 (Woll M 519, 520).

145
The Hearse. Potsdamer Platz
Likvognen. Potsdamer Platz

Plate 1902; impression (between 1902 and 1914)
Intaglio: line etching, drypoint and open bite;
black ink; heavy, stiff wove paper
Image: 231 × 288; paper: 350 × 498
Artist's inscription: Edv. Munch/avant lettre
Secondary inscription: O Felsing Berlin gdr.
NG.K&H.A.19088
Provenance unknown
Sch 156; W 71; Woll G 178 III/III
Printer: Felsing

The impression cannot be dated more precisely
than to the years when Felsing was printing for
Munch. Munch also produced two paintings
with similar subject matter (the intaglio is partly
inverted) in 1902 (Woll M 519, 520).

146
Albert Kollmann

Plate 1902; impression (between 1902 and 1914)
Intaglio: drypoint with plate tone; black ink;
heavy, stiff wove paper
Image: 189 × 141; paper: 499 × 350
Artist's inscription: Edv.Munch/avant lettre
Secondary inscription: O Felsing Berlin gdr.
NG.K&H.A.19089
Provenance unknown
Sch 159; W 74; Woll G 181 I/I
Printer: Felsing

The impression cannot be dated more precisely
than to the years when Felsing was printing for
Munch. Albert Kollmann (1837-1905) was a German mystic, art enthusiast, and ardent spokes-
man for Munch's art starting in 1902. Munch
painted several portraits of Kollmann: two in the
years 1901-02, in one case as solitary subject (Woll
M 499), in the other together with Sten Drewsen,
where the depiction of Kollmann is probably
based on the intaglio (Woll M 500). A further
painted portrait (Woll M 694) and a lithograph
(Woll G 283) are dated to 1906.

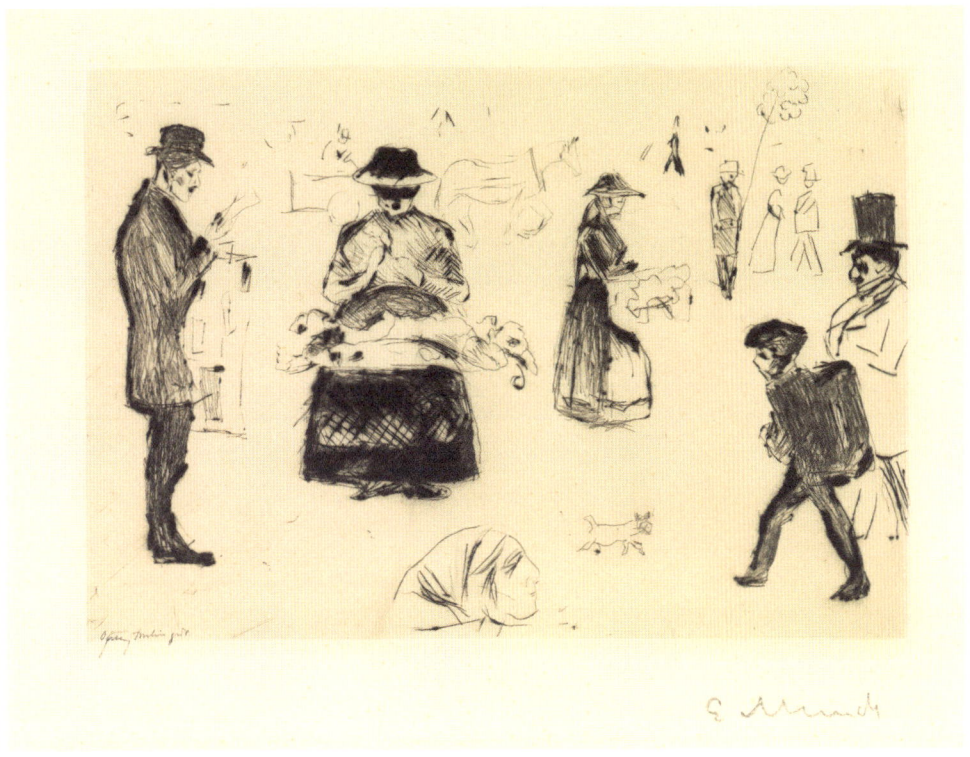

144

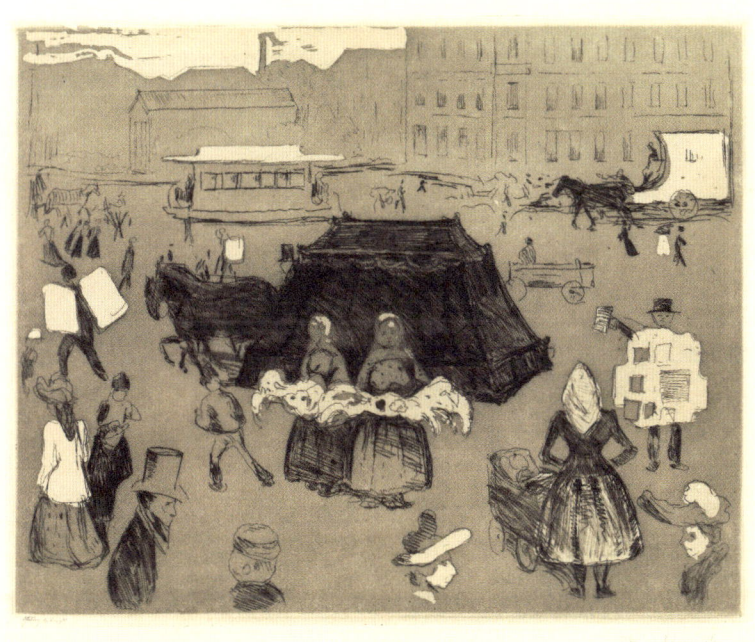

145

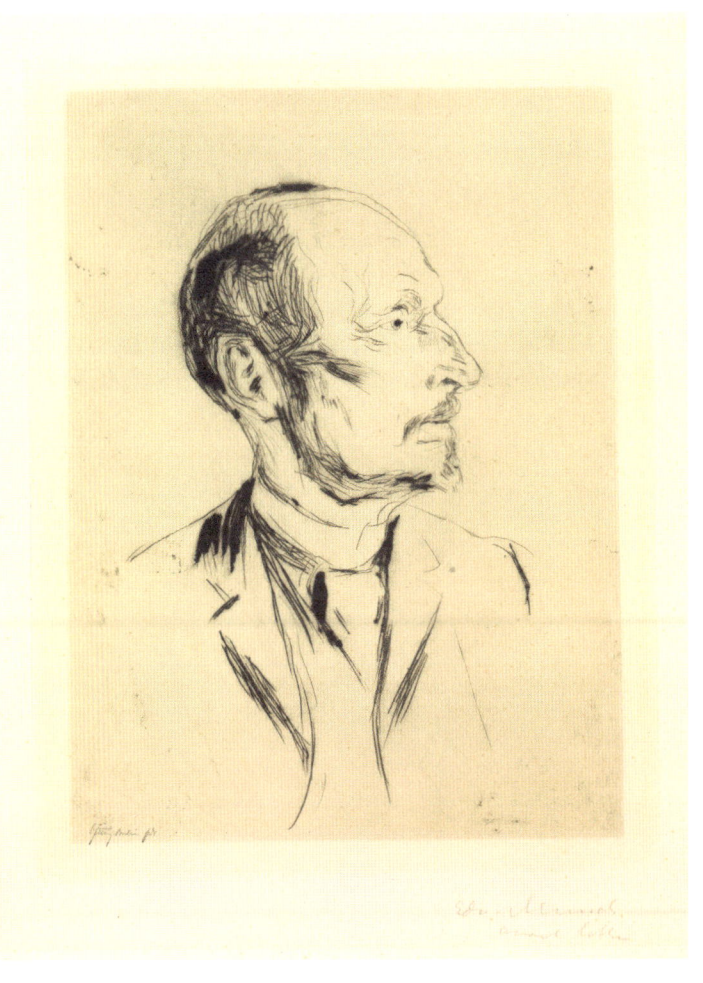

146

147
Café Bauer
Kafé Bauer

Plate 1902; impression (between 1902 and 1914)
Intaglio: drypoint with plate tone; black ink;
heavy, stiff wove paper
Image: 88 × 124; paper: 270 × 350
Artist's inscription: Edv. Munch/avant lettre
Secondary inscription: O Felsing Berlin gdr.
NG.K&H.A.19087
Provenance unknown
Sch 160; W 75; Woll G 182 I/I
Printer: Felsing

The impression cannot be dated more precisely
than to the years when Felsing was printing
for Munch. Café Bauer on the corner of Unter
den Linden and Friedrichstrasse was Munch's
preferred café in Berlin in 1902 and for some time
after.

148
Hopfenblüte

Plate 1902; impression (between 1902 and 1914)
Intaglio: drypoint with plate tone; black ink;
heavy, stiff wove paper
Image: 124 × 241; paper: 350 × 507
Artist's inscription: Edv. Munch/avant lettre
Secondary inscription: O Felsing Berlin gdr.
NG.K&H. A.19090
Provenance unknown
Sch 161; Woll G 183 I/I
Printer: Felsing

The impression cannot be dated more precisely
than to the years when Felsing was printing for
Munch. Hopfenblüte was a café on Unter den
Linden in Berlin.

149
Woman's Head
Kvinnehode

Plate 1902; impression (between 1902 and 1914)
Intaglio: drypoint, with plate tone; black ink;
heavy, stiff wove paper
Image: 268 × 217; paper: 350 × 331
Artist's inscription: Edv. Munch/avant lettre
Secondary inscription: O Felsing Berlin gdr.
NG.K&H.A.19091 (formerly NG.K&H.B.00614)
Purchased at City Auksjon, Oslo, 19 January 1939
(cat. 5)
Sch 162; W 77; Woll G 184 I/I
Printer: Felsing

The impression cannot be dated more precisely
than to the years when Felsing was printing for
Munch. The title *Woman's Head* was given by
Schiefler (*Mädchenkopf*), but in many exhibitions
between 1910 and 1922 Munch used the title
Italienerinde or *Italieninden* (The Italian Woman),
sometimes followed by *Hopfenblüte* in parentheses. *Italienerinnen* was also the title used in the
City Auksjon catalogue.

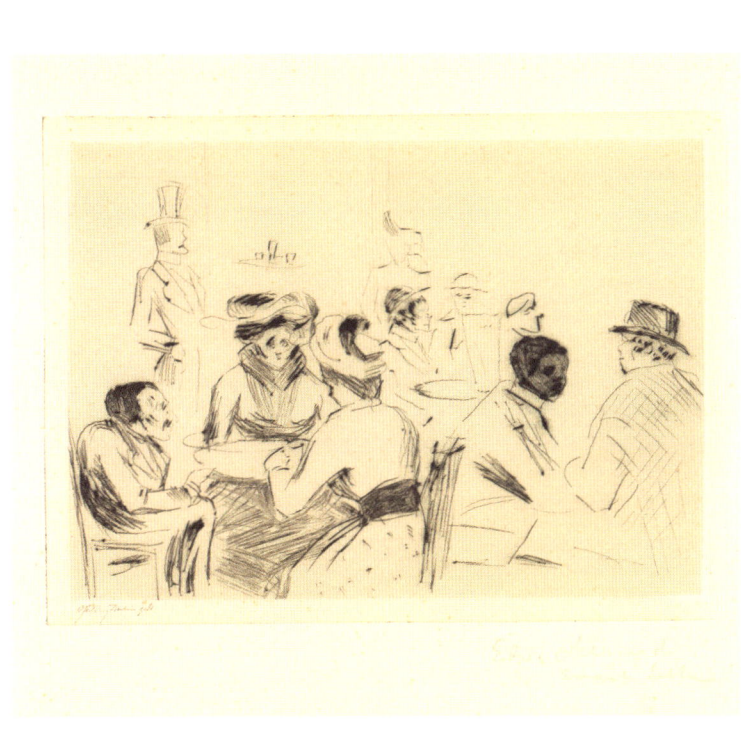

147

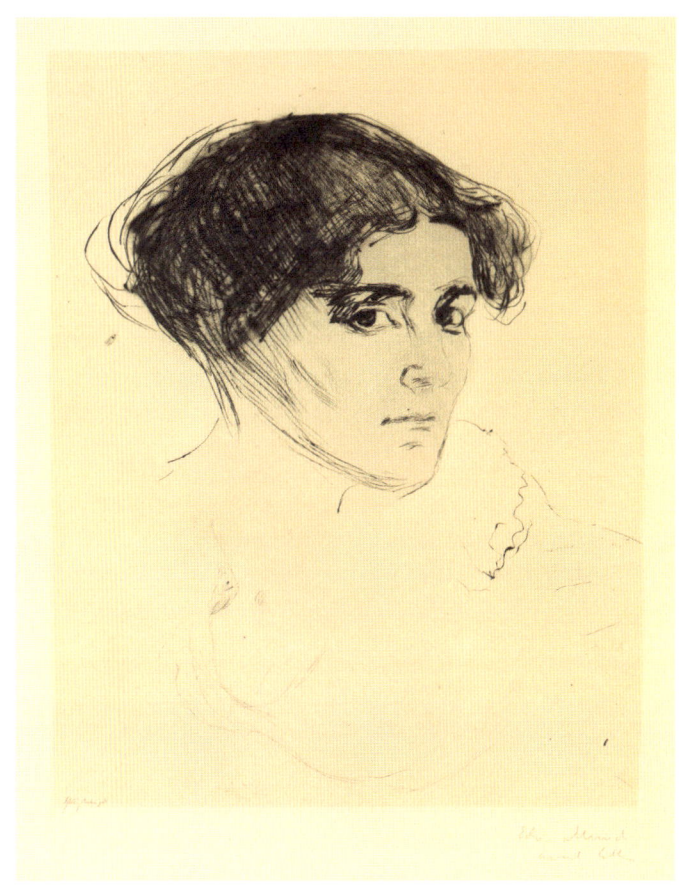

149

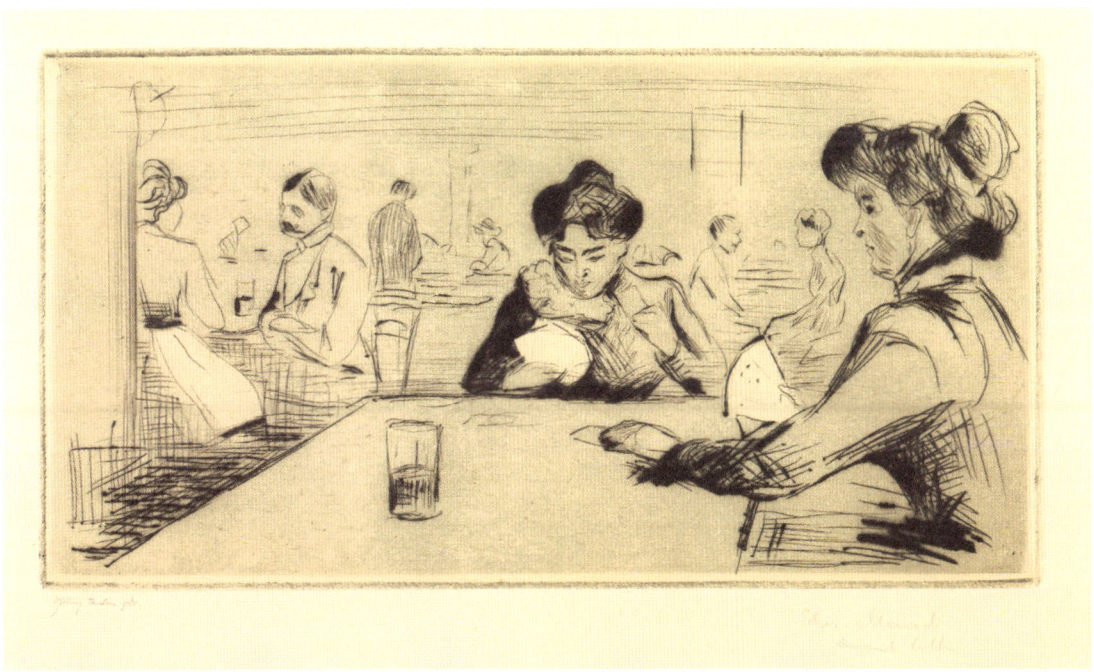

148

150
Old Woman with Umbrella
Gammel dame med paraply

Plate 1902; impression (between 1902 and 1914)
Intaglio: line etching, open bite and burnisher;
black ink; heavy, stiff wove paper
Image: 494 × 320; paper: 643 × 449
Artist's inscription: E Munch
Secondary inscription: O Felsing Berlin gdr.
NG.K&H.A.19092
Provenance unknown
Sch 168; W 83; Woll G 189 III / III
Printer: Felsing

The impression cannot be dated more precisely
than to the years when Felsing was printing for
Munch.

151
Worker
Arbeider

Plate 1902; impression (between 1902 and 1914)
Intaglio: line etching with plate tone; dark brown
ink; heavy, stiff wove paper
Image: 432 × 116; paper: 597 × 440
Artist's inscription: E Munch
Secondary inscription: O Felsing Berlin gdr. //
Kr. 210 [?] [l.r.; pencil]
NG.K&H.A.19084
Provenance unknown
Sch 146; W 61; Woll G 190 I / I
Printer: Felsing

The impression cannot be dated more precisely
than to the years when Felsing was printing for
Munch. Munch's intaglios from 1902-03 include
several depictions of everyday scenes with fisher-
men and workers from Åsgårdstrand.

152
The Fisherman and His Daughter
Fiskeren and hans datter

Zinc plate 1902; impression (between 1906 and
1914)
Intaglio: line etching; dark brown ink;
medium-weight wove paper
Image: 493 × 635; paper: 659 × 961
Artist's inscription: Edv Munch
Secondary inscription: O Felsing Berlin gdr. // Z.
[l.r.; pencil]
NG.K&H.A.19522
Provenance unknown
Sch 147; W 62; Woll G 191 I / I
Printer: Felsing

The inscription "Z" stands for zinc plate. Schiefler
only mentions prints made by Norges Geografiske
Opmaaling (the Norwegian mapping authority).
This means Felsing's imprints are from after 1906.
The intaglio is an inversion of a painting with the
same subject (Woll M 525), also from 1902.

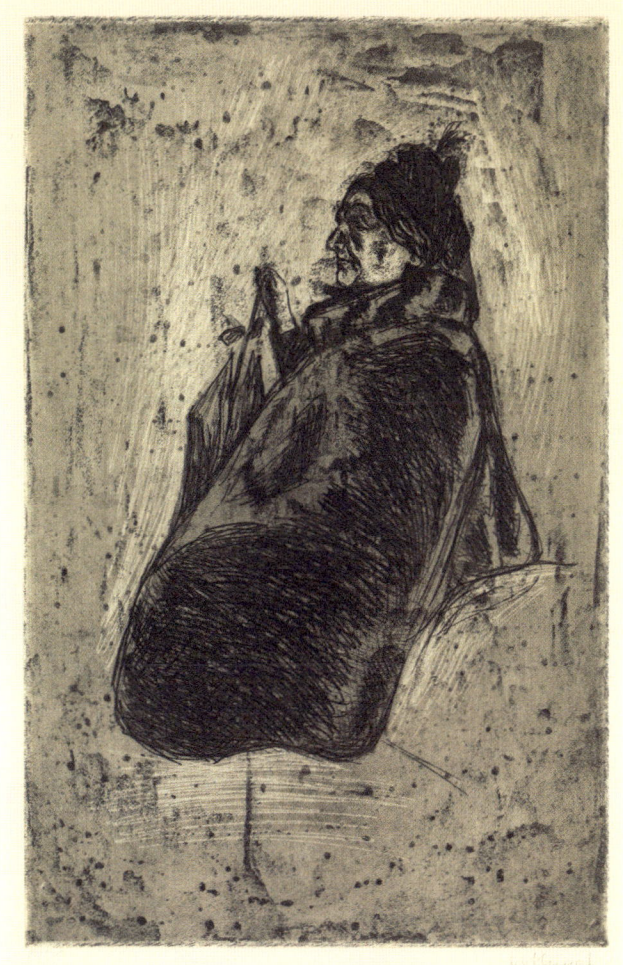

150

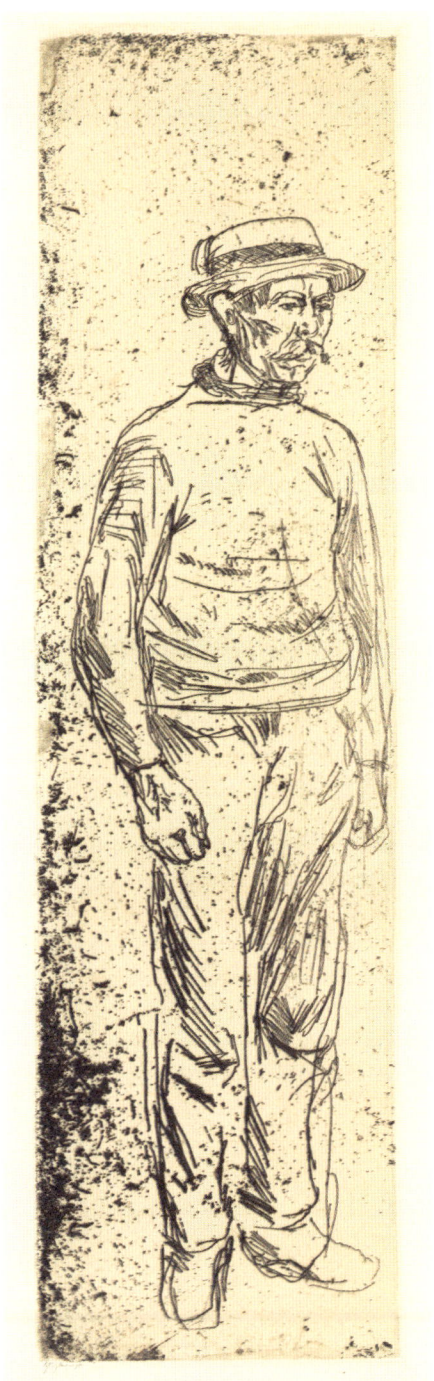

151

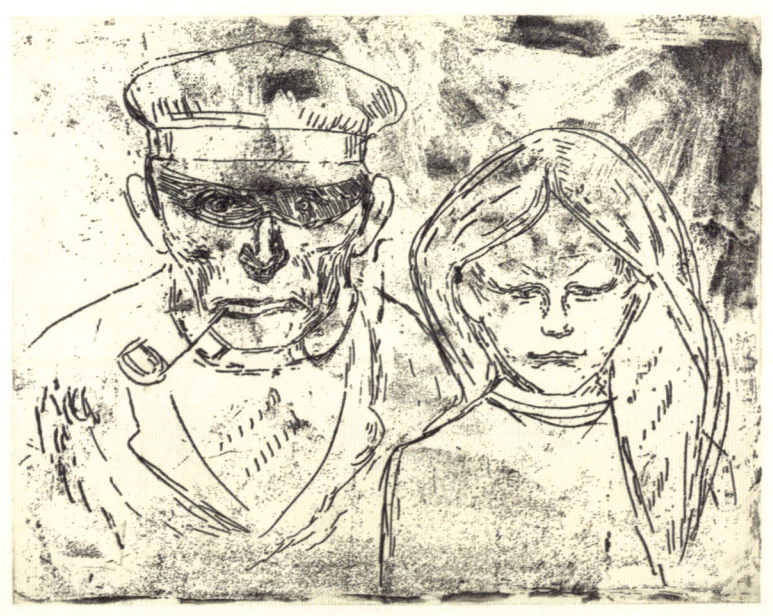

152

153
Anna and Walter Leistikow
Anna og Walter Leistikow

154
Anna and Walter Leistikow
Anna og Walter Leistikow

155
Holger Drachmann

Stones 1902 and 1915; impression (1915)
Lithograph: transfer lithograph from the original
stone (1902): crayon; stone modified with scraper;
black ink; medium-weight, smooth wove paper
Image: 524 × 870; paper: 765 × 1062
Artist's inscription: Edv Munch
Secondary inscription: 13. b. [l.l.; pencil]
NG.K&H.A.19523
Provenance unknown
Sch 170; Woll G 196 II/III
Printer: Nielsen

The stone was first printed by Lassally in Berlin.
Nielsen transferred the image from an impression
Munch had received from Lassally to a duplicate
stone, which was then partially reworked. Under
the date 11.03.1915, Ludvig Ravensberg noted in
his diary that Munch had reworked the lithograph of Leistikow and his wife (original in the
Munch Museum, LR 561). The inscription "13. b."
is probably a numbering by the printer. The edges
of the sheet are folded on all sides. The National
Museum has two impressions of this lithograph
(see cat. 154). Walter Leistikow (1865-1908) was
a German painter and writer. He spoke out in
support of Munch's art in Berlin in 1892 and
assisted in the presentation of the series *Die Liebe*
in 1902. Anna Leistikow (née Mohr) was Danish.
The double portrait is probably based on a photograph taken in Munch's studio in late winter 1902
(Eggum 1987, pp. 100-101).

Stones 1902 and 1915; impression (1915)
Lithograph: transfer lithograph from original
stone (1902): crayon; stone modified with scraper;
black ink; medium-weight, smooth wove paper
Image: 524 × 866; paper: 657 × 984
Unsigned
NG.K&H.A.19523
Provenance unknown
Sch 170; Woll G 196 II/III
Printer: Nielsen

The National Museum has two impressions of
this lithograph, see cat. 153.

Stone 1902; impression (1902)
Lithograph (transfer lithograph): crayon, stone
modified with crayon and tusche; green ink;
heavy, stiff wove paper
Image: 590 × 454; paper: 646 × 501
Artist's inscription: Edv. Munch
Printer: Lassally

Holger Drachmann (1846-1908) was a Danish
writer and painter, and a familiar figure in the
circle of Scandinavian bohemians in Berlin in the
1890s. Munch also painted Drachmann's portrait
in 1898 (Woll M 418).

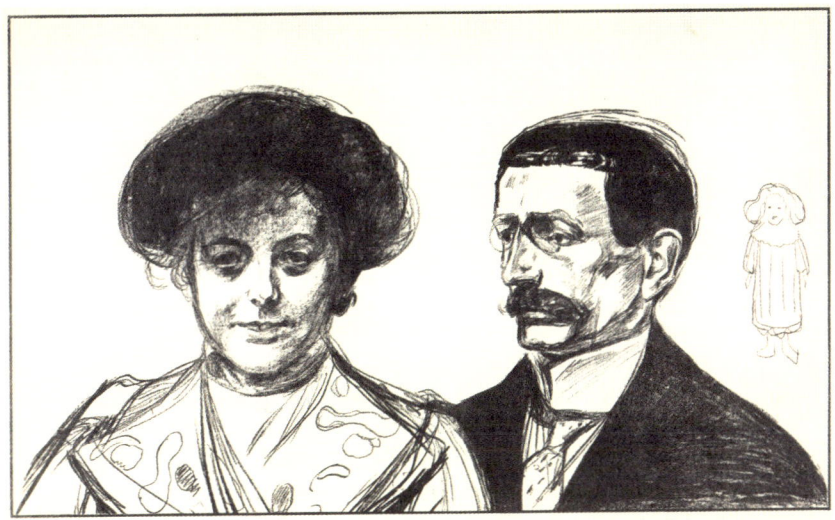

153

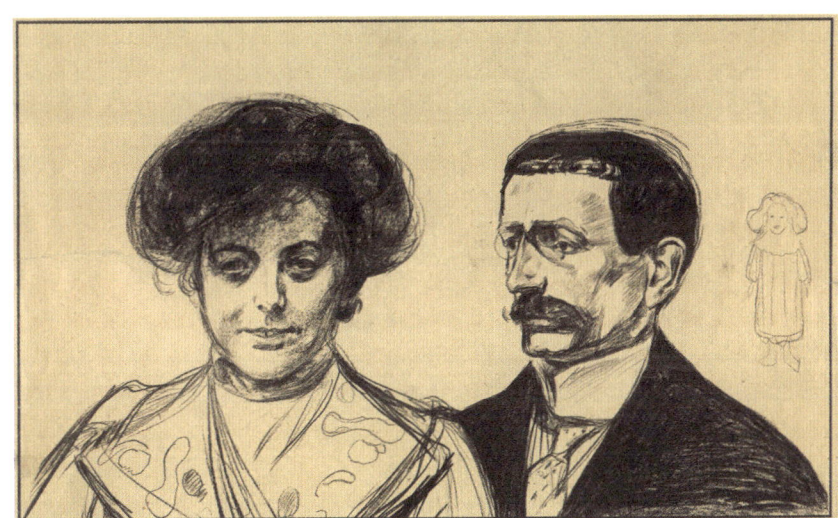

154

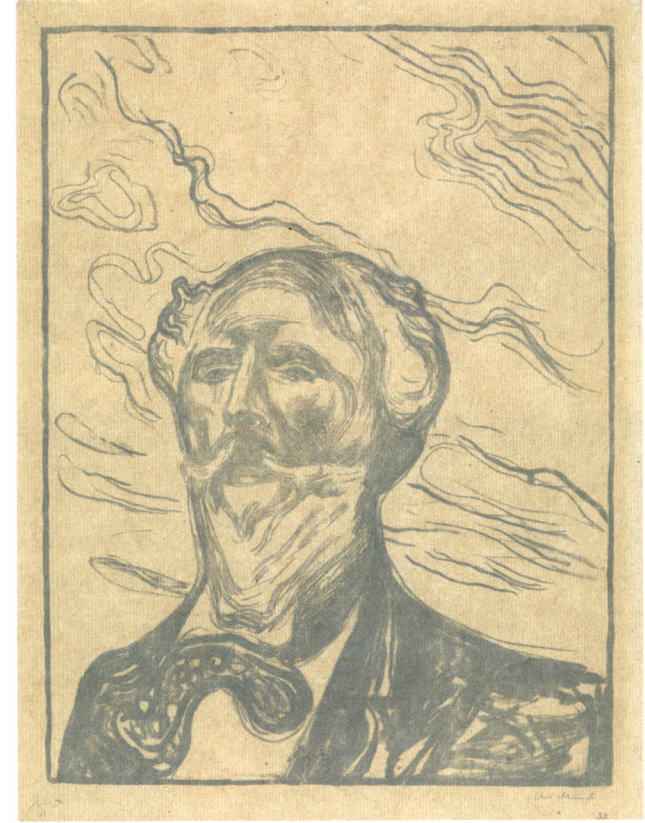

155

156
Nude. The Sin
Akt. Synden

Stone 1902; impression (1902)
Lithograph: crayon and tusche; black ink;
medium-weight, stiff wove paper
Image: 701 × 401; paper: 745 × 451
Artist's inscription: E Munch
NG.K&H.A.19518
Provenance unknown
Sch 142; Woll G 198 I / V
Printer: Lassally

The lithograph exists in both monochrome and
colour versions printed from the original stones
(MM P 165, recto and verso) and from duplicate
stones (not preserved). The National Museum's
impression is an early monochrome print. Schiefler uses the title *Aktfigur*. The colour versions
often have the title *Woman with Red Hair and
Green Eyes*. The secondary title *The Sin* ("... by
the Germans also called 'Die Sünde'," Thiis 1933,
p. 252) indicates that the female figure has been
interpreted as a *femme fatale*. In 1902, Munch
used the same model in a painting (Woll M 503)
and in two photographs (MM.F.6, MM.F.7).

157
Male Nude
Mannsakt

Stone 1902; impression (probably after 1906)
Lithograph: crayon; black ink; light-weight laid
Japan paper
Image: 498 × 369; paper: 617 × 450
Artist's inscription: Edv Munch
NG.K&H.A.19006
Possibly acquired at Munch's exhibition at
Blomqvist in 1902
Sch 169; Woll G 199 I / I
Printer: Lassally

More impressions of this lithograph are registered
today than Schiefler was aware of, indicating that
several date from later than 1906. The National
Museum's impression probably belongs to this
group.

158
Marta Sandal

Stone 1902; impression (1902)
Lithograph (transfer lithograph): crayon; stone
modified with tusche and scraper; reddish brown
ink; heavy, stiff wove paper
Image: 638 × 427; paper: 683 × 477
NG.K&H.A.19938
Provenance unknown
Sch 172; Woll G 201 I / I
Printer: Lassally

The National Museum's impression has no significant inscriptions. Marta Sandal (1878-1931) was a
Norwegian singer. She gave concerts in Berlin in
1902. Munch produced a portrait of her in pastels
in that year (Woll M 502). It is probable that the
lithograph is also from 1902.

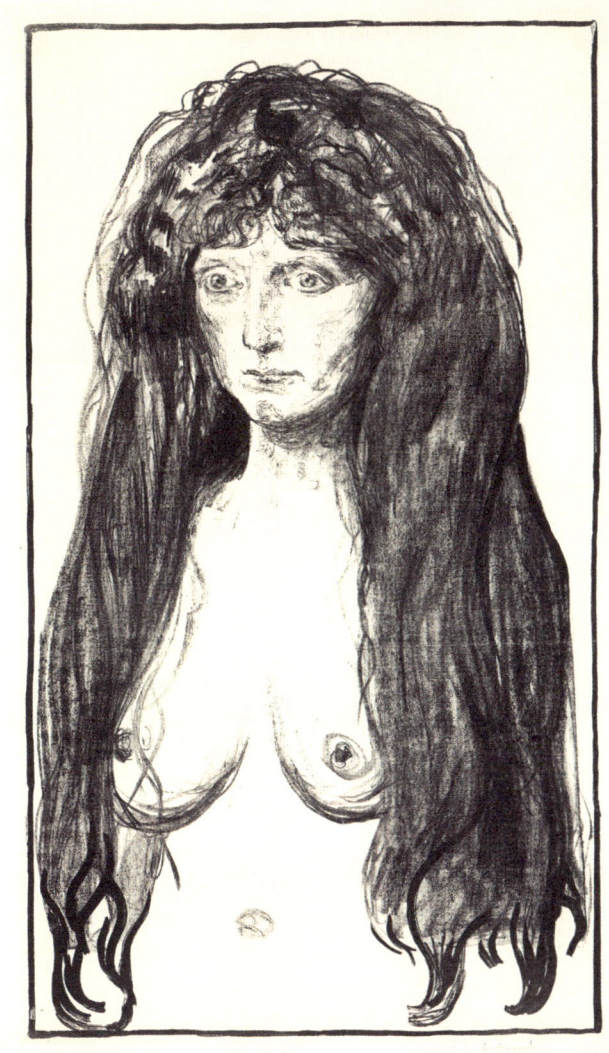

156

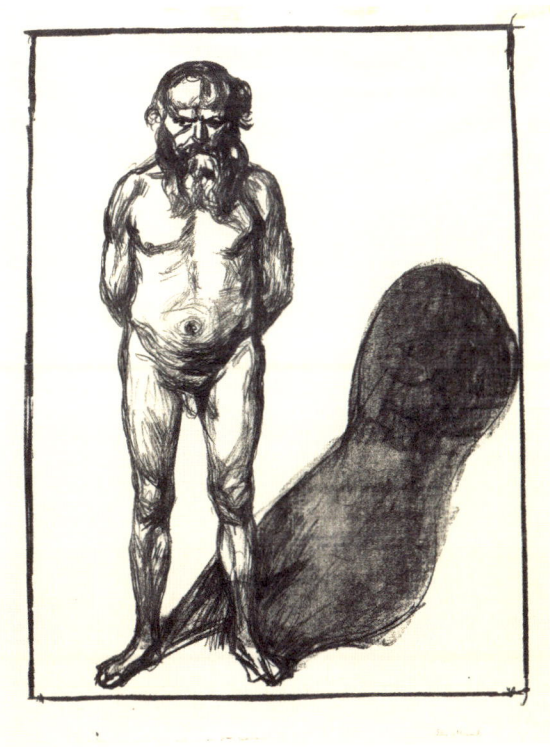

157

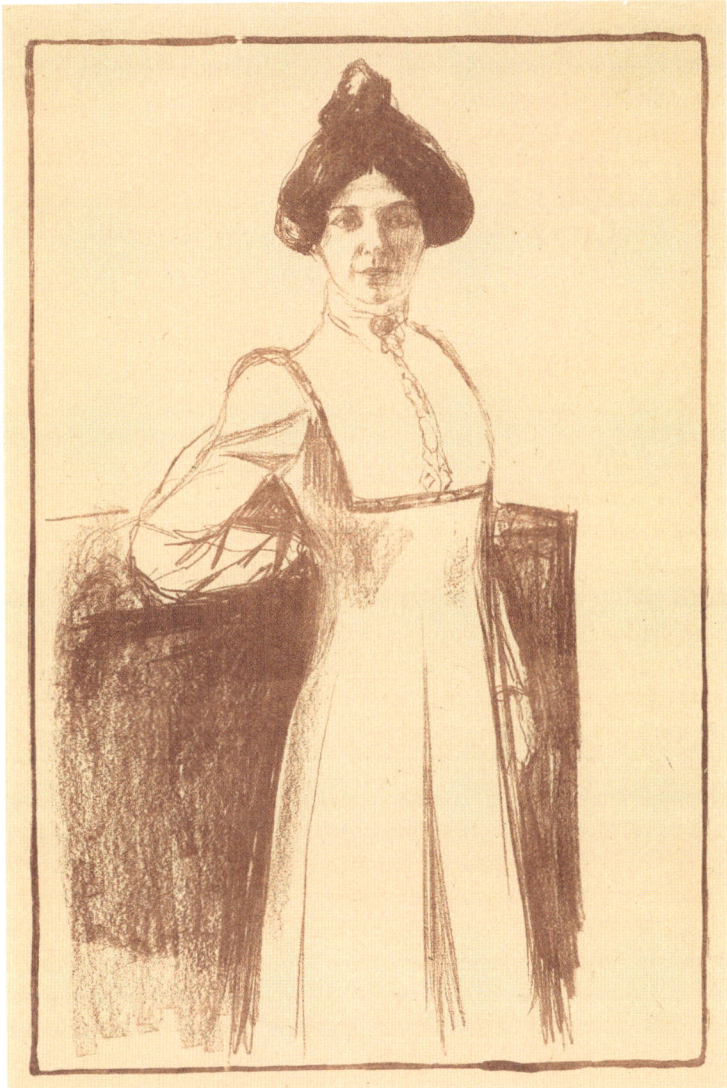

158

263

159
Melancholy III
Melankoli III

160
The Kiss IV
Kyss IV

161
Old Man Praying
Gammel mann i bønn

Woodblock 1902; impression (1902 or slightly later)
Colour woodcut: keyblock: gouges, dark grey ink; colour block: gouges and fretsaw (block cut into three pieces); grey-green and reddish brown ink; heavy, stiff wove paper
Image: 381 × 471; paper: 429 × 567
Artist's inscription: Edv Munch
NG.K&H.A.19104
Provenance unknown
Sch 144; Woll G 203 III 1/III 7
Printer: Lassally

Munch began work on the blocks in winter 1902. These he later reworked, inking them in a variety of colours. The National Museum's impression is on grey wove paper. There is a yellow striped pattern on the recto, which probably stems from a substance that was applied to the paper before it was used for printing, and which has turned yellow over time due to light exposure. A similar effect is present on a number of works with different subjects, suggesting that they can be attributed to the same period and printer. See cat. 89. Munch painted many versions of this subject (Woll M 241, 359, 369, 284, see cat. 19). *Melancholy III* is an inverted reworking of the woodcut version from 1896 (see cat. 120) and therefore has the same orientation as the painted versions.

Woodblock 1902; impression (after 1906)
Woodcut: keyblock: gouges and fretsaw (block cut into two pieces), black ink; colour block: unmodified, grey-green ink; light-weight imitation (?) Japan paper
Image: 471 × 478; paper: 558 × 542
Artist's inscription: Kys [l.l.] // Edv Munch
NG.K&H.A.19517
Provenance unknown
Sch 102 D; Woll G 204 III/IV, 1/3
Printer: probably Lassally

Munch explored this subject as a painting, drawing and print (see cat. 17 and 76). Using the woodcut technique, he produced as many as six compositions with a kissing couple over a forty-six-year period. The first two are dated to 1897. In both, Munch reworked the blocks several times, as was his habit. *Kiss I* (Woll G 114) was initially carved in one state (possibly before he left Paris for Kristiania (Oslo)). The block was then further developed, and finally cut into two pieces (separating out the figure group) using a fretsaw. This block is not preserved. For *Kiss II* (Woll G 115) he used the recto of a spruce panel as a keyblock and the verso as a colour block. The type of wood suggests that this woodcut was produced in Norway. In the next version, *Kiss III* (Woll G 124), dated to 1898, the embracing figures are cut out and printed in black, sometimes on their own, sometimes together with the rest of the block, which is printed in a greyish-green colour. For other impressions the section with the figures is combined with a block for the background in greyish-green. In the various versions with a background, Munch has usually allowed the grain of the wood to feature prominently. *Kiss IV*, which dates from 1902, applies much the same approach. In the National Museum's impression, the section from the keyblock with the figures is superimposed on the imprint of a colour block with conspicuous grain. The use of this visual effect in *Kiss IV* has been frequently highlighted. At the same time, this work is an outstanding example of the woodcut's suitability for simplified yet highly expressive figure compositions. The dark, succinctly captured silhouette of the couple against the flickering greyish-green background has an emblematic quality that makes it an unparalleled image of the duality of the embrace.

Woodblock 1902; impression (1902?)
Colour woodcut (recto and verso of same block): keyblock: gouges; black ink; colour block: greyish yellow ink; heavy, stiff wove paper
Image: 463 × 331; paper: 707 × 526
Artist's inscription: E Munch
NG.K&H.A.19114
Provenance unknown
Sch 173; Woll G 205 II/II
Printer: either the artist or Lassally

On the National Museum's impression, the shade of the printing ink is close to the colour of the paper and consequently only faintly visible. The man's nightshirt is achieved by blind printing (without ink) from the colour block, which has several grooves that are not visible in this section, see cat. 162; in other impressions the corresponding effect is the result of the colour block being printed upside down. The National Museum has two impressions of this woodcut, see cat. 162.

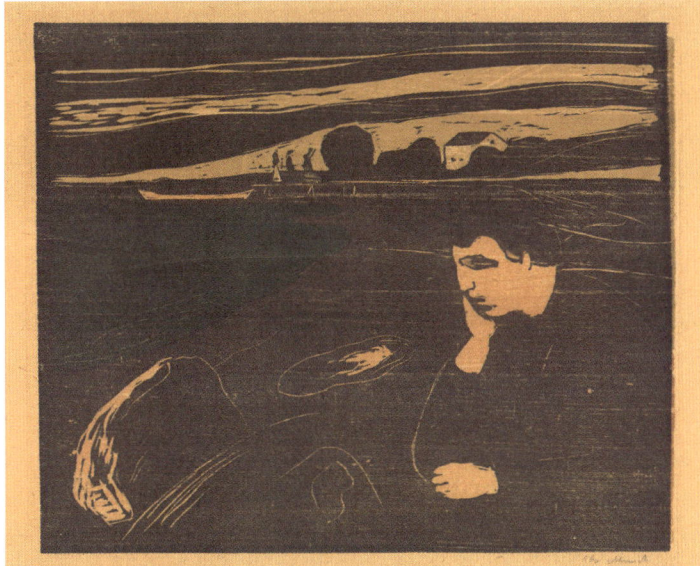

159

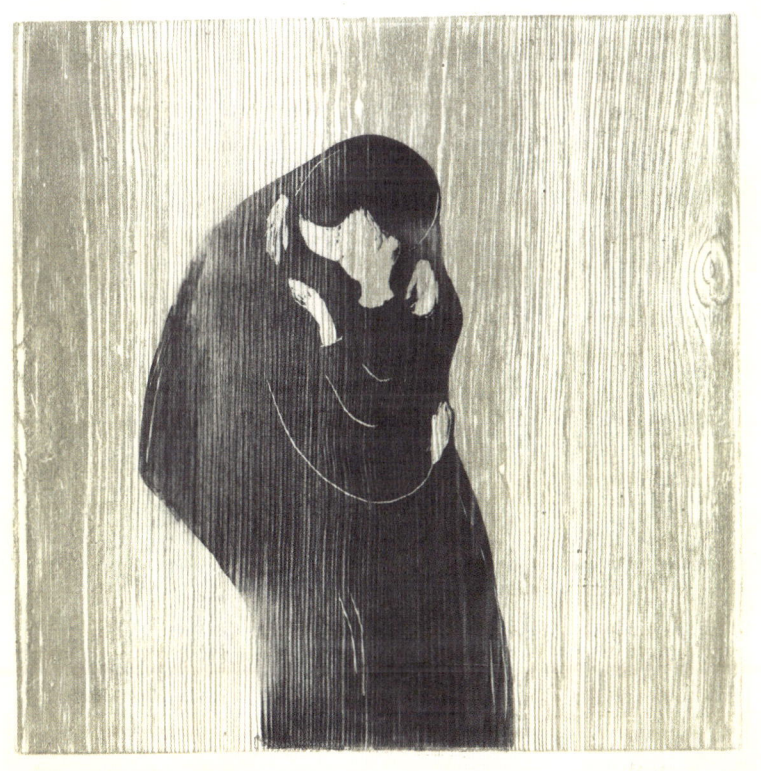

160

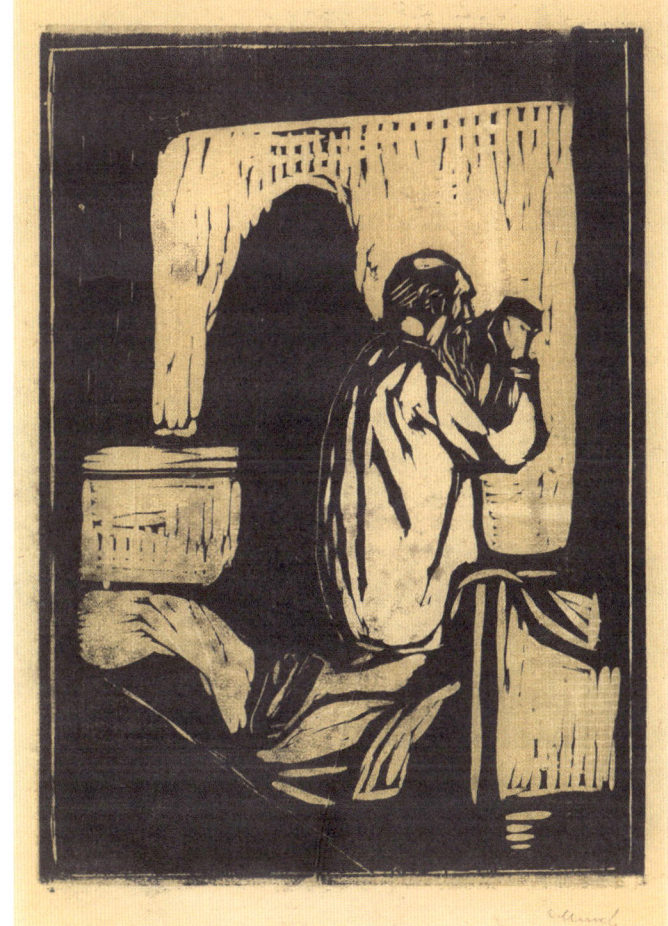

161

162
Old Man Praying
Gammel mann i bønn

Woodblock 1902; impression (between 1906 and 1914)
Colour woodcut (recto and verso of same block): keyblock: gouges; black ink; colour block: gouges, greyish yellow ink; light-weight imitation (?) Japan paper
Image: 461 × 329; paper: 497 × 360
Artist's inscription: E Munch // Betend Mann [l.l.]
NG.K&H.1982.0759
Purchased 1982 from the estate of Ingrid Lindbäck Langaard
Sch 173; Woll G 205 II / II
Printer: Lassally

The National Museum has two impressions of this woodcut, see cat. 161. Both are essentially prints from the blocks in the same state, although the inking of the blocks and the nature of the paper give the impressions different expressive qualities.

163
Head of an Old Man
Hode av gammel mann

Woodblock 1902; impression (1902)
Colour woodcut: gouges and fretsaw (block cut into two pieces); black and red ink; heavy, stiff wove paper
Image: 460 × 325; paper: 711 × 495
Artist's inscription: E Munch
NG.K&H.A.19115
Provenance unknown
Sch 174; Woll G 206 I / II
Printer: the artist or Lassally

Only two impressions of this woodcut in black and red ink are registered. Several monochrome impressions are however registered. Only the section of the block representing the head is preserved (MM P 368).

164
Lübeck

Zinc plate 1902 or 1903; impression (1902 or 1903)
Intaglio: line and soft ground etching; dark brown ink; medium-weight, stiff wove paper
Image: 473 × 622; paper: 654 × 957
Artist's inscription: Edv Munch
Secondary inscription: O Felsing Berlin gdr. //
Z. [l.r.; pencil]
NG.K&H.A.19525
Provenance unknown
Sch 195; W 99; Woll G 227 I / I
Printer: Felsing

In Schiefler and Woll 2012 the plate is dated to 1903. However, Munch visited Lübeck in 1902, and an impression marked "1ste Tryk" (1st print) is dated to that year (MM.G.90-24). The inscription "Z" stands for zinc plate.

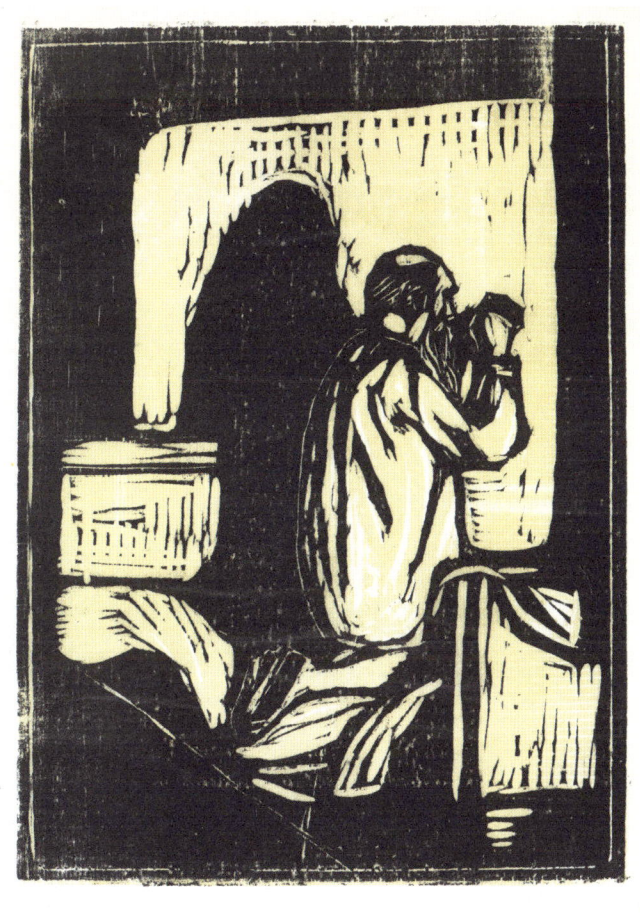

162

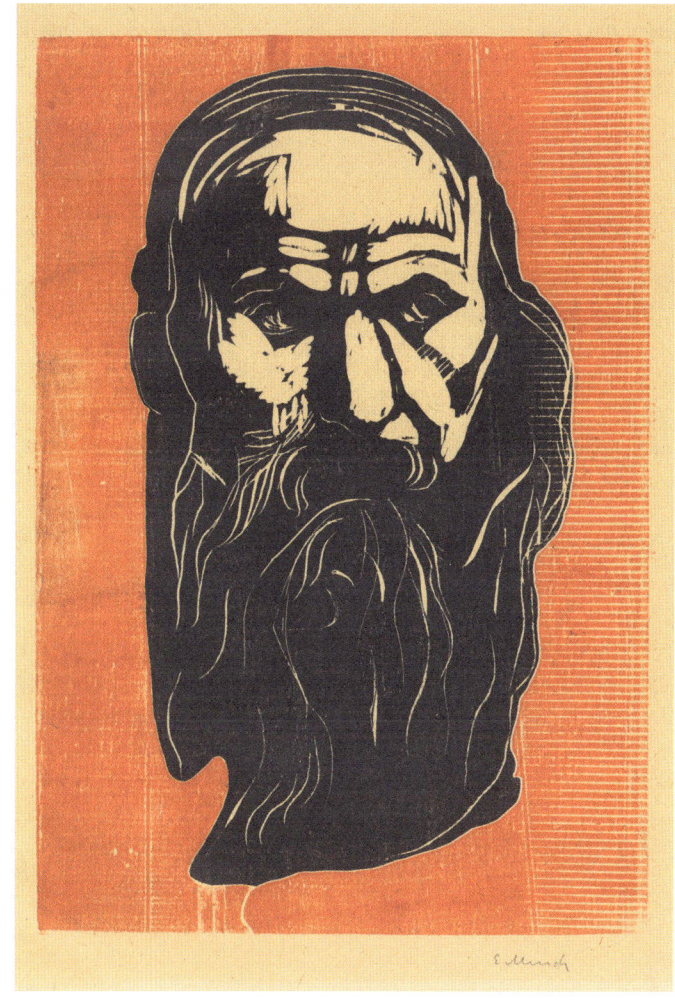

163

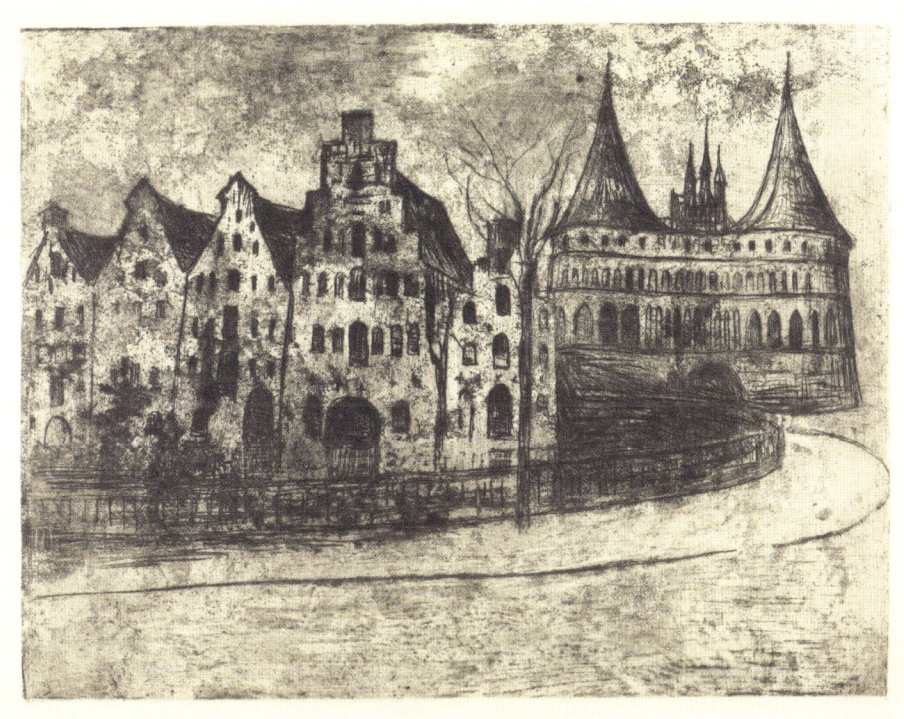

164

165
The Oak
Eken

Zinc plate 1903; impression (1903)
Intaglio: line etching black ink; heavy wove paper
Image: 620 × 479; paper: 775 × 624
Artist's inscription: E Munch
Secondary inscription: O Felsing Berlin gdr.
NG.K&H.A.19526 (formerly NG.K&H.B.00613)
Purchased at City Auksjon, Oslo, September 1938
(cat. 285)
Sch 196; W 103; Woll G 228 I/I
Printer: Felsing

The motif is from Lübeck.

166
Ingse Vibe

Stone 1903; impression (1903 or later)
Lithograph: crayon; black ink; soft wove paper
Image: 484 × 607; paper: 539 × 750
Artist's inscription: Edv Munch
NG.K&H.A.19048
Provenance unknown
Sch 204; Woll G 236 I/I
Printer: probably Petersen & Waitz

Below the portrait of Ingse Vibe and at the top right of the sheet are three small sketches of men's heads, of which the two below can be identified as Ludvig Ravensberg and Munch himself. Schiefler uses the title *Studienblatt*. Ingse (Ingeborg Majory) Vibe-Müller (1882–1943) was an actress and a long-standing friend of Munch. Munch also produced an intaglio (1892, Woll G 193) and a painted portrait of her (1903, Woll M 568).

167
The Brooch. Eva Mudocci
Brosjen. Eva Mudocci

Stones 1903 and 1915; impression (1915)
Lithograph: transfer lithograph from original stone (1903): crayon, tusche and scraper, stone modified with sandpaper; black ink; wove paper
Image: 613 × 471; paper: 698 × 552
Artist's inscription: Edv Munch
Secondary inscription: No 22. III Tilstand [l.l.; pencil]
NG.K&H. B.00816
Bequeathed by Hans Aall, 1947
Sch 212; Woll G 244 V/V
Printer: Nielsen

The inscription "No 22. III Tilstand" (No. 22. IIIrd state) is the printer's. The stone from which the National Museum's impression was pulled has been preserved (MM P 167) and shows the same state as that print. This is a duplicate stone based on Nielsen's transfer of the image by means of an imprint on transfer paper from the original stone (1903, printed by Lassally in Berlin) (see Ludvig Ravensberg's diary, 11 March 1915; original in the Munch Museum, LR 561). Schiefler uses the title *Madonna*. Eva Mudocci (Evangeline Muddock, 1883–1953) was a British violinist and for a time a close friend of Munch. The title *The Brooch* refers to the jewellery the model is wearing, a Norwegian brooch she received from Jens Thiis on the occasion of a concert she gave in Trondheim, together with the pianist Bella (Isabella) Edvards (Thiis 1933, p. 252). Mudocci and Edvards toured Norway in 1902, 1904, 1907 and 1909. Munch depicted them together in the lithograph *Violin Concert*, 1903 (Woll G 243). Another impression of *The Brooch. Eva Mudocci*, owned by the National Gallery, was sold in 1968 to finance the purchase of *Evening. Melancholy I* (cat. 120). This impression was not inventoried, but was entered in the list of works by Munch in the Department of Prints and Drawings' supplementary record "Norwegian Graphics I" (no. 87). Apart from the title, the technique, and the year 1903, no further information about this impression is recorded. Whether pulled from the original stone or a transfer print cannot be determined.

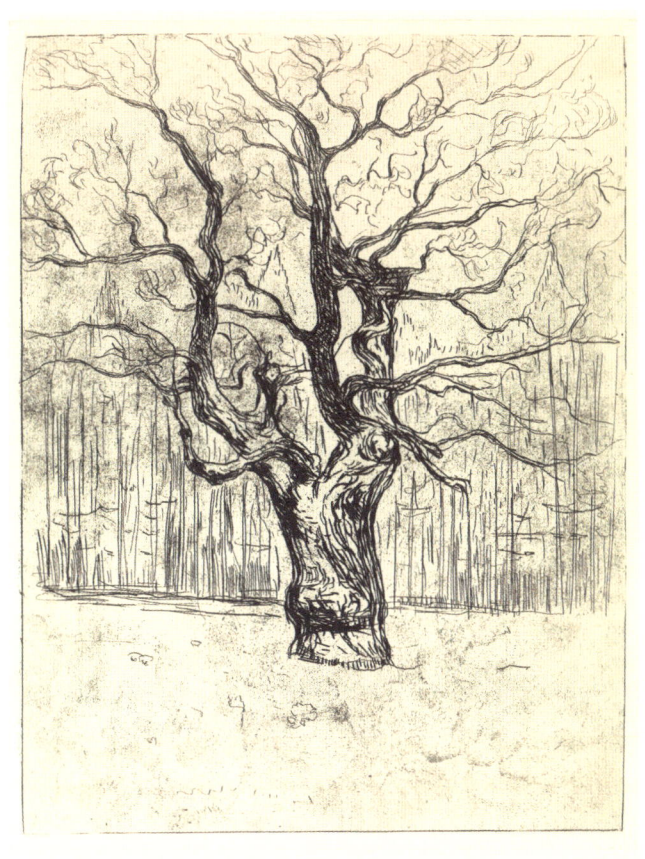

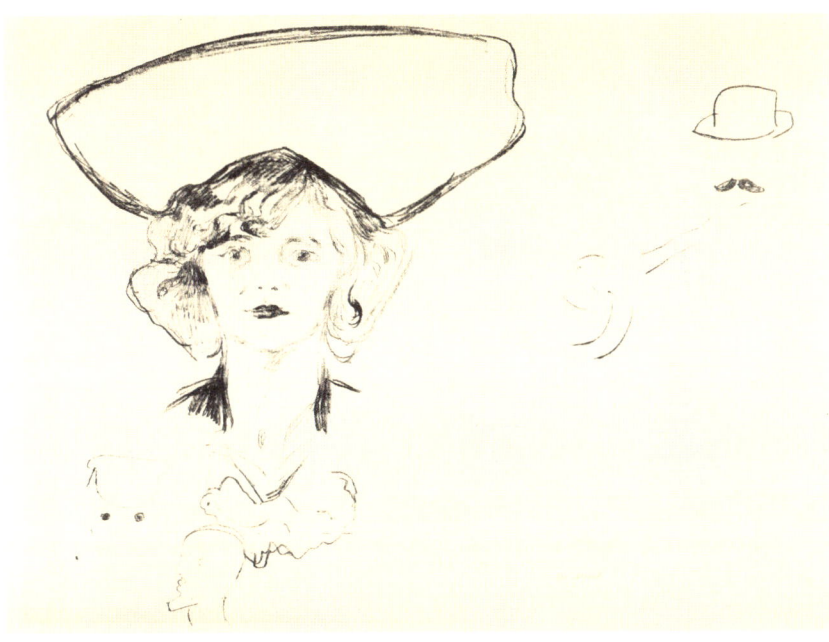

165

166

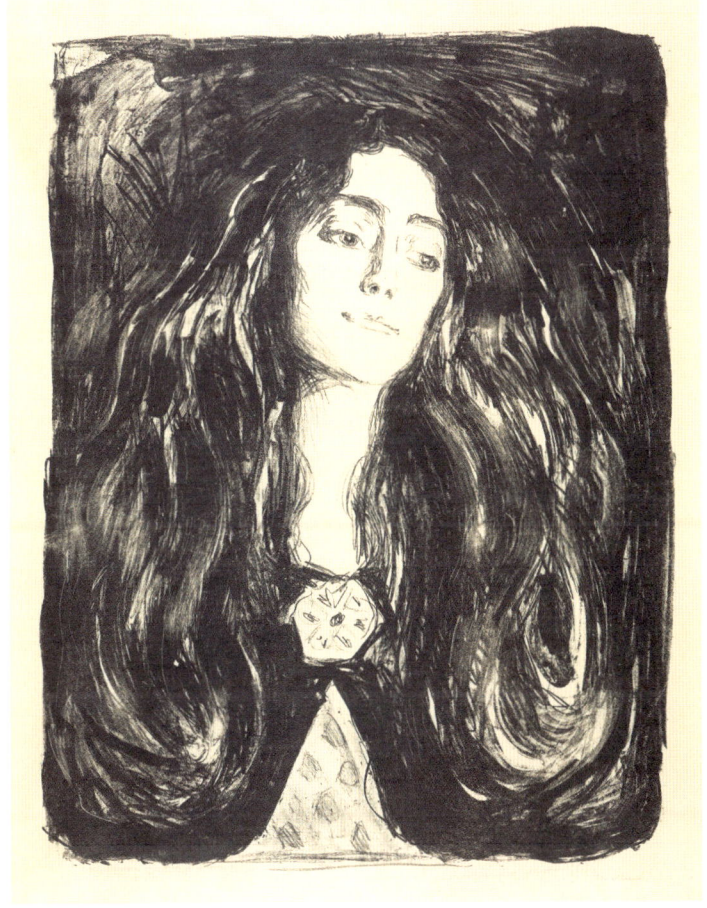

167

168
Salome

Stone 1903; impression (1903)
Lithograph: crayon and scraper; brown ink; heavy, stiff wove paper
Image: 395 × 308; paper: 600 × 397
Artist's inscription: Edv Munch // Salome [l.l.; pencil]
Secondary inscription verso: CV 65/50 [l.l.; blue coloured pencil]
NG.K&H.A.19007 (formerly NG.K&H.B.00613)
Purchased at City Auksjon, Oslo, September 1938 (cat. 153)
Sch 213; Woll G 245 I/I
Printer: Lassally

The woman is undoubtedly Eva Mudocci (see cat. 167), while the male head has usually been regarded as a self-portrait.

169
Amanda

Plate 1904; impression (between 1904 and 1914)
Intaglio: line etching; brown ink; heavy, stiff wove paper
Image: 158 × 226; paper: 307 × 397
Artist's inscription: E Munch / avant lettre // Madchen [sic.; l.l.]
Secondary inscription: O Felsing Berlin gdr.
NG.K&H.A.19093
Provenance unknown
Sch 216; Woll G 249 I/I
Printer: Felsing

The National Museum's impression cannot be dated more precisely than to the period when the plate was executed and Munch's collaboration with Felsing ended. The intaglio has been presented under various titles, but in exhibition catalogues from 1913-17 it was referred to as *Amanda*. The museum had two impressions of this intaglio, see cat. 170.

170
Amanda

Plate 1904; impression (between 1904 and 1914)
Intaglio: line etching; brown ink; paper unknown
Dimensions of plate according to Woll 2012: 178 × 248
Artist's inscription: Edv Munch
Provenance unknown
Sch 216; Woll G 249 I/I
Printer: Felsing
Impression lost

Of this intaglio only impressions printed by Felsing are registered. The museum once had two impressions, see cat. 169. Cat. 170 is recorded in the list of works by Munch in the Department of Prints and Drawings' supplementary record "Norwegian Graphics I" as no. 89, with the information, "Do - " - Do - " - [Sittende pike. Radering. 1904] Edv Munch // [Schiefler] 216" ("Ditto Ditto [Seated Girl. Etching. 1904] ..."). The impression was noted as lost in the collection audits of 1955 and 1969-70 and is not mentioned in Liv I. Jones' catalogue *Norsk grafikk til 1970* (Norwegian Graphics up to 1970) (Oslo: Nasjonalgalleriet, 1971).

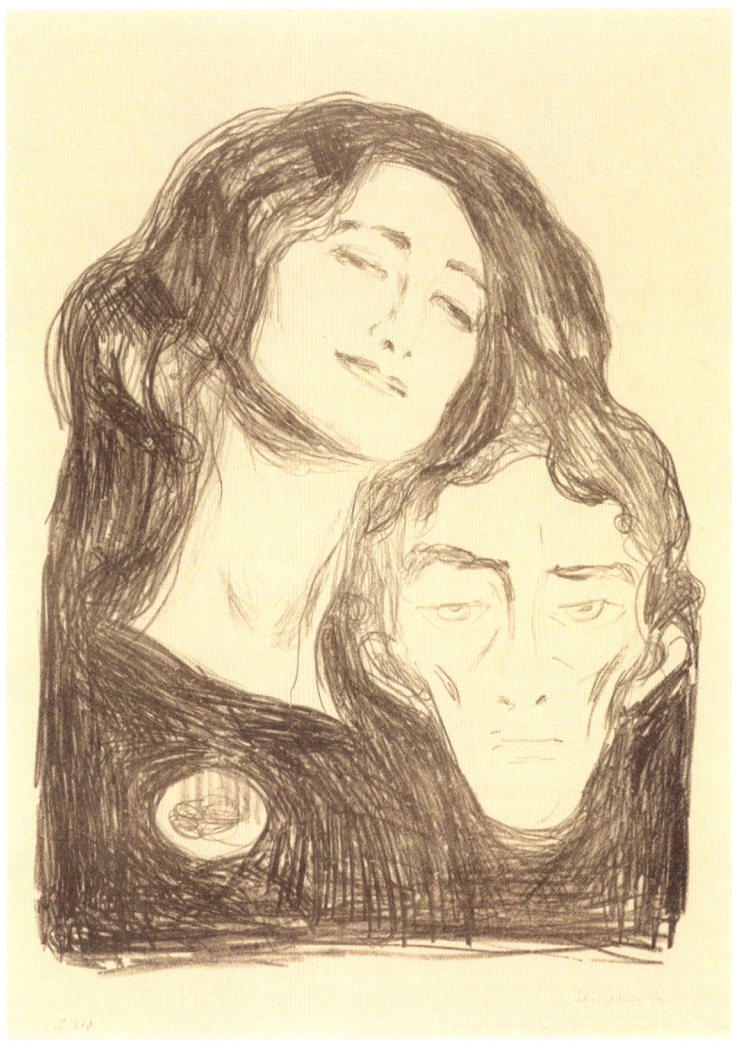

168

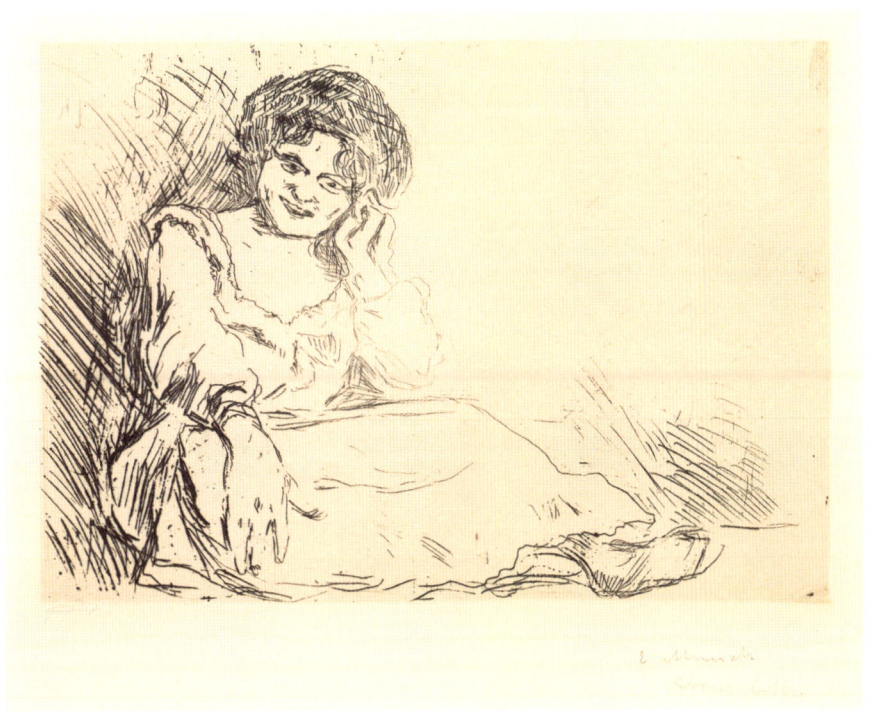

169

171
Gustav Schiefler

172
Old Men and Boys
Gamle menn og gutter

173
Head of a Woman
Kvinnehode

Plate 1905 or 1906; impression (1905 or 1906)
Intaglio: drypoint with plate tone; dark brown
ink; heavy wove paper
Image: 231 × 180; paper: 449 × 322
Artist's inscription: E Munch
Secondary inscription: O Felsing Berlin gdr.//
Landesgerichsdirektor//<kr. 150 > [l.l.; pencil]
NG.K&H.B.00358
Purchased at auction, Wangs Kunst- og Auktions-
forretning, Oslo, 1927
Sch 238; W 108; Woll G 263 I/I
Printer: Felsing

Gustav Schiefler compiled a comprehensive
catalogue of Munch's graphic production
(Schiefler 1907, 1928), on which he began work
in 1904. When he visited Munch at Elgersburg in
the days after Christmas 1905, he had with him
a copper plate, on which Munch began to incise
this portrait on 30 December. It wasn't until
some time later, however, that Schiefler received
finished prints (Munch/Schiefler, *Briefwechsel*, no. 167). Gustav Schiefler (1857-1935) was a
Landesgerichtsdirektor in Hamburg. He and his
wife Luise were prominent connoisseurs and
collectors of expressionist art, and of prints in
particular. Munch painted two portraits of Gustav Schiefler in 1908 (Woll M 818 and 819).

Woodblock 1905; impression (between 1905 and
1914)
Woodcut: gouges; black ink; medium-weight
wove paper
Image: 354 × 443; paper: 415 × 585
Artist's inscription: Edv Munch
NG.K&H.A.19105
Provenance unknown
Sch 235; Woll G 272 II/II
Printer: probably Lassally

The National Museum's impression is probably
from before Munch had the blocks sent from
Berlin to Kristiania (Oslo) following the outbreak
of World War I.

Woodblock 1905; impression (between 1906 and
1914)
Woodcut: gouges; black ink; light-weight imita-
tion (?) Japan paper
Image: 439 × 354; paper: 490 × 396
Artist's inscription: EMunch// Junges Madchen
[sic.][l.l.; pencil]
NG.K&H.A.19108
Provenance unknown
Sch 236; Woll G 273 I/I
Printer: Lassally

Munch pulled some trial proofs from the block
before Lassally took over the printing. Lassally
did not print woodcuts for Munch after 1914.

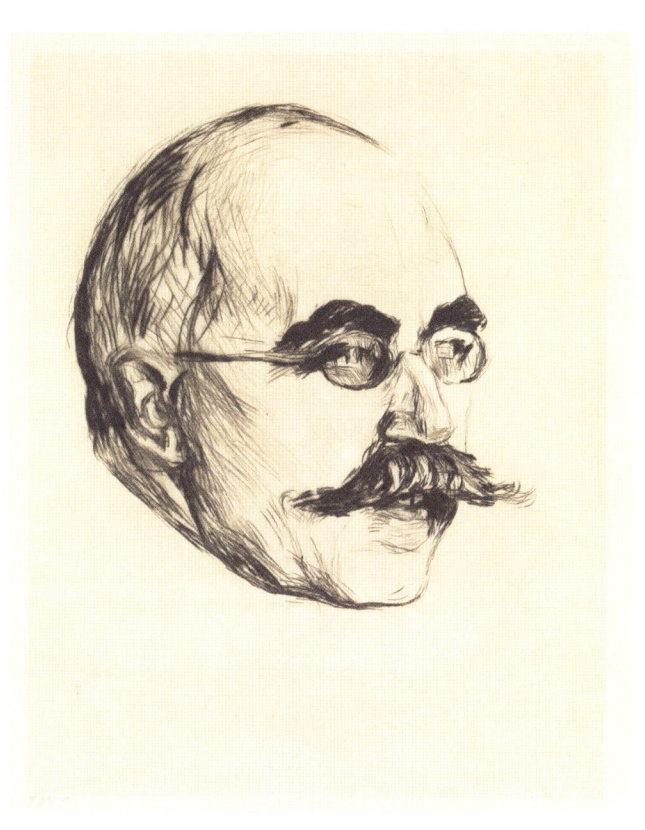

171

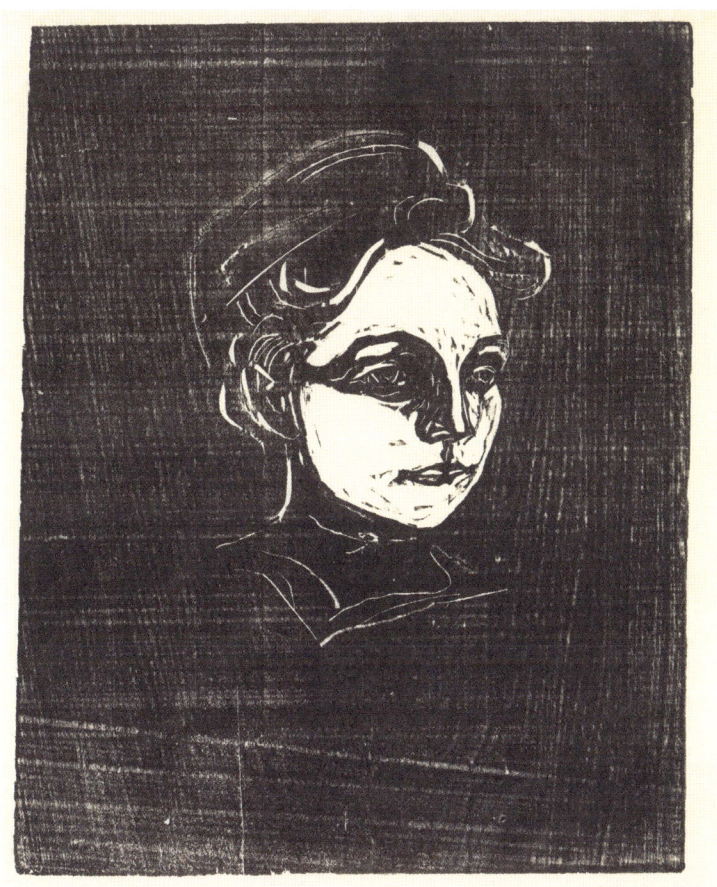

173

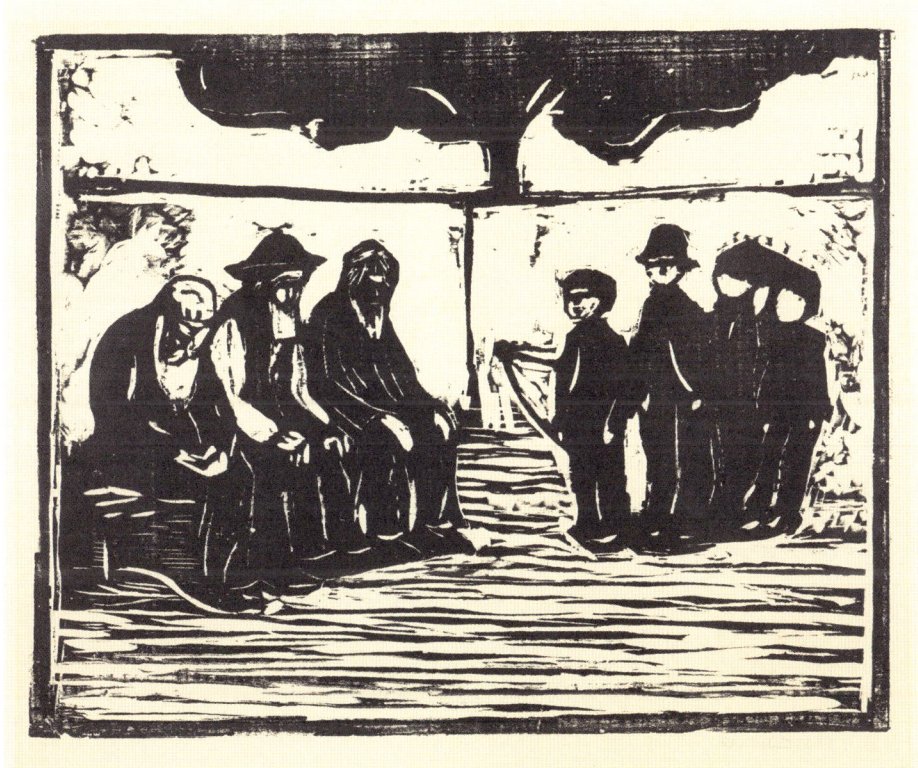

172

174
Mrs Schwarz
Fru Schwarz

Stone 1906; impression (probably 1906)
Lithograph (transfer lithograph): crayon; black
ink; laid papir
Image: 269 × 248; paper: 497 × 399
Artist's inscription: E Munch // Edv. Munch
NG.K&H.1997.1322
Bequeathed by Anna (Vesla) and Jean Heiberg,
1997
Sch 252; Woll G 282 I/I
Printer: Lassally

There exist red and black versions of this lithograph. In December 1907 Schiefler received an
impression in red from Munch (Munch/Schief-
ler, "Tagebuch Schiefler 31. Dezember 1907",
Briefwechsel, p. 268). Munch painted two portraits of the same woman (Woll M 697 and 698)
and produced two lithographs of her son Andreas
(Woll G 280, 281). In 2013, Øystein Ustvedt identified Mrs Schwarz as Helene Flechtheim (née
Kohlstedt, 1882–1971), see cat. 48.

175
Henry van de Velde

Stone 1906; impression (probably 1906)
Lithograph (transfer lithograph): crayon; black
ink; heavy Japan paper
Image: 263 × 174; paper: 478 × 335
Artist's inscription: E Munch
NG.K&H.A.19008
Provenance unknown
Sch 246; Woll G 285 I/I
Printer: Weimarer Kunstschule

Henry van de Velde (1863–1958) was a Belgian
architect, painter and designer. He was a professor at the art school in Weimar (1901–14), for
which he designed a new building in 1906. The
lithograph is an inverted version of a drawing of
van de Velde (private collection).

176
The Death of Marat
Marats død

Stone 1906 or 1907; impression (between 1906 or
1907 and 1914)
Colour lithograph (transfer lithograph): crayon;
green and red ink; heavy, stiff wove paper
Image: 435 × 353; paper: 621 × 481
Artist's inscription: E Munch
Secondary inscription: 16 [l.r.; pencil]
NG.K&H.A.19009
Provenance unknown
Sch 258; Woll G 287 II/II
Printer: Lassally

There are also impressions of this lithograph in
black (Woll G 287 I). It is reasonable to assume
that the composition evolved through the
paintings done in 1906–07 (Woll M 767, 768, 743),
although lithographic impressions exist with
inscriptions that suggest a dating to 1904 or 1905.
The National Museum's impression cannot be
dated more precisely than to the period when
Lassally was printing for Munch. The subject
can be traced back to Munch's final break with
Tulla Larsen in 1902. With the intention of
"talking things over", the two travelled to Munch's
cottage in Åsgårdstrand, where they drank
heavily. During the evening, a shot was fired from
Munch's small revolver, causing injury to two
fingers on his left hand. He was promptly sent to
Rikshospitalet (the National Hospital), where his
hand was operated. This incident was the starting
point for a series of paintings depicting a woman
who has killed a man - as Charlotte Corday did
with Jean-Paul Marat during the French Revolution. In his diary for March 1907 (Munch/Schief-
ler, *Briefwechsel*, no. 299), Schiefler mentions
that Munch used a married couple by the name
of Grävenitz as his models. The lithograph is a
simplified version of the theme as treated in two
of the paintings (Woll M 743, 767), while the composition in the third painted version is somewhat
modified (Woll M 768).

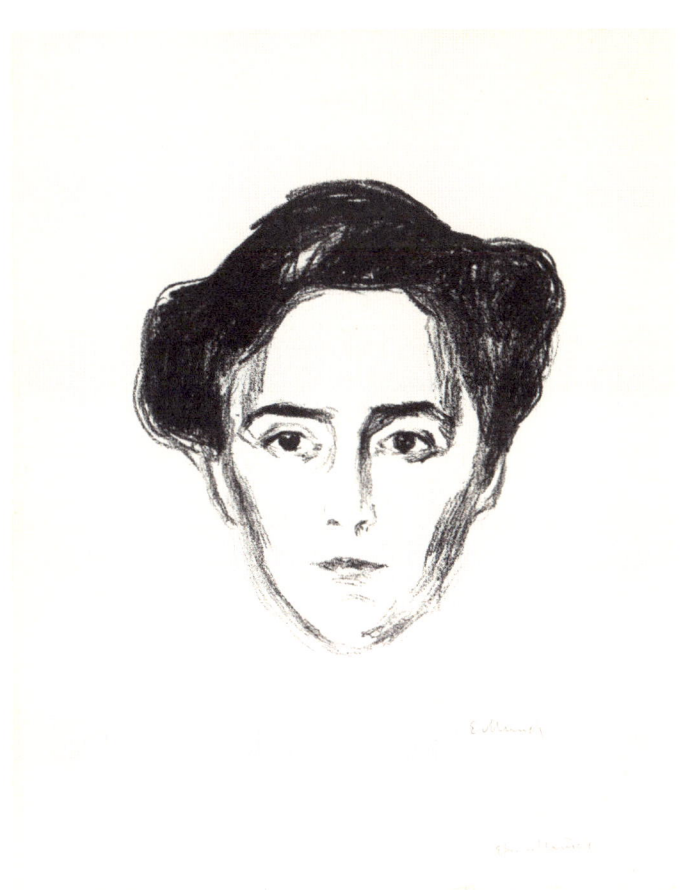

174

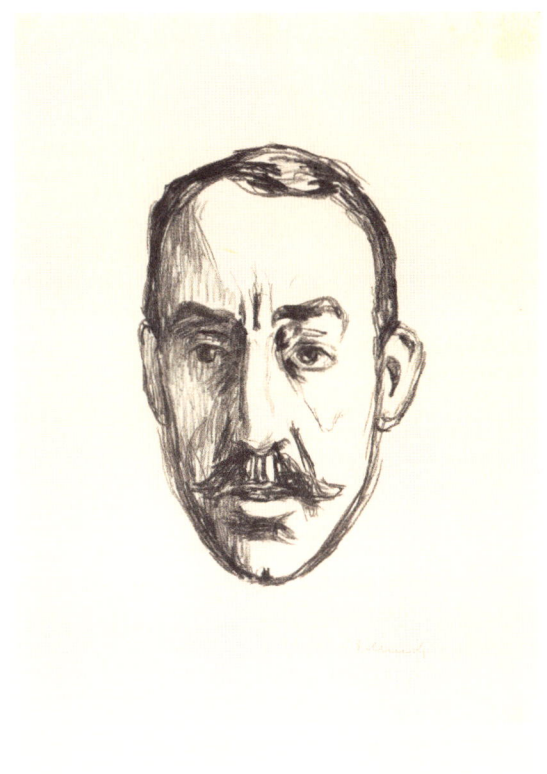

175

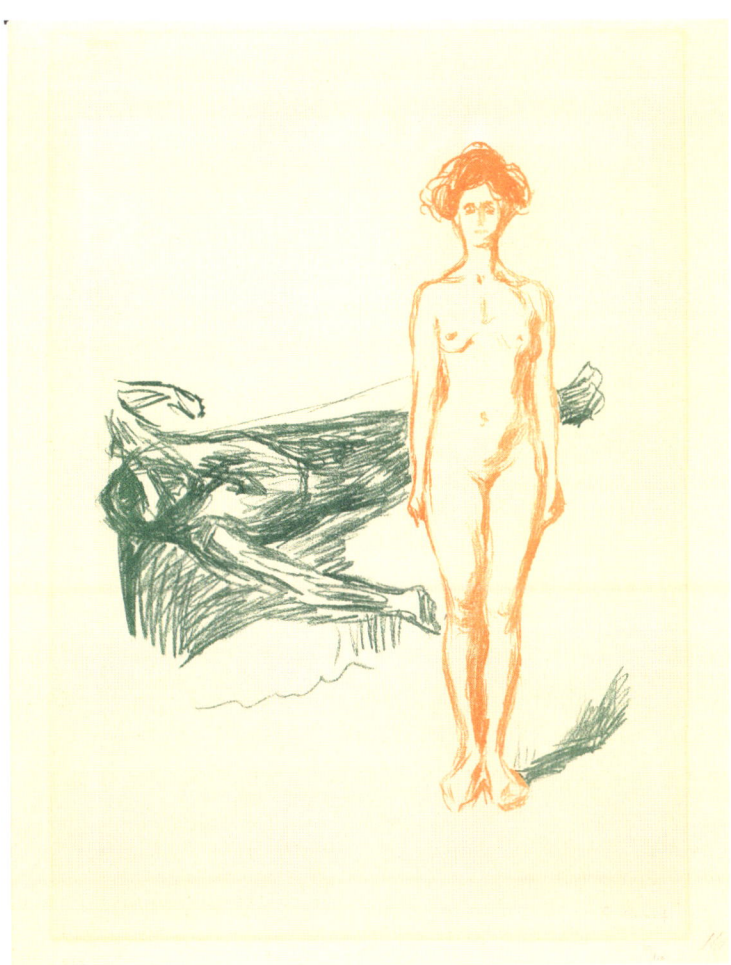

176

177
The Countess
Grevinnen

178
The Beggar
Tiggeren

179
The Nurse
Sykepleiersken

Plate 1907; impression (1907)
Intaglio: drypoint with plate tone; black ink;
heavy wove paper
Image: 230 × 150; paper: 447 × 313
Artist's inscription: Edv Munch [l.r.]
NG.K&H.A.19094
Provenance unknown
Sch 261; W 134; Woll G 290 I / I
Printer: probably Sabo

According to Schiefler, the model was Mrs
Grävenitz, whom Munch called "die Gräfin" (the
Countess) because of her name. Together with
her husband, she was also a model for the paintings *The Death of Marat* (see lithographic version,
cat. 176).

Zinc plate 1908; impression (1908)
Intaglio: line etching with plate tone; dark brown
ink; heavy, stiff wove paper
Image: 581 × 419; paper: 690 × 516
Artist's inscription: EMunch // Betler [sic.] [l.l.]
Secondary inscription: O Felsing Berlin gdr.
NG.K&H.A.19519
Provenance unknown
Sch 272; W 143; Woll G 297 I / I
Printer: Felsing

Plate 1908; impression (1908)
Intaglio: drypoint; black ink; heavy wove paper
Image: 192 × 140; paper: 379 × 315
Artist's inscription: Edv Munch // Portræt af
Sygepleiersken Ch [l.l.]
NG.K&H.A.19095
Provenance unknown
Sch 269; W 140; Woll G 300 II / II
Printer: Dansk Reproduktionsanstalt

The model, Sigrid Schacke Andersen, was a nurse
at Dr. Jacobson's clinic in Copenhagen in the
autumn of 1908. Munch was a patient at the clinic
from October 1908 to April 1909.

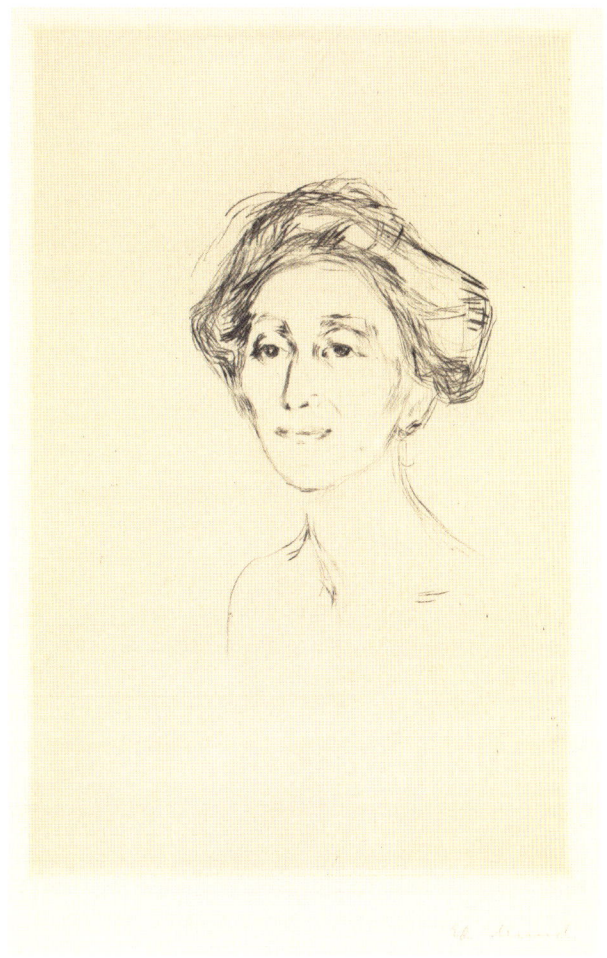

177

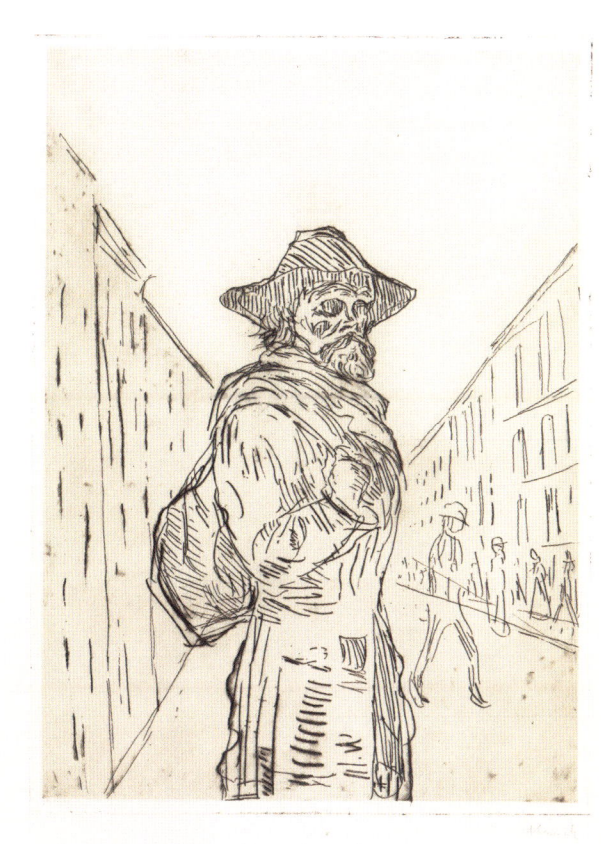

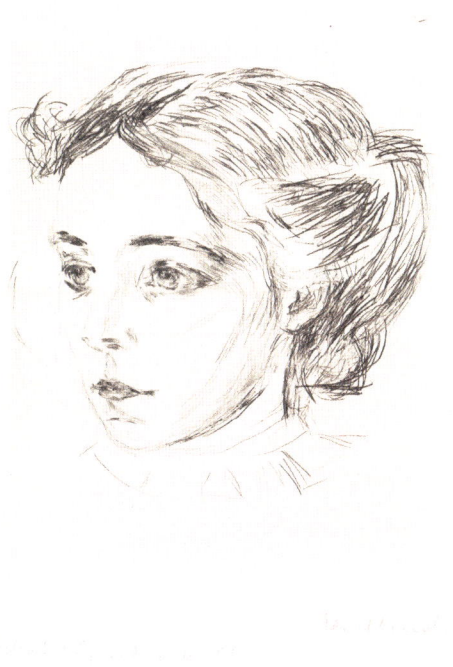

179

178

180

Goldstein Seen Three-Quarter Frontally

Goldstein trekvart en face

Stone 1908 or 1909; impression (1908 or 1909),
Lithograph (transfer lithograph): crayon; black;
heavy wove paper
Image: 324 × 249; paper: 481 × 379
Artist's inscription: Edv Munch
Secondary inscription: 110,- [l.r.; pencil]
NG.K&H.A.19010 (formerly NG.K&H.B.00613)
Purchased at City Auksjon, Oslo, September 1938
(cat. 222)
Sch 276; Woll G 309 I/I
Printer: Dansk Reproduktionsanstalt

Emanuel Goldstein (1860–1921) was a Danish poet
and friend of Munch in 1889–90, when they spent
a lot of time together in Paris. Munch produced a
number of lithographs of Goldstein. The portrait
and the depictions of two panthers were transferred to the same stone, and sometimes all three
motifs were printed on one sheet (Woll G 308).

181

Self-Portrait with a Cigar

Selvportrett med sigar

Stone 1908 or 1909; impression (between 1908 or
1909 and 1912)
Lithograph (transfer lithograph): crayon; black
ink; heavy, stiff wove paper
Image: 567 × 457; paper: 651 × 479
Artist's inscription: E Munch
NG.K&H.A.19039
Provenance unknown
Sch 282; Woll G 313 I/I
Printer: Dansk Reproduktionsanstalt

Schiefler dates the stone to 1908 or 1909; it was
ground down in 1912 (Munch/Schiefler, *Briefwechsel*, no. 581).

182

Tiger's Head I

Tigerhode I

Stone 1908 or 1909; impression (between 1908 or
1909 and 1917)
Lithograph (transfer lithograph): crayon; black
ink; heavy, stiff wove paper
Image: 309 × 259; paper: 373 × 279
Artist's inscription: E Munch
Secondary inscription verso: 180Kr [u.l.; pencil]
NG.K&H.A.19011 (formerly NG.K&H.B.00613)
Purchased at City Auksjon, Oslo, September 1938
(cat. 137)
Sch 287; Woll G 318 I/I
Printer: Dansk Reproduktionsanstalt

Schiefler dates the stone to 1908 or 1909; it was
ground down before October 1917 (exhibition
catalogue, Blomqvist 1917). Munch made drawings of animals at Copenhagen Zoo while an
in-patient at Dr. Jacobson's clinic in 1908-09.

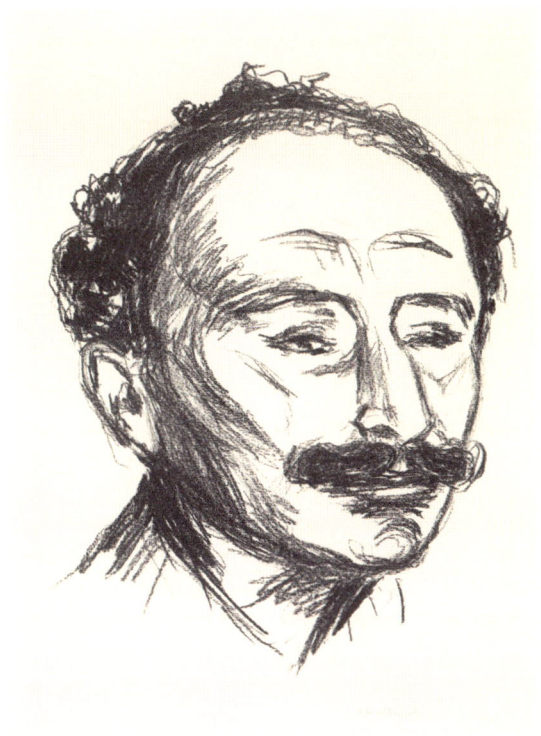

180

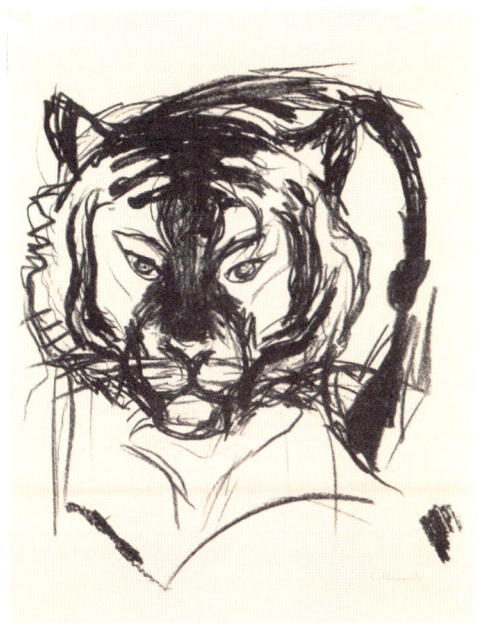

182

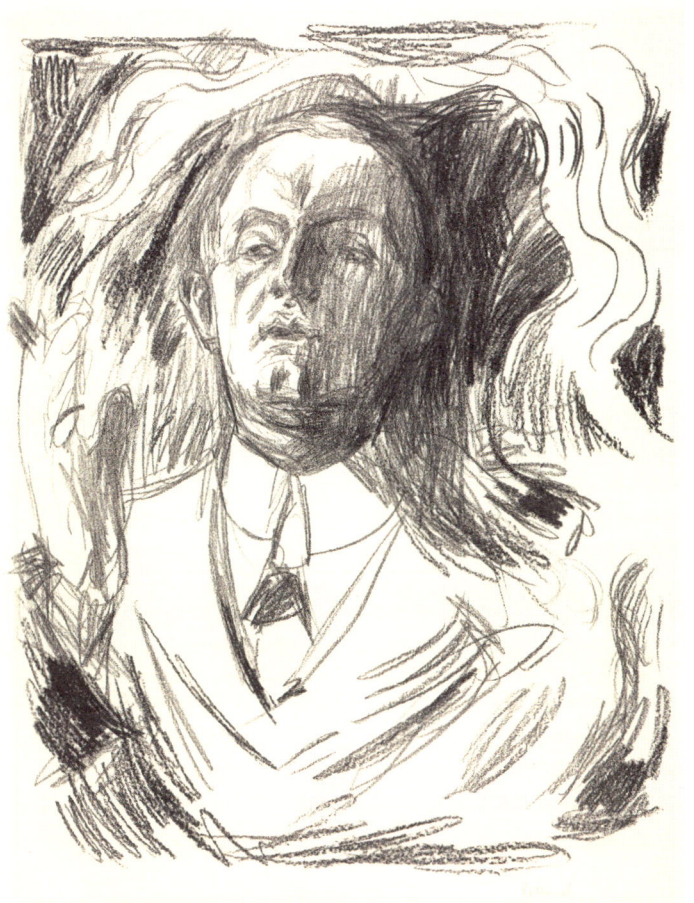

181

183
The Storm
Stormen

Plate 1908 or 1909; impression (1918)
Woodcut: gouges and chisel; blue ink; paper unknown
Dimensions according to Woll G: 371-217 × 325-333
NG.K&H.B.00467
Purchased at auction by Eli Ingebretsen (Greve) (year unknown)
Sch 341; Woll G 371
Printer: the artist or Nielsen
Impression lost

The Department of Prints and Drawings inventoried the impression as No. B.00467 "Stormen, tresnitt blått" (The Storm, woodcut blue). It was noted as missing in the collection audits of 1955 and 1969-70 and is not mentioned in Liv I. Jones' catalogue *Norsk grafikk til 1970* (Norwegian Graphics up to 1970) (Oslo: Nasjonalgalleriet, 1971). All registered early impressions of this print are in black ink. Later impressions are dated on the basis of one in the Munch Museum (MM.G.622-11) that has a date inscription. Munch painted the same scene (inverted) in 1893 (Woll M 324).

184
Jappe Nilssen

Woodblock 1911; impression (probably between 1912 and 1914)
Woodcut: gouges; greyish red ink; heavy wove paper with prominent texture
Image: 320 × 240; paper: 642 × 482
Artist's inscription: Edv Munch
NG.K&H.A.19106 (formerly NG.K&H.B.00613)
Purchased at City Auksjon, Oslo, September 1938 (cat. 106)
Sch 351; Woll G 390 I / I
Printer: the artist or Nielsen

There are also impressions of this woodcut in black. Jappe Nilssen visited Munch at Hvitsten at Christmas 1911. Since one impression (which was probably owned by Gustav Schiefler) has the inscription "Weihnachten 1911", it can be assumed that the portrait dates from that visit. Only a few impressions have been registered; one is dated 1913 (MM.G.626-8) and one 1914 (MM.G.626-1). Jappe (Jakob) Nilssen (1870-1930) was a writer and well-known art critic (writing for *Dagbladet* in 1908-30). Friends since their youth, Munch painted a full-length portrait of Jappe in 1909 (Woll M 832).

185
Self-Portrait
Selvportrett

Woodblock 1911 or 1912; impression (between 1911 or 1912 and 1914)
Woodcut: gouges; black ink; wove paper
Image: 544 × 351; paper: 612 × 432
Artist's inscription: E Munch
Secondary inscription: 110,- [l.c.; pencil]
NG.K&H.A.19116 (formerly NG.K&H.B.00613)
Purchased at City Auksjon, Oslo, September 1938 (cat. 186)
Sch 352; Woll G 391 I / I
Printer: the artist or Nielsen

The National Museum's impression was pulled before the block acquired a number of conspicuous, unintended, vertical lines (damage). One impression dated 1914, in which this damage is visible (MM.G.627-4), provides a *terminus ante quem* for the one in the National Museum.

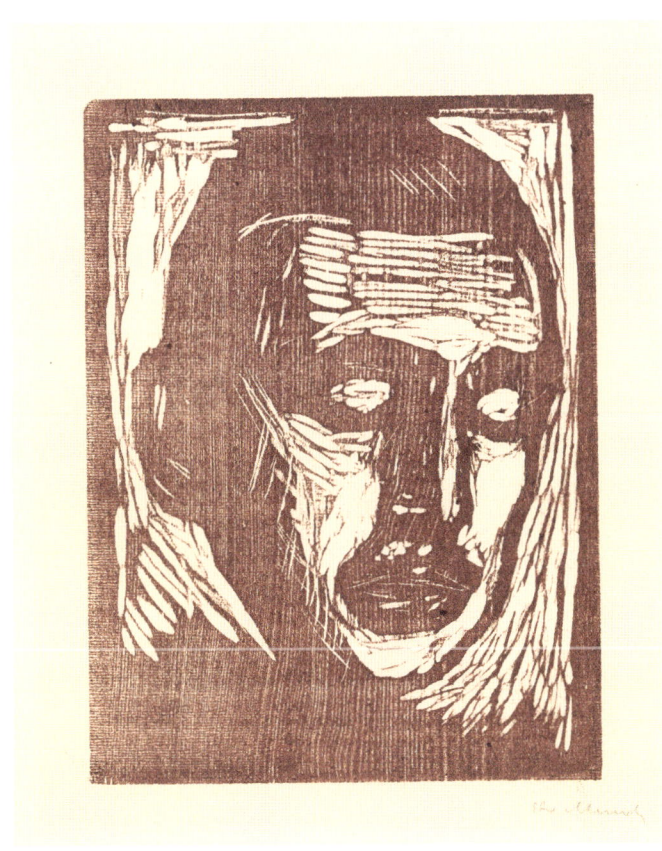

184

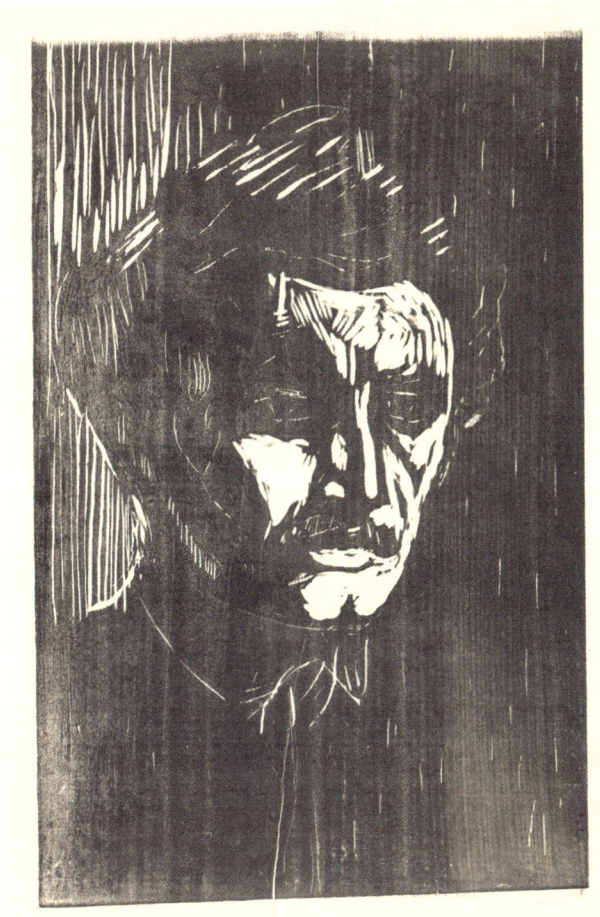

185

186
Self-Portrait in Shadow
Selvportrett i skygge

187
Tor Hedberg

188
Torvald Stang II

Stone 1912; impression (1912)
Lithograph (transfer lithograph): crayon; black ink; medium-weight, stiff wove paper
Image: 311 × 274; paper: 748 × 545
Artist's inscription: Edv Munch
Secondary inscription: 1909. [l.r., pencil]
NG.K&H.A.19041
Provenance unknown
Sch 358; Woll G 395 I / I
Printer: Nielsen

It cannot be determined when the assumed dating 1909 was written on the National Museum's impression. We follow Schiefler's dating.

Stone 1912; impression (1912)
Lithograph (transfer lithograph): crayon; black ink; wove paper
Image: 305 × 268; paper: 750 × 550
Artist's inscription: Edv Munch
Secondary inscription: 1909 [l.r., pencil]
NG.K&H.A.19042
Provenance unknown
Sch 360; Woll G 397 I / I
Printer: Nielsen

It cannot be determined when the assumed dating 1909 was written on the National Museum's impression. Here we follow Schiefler's dating. The drawing that was transferred to the stone is preserved (private collection). Tor Hedberg (1862–1931) was a Swedish author and theatre director.

Stone 1912; impression (1912)
Lithograph (transfer lithograph): crayon; black ink; wove paper
Image: 345 × 336; paper: 411 × 580
Artist's inscription: Edv. Munch
NG.K&H.A.19013
Provenance unknown
Sch 362; Woll G 399 I / I
Printer: Nielsen

The sheet is unevenly cut along the lower edge. Einar Torvald Stang (1865–1914) was a Norwegian lawyer and friend of Munch. Munch produced another lithographic portrait of Stang the same year (Woll G 398) and had painted a full-length portrait of him in 1909 (Woll M 834).

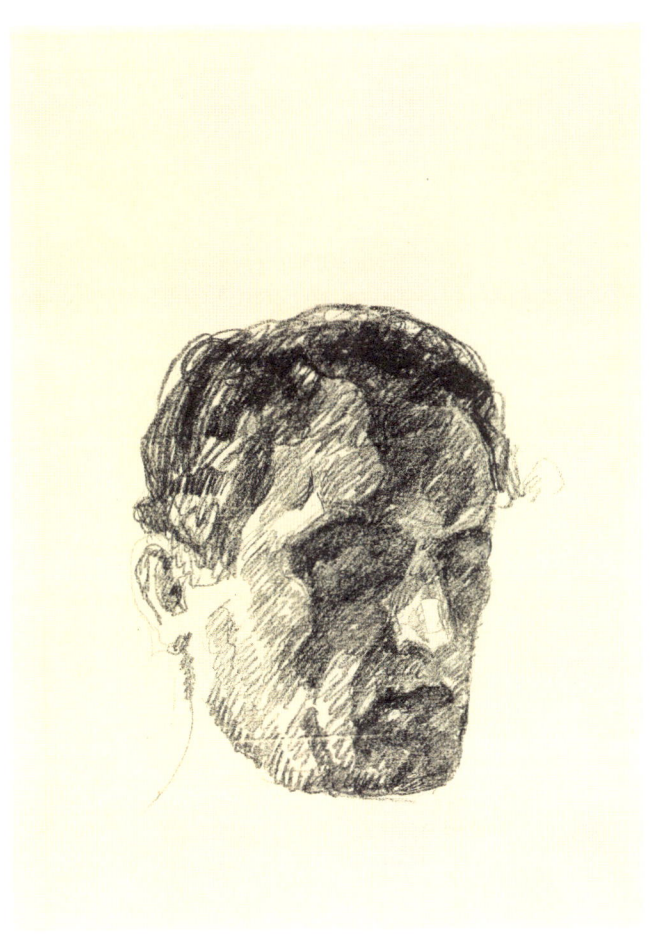

186

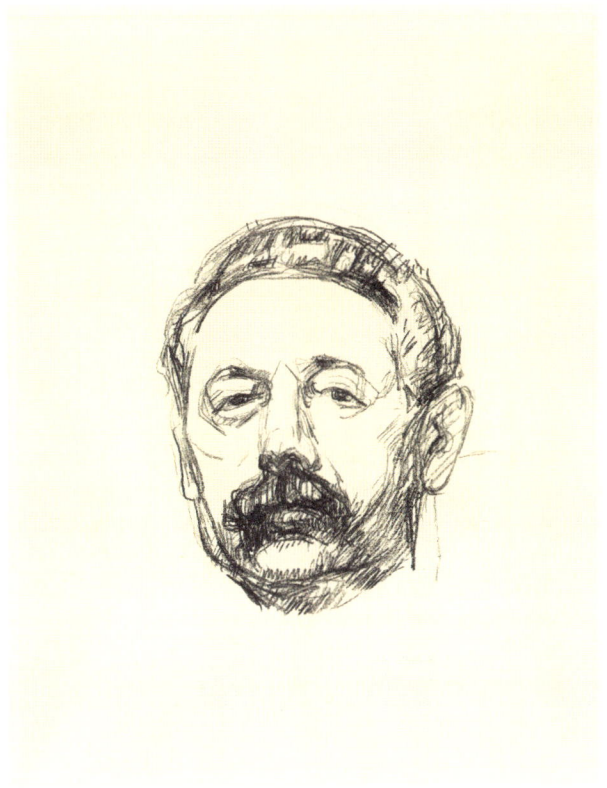

187

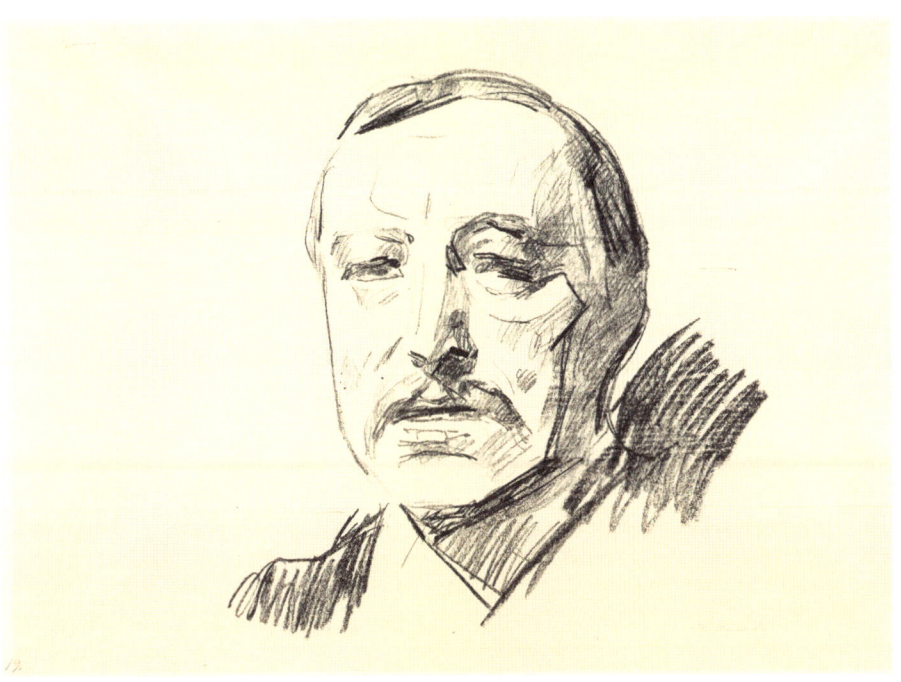

188

189
Wolfgang Gurlitt

Stone 1912; impression (1912)
Lithograph: crayon; blue ink; heavy, stiff wove paper
Image: 477 × 617; paper: 600 × 801
NG.K&H.A.19527 (formerly NG.K&H.B.00613)
Purchased at City Auksjon, Oslo, September 1938 (cat. 64 or 226)
Sch 363; Woll G 400 I/II
Printer: Lassally

The National Museum's impression has no significant inscriptions. Lassally pulled monochrome (in blue or black ink) and multicolour prints (two stones) in 1912. In 1921, Nielsen pulled monochrome prints in black. Wolfgang Gurlitt (1888-1965) was an art dealer in Berlin. The lithograph was made in conjunction with an exhibition Munch held at Gurlitt's gallery in 1912.

190
Jarl

Stone 1912; impression (1912)
Lithograph: crayon; black ink; heavy wove paper with prominent texture
Image: 353 × 351; paper: 480 × 642
Artist's inscription: Edv Munch
Secondary inscription: No 2. [l.l.; pencil]
NG.K&H.A.19015
Provenance unknown
Sch 373; Woll G 409 I/I
Printer: Nielsen

The inscription "No 2" could be the printer's numbering. The model is probably Jarl Barth-Thorbjørnsen. *Seated Man* (see cat. 194) is on the verso of the stone (MM P 193).

191
Seated Nude. The Flea
Sittende akt. Loppen

Stone 1912; impression (1912)
Lithograph: crayon; black ink; wove paper
Image: 351 × 31.7; paper: 635 × 449
Artist's inscription: E Munch
NG.K&H.B.00466
Purchased at auction by Eli Ingebretsen (Greve) (year unknown)
Sch 375; Woll G 411 I/I
Printer: Nielsen

On the same face of the stone (MM P 198) is another representation of the same model (Woll G 410).

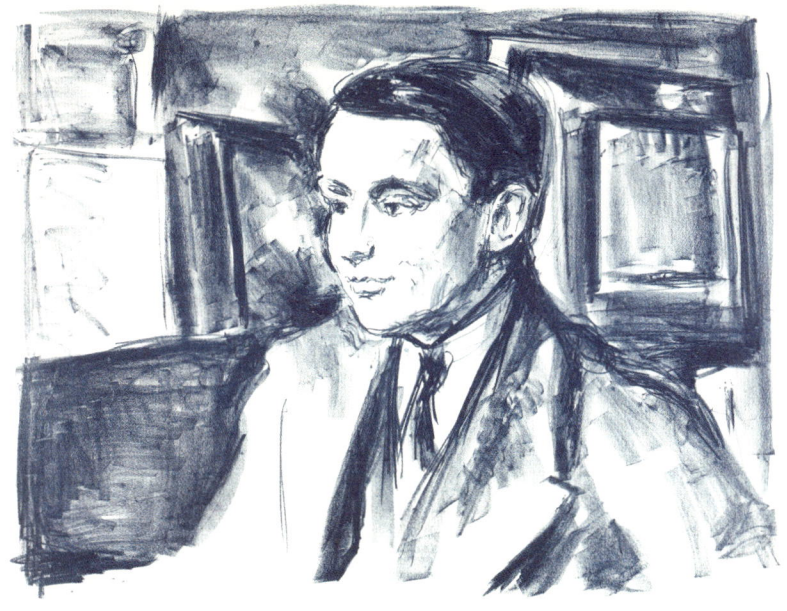

189

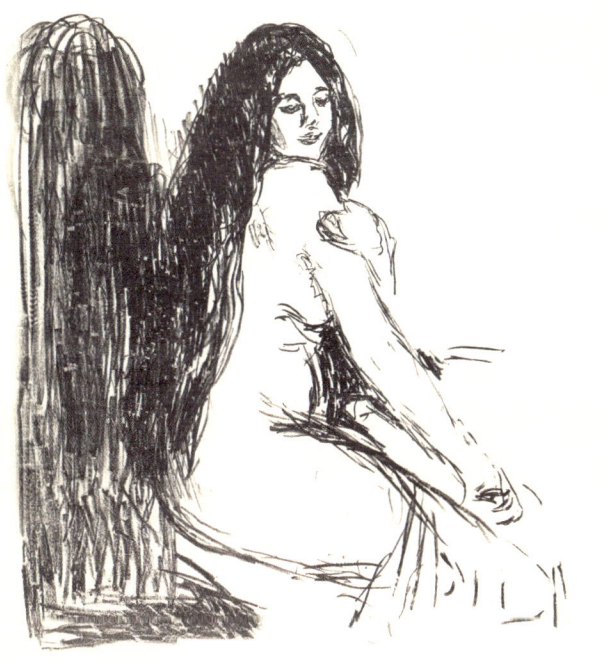

191

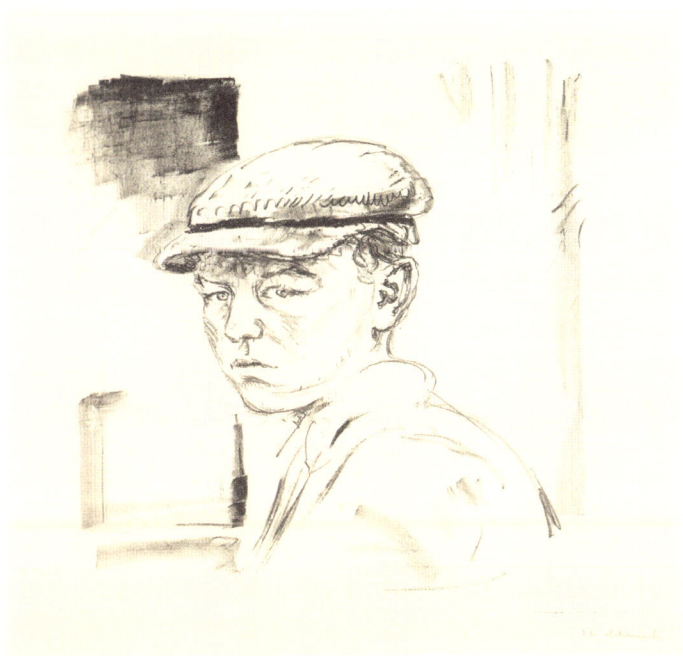

190

192
Workers in Snow
Arbeidere i snø

Stone 1912 or 1913; impression (probably 1915)
Lithograph: crayon; black ink; heavy, stiff wove
paper
Image: 625 × 483; paper: 731 × 500
Artist's inscription: Edv Munch
Secondary inscription: No 13 [l.l.; pencil]
NG.K&H.A.19043
Provenance unknown
Sch 385; Woll G 414 I/III
Printer: Nielsen

The inscription "No 13" is the printer's numbering. Several prints that Nielsen numbered in a
similar manner bear the date 1915 in his hand.
The lithograph was also printed in combination
with a woodblock inked in grey (Woll G 414 II and
III). The subject is an inversion of two paintings
from 1909-10 (Woll M 873, 874). Munch also
produced a woodcut with the same composition
(Woll G 389). In 1913-15, he repeated the subject as
a painting (Woll M 1091) and used it around 1930
as a draft for a monumental decoration of Oslo
City Hall (Woll M 1685).

193
Ducks
Ender

Stone 1912 or 1913; impression (1913)
Lithograph (transfer lithograph): crayon; black
ink; medium-weight Japan paper
Image: 259 × 400; paper: 310 × 520
Artist's inscription: Edv Munch [l.r.]
Secondary inscription: No 13 [l.l.; pencil]
NG.K&H.A.19016
Provenance unknown
Sch 379; Woll G 415 I/I
Printer: Nielsen

The inscription "No 13" is the printer's numbering. Nielsen inscribed another impression
with the date 1913. Around the edges, the fibres
of the sheet are matted together with those of
another sheet of Japan paper; this is probably an
unintended consequence of the printing. In 1913,
Munch produced a painting (Woll M 1041) and a
drawing (MM.T.1428) of the same subject.

194
Seated Man
Sittende mann

Stone between 1912 and 1914; impression (1914)
Lithograph (transfer lithograph): crayon; black
ink; heavy, stiff wove paper
Image: 318 × 253; paper: 483 × 372
Artist's inscription: E Munch
Secondary inscription verso: 90,- [u.l.; pencil]
NG.K&H.A.19014
Provenance unknown
Sch 364; Woll G 417 I/I
Printer: Nielsen

Few impressions of this lithograph have been
registered. One is inscribed "Tidlig Tryk 1914"
(Early print 1914) (MM.G.344-4). *Jarl* (see cat. 190)
is on the verso of the stone (MM P 193).

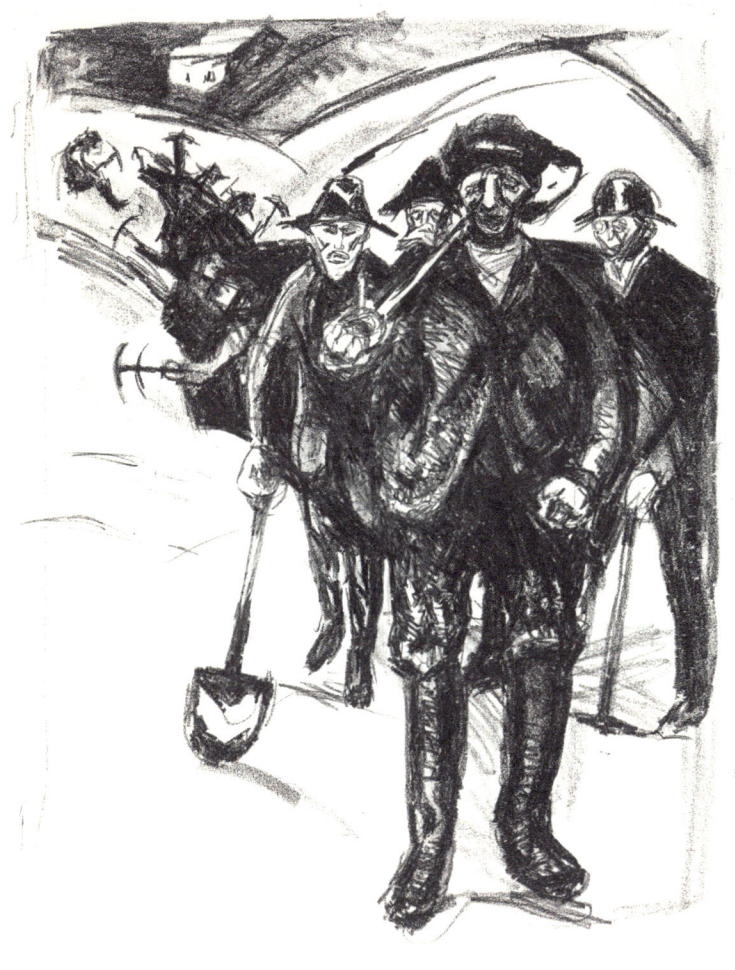

192

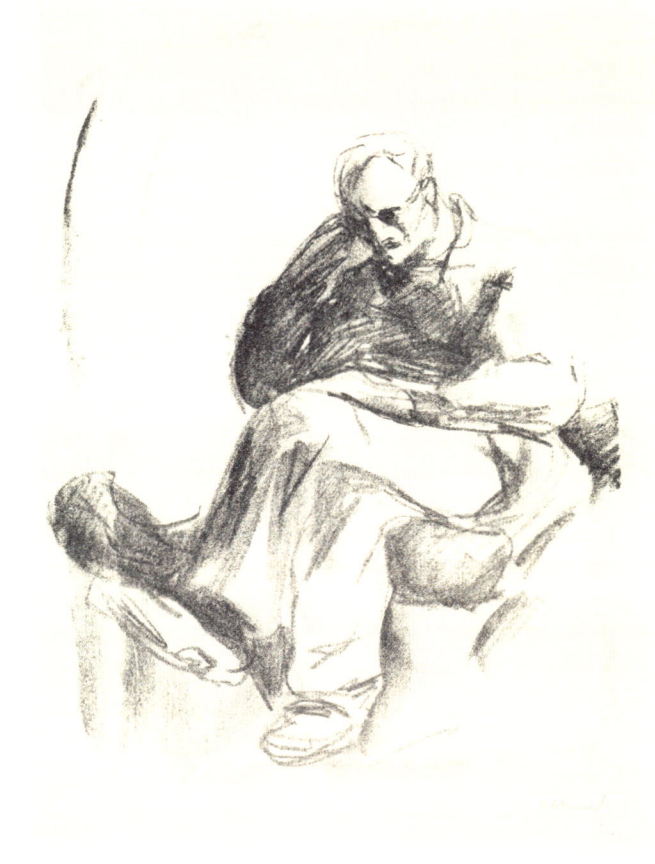

194

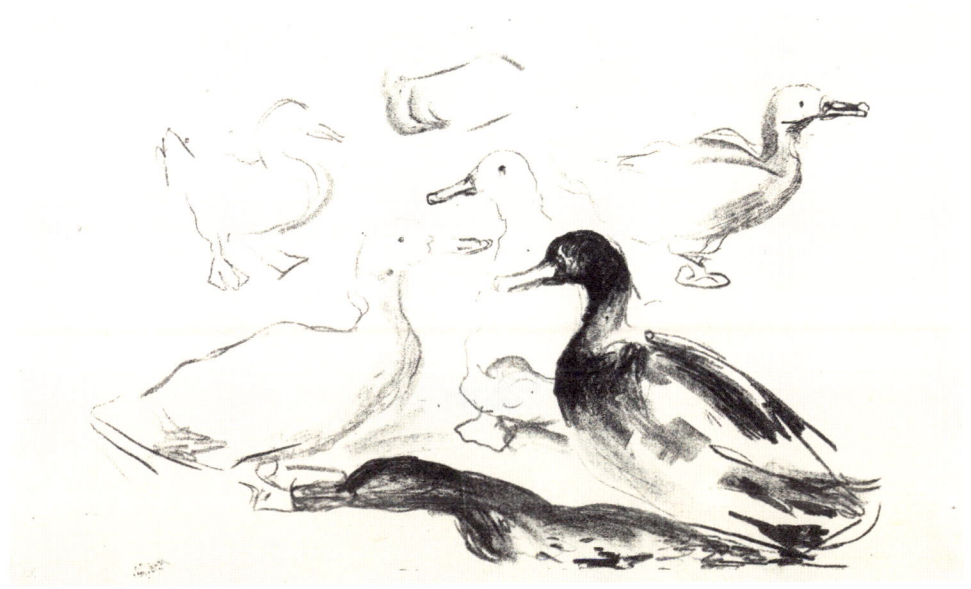

193

195
Hjørdis Gierløff

Plate 1913 or 1914; impression (1914)
Intaglio: drypoint; black ink; heavy wove paper
Image: 231 × 153; paper: 498 × 383
Artist's inscription: Edv Munch
NG.K&H.B.00577
Purchased from Swedish collector, 1935 or 1936
Sch 391; Woll G 438 VI / VI
Printer: the artist

The National Museum's impression is a vague
imprint with a pronounced plate edge (bevelled
plate). Several impressions in states IV, V and
VI are dated 1914. Hjørdis Gierløff (née Nielsen;
1889-1957) married Christian Gierløff (1879-1962)
in 1912. Christian Gierløff was a journalist and
author. He was a long-standing friend of Munch,
who produced several portraits of him and his
family (Woll G 431, 438, 459, 460 and 551; Woll M
836, 1057, 1058, 1190).

196
Street Musicians
Gatemusikanter

Stone 1913; impression (1913)
Lithograph (transfer lithograph): crayon; black
ink; wove paper
Image: 266 × 392; paper: 456 × 643
Artist's inscription: E Munch
NG.K&H.A.19017 (formerly NG.K&H.B.00613)
Purchased at City Auksjon, Oslo, September 1938
(cat. 20)
Sch 406; Woll G 444 I / IV
Printer: Nielsen

The lithograph was made for the silver wedding
of Luise and Gustav Schiefler, which took place in
August 1913. The image of the musicians exists in
only one state, but it occurs in combination with
borders featuring cherubs and written greetings
to the silver wedding couple; the borders and text
are printed from other stones. Concerning Luise
and Gustav Schiefler, see cat. 171.

197
Jens Thiis

Stone 1913; impression (1913 or 1919)
Lithograph (transfer lithograph): crayon; black
ink; medium-weight wove paper
Image: 294 × 236; paper: 401 × 259
Artist's inscription: E Munch [indistinct]
NG.K&H.B.00357
Purchased at auction, Wangs Kunst- og Auktions-
forretning, Oslo, 1927
Sch 410; Woll G 447 I / I
Printer: Nielsen

Probably only a few impressions were printed in
1913, but the inscription on another impression
shows that more were printed on 02.09.1919
(MM.G.371-11). The wood grain in the print originates from a wooden board that Munch used as
a support when drawing the portrait. Jens Thiis
(1870-1942) was an art historian and director of
the National Gallery (1908-41). He was a close
friend of Munch and frequently supported him
from the 1890s on. Munch painted a full-length
portrait of Thiis in 1909 (Woll M 837).

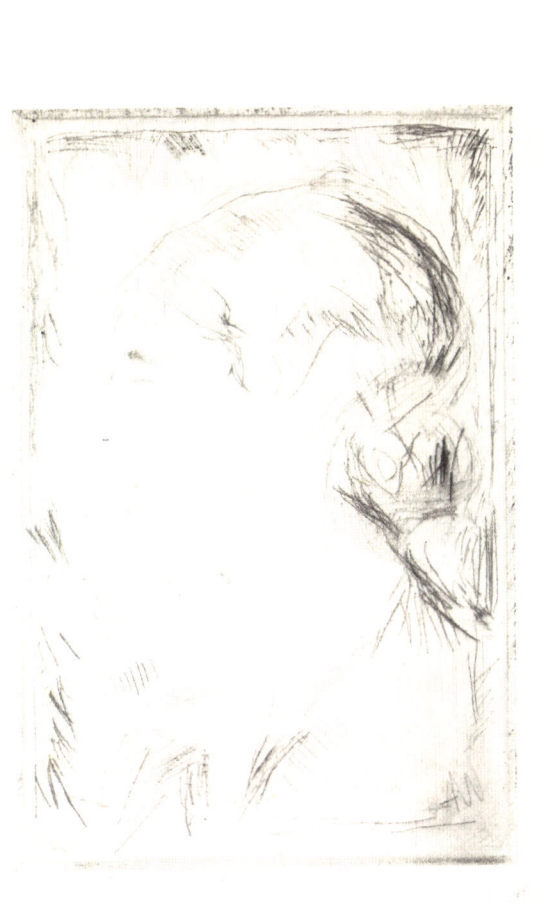

195

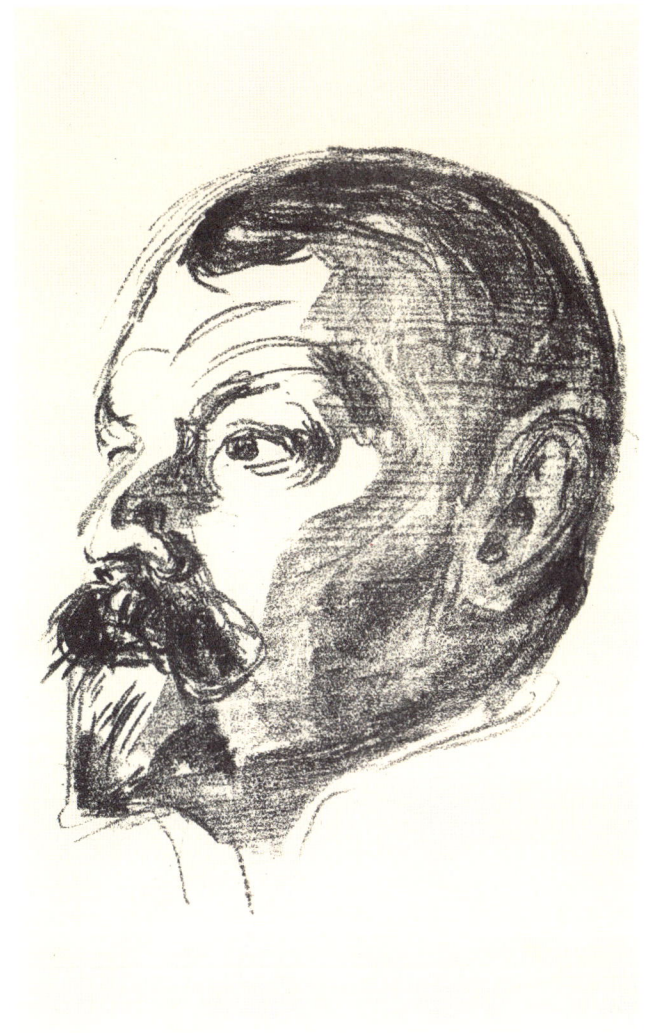

197

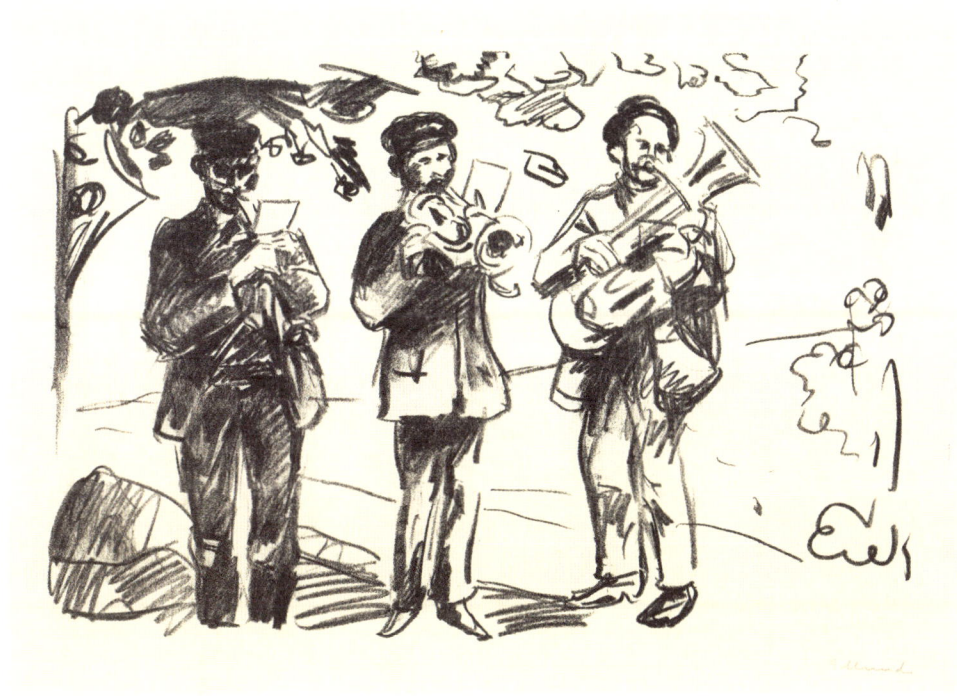

196

198
Turkey, Hens and Peacocks
Kalkun, høns og påfugler

Stone 1913; impression 1915
Lithograph (transfer lithograph): black crayon;
heavy wove paper
Image: 233 × 351; paper: 540 × 731
Artist's inscription: Nilsen [sic.] 1915 [u.r.; brown
coloured pencil]
NG.K&H.A.19040
Provenance unknown
Sch 342; Woll G 455 I/I
Printer: Nielsen

199
Stalking Panther
Snikende panter

Stone 1913; impression (1913)
Lithograph (transfer lithograph): black crayon;
medium-weight imitation (?) Japan paper
Image: 175 × 367; paper: 325 × 458
Artist's inscription: Edv Munch
Secondary inscription: No 1 [l.l.; pencil]
NG.K&H.A.19012
Provenance unknown
Sch 383; Woll G 457 I/I
Printer: Nielsen

The inscription "No 1" is the printer's numbering.
An inscription by Nielsen on the stone (MM P
204) indicates that he printed an edition of 20
impressions in 1913. Impressions are recorded
with numbering up to 20. Munch probably executed the drawing at London Zoo.

200
Garden in Snow II
Hagen i snø II

Woodblock 1913; impression (probably 1913)
Woodcut: gouges; greyish red ink; wove paper
Image: 400 × 502; paper: 544 × 702
Artist's inscription: Edv Munch
Secondary inscription: Winterlandschaft [l.l.;
pencil]
NG.K&H.A.19117 (formerly NG.K&H.B.00613)
Purchased at City Auksjon, Oslo, September 1938
(cat. 32?)
Not in Sch; Woll G 468 I/I
Printer: the artist

Few impressions of this woodcut have been
registered; all are "pale" (sparsely inked). Munch
made another woodcut with a similar composition at the same time (Woll G 467).

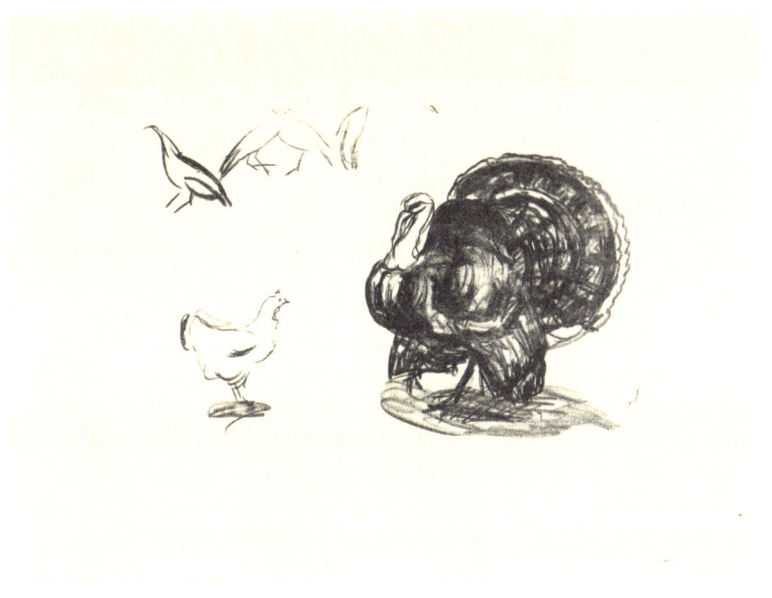

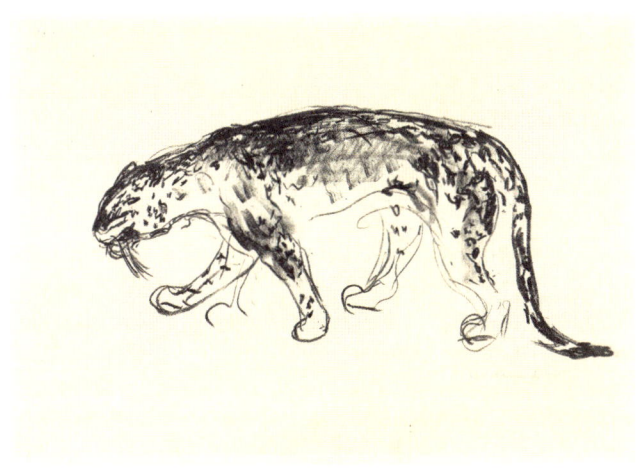

198

199

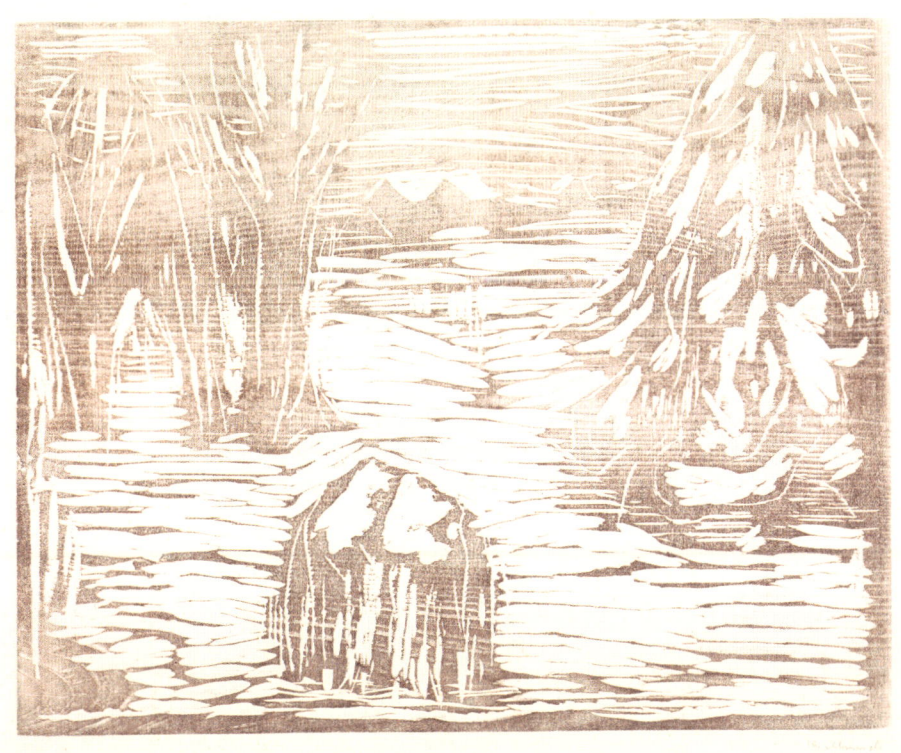

200

201
Céline Nude
Céline naken

Plate 1914; impression (1914)
Intaglio: drypoint and roulette with plate tone;
black ink; wove paper
Image: 266 × 205; paper: 426 × 305 (corners
cropped)
Unsigned
NG.K&H.1960.0054
Purchased at auction, Blomqvist Kunsthandel,
Oslo, autumn auction, 1960, no. 2.
Sch 355; W 144; Woll G 477 I/I
Printer: Wittman

The intaglio was made during Munch's stay in
Paris in 1914. The same model features in two
other intaglios (Woll G 478, 479). A postcard from
the model Céline Cuvelier postmarked "Paris
18.2.14" has been preserved, on which she regrets
not being able to come that morning due to illness
(MM K 1878).

202
Dance of Death
Dødsdans

Stone 1915; impression (1915)
Lithograph (transfer lithograph): crayon; stone
further modified with crayon; black ink; tissue
paper
Image: 364 × 298; paper: 677 × 485
Artist's inscription: Edv Munch // Circa No 15 [l.r.;
pencil]
Secondary inscription: No 3. 2den tilstand [l.l.
pencil]; verso: Døden og maleren K [? ...] [l.c.;
pencil]
NG.K&H.A.19018
Provenance unknown
Sch 432; Woll G 509 III/III
Printer: Nielsen

The inscription "No 3. 2den tilstand" (No. 3.
2nd state) is the printer's. Munch's inscription
"Circa No 15" was probably added after the sheet
had been folded along the bottom in a way that
obscures the printer's inscription. Only two
impressions have been registered beside those
in the Munch Museum (Hamburger Kunsthalle
1954/234, and the National Museum's). Hamburger Kunsthalle's impression is dated 1915. The
title *Dødsdans* (Dance of Death) probably orig-
inated with Schiefler (*Totentanz*), but in exhibitions in 1915 and 1917 the lithograph was referred
to as *Manden og døden* (Man and Death) and
Døden og manden (Death and the Man), respectively. The work can be seen as an ironic allusion
to works from the early 1890s depicting a woman
embracing a skeleton (see cat. 60), and to the
self-portrait from 1895 (cat. 84). But having always
lived with death as a present reality, in 1913, the
year he turned fifty, Munch was in good health
and could afford to approach his own mortality
with a touch of humour.

203
The Tree I
Treet I

Stone 1916; impression (1916 or 1921)
Lithograph (transfer lithograph): crayon; black
ink; stiff wove paper
Image: 223 × 362; paper: 283 × 409
Unsigned
NG.K&H.A.19019 (formerly NG.K&H.B.00613)
Purchased at City Auksjon, Oslo, September 1938
(cat. 316)
Sch 433; Woll G 585 I/I
Printer: Nielsen

Few impressions of this lithograph have been
registered. One is inscribed with the year 1916
(private collection). An inscription by the printer
on the stone (MM P 200) indicates that an edition
was printed in 1921. This and two other lithographic versions of the same subject (Woll G 586
and 587) can be seen as a commentary on the
atrocities of World War I.

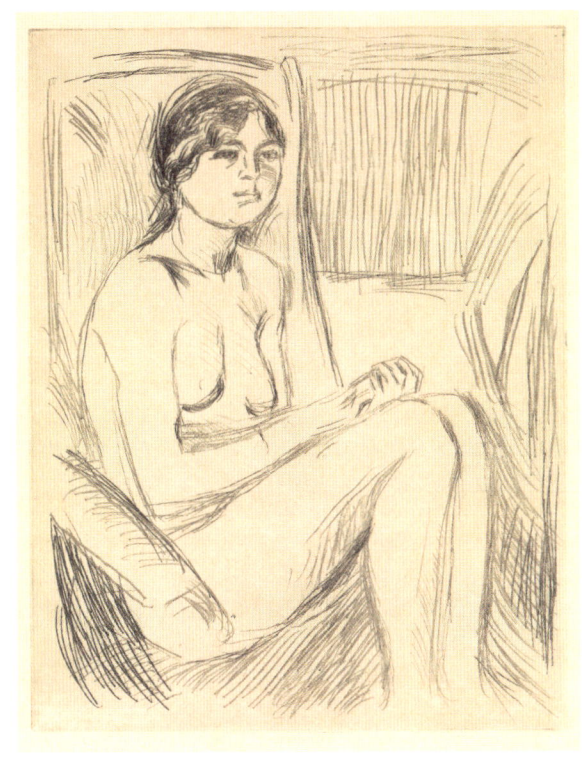

201

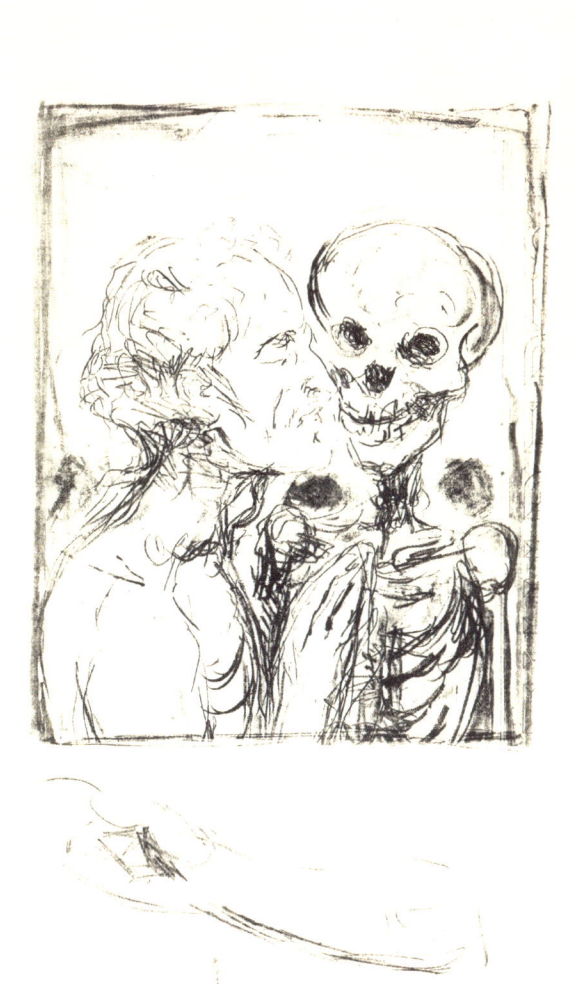

202

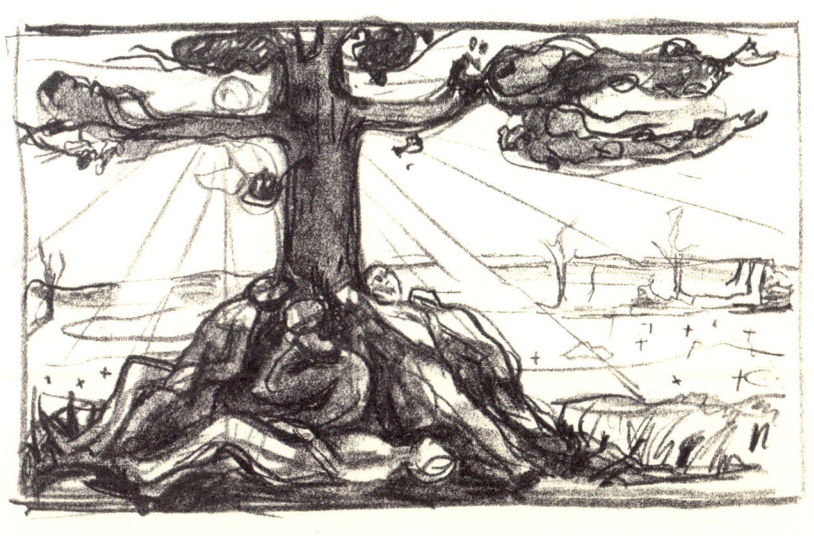

203

204
Richard Strauss

Stone 1917; impression 1917
Lithograph (transfer lithograph): crayon; black
ink; wove paper
Image: 316 × 215; paper: 518 × 365
Artist's inscription: Edv Munch
Secondary inscription: Forsökstryk 5./10/3. 1917.
[l.l.; pencil]
NG.K&H.A.19020 (formerly NG.K&H.B.00613)
Purchased at City Auksjon, Oslo, September 1938
(cat. 259)
Sch 460; Woll G 607 I/I
Printer: Nielsen

The inscription "Forsökstryk 5./10/3. 1917." (Trial
proof 5. 10/3. 1917.) is the printer's, recording the
number and date of the impression. Schiefler
dates the lithograph to 1916, but the portrait was
most likely drawn during Richard Strauss' visit to
Kristiania (Oslo) in March 1917. The drawing that
was transferred to the stone is preserved (private
collection). Richard Strauss (1864-1949) was a
German composer.

205
Self-Portrait with Beard
Selvportrett med skjegg

Stone 1919; impression (1919)
Lithograph (transfer lithograph): crayon; black
ink; medium-weight, stiff wove paper
Image: 430 × 613; paper: 499 × 664
Artist's inscription: Edvard Munch
NG.K&H.A.19044 (formerly NG.K&H.B.00613)
Purchased at City Auksjon, Oslo, September 1938
(cat. 155)
Sch 503; Woll G 630 I/I
Printer: Nielsen

Schiefler uses the title *Selbstporträt, nach einer
Krankheit* (Self-Portrait, after an Illness). The
lithograph resembles a painting from the same
year (Woll M 1297). The portrait was drawn in
1919 during Munch's convalescence, possibly
from an attack of the "Spanish flu", an influenza
pandemic that ravaged many parts of the world
in 1918-20. The drawing that was transferred
to the stone was previously owned by the
printer Nielsen; it is now in the Munch Museum
(MM.T.2766).

206
Arve Arvesen I

Stone 1920; impression (ca. 1920)
Lithograph (transfer lithograph): crayon; black
ink; wove paper
Image: 490 × 666; paper: 700 × 979
Artist's inscription: Edvard Munch
NG.K&H.A.19528 (formerly NG.K&H.B.00611)
Gift from Munch on the occasion of his 70th
birthday exhibition at the Department of Prints
and Drawings. Included in the collection in 1936
or 1937
Sch 471; Woll G 638 I/I
Printer: Nielsen

The ridged structure of the transfer paper is
visible in the imprint. Arve Arvesen (1869-1951),
concert master with the Bergen Philharmonic
Orchestra from 1900 to 1903, founded the string
quartet Kammermusikkforeningen in Kristiania
(Oslo) in 1917 and Arvesens kammertrio, a string
trio, in 1921. Munch painted his portrait in 1891
(Woll M 252) and portrayed him in a second lithograph in 1920 (Woll G 639).

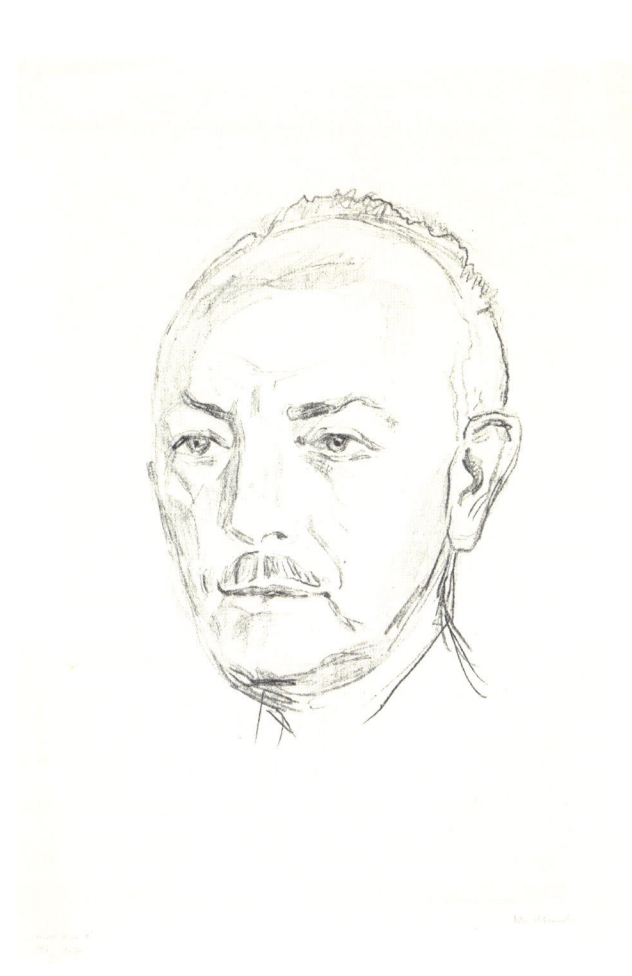

204

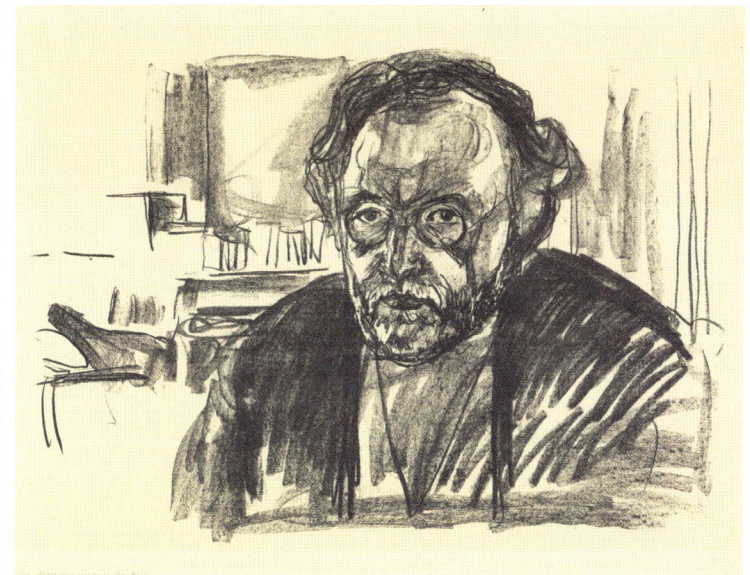

205

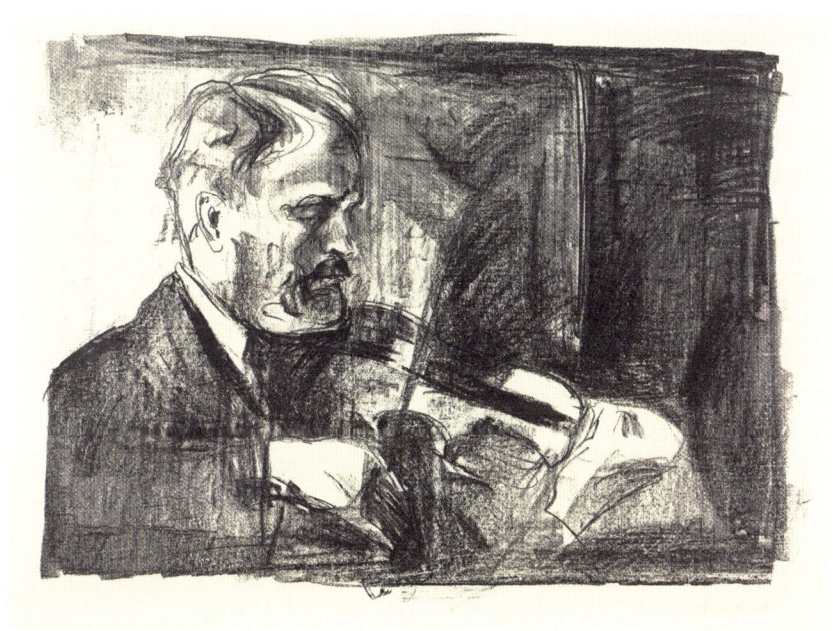

206

207
Frederick Delius

Stone 1919 or 1920; impression (ca. 1920)
Lithograph (transfer lithograph): crayon; black ink; wove paper
Image: 570 × 460; paper: 837 × 621
Artist's inscription: Edv Munch
NG.K&H.A.19529 (formerly NG.K&H.B.00613)
Purchased at City Auksjon, Oslo, September 1938 (cat. 276)
Sch 473; Woll G 640 I/I
Printer: Nielsen (?)

Frederick Delius (1862–1934) was an English composer and friend of Munch. Munch also drew a lithographic portrait of him in Wiesbaden a few years later (Woll G 671).). He had also drawn portraits of Delius in a sketchbook in 1891 (MM.T.00127-25-verso), and an illustration in *Verdens Gang*, 12.10.1891.

208
Woman's Portrait
Kvinneportrett

Stone 1920; impression (1920)
Lithograph (transfer lithograph): crayon; black ink; wove paper
Image: 387 × 266; paper: 447 × 377
Artist's inscription: Edv Munch // Kvinnestudie [l.r.]
Secondary inscription: 28/5 No 6. [l.l.; pencil]
NG.K&H.A.19021 (formerly NG.K&H.B.00611)
Gift from Munch on the occasion of his 70th birthday exhibition at the Department of Prints and Drawings. Included in the collection in 1936 or 1937
Sch 477; Woll G 644 I/I
Printer: Nielsen

The inscription "28/5 No 6." is the printer's dating and numbering of the impression. The subject is probably Helga Rogstad, who worked as a model and housekeeper for Munch in the period 1914–19.

209
Woman with Her Hand by Her Mouth
Kvinne med hånden ved munnen

Stone 1920; impression (probably 1921)
Lithograph (transfer lithograph): crayon; black ink; wove paper
Image: 379 × 272; paper: 500 × 375
Artist's inscription: Edvard Munch
Secondary inscription: No 4. [l.l.]
NG.K&H.A.19022 (formerly NG.K&H.B.00611)
Gift from Munch on the occasion of his 70th birthday exhibition at the Department of Prints and Drawings. Included in the collection in 1936 or 1937
Sch 481; Woll G 645 I/I
Printer: Nielsen

The inscription "No 4." is the printer's numbering of the impression. Schiefler dates the stone to 1920. The printer's inscription on the stone (MM P 231) shows that 20 impressions were printed in 1921. The drawing that was transferred to the stone has been preserved (MM.T.641).

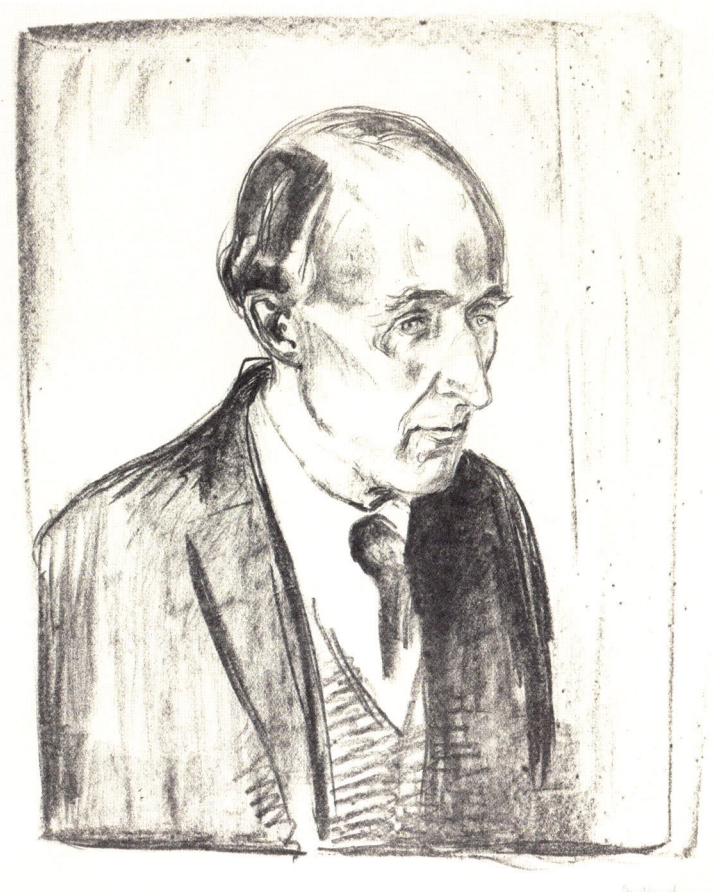

207

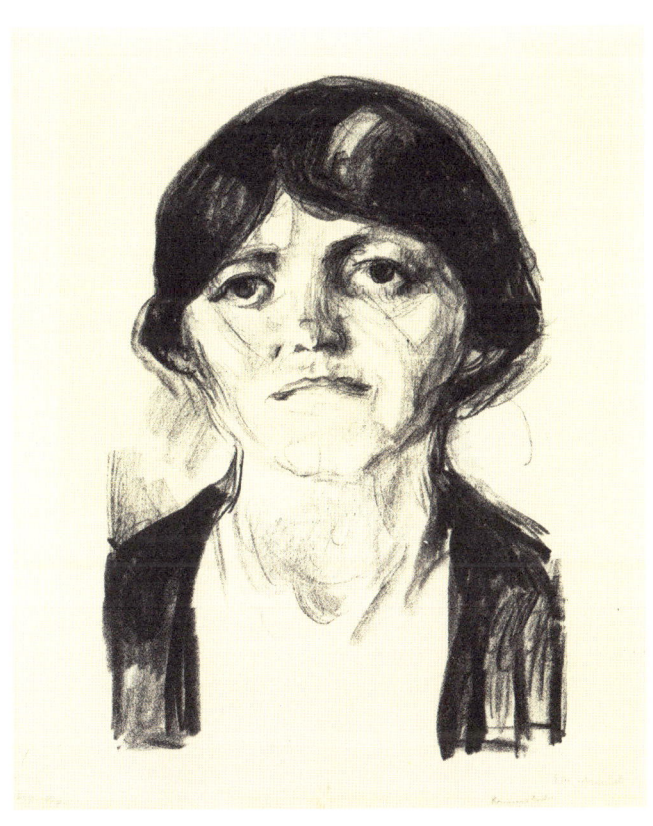

208

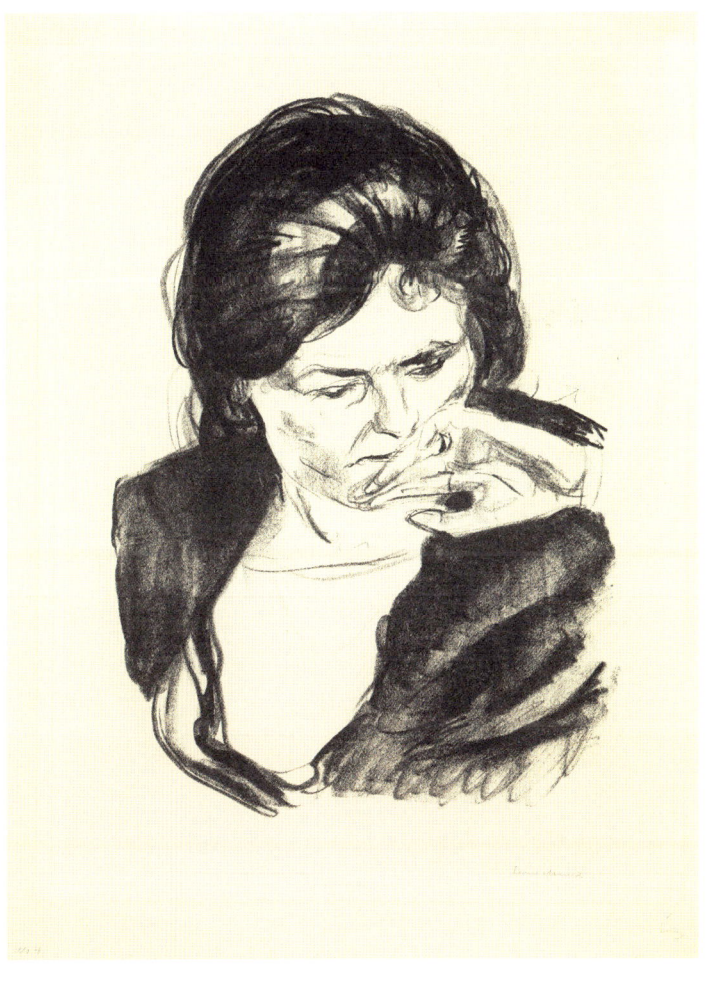

209

210
Fire. Vaterland
Brann. Vaterland

211
Grenadierstrasse in Berlin after the War
Grenadierstrasse i Berlin etter krigen

212
Two People
To mennesker

Stone 1919 or 1920; impression (1919 or 1920)
Lithograph (transfer lithograph): crayon; black ink; wove paper
Image: 550 × 765; paper: 733 × 990
Artist's inscription: Edvard Munch // Brand. Vaterland [l.r.]
NG.K&H.A.19531 (formerly NG.K&H.B.00612)
Gift from Munch on the occasion of his 70th birthday exhibition at the Department of Prints and Drawings. Included in the collection in 1936 or 1937
Sch 483; Woll G 647 I / I
Printer: Nielsen

According to Schiefler, some 100 impressions were printed from the stone, which was then ground down. The work depicts a raging fire at Vaterland in Kristiania (Oslo) in the winter of 1919, which Munch apparently sketched as a direct witness. The location has been referred to as Grønland, which is close to Vaterland. A drawing very similar to the lithograph was originally on a folded sheet together with several other sketches, but was later cut out and sold separately (private collection). Munch also depicted this fire in a painting (Woll M 1353).

Stone 1920 or 1921; impression (1920 or 1921)
Lithograph (transfer lithograph): crayon; black ink; wove paper
Image: 277 × 399; paper: 376 × 500
Artist's inscription: Edvard Munch // Grenadier-strasse. Berlin 1918
NG.K&H.A.19023 (formerly NG.K&H.B.00612)
Gift from Munch on the occasion of his 70th birthday exhibition at the Department of Prints and Drawings. Included in the collection in 1936 or 1937
Sch 496; Woll G 652 I / I
Printer: Nielsen

The lithograph was dated 1921 at exhibitions in Zurich in 1922 and Mannheim in 1926. The year 1918 in the artist's inscription should probably be understood as part of the title, and not as a dating of the print. On several other impressions, Munch has written "efter krigen" or "nach dem Kriege" ("after the war"), indicating that the picture represents a situation in Berlin immediately after World War I. The earliest opportunity Munch had, however, to make such observations would have been his first post-war visit to Berlin, which was in 1920. Schiefler gives the lithograph the title *Grenadierstrasse Berlin*, but Munch also used the title *Gentinerstrasse* both in inscriptions and in the catalogue for the exhibition in Bielefeld in 1931. The latter is also the title used in Woll 2012. Genthiner Strasse was and still is a street in central Berlin. Grenadierstrasse (now Alm-stadtstrasse) was a street in central Berlin before World War II. The street was the religious and cultural centre for Jews who had moved to Berlin from Eastern Europe, hence the characterisation of the figures in the foreground make it probable that the picture represents Grenadierstrasse. The drawing that was transferred to the stone is preserved (MM.T.441). The stone (MM P 228) has another image on the same side (Woll G 637). The printer's inscription on the stone indicates that an edition of both images was printed in 1921.

Stone 1920; impression (between 1925 and 1928)
Lithograph (transfer lithograph): crayon; red ink; wove paper
Image: 644 × 606; paper: 982 × 740
Artist's inscription: Edvard Munch // To menne-sker (Kvinne læner sig til en mand) [l.r.]
NG.K&H.A.19533 (formerly NG.K&H.B.00612)
Gift from Munch on the occasion of his 70th birthday exhibition at the Department of Prints and Drawings. Included in the collection in 1936 or 1937
Sch 504; Woll G 659 I / I
Printer: Nielsen

The impression is dated on the basis of inscriptions on other impressions with similar ink (Woll G 659).

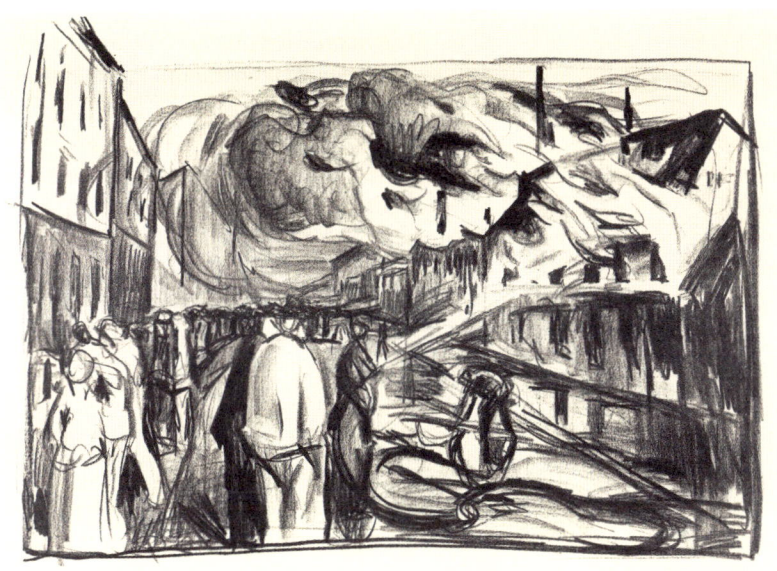

210

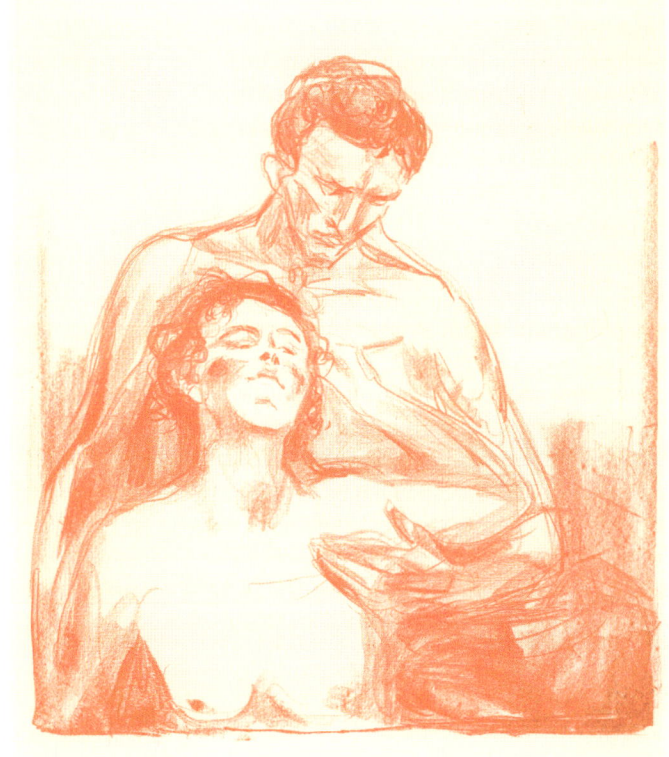

212

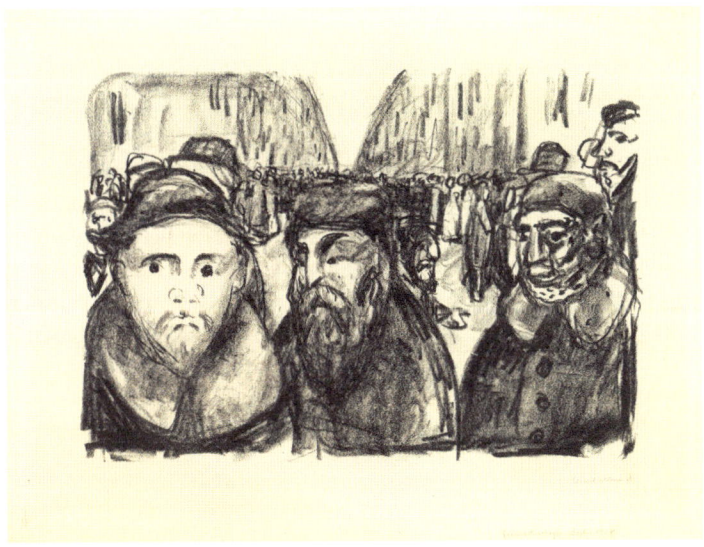

211

213
Peasant Girl
Bondepike

Stone 1920; impression (1920 or 1924)
Lithograph (transfer lithograph): crayon; black
ink, wove paper
Image: 565 × 442; paper: 715 × 501
Artist's inscription: Edvard Munch
NG.K&H.A.19045 (formerly NG.K&H.B.00612)
Gift from Munch on the occasion of his 70th
birthday exhibition at the Department of Prints
and Drawings. Included in the collection in 1936
or 1937
Sch 508; Woll G 660 I/I
Printer: Nielsen

Schiefler states that impressions of this lithograph
were printed in 1920 and 1924.

214
Inger Barth

Stone 1921; impression (1921)
Lithograph (transfer lithograph): crayon; black
ink; wove paper
Image: 588 × 610; paper: 700 × 905
Artist's inscription: Edv Munch // Gedruckt in 30
exemplaren. Stein vernichtet [l.r.]
NG.K&H.A.19530 (formerly NG.K&H.B.00613)
Purchased at City Auksjon, Oslo, September 1938
(cat. 152)
Sch 505; Woll G 663 I/I
Printer: Nielsen

Schiefler uses the title *Die Frau mit der Halskette
(Frau Barth)*. Inger Barth (1885–1950) was the wife
of chief surgeon Dr. Peter Barth. Munch painted
two full-length portraits of her in 1921 (Woll M
1399, 1400).

215
**Frankfurter Bahnhofplatz
during Rathenau's Funeral**
Bahnhofplatz i Frankfurt under Rathenaus likferd

Stone 1922; impression 1922
Lithograph (transfer lithograph): crayon; black
ink; medium-weight wove paper
Image: 299 × 419; paper: 378 × 496
Artist's inscription: Edv Munch // Rathenaus
begravelse. Frankfurt [l.r.; pencil]
Secondary inscription: No 3/29/8 1922 [l.l.; pencil]
NG.K&H. A.19024 (formerly NG.K&H.B.00612)
Gift from Munch on the occasion of his 70th
birthday exhibition at the Department of Prints
and Drawings. Included in the collection in 1936
or 1937
Sch 510; Woll G 673 I/I
Printer: Nielsen

Munch may have added the inscription "Rathenaus begravelse. Frankfurt" (Rathenau's Funeral.
Frankfurt) at the time of donating the print to
the National Gallery. Similar inscriptions can
be found on an impression that belonged to
Gustav Schiefler (Museum of Modern Art, inv.
no. 1217.1968) and one in the Munch Museum
(MM.G.439-4). The inscription "No 3/29/8 1922"
is the printer's numbering and dating of the
impression. Walter Rathenau (1867–1922) was a
German industrialist and politician, and one of
Munch's earliest patrons in Germany. He was shot
dead by radical nationalists on 24 June 1922. The
assassination caused outrage and was followed
by riots. On the day of Rathenau's funeral on 27
June, large demonstrations took place in all major
German cities. Munch heard about the murder
while in Zurich, and probably witnessed the
demonstration when he stopped off in Frankfurt
on his way home.

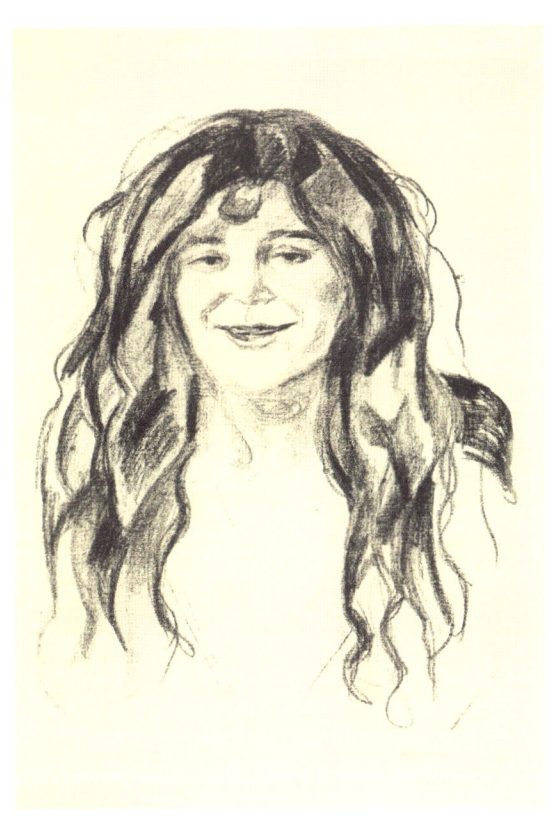

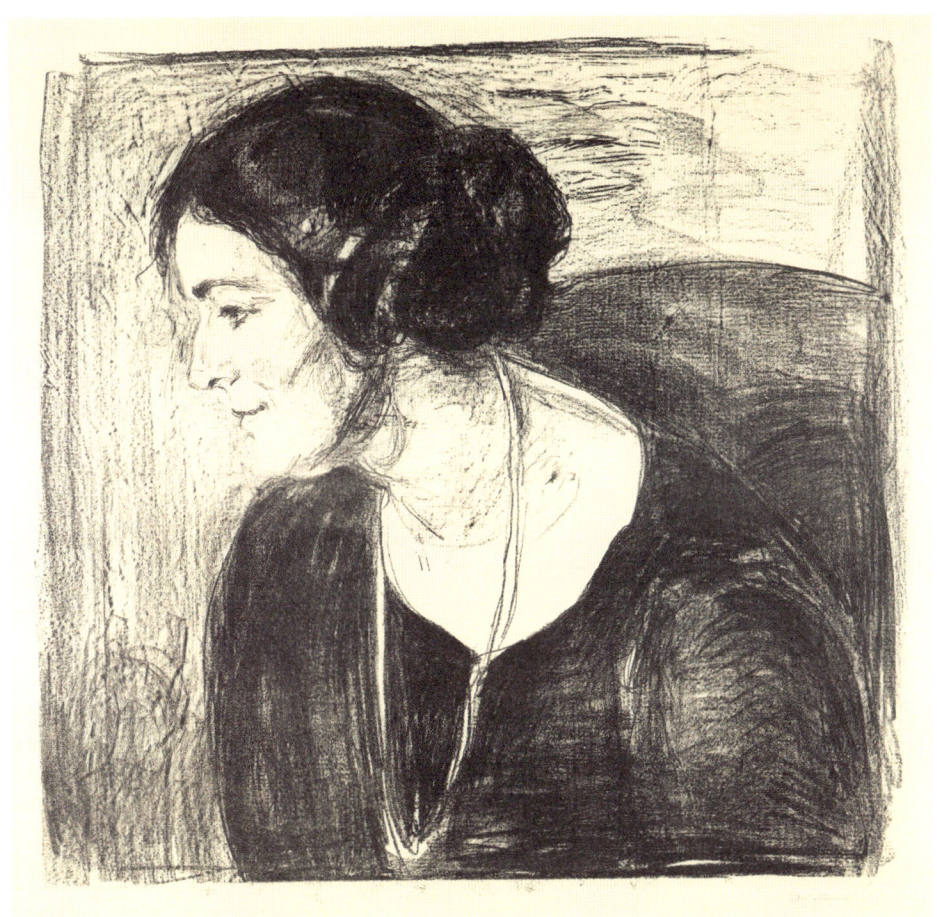

213

214

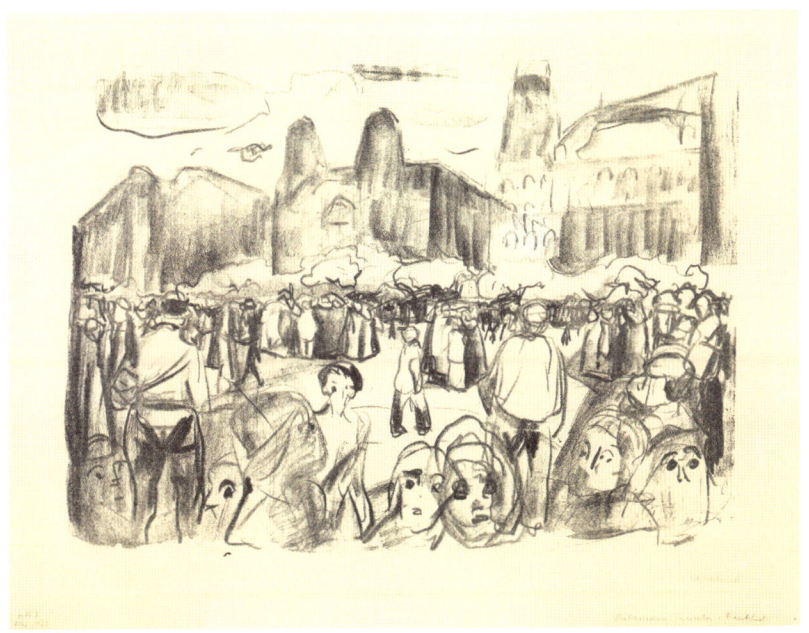

215

216
P.A. Munch's Tombstone in Rome
P.A. Munchs grav i Roma

Stone 1927; impression (1927)
Lithograph (transfer lithograph): crayon; black
ink; stiff wove paper
Image: 267 × 213; paper: 518 × 423
Artist's inscription: Edvard Munch
NG.K&H.A.19026
Provenance unknown
Woll G 680 I/I
Printer: Hagen (?)

The drawing that was transferred to the stone is
preserved (MM.T.1453). Peter Andreas Munch
(1810–63) was a historian and the artist's uncle.
Munch visited his grave in Rome in 1927. He made
two paintings of the same subject in the same
year (Woll M 1623, 1624).

217
Henrik Bull

Stone 1928; impression (1928)
Lithograph (transfer lithograph): crayon; black
ink; heavy, stiff wove paper
Image: 333 × 340; paper: 677 × 500
Artist's inscription: Edvard Munch
NG.K&H.A.19046 (formerly NG.K&H.B.00611)
Gift from Munch on the occasion of his 70th
birthday exhibition at the Department of Prints
and Drawings. Included in the collection in 1936
or 1937
Woll G 685 I/I
Printer: Nielsen

Gustav Schiefler received an impression from
Munch just before Christmas 1928; this provides
a reliable *terminus ante quem* for the dating of the
lithograph. Henrik Bull (1864–1953) was an architect and friend of Munch from childhood. He
designed the so-called Winter Studio at Ekely in
1929. Munch later painted two portraits of Henrik
Bull (Woll M 1745, 1746).

218
Kristian Schreiner

Stone 1928; impression (1928)
Lithograph: transfer lithograph, stone further
modified: crayon; black ink; wove paper
Image: 602 × 502; paper: 959 × 734
Artist's inscription: Edvard Munch
NG.K&H.A.19532 (formerly NG.K&H.B.00611)
Gift from Munch on the occasion of his 70th
birthday exhibition at the Department of Prints
and Drawings. Included in the collection in 1936
or 1937
Woll G 687 III/V
Printer: Nielsen

The drawing that was transferred to the stone
is preserved (MM.T.2880). The lithograph was
included in an exhibition in Stockholm in January
1929. Based on information provided by the artist,
it was dated 1928 in the catalogue of Munch's 1931
exhibition in Bielefeld. There exist monochrome
and two-colour impressions (two stones) of this
lithograph. The National Museum's impression
is pulled from the keystone. Kristian Schreiner
(1874–1957) was a professor of anatomy at the
University of Oslo and a trusted friend of Munch's
in his final years. Munch produced a series of
graphic portraits of him (Woll G 689, 690, 692,
693, 743, 744). He is also the subject of a large
collage that combines sections of lithograph and
watercolour (MM.T.2909).

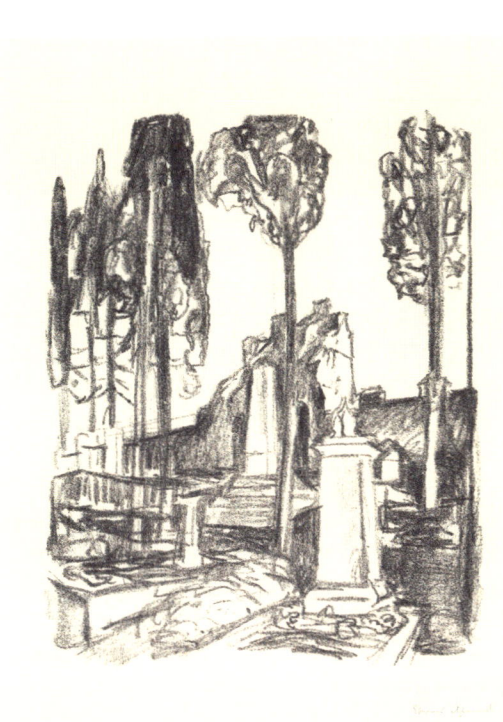

216

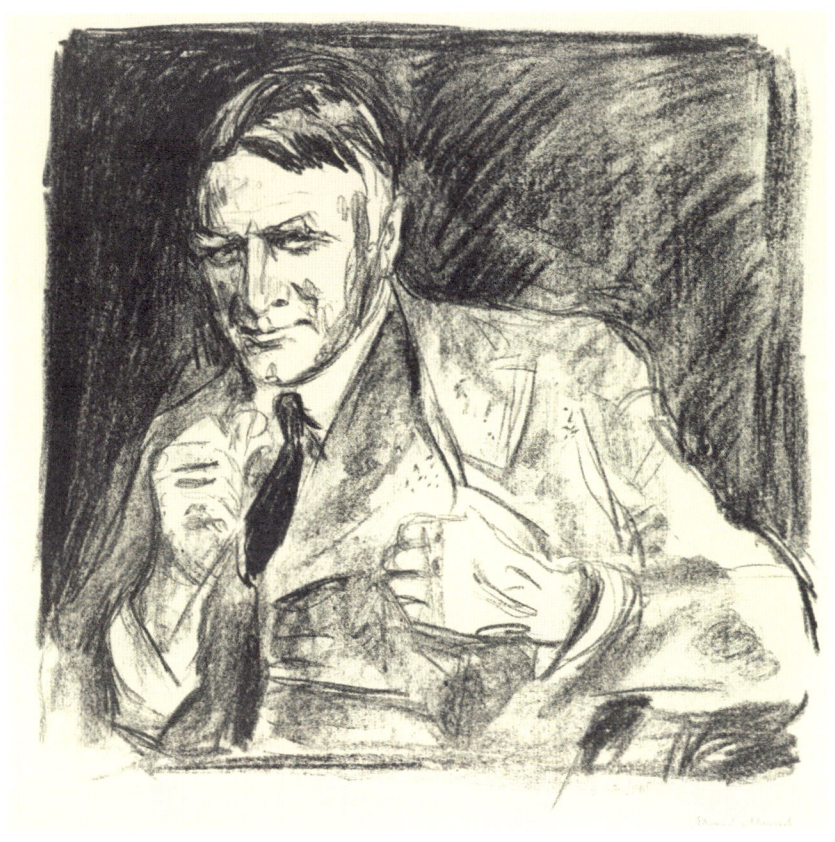

217

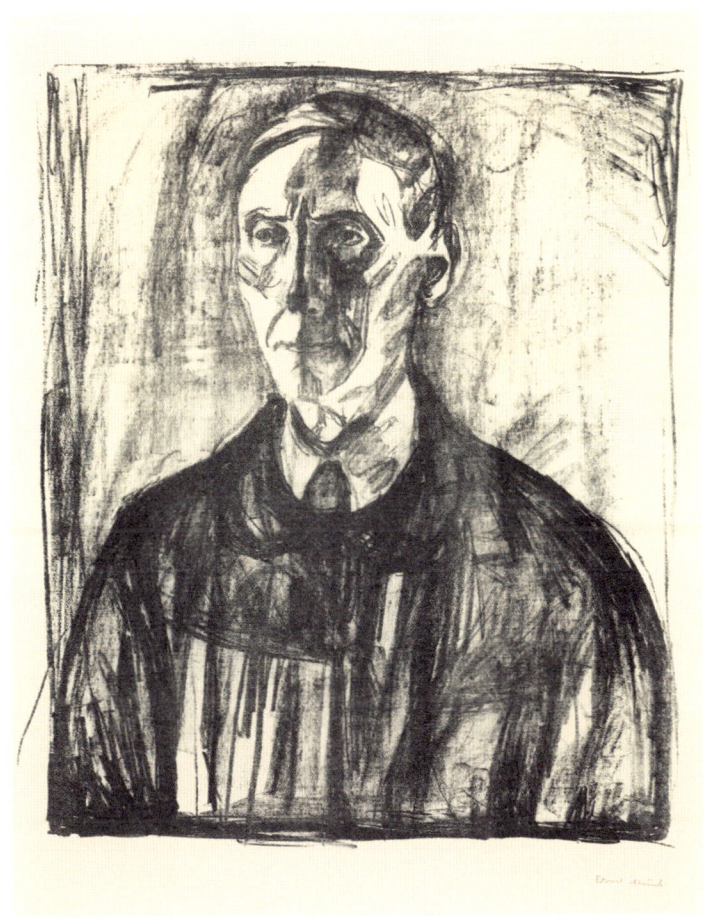

218

219
Brothel Scene
Bordellscene

Stone 1930; impression (1930)
Lithograph: crayon, tusche and scraper; black ink; stiff wove paper
Image: 415 × 541; paper: 485 × 710
Artist's inscription: Edvard Munch // Lokale "Zum lustigen Weibes" [l.r.; pencil]
NG.K&H.A.19047 (formerly NG.K&H.B.00613)
Purchased at City Auksjon, Oslo, September 1938 (not in catalogue)
Woll G 708 IV/IV
Printer: Nielsen

The lithograph was dated 1930 in the catalogue of Munch's 1931 exhibition at Flechtheim in Berlin. Munch had produced a corresponding painting in 1907 (Woll M 781), of which the lithograph is an inversion.

220
Self-Portrait with a Bottle of Wine
Selvportrett ved vinen

Stone 1930; impression (1930)
Lithograph: crayon and scraper; black ink; heavy, stiff papir
Image: 421 × 515; paper: 483 × 656
Artist's inscription: Edv Munch
Secondary inscription: Tryk nr. 20/Kildeborg [l.l.; pencil]
NG.K&H.A.19025 (formerly NG.K&H.B.00613)
Purchased at City Auksjon, Oslo, September 1938 (cat. 97)
Woll G 712 I/I
Printer: Nielsen

The inscription "Tryk nr. 20/Kildeborg" (Print no. 20/Kildeborg) is the printer's numbering and signature (A.P. Nielsen took the name Kildeborg). On the basis of information given by Munch himself, the lithograph was dated to 1930 in the catalogue of his 1931 exhibition in Bielefeld. Munch produced a corresponding painting in 1906 (Woll M 688), of which the lithograph is an inversion.

221
Weeping Woman. Morning
Gråtende kvinne. Morgen

Stone 1930; impression (1930)
Lithograph: crayon; black ink; wove paper
Image: 412 × 370; paper: 644 × 498
Artist's inscription: Edvard Munch // Morgen [l.r.]
NG.K&H.B.00614
Purchased at City Auksjon, Oslo, 19 January 1939 (cat. 6)
Woll G 713 I/I
Printer: Nielsen

The lithograph was included in an exhibition at Galleri Gauguin in Oslo in April 1930. The same scene features in a number of paintings from around 1907 (Woll M 773-777, 829). It is also the subject of one of Munch's very few sculptures (MM S 2). The lithograph is an inversion of the paintings. Several different titles have been applied. The title *Sørgende* (Grieving) was used in City Auksjon's catalogue (and later in the Department of Prints and Drawings' inventory).

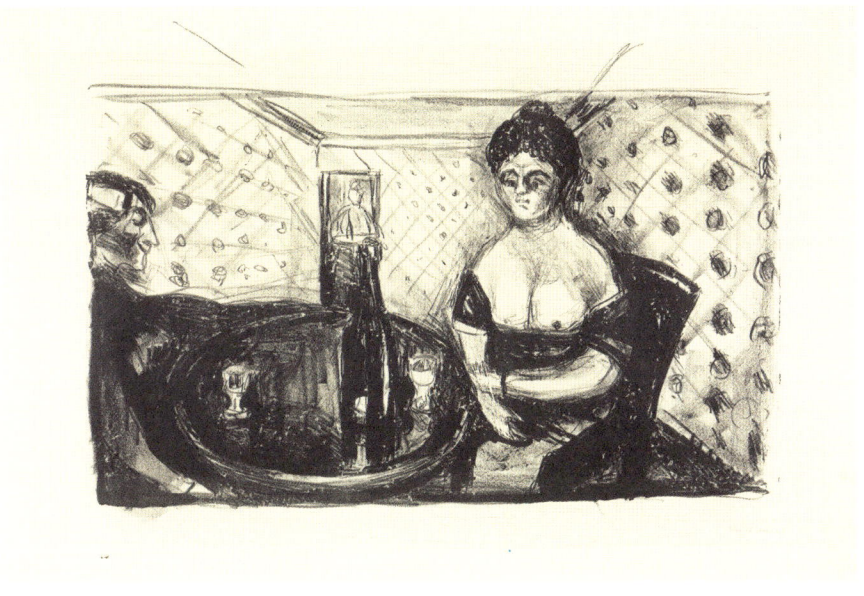

219

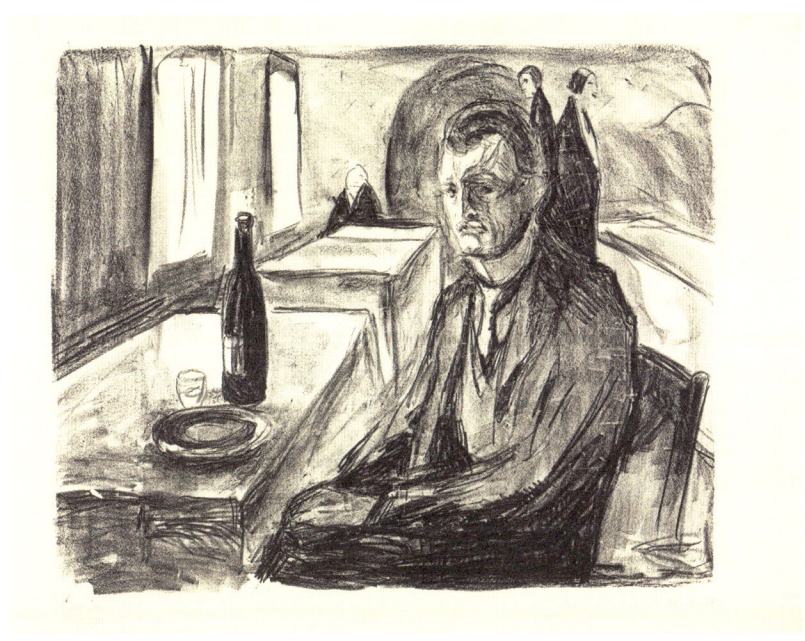

220

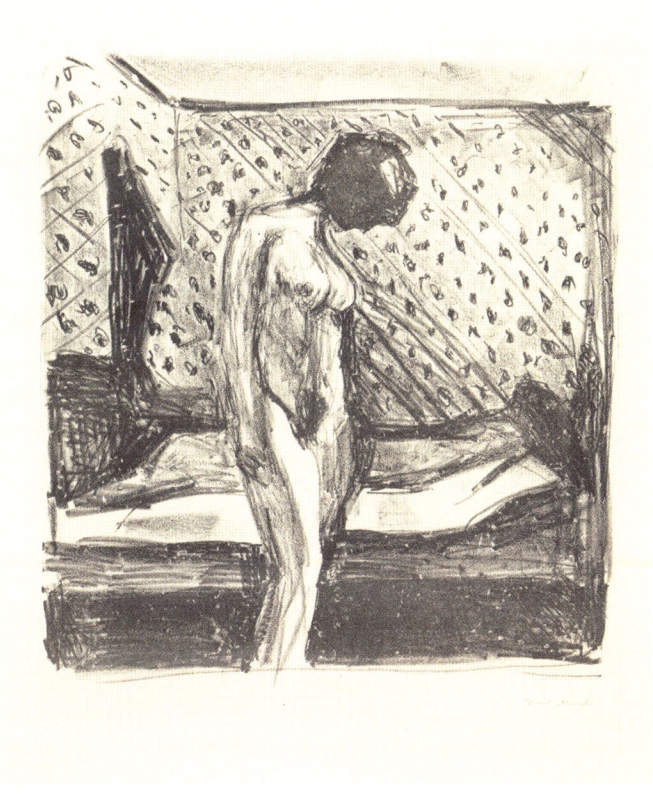

221

Appendix 1
Original prints
in books

222
Head of a Woman
Kvinnehode

Plate 1907; impression (1907)
Intaglio: drypoint
Image: 115 × 88
NG.K&H.B.09817
Sch 259; W132; Woll G 288
Printer: Sabo

Gustav Schiefler, *Verzeichnis des graphischen
Werks Edvard Munchs bis 1906*, Berlin: Bruno
Cassirer 1907 (between pp. VI and 1)

223
From Åsgårdstrand
Fra Åsgårdstrand

Plate 1907; impression (1907)
Intaglio: drypoint
Image: 90 × 128
NG.K&H.B.09818
Sch 260; W 133; Woll G 289
Printer: Sabo

Gustav Schiefler, *Verzeichnis des graphischen
Werks Edvard Munchs bis 1906*, Berlin: Bruno
Cassirer 1907 (between pp. VI and 1)

224
Norwegian Landscape
Norsk landskap

Plate 1908; impression (1919)
Intaglio: drypoint
Image: 105 × 150
NG.K&H.B.09819
Sch 268; W139; Woll G 298 III / III
Printer: PAN-presse

Herman Struck, *Die Kunst des Radierens*, Berlin:
Bruno Cassirer 1919 (between pp. 38 and 39)

225
Head of a Man
Mannshode

Plate 1906; impression (1917)
Intaglio: drypoint
Image: 119 × 88
NG.K&H.B.09820
Sch 243; W 128; Woll G 277

Curt Glaser, *Edvard Munch*, Berlin: Bruno Cas-
sierer, 1917 (frontispiece)

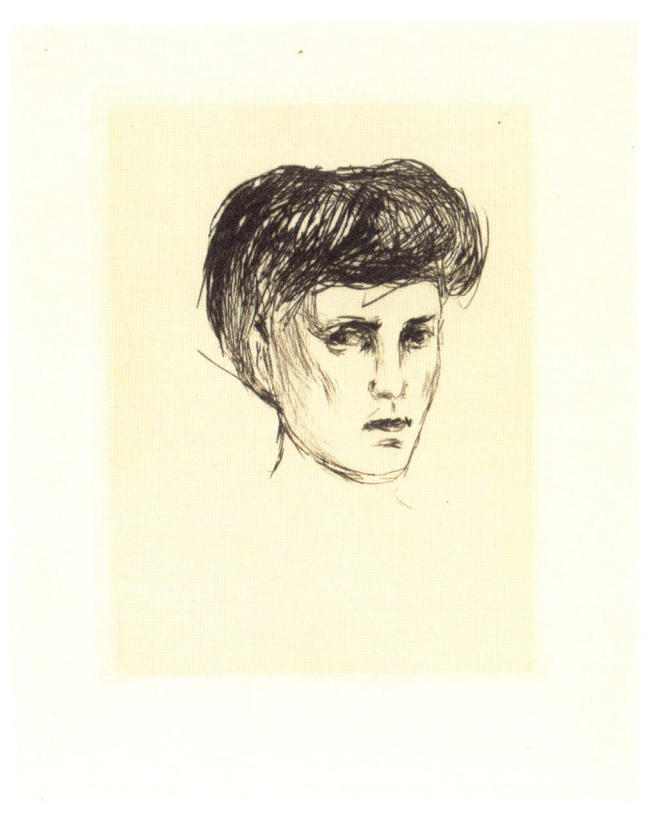

222

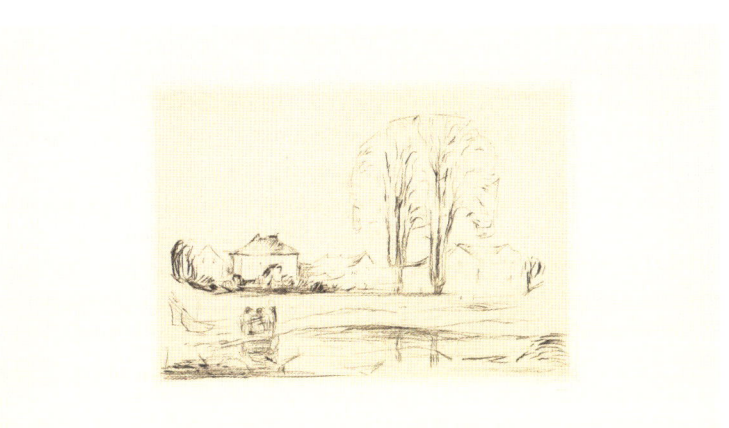

223

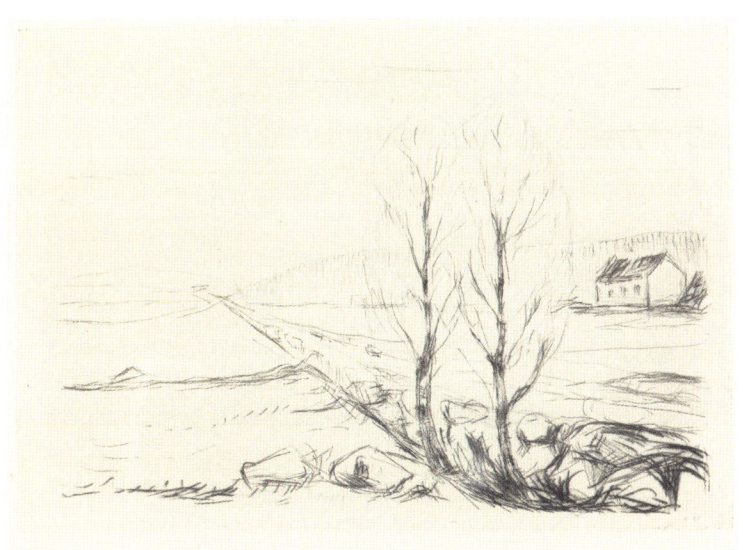

224

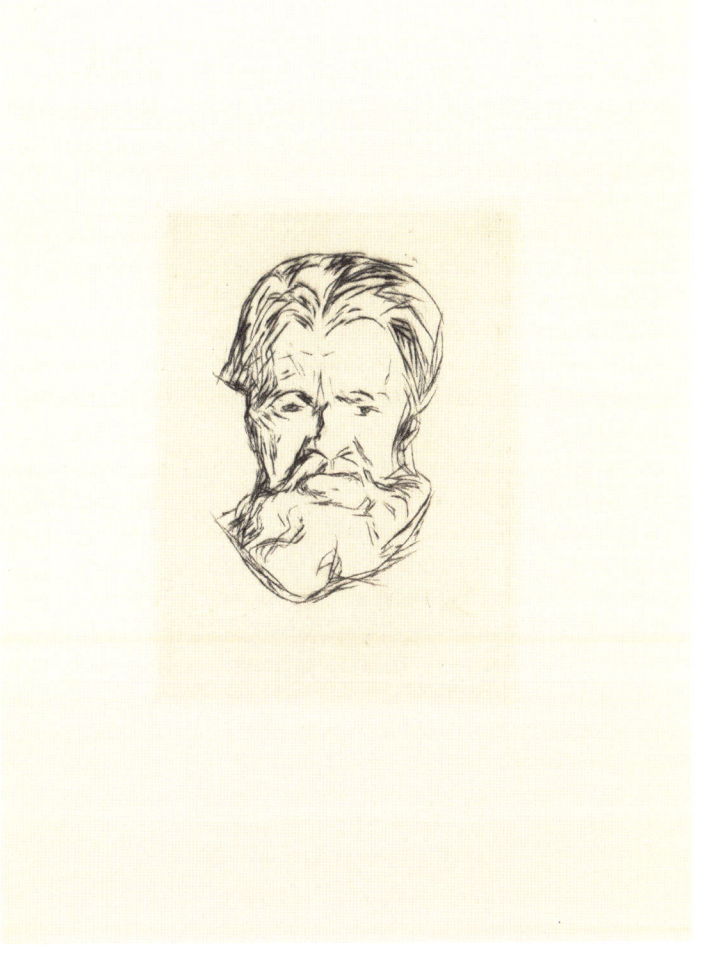

225

Appendix 2
Posters previously in the collection of the Oslo Museum of Decorative Art

The exact number of posters in the collection of the former Oslo Museum of Applied Art, is not known (April 2017), although it probably amounted to some 1,500 items. The collection was inventoried in the late 1990s and is currently being added to the museum's database.

A significant part of the collection was amassed during Henrik Grosch's time as director (1894–1919). His first acquisition, in 1896, of 300 posters from different countries (as well as books about posters) was exhibited at Kristiania Kunstforening in 1897, and detailed in an accompanying catalogue: Henrik Grosch, *Katalog over Kunstindustrimuseets plakatsamling*. Kristiania, 1897. The directors of the newly established museums of decorative art in Bergen and Trondheim, Johan Bøgh and Jens Thiis, also showed their interest in contemporary poster art. In contrast to the purely text-based poster, the picture poster, or art poster, as the genre has been called, emerged in Paris in the 1890s, with Jules Chéret as a notable pioneer and Henri Toulouse-Lautrec as an outstanding practitioner. A major factor in the growth of the genre was the development of colour lithography. In due course, the printing of picture posters also began in Norway, although production did not reach any significant level here until well into the 20th century.

Edvard Munch's poster production is limited and unusual. His first two contributions to the field combine the functions of theatre poster and programme. These small format, black and white designs were printed for Lugné-Poe's productions of Ibsen's *Peer Gynt* (see cat. 113) and *John Gabriel Borkman* (Woll G 108) at the Théâtre de l'Œuvre in Paris in, respectively, 1896 and 1897. Five of Munch's posters were made for his own exhibitions in Kristiania at: Dioramalokalet 1897 (see cat. 226); Hollændergaarden 1901 (*Metabolism*, Woll G 164); Dioramalokalet 1910 (*Chained Eagle*, Woll G 373); Tivoli Festivitetslokale 1914 (two posters, see cat. 227 and 228). He also made a poster for "The Norwegian Art Exhibition" at Charlottenborg, Copenhagen, in 1915 (see cat. 229).

226
Man's Head in Woman's Hair
Mannshode i kvinnehår

Stone 1897, impression (1897)
Colour lithograph: tusche and crayon; black, red, green, and gold inks; wove paper (pasted on canvas)
Image: 706 × 530; paper: 760 × 595
Signed on the stone: E Munch
Secondary inscription: 441. [u.l. recto; red colour pencil]
OK-17622
Provenance unknown
Not in Sch; Woll G 107
Printer: Petersen & Waitz, Kristiania

The image is a rubbing from the woodblock for *Man's Head in Woman's Hair* (see cat. 118), which was then transferred to a lithographic stone and further worked on. The poster was made for Munch's exhibition in the Dioramalokalet, Kristiania, 15 September–19 October 1897.

228
History
Historien

Stone 1914; impression (1914)
Lithograph: crayon; wove paper (pasted on canvas)
Image: 413 × 790; paper: 494 × 845
Artist's inscription: Edv Munch
Secondary inscription: 55 // 623. [l.l. recto; pencil]
OK-17723
Provenance unknown
Sch 426; Woll G 486 I / II
Printer: Nielsen

The lithograph was originally made as a poster for Munch's exhibition of his preparatory paintings for the University's central hall decorations, shown in Tivoli Festivitetslokale, Kristiania, May–June 1914 (see cat. 227); probably made at the time of the augmentation of the exhibition with a number of paintings and prints.

227
Towards the Light
Mot lyset

Stone 1914, impression (1914)
Colour lithograh: crayon and tusche; yellow, red, blue, and violet inks; wove paper (pasted on canvas)
Image: 915 × 720; paper: 890 × 755
Artist's inscription: Edv Munch
Secondary inscription: 624 [l.l. recto; pencil]
OK-17725
Provenance unknown
Not in Sch; Woll G 485 II A / B / III
Printer: unknown (in Kristiania)

The lithograph was originally made as a poster for Munch's exhibition "The University Decorations" in Tivoli Festivitetslokale, Kristiania, May–June 1914. This impression is, however, from an edition printed without text. (See cat. 228.)

229
Neutralia
Nøytralien

Stone1915; impression (1915)
Colour lithograph: tusche and crayon; blue, pink, and three green inks; wove paper (pasted on canvas)
Image: 755 × 485; paper: 926 × 725
Secondary inscription: 641 [l.r. recto; blue colour pencil]
OK-17724
Provenance unknown
Sch 459; Woll G 527A 1/2/B
Printer: Halvorsen & Larsen, Kristiania

Poster for a Norwegian exhibition in Copenhagen, with the text: "Den norske Kunstudstilling Charlottenborg Nov–Dec" (The Norwegian Art Exhibition Charlottenborg Nov–Dec).

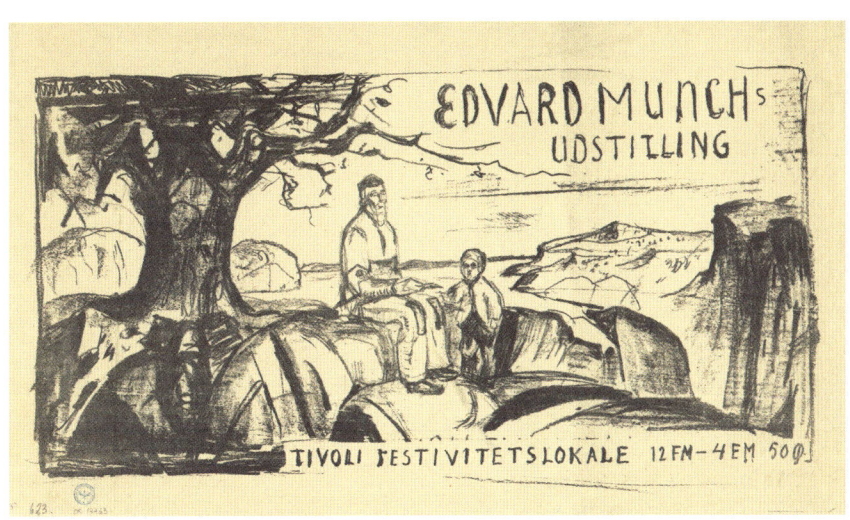

228

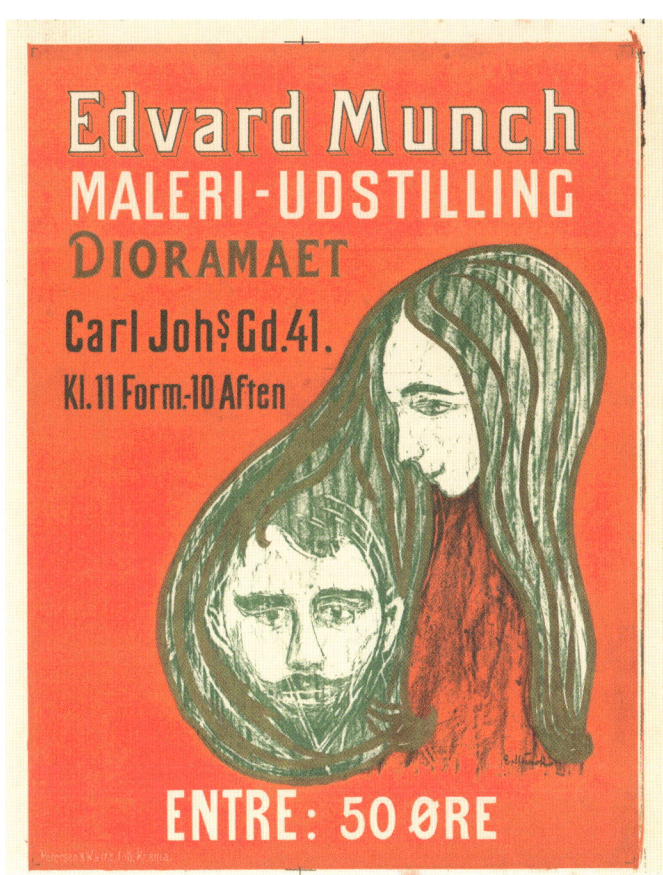

226

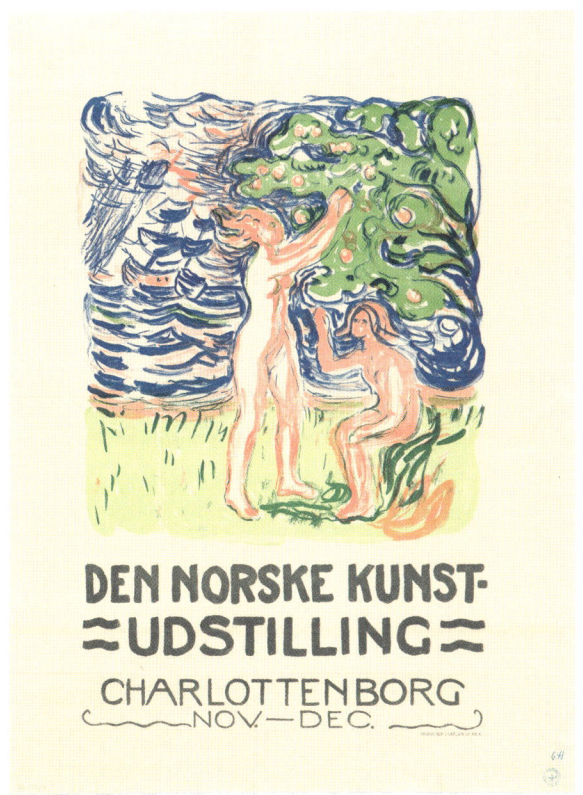

229

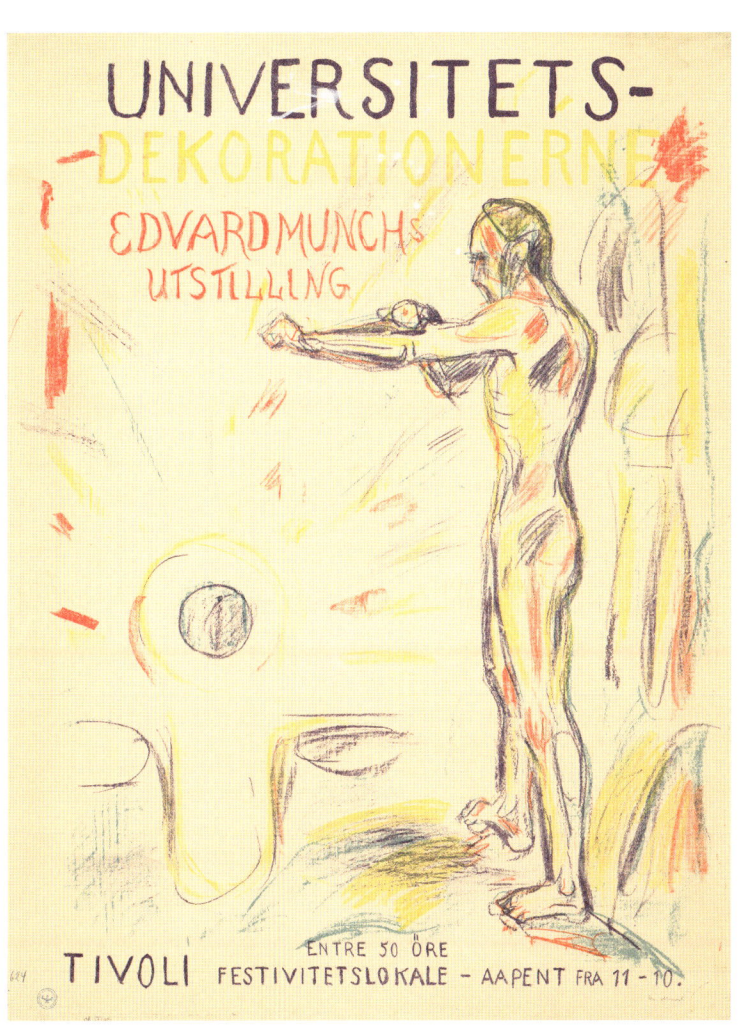

227

Catalogue: Drawings

Dimensions are the sheet of paper in mm height × width.

Inger Munch (1868–1952) was Edvard Munch's sister and the only sibling to outlive him. In his will, Munch bequeathed to her his correspondence and the right to choose 100 graphic works from his artistic estate. In addition, she owned some drawings. The correspondence was later handed over to the Munch Museum/City of Oslo Art Collections.

The National Museum's drawings are included in the Munch Museum's electronic catalogue of Munch's drawings, www.munch. emuseum.com

230
Scene from Bygdøy, (ca. 1881)
Fra Bygdøy

Pencil; wove paper; 152 × 248
Artist's inscription?: Fra Bygdö [l.c.; pencil]
NG.K&H.1953.0004
Purchased at auction, Wangs Kunst- og Auktions-forretning, Oslo, 1953

In his diary for 22 May 1881, Munch mentions a trip to Bygdøy with Henning Kloumann: "Kloumann and I took the boat over to Ladegaardsøen from Skarpsno. Kloumann bought soft drinks. Then walked along the beach at the south end of the island and made a sketch there." Harald Hals has identified the drawing as being of Bygdøy, but also reproduces a small drawing of Bygdøy Kongsgård. Assuming that both were drawn on the occasion noted in Munch's diary, Hals dates them to May 1881. It is possible that the inscription is of later date, which may explain why Munch did not write Ladegaardsøen, as he did in his diary, which was the official name of Bygdøy until 1877, but continued to be used long after.

Literature: Harald Hals II, *Edvard Munch og byen* (Oslo: Oslo Bymuseum, 1955), 21–22.

231
Portrait of a Young Woman, 1883
Portrett av ung kvinne

Pencil; wove paper; 257 × 184
Artist's inscription: 83 [l.r.; pencil]
NG.K&H.B.01039
Purchased from Marie Michelet Holst, widow of Dr. Elling Holst, December 1948

232
Male Head, 1883
Mannshode

Charcoal; wove paper; 455 × 320
Artist's inscription: Edv Munch 1883 [l.r.; pencil]
NG.K&H.B.00484
Purchased from Hans Lyche, 1931

In 1882 and 1883, Munch drew and painted many portrait studies of people with striking features. During this period he was sharing a studio with several other young artists at "Pultosten", the building on the corner at the lower end of Lille Grensen, which was also where Christian Krohg had a studio. Although Krohg was not strictly speaking a teacher to his younger colleagues, his influence can easily be seen in many of their works from this period.

Literature: Sidsel Helliesen, *Tegnekunst. Forarbeid - ferdig kunstverk*. Exhibition catalogue (Oslo: Nasjonalgalleriet, 1991, cat. 7); Sidsel Helliesen, *Tegnekunst. Fra forarbeid til ferdig kunstverk* (Oslo: Labyrinth Press, 1993), 26–27.

233
Two Boys, 1883
To gutter

Charcoal; wove paper; 367 × 457
Artist's inscription: Edv Munch Novb 83 [l.r.; pencil]
Secondary inscription: Blomqvist [u.l. verso; copying pencil]
NG.K&H.B.00446
Purchased from the estate of Eilif Peterssen, 1931

The drawing was shown in the National Annual Autumn Exhibition in 1883, where the twenty-year-old Edvard Munch made his debut with one painting and two drawings. The drawing was praised by Erik Werenskiold in his review in *Dagbladet*, 19.12.1883: "His drawing of two young boys is also highly artistic."

Literature: Eli Ingebretsen [Greve], *Norsk tegnekunst*, Kunst og Kultur's Series, edited by Harry Fett (Oslo: Gyldendal Norsk Forlag, 1932 B), 252.

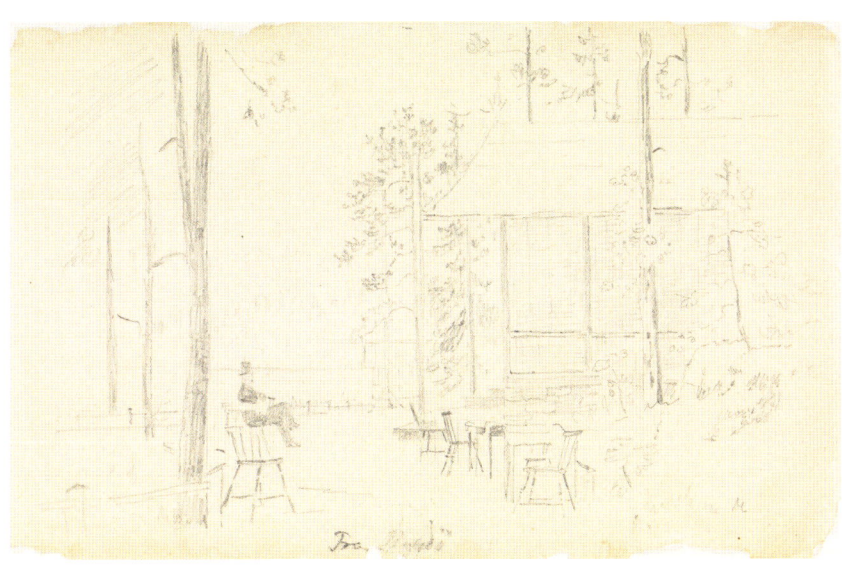

230

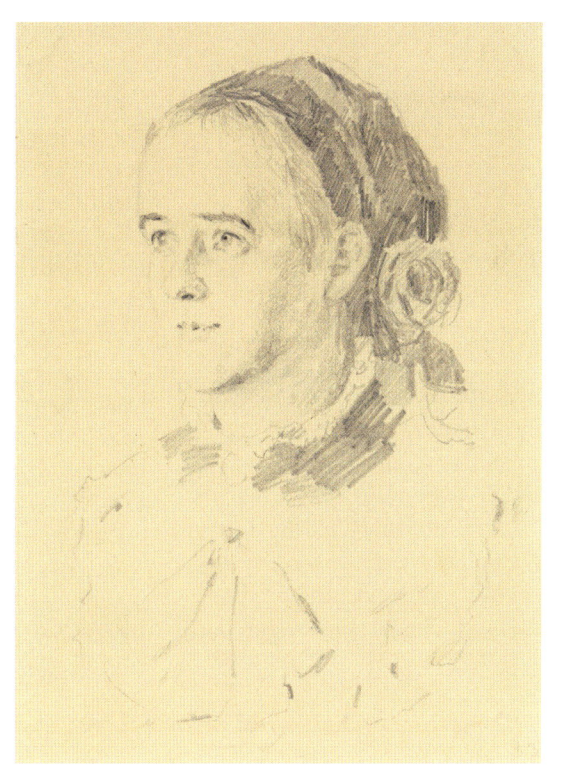

231

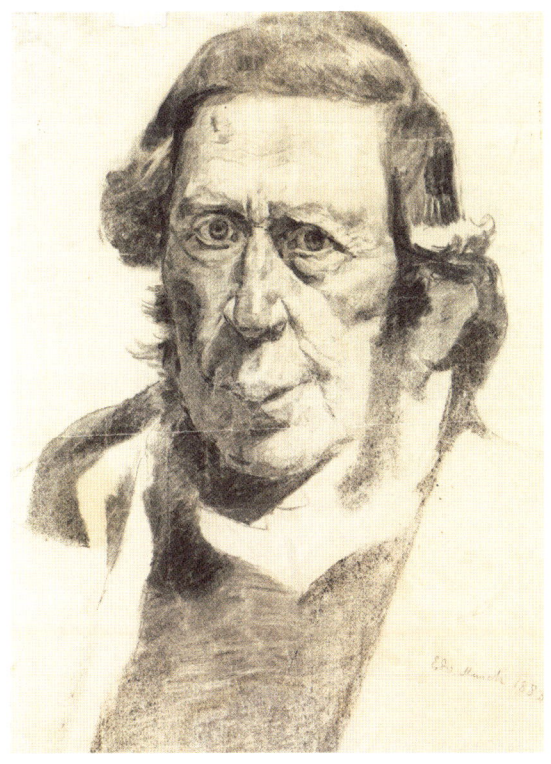

232

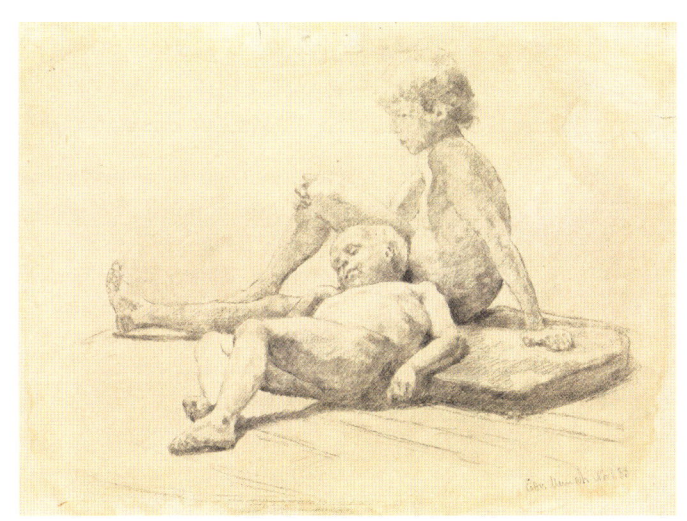

233

234
Naked Woman in Front of a House, (1883 or 1884)
Naken kvinne foran husvegg

Pen, pencil; wove paper; 154 × 157
Secondary inscription: Edvard Munch. 1884. [pen verso]
NG.K&H.1953.0006
Purchased at auction, Wangs Kunst- og Auktionsforretning, Oslo, 1953 (The seller was Ragnar Moltzau, who had acquired the drawing from Inger Munch.)

The inscription on the verso is by Inger Munch. She dated many of the drawings in her brother's estate, and her memory is impressive. Nonetheless, the inscriptions were made some fifty years after Munch made the drawings, and her datings are not entirely reliable. The image is ambiguous, and the National Museum previously used the title *Kvinneakt i interiør* (Female Nude in Interior).

235
Two Children by the Window; Fighting couple and a Devil; Girl seeing a Devil's feet, (ca. 1884)
To barn ved vinduet; Kranglende par og djevel; Jente som ser bukkeføtter

Pen; laid paper; 220 × 141
Secondary inscription: Ingløv fra / Inger. / 1882. [l.l. pen] // Tegning av E. Munch [l.r. pen]
NG.K&H.1951.0017 recto
Purchased from Ole Tronhuus, 1951 (Ole Tronhuus was the brother of Ingløv Munch Tronhuus, who was given the drawing by Inger Munch.)

Sketchbook sheet with three motives. The secondary inscription is by Inger Munch. She dated the drawing to 1882, but the style is more typical of 1884, which is also more probable for the drawing on the verso of the sheet (see cat. 236). The subjects can be linked to childhood recollections and descriptions in one of Munch's so-called literary diaries (MM.T.02761 p. 7-8).

236
Scene from Karl Johan Street, (ca. 1884)
Fra Karl Johan

Penn; laid paper; 141 × 220
NG.K&H.1951.0017 verso
Purchased from Ole Tronhuus, 1951 (Ole Tronhuus was the brother of Ingløv Munch Tronhuus, who was given the drawing by Inger Munch.)

Two paintings titled *Music on Karl Johan* (Munchmuseet, Woll M 175 and Kunsthaus Zurich, Woll M 176) were painted in 1889, but Munch had sketched and painted scenes from the same street many times before in the 1880s. Cat. 235 is on the recto of the same sheet.

237
Female Nude, 1887
Kvinneakt

Pencil; wove paper. The sheet has torn edges on all sides; 453 × 350
Artist's inscription: Edv Munch 87 [l.r.; pencil]
NG.K&H.B.00161
Anonymous gift, 1918

According to the inscription, this female nude was drawn in 1887. Munch drew and painted several nude studies in 1886 and 1887.

238
Karen Bjølstad, 1889

Pencil and black crayon; wove paper; 350 × 282
Artist's inscription: Edv Munch 89 [l.l.; pencil]
NG.K&H.B.00896
Purchased from Marie Michelet Holst, widow of Dr. Elling Holst, December 1948

Karen Bjølstad (1839-1931) was Edvard Munch's aunt, who took care of the children and the household after the death of her sister in 1868. She is identifiable in many of Munch's drawings and paintings.

239
Beach Landscape, (1891 or 1892)
Strandmotiv

Pencil; wove paper; 238 × 351
NG.K&H.1952.0025
Gift from Ragnar Moltzau, 1952 (Moltzau had acquired the drawing from Inger Munch.)

The coastline is the same as Munch used in his various versions of *Melancholy*, although here the male figure in the foreground is missing. (See the woodcut cat. 120, and the painting cat. 19)
   Literature: Arne Eggum, *Edvard Munch. Livsfrisen fra maleri til grafikk* (Oslo: J.M. Stenersen Forlag, 2000), reprint of 1990 edition, p. 117; Arne Eggum, *Edvard Munch: Malerier - Skisser og studier* (Oslo: Stenersen, 1983A), 74.

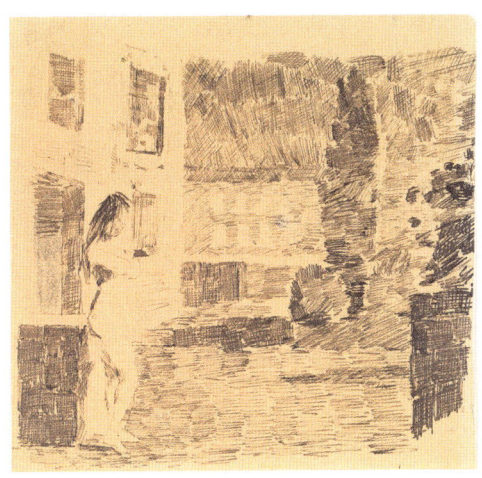

234

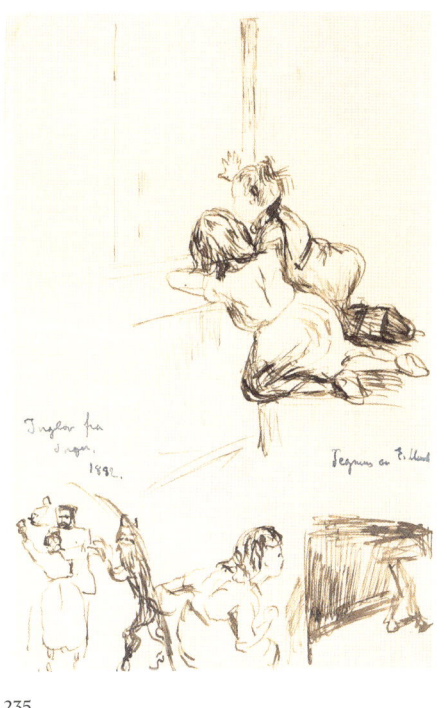

235

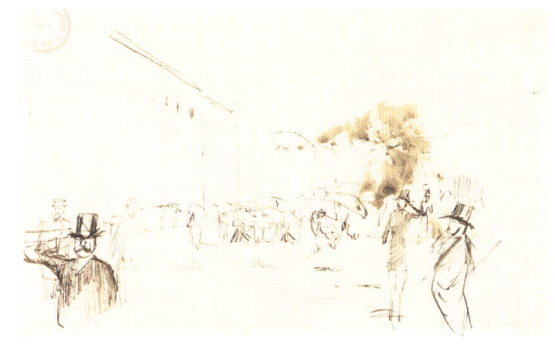

236

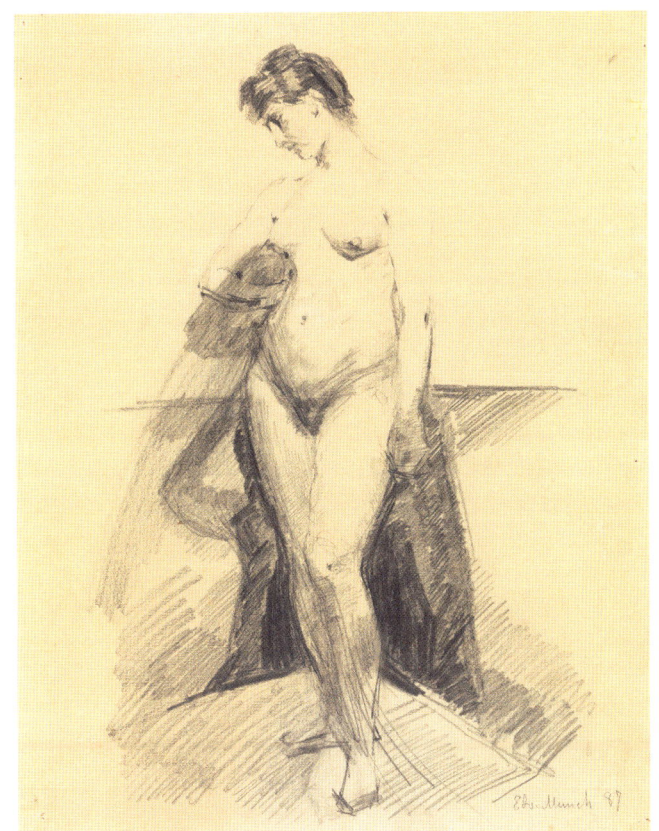

237

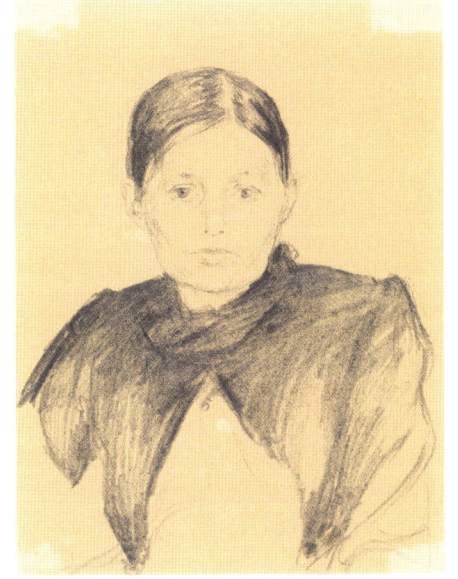

238

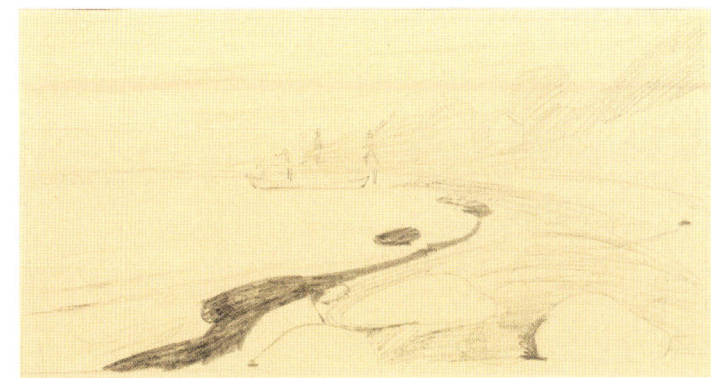

239

240
Woman, (ca. 1894)
Kvinnen

Penn; wove paper; 168 × 207
NG.K&H.1952.0026
Gift from Ragnar Moltzau, 1952 (Moltzau had acquired the drawing from Inger Munch.)

Munch probably developed the subject in paint in summer 1894 (Woll M 361 and 262), later repeating it in several paintings, as a lithograph (Woll 147), and two intaglios (Woll 21 and 22, see cat. 75). Like many other treatments of the subject, the drawing has often gone by the title *Kvinnen i tre stadier* (The Woman in Three Stages).
Literature: Arne Eggum, *Edvard Munch. Livsfrisen fra maleri til grafikk* (Oslo: J.M. Stenersen Forlag, 1990), 97.

241
Tupsy Jebe, (1896)

Charcoal and crayon; wove paper; 325 × 460
NG.K&H.A.19001 verso
Provenance unknown

The drawing is on the verso of a lithographic portrait of Sigbjørn Obstfelder (see cat. 117), and it is reasonable to assume that it was done shortly after the production of the print, which is dated to 1896. The woman is probably Tupsy Jebe, who was together with Munch in Paris for a few months in spring 1896, before she returned to Norway in June. Munch also portrayed her in a couple of other drawings (MM.T.00129-31 verso, MM.T.00129-47 recto) and an etching (cat. 98). Tupsy (Martha Caroline) Jebe (1871-1959) was a student of Hans Heyerdahl in Kristiania in 1895 and there is a portrait of her attributed to him (Sotheby's lot 98, 3 June 2009). Being one of the items in Munch's bequest to the City of Oslo, the portrait was sold at auction in 1947. Tupsy Jebe took the name Clement on marrying the Danish painter Gad Frederik Clement in 1902.

242
Street in Kragerø with Children, (1910)
Kragerøgate med barn

Watercolour, gouache and charcoal; heavy watercolour paper; 470 × 645
NG.K&H.B.08186
Purchased from Anne Birgitte Bjerke, 1967

Munch painted (Woll M 902 and 903) and drew the same street many times in the period 1910-15.
Literature: Hans-Martin Frydenberg Flaatten, *Soloppgang i Kragerø* (Kragerø: Kragerø kommune og Kragerø og Skåtøy historielag, 2009), 60–63.

243
Café Scene, (ca. 1925)
Kaféscene

Pen, laid envelope paper; 217 × 218
NG.K&H.1953.0005
Purchased at auction, Wangs Kunst- og Auktionsforretning, Oslo, 1953 (The seller was Ragnar Moltzau, who had acquired the drawing from Inger Munch.)

The drawing is made on an unfolded envelope and has an inscription by Inger Munch. There is no clear evidence for dating, but there is reason to believe the drawing is relatively late, probably from the 1920s.

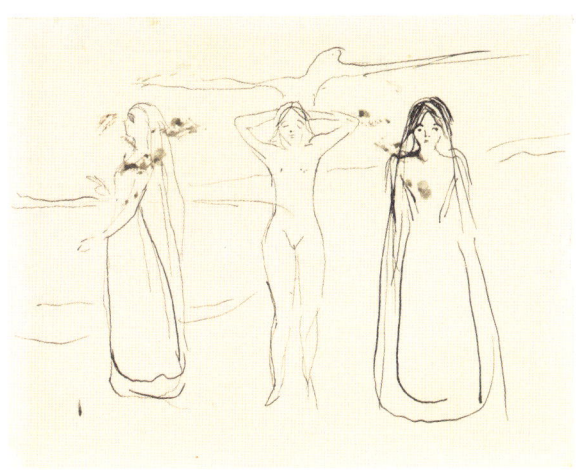

240

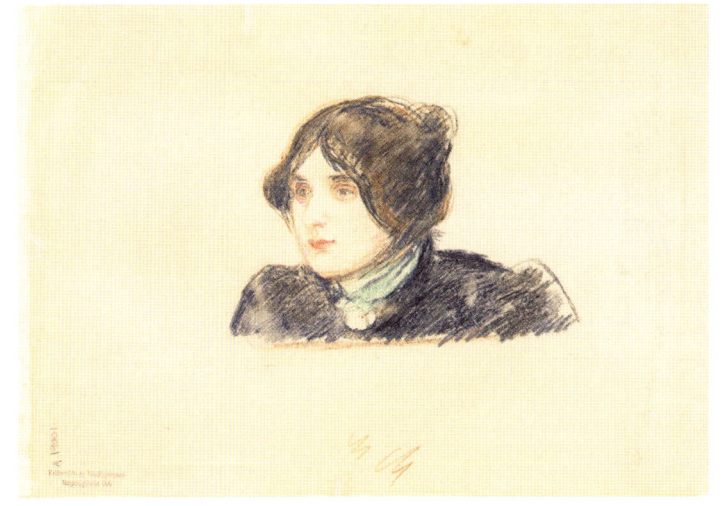

241

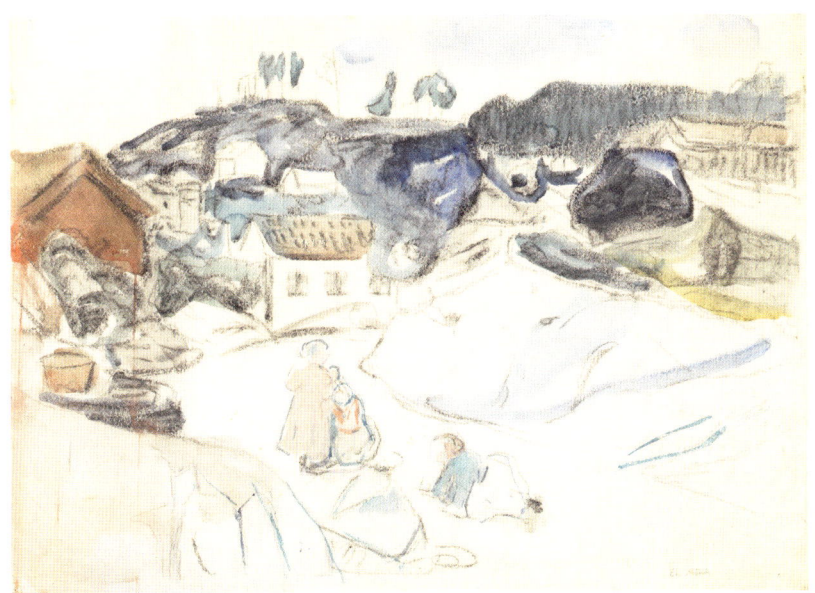

242

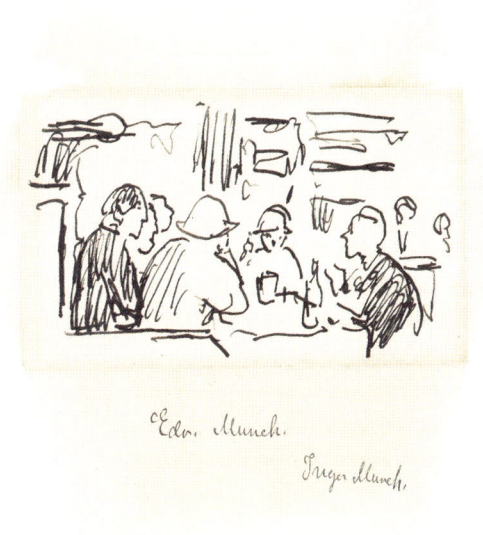

243

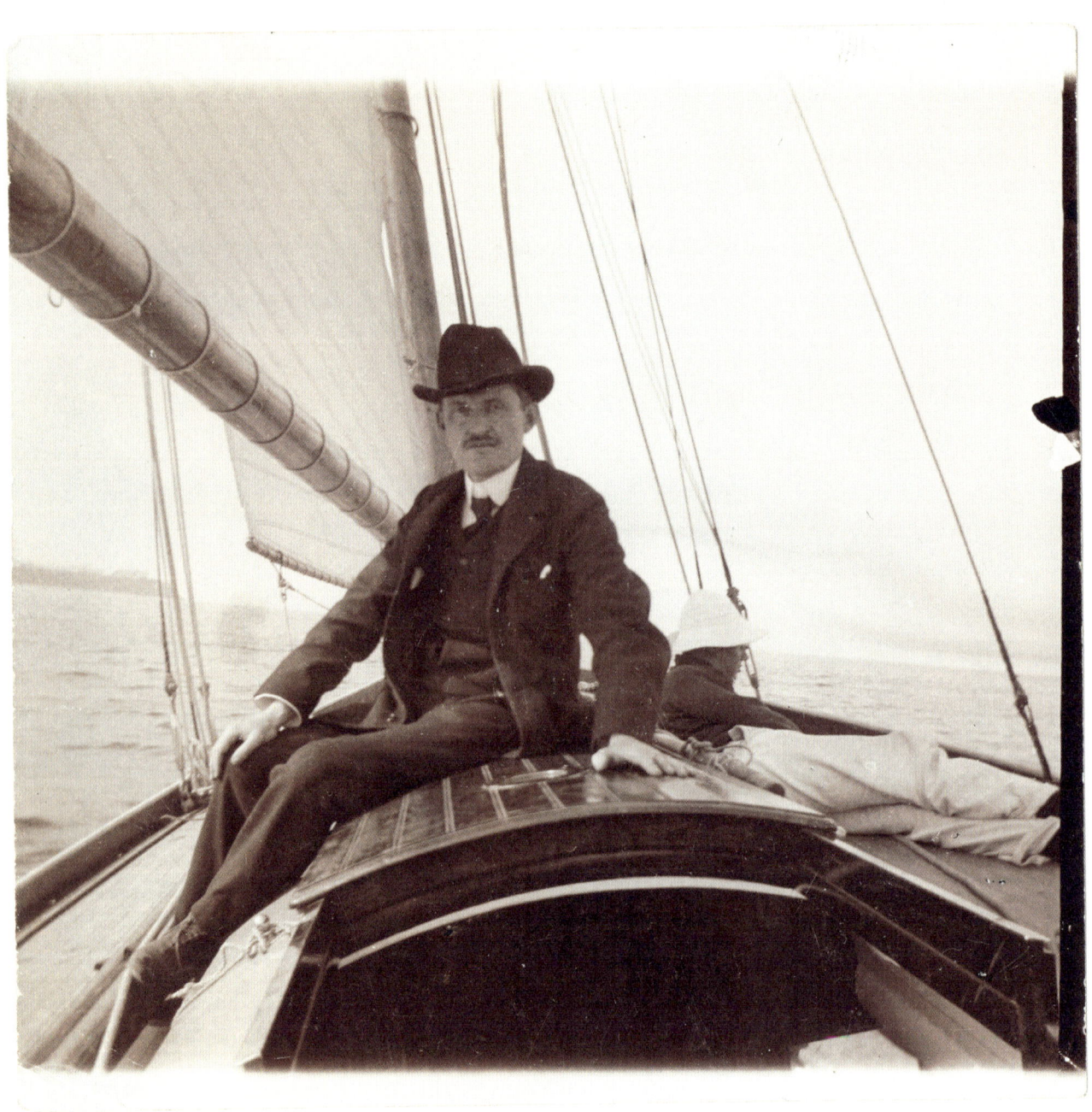

Edvard Munch:
Self-Portrait on a Sailboat, Åsgårdstrand, 1903
Collodion photography
Munchmuseet
MM.F.00029.01

1836–1837
In 1836, the Storting approves the establishment of a national art museum. The following year the Norwegian State Central Museum of Art is founded, later the National Gallery. In 2003, the institution is incorporated into the new National Museum of Art, Architecture and Design.

1863
Edvard Munch is born on 12 December on the Engelhaug farm, Løten, Hedmark. Parents: military doctor, later corps doctor, Christian Munch and Laura Cathrine Bjølstad.

1864
The family moves to Christiania (later Kristiania).

1868
Munch's mother Laura dies of tuberculosis. Her sister Karen Bjølstad moves in with the family and assumes responsibility for the household.

1877
Munch's older sister Johanne Sophie dies of tuberculosis.

1880
After a year at Kristiania Technical College, Munch decides to become a painter. He enrols at the Royal School of Design in Kristiania in December.

1882
The National Gallery moves into the Sculpture Museum, renting rooms on the upper floor. Munch shares a studio with six fellow artists of similar age in "Pultosten" at Stortings Plass in Kristiania. For a period the group receive free tuition from the painter Christian Krohg.

1883
Makes his debut at the Norwegian Industry and Art Exhibition in Kristiania with the painting *Study of a Head*. Participates in the National Annual Autumn Exhibition, where he receives praise for his *Early in the Morning*.

1884
The National Gallery's board approves a stipend for Munch from the Schäffer Legacy. This enables him to make his first study trip abroad, to Antwerp and to Paris the following year.

1885
Participates in the World Fair in Antwerp with a portrait of his sister Inger (cat. 6).

1886
The painting *The Sick Child* (cat. 8) is shown at the National Gallery as part of the National Annual Autumn Exhibition, under the title *Study*.

1889
First solo exhibition in Kristiania. Spends his first summer in Åsgårdstrand. The National Gallery's board recommends Munch for a government travel stipend. In the following years, he receives this stipend three times. Travels to Paris again. His father dies in November.

1891
The National Gallery purchases its first painting by Munch, *Night in Nice* (cat. 15).

1892
Major solo exhibition in Tostrupgården, Kristiania. His solo exhibition at the Verein Berliner Künstler in Berlin causes uproar and is closed after less than a week. The same exhibition is later shown in Düsseldorf and Cologne. In December he mounts a new exhibition in Berlin, this time renting rooms in the Equitable Palast. He remains in Berlin.

1894
The first book about Munch is published in June, *Das Werk des Edvard Munch*, with texts by Stanisław Przybyszewski, Franz Servaes, Willy Pastor, and Julius Meier-Graefe. Munch begins to work with prints and makes his first etchings.

1895
The painting *Self-Portrait with Cigarette* (cat. 32) is purchased for the collection. The painting *Jørgen Sørensen* (cat. 7) is received as a gift from Nikolai J. Sørensen, following the death of the portrait's subject the previous year. Munch spends the summer and the rest of the year in Norway, with an exhibition in Kristiania in October. In December, his brother Peter Andreas dies.

1896
Participates in an exhibition at the Salon des Artistes Indépendants in Paris in April and one at Bing's Salon de l'Art Nouveau in May. Produces his first woodcuts and prints colour lithographs in the workshop of Auguste Clot.

1897
The painting *Hans Jæger* (cat. 13) is purchased for the collection. In October, Munch has a major exhibition in the Dioramalokalet on Karl Johans gate in Kristiania.

1898
Rents a house in Åsgårdstrand together with Alfred Hauge for the summer. Later in the year, Munch buys a small house in the same place.

1899
The paintings *Spring* (cat. 12) and *Inger in Black and Violet* (cat. 20) are purchased for the collection.

1901
The paintings *Winter in the Woods* (cat. 37) and *White Night* (cat. 41) are purchased for the collection. In the autumn, a major exhibition is arranged in Kristiania, in the so-called Hollendergården in Stortingsgaten. By the end of the year, Munch is represented in the collection of the National Gallery with eight paintings and a large number of graphic works.

1902
At the Berliner Secession in April–May, Munch exhibits "a number of pictures of life". He spends the summer in Åsgårdstrand. Visits the art collector and oculist Max Linde in Lübeck and meets the art collector and critic Gustav Schiefler.

1904
Signs a contracts with Bruno Cassirer giving him the exclusive right to sell Munch's graphic works for the next three years.

1907
Gustav Schiefler publishes a catalogue of Munch's graphic works.

1908
Jens Thiis is appointed as the first director of the National Gallery. Thiis is already as an expert on and advocate for Munch's art. In the autumn, Munch travels to Copenhagen. There he is admitted to Dr. Daniel Jacobson's private clinic following a nervous breakdown. In the same year he is awarded the Norwegian Order of St. Olav.

1909
With financial support from the A.C. Houen foundation, the National Gallery purchases five paintings from Munch's major solo exhibition at Blomqvist Kunsthandel in Kristiania: *Puberty* (cat. 26), *The Day After* (cat. 27), *Ashes* (cat. 30), *On the Veranda* (cat. 45), and *The Frenchman* (cat. 46). Munch moves back to Norway and rents the property Skrubben near Kragerø. Prepares preliminary sketches for the competition to decorate the Aula (central hall) at Kristiania University.

1909–1910
Buys the property Nedre Ramme in Hvitsten. Olaf Schou donates a large collection of art to the National Gallery. The gift includes ten paintings by Munch: *Betzy Nilsen* (cat. 10), *Moonlight by the Mediterranean* (cat. 18), *Death in the Sickroom* (cat. 22), *The Sick Child* (second version from 1896, now in the Gothenburg Museum of Art), *The Scream* (cat. 23), *Madonna* (cat. 29), *Young Woman Washing* (cat. 33), *Mother and Daughter* (cat. 35), *The Dance of Life* (cat. 40) and *The Girls on the Bridge* (cat. 42).

1910
Major exhibition in the Dioramalokalet in Kristiania with around 100 paintings and 200 graphic works.

1912
The National Gallery receives the painting *Julius Meier-Graefe* (cat. 24) as a gift from the eponymous subject. In May, Munch travels to Paris via Copenhagen. Then to Cologne, where he is one of the main exhibitors at the Sonderbund exhibition, alongside Vincent van Gogh, Paul Gauguin, Paul Cézanne, and Pablo Picasso.

1913
Major celebrations to mark Munch's 50th birthday in December.

1914
In May, Kristiania University accepts Munch's decorations for the Aula. World War I breaks out in late summer.

1915
The museum receives the painting *Midsummer* (cat. 51) as a gift from Olaf Schou. Munch spends spring and summer in Hvitsten, where he works on the Aula decorations.

1916

Buys the property Ekely on the outskirts of Kristiania, moving there in the spring. It becomes his principal residence for the remainder of his life. Completes the decorations for the university Aula, which are unveiled on 19 September.

1917

The museum purchases the painting *Night in Saint-Cloud* (cat. 14) for the collection. Curt Glaser publishes the book *Edvard Munch* in Berlin. In November, Munch exhibits 27 paintings and some 150 graphic works in Copenhagen.

1918

Large exhibition at Blomqvist Kunsthandel, Kristiania, in February, where Munch shows paintings from what he now refers to as the Frieze of Life. For the occasion, he publishes a booklet with the same title.

1919

Munch falls seriously ill, possibly with the Spanish flu. Creates several works that address his illness (see cat. 55).

1920

Munch commissions the construction of a winter studio at Ekely, designed by Arnstein Arneberg. Visits Berlin and Paris for the first time since World War I.

1921

The museum buys the work *Self-Portrait* (cat. 47) for the collection. The painting *Flowery Meadow at Veierland* (cat. 11) is received as a gift from Jacob Woxen. Munch exhibits paintings and works on paper in Berlin, Dresden, Chemnitz, and Hamburg. Makes sketches for the decoration of the dining hall at the Freia chocolate factory, Kristiania.

1922

Kunsthaus Zürich mounts a substantial retrospective with 73 paintings and 433 graphic works. Munch completes the Freia decorations.

1923

Munch is guest of honour at the Anniversary Exhibition of Nordic Art in Gothenburg, alongside the Danish painter J.F. Willumsen. Munch participates with 29 paintings.

1924

In Bergen, the Rasmus Meyer Collection opens as a public museum in March, where a significant number of works are by Munch. In the same year, the National Gallery inaugurates a room devoted to Munch.

1925

Kristiania changes its name to Oslo. Munch visits Lübeck, Berlin, Venice, Munich, and Wiesbaden. He makes copies of his own paintings *Ashes* and *The Dance of Life* in the National Gallery collection. After a summer in Norway, he travels to Paris in October, stopping at various other destinations en route.

1926

Munch's sister Laura dies. In January, the Thiel Gallery opens in Stockholm, with many works by Munch. Major exhibition in Mannheim, with 74 paintings and some 150 graphic works (1926-1927).

1927

To Berlin in February in connection with a major retrospective in the Nationalgalerie, with a total of 244 works by Munch. In Oslo, a slightly expanded version of the same exhibition opens in the National Gallery on 8 June. The museum receives the painting *Bathing Man* (cat. 54) as a gift from the artist. Munch starts sketching ideas for the decoration of the new City Hall in Oslo.

1928

Prepares several proposals for the decorations for Oslo City Hall. The second volume of Gustav Schiefler's catalogue of Munch's graphic works is published.

1929

Rebuilds and extends his winter studio at Ekely, based on drawings by architect Henrik Bull.

1931

The first painted version of *The Sick Child* (cat. 8) is acquired for the collection in exchange for the second painted version, which is now in the Gothenburg Museum of Art. Munch's aunt Karen Bjølstad dies.

1933

The painting *Rue Lafayette* (cat. 16) is purchased for the collection. The National Gallery marks Munch's 70th birthday in December with an exhibition of his graphic works. On the same occasion he is awarded the Grand Cross of the Order of St. Olav. Jens Thiis and Pola Gauguin each publish a monograph on Munch.

1935

The museum receives two paintings as a gift from Harald Nørregaard: *Aase Nørregaard* (cat. 38) and *Aase and Harald Nørregaard* (cat. 39).

1936

The Norwegian author, art collector, and financier Rolf E. Stenersen offers his art collection to the municipality of Aker (later part of Oslo). It includes more than 20 paintings and around 400 graphic works by Munch.

1937

On the occasion of its centenary celebration, the National Gallery receives seven paintings as a gift from Charlotte and Christian Mustad: *Inger Munch in Black* (cat. 6), *Bathing Boys* (cat. 28), *Two Nudes* (cat. 44), *Winter on the Fjord* (cat. 50), *Man in the Cabbage Field* (cat. 52), *Self-Portrait with the Spanish Flu* (cat. 55), and *Autumn Ploughing* (cat. 56). A spacious new top-lit hall devoted to Munch's art on the museum's upper floor is inaugurated. In Germany, his art is labelled as "entartet" (degenerate) and 82 of his works are confiscated from German museums.

1938-39

With financial support from the Olaf Schou endowment fund, the museum purchases the paintings *Thorvald Torgersen* (cat. 2), *Self-Portrait* (cat. 9), *Moonlight* (cat. 21), and *House with Red Virginia Creeper* (cat. 36).

1940

War breaks out and Norway is occupied by Germany. Munch writes a will in which he leaves his entire art collection to the City of Oslo.

1942

Under the directors appointed by the government of occupation, the National Gallery mounts the exhibition "Kunst og ukunst" (Art and Non-Art), which includes several paintings by Munch.

1943

Munch's 80th birthday is celebrated on 12 December.

1944

Munch dies at Ekely on 23 January.

1945

The National Gallery exhibits Munch's bequest to the City of Oslo. This later forms the basis for the Munch Museum, which opens in Oslo in 1963.

1946

The National Gallery mounts a major exhibition of Munch's woodcuts. The museum receives the painting *Thorvald Løchen* (cat. 53) as a bequest from Ingeborg and Thorvald Løchen.

1947

The museum purchases 26 works on paper by other artists from Edvard Munch's estate, including works by Henri Toulouse-Lautrec, Lovis Corinth, Max Beckmann, Erich Heckel, and Paul Klee.

1951

The museum receives the painting *Enchanted Forest* (cat. 43) as a bequest from Alfred Larsen.

1958

The painting *From Vestre Aker* (cat. 1) is purchased for the museum's collection.

1959

The museum enters an agreement for a major bequest from Charlotte and Christian Mustad. The bequest is enacted on the latter's death in 1970.

1964

The painting *Study of a Head* (cat. 4) is purchased for the collection.

1970

The museum receives the last part of Charlotte and Christian Mustad's bequest, consisting of the paintings *Andreas Reading* (cat. 3), *Around the Paraffin Lamp* (cat. 5), *The Kiss* (cat. 17), *Melancholy* (cat. 19), *Ragnhild Bäckstsröm* (cat. 24), *Moonlight* (cat. 31), *Parisian Model* (cat. 34), *Mrs Schwarz* (cat. 48), *Seated Nude* (cat. 49), and *Workers Returning Home* (cat. 57).

1994

The painting *The Scream* (cat. 23) is stolen. The work is found and returned later the same year.

2009

The National Museum presents an exhibition devoted to *The Sick Child* (cat. 8) in the National Gallery, which brings together all versions of the painting.

2013

In collaboration with the Munch Museum in Oslo, the National Museum marks the 150th anniversary of Munch's birth with an extensive exhibition in the National Gallery and the Munch Museum.

2022

A catalogue detailing all the works by Munch in the collection of the National Museum is published in connection with the opening of the museum's new home at Vestbanen in Oslo.

Exhibitions 1883-2019

1883 Kristiania. Den norske Industri- og Kunstudstilling. 16 June–21 October
1885 Antwerp. *L'exposition universelle.* 2 May–2 November
1886 Kristiania. Nationalgalleriet, Kunstudstillingen [National Annual Autumn Exhibition]. 18 October–5 December
1888 Copenhagen. Den Nordiske Industri-, Landbrugs- og Kunstudstilling. From 18 May 1888
1889 Kristiania. Studentersamfundets lille sal, *Edv. Munchs Maleriudstilling.* 20 April–12 May
1890 Kristiania. Tivolis Udstillingsbygning, *Kunstudstillingen* [National Annual Autumn Exhibition]. 6 October–9 November
1891 Munich. Glaspalast, *Münchener Jahresausstellung von Kunstwerken aller Nationen.* From 24 July
1891 Kristiania. Tivolis Udstillingsbygning. *Statens Kunstudstilling* [National Annual Autumn Exhibition]. 8 November–13 December
1892 Kristiania. Juveler Tostrups Gaard, *Edvard Munchs maleriudstilling.* 14 September–4 October
1892 Berlin. Verein Berliner Künstler. Architektenhaus, *Sonderausstellung des Malers Eduard Munch.* 5–12 November; Düsseldorf. Eduard Schulte. From 20 November; Cologne. Eduard Schulte December; Berlin. Equitable-Palast. 26 December–January 1893; Copenhagen. Georg Kleis. Skandinavisk Kunstudstillings lokaler, *Eduard Munch's samlede arbejder.* 24 February–14 March 1893; Breslau. Kunstverein Lichtenberg, *Sonderausstellung des Malers Eduard Munch April.* 1893; Dresden. Theodor Lichtenberg Nachfolger. Victoriahaus. May; Munich. Kunstverein Lichtenberg. June 1893
On the initiative of the painter Adelsteen Normann, the Verein Berliner Künstler invited Munch to mount a solo exhibition at the Architektenhaus in November 1892. The exhibition created a scandal and was closed after less than a week. It was subsequently shown in Düsseldorf and Cologne. In late December Munch hired the Equitable-Palast to present the exhibition again in Berlin. It was in essence the same exhibition that was shown in Copenhagen, Breslau, Dresden and Munich in 1893.
1893 Berlin. Unter den Linden, *Eduard Munch Gemäldeausstellung.* From 3 December

1894 Stockholm. Konstföreningens lokale (arranged by the art dealer Theodor Blanch), *Edvard Munchs utställning.* 1–31 October
1895 Berlin. Ugo Barroccio, Unter den Linden, *Edvard Munch und Axel Gallen.* 3–24 March
1895 Kristiania. Blomqvist Kunsthandel, *Edvard Munch.* From 1 October [14 new pictures were added to the exhibition on 22 October]; Bergen. Bergens Kunstforening. 24 November–15 December; Stavanger. Stavanger Kunstforening. May 1896
1896 Paris A. *12e Exposition - Salon des Artistes Indépendants.* 1 April–31 May
1896 Paris B. Salon de l'Art Nouveau. S. Bing, *Edouard Munch.* From 19 May
1897 Paris. *13e Exposition - Salon des Artistes Indépendants.* 3 April–31 May
1897 Stockholm. *Almänna Konst- och Industri-utställningen.* 15 May–3 October
1897 Kristiania. Dioramalokalet, *Edvard Munch - Maleriudstilling.* 15 September–17 October
1897 St. Petersburg. Det Russiske Selskabs Lokaler, *Skandinavisk Udstilling.* From 23 October
1898 Copenhagen. *Den Frie Udstilling.* From 26 March
1898 Dresden. Dresdner Kunst-Salon. Galerie Arno Wolfframm, *Eduard Munch* December
1900 Dresden. Dresdner Kunst-Salon. Galerie Arno Wolfframm, *Sonder-Ausstellung von Edvard Munch.* 22 April–May
1900 Kristiania. Dioramalokalet. December
1901 Kristiania. Hollændergården, *Edvard Munchs Maleriudstilling.* From 23 September–ca. 20 October [A new hanging from 5 October]
1902 Berlin. Kurfürstendamm, *Fünfte Kunstausstellung der Berliner Secession.* 26 April–May
1902 Kristiania. Blomqvist Kunsthandel. *Edv. Munch - Th. Kittelsen.* 24 September–17 October. The exhibition travelled on to Drammen, Hamar, Trondheim and Bergen.
1903 Berlin. Paul Cassirer. 17–31 January
1903 Hamburg. Paul Cassirer. April
1903 Leipzig. P.H. Beyer & Sohn February–March
1903 Paris. *19e Exposition - Salon des Artistes Indépendants.* 20 March–25 April
1904 Vienna. *Vereinigung bildender Künstler Österreichs Secession. XIX Kunst-Ausstellung.* 16 January–6 March
1904 Hamburg. Paul Cassirer. 16 May–June

1904 Copenhagen. Den Frie Udstillings lokale ved Nørrebanegaarden. 4–30 September
1904 Kristiania. Dioramalokalet, *Edvard Munch udstilling.* From 16 October
1904 Berlin. Paul Cassirer. December–January 1905
1905 Prague. Umelcú "Manes" V Praze (Galerie Manes), *Edvard Munch.* 5 February–12 March
1906 Dresden. Sächsischer Kunstverein. Ca. 11–25 February
1906 Hamburg. Galerie Commeter. From 7 March
1906 Chemnitz. Kunsthütte zu Chemnitz, *Kollektion des Norwegers Munch.* From 17/18 March
1906 Berlin. Eduard Schulte. 13 May–7 July
1906 Hagen. Museum Folkwang. From 1 October
1906 Copenhagen. Charlottenborg, *Den norske Udstilling.* From 1 October
1906 Weimar. Grossherzogliches Museum für Kunst und Kunstgewerbe, *Werken von Edvard Munch in Kösen.* From 11 November
1907 Berlin. Paul Cassirer, *Edvard Munch.* 24 January–18 February
1907 Bielefeld. Kunst-Salon Fischer, *Collectiv-Ausstellung von Edvard Munch.* 6–18 April. [2nd hanging: 19–30 April]
1907 Hamburg. Salon Clematis. From 30 October
1908 Breslau. Franz Hancke, 22 November–ca. 5 December
1908 Copenhagen. Kunstforeningen. 22 November–20 December
1909 Helsinki. Ateneum Taidemuseo, *Edv. Munch.* 3–31 January
1909 Bremen. Kunsthalle Bremen. 7 February–ca. 7 March
1909 Kristiania. Blomqvist Kunsthandel. From 1 March
1909 Trondheim. Trondhjem Kunstforening. April
1909 Bergen. Bergens Kunstforening. From 28 May
1910 Kristiania. Dioramalokalet, *Edvard Munchs udstilling.* 5 March–7 April
1911 Helsinki. Ateneum Taidemuseo, *Den norske utstilling i Helsingfors.* 21 February–26 March
1911 Rome, *Esposizione internazionale.* From 27 March
1912 Munich. Thannhäuser Moderne Galerie, *Kollektiv-Ausstellung Edvard Munch.* 13 February–10 March
1912 Gothenburg. Konstforeningen Valand. 31 October–ca. 1 December

1913 Kristiania. Kunstforeningen, *Edvard Munch.* 2–23 February
1913 Stockholm A. Salong Joël, *Målningar och grafisk konst af Edvard Munch.* From 4 February
1913 Stockholm B. Konstnärshuset, *Edvard Munch - Målningar.* From 3 September
1914 Berlin. Gurlitt Kunst-Salon, *Kollektiv-Ausstellung Edvard Munch.* February–March
1914 Kragerø. Solo exhibition in aid of fund for needy mariners. March
1914 Kristiania. Tivoli Festivitetslokale, *Edvard Munchs utstilling* [Study for the Aula decorations]. 9 May–June
1915 Kristiania. Blomqvist Kunsthandel, *Edvard Munch.* From 22 October
1915 Copenhagen. Charlottenborg, *Den Norske Kunst-udstilling.* 11 November–December
1916 Kristiania. Blomqvist Kunsthandel. 1–20 October
1917 Copenhagen. Georg Kleis, *Edvard Munch.* From 10 November
1918 Kristiania. Blomqvist Kunsthandel, *Edvard Munch.* From 16 February
1919 Kristiania A. Kunstforeningen, *To privatsamlinger.* From 10 May–June
1919 Kristiania B. Blomqvist Kunsthandel, *Edvard Munch.* From 2 October
1921 Kristiania. Blomqvist Kunsthandel, *Edv. Munch.* From 18 January
1922 Zürich. Kunsthaus Zürich, *Edvard Munch in Zürcher Kunsthaus.* 18 June–2 August. Parts of the exhibition travelled on to Bern and Basel.
1922 Bern. Kunsthalle Bern, *Ausstellung Edvard Munch.* 3–24 September; Basel. Kunsthalle Basel. 8–29 October. The selection had previously been shown in Zürich.
1923 Gothenburg. Göteborg Konsthall, *Jubileumsutställning - Nordisk Konst.* 8 May–15 October
1926 Munich. Glaspalast, *Allgemeine Kunst-Ausstellung.* 1 June–ca. 1 October
1926 Mannheim. Kunsthalle Mannheim, *Edvard Munch - Gemälde und Graphik.* 7 November–9 January 1927
1927 Berlin. Nationalgalerie, *Edvard Munch.* 12 March–15 May. Most of the selection travelled on to Oslo.
1927 Oslo. Nasjonalgalleriet, *Edvard Munch.* 8 June–27 July. The selection is largely the same as in Berlin, but with additional works from many Norwegian collections.
1927 Pittsburgh. Carnegie Institute,

Twenty-sixth annual international exhibition of paintings organized by the Carnegie Institute, Pittsburgh. 13 October-4 December; New York. Brooklyn Museum. 9 January-19 February 1928; San Francisco. California Palace of the Legion of Honor. 2 April-13 May 1928

1929 Kiel. Kunsthalle Kiel, *Ausstellung Nordischer Kunst*. 15 June-1 August

1931 Budapest. Nemzeti Szalon, *Az Elsö Norvég representativ Képzömüvészeti kiállitás*. 15 February-4 March; Vienna, *Norwegische Kunst. Vereinigung bildender Künstler Wiener Secession. CXVI Kunst-Ausstellung*. 15 March-6 April.

1932 Oslo A. Kunstnernes Hus, *Høst-utstillingen gjennom de første 25 år, 1882-1907*. 5 September-2 October

1932 Oslo B. Blomqvist Kunsthandel, *Thv. Torgersen*. 17 September-1 October

1934 Copenhagen. Charlottenborg, *Grønningen 1934*. 20 January-11 February

1937 Paris. *L'exposition universelle* [International Exposition]. From 25 May

1938 Oslo. Wangs Kunst- og Antikvitetshandel, *Harald Nørregaards samling* [auction]. 24-26 September

1942 Oslo. Nasjonalgalleriet, *Kunst og ukunst. Oppryddingen april 1942*. 24 April-16 May

1950 USA. Touring exhibition. *Edvard Munch*. Washington, DC. Phillips Gallery. 28 May-29 June; New York. Museum of Modern Art. 30 June-13 August; Detroit. Detroit Institute of Arts. From 1 September; Minneapolis. Minneapolis Institute of Arts. To 9 November; Denver. From 24 November; Los Angeles. Los Angeles County Museum. Ca. 10 January-11 February 1951; San Francisco. M.H. De Young Memorial Museum. From ca. 15 February; Chicago. Art Institute of Chicago. 8 May-10 June; St. Louis. City Art Museum. 18 June-15 July 1951

1951 Oslo. Kunstnernes Hus, *Edvard Munch utstilling: Malerier, akvareller, tegninger, grafikk*. 10 November- 16 December

1951 Brighton. Brighton Art Gallery, *Edvard Munch: An Exhibition of Paintings, Etchings, Lithographs*. 1-22 September; Glasgow, Kelvingrove Gallery. 1-22 October; London. Tate Gallery. 31 October-1 December; Haag. Gemeentemuseum. 12 December-15 February 1952; Paris. Petit Palais. 28 March-30 April 1952. Touring exhibition organised by The Arts Council of Great Britain

1952 Zürich. Kunsthaus Zürich, *Edvard Munch*. 22 June-17 August

1952 Brussels. Palais des Beaux-Arts, *Edvard Munch. Peintures, oeuvre gravé*. 11 October-2 November

1954 Venice. *La biennale di Venezia*. 19 June-17 October

1954 Munich. Haus der Kunst, *Ausstellung Edvard Munch*. 12 November-19 December; Cologne. Wallraff-Richartz-Museum. 3 January- 20 February 1955

1955 Copenhagen. Statens Museum for Kunst, *Kunstforeningens Edvard Munch udstilling*. 5-27 March; Odense. Fyn Stiftsmuseum, *Fyns Stiftsmuseums Edvard Munch udstilling*. 3-17 April

1955 Rome. Palazzo delle Esposizioni, *Arte Nordica Contemporanea*. 2 April-20 May

1958 Bern. Kunstmuseum Bern, *Edvard Munch*. 7 October-30 November

1958 Rotterdam. Museum Boymans-van-Beuningen, *Edvard Munch*. 10 December-8 February 1959

1958 Brussels. Palais des Beaux-Arts. *50 ans d'art moderne: Exposition universelle et internationale de Bruxelles* [Brussels World's Fair]. 17 April-21 July

1959 Vienna. Akademie der Bildende Künste, *Edvard Munch. Wiener Festwochen*. 22 May-5 July

1959 Warsaw. Muzeum Narodowe, *Edvard Munch. Malarstwo i grafika*. 2 November-15 December

1960 New York. Museum of Modern Art. *Art nouveau: art and design at the turn of the century*. 6 June-6 September; Pittsburgh. Carnegie Institute. 13 October-12 December; Los Angeles. Los Angeles County Museum. 17 January-5 March 1961; Baltimore. Baltimore Museum of Art. 1 April-15 May 1961

1960 Paris. Musée national d'art moderne, *Les sources du XXe siècle. Les arts en Europe de 1884 à 1914*. 4 November-23 January 1961

1960 Recklinghausen. Ruhrfestspiele, *Berlin, Ort der Freiheit in die Kunst*. 2 June-17 July; Vienna, Wiener-Secession. 2 August-4 September; Berlin. Berliner-Festspiele. 18 September-6 November; Oslo. Kunstnernes hus, *Berlin-kunst. Stadier i utviklingen fra 1892 til i dag*. 14 January-5 February 1961; Helsinki. Taidehalli, *Taidetta Berliinissä. Kehityksen tie 1892-1960*. 17 March-9 April 1961

1962 Frankfurt am Main. Steinernes Haus, Römerberg, *Edvard Munch*. 9 November-6 January 1963

1963 Humlebæk. Louisiana, *100 års norsk kunst*. 18 January-17 February

1963 Darmstadt. Mathildenhöhe, *Zeugnisse der Angst in der modernen Kunst*. 29 June-1 September

1964 Munich. Haus der Kunst, Secession. *Europäische Kunst um die Jahrhundertwende*. 14 March-10 May

1964 Oslo. Nasjonalgalleriet, *Jubileumsutstilling 1814-1964*. 5 May-7 June

1964 Firenze. Palazzo Strozzi, *L'Espressionismo. Pittura, Scultura, Architettura*. May-June

1964 Kiel. Kunsthalle zu Kiel, *150 Jahre Norwegische Malerei*. 21 June-26 July

1964 Dublin. National Gallery of Ireland, *1864-1964: Centenary Exhibition*. 1 October-December

1965 New York A. The Gallery of Modern Art, *Scandinavian Painters*. 23 March-25 April

1965 Recklinghausen. Städtische Kunsthalle Recklinghausen, *Signale - Manifeste - Proteste im 20. Jahrhundert*. 12 June-25 June

1965 New York B. The Solomon R. Guggenheim Museum, *Edvard Munch*. 14 October-20 February 1966

1967 Montreal. National Gallery of Canada, *Man and his World. International Fine Arts Exhibition. Expo 67*. 28 April-27 October

1968 Schaffhausen. Museum zu Allerheiligen, *Edvard Munch*. 30 March-9 June

1968 Stockholm. Nationalmuseum, *Höjdpunkter i norsk konst*. 19 September-8 December

1970 Munich. Haus der Kunst, *Europäischer Expressionismus*. 7 March-10 May; Paris, Musée National d'Art Moderne, *L'Expressionisme Européen*. 26 May-27 July

1970 Japan. Touring exhibition. *Edvard Munch*. Kamakura. Kanagawa Prefectural Modern Art Museum. 25 September-18 October; Nagoya. Aichi Prefectural Art Museum. 21 October-8 November; Kobe. Hyogo Prefectural Modern Art Museum. 21 November-20 December; Kyoto. National Museum of Modern Art. 20 January-14 February 1971

1971 Oslo. Munchmuseet, *Edvard Munch og den tsjekkiske kunst*. 27 February-30 April

1972 Kristiansand. Christianssands Kunstforening, *Norsk malerkunst fra 1800 til 1930-årene*. 16 September-1 October

1973 Oslo. Munchmuseet, *Edvard Munch - tegninger, skisser og studier*. 14 February-29 April

1973 Munich. Haus der Kunst, *Edvard Munch 1863-1944*. 6 October-16 December; London. Hayward Gallery, Arts Council of Great Britain. 12 January-3 March 1974; Paris. Musée National d'Art Moderne. 22 March-13 May 1974

1974 Høvikodden. Henie Onstad Kunstsenter, *Impresjonismen 100 år*. 1 November-19 January 1975

1975 Århus. Aarhus Kunstmuseum, *Edvard Munch*. 13 September-5 October; Humlebæk. Louisiana. 11 October-4 January 1976

1975 Rotterdam. Museum Boymans-van-Beuningen, *Het symbolism in Europa*. November-January 1976; Brussels. Musées royaux des Beaux-Arts de Belgique January-mars; Baden-Baden. Staatliche Kunsthalle, *Symbolismus in Europa*. 20 March-9 May; Paris. Grand Palais. 21 May-19 July 1976

1976 Darmstadt. Kunsthalle Darmstadt, *Ein Dokument Deutscher Kunst Darmstadt 1901-1976. Band 3. Akademie - Sezession - Avantgarde um 1900*. 22 October-30 January 1977

1977 Warsaw. Muzeum Narodowe w Warszawie, *Edvard Munch 1863-1944. Wystawa obrazów olejnych, akwarel, rysunków, i grafiki ze zbiorów Muzeum Muncha i Galerii Narodowej w Oslo*. January-February

1977 Stockholm. Liljevalchs & Kulturhuset, *Edvard Munch 1863-1944*. 25 March-15 May

1977 Oslo. Munchmuseet, *Edvard Munchs arbeiderbilder*. 30 September-ca. 21 February 1978. Part of the exhibition shown in Stockholm.

1978 Hamburg. Kunstverein in Hamburg, *Edvard Munch. Arbeiterbilder 1910-1930*. 11 May-9 July; Stuttgart. Württembergischer Kunstverein. 19 July-27 August; Berlin. Staatliche Kunsthalle. 4-27 September; Frankfurt am Main. Frankfurter Kunstverein. 24 November-21 January 1979

1978 Madison. Elvehjem Museum of Art, University of Wisconsin, *The Art of Norway 1750-1914*. 5 November-7 January 1979; Minneapolis. Minneapolis Institute of Arts. 17 February-1 April; Seattle. Seattle Art Museum. 5-17 June 1979

1978 Washington. National Gallery of Art, *Edvard Munch. Symbols & images*. 11 November-19 February 1979

1979 New York. Museum of Modern Art, *The masterworks of Edvard Munch*. 15 March-24 April

1979 Nykøbing. Annebergsamlingerne, *Edvard Munch. Malerier fra eventyrskoven samt raderinger, litografier og tegninger*. 1 June-31 August; Copenhagen. Kastrupgårdsamlingen. 16 September-14 October

1979 Milan. Castello Storzesco, *Origini dell'Astrattismo - Verso altri orizzonti del reale*. 18 October-18 January 1980

1979 London. Royal Academy of Arts, *Post-impressionism. Cross-currents in European painting*. 17 November-16 March 1980

1979 Oslo. Munchmuseet, *Edvard Munch og hans bilder fra eventyrskogen*. 1 December 1979-June 1980

1980 Liège. Musée Saint-Georges, *Edvard Munch: Images du travailleur: 1910-1930*. 15 March-27 April

1980 Washington. National Gallery of Art, *Post-Impressionism. Cross-currents in European and American Painting 1880-1906*. 25 May-11 September

1980 Oslo. Kunstnerforbundet, *Norske sommerlandskap i 100 år*. 20 June-16 August

1980 Berlin. Nationalgalerie, Staatliche Museen Preussischer Kulturbesitz, *Bilder vom Menschen in der Kunst des Abendlandes. Jubiläumsausstellung der Preussischen Museen Berlin 1830-1980*. 5 July-28 September

1981 Tokyo. National Museum of Modern Art, *Munch exhibition*. 9 October-23 November; Sapporo. Hokkaido Museum of Modern Art. 28 November-25 December; Nara. Nara Prefectural Museum of Art. 9 January-21 February 1982; Nagoya. Aichi Prefectural Art Gallery. 24 February-17 March 1982; Leningrad. Hermitage Museum, *Живопись и графика Эдварда Мунка* [Paintings and Graphic Works by Edvard Munch]. 27 April- 25 May 1982; Moscow. June 1982

1982 Oslo A. Munchmuseet, *Edvard*

Munch – De første studieår. 23 August–25 November. Later repeated on several occasions: 22 March–30 August 1984; summer and autumn 1985

1982 Washington, DC. Corcoran Gallery of Art, *Northern light. Realism and symbolism in Scandinavian painting 1880–1910.* 8 September–17 October; New York, The Brooklyn Museum. 10 November–6 January; Minneapolis, The Minneapolis Institute of Arts. 6 February–10 April 1983

1982 Oslo B. Munchmuseet, *Lindefrisen.* 15 September–6 October

1983 Dresden. Gemäldegalerie Neue Meister, *Edvard Munch.* 13 December–22 February 1984

1984 Toronto. Art Gallery of Ontario, *The mystic north. Symbolist landscape painting in northern Europe and north America 1890–1940.* 13 January–11 March; Cincinnati. Cincinnati Art Museum. 31 March–13 May

1984 Paris. Grand Palais, Centenaire de la Société des artistes indépendants. 8 April–2 May

1984 Berlin. Berlinische Galerie, *Berlin um 1900.* 9 September–28 October

1984 Newcastle. Polytechnic Gallery, *Munch and the workers.* 8 October–30 November; London. The Barbican Art Centre. 14 February–8 April 1985; Edinburgh. City Art Centre. 17 April–18 May 1985; Belfast. Ulster Museum. 30 May–24 June 1985; Liverpool. Walker Art Gallery. 4 July–18 August 1985; Dublin. National Gallery of Ireland. September–October 1985

1984 Tromsø. Tromsø Kunstforening, *Edvard Munch.* 20 October–11 November

1985 Moss. Galleri F 15, *Ungdomsutstillingen.* 24 August–22 September

1985 Oslo. Nasjonalgalleriet, *1880-årene i nordisk maleri.* 24 August–13 October; Stockholm. Nationalmuseum. 25 October–6 January 1986; Helsinki. Amos Andersons Kunstmuseum. 19 January–9 March 1986; Copenhagen. Statens Museum for Kunst. 22 March–18 May 1986

1985 Milan. Palazzo Reale and Palazzo Bagatti Valsecchi, *Munch.* 4 December–16 March 1986; Rome. Palazzo Braschi. 26 March–1 June 1986

1986 West Palm Beach. The Norton Gallery of Art, *Edvard Munch. Mirror reflections.* 20 February–13 April

1986 Hamburg. Hamburger Kunsthalle, *Eva und die Zukunft. Das Bild der Frau seit der Französischen Revolution.* 11 June–14 September

1986 London. Hayward Gallery, *Dreams of a summer night. Scandinavian painting at the turn of the century.* 10 July–5 October; Düsseldorf. Kunstmuseum Düsseldorf. *Im Lichte des Nordens. Skandinavische Malerei um die Jahrhundertwende.* 26 October–1 February 1987; Paris, Musée du Petit Palais, *Lumières du Nord, La peinture scandinave.* 21 February–17 May 1987; Oslo. Nasjonalgalleriet,

Nordiske stemninger. Nordisk maleri ved århundreskiftet. 20 June–16 August 1987

1987 Barcelona. Centre Cultural de la Fundació Caixa de Pensions, *Munch 1863–1944.* 27 January–22 March

1987 Berlin. Staatliche Museen zu Berlin (Alten Museum). *Kunst in Berlin 1648–1987.* 10 June–25 October

1987 Kongsvinger. Kongsvinger Museum, *Dagny Juel-uken.* 5–11 August

1987 Essen. Museum Folkwang, *Edvard Munch.* 18 September–8 November. Largely the same exhibition travelled on to Zürich.

1987 Tokyo. The Seibu Museum of Art, *Scandinavian Art. 19 artists from Denmark, Finland, Iceland, Norway, Sweden: seeing the silence and hearing the scream.* 17 October–17 November

1987 Oslo A. Kunstnernes Hus, *Høstutstillingens 100-års jubileum.* 24 August–11 October

1987 Oslo B. Nasjonalgalleriet, *Olaf Schous gaver til Nasjonalgalleriet.* 14 November–7 February 1988

1987 Zürich. Kunsthaus Zürich, *Edvard Munch.* 19 November–14 February 1988. Largely the same exhibition as in Essen.

1988 Humlebæk. Louisiana, *Edvard Munch. Maler og fotograf. Kunstneren og fotografiet.* 20 February–15 May

1988 Mannheim. Städtische Kunsthalle, *Edvard Munch. Sommernacht am Oslofjord um 1900.* 27 February–17 April

1988 Oslo. Galleri K, *Yngre realister rundt Christian Krohg.* 10 May–14 June

1989 Vienna. Ehemalig Hofstallungen Messepalast, *Wunderblock. Eine Geschichte der Modernen Seele.* 27 April–6 August

1989 Dal (Eidsvoll). Galleri Unique, *Fra grunnlov til velferdssamfunn.* 28 April–11 June

1989 Høvikodden. Henie Onstad Kunstsenter, *Norge i bilder – Natur og naturfølelse i norsk malerkunst gjennom 175 år.* 17 May–17 September

1990 Cologne. Wallraf-Richartz-Museum, *Landschaft im Licht: impressionistische Malerei in Europa und Nordamerika 1860–1910.* 6 April–1 July

1991 Paris. Musée d'Orsay, *Munch et la France.* 24 September–5 January 1992; Oslo, Munchmuseet. *Munch og Frankrike.* 3 February–21 April; Frankfurt am Main. Schirn Kunsthalle, *Munch in Frankreich.* 30 May–9 August 1992

1991 Kristiansand. Christianssands Kunstforening, *Sørlandet og malerne.* 6 December–12 January 1992

1992 London. The National Gallery, *Edvard Munch. The Frieze of Life.* 12 November–7 February

1993 Atlanta. The Fernbank Museum of Natural History, *Winterland.* 11 February–4 April; Tokyo. The National Museum of Western Art. 26 April–30 June; Barcelona. Fundació "la Caixa". 1 August–1 October; Munich. Kunsthalle München. 18 November–16 January 1994; Lillehammer. Lille-

hammer Bys Malerisamling, *Vinterland.* 8 February–31 March 1994

1993 Lillehammer. Lillehammer Bys Malerisamling, *Edvard Munch. Monumentale prosjekter 1909–30.* 3 June–22 August

1993 Tokyo. Idemitsu Museum of Arts, *Edvard Munch. The Frieze of Life.* 5 October–7 November; Osaka. Idemitsu Museum of Arts. 16 November–12 December

1994 Munich. Kunsthalle der Hypo-Kulturstiftung, *Munch und Deutschland.* 23 September–27 November; Hamburg. Hamburger Kunsthalle. 9 December–12 February 1995; Berlin. Nationalgalerie. 24 February–23 April 1995

1994 Oslo. Nasjonalgalleriet, *Tradisjon og fornyelse. Norge rundt århundreskiftet.* 22 October–15 January 1995

1995 Madrid. Museo Nacional Centro de Arte Reina Sofia, *Luz del Norte/Llum del nord.* 30 March–15 May; Barcelona. Museu d'Art Modern del MNAC. 2 June–16 July; Reykjavik. Listasafn Íslands, *Ljós úr Norðri.* 11 August–24 September; Stockholm. Nationalmuseum, *Nordiskt sekelskifte/The light of the north.* 20 October–7 January 1996

1995 Montreal. Museum of Fine Arts, *Lost Paradise: Symbolist Europe.* 8 June–15 October

1995 Venezia. La Biennale di Venezia, *Identità e alterità. Figure del corpo 1895/1995.* 11 June–15 October

1995 New York. National Academy of Design, *Edvard Munch and Harald Sohlberg. Landscapes of the Mind.* 15 October–15 January 1996. Parts of the exhibition travelled on to Høvikodden. Henie Onstad Kunstsenter. 27 January–25 February 1996

1996 Tokyo. Museum of Contemporary Art. *La ville moderne en Europe. Visions urbaines d'artistes et d'architectes 1870–1996.* 24 July–16 September

1996 Berlin. Nationalgalerie. *Manet bis van Gogh – Hugo von Tschudi und der Kampf um die Moderne.* 20 September–6 January 1997; Munich. Neue Pinakothek. 24 January–11 May 1997

1997 Tokyo. Setagaya Art Museum, *Munch and Photography.* 5 April–8 June

1998 Paris. Musée d'Art modern de la Ville de Paris, *Visions du nord. Lumière du monde, lumière du ciel.* 5 February–17 May

1998 Cologne. Wallraf-Richartz-Museum, *Landschaft als Kosmos der Seele. Malerei des nordischen Symbolismus bis Munch 1880–1910.* 4 April–7 June

1998 Lugano. Museo d'Arte Moderna, *Edvard Munch.* 19 September–13 December

1998 Munich. Haus der Kunst, *Die Nachte.* 1 November–7 February 1999

1998 Oslo. Munchmuseet, *Munch og Ekely.* 22 November–28 February 1999

1999 Modum. Blaafarveværket, *Sommeren med Edvard Munch og Arne Kavli.* 22 May–30 September

1999 Florence. Galleria Palatina di Palazzo Pitti, *Edvard Munch. Dal realismo*

all'espressionismo. 30 October–13 February 2000

2000 Vienna. Österreichischen Galerie Belvedere, *Klimt und die Frauen.* 20 September–7 January 2001

2000 London. Royal Academy of Arts, *1900: Art at the Crossroad.* 16 January–3 April; New York. Solomon R. Guggenheim Museum. 18 May–13 September

2001 Boston. McMullen Museum of Art Boston College, *Edvard Munch. Psyche, Symbol and Expression.* 5 February–20 May

2001 Berlin. Neue Nationalgalerie, *Der Potzdamer Platz. Ernst Ludwig Kirchner und der Untergang Preussens.* 24 April–12 August

2001 Darmstadt. Instituts Mathildenhöhe, *Die Lebensreform. Entwürfe zur Neugestaltung von Leben und Kunst um 1900.* 21 October–24 February 2002

2001 Ferrara. Palazzo dei Diamanti, *Da Dahl a Munch. Romanticismo, realismo e simobolismo nella pittura di paesaggio norvegese.* 25 October–3 January 2002

2002 Venice. Palazzo Grassi, *Verso l'Arte Moderna: Da Puvis de Chavannes a Matisse e Picasso.* 10 February–16 June

2002 Turin. GAM, *Guiseppe De Nittis e la pittura della vita moderna in Europa.* 16 February–26 May

2002 Oslo. Nasjonalgalleriet, *Bilder fra familielivet.* 17 February–4 April

2002 Stockholm. Nationalmuseum, *Impressionismen och Norden. Det sena 1800-talets franska avantgardekonst och konsten i norden 1870–1920.* 25 September–19 January 2003; Copenhagen. Statens museum for kunst. 21 February–25 May 2003

2002 Gothenburg. Göteborgs Konstmuseum, *Edvard Munch.* 28 September–6 January 2003

2003 Vienna. Albertina, *Edvard Munch – Thema und Variation.* 15 March–22 June

2003 Basel. Foundation Beyeler, *Expressive!* 30 March–10 August

2003 Treviso. Fondazione Cassamarca, *L'Oro e l'Azzurro – I colori del Sud da Cézanne á Bonnard.* 11 October–7 March 2004

2003 Rovereto. Museo di Arte Moderna e Contemporanea di Trento e Rovereto. *Montagna. Arte, scienzia, mito da Dürer a Warhol.* 19 December–17 April 2004

2004 Melbourne. National Gallery of Victoria, *Edvard Munch. The Frieze of Life.* 13 October–12 January 2005

2004 Turin. Palazzina della Promotrice delle Belle Arti, *Gli Impressionisti e la neuve: La Francia e l'Europa.* 27 November–25 April 2005

2004 London. Whitechapel Art Gallery, *Faces in the Crowd. Picturing Modern Life.* 3 December–6 March 2005; Turin. Castello di Rivoli Museo d'Arte Contemporanea, *Volti nella folla. Immagini della vita moderna.* 6 April–10 July 2005

2005 Dortmund. Museum für Kunst und Kulturgeschichte, *Munch revisited.*

Edvard Munch und die heutige Kunst. 30 January-1 May; Høvikodden. Henie Onstad Kunstsenter, *Møter med Munch. Revisited.* 17 June-18 September
2005 Stockholm. Moderna Museet, *Munch själv.* 19 February-15 May; Oslo. Munchmuseet, *Munch selv.* 11 June-28 August; London. Royal Academy of Arts, *Munch by himself.* 17 September-11 December
2005 Rome. Complesso del Vittoriano, *Munch 1863-1944.* 10 March-19 June
2005 Oslo. Nasjonalmuseet, *Museumsfeber.* 24 September 2005-1 January 2006
2005 Philadelphia. The Philadelphia Museum of Art, *Edvard Munch's "Mermaid".* 24 September-31 December
2006 New York. Museum of Modern Art, *Edvard Munch. The modern life of the soul.* 17 February-8 May
2006 Helsinki. Ateneum, *Naturens spegel. Nordiskt landskapsmåleri 1840-1910.* 21 April-27 August; Stockholm. Nationalmuseum. 30 September-14 January 2007; Oslo. Nasjonalmuseet, *Naturens speil. Nordisk landskapsmaleri 1840-1910.* 15 February-20 May 2007; Copenhagen. Statens Museum for Kunst. 6 October-20 January 2008; Minneapolis. The Minneapolis Institute of Arts. *A Mirror of Nature. Nordic Landscape Painting 1840-1910.* 23 June-2 September 2008
2007 Ferrara. Palazzo dei Diamanti, *Il Simbolismo. Da Moreau a Gauguin a Klimt.* 18 February-20 May; Rome. Galleria Nazionale d'Arte Moderna. 6 June-16 September
2007 Basel. Fondation Beyeler, *Edvard Munch. Zeichen der Moderne.* 18 March-15 July
2007 Tokyo. The National Museum of Western Art, *Edvard Munch. The Decorative Projects.* 6 October-6 January 2008; Kobe. Hyogo Prefectural Museum of Art. 19 January-30 March 2008
2008 Oslo. Munchmuseet, *Munch blir "Munch". Kunstneriske strategier 1880-1892.* 10 October-11 January 2009
2009 Chicago. The Art Institute of Chicago, *Becoming Edvard Munch: Influence, Anxiety and Myth.* 15 February-26 April
2009 Oslo. Nasjonalgalleriet, *Edvard Munch. Det syke barn. Historien om et mesterverk.* 16 January-3 May
2009 Copenhagen. Ordrupgaardgård, *Edvard Munch og Danmark.* 3 September-6 December; Oslo. Munchmuseet. 22 January-18 April 2010
2010 Codroipo. Passariano di Codroipo, *Munch e lo spirito del Nord. Scandinavia nel second Ottocento.* 25 September-6 March 2011
2011 Valencia. Consorcio de Museos de la Comunidad Valenciana, *Retratos de la Belle Epoque.* 5 April-26 June; Barcelona. Fundació "la Caixa". 19 July-9 October
2011 Paris. Centre Pompidou, *Edvard Munch: L'Œil Moderne.* 22 September-9 January 2012; London. Tate Modern, *Edvard Munch. The Modern Eye.*

28 June-12 October 2012; Frankfurt am Main. Schirn Kunsthalle, *Edvard Munch. Der moderne Blick.* 9 February-28 May 2013; Oslo. Munchmuseet, *Edvard Munch. Det moderne øye.* 31 October 2012-17 February 2013
2012 Essen. Museum Folkwang, *The Ecstasy of Colour - Munch, Matisse and the Expressionists.* 29 September-20 January
2012 Århus. Aros, *Edvard Munch. Angst.* 6 October-17 February 2013
2012 Budapest. Museum of Fine Arts, *Cézanne and the Past: Tradition and Creativity.* 25 October 2012-17 February 2013
2012 Groningen. Groninger museum, *Nordic Art. The Modern Breakthrough 1860-1920.* 9 December-5 May 2013; Munich. Kunsthalle der Hypo-Kulturstiftung. 30 May-6 October
2012 Norway. Touring exhibition. *Munch i koffert.* 12 December-21 May 2013
2013 Stockholm. Thielska Galleriet. *MUNCH! Nietzsche, Thiel och Nordens största konstnär.* 9 February-12 May
2013 Modum. Blaafarveværket, *Munch og malervennene på Modum.* 11 May-22 September
2013 Oslo. Nasjonalmuseet/Munchmuseet, *Munch 150.* 2 June-13 October
2014 Wiesbaden. Museum Wiesbaden, *The Jawlensky Horizon. Alexej von Jawlensky in the Reflection of his Encounters from 1900 to 1914.* 14 February-1 June; Emden. Kunsthalle Emden. 21 June-19 October
2014 Helsinki. Didrichsen Konstmuseum, *Edvard Munch - Livets dans/Edvard Munch - The Dance of Life.* 6 September-1 February 2015
2015 Oslo. Nasjonalmuseet, *Det magiske nord. Finsk og norsk kunst omkring 1900.* 30 January-16 May; Helsinki. Ateneum kunstmuseum. 18 June-7 September
2015 Oslo. Munchmuseet, *Munch - Van Gogh.* 7 May - 6 September; Amsterdam, Van Gogh-museet. 24 September-18 January 2016
2015 Madrid. Museo Thyssen-Bornemisza, *Edvard Munch. Archetypes.* 6 October-17 January 2016
2015 Münster. LWL-Museum für Kunst und Kultur, *Wilhelm Morgner und die Moderne.* 14 November-6 March 2016
2016 New York. Neue Galerie, *Munch and Expressionism.* 18 February-13 July
2016 Paris. Musée Marmotta Monet, *Hodler, Monet, Munch: Peindre l'impossible/Painting the Impossible.* 15 September- 22 January 2017; Martigny. Fondation Pierre Gianadda. 3 February-11 June 2017
2016 Oslo. Munchmuseet, *Jorn + Munch.* 15 October-18 January 2017
2017 San Francisco. San Francisco Museum of Modern Art, *Edvard Munch: Between the Clock and the Bed.* 24 June-9 October 2017; New York. The Metropolitan Museum. 14 November-4 February; Oslo. Munchmuseet. 12 May-9 September 2018
2018 Oslo. Munchmuseet, *Moonrise.*

Marlene Dumas & Edvard Munch. 29 September 2018-13 January 2019
2019 Bergen. KODE Kunstmuseer og komponisthjem, *Edvard Munch. I oss er verdener.* 7 September 2019-19 January 2020
2019 Düsseldorf. Kunstsammlung Nordrhein-Westfalen, *Munch seen by Karl Ove Knausgård.* 12 October 2019-1 March 2020

Bibliography

A

Affentranger-Kirchrath, Angelika. "Die Frage nach dem Menschen. Porträtmalerei um 1900 am Beispiel Ferdinand Hodlers und Edvard Munchs". *Zeitschrift für Schweizerische Archäologie und Kunstgeschichte* 51, no. 4 (1994): 295-308.

Ahtola-Moorhouse, Leena. "Edvard Munch. Theatre of the eye". In *Border Crossings. Fourteen Scandinavian Artists* [exhibition catalogue], 44-61. London: Barbican Art Gallery, 1992.

Ahtola-Moorhouse, Leena. "Elämän tanssin maalari = Målaren och livets dans". In *Edvard Munch: Elämän tanssi = Livets dans = The Dance of Life* [exhibition catalogue], 15-79. Helsinki: Didrichsen Art Museum, 2014.

Aitken, Geneviève. "Edvard Munch et la scène française". In *Munch et la France* [exhibition catalogue], 222-239. Paris: Réunion des Musées nationaux, 1991 A.

Aitken, Geneviève. "Edvard Munch og det franske teater". In *Munch og Frankrike* [exhibition catalogue], 222-237. Oslo: Munchmuseet, 1991 B. [Also published Paris 1991]

Alarcó, Paloma, et al. "Edvard Munch. Archetypes". In *Edvard Munch. Archetypes* [exhibition catalogue], 14-52. Madrid: Museo Thyssen-Bornemisza, 2015.

Albrecht, Thorsten. "Entartet oder Nordische Kunst. Das Schicksal der Werke Edvard Munchs in Lübeck nach 1933". In *Edvard Munch und Lübeck* [exhibition catalogue], 43-51. Lübeck: Museum für Kunst und Kulturgeschichte der Hansestadt, 2003.

Alessandrini, Marco. *La mente spiegata da Edvard Munch. Psicoanalisi in dialogo con un artista*. Rome: Edizione Magi, 2009.

Andersen, Christine Buhl. "Menneskebjerget". In *Edvard Munch og Henrik Ibsen* [exhibition catalogue], 10-19. Copenhagen: Kunstforeningen, 1998.

Anderson, Katherine A. *The landscapes of Edvard Munch. A medium of communication and the continuation of a tradition* [unpublished thesis, Master of Art]. Chicago: Michigan State University, 1984.

Andral, Jean-Louis. "Das Irdische verlieren". In *Edvard Munch in Chemnitz* [exhibition catalogue], 301-309. Chemnitz: Wienand, 1999.

Arnold, Mathias. "Gemalte Biographie. Die Selbstbildnisse Edvard Munchs". *Kunst und Antiquitäten*, no. 4 (1986): 70-79.

Asendorf, Christoph. "Kraft, Trieb, Wille

- Munchs energetisches Welttheater im Kontext des Fin de Siècle = Power, instinct, will - Munch's energetic world theater in the context of Fin de Siècle". In *Edvard Munch. Thema und Variation = Edvard Munch. Theme and variation* [exhibition catalogue], 83-90. Vienna: Albertina, 2003.

Askeland, Jan. "Angstmotivet i Edvard Munchs kunst". *Kunsten idag*, no. 4 (1966), 1-47.

Aslaksby, Trond. "La conservació de la collectió d'Eduard Munch. Una historia de 50 anys = The conservation of the Edvard Munch collection. A 50 years' story". In *Conservació i restauració d'art contemporani*, 35-43. Barcelona: Universitat de Barcelona, 1996.

Aslaksby, Trond. "*The Sick Child* - a closer look". In *Conservare necesse est. Festskrift til Leif Einar Plahter på hans 70-årsdag*, 139-143. Oslo: Nordisk konservatorforbund, Den norske seksjon, 1999.

Aslaksby, Trond. "The Weathered Paintings of Edvard Munch. Artistic Intention, Conservation, Display - A Triangle of Conflicts". In *El Guernica y los problemas éticos y técnicos de la manipulación de obras de arte*, 285-291. Madrid: Fundatión Marcelino Botin, 2002.

Aslaksby, Trond. "Det syke barn. Et maleri i forvandling - teknikk og behandling". In *Edvard Munch: "Det syke barn": Historien om et mesterverk = Edvard Munch: The Sick Child: The Story of a Masterpiece*, 57-79. Oslo: Nasjonalmuseet, 2009.

Aslaksby, Trond. "Edvard Munch's painting 'The Scream' (1893): Notes on technique, materials and condition". In *Public Paintings by Edvard Munch and his Contemporaries: Change and Conservation Challenges*, 52-71. London: Archetype, 2015.

Aubert, Andreas. "Universitetets nye festsal og den norske kunst og kultur". *Kunst og Kultur* 1, no. 2 (1910): 166-180.

Autin-Grenier, Pierre. "Edvard Munch, une anecdote". In *Edvard Munch au Centre Pompidou*, 72-75. Paris: Télérama, 2011.

B

Bal, Mieke. *Emma & Edvard Looking Sideways. Loneliness and the Cinematic*. Oslo: Munchmuseet, 2017.

Bang, Erna Holmboe. *Edvard Munch og Jappe Nilssen. Efterlatte brev og kritikker*. Oslo: Dreyer, 1946.

Bang, Erna Holmboe. *Edvard Munchs kriseår. Belyst i brever*. Oslo: Gyldendal, 1963.

Bardon, Annie. "Warnemünde. Hvordan Edvard Munch kunne oppleve badestedet i årene 1907-1908 = Warnemünde - wie Edvard Munch das Seebad 1907-1908 erleben konnte". In *Munch og Warnemünde 1907-1908 = Munch und Warnemünde* [exhibition catalogue], 9-24. Rostock: Kunsthalle Rostock; Oslo: Munchmuseet, 1999.

Bartrum, Giulia. "The inner soul of an artist. Munch's background and the development of his Frieze of Life" [34-57]; "Munch and the world of printmaking" [58-95]. In *Edvard Munch. Love and angst* [exhibition catalogue]. London: Thames & Hudson, 2019.

Baselitz, Georg. "Erfundene Bilder. Georg Baselitz über Edvard Munch, Derneburg, 17. März 1985". In *Edvard Munch. Sein Werk in Schweizer Sammlungen* [exhibition catalogue], 145-166. Basel: Öffentliche Kunstsammlung Basel, 1985.

Becker, Hans. "Maltechnische Aspekte zu einigen Werken Munchs". In *Edvard Munch. Sommernacht am Oslofjord, um 1900* [exhibition catalogue], 51-59. Mannheim: Städtische Kunsthalle Mannheim, 1988.

Beitin, Andreas. *Der Schrei: Kunst- und Kulturgeschichte eines Schlüsselmotivs in der deutschen Malerei und Graphik des 20. Jahrhunderts* [thesis, PhD]. Münster: Westfälische Wilhelms-Universität, 2004.

Benesch, Otto. *Edvard Munch*. London: Phaidon, 1960.

Benesch, Otto. "Hodler, Klimt und Munch als Monumentalmaler". *Wallraf-Richartz Jahrbuch* XXIV (1962): 333-358.

Benesch, Otto. "Edvard Munchs tro/Edvard Munchs Glaube". *Oslo kommunes kunstsamlinger. Årbok 1963* (1963): 9-23/102-112.

Berg, Knut. "Om dateringen av et Munch-maleri". *Kunst og Kultur* 76, no. 4 (1993): 213-222.

Bergan, Bodil. "80 år med Munch". *Panorama*, no. 3 (2003): 8-9.

Berman, Patricia G. "Edvard Munch's photography". In *Edvard Munch. Mirror reflections* [exhibition catalogue], 105-113. West Palm Beach: Norton Gallery, 1986.

Berman, Patricia G. *Monumentality and historicism in Edvard Munch's University of Oslo Festival Hall paintings* [unpublished thesis, doctoral]. New York: New York University, 1989.

Berman, Patricia G. "Body and body politic in Edvard Munch's Bathing Men". In *The body imaged. The human form and visual culture since the Renaissance*, 71-83. Cambridge: Cambridge University Press, 1993 A.

Berman, Patricia G. "Edvard Munch's Self-Portrait with Cigarette. Smoking and the bohemian persona". *Art Bulletin* LXXV, no. 4 (1993 B): 627-646.

Berman, Patricia G. "Edvard Munch's Portrait of Irmgard Steinbart". In *A Gallery of Modern Art* [exhibition catalogue], 96-97. St. Louis: Washington University Gallery of Art, 1994 A.

Berman, Patricia G. "(Re-)Reading Edvard Munch. Trends in the current literature". *Scandinavian Studies* 66, no. 1 (1994 B): 45-67.

Berman, Patricia G. "The Invention of History. Julius Meier-Graefe, German Modernism, and the Genealogy of Genius". In *Imagining Modern German Culture: 1889-1910, Studies in the History of Art 53, Symposium Papers XXXI*, 91-105. Washington D.C.: National Gallery of Art and University Press of New England, 1996.

Berman, Patricia G. "Edvard Munch. Women, woman, and the genesis of an artist's myth". In *Munch and Women. Image and Myth* [exhibition catalogue], 11-40. Alexandria: Art Services International, 1997 A.

Berman, Patricia G. "Edvard Munch's Bohemian Identity and the Metaphor of Pain at the Fin de Siècle". In *Edvard Munch* [exhibition catalogue], 211-215. Tokyo: Setagaya Art Museum, 1997 B.

Berman, Patricia G. "Edvard Munch's Peasants and the Invention of Norwegian Culture". In *Nordic Experiences. Exploring Scandinavian Cultures*, 213-223. Westport: Greenwood Press, 1997 C.

Berman, Patricia G. "Kropp och kroppspolitik i Edvard Munchs Badande män". In *Den maskulina mystiken. Konst, kön och modernitet*, 117-136. Lund: Studentlitteratur, 2002.

Berman, Patricia G. "Making Family Values. Narratives of Kinship and Peasant Life in Norwegian Nationalism". In *Art, Culture, and National Identity in Fin-de-Siècle Europe*, 207-228. Cambridge: Cambridge University Press, 2003.

Berman, Patricia G. "Bodies of uncertainty. Edvard Munch's 'new men' in the 1890s". In *Edvard Munch. An anthology*, 121-140. Oslo: Unipub, 2006 A.

Berman, Patricia G. "Edvard Munch's 'modern life of the soul'". In *Edvard Munch. The modern life of the soul* [exhibition catalogue], 34–50. New York: Museum of Modern Art, 2006 B.

Berman, Patricia G. "Mens sana in corpore sano. Munchs vitale kropper". In *Livskraft. Vitalismen som kunstnerisk impuls 1900–1930* [exhibition catalogue], 45–64. Oslo: Munchmuseet, 2006 C.

Berman, Patricia G. "Dionysus with Tan Lines. Edvard Munch's Discursive Skin". In *A Fine Regard: Essays in Honor of Kirk Varnedoe*, 68–85. Aldershot and Burlington: Ashgate, 2008 A.

Berman, Patricia G. "Den sublime storbyen og dannelsen av den moderne kunstner". In *Munch blir Munch: Kunstneriske strategier 1880–1892 = Munch Becoming "Munch". Artistic Strategies 1880–1892* [exhibition catalogue], 139–158. Oslo: Munchmuseet, 2008 B.

Berman, Patricia G. "Çoğaltma, ekleme, çikarma. Warhol, Munch ve çoğaltilmiş baski". In *Munch/Warhol* [exhibition catalogue], 9–48. Ankara: CerModern, 2013.

Berman, Patricia G. "Edvard Munch's Woman: The Construction of an Archetype". In *Edvard Munch. Archetypes* [exhibition catalogue], 84–99. Madrid: Museo Thyssen-Bornemisza, 2015.

Berman, Patricia G. "Self-Portraits 'As': Expressionist Embodiments". In *Munch and Expressionism* [exhibition catalogue], 81–95. Munich: Prestel, 2016.

Berman, Patricia G. "The Business of Being Edvard Munch". In *Edvard Munch: Between the Clock and the Bed* [exhibition catalogue], 45–47. New York: Metropolitan Museum of Art, 2017.

Bernau, Nikolaus. "Wo hing Munchs 'Lebens-Fries'? Zu dem Bau der Kammerspiele und ihrem berühmtesten Schmuck". In *Max Reinhardt und das deutsche Theater. Blätter des deutschen Theaters* 2, 65–77. Berlin: Deutsches Theater; Leipzig: Henschel, 2005.

Beuys, Joseph. "Nicht blosse Bilder. Joseph Beuys über Edvard Munch, Düsseldorf, 16 März 1985". In *Edvard Munch. Sein Werk in Schweizer Sammlungen* [exhibition catalogue], 135–144. Basel: Öffentliche Kunstsammlung Basel, 1985.

Billeter, Erika. "Aspekte der Melancholie. Zu Nachtbildern von Edvard Munch und Edward Hopper". In *Die Nacht* [exhibition catalogue], 119–134. Munich: Haus der Kunst; Wabern-Bern: Benteli, 1998.

Bisanz, Hans. *Edvard Munch und seine Bedeutung für den mitteleuropäischen Expressionismus* [thesis, doctoral]. Vienna: Universität Wien, 1959.

Bisanz, Hans. "Edvard Munch og portrettkunsten i Wien etter 1900/Edvard Munch und die Wiener Porträtmalerei nach 1900". *Oslo kommunes kunstsamlinger. Årbok 1963* (1963): 68–101/136–144.

Bischoff, Ulrich. *Edvard Munch. Gemälde und Zeichnungen aus einer norwegischen Privatsammlung* [exhibition catalogue]. Kiel: Kunsthalle, 1979.

Bischoff, Ulrich. "Die Rolle Edvard Munchs beim Einzug der Moderne in die deutschen Museen - Anmerkungen zu acht Bildern aus einer norwegischen Privatsammlung". *Pantheon* (1985): 126–140.

Bischoff, Ulrich. *Edvard Munch. 1863–1944.* Cologne: Benedict Taschen, 1993.

Bischoff, Ulrich. "Munchs Einzug in die deutschen Museen bis 1937". In *Munch und Deutschland* [exhibition catalogue], 112–126. Stuttgart: Gerd Hatje Verlag, 1994.

Bischoff, Ulrich. *Edvard Munch 1863–1944: Images of Life and Death.* Cologne: Taschen, 2011.

Bjerke, Øivind Storm. *Edvard Munch, Harald Sohlberg. Landscapes of the Mind* [exhibition catalogue]. New York: National Academy of Design, 1995.

Bjerke, Øivind Storm. "La sviluppo di Munch pittore 1880–1893 = Munchs Entwicklung als Maler 1880–1893". In *Edvard Munch = Edvard Munch* [exhibition catalogue], 19–42. Lugano: Museo d'arte moderna and Città di Lugano; Milan: Skira, 1998.

Bjerke, Øivind Storm. "Edvard Munch. L'opera come testo". In *Edvard Munch. L'io e gli altri* [exhibition catalogue], 47–61. Milan: Electa Palazzo forti, 2001.

Bjerke, Øivind Storm. "Skrik - Angst - Døden og barnet - Dødskamp - Moderen og de badende børn". In *Edvard Munchs Livsfrise. En rekonstruksjon av utstillingen hos Blomqvist 1918* [exhibition catalogue], 125–136. Oslo: Munchmuseet and Labyrinth Press, 2002.

Bjerke, Øivind Storm. "Il maestro del 'non finito'". In *Munch 1863–1944* [exhibition catalogue], 21–33. Milan: Skira, 2005.

Bjerke, Øivind Storm. "The Sick Child. Form as content". In *Edvard Munch. An anthology*, 65–86. Oslo: Unipub, 2006.

Bjerke, Øivind Storm. "The Scream as image of a 'scream'". *Kunst og Kultur* 90, no. 3 (2007): 175–185.

Bjerke, Øivind Storm. "Skrik som del av den kunsthistoriske kanon = The Scream as Part of the Art Historical Canon". In *Skrik = The Scream* [exhibition catalogue], 13–55. Oslo: Vigmostad & Bjørke, 2008 A.

Bjerke, Øivind Storm. "Stil og teknikk som strategiske virkemidler innenfor 'Mellomgenerasjonen' 1882–86". In *Munch blir "Munch". Kunstneriske strategier 1882–1892 = Munch Becoming "Munch". Artistic Strategies 1880–1892* [exhibition catalogue], 35–60. Oslo: Munchmuseet, 2008 B.

Bjerke, Øivind Storm. "Edvard Munch og Røros". In *Kunst i Bergstaden* [exhibition catalogue], 15–22. Røros: Kunst i Bergstaden, 2013.

Bjørnstad, Ketil. *Historien om Edvard Munch.* Oslo: Gyldendal, 1993.

Bjørnstad, Ketil. *Edvard Munch. Die Geschichte seines Lebens.* Frankfurt am Main: Insel-Verlag, 1995.

Bjørnstad, Ketil. *The story of Edvard Munch.* London: Arcadia, 2001.

Blegvad, Maria Kappel. "Edvard Munch - kunstneriske og litterære inspirationskilder / Edvard Munch - artistic and literary inspirations". In *Edvard Munch. Angst = Anxiety* [exhibition catalogue], 65–79. Aarhus: ARoS Aarhus Kunstmuseum, 2012.

Blomberg, Erik. "Munch flyttar hem från Tyskland". *Konstrevy*, no. 1 (1939): 14–16.

Bock, Henning. "Farbe als Ausdruck. Zur Deutung von Bildern Edvard Munchs". In *Edvard Munch. Probleme - Forschungen - Thesen*, 69–76. Munich: Prestel, 1973.

Boe, Roy A. "Jealousy. An important painting by Edvard Munch". *The Minneapolis Institute of Arts Bulletin* XLV, no. 1 (1956): 3–11.

Boe, Roy A. "Edvard Munch og J.P. Jacobsens 'Niels Lyhne'". *Oslo kommunes kunstsamlinger. Årbok 1852–1959* (1960 A): 9–12.

Boe, Roy A. "Edvard Munch's Murals for the University of Oslo". *The Art Quarterly* XXIII, no. 3 (1960 B): 233–246.

Boe, Roy A. *Edvard Munch. His life and work from 1880 to 1920* [unpublished thesis, doctoral]. New York: New York University, 1970.

Boersma-Pappenheim, A.M. Roorda. "Verslag van de restauratie van een schilderij van Edvard Munch". *IIC Nederland - Mededelingsblad N*, no. 3 (1989): 8–13.

Bolin, Asta. "Människan - ett tecken?" *Vår Lösen* 89, no. 7 (1998): 569–571.

Brandtzæg, Kari. "Edvard Munch's impact on Norwegian modern art after WWI". In *The Nordic Avant-gardes in the European Context of the Early 20th Century*, 41–51. Bari: Edizioni di Pagina, 2017.

Brandtzæg, Kari (ed.). *Hode ved hode. Cronqvist, Bjørlo, Munch. Kunsten og livet = Head by head. Cronqvist, Bjørlo, Munch. Art and Life* [exhibition catalogue]. Oslo: Munchmuseet, 2017.

Borgmann, Verena. "Oda Krohg und Edvard Munch - Seelenlandschaften". In *Oda Krohg. Malerin und Muse im Kreis um Edvard Munch* [exhibition catalogue], 40–51. Cologne: Weinand, 2011.

Brengmann, Hedwig. *Edvard Munch und Frankreich* [thesis, magister]. Bonn: Rheinische Friedrich-Wilhelms-Universität, 1990.

Brenna, Arne. "Hans Jægers fengselsfrise". *St. Hallvard* (1972): 238–66.

Brenna, Arne. "Hans Jæger og Edvard Munch, I og II". *Nordisk Tidskrift* (1976): 89–115, 188–215.

Brenna, Arne. "Edvard Munch og Dagny Juell". *Samtiden* 87, no. 1 (1978 A): 51–64.

Brenna, Arne. "Edvard Munchs arbeiderbilder 1909–15". *Kunst og Kultur* 61, no. 4 (1978 B): 197–220.

Brennecke, Detlef. *Die Nietzsche-Bildnisse Edvard Munchs.* Berlin: Berlin Verlag Arno Spitz, 2000.

Broby-Johansen, Rudolf. "Edvard Munch". *Samleren* 10 (1926): 173–178.

Broby-Johansen, Rudolf. "Besuch bei Munch". *Der Querschnitt* 9 (1931): 623–626.

Brunner, Werner. "Der halbierte Edvard Munch. Zu den Arbeiterbildern". *Spuren* 4 (1978): 46–48.

Bruno, Gianfranco. "Edvard Munch - il poema dell'immaginario". In *Munch* [exhibition catalogue], 29–50. Milan: Mazzotta, 1985.

Bruteig, Magne. "Munch as a Graphic Artist/Edvard Munch graafikkon". In *Edvard Munch 1863–1944. Puupiirroksia ja litografioita Oslon Munch-museon kokoelmista* [exhibition catalogue], 8–13/31–35. Riihimäki: Riihimäen taidemuseo, 1999.

Bruteig, Magne. "Bilder underveis. Tre tegninger av Edvard Munch = Images on the way. Three drawings by Edvard Munch". In *Skrigets Ekko = Echoes of the Scream* [exhibition catalogue], 124–135. Ishøj: Arken, 2001 A.

Bruteig, Magne. "Edvard Munch. Det forbudte og det fellesmenneskelige". In *Skrigets Ekko = Echoes of the Scream* [exhibition catalogue], 23–33. Ishøj: Arken, 2001 B.

Bruteig, Magne. "… Det skjønneste av alt …" In *Edvard Munchs Livsfrise. En rekonstruksjon av utstillingen hos Blomqvist 1918* [exhibition catalogue], 79–84. Oslo: Munchmuseet and Labyrinth Press, 2002.

Bruteig, Magne. "Models and muses". In *Edvard Munch. The Frieze of Life* [exhibition catalogue], 141–155. Melbourne: National Gallery of Victoria, 2004 A.

Bruteig, Magne. *Munch. Tegneren.* Oslo: Aschehoug, 2004 B.

Bruteig, Magne. "Als wenn viele Geigen… Die frühe 'Brücke'- Graphik und Edvard Munch". In *Frühe Druckgraphik der "Brücke"* [exhibition catalogue], 48–58. Berlin: Hirmer, 2005 A.

Bruteig, Magne. "Over var stjernene med sin himmel". In *Edvard Munch: Smertens blomst: Blossom of Pain* [exhibition catalogue], 13–91. Lemvig: Museet for religiøs kunst, 2005 B.

Bruteig, Magne. "Han er i sannhet en dyreven. Om Munch og hans hunder = He is a genuine animal lover! On Munch and his dogs". In *Munch & Maning: mellom klokken og veggen* [exhibition catalogue], 83–105. Oslo: Munchmuseet, 2006.

Bruteig, Magne. "Mangfold og enhet. Litografiet Madonna = Diversity and Unity. Munch's lithograph Madonna". In *Madonna = Madonna* [exhibition catalogue], 61–71. Bergen: Vigmostad & Bjørke, 2008 A.

Bruteig, Magne. "Umalte tegninger". In Munch blir "Munch". Kunstneriske strategier 1888–1892 = Munch Becoming "Munch". *Artistic Strategies 1880–1892* [exhibition catalogue] 63–82. Oslo: Munchmuseet, 2008 B.

Bruteig, Magne, Maite van Dijk and Leo Jansen. "Van Gogh + Munch. En innføring". In *Van Gogh + Munch* [exhibition catalogue], 11–32. Oslo and Brussels: Mercatorfonds, Orfeus, Munchmuseet and Van Gogh Musum, 2015.

Brynildsen, Aasmund. "Giganten og tiden. En Munchstudie". *Janus* 7, no. 6 (1939): 503-527.

Buchhart, Dieter. "Das Verschwinden – Experimente mit Material und Motiv = Disappearance – Experiments with material and motif". In *Edvard Munch. Thema und Variation = Edvard Munch. Theme and variation* [exhibition catalogue], 23-40. Vienna: Albertina, 2003.

Buchhart, Dieter. *Das verschwinden im Werk Edvard Munchs. Experimente mit Materialisierung und Dematerialisierung* [unpublished thesis, doctoral]. Vienna: Universität Wien, 2004.

Buchhart, Dieter. *Edvard Munch. Zeichen der Moderne* [exhibition catalogue]. Ostfildern: Hatje Cantz Verlag, 2007.

Buchhart, Dieter. "Edvard Munch og Danmark. København, en bro til moderniteten". In *Edvard Munch og Danmark* [exhibition catalogue], 11-30. Copenhagen: Ordrupgaard; Ostfildern: Hatje Cantz Verlag, 2009.

Buchhart, Dieter. "Edvard Munch - du 'traitement de cheval', de la photographie et du film muet en tant qu'expression de la peinture moderne du XXème siècle". In *Edvard Munch, ou l'"Anti-Cri"* [exhibition catalogue], [unpaginated]. Paris: Éditions Pinacothèque de Paris, 2010.

Buchhart, Dieter. "Edvard Munch - Ernst Ludwig Kirchner". In *Edvard Munch, Ernst Ludwig Kirchner* [exhibition catalogue], 23-39. Munich: Galerie Thomas, 2012 A.

Buchhart, Dieter. "Chapter III Exhibited works - SELF-PORTRAIT". In *Edvard Munch, Ernst Ludwig Kirchner* [exhibition catalogue], 75-77. Munich: Galerie Thomas, 2012 B.

Buchhart, Dieter. "Zusammenbruch und Aufbruch Edvard Munchs in Kopenhagen 1908/1909 = Edvard Munch's Collapse and New Beginning in Copenhagen, 1908/1909". In *Edvard Munch. Alpha & Omega* [exhibition catalogue], 23-47. Alkersum: Museum Kunst der Westküste, 2013.

Buchholz, Kai (ed.). *Die Lebensreform. Entwurfe zur Neugestaltung von Leben und Kunst um 1900*, vol. 2. Darmstadt: Institut Mathildenhöhe, 2001.

Buenger, Barbara C. "Edvard Munch looks at children. Two paintings lent to Elvehjem by the Munch-museum". *Elvehjem Museum of Art Bulletin*, 1978-80 (1980): 44-63.

Buenger, Barbara C. "Junge Männer am Meer". *Pantheon* XLI (1983): 134-144.

Bugge, Anders. *Munchs Aula-billeder.* Oslo: A. Bugge, 1938.

Burzacka, Irene. "Kunstnerisk dialog. Om maleriet Skrik av Edvard Munch og romanen Skrik av Stanislaw Przybyszewski". *Edda*, no. 1 (1989): 3-8.

Busch, Günter. "Über Gegenwart und Tod - Edvard Munch und Paula Modersohn-Becker". In *Edvard Munch. Probleme - Forschungen - Thesen*, 161-176. Munich: Prestel, 1973.

Buschhoff, Anne. "Liebe, Angst und Tod in Werken von Edvard Munchs Zeitgenossen". In *Edvard Munch - Rätsel hinter der Leinwand* [exhibition catalogue], 220-237. Cologne: DuMont, 2011.

Buvik, Per. "Kunst, ideologi og historie. Omkring eit maleri av Munch. Vampyr". In *Med og utan rammar. Sytten artiklar om bilde*, 55-66. Oslo: Samlaget, 1984.

Buvik, Per. "Munch og kvinnen". In *Munch og kvinnen = Munch and women* [exhibition catalogue], 9-11. Bergen: Bergen kunstmuseum, 2001.

Bøe, Alf. *Edvard Munch.* Oslo: Aschehoug, 1992.

Bøe, Alf. "The winter paintings of Edvard Munch". In *Winterland. Norwegian visions of winter* [exhibition catalogue], 41-48. Oslo: De norske bokklubbene, 1993.

C

Callen, Anthea. "The Unvarnished Truth: Mattness, 'Primitivism' and Modernity in French Painting, c. 1870-1907", *Burlington Magazine* 136, art. no. 1100 (1994): 738-746.

Carey, Frances. "Is art influenced by too much business?" In *Edvard Munch. Love and angst* [exhibition catalogue], 128-149. London: Thames & Hudson, 2019.

Carstensen, Richard. "Edvard Munchs Kinderbilder". *Der Wagen* (1980): 44-62.

Cassou, Jean. "Munch i Frankrike / Munch en France". *Oslo kommunes kunstsamlinger. Årbok 1963* (1963): 47-55 / 121-125.

Cathrine, Arnaud. "Itinéraire d'un enfant terrible". In *Edvard Munch au Centre Pompidou*, 18-26. Paris: Télérama, 2011.

Cernuschi, Claude. "Sex and psyche, nature and nurture, the personal and the political. Edvard Munch and German expressionism". In *Edvard Munch. Psyche, symbol and expression* [exhibition catalogue], 134-167. Chestnut Hill: McMullen Museum of Art, 2001.

Chang, Alison. *Negotiating Modernity: Edvard Munch's Late Figural Work 1900-1925* [unpublished thesis, PhD]. Philadelphia: University of Pennsylvania, 2010.

Chéroux, Clément. "Depth of Field". In *Edvard Munch. The Modern Eye = Der Moderne Blick = L'oeil moderne* [exhibition catalogue], 83-95. London: Tate Publishing, 2012. [Also published Paris 2011 and Frankfurt 2012]

Clarke, Jay. "Munch, Liebermann, and the question of etched 'reproductions'". *Visual Resources* XVI (2000): 27-63.

Clarke, Jay. "Meier-Graefe sells Munch. The critic as dealer". In *Festschrift für Eberhard W. Kornfeld zum 80. Geburtstag*, 181-194. Bern: Kornfeld & Cie, 2003.

Clarke, Jay. "Munch's critical reception in the 1890s and his 'place' in history". In *Seeing and Beyond. Essays on eighteenth to twenty-first century art in honor of Kermit S. Champa*, 185-209. New York: Peter Lang, 2005.

Clarke, Jay. "Originality and repetition in Edvard Munch's *Sick Child*". In *Edvard Munch. An anthology*, 43-64. Oslo: Unipub, 2006.

Clarke, Jay. *Becoming Edvard Munch. Influence, Anxiety, and Myth* [exhibition catalogue]. Chicago: Art Institute of Chicago, 2009.

Clarke, Jay. "Munchs *Pubertet* som fiksert forvandling = Munch's *Puberty* as Metabolic Moment". In *Edvard Munch: Pubertet = Edvard Munch: Puberty* [exhibition catalogue], 32-54. Oslo: Munchmuseet and Orfeus Publishing, 2012.

Clarke, Jay. "Kunst = Liv? Munch og biografiens problem". In *Edvard Munch 1863-1944*, 50-61. Milan: Skira; Oslo: Nasjonalmuseet and Munchmuseet, 2013.

Clarke, Jay. "Art and Life - Munch and Biography". In *Edvard Munch and the Modern Soul* [exhibition catalogue], 52-67. Seoul: Seoul Arts Center, 2014.

Clark, Kenneth. "Edvard Munch". In *Edvard Munch 1863-1944* [exhibition catalogue], 6-8. Munich: Haus der Kunst, 1973.

Coppel, Stephen. "Munch and the theatre in Paris". In *Edvard Munch. Love and angst* [exhibition catalogue], 96-127. London: Thames & Hudson, 2019.

Cordulack, Shelley Wood. *Edvard Munch's Frieze of Life in the context of nineteenth-century physiology* [thesis, PhD]. Urbana: University of Illinois at Urbana, 1996.

Cordulack, Shelley Wood. *Edvard Munch and the physiology of symbolism*. Madison: Fairleigh Dickinson University Press, 2002.

Cox, Jan Deryck. *The impact of Nordic art in Europe 1878-1889* [thesis, PhD]. Leeds: University of Leeds, 2014.

Crockett, Campbell. "Psychoanalysis in art criticism". *The Journal of Aestethics and Art Criticism* XVII, no. 1 (1958): 34-44.

Cummings, Scott T. "A strange boulder in the whirlpool of theater. Edvard Munch, Max Reinhardt, and Ghosts". In *Edvard Munch. Psyche, symbol and expression* [exhibition catalogue], 111-131. Chestnut Hill: McMullen Museum of Art, 2001.

Czymmek, Götz. "Edvard Munchs Weg zur symbolistischen Landschaft". In *Landschaft als Kosmos der Seele. Malerei des nordischen Symbolismus bis Munch 1880-1910* [exhibition catalogue], 67-76. Heidelberg: Braus, 1998.

D

Dagen, Philippe. *Hodler, Monet, Munch. Peindre l'impossible = Hodler, Monet, Munch. Painting the Impossible* [exhibition catalogue]. Vanves: Hazan; Paris: Musée Marmottan Monet, 2016.

Dahl, Chrix. "Mesteren på Ekely, Edvard Munch". In *Edvard Munch. Mennesket og kunstneren*, 145-156. Oslo: Gyldendal, 1946.

Dahlan, Abdul Ghani. "The Scream & Starry Night: emotions, symbol & motives". *Estudios sobre sel Mensaje Periodístico* 20, no. 1 (2014): 331-339.

Dalgard, Olav. "Edvard Munch". *Syn og Segn* 40 (1934): 395-409.

Dam, Anders Ehlers. "Panteren Goldstein. Edvard Munchs danske ven og hans forfatterskab". In *Munch og Goldstein. Intense linjer* [exhibition catalogue], 151-179. Aarhus: Aarhus University Press, 2019.

Dedekam, Hans. "Edvard Munch". In *Kunst og Kultur. Lorentz Dietrichson tilegnet i anledning af hans 75-aarige fødselsdag fra Kunsthistorisk forening. Studier og afhandlinger*, 288-310. Kristiania: Cammermeyer, 1908.

Dedichen, Jens. *Tulla Larsen og Edvard Munch*. Oslo: Dreyer, 1981.

Deknatel, Frederick B. *Edvard Munch*. New York: Museum of Modern Art; Boston: Institute of Contemporary Art, 1950.

Deri, Max. *Die Malerei im XIX Jahrhundert*, vol. 1. Berlin: P. Cassirer, 1923.

Dery, Mark. "Have an angst day. The Scream meme". In *The pyrotechnic insanitarium. American culture on the brink*, 45-59. New York: Grove Press, 1999.

Diana, Roberta. "Il rinascimento italiano secondo Munch: i viaggi in Italia e le riflessioni negli appunti dell'artista norvegese". *Studi Nordici* XVII (2010): 11-26.

Dijk, Maite van. "International artists at the Salon des Indépendants in Paris: the case of Edvard Munch (1896 and 1897)". In *Foreign Artists and Communities in Modern Paris, 1870-1914: Strangers in Paradise*, 43-52. Farnham, Surrey, and Burlington: Ashgate, 2015 A.

Dijk, Maite van. "Slektskapet oppdages" [200-216]; "Vive la France! Munch, Van Gogh og moderne fransk kunst" [100-122]. In *Van Gogh + Munch* [exhibition catalogue]. Oslo and Brussels: Mercatorfonds, Orfeus, Munchmuseet and Van Gogh Musum, 2015 B.

Dijk, Maite van. *Foreign Artists versus French Critics: Exhibition Strategies and Critical Reception at the Salon des Indépendants in Paris (1884-1914)* [thesis, PhD]. Amsterdam: University of Amsterdam, 2017.

Dine, Jim. "Jim Dine on Edvard Munch". In *Artists' journeys*, 11-17. London: BBC Education, 1992.

Ditteney, Eva. *Skandinavier in Berlin. Untersuchung zur Malerei von Lovis Corinth, Akseli Gallen-Kallela, Walter Leistikow, Max Liebermann, Edvard Munch und Anders Zorn anhand ihrer Ausstellungstätigkeit in Berlin zwischen 1892 und 1910* [unpublished thesis, doctoral]. Freiburg: Albert-Ludwigs-Universität, 2009.

Dittmann, Reidar. *Eros and Psyche. Strindberg and Munch in the 1890s* [unpublished thesis, doctoral]. Seattle: University of Washington, 1976.

Dobai, Johannes. "Randbemerkungen zum Thema der Erotik bei Munch und einigen Zeitgenossen". In *Edvard Munch. Probleme - Forschungen - Thesen*, 77–98. Munich: Prestel, 1976.

Dolnick, Edward. *The Rescue Artist: A True Story of Art, Thieves, and the Hunt for a Missing Masterpiece*. New York: HarperCollins Publishers, 2005.

Dorn, Roland. "Edvard Munch in Paris" [39–43]; "Edvard Munch in Mannheim" [257–291]. In *Edvard Munch. Sommernacht am Oslofjord, um 1900* [exhibition catalogue]. Mannheim: Städtische Kunsthalle Mannheim, 1988.

Dorn, Roland. "Ein befreiender Akt in dieser kampfhaften Zeit. Edvard Munchs Ausstellung bei Gustav Gerstenberger 1921". In *Edvard Munch in Chemnitz* [exhibition catalogue], 175–185. Chemnitz: Wienand, 1999.

Dorra, Henri. "Munch, Gauguin and Norwegian painters in Paris". *Gazette des Beaux-Arts*, November (1976): 175–180.

Drechsel, Kerstin. "Edvard Munch im Sammlungsbestand der Kunstsammlungen Chemnitz". In *Edvard Munch in Chemnitz* [exhibition catalogue], 269–283. Chemnitz: Wienand, 1999.

Dreier, Franziska. *Landschaft als Spiegel der Seele. Edvard Munch: Sternennacht, 1923/24 (Munch-museet M 9)* [unpublished thesis, magister]. Göttingen: Georg-August-Universität, 2000.

Dresdner, Albert. "Edvard Munchs Aulabilder und ihre Stellung in der norwegischen Kunst". *Der Kunstwanderer* 3, 2nd July edition (1921): 450–453.

Drost, Wolfgang. "Der stumme Schrei. Der Romancier als Interpret. Munch und Przybyszewski". In *Artefakte, Artefiktionen: Transformationsprozesse zeitgenössischer Literaturen, Medien, Künste, Architekturen = Artefacts, Artefictions: crossovers between contemporary literatures, media, arts and architectures*, 167–173. Heidelberg: C. Winter, 2000.

E

Eggum, Arne. "Edvard Munchs första utställning i Sverige". In *Edvard Munch* [exhibition catalogue], 19–32. Malmö: Malmö konsthall, 1975.

Eggum, Arne. "Det gröna rummet" [62–102]; "En fris för en aula" [124–133]; "Kristianiabohemen" [116–119]; "Munchs sena livsfris" [19–25]; "Sovrummet" [104–112]. In *Edvard Munch 1863-1944* [exhibition catalogue]. Stockholm: Liljevalchs, 1977.

Eggum, Arne. *Die Brücke: Edvard Munch* [exhibition catalogue]. Oslo: Munchmuseet, 1978 A.

Eggum, Arne. "Munch's self-portraits" [11–32]; "The Major Paintings" [33–76]; "The Theme of Death" [143–183]. In *Edvard Munch. Symbols & Images* [exhibition catalogue]. Washington: National Gallery of Art, 1978 B.

Eggum, Arne and Gerd Woll. *Edvard Munch. Malerier fra eventyrskoven. Samt raderinger, litografier, træsnit* [exhibition catalogue]. Copenhagen: Kastrupgårdsamlingen, 1979.

Eggum, Arne. "Munch og musikken". In *Frederick Delius og Edvard Munch* [exhibition catalogue], 51–62. Oslo: Oslo kommunes kunstsamlinger, 1979 A.

Eggum, Arne. "Commentaries". In *The Masterworks of Edvard Munch*, 12–57. New York: Museum of Modern Art, 1979 B.

Eggum, Arne. "Children with Nature. The Landscapes of Edvard Munch". In *Edvard Munch. Paintings from the Munch-museum* [exhibition catalogue], 9–21. Newcastle upon Tyne: Polytechnic Art Gallery, 1980.

Eggum, Arne (ed.). *Edvard Munch. Liebe, Angst, Tod: Themen und Variationen* [exhibition catalogue]. Bielefeld: Kunsthalle Bielefeld, 1980 A.

Eggum, Arne. "Edvard Munchs tidlige barneportretter". *Kunst og Kultur* 63, no. 4 (1980 B): 241–256.

Eggum, Arne. "James Ensor and Edvard Munch. Mask and Reality". In *James Ensor. Edvard Munch. Emil Nolde* [exhibition catalogue], 21–29. Regina, Alberta: Norman Mackenzie Art Gallery, 1980 C.

Eggum, Arne. *Edvard Munch. Alfa og Omega* [exhibition catalogue]. Oslo: Oslo kommunes kunstsamlinger, 1981.

Eggum, Arne. *Der Linde-Fries. Edvard Munch und sein erster deutscher Mäzen, Dr. Max Linde*. Lübeck: Senat der Hansestadt Lübeck, Amt für Kultur, 1982 A.

Eggum, Arne. "Litteraturen om Edvard Munch gjennom nitti år". *Kunst og Kultur* 65, no. 4 (1982 B): 270–279.

Eggum, Arne. *Edvard Munch. Malerier - skisser - studier = Edvard Munch. Peintures - esquisses - études*. Paris: Berggruen; Oslo: Fabritius, 1983 A. [Also published London 1984 and Stockholm 1985]

Eggum, Arne. "Edvard Munch". In *Norsk Kunstnerleksikon*, vol. 2, 979–995. Oslo: Universitetsforlaget, 1983 B.

Eggum, Arne. "Das grüne Zimmer" [33–41]; "Edvard Munch und die Fauves. Vorläufer des Expressionismus im 20. Jahrhundert" [29–31]. In *Edvard Munch. Höhepunkt des malerischen Werks im 20. Jahrhundert* [exhibition catalogue]. Hamburg: Frölich & Kaufmann, 1984 A.

Eggum, Arne. *Edvard Munch. La vita e le opere*. Oslo: Stenersen, 1984 B.

Eggum, Arne. "Edvard Munch - la sua vita e la sua arte". In *Munch* [exhibition catalogue], 51–64. Milan: Mazzotta, 1985.

Eggum, Arne. *Edvard Munch. Gemälde, Zeichnungen und Studien*. Stuttgart: Clett Cotta, 1986 A.

Eggum, Arne. "Landscape Motif". In *Edvard Munch* [exhibition catalogue], 33–40. Vancouver: Vancouver Art Gallery, 1986 B.

Eggum, Arne. *Munch og fotografi*. Oslo: Gyldendal, 1987 A. [Also published New Haven 1988 and Bern 1991]

Eggum, Arne. "Über Munch und die Schweiz". In *Edvard Munch* [exhibition catalogue], 351–359. Essen: Museum Folk-wang Essen; Zürich: Kunsthaus Zürich, 1987 B.

Eggum, Arne. *Edvard Munch og hans modeller, 1912-1943* [exhibition catalogue]. Oslo: Munchmuseet, 1988 A.

Eggum, Arne. "Edvard Munchs eksperimentelle fotografier". *Louisiana Revy* 28, no. 2 (1988 B): 24–38.

Eggum, Arne. *Edvard Munch. Livsfrisen fra maleri til grafikk*. Oslo: Stenersen, 1990.

Eggum, Arne. "Den unge Munch i lys av den franske naturalismen og impresjonisme" [33–61]; "Om betydningen av Munchs to opphold i Frankrike, 1891 og 1892" [106–147]; "Edvard Munchs forsøk på å erobre Paris 1896-1898" [188–221]; "Edvard Munchs fargekunst og fauvismen" [288–309]. In *Munch og Frankrike* [exhibition catalogue]. Oslo: Munchmuseet, 1991. [Also published Paris 1991]

Eggum, Arne. "Edvard Munch. A Biographical Background". In *Edvard Munch. The Frieze of Life* [exhibition catalogue], 15–24. London: National Gallery Publications, 1992.

Eggum, Arne. "Edvard Munch und seine Modelle". In *Edvard Munch und seine Modelle* [exhibition catalogue], 13–154. Stuttgart: Verlag Gerd Hatje, 1993.

Eggum, Arne. *Edvard Munch. Portretter* [exhibition catalogue]. Oslo: Munchmuseet and Labyrinth Press, 1994 A.

Eggum, Arne. "Döden och kärleken. Ett centralt tema i Edvard Munchs konst". In *Kärleken och Döden. Två odödliga teman speglade i konsten under fyra sekler* [exhibition catalogue], 26–31. Gothenburg: Göteborgs konstmuseum, 1994 B.

Eggum, Arne. "Edvard Munch. Skulpturalen Arbeiten und Ideen". In *Die Maler und ihre Skulpturen: von Edgar Degas bis Gerhard Richter* [exhibition catalogue], 98–102. Essen: Museum Folkwang Essen; Cologne: DuMont, 1997.

Eggum, Arne. *Edvard Munchs sene Livsfrise og Lindefrisen* [unpublished exhibition catalogue]. Oslo: Munchmuseet, 1998 A.

Eggum, Arne. "Ekelyperioden i Edvard Munchs kunst 1916-1944". In *Munch og Ekely: 1916-1944* [exhibition catalogue], 9–92. Oslo: Munchmuseet and Labyrinth Press, 1998 B.

Eggum, Arne. "Henrik Ibsen som dramatiker i Edvard Munchs perspektiv". In *Edvard Munch og Henrik Ibsen* [exhibition catalogue], 20–34. Copenhagen: Kunstforeningen, 1998 C.

Eggum, Arne. *Munch i Munch-museet*. Oslo: Messel forlag, 1998 D.

Eggum, Arne. "Speilinger fra Auguste Rodin i Edvard Munchs kunst = Les reflets d'Auguste Rodin dans l'art d'Edvard Munch". In *Rodin og Norge* [exhibition catalogue], 110–119. Oslo: Orfeus, 1998 E.

Eggum, Arne. "Anarkistiske impresjoner fra Edvard Munchs pensel". In *Sommeren med Edvard Munch og Arne Kavli* [exhibition catalogue], 7–37. Vikersund: Blaafarveværket, 1999 A.

Eggum, Arne. "Edvard Munch, der Universalkünstler". In *Edvard Munch in Chemnitz* [exhibition catalogue], 13–19. Chemnitz: Wienand, 1999 B.

Eggum, Arne. "Munch og Warnemünde". In *Munch og Warnemünde 1907-1908 = Munch und Warnemünde* [exhibition catalogue], 25–107. Rostock: Kunsthalle Rostock, Oslo: Munchmuseet, 1999 C.

Eggum, Arne. *Edvard Munch. The Frieze of Life from painting to graphic art*. Oslo: Stenersens forlag, 2000.

Eggum, Arne. "Edvard Munch - the forbidden and the universal". In *Skrigets Ekko = Echoes of The Scream* [exhibition catalogue], 23–33. Ishøj: Arken, 2001.

Eggum, Arne. "Livsfrisen som den var utstilt hos Blomqvist i 1918". In *Edvard Munchs Livsfrise. En rekonstruksjon av utstillingen hos Blomqvist 1918* [exhibition catalogue], 13–36. Oslo: Munchmuseet and Labyrinth Press, 2002.

Eggum, Arne. "Munch på vei til Thielska Galleriet. En vandring med Nietzsche langs stupet". In *Edvard Munch og Thielska Galleriet*, 17–23. Oslo: Labyrinth Press, 2007.

Eggum, Arne. "'The woman, he must weep'". In *Edvard Munch. The Modern Eye = Der Moderne Blick = L'oeil moderne* [exhibition catalogue], 131–143. London: Tate Publishing, 2012. [Also published Paris 2011 and Frankfurt 2012]

Eggum, Arne. "The Scream as a vision of despair". In *Keys to a Passion* [exhibition catalogue], 192–199. Paris: Hazan, 2015.

Ekelöf, Gunnar. "Edvard Munch. Reflexioner med anledning av utställningen i Konstakademien". *Konstrevy* 3 (1937): 79–83.

Elsen-Schwedler, Beate. "Lesarten zu Edvard Munchs Vampir, einem Schlüsselbild der beginnenden Moderne". In *Edvard Munch, Vampir* [exhibition catalogue], 9–49. Schwäbisch Hall: Kunsthalle Würth Swiridoff, 2003.

Endresen, Signe. "Sol, sjø og nakne menn". In *Motiver, Mennesker. Studenter velger Munch* [exhibition catalogue], 25–27. Oslo: Munchmuseet, 2003.

Endresen, Signe. "Mannen og kunstneren. Den mørke mannsfiguren i Edvard Munchs malerier 1891-1908". In *Kjønnsforhandlinger. Studier i kunst, film og litteratur*, 216–230. Oslo: Pax, 2013.

Endresen, Signe. *Serial Experiments: Close Readings of Edvard Munch's Det Grønne Værelset* [thesis, PhD]. Oslo: Universitetet i Oslo, 2015.

Enoksen, Bjørn et al. (eds.). *Nordisk kriminalkrønike 2009*. Strømmen: Nordisk kriminalkrønike A/S and Nordisk politi-idrettsforbund, 2009.

Epstein, Sarah. *The Prints of Edvard Munch. The Mirror of His Life* [exhibition catalogue]. Oberlin: Oberlin College, 1983.

Esswein, Hermann. *Edvard Munch*. Munich and Leipzig: R. Piper & Co, 1905.

F

Faxneld, Per. "Blod, sæd og astrale energisugere. Edvard Munchs *Vampyr*". In *eMunch.no - tekst og bilde* [exhibition catalogue], 187-198. Oslo: Munchmuseet, 2011.

Feller, Gerd Udo. "Die Bilder von Edvard Munch als Bühne der Innenwelt betrachtet". In *Edvard Munch. Liebe, Angst, Tod: Themen und Variationen* [exhibition catalogue], 445-464. Bielefeld: Kunsthalle Bielefeld, 1980.

Ferus, Katharina. "Gesicht - Maske - Farbe. Frauenbilder des frühen zwanzigsten Jahrhunderts". In *Gesicht - Maske - Farbe* [exhibition catalogue], 9-92. Münster: Westfälisches Landesmuseum für Kunst und Kulturgeschichte; Nordrhein-Westfalen: Landschaftsverband Westfalen-Lippe, 2003.

Filla, Emil. "Tsjekkerne og Edvard Munch". *Kunst og Kultur* 25, no. 2 (1939): 65-71.

Flor, Harald. "Skrikets Ekko". *Vi ser på Kunst*, no. 2 (2001): 18-21.

Fluck, Andreas. "'... Jenseits von Zwist und Lärm' - Emil Nolde und Edvard Munch". In *Emil Nolde. Druckgraphik. Aus der Sammlung der Nolde-Stiftung Seebüll* [exhibition catalogue], 35-78. Munich: Hirmer, 1999.

Flaatten, Hans-Martin Frydenberg. "Skrik som ikon og dikt". In *Edvard Munchs Livsfrise. En rekonstruksjon av utstillingen hos Blomqvist 1918* [exhibition catalogue], 67-78. Oslo: Munchmuseet and Labyrinth Press, 2002.

Flaatten, Hans-Martin Frydenberg. "Dikteren, direktøren, maleren". In *Motiver, Mennesker. Studenter velger Munch* [exhibition catalogue], 13-15. Oslo: Munchmuseet, 2003.

Flaatten, Hans-Martin Frydenberg. "Politikk og privatliv. Peter Watkins' Edvard Munch". *Kunstmagasinet*, no. 3 (2007): 50-52.

Flaatten, Hans-Martin Frydenberg. "Frå 'romanfragment' til prosadikt - Edvard Munch og den moderne pessimismens Medusahode". In *Munch blir "Munch": Kunstneriske strategier 1880-1892 = Munch Becoming "Munch". Artistic Strategies 1880-1892* [exhibition catalogue], 105-120. Oslo: Munchmuseet, 2008.

Flaatten, Hans-Martin Frydenberg. *Soloppgang i Kragerø. Historien om Edvard Munchs liv på Skrubben 1909-1915*. Kragerø: Kragerø kommune and Kragerø og Skåtøy historielag, 2009.

Flaatten, Hans-Martin Frydenberg. "Edvard Munch og Åsgårdstrand - en kronologisk oversikt". In *Kjærlighetens strand. Edvard Munch og Åsgårdstrand* [exhibition catalogue], 81-98. Oslo: Labyrinth Press, 2010 A.

Flaatten, Hans-Martin Frydenberg. "Schede critiche". In *Munch e lo spirito del Nord. Scandinavia nel secondo ottocento* [exhibition catalogue], 323-342. Treviso: Linea d'ombra, 2010 B.

Flaatten, Hans-Martin Frydenberg. *Edvard Munch. Måneskinn i Åsgårdstrand - Edvard Munchs sjelelandskap, scener, stemmer og stemninger i en småby ved sjøen*. Oslo: Sem & Stenersen, 2013 A.

Flaatten, Hans-Martin Frydenberg. "Byen, fjorden og landskapet. Edvard Munchs søken etter stedets sjel". In *Edvard Munch 1863-1944* [exhibition catalogue], 88-101. Milan: Skira; Oslo: Nasjonalmuseet and Munchmuseet, 2013 B.

Flaatten, Hans-Martin Frydenberg. *Edvard Munch i Moss: Kunst, krig og kapital på Jeløy 1913-1916*. Oslo: Sem & Stenersen, 2014 A.

Flaatten, Hans-Martin Frydenberg. "Mestari ja meklari - Edvard Munch ja Rolf E. Stenersen = Mästaren och mäklaren - Edvard Munch och Rolf E. Stenersen". In *Edvard Munch: Elämän tanssi = Livets dans = The Dance of Life* [exhibition catalogue], 83-119. Helsinki: Didrichsen Art Museum, 2014 B.

Flaatten, Hans-Martin Frydenberg. *Edvard Munch. Høysommer i Hvitsten - Hans kunstnerliv på Nedre Ramme 1910-44*. Vestby: Vestby kommune, 2016.

Flaatten, Hans-Martin Frydenberg. "Rasmus Meyer: Den 'umættelige' Munch-samleren". In *I oss er verdener* [exhibition catalogue], 68-78. Bergen: KODE, 2019.

Ford, Thierry, Adriana Rizzo, Ella Hendriks, Tine Frøysaker and Francesco Caruso. "A non-invasive screening study of varnishes applied to three paintings by Edvard Munch using portable diffuse reflectance infrared Fourier transform spectroscopy (DRIFTS)". *Herit Sci* 7, art. no. 84 (2019): https://doi.org/10.1186/s40494-019-0327-1.

Ford, Thierry. "An Integrated Conservation Approach to a Historic Collection: The Controversial Varnishing of Munch's Paintings". In *Transcending Boundaries: Integrated Approaches to Conservation*, 17.-21. May. Beijing: ICOM-CC 19th Triennial Conference Preprints, 2021.

Ford, Thierry, Magdalena Iwanickca, Elena Platania, Piotr Targowoski and Ella Hendriks. "Munch and optical coherence tomography: unravelling historical and artist applied varnish layers in painting collections". *European Physical Journal Plus* 136, art. no. 899 (2021): https://doi.org/10.1140/epjp/s13360-021-01758-5.

Forsman, Erik. "'Alpha und Omega'. Edvard Munch als Erzähler". In *Bild und Gedanke. Festschrift für Gerhart Baumann zum 60. Geburtstag*, 120-132. Munich: Fink, 1980.

Forsman, Erik. "Menschen auf der Strasse - ein Bildthema bei Edvard Munch". In *Studier i konstvetenskap tillägnade Brita Linde*, 55-65. Stockholm: Konstvetenskapliga institutionen vid Stockholms Universitet, 1985.

Forsman, Erik. "Tanz und Tod im Werk Edvard Munchs". In *Tanz und Tod in der Kunst und Literatur*, 299-315. Berlin: Dunker und Humblot, 1993.

Forsman, Erik. "Edvard Munch. Sein Werk und die Kunstwissenschaft heute". *Zeitschrift für Kunstgeschichte* 57, no. 3 (1994): 521-532.

Fosli, Halvor. *Kristianiabohemen. Byen, miljøet, menneska*. Oslo: Samlaget, 1994.

Franke, Carola. *Edvard Munch und sein erster Berlin-Aufenthalt in den Jahren 1892-1895* [unpublished thesis, magister]. Tübingen: Universität Tübingen, 1980.

Fredlund, Björn (ed.). *Edvard Munch* [exhibition catalogue]. Gothenburg: Göteborgs konstmuseum, 2002.

Fredly, Janne. "Fire malerier". In *Motiver, Mennesker. Studenter velger Munch* [exhibition catalogue], 37-38. Oslo: Munchmuseet, 2003.

Frosterus, Sigurd. "Edvard Munchs utställning i Ateneum". In *Solljus och slagskugga*, 128-138. Helsinki: Söderström & Co förlagsaktiebolag, 1917.

Frosterus, Sigurd. *Nordiskt i dur och moll*. Helsinki: Søderstrøm, 1946.

Frøysaker, Tine. "The paintings of Edvard Munch in the Assembly Hall of Oslo University. Their treatment history and the Aula-project". *Restauro*, June (2007): 246-257.

Frøysaker, Tine. "Bevaring av Edvard Munchs Aula-malerier før og nå". *Kunst og Kultur* 91, no. 1 (2008): 2-17.

Frøysaker, Tine (ed.). *Public Paintings by Edvard Munch and His Contemporaries: Change and Conservation Challenges*. London: Archetype, 2015.

Fuchs, Rudi. "Standhaftighet = obstinacy". In *Munch og etter Munch, eller Maleres standhaftighet = Munch and after Munch, or The obstinacy of painters* [exhibition catalogue], 11-27. Amsterdam: Stedelijk Museum; Oslo: Munchmuseet, 1996.

Fugl, Alexander. "Edvard Munch 70 år". *Samleren* 10 (1933): 165-180.

Fåhræus, Klas. "Edvard Munch". *Konstrevy* 4 (1927): 3-14.

G

Gaillard, Nicole. "Munch: le triomphe de Carmen". In *Couples peints. Esthètique de la réception et peinture figurative*, 91-109. Lausanne: Éditions Antipodes, 2013.

Gauguin, Pola. *Edvard Munch*. Oslo: Aschehoug, 1933.

Gauguin, Pola. *Edvard Munch* [new edition]. Oslo: Aschehoug, 1946 A.

Gauguin, Pola. *Grafikeren Edvard Munch. Litografier*. Trondheim: F. Bruns bokhandels forlag, 1946 B.

Gauguin, Pola. *Grafikeren Edvard Munch. Tresnitt og raderinger*. Trondheim: F. Bruns bokhandels forlag, 1946 C.

Gauguin, Pola. "Mennesket Edvard Munch". *Kunst og Kultur* 29, nos. 3-4 (1946 D): 103-126.

Gauguin, Pola. *Edvard Munch*. Stockholm: Albert Bonniers Förlag, 1947.

Geelhaar, Christian. "Katalog und Kommentare zu den Gemälden". In *Edvard Munch. Sein Werk in Schweizer Sammlungen*, 11-65. Basel: Öffentliche Kunstsammlung Basel, 1985.

Georgi, Walter. "Herbstausstellung Berlin 1913". *Deutsche Kunst und Dekoration* 5, February (1914): 357-364.

Gerard, Edouard. "Edvard Munchs kunst". In *Edvard Munch. Maleriudstilling i Dioramalokalet, Karl Johans Gd. 41* [exhibition catalogue], 3-6. Kristiania: Johannes Bjørnstads Bogtrykkeri, 1897.

Gercken, Günther. "Todesangst und Todesvisionen im Werk von Edvard Munch". In *Todesbilder in der zeitgenössischen Kunst mit einem Rückblick auf Hodler und Munch* [exhibition catalogue], 9-15. Hamburg: Kunstverein, 1983.

Gercken, Günther. "Keime des Zukünftigen. Baselitz und Munch". In *Edvard Munch. Höhepunkt des malerischen Werks im 20. Jahrhundert* [exhibition catalogue], 77-84. Hamburg: Frölich & Kaufmann, 1984.

Gerkens, Gerhard. "Munch und Vuillard". In *Edvard Munch. Probleme - Forschungen - Thesen*, 133-146. Munich: Prestel, 1973.

Gerkens, Gerhard. "Edvard Munch. Die tote Mutter, um 1900". In *Bilder Entstehen* [exhibition catalogue], 32-39. Bremen: Kunsthalle Bremen, 1975.

Gerner, Cornelia. *Edvard Munch: Die Madonna: Untersuchungen zu einer für die künstlerische Persönlichkeit und die psychologischen Wurzeln seiner Thematik aufschlussreiche Werkgruppe Munchs* [thesis, magister]. Munich: Ludwig-Maximilians-Universität, 1982.

Gerner, Cornelia. "Die Beschlagnahmung der Werke Munchs im Nationalsozialismus" [340-350]; "Zur Munch-Rezeption nach 1945 in Deutschland" [351-356]. In *Edvard Munch. Sommernacht am Oslofjord, um 1900* [exhibition catalogue]. Mannheim: Städtische Kunsthalle Mannheim, 1988.

Gerner, Cornelia. *Die "Madonna" in Edvard Munchs Kunst. Frauenbilder und Frauenbild im ausgehenden 19. Jahrhundert* [thesis, doctoral]. Berlin: Technische Universität, 1990.

Gerner, Cornelia. *Die "Madonna" in Edvard Munchs Kunst. Frauenbilder und Frauenbild im ausgehenden 19. Jahrhundert*. Morsbach: Literaturverlag Norden Reinhardt, 1993.

Gerner, Cornelia. "Salome, Vampir und Madonnen. Zu Munchs Frauenbildern". In *Munch revisited. Edvard Munch und die heutige Kunst* [exhibition catalogue], 26-34. Dortmund: Kerber Verlag, 2005.

Geskó, Judit (ed.). *Cézanne and the Past. Tradition and Creativity*. Budapest: Museum of Fine Arts, 2012.

Gether, Christian. "Edvard Munchs vitalisme". In *Edvard Munch. Det nære liv - malerier fra Ekely 1916-1944* [exhibition catalogue], 11-20. Ishøj: Arken, 2000.

Gether, Christian. "Broen til det 20. århundre = The bridge to the 20th century". In *Skrigets Ekko = Echoes of The Scream* [exhibition catalogue], 11–22. Ishøj: Arken, 2001.

Gether, Christian. "Kroppen, den ny tids katedral. Om Edvard Munchs Badende menn, 1907–08". In *500 års verdenskunst*, 156–163. Copenhagen: Gyldendal, 2004.

Gierløff, Christian. "Munch selv". *Kunst og Kultur* 4 (1913): 102–116.

Gierløff, Christian. "Munch i Åsgård-strand sommeren 1904". In *Åsgårdstrand. Om hvite hus og løvkroner. Spredt historikk*, 86–100. Bergen: J.W. Eide, 1946.

Gierløff, Christian. *Edvard Munch selv*. Oslo: Gyldendal, 1953.

Ginzburg, Natalia. "L'Urlo". In *Mai devi domandarmi*, 96–101. Milan: Garzanti, 1971.

Gjessing, Oda Wildhagen. "Edvard Munch - tolkningsstrategier". *En Face. Kunsthistorisk tidsskrift*, no. 2 (2004 A): 63–71.

Gjessing, Oda Wildhagen. "Tanker omkring et konsept og en akt". In *Avkledd. Studenter velger Munch* [exhibition catalogue], 5–7. Oslo: Munchmuseet, 2004 B.

Gjessing, Oda Wildhagen. "Asger Jorn og Edvard Munch". *Kunst og Kultur* 90, no. 4 (2007): 210–229.

Gjessing, Oda Wildhagen. "Jorn + Munch". In *Jorn + Munch* [exhibition catalogue], 27–55. Brussels: Mercatorfonds; Oslo: Munchmuseet, 2016.

Glaser, Curt. "Edvard Munchs Wand-gemälde für die Universität in Kristiania". *Zeitschrift für bildende Kunst*, Sonder-drück N.F. (1914): 61–66.

Glaser, Curt. *Edvard Munch*. Berlin: Bruno Cassirer, 1917. [Revised editions 1918 and 1922]

Glaser, Curt. "Edvard Munch". *Der Quer-schnitt* 12, December (1926): 924–929.

Glaser, Curt. "Besuch bei Munch". *Kunst und Künstler* XXV (1927): 203–209.

Glosli, Sven Arne. "Edvard Munchs tre kvinner i St. Cloud". *Agora* 3–4 (1995): 112–123.

Gluchowska, Lidia. "Munch, Przybysze-wski and 'The Scream'". *Kunst og Kultur* 96, no. 4 (2013): 182–191.

Gløersen, Inger Alver. *Den Munch jeg møtte*. Oslo: Gyldendal, 1962.

Gløersen, Inger Alver. *Lykkehuset. Edvard Munch og Åsgårdstrand*. Oslo: Gyldendal, 1970.

Gløersen, Inger Alver. *Munch as I knew him*. Hellerup: Edition Bløndal, 1994.

Gohr, Siegfried. "Warhol and Munch". In *Warhol after Munch* [exhibition catalogue], 32–40. Humlebæk: Louisiana Museum of Modern Art, 2010.

Goldberg, Itzhak. "Les autoportraits de Munch: Une obsession autobi-ographique". In *Edvard Munch. L'oeil moderne* [exhibition catalogue], 42–49. Issy-les-Moulineaux: Beaux Arts, 2011.

Goldin, Marco (ed.). *Munch e lo spirito del Nord. Scandinavia nel secondo ottocento* [exhibition catalogue]. Treviso: Linea d'ombra, 2010.

Gordon, Donald E. "'Kirchner in Dresden'". *The Art Bulletin*, vol. 48 (1966): 335–366.

Graen, Monika. *Das Dreifrauenthema bei Edvard Munch*. Frankfurt am Main: Peter Lang, 1985.

Gran, Henning. "Edvard Munchs møte med norsk kritikk 1895". *Kunst og Kultur* 46, no. 4 (1963): 205–226.

Greenberg, Clement. "Complaints of an art critic". In *The collected essays and criticism. Modernism with a vengeance* 4, 265–272. Chicago: University of Chicago Press, 1993.

Grelland, Hans Herlof. *Tausheten og øyeblikket. Kierkegaard - Ibsen - Munch*. Kristiansand: Høyskoleforlaget, 2007.

Greve, Eli Ingebretsen. *Edvard Munch (grafikk)*. Oslo: Nasjonalgalleriet, 1932 A.

Greve, Eli Ingebretsen. *Norsk tegnekunst*. Oslo: Gyldendal Norsk Forlag, 1932 B.

Greve, Eli Ingebretsen. *Edvard Munchs tresnitt*. Oslo: Nasjonalgalleriet, 1946.

Greve, Eli Ingebretsen. *Edvard Munch. Liv og verk i lys av tresnittene*. Oslo: Cap-pelen, 1963.

Grimschitz, Bruno. "Männer am Meer". *Die Bildende Kunste. Wiener Jahrbuch*, no. 4 (1921): 57–58.

Grimstad, Inger. *Menneskeberget, en studie av Edvard Munch. Undersøkelses-og konserveringsrapport for MM M935* [unpublished thesis, technical conserva-tor]. Oslo: I. Grimstad, 2000.

Grimstad, Inger. "Menneskeberget - en studie av Edvard Munch". *Norske Kon-serves* 13, no. 1 (2002): 9–10.

Grisebach, Lucius. "Munch-Ausstel-lungen". In *Edvard Munch. Probleme - Forschungen - Thesen*, 239–248. Munich: Prestel, 1973.

Gropp, Birgit. *Das Kunstwerk des Monats. Februar 2004. [Edvard Munch: Zwei weibli-che Akte, 1903]*. Münster: Landesmuseum für Kunst und Kulturgeschichte, 2004.

Grøgaard, Stian. *Edvard Munch. Et utsatt liv*. Oslo: Akademika, 2013 A.

Grøgaard, Stian. "The lure of memory in The sick child". *Scandinavian Psychoana-lytic Review* 36, no. 2 (2013 B): 74–79.

Guenther, Peder W. "Edvard Munch und der Symbolismus". In *Edvard Munch. Liebe, Angst, Tod: Themen und Variationen* [exhibition catalogue], 387–392. Bielefeld: Kunsthalle Bielefeld, 1980.

Guleng, Mai Britt. "Utstillingsstrategi og kunstnerisk individualitet. Edvard Munchs kritikere 1892". In *Munch blir "Munch". Kunstneriske strategier 1880–1892 = Munch Becoming "Munch". Artistic Strategies 1880–1892* [exhibition catalogue], 211–230. Oslo: Munchmuseet, 2008.

Guleng, Mai Britt. "Edvard Munch - fortelleren", i *eMunch.no - tekst og bilde* [exhibition catalogue], 219–236. Oslo: Munchmuseet, 2011.

Guleng, Mai Britt. "Livsfrisens for-tellinger. Edvard Munchs bildeserier". In *Edvard Munch 1863-1944*, 128–139. Milan: Skira; Oslo: Nasjonalmuseet and Munchmuseet, 2013.

Guleng, Mai Britt. "Edvard Munch and Authentic Expression". In *Anxiety and Exploration. Polish and Norwegian Artists at the Points of Breakthrough* [exhibition catalogue], 354–372. Warsaw: The Fry-deryk Chopin Institute, 2014.

Gurlitt, Fritz. *See* "Kunstsalon Fritz Gurlitt". 1914.

Göpel, Erhard. *Edvard Munch. Selbst-bildnisse und Dokumente*. Munich: Albert Langen & Georg Müller, 1955.

Göschel, Detlef. "Der konservatorische und maltechnische Zustand des Gemäl-des". In *Edvard Munch, Käte und Hugo Perls 1913* [exhibition catalogue], 49–50. Chemnitz: Wienand, 2003.

H

Halkes, Petra. "'The Scream' in the age of mechanical reproduction". *Parallax* 5, no. 3 (1999): 114–128.

Hals, Harald. "Edv. Munch og Åsgård-strand". *Vestfoldminne* 5 (1946): 65–79.

Hals, Harald. *Edvard Munch og byen. Oslo-bilder fra kunstnerens ungdom*. Oslo: Oslo bymuseum, 1955.

Halvorsen, Harald Holst. *Endel av Edv. Munchs kunstverker, som jeg har samlet, og for de flestes vedkommende dessverre også solgt igjen fra 1915-1950*. Oslo: Holst Halvorsens kunsthandel, 1952.

Hamran, Ulf. "Edvard Munchs Krag-erø-bilder". *Historieglimt. Årsskrift for Kragerø og Skåtøy Historielag* (2009): 118–133.

Hansen, Dorothee, Barbara Nier-hoff-Wielkog Katharina Groth. "Die ausgestellten Werke". In *Edvard Munch - Rätsel hinter der Leinwand* [exhibition catalogue], 42–173. Cologne: DuMont, 2011.

Hansen, Dorothee. "Die Munch-Ausstel-lung im Februar/März 1909 in Bremen". In *Edvard Munch - Rätsel hinter der Leinwand* [exhibition catalogue], 212–213. Cologne: DuMont, 2011 A.

Hansen, Dorothee. "Munchs Werke in der Internationalen Ausstellung in der Kunsthalle Bremen, 1. Februar bis 31. März 1914". In *Edvard Munch - Rätsel hinter der Leinwand* [exhibition catalogue], 214. Cologne: DuMont, 2011 B.

Hansen, Jan Erik Ebbestad. "Munch". In *Mesterverk. Odd Nerdrums kanon*, 233–237. Oslo: Gyldendal fakta, 2002.

Hansen, Vibeke Waallann. "Landskap som sjelstilstand". In *Det magiske nord. Finsk og norsk kunst omkring 1900* [exhi-bition catalogue], 163–167. Oslo: Nasjonal-museet, 2015.

Hardeberg, John Yngve et al. "Spectral 'scream': hyperspectral image acquisi-tion and analysis of a masterpiece". In *Public paintings by Edvard Munch and his contemporaries. Change and conservation challenges*, 72–83. London: Archetype, 2015.

Haugerud, Helge. *Edvard Munch - årene 1902-09. Spesialoppgave i psykiatri* [unpublished thesis]. Oslo: Universitetet i Oslo, 1985.

Hauptmann, Ivo. "Minner om Edvard Munch" [62–67]; "Erinnerungen an Edvard Munch" [131–132]. *Oslo kommunes kunstsamlinger. Årbok 1963* (1963).

Hedin, Gry. "Missing links. Om korre-spondansen mellom Edvard Munchs *Skrik* og Charles Darwins *The Expression of the Emotions in Man and Animals*". *Kunst og kultur* 94, no. 3 (2011 A): 134–143.

Hedin, Gry. *Skrig, sult og frugtbarhed: Darwins fortællinger og metoder som katalysator for værker af J. P. Jacobsen, Knut Hamsun, J. F. Willumsen, Edvard Munch og August Strindberg* [thesis, PhD]. Copenhagen: Københavns Universitet: 2011 B.

Heere, Heribert. "Edvard Munch. Ein Naturalist der Seele?" In *Edvard Munch. Liebe, Angst, Tod: Themen und Variationen* [exhibition catalogue], 393–406. Bielefeld: Kunsthalle Bielefeld, 1980.

Heilbut, Emil. "Die Sammlung Linde in Lübeck". *Kunst und Künstler* 2 (1903): 6–20.

Heilbut, Emil. "Die Sammlung Linde in Lübeck (Schluss)" [302–325]; "Einige neue Bildnisse von Edvard Munch" [489–492]. *Kunst und Künstler* 2 (1904).

Heise, Carl Georg. "Edvard Munchs Selb-stbildnisse". *Ostsee-Rundschau*, November (1933): 128–137.

Heise, Carl Georg. *Die vier Söhne des Dr. Max Linde*. Stuttgart: Philipp Reclam jun., 1956.

Heise, Carl Georg. "Erinnerungen an Edvard Munch". In *Edvard Munch. Probleme - Forschungen - Thesen*, 9–13. Munich: Prestel, 1973.

Helleland, Allis. "Edvard Munch - et liv i angst = Edvard Munch - A Life in Anx-iety". In *Edvard Munch. Angst = Anxiety* [exhibition catalogue], 17–35. Aarhus: ARoS Aarhus Kunstmuseum, 2012.

Heller, Reinhold. "Strømpefabrikanten, van de Velde og Edvard Munch". *Kunst og Kultur* 51, no. 2 (1968): 89–104.

Heller, Reinhold. "'Affæren Munch' Berlin 1892–1893". *Kunst og Kultur* 52, no. 3 (1969 A): 175–191.

Heller, Reinhold. *Edvard Munch's "Life Frieze". Its beginnings and origins* [unpub-lished thesis, doctoral]. Bloomington: Indiana University Bloomington, 1969 B.

Heller, Reinhold. "The Iconography of Edvard Munch's 'The Sphinx'". *Art Forum*, October (1970): 72–80.

Heller, Reinhold. "Edvard Munch and the clarification of life". In *The Epstein Collection* [exhibition catalogue], 121–129. Oberlin: Oberlin College, 1972.

Heller, Reinhold. "Edvard Munch's 'Vision' and the Symbolist Swan". *Art Quarterly* (1973 A): 209–249.

Heller, Reinhold. *The Scream*. London: Allen Lane, 1973 B.

Heller, Reinhold. "Edvard Munch's Night,

the aesthethics of decadence and the content of biography". *Arts Magazine* 53 (1978 A): 80-105.

Heller, Reinhold. "Love as a Series of Paintings". In *Edvard Munch. Symbols & Images* [exhibition catalogue], 87-111. Washington: National Gallery of Art, 1978 B.

Heller, Reinhold. "Edvard Munch. Die Liebe und die Kunst". In *Edvard Munch. Liebe, Angst, Tod: Themen und Variationen* [exhibition catalogue], 297-306. Bielefeld: Kunsthalle Bielefeld, 1980.

Heller, Reinhold. "Some observations concerning grim ladies, dominating women, and frightened men around 1900". In *The earthly chimera and the femme fatale. Fear of woman in nineteenth-century art* [exhibition catalogue], 7-14. Chicago: University of Chocago and David and Alfred Smart Gallery, 1981.

Heller, Reinhold. *Munch. His Life and Work*. London: John Murray, 1984.

Heller, Reinhold. "Concerning Symbolism and the Structure of Surface". *Art Journal* XLV, no. 2 (1985): 146-153.

Heller, Reinhold. "Form and Formation of Edvard Munch's Frieze of Life". In *Edvard Munch. The Frieze of Life* [exhibition catalogue], 25-37. London: National Gallery Publications, 1992.

Heller, Reinhold. "Anton von Werner, der Fall Munch und die Moderne im Berlin der 1890er Jahre". In *Anton von Werner. Geschichte in Bildern*, 101-109. Munich: Hirmer, 1993 A.

Heller, Reinhold. *Edvard Munch. Leben und Werk*. Munich: Prestel, 1993 B.

Heller, Reinhold. "Å se Edvard Munch". *Agora. Journal for metafysisk spekulasjon*, nos. 3-4 (1995): 4-22.

Heller, Reinhold. "Krankheit, Kunst und Keuschheit. Edvard Munch am Ende des 19. Jahrhunderts = Malattia, arte e castità. Edvard Munch alla fine del XIX secolo". In *Edvard Munch = Edvard Munch* [exhibition catalogue], 93-110. Lugano: Museo d'arte moderna and Città di Lugano; Milan: Skira, 1998.

Heller, Reinhold. "'Ich glaube, ich male nur noch Frauen.' Die Aktdarstellung im Werk von Edvard Munch". In *Edvard Munch in Chemnitz* [exhibition catalogue], 285-292. Chemnitz: Wienand, 1999.

Heller, Reinhold. "Mondo meraviglioso". In *Edvard Munch. L'io e gli altri* [exhibition catalogue], 33-46. Milan: Electa Palazzo forti, 2001.

Heller, Reinhold. "'Could only have been painted by a madman', or could it?" In *Edvard Munch. The modern life of the soul* [exhibition catalogue], 16-33. New York: Museum of Modern Art, 2006.

Heller, Reinhold (ed.). *Brücke. The Birth of Expressionism in Dresden and Berlin, 1905-1913* [exhibition catalogue]. Ostfildern: Hatje Cantz, 2009.

Heller, Reinhold. "'Delvis meg selv': En sammenligning mellom Edvard Munch og Vincent van Gogh". In *Van Gogh + Munch* [exhibition catalogue], 62-80. Oslo and Brussels: Mercatorfonds, Orfeus, Munchmuseet and Van Gogh Musum, 2015.

Heller, Reinhold. "Edvard Munch, Germany and Expressionsim". In *Munch and Expressionism* [exhibition catalogue], 35-53. Munich: Prestel, 2016.

Helliesen, Sidsel. *Tegnekunst. Forarbeid - ferdig kunstverk* [exhibition catalogue]. Oslo: Nasjonalgalleriet, 1991.

Helliesen, Sidsel. *Tegnekunst. Fra forarbeid til ferdig kunstverk*. Oslo: Labyrinth Press, 1993.

Helliesen, Sidsel. *Norsk grafikk gjennom 100 år*. Oslo: Aschehoug, 2000.

Henningsen, Rune. "Åsgårdstrand 1967". In *Broen: Aasgaardstrandiana*, 88-103. Åsgårdstrand: Aasgaardstrand og omegn historielag, 2010.

Henningsen, Rune (ed.). *Edvard Munch i Åsgårdstrand. En fotografisk vandring i Munchs Åsgårdstrand = Edvard Munch in Åsgårdstrand. A photographic Tour in Munch's Åsgårdstrand = Edvard Munch in Åsgårdstrand. Ein photographischer Blick aus Munchs Åsgårdstrand*. Åsgårdstrand: Aasgaardstrand og omegn historielag, 2014.

Hodin, J.P. "Ett möte med Edvard Munch". *Konstrevy* (1939): 9-13.

Hodin, J.P. "Strindberg om Edvard Munch". *Konstrevy* (1940): 199-202.

Hodin, J.P. *Edvard Munch. Nordens genius*. Stockholm: Ljus, 1948.

Hodin, J.P. "Munch and expressionism". *Art News* XLIX, no. 3 (1950): 26-29/55-56.

Hodin, J.P. *Edvard Munch*. London: Thames & Hudson, 1972.

Hoershelmann, Antonia. "Crossover - Munch und die Moderne = Crossover - Munch and modernism". In *Edvard Munch. Thema und Variation = Edvard Munch. Theme and variation* [exhibition catalogue], 13-22. Vienna: Albertina, 2003.

Hofer, Gunter. "Edvard Munch. 'Anziehung' und 'Loslösung'". In *Edvard Munch. Liebe, Angst, Tod. Themen und Variationen* [exhibition catalogue], 307-314. Bielefeld: Kunsthalle Bielefeld, 1980.

Hofstätter, Hans H. *Jugendstil*. Stuttgart: Klett, 1982.

Hougen, Pål. "Kunstneren som stedfortreder". In *Höjdpunkter i norsk konst. En konstbok från Nationalmuseum*, 123-140. Stockholm: Rabén & Sjögren, 1968.

Hougen, Pål. *Edvard Munch. Tegninger, skisser, studier* [exhibition catalogue]. Oslo: Munchmuseet, 1973.

Hougen, Pål. *Edvard Munch og Henrik Ibsen* [exhibition catalogue]. Bergen: Vestlandske kunstindustrimuseum, 1975.

Hougen, Pål. *Munch und Ibsen* [exhibition catalogue]. Zürich: Kunsthaus Zürich, 1976.

Hougen, Pål. "Munch and Ibsen". In *Edvard Munch and Henrik Ibsen* [exhibition catalogue], 11-29. Northfield: St. Olaf College, 1978.

House, John. "That Magical Light". In *Impressions of the Riviera. Monet, Renoir, Matisse and their Contemporaries* [exhibition catalogue], 10-26. Portland: Portland Museum of Art, 1998.

Hovdenakk, Per. "Edvard Munch og Norge. Fortolkningsproblemer = Edvard Munch and Norway. Problems of interpretation". In *Skrigets Ekko = Echoes of The Scream* [exhibition catalogue], 86-103. Ishøj: Arken, 2001.

Hovdenakk, Per. "Skrikets Ekko". *Nettverk*, no. 1 (2001): 26-28.

Howe, Jeffrey. "Munch in context" [11-19]; "Nocturnes: The music of melancholy, and the mysteries of love and death" [48-74]. In *Edvard Munch. Psyche, symbol and expression* [exhibition catalogue]. Chestnut Hill: McMullen Museum of Art, 2001.

Howoldt, Jenns E. "Bildersturm im Behnhaus. Die Aktion 'Entartete Kunst' 1937 und ihre Vorgeschichte". In *Bildersturm im Behnhaus* [exhibition catalogue], 3-12. Lübeck: Museum für Kunst und Kulturgeschichte der Hansestadt, 1987.

Hübener, Kristin. *Edvard Munch und Henrik Ibsen: Bild- und texthermeneutische Studien zu Munchs "Die Frau in drei Stadien" und Ibsens "Wenn wir Toten erwachen" vor dem Hintergrund der Künstler - Leben - Problematik un 1900* [thesis, magister]. Frankfurt am Main: Johann Wolfgang Goethe-Universität, 1994.

Huber, Hans Dieter. "Farbgestalt und Farbsymbolik in Munchs 'Sommernacht am Oslofjord'". In *Edvard Munch. Sommernacht am Oslofjord, um 1900* [exhibition catalogue], 60-69. Mannheim: Städtische Kunsthalle Mannheim, 1988.

Huber, Hans Dieter. "Edvard Munch porträtiert Käte und Hugo Perls". In *Edvard Munch. Käte und Hugo Perls* [exhibition catalogue], 7-40. Chemnitz: Wienand, 2003.

Huber, Hans Dieter. *Edvard Munch. Tanz des Lebens. Eine Biographie*. Stuttgart: Reclam, 2013.

Huusko, Timo. "I spenningsfeltet mellom kunst og kjød. Edvard Munch, Badende menn og Finland = Im Spannungsfeld von Kunst und Trieb. Edvard Munch, Badende Männer und Finnland". In *Munch og Warnemünde = Munch und Warnemünde* [exhibition catalogue], 109-117. Rostock: Kunsthalle Rostock; Oslo: Munchmuseet, 1999.

Huusko, Timo. "Naturopplevelse og folketro som kunstnerisk drivkraft". In *Det magiske nord. Finsk og norsk kunst omkring 1900* [exhibition catalogue], 69-83. Oslo: Nasjonalmuseet, 2015.

Høifødt, Frank. "Rød Villvin". *Vi ser på Kunst*, no. 4 (1989): 26-27.

Høifødt, Frank. "Smertens blomst - et supplement". *Kunst og Kultur* 72, no. 4 (1989): 219-231.

Høifødt, Frank. "Livets dans". *Kunst og Kultur* 73, no. 3 (1990): 166-181.

Høifødt, Frank. *Kvinnen, kunsten, korset.*

Edvard Munch anno 1900 [unpublished thesis, doctoral]. Oslo: Universitetet i Oslo, 1995 A.

Høifødt, Frank. "Munch - og skriket fra Marsyas". *Agora. Journal for metafysisk spekulasjon*, nos. 3-4 (1995 B): 61-72.

Høifødt, Frank. "Edvard Munchs 'Rødt og hvitt' - 1894 eller 1900?" *Kunst og Kultur* 81, no. 2 (1998): 89-103.

Høifødt, Frank. "Edvard Munchs Stoffveksling - frisens 'beltespenne'". *Kunst og Kultur* 84, no. 3 (2001): 124-147.

Høifødt, Frank. "Kvinnen - Kjærlighet og død - Dommedag". In *Edvard Munchs Livsfrise. En rekonstruksjon av utstillingen hos Blomqvist 1918* [exhibition catalogue], 97-114. Oslo: Munchmuseet and Labyrinth Press, 2002 A.

Høifødt, Frank. *Munch i Oslo = Munch in Oslo*. Oslo: N.W. Damm & Søn, 2002 B.

Høifødt, Frank. "Edvard Munch - Stil und Tema um 1900 = Edvard Munch - style and theme around the year 1900". In *Edvard Munch. Thema und Variation = Edvard Munch. Theme and variation* [exhibition catalogue], 53-66. Vienna: Albertina, 2003.

Høifødt, Frank. "Skuddet i Åsgårdstrand. Tema med variasjoner". *En Face*, no. 2 (2004): 54-61.

Høifødt, Frank. "The Kristiania bohemia reflected in the art of the young Edvard Munch". In *Edvard Munch. An anthology*, 15-42. Oslo: Unipub, 2006.

Høifødt, Frank. "The riddle in Bremen". *Kunst og Kultur* 90, no. 3 (2007): 197-207.

Høifødt, Frank. "Munchs Madonna - drøm og visjon = Munchs Madonna - Dream and Vision". In *Madonna = Madonna* [exhibition catalogue], 13-59. Bergen: Vigmostad & Bjørke, 2008.

Høifødt, Frank. *Kunsten, kvinnen og en ladd revolver. Edvard Munch anno 1900*. Oslo: Press, 2010 A.

Høifødt, Frank. "Munken og det tomme kors - Edvard Munch (1863-1944) og kristendommen". *Kirke og Kultur: Religon og Samfunn* 114, no. 2 (2010 B): 114-123.

Høst, Sigurd. "Edvard Munch. Minder og indtryk". *Kunst og Kultur* 4 (1914): 117-121.

Høst, Sigurd. "Edvard Munch". *The American Scandinavian Review* VII, no. 6 (1919): 432-442.

Haaland, Øivind. *Melankoliens pedagogikk - en fortelling om kjærlighet og kunst*. Lillehammer: Høgskolen i Lillehammer, 2000.

Haaland, Øivind and Stephen Dobson. "Den postmoderne melankoli - Edvard Munchs livsfrise med Julia Kristevas tekst". *Sosiologisk årbok* 5, no. 2 (2000): 181-229.

I

Ito, Fumiko. "Historien - utviklingen av et motiv". In *Motiver. Mennesker. Studenter velger Munch* [exhibition catalogue], 31-33. Oslo: Munchmuseet, 2006 A.

Ito, Fumiko. "Kojiro Matsukata and

Edvard Munch". *Journal of the National Museum of Western Art* 10 (2006 B): 25–62.

J

Jacob, Carmen Fernández. "Edvard Munch (Löten 1863 – Skoyen 1944). Biografía, obra pictórica". In *La patología ocular en la pintura a través de la historia clínica oftalmológica*, 167–188. Zaragoza: Sociedad Española de Oftalmológica, 2017.

Jacobsen, Lasse. "Livsfrisen og Livsfrisens tilblivelse – maleren griper til sverdet og pennen". In *Edvard Munchs Livsfrise. En rekonstruksjon av utstillingen hos Blomqvist 1918* [exhibition catalogue], 62–66. Oslo: Munchmuseet and Labyrinth Press, 2002.

Jacobsen, Lasse. "Edvard Munchs fotoalbum fra atelier Marschalk, Berlin 1892–93 – og 'Det syke barn'" [199–205]; "Verein Berliner Künstler og utstillingslokalene i Architektenhaus – Rotunden" [207–208]. In *Munch blir "Munch". Kunstneriske strategier 1888–1892 = Munch Becoming "Munch". Artistic Strategies 1880–1892* [exhibition catalogue]. Oslo: Munchmuseet, 2008.

Jacobsen, Lasse. "Edvard Munchs egne publikasjoner". In *eMunch.no – tekst og bilde* [exhibition catalogue], 109–120. Oslo: Munchmuseet, 2011.

Jacobsen, Lasse. "Edvard Munchs søknader til legatene og til Statens kunstnerstipend". *www.emunch.no. Edvard munchs tekster, digitalt arkiv* https://www.emunch.no/ART_applications.xhtml.

JAMA. "Edvard Munch painted the Inheritance". *The Journal of the American Medical Association* 212, no. 2 (1970): 232.

Janda, Annegret and Jörn Grabowski. *Kunst in Deutschland 1905–1937. Die verlorene Sammlung der Nationalgalerie im ehemaligen Kronprinzen-Palais*. Berlin: Staatliche Museen zu Berlin Preussischer Kulturbesitz, 1992.

Janssen, Hans. "Harry Graf Kessler und Edvard Munch". *Weltkunst* 11 (1990): 1706–1709.

Jaworska, Wladyslawa. "Munch und Przybyszewski". In *Edvard Munch. Probleme - Forschungen - Thesen*, 47–68. Munich: Prestel, 1973.

Jedlicka, Gotthard. "Über einige Selbstbildnisse von Edvard Munch". *Wallraf-Richartz-Jahrbuch* XX (1958): 225–260.

Johannesen, Ina. "Ritratto di donna in camicetta verde". In *Edvard Munch. Dal realismo all'espressionismo: dipinti e opere grafiche dalla Galleria nazionale di Oslo* [exhibition catalogue], 60. Livorno: Sillabe, 1999.

Johannesen, Ina. "Collections particulières". In *Edvard Munch, ou l'"Anti-Cri"* [exhibition catalogue], [unpaginated]. Paris: Éditions Pinacothèque de Paris, 2010.

Johannesen, Ina. "Munch på Ekely". In *Ekely. Historien om Munchs Ekely og kunstnerkolonien i Munchs hage*, 22–61. Oslo: Opera forlag, 2019.

Johannesen, Ole Rønning. "Edvard Munch og Bergen". *Oslo kommunes kunstsamlinger. Årbok 1852–1959* (1960): 18–37.

Jones, Liv Inger. *Norsk grafikk til 1970*. Oslo: Nasjonalgalleriet, 1971.

Junillon, Ingrid. *Le théâtre d'Henrik Ibsen dans l'oeuvre d'Edvard Munch : Scénographie, "illustration" et variations graphiques* [unpublished thesis, doctoral]. Lyon: Université Lumière, 2000.

Junillon, Ingrid. "Les autoportraits d'Edvard Munch à la lumiere du mythe de narcisse". *Textures*, no. 9 (2003): 147–179.

Junillon, Ingrid. "Deux Ragnarok du XXe siècle. Une série graphique d'Edvard Munch (1915–1916) et une fresque de Per Krohg (1933)". *Cahiers d'Études Germaniques*, no. 51 (2006): 21–41.

Junillon, Ingrid. *Edvard Munch face à Henrik Ibsen: impressions d'un lecteur*. Leuven: Peeters, 2009.

K

Karpf, Eva-Maria. *Karriereförderung in der Boheme: Munch, Strindberg, Przybyszewski und Meier-Graefe in Berlin und Paris* [thesis, magister]. Kiel: Christian-Albrecht-Universität, 1996.

Karpinski, Caroline. "Munch and Lautrec". *The Metropolitan Museum of Art Bulletin*, November (1964): 125–134.

Kaspers, Asja. "In Szene gesetzt – Figuren und Stilleben". In *Im Farbenrausch: Munch, Matisse und die Expressionisten* [exhibition catalogue], 252–255. Göttingen: Edition Folkwang/Steidl, 2012.

Kassay, Anne Marie. "Die Arbeiterbilder Edvard Munchs". *Tendenzen* 19, no. 122 (1978): 25–29.

Kaufmann, Bettina. "Eva Mudocci. Munchs 'søster-kjærlighet'?" In *Motiver, mennesker. Studenter velger Munch* [exhibition catalogue], 16–21. Oslo: Munchmuseet, 2003.

Kaufmann, Bettina. *Symbol und Wirklichkeit. Ernst Ludwig Kirchners "Bilder aus der Phantasie" und Edvard Munchs "Lebensfries"* [unpublished thesis, doctoral]. Freiburg: Universität Freiburg, 2004.

Kaufmann, Bettina. "Ernst Ludwig Kirchner and Edvard Munch". In *Edvard Munch. An anthology*, 179–190. Oslo: Unipub, 2006.

Kellein, Thomas. "Munch 1912 in Deutschland". In *Edvard Munch 1912 in Deutschland* [exhibition catalogue], 13–39. Bielefeld: Kunsthalle Bielefeld, 2002.

Ketterer, Roman Norbert. *Dialoge*. Stuttgart: Belser, 1988.

Kingwell, Mark. "Commodity and Culture: The object in question". *Queens quarterly* 5, no. 4 (1998): 489–510.

Kirkeby, Per. *Munch*. Hellerup: Edition Bløndal, 1997.

Kirsch, Andrea. "Edvard Munch: Self-portrait beneath a woman's mask" [148]; Edvard Munch: Death and the maiden" [235]. In *Seeing Through Paintings: Physical Examination in Art Historical Studies*, Materials and Meaning in the Fine Arts 1. New Haven: Yale University Press, 2000.

Kisch-Arendt, Ruth. "A portrait of Felix Auerbach by Munch". *The Burlington Magazine*, March (1964): 131–132.

Kivelitz, Christoph and Regina Selter. "Looking in – Looking out". In *Munch revisited* [exhibition catalogue], 17–25. Dortmund: Kerber Verlag, 2005.

Klein, Janine. "Edvard Munch und Anton von Werner". In *Wahlverwandtschaft. Skandinavien und Deutschland 1800 bis 1914* [exhibition catalogue], 363–366. Berlin: Jovis, 1997.

Knausgård, Karl Ove. *Så mye lengsel på så liten flate. En bok om Edvard Munchs bilder*. Oslo: Oktober, 2017 A.

Knausgård, Karl Ove. "Preface: On Edvard Munch". In *Edvard Munch. Between the Clock and the Bed* [exhibition catalogue], 11–15. New York: Metropolitan Museum of Art, 2017 B.

Kneher, Jan. "Munch-Ausstellungen von 1883 bis zur Retrospektive 1926 in der Kunsthalle Mannheim". In *Edvard Munch. Sommmernacht am Oslofjord, um 1900* [exhibition catalogue], 234–256. Mannheim: Städtische Kunsthalle Mannheim, 1988.

Kneher, Jan. *Edvard Munch in seinen Ausstellungen zwischen 1892 und 1912. Eine Dokumentation der Ausstellungen und Studie zur Rezeptionsgeschichte von Munchs Kunst* [thesis, PhD]. Worms: Wernersche Verlagsgesellschaft, 1994.

Kokoschka, Oskar. *Der Expressionismus Edvard Munchs*. Vienna: Gurlitt-Verlag, 1953.

Kongssund, Anita. "Kunst og ukunst. En moderne ikonoklasme = Art and Non-Art. A Modern Iconoclasm". In *Kunst i kamp = Art in Battle* [exhibition catalogue], 76–97. Bergen: KODE, 2015.

Krämer, Felix. "The Blackness of Night/Die Schwärze der Nacht". In *Unheimlich. Innenräume von Edvard Munch bis Max Beckmann = The Uncanny Home. Interiors from Edvard Munch to Max Beckmann* [exhibition catalogue], 109–126. Bonn: Kunstmuseum Bonn; Munich: Hirmer, 2016.

Krause-Zimmer, Hella. "Edvard Munch im Hause Linde". *Die Drei. Zeitschrift für Wissenschaft* 49 (1979): 713–719.

Kress, Annelise. "Van Gogh and Munch". *Vincent. Bulletin of the Rijkmuseum Vincent van Gogh* 4, no. 3 (1975): 27–40.

Krieger, Peter. "Aus den Galerien Edvard Munch Selbstbildnis unter den Frauenmaske". *Westermanns Monatshefte* 109, no. 6 (1968): 4, 6.

Krieger, Peter. *Edvard Munch. Der Lebensfries für Max Reinhardts Kammerspiele* [exhibition catalogue]. Berlin: Nationalgalerie Berlin, 1978.

Krisch, Monika. *Die Munch-affäre. Rehabilitierung der Zeitungskritik. Eine Analyse ästhetischer und kulturpolitischer Beurteilungskriterien in der Kunstberichterstattung der Berliner Tagespresse zu Munchs Ausstellung 1892*. Mahlow bei Berlin: Tenea, 1997.

Kristensen, Rolf. "Malerimodellene i Åsgårdstrand". In *Broen: Aasgaardstrandiana* 56–69. Åsgårdstrand: Aasgaardstrand og omegn historielag, 2010.

Kristoffersen, Sigrid Fløttum. "Jobs Skrik? Et bidrag til tolkningen av Edvard Munchs maleri". *Kunst og Kultur* 83, no. 1 (2000): 50–61.

Krohg, Christian. "Fernis". *Dagens Nyt*, 17.06.1909.

Kruskopf, Erik. *Edvard Munch och Finland*. Oslo: Munchmuseet, 1968.

Kuhn, Alfred. "Edvard Munch und der Geist seiner Zeit. Anlässlich der grossen Munch-Ausstellung der Nationalgalerie zu Berlin". *Der Cicerone* XIX, no. 5 (1927): 139–147.

Kunstsalon Fritz Gurlitt. *Edvard Munch* [print portfolio]. Berlin: F. Gurlitt, 1914.

Kuuva, Sari. *Symbol, Munch and Creativity. Metabolism of Visual Symbols* [thesis, PhD]. Jyväskylä: University of Jyväskylä, 2010.

Körber, Lill-Ann. "Vampire und Décadents. Re-vision der Geschlechterverhältnisse im Werk Edvard Munchs". *Norrøna*, no. 32 (2002): 15–28.

Körber, Lill-Ann. *Männlichkeit, Arbeit und Nation bei Edvard Munch* [unpublished thesis, magister]. Berlin: Humboldt-Universität, 2003.

Körber, Lill-Ann. "Munch and men. Work, nation, and reproduction in Edvard Munch's later works". In *Edvard Munch. An anthology*, 163–178. Oslo: Unipub, 2006 A.

Körber, Lill-Ann. "Sunnhet versus homoerotikk? Badende menn, nakenhet og den mannlige akt rundt 1905". In *Livskraft. Vitalismen som kunstnerisk impuls 1900–1930* [exhibition catalogue], 79–94. Oslo: Munchmuseet, 2006 B.

Kaaring, Liza. "Et vekselspil. Venskabet mellom Edvard Munch og Emanuel Goldstein". In *Munch og Goldstein. Intense linjer* [exhibition catalogue], 11–40. Aarhus: Aarhus University Press, 2019.

L

La Nasa, Jacopo, Brenda Doherty and Francesca Rosi et al. "An integrated analytical study of crayons from the original art materials collection of the MUNCH museum in Oslo". *Sci Rep* 11, art. no 7152 (2021): https://doi.org/10.1038/s41598-021-86031-6.

Lachana, Evanghélia. *Edvard Munch: le peintre face au theatre* [thesis, PhD]. Paris: Université de la Sorbonne nouvelle, 1997.

Lahelma, Marja. *Ideal and disintegration: Dynamics of the self and art at the fin-de siècle* [thesis, PhD]. Helsinki: Helsingfors universitet, 2014.

Lahelma, Marja. "Symbolisme i Norge

og Finland". In *Det magiske nord. Finsk og norsk kunst omkring 1900* [exhibition catalogue], 11-41. Oslo: Nasjonalmuseet, 2015.

Lampe, Angela. "Dislocated Motifs: Munch's Tendency Towards Repetition". In *Edvard Munch. The Modern Eye = Der Moderne Blick = L'oeil moderne* [exhibition catalogue], 29-53. London: Tate Publishing, 2012. [Also published Paris 2011 and Frankfurt 2012]

Lande, Marit. " - for aldrig meer at skilles -". Fra Edvard Munchs barndom og ungdom i Christiania. Oslo: Universitetsforlaget, 1992.

Lande, Marit. *Edvard Munch. His life and works*. Oslo: Aventura and Munchmuseet, 1995.

Lande, Marit. *På sporet av Edvard Munch. Mannen bak mytene*. Oslo: Messel, 1996.

Landro, Gry, Biljana Topalova-Casadiego and Magdalena Ufnalewska-Godzimirska. "Konserveringen av Munch-museets Skrik. Undersøkelser og betraktninger = The Conservation of the Munch Museum's Scream. Examinations and Observations". In *Skrik = The Scream* [exhibition catalogue], 57-74. Oslo: Vigmostad & Bjørke, 2008.

Lange, Marit and Tone Skedsmo. *Norske malerier: Katalog*. Oslo: Nasjonalgalleriet, 1992.

Lange, Marit. "Edvard Munch og Max Klinger. Forbudt område". *Konsthistorisk Tidskrift* LXIII, nos. 3-4 (1994): 233-249.

Lange, Marit. "Die Neuromantik in der Norwegischen Landschaftsmalerei". In *Landschaft als Kosmos der Seele. Malerei des nordischen Symbolismus bis Munch 1880-1910* [exhibition catalogue], 51-59. Heidelberg: Braus, 1998.

Lange, Marit. "Edvard Munch. Från realism til expressionism". In *Edvard Munch* [exhibition catalogue], 8-15. Gothenburg: Göteborgs konstmuseum, 2002.

Lange, Marit. "Edvard Munchs 'Natt i Saint Cloud'. Fortolkninger og forvrengninger". In *Fra romersk barokk til norsk nyromantikk. Utvalgte artikler*, 79-91. Oslo: Ortiz, 2003.

Lange, Marit. "Munch's self-portraits" [113-123]; "Munch as a portrait painter" [125-139]. In *Edvard Munch. The Frieze of Life* [exhibition catalogue]. Melbourne: National Gallery of Victoria, 2004.

Lange, Marit. "Skrik etc. Nok engang kontrafaktisk kunsthistorie". *Kunst og Kultur* 88, no. 4 (2005): 241-253.

Lange, Marit. "The young Munch. Max Klinger's impact on his imagery". *Kunst og Kultur* 90, no. 3 (2007): 161-173.

Langslet, Lars Roar. *Henrik Ibsen - Edvard Munch. To genier møtes = Two Geniuses Meet*. Oslo: Cappelen, 1994.

Langaard, Ingrid Lindbäck. *Edvard Munch. Modningsår. En studie i tidlig ekspresjonisme og symbolisme*. Oslo: Gyldendal, 1960.

Langaard, Johan H. "5 malerier av Edvard Munch". *Kunstmuseets Aarskrift 1946-47* (1946): 81-98.

Langaard, Johan H. *Edvard Munchs selvportretter*. Oslo: Gyldendal, 1947.

Langaard, Johan H. "Edvard Munchs formler. Et lite forsøk på en formanalyse". *Samtiden* 58, no. 1 (1949): 50-58.

Langaard, Johan H. and Reidar Revold. *Edvard Munch som tegner*. Oslo: Kunsten idag, 1958.

Langaard, Johan H. and Reidar Revold. *Edvard Munch. Auladekorasjonene. Et billedverk*. Oslo: Norsk kunstreproduksjon, 1960.

Langaard, Johan H. "Munch og Baudelaire". *Oslo kommunes kunstsamlinger. Årbok 1852-1959* (1960): 13-17.

Langaard, Johan H. and Reidar Revold. *Edvard Munch fra år til år. En håndbok = A year by year record of Edvard Munch's life. A handbook*. Oslo: Aschehoug, 1961.

Langaard, Johan H. and Reidar Revold. *Edvard Munch. Mesterverker i Munch-museet, Oslo*. Oslo: Forlaget norsk kunstreproduksjon Stenersen, 1963.

Langaard, Johan H. "The late Munch". In *Edvard Munch* [exhibition catalogue], 18-22. New York: The S.R. Guggenheim Foundation, 1965.

Langaard, Johan H. *Edvard Munch. I familien Sigval Bergesen d.y.s eie. Katalog*. Oslo: Bergesens samling, 1967.

Langaard, Johan H. *Malerier og grafikk. I familien Sigval Bergesen d.y.s eie. Katalog*. Oslo: Bergesens samling, 1971.

Larsen, Peter Nørgaard (ed.). *Sjælebilleder. Symbolismen i dansk og europæisk maleri 1870-1910*. Copenhagen: Statens Museum for Kunst, 2000.

Larsen, Øivind. "Den andre puberteten". *Tidsskrift for Den norske lægeforening* 121, no. 6 (2001): 7-8.

Larsson, Lars Olof. "August Strindberg und Edvard Munch in Berlin". In *Grenzgänge. Skandinavisch-deutsche Nachbarschaften*, 161-178. Göttingen: Wallstein, 1996.

Larsson, Lars Olof. "Die Weissen Nächte als Thema der Skandinavischen Malerei um 1900". In *Landschaft als Kosmos der Seele. Malerei des nordischen Symbolismus bis Munch 1880-1910* [exhibition catalogue], 21-26. Heidelberg: Braus, 1998.

Lathe, Carla. *The Group Zum Schwarzen Ferkel. A study in early modernism* [unpublished thesis, PhD]. Norwich: University of East Anglia, 1972.

Lathe, Carla. *Edvard Munch and his Literary Associates* [exhibition catalogue]. Norwich: University of East Anglia, 1979 A.

Lathe, Carla. "Edvard Munch and the concept of 'Psychic Naturalism'". *Gazette des Beaux Arts* (1979 B): 135-146.

Lathe, Carla. "Edvard Munch's dramatic images 1892-1909". *Journal of the Warburg and Courtauld Institutes* 46 (1983): 191-206.

Lathe, Carla. "Munch and Modernism in Berlin". In *Edvard Munch. The Frieze of Life* [exhibition catalogue], 38-44. London: National Gallery Publications, 1992.

Laux, Walter Stephan. "Edvard Munch und Walter Leistikow" [48-50]; "Land-schaftsstudien Edvard Munchs in Zeichnungen und Aquarellen" [70-85]; "Munchs graphische Portraits seiner Zeitgenossen" [186-233]. In *Edvard Munch. Sommernacht am Oslofjord, um 1900* [exhibition catalogue]. Mannheim: Städtische Kunsthalle Mannheim, 1988.

Lenz, Christian. "Das Verhältnis von Max Beckmann zu Edvard Munch". In *Edvard Munch in Chemnitz* [exhibition catalogue], 293-299. Chemnitz: Wienand, 1999.

Lexow, Einar. "Edvard Munch og Tyskland". *Kunst og Kultur* 4 (1913): 125-128.

Lieberg, Tonje. "Pregnante positurer". In *Avkledd. Studenter velger Munch* [exhibition catalogue], 47-49. Oslo: Munchmuseet, 2004.

Lind, Ebba. "På sporet av 'skrik'". *Kunst og Kultur* 80, no. 2 (1997): 98-105.

Linde, Max. *Edvard Munch und die Kunst der Zukunft*. Berlin: Friedrich Gottheiner, 1902.

Linde, Max. *Edvard Munchs brev fra dr. med. Max Linde*. Oslo: Dreyer, 1954.

Linde, Ulf. *Edvard Munch og Thielska Galleriet*. Oslo: Labyrinth Press, 2007.

Lindhagen, Nils. *Konst hos Freia och Marabou*. Oslo: Freia; Stockholm: Marabou, 1955.

Lippincott, Louise. *Edvard Munch. Starry Night*. Malibu: J. Paul Getty Museum, 1988.

Llorens, Tomàs and Boye Llorens. *Retratos de la Belle Époque*. Valencia: Consorcio de Museos de la Comunidad Valenciana, 2011.

Lloyd, Jill. "Van Gogh og Munch: Et spørsmål om stil". In *Van Gogh + Munch* [exhibition catalogue], 124-147. Oslo and Brussels: Mercatorfonds, Orfeus, Munchmuseet and Van Gogh Musum, 2015.

Lloyd, Jill. "Edvard Munch and the Expressionsts: Influence and Affinity". In *Munch and Expressionism* [exhibition catalogue], 13-33. Munich: Prestel, 2016.

Lomas, Davis. "Sick Art". In *Melgaard + Munch - The End of It All Has Already Happened* [exhibition catalogue], 215-227. Ostfildern-Ruit: Hatje Cantz Verlag; Oslo: Munchmuseet, 2015.

Loshak, David. "Space, time and Edvard Munch". *Burlington Magazine* 131, April (1989): 273-281.

López, Horacio. *Grandes maestros de la pintura: Munch*. Barcelona: Editorial Sol 90 S.L., 2008.

Lubow, Arthur. "Edvard Munch. Beyond The Scream". *Smithsonian* 36, no. 12 (2006): 58-67.

Lund, Hans. "Edvard Munchs Skrik som kulturelt ikon". *Agora* 19, nos. 2/3 (2001): 20-41.

Lund, Hans. *Kulturella ikoner i text, musik och bild*. Stockholm: Carlsson, 2012.

Løchen, Ingeborg Motzfeldt. "Mine samtaler med Edvard Munch". In *Edvard Munch som vi kjente ham*. Oslo: Dreyer, 1946.

Løchen, Rolf. "Skikkelser i bohêmetiden". *Byminner*, no. 1 (1970): 3-23.

Løchen, Rolf. "Nytt om Edvard Munch og hans krets. Et kunsthistorisk detektivarbeide". *Byminner*, no. 4 (1971): 5-29.

Løchen, Rolf. "Ennå mer 'Nytt om Edvard Munch og hans krets'. 'Men Rocambole var ikke død'". *Byminner*, no. 1 (1972): 35-39.

M

Marcellàn, Clara. "Munch before the Mirror: A Biography". In *Edvard Munch. Archetypes* [exhibition catalogue], 207-221. Madrid: Museo Thyssen-Bornemisza, 2015.

Magnaguagno, Guido. "Munch als Maler". In *Edvard Munch* [exhibition catalogue], 63-75. Essen: Museum Folkwang Essen; Zürich: Kunsthaus Zürich, 1987.

Malmanger, Magne. "L'arte di Edvard Munch tra Norvegia ed Europa". In *Nord ed Europa. Identità Scandinava e rapporti culturali con il continente nel corso dei secoli = The North and Europe. Scandinavian identity and cultural relations with the continent through the centuries*, 205-220. Genoa: Tilgher, 2004.

Malmanger, Magne. "En ung norsk maler. Edvard Munch". In *Munch og malervennene på Modum* [exhibition catalogue], 161-205. Åmot i Modum: Blaafarveværket, 2013.

Marjanovic, Marianne Berger. "Fortellerstrategi og iscenesettelse". In *Avkledd. Studenter velger Munch* [exhibition catalogue], 51-53. Oslo: Munchmuseet, 2004.

Marten, Miloš. *Edvard Munch*. Prague: Zdenka Braunerová, 1905.

Marx, Werner. "Weisse Nacht" [120]; "Berlin und die Sehnsucht nach dem Norden" [163-185]. In *Edvard Munch. Sommernacht am Oslofjord, um 1900* [exhibition catalogue]. Mannheim: Städtische Kunsthalle Mannheim, 1988.

Maurer, Emil. "Munch, international". In *Edvard Munch* [exhibition catalogue], 49-61. Essen: Museum Folkwang Essen; Zürich: Kunsthaus Zürich, 1987.

Meier-Graefe, Julius. "Das Werk von Edvard Munch". In *Das Werk von Edvard Munch. Vier Beiträge / Herausgegeben von Stanisław Przybyszewski*, 75-95. Berlin: Fischer, 1894.

Meier-Graefe, Julius. *Edvard Munch. Acht Radierungen*. Berlin: J. Meier-Graefe, 1895 A.

Meier-Graefe, Julius. *Edvard Munch. Geleitwort einer Mappe mit 8 Radierungen*. Berlin: J. Meier-Graefe, 1895 B.

Meissel, Franz-Stefan. "Edvard Munchs 'Sommernacht am Strand' und das Restitutionsverfahren Alma Mahler-Werfels gegen die Republik Österreich". In *Mit den Augen der Rechtsgeschichte*, 473-501. Vienna: LIT, 2007.

Messel, Nils. "Fra Munchs have til Matisse' atelier. En impresjonistisk presentasjon av Ludvig Karsten og andre 'munchianere'". *Kunst og Kultur* 72, no. 3 (1989): 122-136.

Messel, Nils. *Norske forfatterportretter.* Oslo: Nasjonalgalleriet, Aschehoug and Gyldendal, 1993.

Messel, Nils. "Edvard Munch and his critics in the 1880s". *Kunst og Kultur* 77, no. 4 (1994): 213-227.

Messel, Nils. "Edvard Munch og hans kritikere i 1880-årene". *Munch blir "Munch". Kunstneriske strategier 1880-1892 = Munch Becoming "Munch". Artistic Strategies 1880-1892* [exhibition catalogue], 159-170. Oslo: Munchmuseet, 2008.

Messel, Nils. "Den smakfuldeste dekoratør i Norden; Jens Thiis i Nasjonalgalleriet". *Kunst og Kultur* 95, no. 4 (2012): 200-217.

Metzger, Othmar. "Vier Mädchen in der Staatsgalerie Stuttgart". *Weltkunst* XXVI, no. 24 (1956): 6-7.

Midbøe, Hans. "Max Reinhardts iscenesettelse av Ibsens 'Gespenster'". In *Kammerspiele des Deutschen Theaters Berlin 1906. Dekor - Edvard Munch.* Trondheim: Brun, 1969.

Milnes, Anne and Biljana Topalova-Casadiego. "Konserveringen av Munch-museets Madonna. Undersøkelser og betraktninger = The Conservation of the Munch Museum's Madonna. Examinations and Observations". In *Madonna = Madonna* [exhibition catalogue], 73-89. Bergen: Vigmostad & Bjørke, 2008.

Moen, Arve. *Edvard Munch. Tier und Landschaft. Ein Bildwerk.* Munich: F. Bruckmann, 1959.

Mohr, Otto Lous. *Edvard Munchs Auladekorasjoner i lys av ukjente utkast og sakens akter.* Oslo: Gyldendal, 1960.

Monrad, Kasper (ed.). *Luz del norte / Llum del nord / The light of the north.* Madrid: Ministerio de Cultura; Copenhagen: Nordisk ministerråd; Barcelona: Generalitat de Catalunya, 1995.

Morehead, Allison. "Madness in method. Edvard Munch and the problem of pathological form". In *Creative pathologies. French experimental psychology and symbolist Avant-gardes* [unpublished thesis, PhD], 372-493. Chicago: University of Chicago, 2007.

Morehead, Allison. "The Untimely Face of Munch". In *Edvard Munch: Between the Clock and the Bed* [exhibition catalogue], 21-29. New York: Metropolitan Museum of Art, 2017 A.

Morehead, Allison. "Munch: A modern Velázquez?" *Kunst og Kultur* 100, nos. 1-2 (2017 B): 6-19.

Munch, Edvard. *Eduard Munch Gemälde-Ausstellung* [exhibition catalogue]. Berlin: Unter den Linden 19, 1893.

Munch, Edvard. *Förteckning öfver Edvard Munch Utställningen.* Stockholm: Konstföreningens Lokal, 1894.

Munch, Edvard. "Alfa og Omega = Alpha et Omega". In *Katalog over grafisk kunst* [exhibition catalogue], 11-14. Kristiania: Johannes Bjørnstads boktrykkeri, 1914?.

Munch, Edvard. *Blomqvists kunstud-stilling* [exhibition catalogue]. Kristiania: Blomqvist, 1918.

Munch, Edvard. *Livs-frisen.* Kristiania: E. Munch, 1919.

Munch, Edvard. *Livsfrisens tilblivelse.* Kristiania: E. Munch, 1928.

Munch, Edvard. "1889-1929. Små utdrag fra min dagbok". In *Edvard Munch utstilling. Blomqvist Kunsthandel* [exhibition catalogue], 1-2. Oslo: Blomqvist, 1929.

Munch, Edvard. *Edvard Munchs brev. Familien / Et utvalg av Inger Munch.* Oslo: Tanum, 1949.

Munch, Edvard and Max Linde. *Edvard Munch - Dr. Max Linde. Briefwechsel 1902-1928 / Herausg. von Gustav Lindtke.* Lübeck: Senat der Hansestadt, Amt für Kultur, 1974.

Munch, Edvard. *Words and Images of Edvard Munch / translated and edited by Bente Torjusen.* Chelsea: Chelsea Green Publishing Company, 1986.

Munch, Edvard and Gustav Schiefler. *Edvard Munch / Gustav Schiefer. Breifwechsel. Band 1 1902-1914.* Hamburg: Verein fur Hamburgische Geschichte, 1987.

Munch, Edvard and Gustav Schiefler. *Edvard Munch / Gustav Schiefler. Briefwechsel*, vol. 2. Hamburg: Verlag Verein, 1987-1990.

Munch, Edvard. "Journal inédit". In *Munch et la France* [exhibition catalogue], 341-361. Paris: Réunion des Musées Nationaux, 1991.

Munch, Edvard. "Et utvalg av Edvard Munchs nedtegnelser i Frankrike". In *Munch og Frankrike* [exhibition catalogue], 341-363. Oslo: Munchmuseet, 1991. [Also published Paris 1991]

Munch, Edvard. "Auszügeaus Munchs unveröffentlichtem Tagebuch in Frankreich". In *Munch in Frankreich* [exhibition catalogue], 361-386. Franfurt am Main: Schirn Kunsthalle, 1992.

Munch, Edvard. *Munch. Med egne ord / red. Poul Erik Tøjner.* Oslo: Press, 2000.

Munch, Edvard. *Munch. In his own words / ed. Poul Erik Tøjner.* Munich: Prestel, 2001.

Munch, Edvard. *The private journals of Edvard Munch. We Are Flames Which Pour Out of the Earth / Edited and translated by J. Gill Holland.* Madison: University of Wisconsin Press, 2005.

Munch, Edvard. *Být sám. Obrazy - deniky - ohlasy / vybrali, sestavili a komentárem opatrili Otto M. Urban, Jarka Vrbová a Thomás Vrba.* Prague: Arbor Vitae, 2006.

Müller-Westermann, Iris. "Edvard Munchs Selbstbildnisse. Widersprüche als Herausforderung". In *Wunderblock. Eine Geschichte der modernen Seele* [exhibition catalogue], 517-527. Vienna: Löcker, 1989.

Müller-Westermann, Iris. "Huden som speilbilde for selvopplevelsen". *UKS*, nos. 3/4 (1991): 4-7.

Müller-Westermann, Iris. "Edvard Munch. Marats Tod 1902-1930". In *Die Metamorphosen der Bilder* [exhibition catalogue], 224-228. Hanover: Sprengel Museum Hannover, 1992.

Müller-Westermann, Iris. "Im männlichen Gehirn. Das Verhältnis der Geschlechter im Lebensfries" [30-38]; "Mit Kopf und Hand. Zu Munchs Selbstverständnis als Künstler" [39-45]. In *Munch und Deutschland* [exhibition catalogue]. Stuttgart: Gerd Hatje Verlag, 1994.

Müller-Westermann, Iris. "Edvard Munch und Wien. Österreichs Begegnung mit dem Werk Edvard Munchs 1901-1918". In *Sehnsucht nach Glück: Wiens Aufbruch in die Moderne* [exhibition catalogue], 224-227. Frankfurt am Main: Schirn Kunsthalle, 1995.

Müller-Westermann, Iris. "The Head in the Hand - and the Hand in his Blood. Munch's Self-Comprehension as an Artist from 1895 until 1905". In *Totenmesse. Modernism in the Culture of Northern and Central Europe*, 79-87. Warsaw: Institute of Art, Polish Academy of Science, 1996.

Müller-Westermann, Iris. *Edvard Munch. Die Selbstbildnisse* [thesis, PhD]. Hamburg: Universität Hamburg, 1997.

Müller-Westermann, Iris. "I mannens hjerne, forholdet mellom kjønnene i Livsfrisen". In *Munch og kvinnen* [exhibition catalogue], 25-28. Bergen: Bergen Kunstmuseum, 2001.

Müller-Westermann, Iris. "Die Zeit von 'Carmen' - Zum Verhältnis der Geschlechter im Werk Edvard Munchs 1890-1920". In *Edvard Munch. Thema und Variation = Edvard Munch. Theme and Variation* [exhibition catalogue], 67-82. Vienna: Albertina, 2003.

Müller-Westermann, Iris. *Munch själv = Munch by himself = Edvard Munch. Die Selbstbildnisse* [exhibition catalogue]. Stockholm: Moderna Museet; London: Royal Academy of Arts; Munich: Schirmer Mosel, 2005.

Müller-Westermann, Iris. "A Modern Eye: Edvard Munch's Self-Portraits after 1908". In *Edvard Munch. The Modern Eye = Der Moderne Blick = L'oeil moderne* [exhibition catalogue], 281-291. London: Tate Publishing, 2012. [Also published Paris 2011 and Frankfurt 2012]

Myre, Olav. *Edvard Munch og hans boksamling.* Oslo: N.W. Damm & Søn, 1946.

März, Roland. "'Das Urbild eines nordischen Künstlers'. Germanenmythos, Nationalsozialismus und Edvard Munch". In *Munch und Deutschland* [exhibition catalogue], 131-138. Stuttgart: Gerd Hatje Verlag, 1994.

März, Roland. *Edvard Munch. Melancholie aus dem Reinhardt-Fries 1906-07.* Berlin: Kulturstiftung der Länder, 1998.

März, Roland. "Porträt eines Weltmannes. Edvard Munch malt Harry Graf Kessler in Weimar". In *Aufstieg und Fall der Moderne* [exhibition catalogue], 182-193. Ostfildern-Ruit: Hatje Cantz Verlag, 1999.

Mørstad, Erik. "Kjærlighetens forvandlinger". In *Edvard Munchs Livsfrise. En rekonstruksjon av utstillingen hos Blomqvist 1918* [exhibition catalogue], 85-96. Oslo: Munchmuseet and Labyrinth Press, 2002.

Mørstad, Erik. "Edvard Munch under Medusas hode". *En Face. Kunsthistorisk Tidsskrift*, no. 1 (2003 A): 5-17.

Mørstad, Erik. "Edvard Munchs bruk av slagskygger". *Kunst og Kultur* 86, no. 2 (2003 B): 66-97.

Mørstad, Erik. "Edvard Munchs Livsfrise. Struktur, kontekst og kritikk". *Kunst og Kultur* 87, no. 3 (2004 A): 122-125.

Mørstad, Erik. "Edvard Munchs maleri Aske. Analyse, tolkninger og kontekst". *En Face. Kunsthistorisk Tidsskrift*, no. 2 (2004 B): 38-53.

Mørstad, Erik. "Munch og Böcklin. En komparativ analyse". *Kunst og Kultur* 87, no. 3 (2004 C): 156-174.

Mørstad, Erik. "Il linguaggio formale di Edvard Munch. Formule e caricature". In *Munch 1863-1944* [exhibition catalogue], 41-55. Milan: Skira, 2005.

Mørstad, Erik. "Badende menn. Kroppspolitikk, kroppsteknikk og kroppspleie". In *Livskraft. Vitalismen som kunstnerisk impuls 1900-1930* [exhibition catalogue], 65-78. Oslo: Munchmuseet, 2006 A.

Mørstad, Erik. "Responding to Self-portrait with Cigarette. A case history". In *Edvard Munch. An anthology*, 87-120. Oslo: Unipub, 2006 B.

Mørstad, Erik. "The improvisations of Edvard Munch". *Kunst og Kultur* 90, no. 3 (2007): 139-159.

Mørstad, Erik. "Edvard Munch. Dannelse og utdannelse". *Kunst og Kultur* 91, no. 1 (2008): 19-31.

Mørstad, Erik. "Munch and the Literary". *Kunst og Kultur* 96, no. 4 (2013): 205-217.

Mørstad, Erik. *Edvard Munch: Formative år 1874-1892. Norske og franske impulser* [thesis, PhD]. Oslo: Universitetet i Oslo, 2016.

Mössinger, Ingrid. "Edvard Munch in Chemnitz" [9-11]; "Herbert Eugen Esche und Hanni Esche" [21-24]. In *Edvard Munch in Chemnitz* [exhibition catalogue]. Chemnitz: Wienand, 1999.

N

Nag, Martin. "Dostojevskij og Edvard Munch". *Kunst og Kultur* 76, no. 1 (1993): 41-55.

Nahum, Katherine. "'In wild embrace'. Attachment and loss in Edvard Munch". In *Edvard Munch. Psyche, symbol and expression* [exhibition catalogue], 31-47. Chestnut Hill: McMullen Museum of Art, 2001.

Nasgaard, Roald. *The Mystic North. Symbolist Landscape Painting in Northern Europe and North America 1890-1940* [exhibition catalogue]. Toronto: Art Gallery of Ontario and University of Toronto Press, 1984.

Natanson, Thadée. "M. Edvard Munch".

La Revue Blanche 6, vol. IX, no. 59 (1895): 477-478; no. 60 (1895): 527-528.

Nerdrum, Nora Ceciliedatter. "Kunstranet som skapte et ikon". In *EXIT! Historier fra Munchmuseet* [exhibition catalogue], 235-248. Oslo: Munchmuseet, 2019.

Nergaard, Trygve. "Edvard Munchs visjon. Et bidrag til Livsfrisens historie". *Kunst og Kultur* 50, no. 2 (1967): 69-92.

Nergaard, Trygve. *Refleksjon og visjon. Naturalismens dilemma i Edvard Munchs kunst 1889-1894* [unpublished thesis, magister]. Oslo: Universitetet i Oslo, 1968.

Nergaard, Trygve. "Kunsten som det evig kvinnelige - en vampyrgåte". *Kunst og Kultur* 57, no. 3 (1974): 251-262.

Nergaard, Trygve. "Emanuel Goldstein og Edvard Munch". *Louisiana Revy* 16, no. 1 (1975): 16-18.

Nergaard, Trygve. "Despair". In *Edvard Munch. Symbols & Images* [exhibition catalogue], 113-141. Washington: National Gallery of Art, 1978.

Nergaard, Trygve. "Tema med variasjoner: Kyss - Piken og døden - Vampyr - Trøst". In *Edvard Munchs Livsfrise. En rekonstruksjon av utstillingen hos Blomqvist 1918* [exhibition catalogue], 115-124. Oslo: Munchmuseet and Labyrinth Press, 2002.

Ness, Nina Denney. "Om en illustrasjon av Erik Werenskiold: og dens relasjon til motiver av Edvard Munch". *Kunst og Kultur* 96, no. 1 (2013): 2-12.

Nielsen, Trine Otte Bak. "Vitalisme og Badende Menn". In *Avkledd. Studenter velger Munch* [exhibition catalogue], 19-21. Oslo: Munchmuseet, 2004.

Nielsen, Trine Otte Bak. "Vigeland + Munch. Bak mytene". In *Vigeland + Munch. Bak mytene* [exhibition catalogue], 22-55. Oslo: Mercatorfonds and Munchmuseet, 2015.

Nierhoff-Wielk, Barbara. "Der Lebensfries". In *Edvard Munch - Rätsel hinter der Leinwand* [exhibition catalogue], 38-41. Cologne: DuMont, 2011.

Nilssen, Jappe. "Hærverk". *Dagens Nyt*, 14.6.1909.

Nilssen, Jappe. "Edvard Munch i sit hjem". *Julehelg* (1912): 36-39.

Nilssen, Jappe. "Edvard Munch 163 - 12. desember - 1913". *Kunst og Kultur* 4 (1913): 81-101.

Nilssen, Jappe. *Edvard Munch. A/S Freia Chocolade Fabriks spisesalsdekorationer*. Kristiania: Freia Chocolade Fabrik, 1922.

Nimmen, Jan Van. "Loving Edvard Munch. Women who were his patrons, collectors, admirers". In *Munch and Women. Image and Myth* [exhibition catalogue], 43-59. Alexandria: Art Services International, 1997.

Nome, Paul. *Kunst som "krystallisasjon": en studie i Edvard Munchs notater om hans tro, livssyn og kunstforståelse* [thesis, PhD]. Oslo: Universitetet i Oslo, 2000.

Nordhagen, Per Jonas. "I grenseland. Edvard Munchs Dansemoro". *Kunst og Kultur* 65, no. 1 (1982): 47-53.

Nordkvelle, Trine. "Fra Japan til Munch". *Kunst og Kultur* 95, no. 1 (2012): 30-43.

Nordkvelle, Trine. "Gjentatte Kyss - visuelle fortellinger. Et narratologisk eksperiment". In *Edvard Munch 1863-1944* [exhibition catalogue], 264-271. Milan: Skira; Oslo: Nasjonalmuseet and Munchmuseet, 2013.

Norem, Johs. "Hans Jæger på Hisøy ved Arendal". *Kunst og Kultur* 41, no. 1 (1958): 63.

Nummelin, Rolf. "Munchs inflytande på Finländsk måleri 1909-1914". In *Edvard Munch. Målningar och grafik* [exhibition catalogue], 25-28. Helsinki: Föreningen Konstsamfundet, 1979.

Nyaas, Tone Lyngstad (ed.). *Munch by Others*. Stockholm: Arvinius and Orfeus, 2013.

Nygård-Nilsen, Arne. "Munch Litteraturen". *Kunst og Kultur* 20, no. 1 (1934 A): 59-64.

Nygård-Nilsen, Arne. "Næringslivet i norsk kunst". *Kunst og Kultur* 20, no. 4 (1934): 209-288.

Næss, Atle. *Munch. En biografi*. Oslo: Gyldendal, 2004. [Also published in Danish, Finnish, Russian and Polish 2005-2007]

Næss, Trine. "Edvard Munch og 'Den fri Kjærligheds By'". *Kunst og Kultur* 56, no. 3 (1973): 145-160.

O

Obstfelder, Sigbjørn. "Edvard Munch. Et forsøg". *Samtiden* (1896): 17-22. Gjengitt i Obstfelder. *Samlede skrifter 3*, 202-209. Oslo: Gyldendal Norsk Forlag, 2000.

Oftedahl, Sophia. "Under stjernene". In *Motiver, Mennesker. Studenter velger Munch* [exhibition catalogue], 7-9. Oslo: Munchmuseet, 2003.

Ohlsen, Nils. "Ein Jahresfries. Die Landschaft im Spätwerk von Edvard Munch". In *Edvard Munch. Bilder aus Norwegen* [exhibition catalogue], 14-29. Ostfildern-Ruit: Hatje Cantz Verlag, 2004.

Ohlsen, Nils. "Edvard Munchs visuelle retorikk - en tilnærming med utgangspunkt i utvalgte interiører". In *Edvard Munch 1863-1944* [exhibition catalogue], 196-207. Milan: Skira; Oslo: Nasjonalmuseet and Munchmuseet, 2013.

Ohlsen, Nils. "Beckmann and Munch: Distant and Yet Quite Close". In *Munch and Expressionism* [exhibition catalogue], 55-67. Munich: Prestel, 2016.

Oliva, Achille Bonito. "Forme di dolore insite nella vita stessa 'il mondo stesso è il Giudizio Universale'". In *Munch 1863-1944* [exhibition catalogue], 35-39. Milan: Skira, 2005.

Olson, Donald W., Russell L. Doescher and Marilynn S. Olson. "When the sky ran red. The story behind The Scream". *Sky & Telescope*, February (2004): 29-35.

Ormhaug, Knut. "Angst and Melancholy". In *The Frieze of Life* [exhibition catalogue], 47-57. Melbourne: National Gallery of Victoria, 2004.

Owesen, Ingeborg W. "Edvard Munch mellom kvinnesak, kjønn og kjærlighet". In *Edvard Munch 1863-1944* [exhibition catalogue], 297-305. Milan: Skira; Oslo: Nasjonalmuseet and Munchmuseet, 2013.

P

Parke-Taylor, Michael. "'The scarlet trail of the serpent'. The reception of Edvard Munch in America". In *The Symbolist print of Edvard Munch* [exhibition catalogue], 23-48. Toronto: Art Gallery of Ontario; London: Yale University Press, 1997.

Pastor, Willy. "Das Werk von Edvard Munch". In *Das Werk von Edvard Munch. Vier Beiträge / Herausgegeben von Stanisław Przybyszewski*, 57-74. Berlin: Fischer, 1894.

Paz, Octavio. "Edvard Munch: La dama y el esqueleto". *Vuelta*, no. 137 (1988): 50-52.

Pedersen, Arild. "Does The Scream just scream, or does it also give a lecture in philosophy?" *Kunst og Kultur* 80, no. 3 (2007): 187-195.

Pedersen, Gustav Jørgen. *On the Pictorial Thinking of Death: A Study in Martin Heidegger's Unthought Art History of Being Regarding Edvard Munch's The Sick Child and Metabolism* [thesis, PhD]. Oslo: Universitetet i Oslo, 2017.

Perls, Hugo. "Erindringer om Edvard Munch". *Kunst og Kultur* 45, no. 1 (1962): 27-46.

Perron, Janine. "Between Fear and Sex. The Odyssey of Edvard Munch". In *Edvard Munch Paintings 1892-1917* [exhibition catalogue], 3-7. Copenhagen: Galleri Faurschou, 2000.

Pessler, Monica and Thomas Trummer. "Porträt der Ragnhild Bächström". In *Klimt und die Frauen* [exhibition catalogue], 173. Vienna: Österreichische Galerie; Cologne: DuMont, 2000.

Peters, Hans Albert. "Edvard Munch: Vier Mädchen auf der Brücke". In *Wallraf-Richartz-Museum. Zur Kunst des 19. Jahrhunderts*, 100-103. Cologne: Wallraf-Richartz-Museum, 1980.

Petrusevičiūtė, Laima Marija. *Melancholy and Sun. Munch and Čiurlionis*. Vilnius: Mintis, 2010.

Pettersen, Petra. "Et innblikk i Munchs utstillingsvirksomhet og hans anseelse i Ekelyperioden". In *Munch og Ekely: 1916-1944* [exhibition catalogue], 123-140. Oslo: Munchmuseet and Labyrinth Press, 1998.

Pettersen, Petra. "Angst = Angst". In *Skrigets ekko = Echoes of the Scream* [exhibition catalogue], 114-123. Ishøj: Arken, 2000.

Pettersen, Petra. "Livsfrisen 1918 i Munch-museet 2002 - en kort redegjørelse for billedutvalget". In *Edvard Munchs Livsfrise. En rekonstruksjon av utstillingen hos Blomqvist 1918* [exhibition catalogue], 137-142. Oslo: Munchmuseet and Labyrinth Press, 2002.

Pettersen, Petra. "Munch a Nizza". In *L'oro e l'azzurro. I colori del sud da Cézanne a Bonnard* [exhibition catalogue], 187-207. Conegliano: Linea d'ombra libri, 2003.

Pettersen, Petra and Elizabeth Cross. "Nordic light and landscape". In *Edvard Munch. The frieze of life* [exhibition catalogue], 157-171. Melbourne: National Gallery of Victoria, 2004.

Pettersen, Petra. "Berlin 1892 - Forsøk på rekonstruksjon". In *Munch blir "Munch". Kunstneriske strategier 1880-1892 = Munch Becoming "Munch". Artistic Strategies 1880-1892* [exhibition catalogue], 173-193. Oslo: Munchmuseet, 2008.

Pettersen, Petra. "Munch. Un 'outsider' del suo tempo". In *Munch e lo spirito del Nord. Scandinavia nel secondo ottocento* [exhibition catalogue], 101-114. Treviso: Linea d'ombra, 2010.

Pettersen, Petra. "Betraktninger over to livsfriser". In *Vigeland + Munch. Bak mytene* [exhibition catalogue], 120-133. Oslo: Mercatorfonds and Munchmuseet, 2015.

Pienkos, Andrzej. "Naturalism, Symbolism aud Expressionism. The question of Edvard Munch's painting technique". In *Totenmesse. Modernism in the culture of northern and central Europe*, 89-100. Warsaw: Institute of Art, Polish Academy of Science, 1996.

Pietsch, Ulrich. "Edvard Munch". In *Das Licht des Nordens* [exhibition catalogue], 28-36. Hamburg: Altonaer Museum in Hamburg, Norddeutsches Landesmuseum, 1993.

Piontek, Roya. *Edvard Munchs Wirkung auf die Maler der "Brücke"* [thesis, magister]. Münster: Westfälischen Wilhelms-Universität, 2005.

Plahter, Leif Einar. "Det syke barn og Vår. En røntgenundersøkelse av to Munch-bilder". *Kunst og Kultur* 57, no. 2 (1974): 103-115.

Plahter, Leif Einar. "Det syke barn. Spekulasjoner og fakta om maleriets opprinnelige utseende". *Kunst og Kultur* 75, no. 2 (1992): 85-99.

Plahter, Leif Einar. "Atelierleder Leif Einar Plahters rapport". *Kunst og Kultur* 76, no. 4 (1993): 222-223.

Plahter, Leif Einar. *Munch under overflaten. Teknisk undersøkelse av fire malerier av Edvard Munch = Below the surface of Edvard Munch. Technical examination of four paintings by Edvard Munch* [exhibition catalogue]. Oslo: Nasjonalgallereiet, 1994.

Plahter, Leif Einar. "Beneath the surface of Edvard Munch. Technical examinations of four paintings by Edvard Munch". In *Conservare necesse est. Festskrift til Leif Einar Plahter på hans 70-årsdag*, 111-127. Oslo: Nordisk konservatorforbund, Den norske sekjson, 1999.

Plahter, Leif Einar. "Munch". In *Norsk signaturleksikon. Malere født før 1920*, 97, 177. Oslo: Nasjonalgalleriet, 2000.

Plahter, Leif E. and Unn Plahter.

"Munch's Paintings: Scientific Research Both Recent and in Retrospect". In *Public Paintings by Edvard Munch and His Contemporaries. Change and Conservation Challenges*, 3-35. London: Archetype, 2015.

Prelinger, Elizabeth. *Edvard Munch. Master Printmaker. An Examination of the Artist's Works and Techniques based on the Philip and Lynn Straus Collection*. New York and London: W.W. Norton, 1983.

Prelinger, Elizabeth. "When the halted traveler hears the scream in nature. Preliminary thoughts on the transformation of some romantic motifs". In *Shop talk. Studies in honor of Seymour Slive*, 198-203. Cambridge: Harvard University Art Museums, 1995.

Prelinger, Elizabeth. "Edvard Munch and the techniques of Symbolist graphics". In *The Symbolist print of Edvard Munch* [exhibition catalogue], 1-22. Toronto: Art Gallery of Ontario; London: Yale University Press, 1997.

Prelinger, Elizabeth. "Music to our ears? Munch's Scream and romantic music theory". In *The Arts Entwined. Music and painting in the nineteenth century*, 209-225. New York: Garland; London: Routledge, 2000.

Prelinger, Elizabeth. *After The Scream. The late paintings of Edvard Munch* [exhibition catalogue]. Atlanta: High Museum of Art and Yale University Press, 2002.

Prelinger, Elizabeth. "Metal, stone, and wood. Matrices of meaning in Munch's graphic work". In *Edvard Munch. The modern life of the soul* [exhibition catalogue], 56-62. New York: Museum of Modern Art, 2006.

Presler, Gerd. *Edvard Munch: Werksverzeichnis der Skizzenbücher*. Karlsruhe: Engelhardt und Bauer, 2004.

Presler, Gerd. "What have I got to do with Munch: Ernst Ludwig Kirchner and Edvard Munch". In *Ernst Ludwig Kirchner - Edvard Munch* [exhibition catalogue], 61-73. Munich: Galerie Thomas, 2012.

Presler, Gerd. *Edvard Munch. Der Schrei - Ende eines Irrtums = The Scream - End of an error*. Weingarten: Gerd Presler, 2015.

Prestøe, Birgit. "Minner om Edvard Munch". In *Edvard Munch som vi kjente ham. Vennene forteller*, 100-106. Oslo: Dreyer, 1946.

Przybyszewski, Stanisław. "Das Werk von Edvard Munch". In *Das Werk des Edvard Munch. Vier Beiträge / Herausgegeben von Stanisław Przybyszewski*, 9-31. Berlin: Fischer, 1894 A.

Przybyszewski, Stanisław. "Psychischer Naturalismus". *Neue Deutsche Rundschau (Freie Bühne)* V (1894 B): 150-156.

Przybyszewski, Stanisław. "Edvard Munch". *Moderni Revue (Praha)*, March (1897): 99-104, 131-133, 161-165.

R

Rapetti, Rodolphe. "Munch face à la critique française 1893-1905" [17-31]; "Le naturalisme français, l'impressionnisme et le jeune Munch" [33-61]; "Munch et Paris, 1889-1891" [64-105]; "1896-1898, Boulevard parisien" [276-279]; "Bonnard et Munch. L'exemple de La Mort de Marat" [310-317]. In *Munch et la France* [exhibition catalogue]. Paris: Réunion des Musées nationaux, 1991 A.

Rapetti, Rodolphe. "Munchs møte med den franske kritikken, 1893-1905" [16-31]; "Munch og Paris, 1889-1991" [64-104]; "Munch og symbolismen. Den franske innflytelsen" [148-185]; "1896-1898, Pariser-boulevard" [276-279]; "Bonnard og Munch. Eksemplet Marats død" [310-316]. In *Munch og Frankrike* [exhibition catalogue]. Oslo: Munchmuseet, 1991 B. [Also published Paris 1991]

Rasch, Wolfdietrich. "Edvard Munch und das literarische Berlin der neunziger Jahre". In *Edvard Munch. Probleme - Forschungen - Thesen*, 14-23. Munich: Prestel, 1973.

Ravenal, Carlo M. "Three Faces of Mother. Madonna, Martyr, Medusa in the Art of Edvard Munch". *The Journal of Psychology* 13, no. 4 (1986): 371-412.

Ravenal, John B. *Jasper Johns + Edvard Munch. Inspirasjon og forvandling* [exhibition catalogue]. Richmond and Oslo: Virginia Museum of Fine Arts, Yale University Press and Munchmuseet, 2016.

Read, Herbert. "Edvard Munch". *Oslo kommunes kunstsamlinger. Årbok 1963* (1963): 56-62, 126-130.

Reenberg, Holger. "Edvard Munch. Det nære liv". In *Edvard Munch. Det nære liv - Malerier fra Ekely 1916-1944* [exhibition catalogue], 7-10. Ishøj: Arken, 2000.

Reenberg, Holger. "Skrigets Ekko = Echoes of The scream". In *Skrigets Ekko = Echoes of The Scream* [exhibition catalogue], 34-85. Ishøj: Arken, 2001.

Réja, Marcel. "Symbolisme pictoral. H. Héran - E. Munch - O. Redon". *La Critique* 6, no. 118 (1900): 9-11.

Revold, Reidar. 1958, 1960, 1961 and 1963. *See* Langaard, Johan. 1958, 1960, 1961 and 1963.

Revold, Reidar. "Omkring en motivgruppe hos Edvard Munch". *Oslo kommunes kunstsamlinger. Årbok 1952-1959* (1960): 38-51.

Revold, Reidar. "Edvard Munch und Deutschland". *Jahrbuch der Stiftung Preussischer Kulturbesitz* (1966): 225-236.

Richard, Lionel. "Une vie exaltée et depressive. 'J'aime la vie, la vie, même malade'". In *Edvard Munch. L'oeil moderne* [exhibition catalogue], 10-17. Issy-les-Moulineaux: Beaux Arts, 2011.

Richardson, John. "Crimes against the Cubists". *The New York Review of Books*, 16 June (1983): https://www.nybooks.com/articles/1983/06/16/crimes-against-the-cubists/.

Ringbom, Sixten. "Färg - Form - Känsla.

Munch och bildens yttersta uttrycksmedel". In *Edvard Munch. Målningar och grafik* [exhibition catalogue], 39. Helsinki: Föreningen Konstsamfundet, 1979.

Ritter, Beate. "Die 'Kollektion des Norwegers Edvard Munch' in der Kunsthütte Chemnitz 1906" [157-167]; "Immer wieder Munch. Der norwegische Künstler und seine Ausstellungen im Museum am Theaterplatz" [197-225]. In *Edvard Munch in Chemnitz* [exhibition catalogue]. Chemnitz: Wienand, 1999.

Ritter, William. "Un peintre norvégien. M. Edvard Munch". In *Études d'art étranger*, 81-122. Paris: Société du Mercure de France, 1906.

Rognerud, Hilde Marie Jamessen. "'Zarathustra-Nietzsche med vinger'. Edvard Munch maler samtidens motefilosof". *Kunst og Kultur* 94, no. 3 (2011): 146-160.

Rognerud, Hilde. *Nordens störste konstnär* [exhibition catalogue]. Stockholm: Thielska galleriet, 2013.

Rognerud, Hilde Marie Jamessen. "Nietzsche, zarathustrisch und geflügelt. Edvard Munchs Visionen eines Philosophen der Moderne". *Zeitschrift für Kunstgeschichte* 77 (2014): 101-116.

Romdahl, Axel. "Edvard Munch i Konstmuseet". *Göteborgs Musei Årstryck* (1944): 89-98.

Romdahl, Axel. "Edvard Munchs stil. Et utkast till en undersökning". *Kunst og Kultur* 29, nos. 3-4 (1946): 79-102.

Romdahl, Axel. "Edvard Munch som expressionist". *Tidskrift för konstvetenskap* (1947): 165-186.

Rosenblum, Robert. "Munch and Hodler". In *Modern Painting and the Northern Romantic Tradition*, 101-128. London: Thames & Hudson, 1975.

Rosenblum, Robert. "Edvard Munch. Some changing contexts". In *Edvard Munch. Symbols & Images* [exhibition catalogue], 1-9. Washington: National Gallery of Art, 1978.

Rosenblum, Robert. "Edvard Munch. Charting the psyche". In *Love, isolation, darkness. The art of Edvard Munch* [exhibition catalogue], 7-32. Greenwich: Bruce Museum, 1996.

Rumble, Vanessa. "The Scandinavian Conscience. Kierkegaard, Ibsen and Munch". In *Edvard Munch. Psyche, Symbol and Expression* [exhibition catalogue], 20-30. Chestnut Hill: McMullen Museum of Art, 2001.

Rutkowski, Eva. *Edvard Munch's Frauen: Frauendarstellung in den frühen Gemälden des norwegischen Malers Edvard Munch*. Saarbrücken: WDM Müller, 2008.

Rød, Johannes. "Harald Brun; Konservator ved Nasjonalgalleriet 1905-21". *Kunst og Kultur* 76, no. 2 (1993): 89-107.

Rød, Johannes. "Cleaning of Paintings at the National Gallery in Oslo - An Historical Overview". In *Congress Preprints Surface Treatments: Cleaning, Stabiliza-

tion and Coatings*, 15-25. Lyngby: Nordisk konservatorforbund, 1994.

Rød, Johannes. "The Cleaning Controversy and the Keeping of Secrets at the National Gallery in Oslo 1917-1921". In *Preprints, 11th Triennial Meeting: Edinburgh, Scottland, 1-6 September 1996*, vol. 1: 172-176. London: James, 1996.

Rød, Johannes. "'Hestekur', Aulamalerier og Nasjonalgalleriet. Om kunstneren og konservatoren Ole Dørje Haug (1888-1952)". *Kunst og Kultur* 80, no. 1 (1997): 54-66.

Rød, Johannes. "Er mesteren Edvard Munch?" In *Falsk. Kunst som forfalskning, forfalskning som kunst*, 164-167. Oslo: Gyldendal fakta, 2000.

S

Sadowsky, Thorsten. "Sjælens skygger". In *Den sene Munch. Malerier fra Ekely 1916-1944* [exhibition catalogue], 7-15. Kolding: Trapholt, 2000.

Salda, F.X. "Den voldsomme drømmer. Noen tanker om Edvard Munchs arbeider". *Kunst og Kultur* 52, no. 1 (1969): 40-48.

Sandberg, Inger. "Edvard Munch maler barn i Kragerø". *Historieglimt. Årsskrift for Kragerø og Skåtøy Historielag* (1994): 101-105.

Sandberg, Inger. "Gate i Kragerø". *Historieglimt. Årsskrift for Kragerø og Skåtøy Historielag* (2002): 75-76.

Schacht, Roland. "Edvard Munchs utstilling i Berlin". *Kunst og Kultur* 14, 2 (1927): 65-76.

Schemm, Jürgen V. "Edvard Munchs Gemälde 'Sommernacht am Oslofjord', um 1900" [9-14]; "Zur Entwicklung der Landschaftsmalerei im Werk Edvard Munchs" [15-38]; "Edvard Munch und Arnold Böcklin" [44-47]. In *Edvard Munch. Sommernacht am Oslofjord, um 1900* [exhibition catalogue]. Mannheim: Städtische Kunsthalle Mannheim, 1988.

Schiefler, Gustav. *Verzeichnis des graphischen Werks Edvard Munchs bis 1906*. Berlin: Bruno Cassirer, 1907.

Schiefler, Gustav. "Edvard Munchs Alfa und Omega". *Kunst und Künstler* VIII, no. 8 (1910): 409-413.

Schiefler, Gustav. "Einführung". In *Edvard Munch. Ausstellung von Originalradierungen, Lithographien, Holzschnitten* [exhibition catalogue], 5-21. Hamburg: Galerie Commeter, 1913.

Schiefler, Gustav. "Das Werk von Edvard Munch". *Das Kunstblatt*, January (1917): 9-18.

Schiefler, Gustav. *Edvard Munchs Graphische Kunst*. Dresden: Ernst Arnold, 1923.

Schiefler, Gustav. *Edvard Munch. Das graphische Werk: 1906-1926*. Berlin: Euphorion, 1928.

Schiefler, Gustav. *Das graphische Werk: 1906-1926* [facsimile edition]. Oslo: Cappelen, 1974 A.

Schiefler, Gustav. *Meine Graphiksammlung*. Hamburg: Christian, 1974 B.

Schiefler, Gustav. *Verzeichnis des graphischen Werks Edvard Munchs bis 1906* [facsimile edition]. Oslo: Cappelen, 1974 C.

Schiefler, Gustav. *Briefwechsel. See* Munch, Edvard. *Briefwechsel* (1987-1990).

Schinnerer, Adolf. "Edvard Munch, der Maler". *Die Kunst* 28, no. 3 (1926): 73-81.

Schinnerer, Adolf. "Zu den Bildern von Edvard Munch". *Die Kunst* 71, no. 5 (1935): 131-140.

Schjeldal, Peter. "Munch. The missing master". *Art in America*, May-June (1979): 80-95.

Schlagheck, Irma. "Ein gutes Bild hält eine Rosskur aus". *Art - das Kunstmagazin*, no. 3 (1995): 82-85.

Schlittgen, Hermann. "Im 'Schwarzen Ferkel'". In *Erinnerungen*, 235-248. Munich: A. Langen, 1926.

Schloesser, Stephen. "From spiritual naturalism to psychical naturalism. Catholic decadence, Lutheran Munch, and Madone mystérique". In *Edvard Munch. Psyche, symbol and expression* [exhibition catalogue], 75-110. Chestnut Hill: McMullen Museum of Art, 2001.

Schmitz, Regine. *Naturalistische und Symbolistische Tendenzen bei Hans Jaeger und Edvard Munch* [thesis, magister]. Bonn: Rheinische Friedrich-Wilhelms-Universität, 1985.

Schmoll, J.A. (Eisenwerth). "Munch, Edward". In *Malerei nach Fotografie* [exhibition catalogue], 125-131, pl. 49-51. Munich: Karl M. Lipp Verlag, 1970.

Schmoll, J.A. (Eisenwerth). "Munch und Rodin" [99-132]; "Munchs fotografische Studien" [187-225]. In *Edvard Munch. Probleme - Forschungen - Thesen*. Munich: Prestel, 1973.

Schneede, Uwe M. *Edvard Munch. Arbeiterbilder 1910-1930* [exhibition catalogue]. Hamburg: Kunstverein in Hamburg, 1978.

Schneede, Uwe M. *Das kranke Kind. Arbeit an der Erinnerung*. Frankfurt am Main: Fischer Taschenbuch Verlag, 1984 A.

Schneede, Uwe M. "Selbstprüfungen in schwierigen Jahren". In *Edvard Munch. Höhepunkt des malerischen Werks im 20. Jahrhundert* [exhibition catalogue], 65-74. Hamburg: Frölich & Kaufmann, 1984 B.

Schneede, Uwe M. "Das Freia-Projekt. Zu Edvard Munchs Fries-Konzept". In *Kunstsplitter. Beiträge zur nordeuropäischen Kunstgeschichte. Festschrift für Wolfgang J. Müller zum 70. Geburtstag*, 180-191. Husum: Husum Druck- und Verlagsgesellschaft, 1984 C.

Schneede, Uwe M. *Edvard Munch. The Early Masterpieces*. Munich: Schirmer and Mosel, 1988.

Schneede, Uwe M. "Munch in Deutschland = Munch in Germania". In *Edvard Munch = Edvard Munch* [exhibition catalogue], 43-70. Lugano: Museo d'arte moderna and Città di Lugano; Milan: Skira, 1998.

Schneede, Uwe M. *Die Geschichte der Kunst im 20. Jahrhundert: von den Avantgarden bis zur Gegenwart*. Munich: Beck, 2001.

Schneede, Uwe M. "Der Klassiker und die Wilden. Munch in Deutschland". In *Im Farbenrausch. Munch, Matisse und die Expressionisten* [exhibition catalogue], 61-71. Göttingen: Edition Folkwang/Steidl, 2012.

Schneede, Uwe M. "Bilder i samklang: Van Goghs 'dekorasjon' og Munchs Livsfrise". In *Munch + Van Gogh* [exhibition catalogue], 152-168. Brussels: Mercatorfonds and Orfeus Publishing, 2015.

Schroll, Elena. "Whore or Saint? The Image of Women in the Works of Edvard Munch". In *Battle of the Sexes. Franz von Stuck to Frida Kahlo* [exhibition catalogue], 177-182. Munich: Prestel, 2016.

Schultze, Jürgen. "Beobachtungen zum Thema 'Munch und der deutsche Expressionismus'". In *Edvard Munch. Probleme - Forschungen - Thesen*, 147-160. Munich: Prestel, 1973.

Schultze, Jürgen. "Deutschland - 'die zweite Heimat'". In *Edvard Munch* [exhibition catalogue], 343-350. Essen: Museum Folkwang Essen; Zürich: Kunsthaus Zürich, 1987.

Schultze, Sabine (ed.). *Sehnsucht nach Glück: Wiens Aufbruch in die Moderne* [exhibition catalogue], Frankfurt am Main: Schirn Kunsthalle, 1995.

Schütz, Barbara. *Farbe und Licht bei Edvard Munch* [unpublished thesis, PhD]. Saarbrücken: Universität des Saarlandes, 1985.

Schütz, Barbara. "Die Farbe bei Edvard Munch". In *Edvard Munch* [exhibition catalogue], 77-87. Essen: Museum Folkwang Essen; Zürich: Kunsthaus Zürich, 1987.

Schröder, Klaus Albrecht and Antonia Hoerschelmann (eds.). *Edvard Munch. Thema und Variation = Edvard Munch. Theme and variation* [exhibition catalogue]. Vienna: Albertina, 2003.

Seiler, Harald. "Edvard Munch. Dorfplatz in Elgersburg". *Niederdeutsche Beiträge zur Kunstgeschichte* IX (1970): 235-242.

Sejersted, Ingebjørg Strønø. "Kvinnen - En deilig skapning?" In *Avkledd. Studenter velger Munch* [exhibition catalogue], 9-11. Oslo: Munchmuseet, 2004.

Selber, Walter (pseudonym for Leistikow). "Edvard Munch i Berlin". *Samtiden* (1893): 38-43.

Selz, Jean. *E. Munch*. Munich: Sydwest verlag, 1974.

Servaes, Franz. "Das Werk von Edvard Munch". In *Das Werk von Edvard Munch. Vier Beiträge/Herausgegeben von Stanisław Przybyszewski*, 33-56. Berlin: Fischer, 1894.

Sherman, Ida. "Edvard Munchs 'Alma Mater'. Tretti år i kamp med et motiv". *Kunst og Kultur* 58, no. 3 (1975): 137-153.

Sherman, Ida. "Edvard Munch og Felicien Rops". *Kunst og Kultur* 59, no. 4 (1976): 243-258.

Shiff, Richard. "Vibrations". In *Edvard Munch, ou l'"Anti-Cri"* [exhibition catalogue], [unpaginated]. Paris: Éditions Pinacothèque de Paris, 2010.

Shiff, Richard. "Munch on the Periphery". In *Edvard Munch: Between the Clock and the Bed* [exhibition catalogue], 59-73. New York: Metropolitan Museum of Art, 2017.

Singer, Brian et al. "Investigation of Materials Used by Edvard Munch". *Studies in Conservation* 55, no. 4 (2013): 274-292.

Sjåstad, Øystein. "Absorbert og teatralt i Christian Krohgs og Edvard Munchs kunst". *Kunst og Kultur* 93, no. 3 (2010): 172-179.

Sjåstad, Øystein. "Das Bild von Oda Krohg als 'eine wahre Boheme-Prinzessin'". In *Oda Krohg. Malerin und Muse im Kreis um Edvard Munch* [exhibition catalogue], 23-39. Cologne: Wienand, 2011.

Skaug, Erling, Françoise Hanssen-Bauer and Kaja Kollandsrud (eds.). *Conservare necesse est: Festskrift til Leif Einar Plahter på hans 70-årsdag*. Oslo: Nordisk Konservatorforbund, Den norske seksjon, IIC Nordic Group, 1999.

Skedsmo, Tone. *To norske kunstsamlere ved århundreskiftet. Olaf Schou og Rasmus Meyer* [unpublished thesis, magister]. Oslo: Universitetet i Oslo, 1976.

Skedsmo, Tone (ed.). *Norske mesterverker i Nasjonalgalleriet*. Oslo: J.M. Stenersens forlag, 1981.

Skedsmo, Tone. "Tautrekking om Det syke barn". *Kunst og Kultur* 68, no. 3 (1985): 184-195.

Skedsmo, Tone. "Edvard Munch". In *Nordiske stemninger. Nordisk maleri fra århundreskiftet* [exhibition catalogue], 218-226. Oslo: Nasjonalgalleriet, 1987 A.

Skedsmo, Tone. *Edvard Munch* [exhibition catalogue]. Essen: Museum Folkwang Essen; Zürich: Kunsthaus Zürich, 1987 B.

Skedsmo, Tone. *Olaf Schous gaver til Nasjonalgalleriet*. Oslo: Nasjonalgalleriet, 1987 C.

Skedsmo, Tone. "Nasjonalgalleriets Munch-samling. En historikk". In *Edvard Munch i Nasjonalgalleriet*, 5-15. Oslo: Nasjonalgalleriet, 1989. [New edition 1998]

Skredsvig, Christian. "Edvard Munch i Monte Carlo". In *Dage og nætter blandt kunstnere*, 111-119. Kristiania and Copenhagen: Nordisk forlag, 1908.

Skårderud, Finn. "For første gang. Kroppstanker om ungdomsliv = For the First Time - Bodily Reflections about Youth". In *Edvard Munch: Pubertet = Edvard Munch: Puberty* [exhibition catalogue], 54-65. Oslo: Munchmuseet and Orfeus Publishing, 2012.

Skårderud, Finn. "I skjønneste uorden. Møter med Edvard Munchs maleri PUBERTET fra 1894". In *I skjønneste uorden. Møter med Edvard Munchs maleri Pubertet*, 7-56. Oslo: Munchmuseet and Orfeus Publishing, 2018.

Smith, Alison. "Edvard Munchs dobbeltportretter". In *I oss er verdener* [exhibition catalogue], 62-66. Bergen: KODE, 2019.

Smith, John Boulton. "Edvard Munch og Frederick Delius". *Kunst og Kultur* 48, no. 3 (1965): 137-158.

Smith, John Boulton. "Portrait of a friendship. Edvard Munch and Frederick Delius". *Apollo* (1971): 38-47.

Smith, John Boulton. *Frederick Delius and Edvard Munch. Their Friendship and Their Correspondence*. Rickmansworth: Triad Press, 1983.

Sommer, Achim. "Aspekte des Figurenbildes im Spätwerk von Edvard Munch". In *Edvard Munch. Bilder aus Norwegen* [exhibition catalogue], 70-89. Ostfildern-Ruit: Hatje Canz Verlag, 2004.

Southgate, M. Therese. "Death of Marat". *JAMA. Journal of the American Medical Association* 267, no. 2 (1992): cover.

Stabell, Waldemar. "Edvard Munch og Eva Mudocci". *Kunst og Kultur* 56, no. 4 (1973): 209-236.

Stafne-Pfisterer, Lin. "Norske og finske forbindelser i kunstlivet omkring 1900". In *Det magiske nord. Finsk og norsk kunst omkring 1900* [exhibition catalogue], 87-95. Oslo: Nasjonalmuseet, 2015.

Stang, Nic. *Edvard Munch*. Oslo: Johan Grundt Tanum, 1971.

Stang, Ragna. *Edvard Munch. Mennesket og kunstneren*. Oslo: Aschehoug, 1977.

Stang, Ragna. "The aging Munch. New creative power". In *Edvard Munch. Symbols & Images* [exhibition catalogue], 77-85. Washington: National Gallery of Art, 1978.

Stang, Ragna. *Edvard Munch. Der Mensch und der Künstler = Edvard Munch. Leven en werk = Edvard Munch. The Man and His Art*. Königstein im Taunus: Langewiesche; Amsterdam: Meulenhoff; New York: Abbeville, 1979.

Statens Kunstutstilling 1891. *Katalog over statens kunstudstilling: [Høstutstillingen] 1891*. Kristiania: BKS, 1891.

Steihaug, Jon-Ove. "Edvard Munchs performative selvportretter". In *Edvard Munch 1863-1944* [exhibition catalogue], 12-23. Milan: Skira; Oslo: Nasjonalmuseet and Munchmuseet, 2013 A.

Steihaug, Jon-Ove. "Fra Munch til Slettemark og tilbake igjen". In *Fra Munch til Slettemark: 200 kunstverk fra en norsk privatsamling* [exhibition catalogue], 212-214. Oslo: Munchmuseet, 2013 B.

Steihaug, Jon-Ove. "Edvard Munch's Dramatic Art". In *Edvard Munch and the Modern Soul* [exhibition catalogue], 26-35. Seoul: Seoul Arts Center, 2014.

Steihaug, Jon-Ove. "Edvard Munch's Dramatic Art". In *Edvard Munch. Archetypes* [exhibition catalogue], 151-163. Madrid: Museo Thyssen-Bornemisza, 2015.

Steihaug, Jon-Ove. "Mappelthorpe + Munch". In *Mappelthorpe + Munch* [exhibition catalogue], 8-175. Oslo: Mercatorfonds and Munchmuseet, 2016.

Steihaug, Jon-Ove. "Radikalt maleri - et bilde i samtiden". In *I skjønneste uorden. Møter med Edvard Munchs maleri Pubertet*, 57-86. Oslo: Munchmuseet and Orfeus Publishing, 2018.

Stein, Mille. "Edvard Munch for fremtiden?" In *Kulturminner - en ressurs i tiden*, 170-184. Oslo: NIKU, 2005.

Stein, Mille, Vegar Bakkestuen, Lars Eriksted and Inger Grimstad. "A conservation plan for 1158 paintings by Edvard Munch". *Zeitschrift für Kunsttechnologie und Konservierung* 20, no. 2 (2006): 353-360.

Stein, Mille and Johannes Rød. "A contribution to the varnish history of the paintings by Edvard Munch at the National Museum and Munch Museum". In *Public paintings by Edvard Munch and his contemporaries. Change and conservation challenges*, 257-270. London: Archetype, 2015.

Stein, Mille. "Edvard Munch og 'hestekuren'. En revurdering". *Kunst og Kultur* 100, nos. 1-2 (2017 A): 48-74.

Stein, Mille. "Patterns in Munch's Painting Technique". In *Edvard Munch: Between the Clock and the Bed* [exhibition catalogue], 31-43. New York: Metropolitan Museum of Art, 2017 B.

Stein, Mille. "Sjalusiens farger. Edvard Munchs maleriske virkemidler". In *I oss er verdener* [exhibition catalogue], 31-41. Bergen: KODE, 2019.

Steinberg, Stanley and Joseph Weiss. "The Art of Edvard Munch and its Function in his Mental Life". *The Psychoanalytic Quarterly*, no. 3 (1954): 409-423.

Steltner, Ulrich. "Krzyk - Der Schrei. Stanisław Przybyszewski und Edvard Munch". *Bulletin der Deutschen Slavistik*, no. 2 (1996): 8-10.

Stene-Johansen, Knut. "'Trang til krystalisation': Om Edvard Munchs og Asger Jorns litterære produksjon". In *Jorn + Munch* [exhibition catalogue], 77-87. Brussels: Mercatorfonds; Oslo: Munchmuseet, 2016.

Stenersen, Rolf. *Edvard Munch. Närbild av ett geni*. Stockholm: Wahlström & Widstrand, 1944.

Stenersen, Rolf. *Edvard Munch. Nærbilde av et geni*. Oslo: Gyldendal, 1945. [New editions 1946, 1964, 1968, 1994, 2005 and 2012]

Stenersen, Rolf. *Edvard Munch. Close-up of a genius*. Oslo: Gyldendal, 1969.

Stenerud, Karl. "Edvard Munchs testamente". *Kunst og Kultur* 29, nos. 3-4 (1946): 73-78.

Stenseth, Bodil. *Pakten. Munch - en familiehistorie*. Oslo: Aschehoug, 2004.

Stensman, Mailis. *Konst i industrimiljö*. Saltsjöbaden: Apel, 1989.

Stokkan, Torill. *Tante Karen. Kvinnen bak Edvard Munch*. Oslo: Orfeus, 2013.

Strindberg, August. "L'exposition d'Edvard Munch". *Revue Blanche* (1896): 525-526.

Stubbe, Wolf. "Den sørgende pike var ikke sørgmodig. Edvard Munch og hans modell". *Kunst og Kultur* 55, no. 2 (1972): 105-108.

Stubbe, Wolf. "Munchs Bild-Ideen und die Technik seiner Druckgraphik". In

Edvard Munch. Probleme - Forschungen - Thesen, 177-186. Munich: Prestel, 1973.

Sturgis, Alexander. "Moment and Movement". In *Telling Time* [exhibition catalogue], 35-59. London: National Gallery and Yale University Press, 2000.

Svenæus, Gösta. *Idé och innehåll i Edvard Munchs konst: en analys av aulamålningarna*. Oslo: Gyldendal, 1953.

Svenæus, Gösta. "Trädet på berget. En studie i förhållandet Munch-Nietzsche" [24-46]; "Der Baum auf dem Berg" [113-120]. *Oslo kommunes kunstsamlinger. Årbok 1963* (1963).

Svenæus, Gösta. "Strindberg och Munch i Inferno". *Kunst og Kultur* 50, no. 1 (1967): 1-30.

Svenæus, Gösta. *Edvard Munch. Das Universum der Melancholie*. Lund: Vetenskaps-societeten, 1968.

Svenæus, Gösta. "Munch og Strindberg. Quickborn-episoden, 1898". *Kunst og Kultur* 52, no. 1 (1969): 13-36.

Svenæus, Gösta. "Der heilige Weg. Nietzsche-Fermente in der Kunst Edvard Munchs". In *Edvard Munch. Probleme - Forschungen - Thesen*, 25-46. Munich: Prestel, 1973 A.

Svenæus, Gösta. *Edvard Munch. Im Männlichen Gehirn*. Lund: Gleerup, 1973 B.

Sæther, Astrid. "Ibsen som billedmaker". In *Edvard Munch og Henrik Ibsen* [exhibition catalogue], 36-43. Copenhagen: Kunstforeningen, 1998.

Sørbø, Tommy. "Edvard Munchs sene malerier". In *Edvard Munch - Asger Jorn - Per Kirkeby* [exhibition catalogue], 1-2. Moss: Galleri F 15, 1984.

Sørbø, Tommy. "En hyllest til livet". *Kunst* 58, no. 1 (2011): 94-95.

Sørbø, Tommy. *For et vær! Vår lidenskap for været*. Oslo: Font forlag, 2013.

Sørensen, Bengt Algot. "Der Fall Munch und seine Auswirkungen". In *Spurensuche in Sprach- und Geschichtslandschaften. Festschrift für Ernst Erich Metzner*, 519-534. Münster: LIT, 2003.

Sørensen, Gunnar. "Vitalismens år?" *Cras*, no. 24 (1981): 26-42.

Sørensen, Gunnar. "Kunstnerisk enhet og felleskap". In *Det store løftet. Rådhuset i Oslo*, 257-436. Oslo: Aschehoug and Oslo kommune, 2000.

Sørensen, Gunnar. *Bjørn Carlsen - møte med Munch* [exhibition catalogue]. Oslo: Munchmuseet, 2004 A.

Sørensen, Gunnar. "Vitalismens år." In *Livskraft. Vitalismen som kunstnerisk impuls 1900-1930* [exhibition catalogue], 13-44. Oslo: Munchmuseet, 2004 B.

Sørensen, Jens Erik. "Eventyrskogen". In *Edvard Munch. Angst = Anxiety* [exhibition catalogue], 189. Aarhus: AROS Aarhus Kunstmuseum, 2012.

Sørlie, Nina. "Edvard Munch møter publikum i Kristiania". In *Edvard Munchs Livsfrise. En rekonstruksjon av utstillingen hos Blomqvist 1918* [exhibition catalogue], 50-61. Oslo: Munchmuseet and Labyrinth Press, 2002.

T

Tanaka, Masayuki. "Edvard Munch, the decorative challenge". In *Edvard Munch. The decorative projects* [exhibition catalogue], 177-183. Tokyo: National Museum of Western Art, 2007.

Temkin, Ann. *The Scream: Edvard Munch* [exhibition catalogue]. New York: Museum of Modern Art, 2012.

Templeton, Joan. "The Munch-Ibsen connection. Exposing a critical myth". *Scandinavian Studies* 72, no. 4 (2011): 445-462.

Templeton, Joan. *Munch's Ibsen. A Painter's Visions of a Playwright*. Seattle: Museum Tusculanum Press and University of Washington Press, 2008.

Thiis, Jens. "Edvard Munch". In *Norske malere og billedhuggere*, vol. 2, 413-441. Bergen: John Griegs forlag, 1907 A.

Thiis, Jens. "Edvard Munch. Et foredrag holdt i anledning af en udstilling af kunstnerens arbeider i Kristiania". *Ord och Bild* 16 (1907 B): 533-546.

Thiis, Jens. "Den internationale kunstutstilling i Köln". *Kunst og Kultur* 2 (1912 A): 234-237.

Thiis, Jens. *Norsk malerkunst i Nationalgalleriet. Halvhundrede gjengivelser av norske maleres arbeider*. Kristiania: Mittet, 1912 B.

Thiis, Jens. "Edvard Munch. I. Om indholdet i hans kunst (1901). II. Om utviklingslinjen i hans kunst (1913)". *Kunst og Kultur* 4 (1913): 67-80.

Thiis, Jens. *Edvard Munch* [exhibition catalogue]. Oslo: Nasjonalgalleriet, 1927 A.

Thiis, Jens. "Malerkunsten i det 19. og 20. aarhundrede". In *Norsk kunsthistorie*, vol. 2, 389-598. Oslo: Gyldendal, 1927 B.

Thiis, Jens. *Edvard Munch og hans samtid. Slekten, livet og kunsten, geniet*. Oslo: Gyldendal, 1933.

Thiis, Jens. *Edvard Munch. Ein Nordischer Maler*. Berlin: Rembrandt-Verlag, 1934.

Thiis, Jens. "Minneord om Helge Rode". In *Festskrift til Francis Bull på 50-årsdagen*, 301-323. Oslo: Gyldendal, 1937.

Thiis, Jens. "Munch, Edvard, 1863-". In *Norsk Biografisk Leksikon*, vol. IX, 408-430. Oslo: Aschehoug, 1940.

Thomsen, Ingrid Reed. "Skredsvig og Munch på Rivieraen 1891-1892". *Kunst og Kultur* 82, no. 3 (1999): 163-179.

Thormaehlen, Ludwig. "Drei neu erworbene Bilder von Munch in der National-Galerie". *Museum der Gegenwart*, no. 3 (1930): 124-134.

Thue, Oscar. "Edvard Munch og Christian Krohg". *Kunst og Kultur* 56, no. 4 (1973): 237-255.

Thue, Oscar. "Tidligere upubliserte brev fra Erik Werenskiold". *Kunst og kultur* 72, no. 4 (1989): 232-243.

Thune, Jens Christian. *Med et skrik*. Oslo: Aschehoug, 1996.

Thurmann-Moe, Jan. "Note sulla tecnica pittorica di Edvard Munch". In *Munch* [exhibition catalogue], 65-75. Milan: Mazzotta, 1985.

Thurmann-Moe, Jan. "Bemerkungen zu Munchs Maltechnik". In *Edvard Munch* [exhibition catalogue], 89-99. Essen: Museum Folkwang Essen; Zürich: Kunsthaus Zürich, 1987 A.

Thurmann-Moe, Jan. "'Rosskur' und Firnis bei Edvard Munch". In *Das 19. Jahrhundert und die Restaurierung. Beiträge zur Malerei, Maltechnik und Konservierung*, 112-121. Munich: Callwey, 1987 B.

Thurmann-Moe, Jan. *Munchs "Rosskur". Experimente mit Technik und Material*. Hamburg: Dölling und Galitz, 1994.

Thurmann-Moe, Jan. *Edvard Munchs "hestekur". Eksperimenter med teknikk og materialer* [exhibition catalogue]. Oslo: Munchmuseet, 1995.

Thurmann-Moe, Jan. "Edvard Munchs opphold i Kolbjørnsvik på Hisøy ved Arendal sommeren 1886". *Kunst og Kultur* 84, no. 4 (2001): 247-254.

Thurmann-Moe, Jan. "Edvard Munchs 'Rosskur' als Vorläufer informeller Techniken". *Informel. Material und Technik. Schriftenreihe des Museums am Ostwall*, vol. IV (2004): 27-34.

Thurmann-Moe, Jan. "Markens grøde. Edvard Munchs malerier fra nordre Ålerud gård i Vestby". *Follominne, Årbok 2004* (2004): 48-70.

Tiala, Crystal. "Notes on the reconstruction of scenic designer's model for Ibsen's Ghosts". In *Edvard Munch. Psyche, symbol and expression* [exhibition catalogue], 132-133. Chestnut Hill: McMullen Museum of Art, 2001.

Timm, Ingo. "Edvard Munch: Das Walther-Rathenau-Bildnis. Bemerkungen zur Maltechnik des Berliner Porträts". *Restauro. Zeitschrift für Kunsttechniken, Restaurierung und Museumsfragen*, no. 4 (1996): 248-252.

Timm, Werner. *Edvard Munch. Graphik*. Berlin: Henschelverlag Kunst und Gesellschaft, 1969.

Titus-Carmel, Gérard. *Edvard Munch entre chambre et ciel*. Besançon: Éditions Virgile, 2007.

Toft-Eriksen, Lars. "Den virile protest". In *Avkledd. Studenter velger Munch* [exhibition catalogue], 23-25. Oslo: Munchmuseet, 2004.

Toft-Eriksen, Lars. "A Few Thoughts on a Rubber House". In *Melgaard + Munch - The End of It All Has Already Happened* [exhibition catalogue], 206-213. Ostfildern-Ruit: Hatje Cantz Verlag; Oslo: Munchmuseet, 2015.

Topalova-Casadiego, Biljana. "Studie av maleriteknikk i et utvalg av Edvard Munchs malerier" [part of unpublished thesis, PhD]. Prague: Academy of Fine Arts, 2002.

Topalova-Casadiego, Biljana. "Edvard Munchs Løsrivelse, 1896. Aspekter ved maleteknikken". *Norske Konserves*, no. 2 (2004 A): 13-14.

Topalova-Casadiego, Biljana. "Noen aspekter ved Edvard Munchs Piken og døden, 1893". *Meddelelser om Konservering*, no. 1 (2004 B): 25-29.

Topalova-Casadiego, Biljana and Kirsten Korff. "Preliminær undersøkelse av Edvard Munchs Skrik 1893 (?). Munch-museets reg. nr. 514". *Meddelelser om Konservering*, no. 1 (2005 A): 3-15.

Topalova-Casadiego, Biljana and Kirsten Korff. "Tekniske undersøkelser av Munchs Skrik". *Norske Konserves*, no. 1 (2005 B): 12.

Topalova-Casadiego, Biljana. "Kort om en nyoppdaget Munch". *Norske Konserves*, no. 1 (2006): 15-16.

Topalova-Casadiego, Biljana. "De to malte versjonene av Skrik. Forsøk på en maleteknisk sammenligning = The Two Painted Versions of Scream. An Attempt at a Comparison Based on Technical Painting Characteristics". In *Skrik = The Scream* [exhibition catalogue], 87-99. Oslo: Vigmostad & Bjørke, 2008.

Topalova-Casadiego, Biljana. "'Versteckte' Bilder - Doppelbespannungen, Rückseitenbearbeitungen und Übermalungen im Werk von Edvard Munch". In *Edvard Munch - Rätsel hinter der Leinwand* [exhibition catalogue], 186-197. Cologne: DuMont, 2011.

Topalova-Casadiego, Biljana. "Aspekter ved *Pubertet*. Resultater fra nyere studier/Painterly Aspects of *Puberty*. The Results of Recent Studies". In *Edvard Munch: Pubertet = Edvard Munch: Puberty* [exhibition catalogue], 66-84. Oslo: Munchmuseet and Orfeus Publishing, 2012.

Torjusen, Bente. *Edvard Munch og den tsjekkiske kunst* [exhibition catalogue]. Oslo: Munchmuseet, 1971 A.

Torjusen, Bente. "Edvard Munchs utstilling i Praha i 1905. Samtidskritikkens og kunstnernes reaksjoner". *Kunsten idag*, no. 3 (1971 B): 4-51.

Torjusen, Bente. "The mirror". In *Edvard Munch. Symbols & Images* [exhibition catalogue], 185-212. Washington: National Gallery of Art, 1978.

Torjusen, Bente. "'Der Spiegel'. Eine graphische Folge und ein Graphik-Blatt". In *Edvard Munch. Liebe, Angst, Tod: Themen und Variationen* [exhibition catalogue], 377-386. Bielefeld: Kunsthalle Bielefeld, 1980.

Trabuco, Luca. "Munch: morte e follia". In *Arte, genio, follia: il giorno e la notte dell'artista* [exhibition catalogue] 134-149. Milan: Mazzotta, 2009.

Tschudi-Madsen, Stephan. *Sources of Art Nouveau* [thesis, doctoral]. Oslo: Universitetet i Oslo, 1956.

Tschudi-Madsen, Stephan. *An Introduction to Edvard Munchs wallpaintings in the Oslo University Aula*. Oslo: University Press, 1959.

Tucker, Mark S. and Suzanne Penn. "The 1938 alteration of Edvard Munch's Mermaid. Circumstances, implications, and challenges". In *Edvard Munch's Mermaid* [exhibition catalogue], 48-53.

Philadelphia: Philadelphia Museum of Art and Pennsylvania State University Press, 2005.

Tøjner, Poul Erik. "Helt igennem primitiv – om Edvard Munch". In *Verdenskunst: Fra Tizian til i dag*, 135-145. Copenhagen: Kunstbogklubben, 1997.

Tøjner, Poul Erik. "Overfladisk, dypest sett". In *Munch. Med egne ord*, 11-54. Oslo: Press, 2000.

Tøjner, Poul Erik and Bjarne Riiser Gundersen. *Skrik: Historien om et bilde*. Oslo: Press, 2013.

Törsleff, Hans. "Edvard Munch ... der Einsiedler von 'Ekely'". *Die Dame*, no. 4, November (1930): 7-9, 42, 44.

U

Ulferts, Gerd-Dieter. "Edvard Munch in Thüringen – Ansichten von Menschen und Landschaften". In *Aufstieg und Fall der Moderne* [exhibition catalogue], 194-207. Ostfildern-Ruit: Hatje Cantz Verlag, 1999.

Usselmann, Henri. "Edvard Munch et De la Bohème de Christiania". *Gazette des Beaux-Arts*, September (1992): 89-96.

Ustvedt, Øystein. "Nærbilde av Stenersen". In *Stenersens Munch. Edvard Munch i Stenersenmuseet* [exhibition catalogue], 23-30. Oslo: Stenersenmuseet, 2003.

Ustvedt, Øystein. "Historien om et mesterverk". In *Edvard Munch: "Det syke barn": Historien om et mesterverk = Edvard Munch: The Sick Child: The Story of a Masterpiece*, 9-54. Oslo: Nasjonalmuseet, 2009.

Ustvedt, Øystein and Trond Aslaksby (eds.). *Edvard Munch: "Det syke barn": Historien om et mesterverk = Edvard Munch: The Sick Child: The Story of a Masterpiece*. Oslo: Nasjonalmuseet, 2009.

Ustvedt, Øystein. "Edvard Munchs portretter. Kunstnerisk plattform og kilde til fornyelse". In *Edvard Munch 1863-1944* [exhibition catalogue], 232-241. Milan: Skira; Oslo: Nasjonalmuseet and Munchmuseet, 2013 A.

Ustvedt, Øystein. "Who was Mrs. Schwarz? On a Portrait by Edvard Munch. *Kunst og Kultur* 96, no. 4 (2013 B): 218-229.

Ustvedt, Øystein. "The Vitalist Impulse: Munch's Renewal and the German Expressionists". In *Munch and Expressionism* [exhibition catalogue], 69-77. Munich: Prestel, 2016.

Ustvedt, Øystein. *Edvard Munch. En introduksjon til bildene og livet*. Oslo: Stenersens forlag, 2018.

V

Varnedoe, Kirk. "Christian Krohg and Edvard Munch". *Arts Magazine* 59, no. 8 (1979): 88-95.

Varnedoe, Kirk. *Northern Light. Realism and Symbolism in Scandinavian Painting* [exhibition catalogue]. Washington: The Brooklyn Museum, 1982.

Vassenden, Erik. "Liv, bilde, fortelling. Narrative mønstre i Edvard Munchs 'Livsfrise'". In *I oss er verdener* [exhibition catalogue], 24-29. Bergen: KODE, 2019.

Vehmas, E.J. "Edvard Munchs badande män". *Ateneumin Taidemuseo*, nos. 1-2 (1964): 2-9, 23-26.

Velsand, Torstein. *Norges nasjonalarv: Edvard Munch = Norwegian Heritage: Edvard Munch - Life and Art*. Nesøya: Font forlag, 2010.

Vidalenc, Georges. "Edvard Munch". *Kunst og Kultur* 8 (1920): 130-144.

Vigtel, Gudmund. "The Impact of Early Munch". In *After the Scream. The Late Paintings of Edvard Munch* [exhibition catalogue], 15-35. Atlanta: High Museum of Art and Yale University Press, 2002.

Volle, Wenche. *Munchs rom* [thesis, PhD]. Oslo: Arkitektur- og designhøgskolen i Oslo, 2012 A.

Volle, Wenche. "Nolde og Munch". In *Emil Nolde. Jakten på det autentiske = In search of the authentic* [exhibition catalogue], 22-28. Oslo: Nasjonalmuseet, 2012 B.

W

Wahl, Volker. "Edvard Munch in Thüringen. Der norwegische Maler im Thüringer Wald 1905/06". *Mitteldeutsches Jahrbuch für Kultur und Geschichte* 9 (2002): 113-141.

Warick, Lawrence and Elaine. "Transitional Process and Creativity in the Life and Art of Edvard Munch". *Journal of the American Academy of Psychoanalysis* 12, no. 3 (1984): 413-424.

Warick, Lawrence and Elaine. "Edvard Munch. The Creative Search for Self". *Psychoanalytic Perspectives on Art*, no. 2 (1987): 275-305.

Weaver, J.R.H., George Stout and Paul Coremans. "The Weaver report on the cleaning of pictures in the National Gallery". *Museum International*, 3(2) (1950): 113-176.

Weinstein, Arnold. *Northern Arts. The Breakthrough of Scandinavian Literature and Art, from Ibsen to Bergman*. Princeton: Princeton University Press, 2008.

Weisberg, Gabriel P. "S. Bing, Edvard Munch and l'Art Nouveau". *Arts Magazine* 61, no. 1 (1968): 58-64.

Weisner, Ulrich. "Munchs Inszenierung symbolischer Konstellationen". In *Edvard Munch. Liebe, Angst, Tod: Themen und Variationen* [exhibition catalogue], 433-444. Bielefeld: Kunsthalle Bielefeld, 1980.

Wennerberg, Tor. *Edvard Munch - anknytningstrauma i konst och liv: en traumapsykolgisk analys av tre centrala verk ur Edvard Munchs 1890-talsproduktion* [thesis (essay for psychologist exam)]. Stockholm: Stockholms Universitet, 2010.

Wense, Stephanie von der. "Dorfplatz in Elgersburg, Thüringen, 1905/1906. Strasse in Kragerö. Jugendliche und Enten, 1910/1911". In *Die Metamorphosen*

der Bilder [exhibition catalogue], 234-236. Hanover: Sprengel Museum Hannover, 1992.

Werenskiold, Marit. "Die Brücke und Edvard Munch". *Zeitschrift des deutschen Verein für Kunstwissenschaft* XXVIII, nos. 1-4 (1974): 140-152.

Warick, Lawrence and Elaine. *Ekspresjonisme-begrepets opprinnelse og forvandling* [thesis, doctoral]. Oslo: Universitetet i Oslo, 1984.

Willoch, Sigurd. *Nasjonalgalleriet gjennem hundre år*. Oslo: Gyldendal, 1937.

Willoch, Sigurd. *Edvard Munchs raderinger = Edvard Munch: Etchings*. Oslo: Johan Grundt Tanum, 1950.

Willoch, Sigurd. "The early Munch". In *Edvard Munch* [exhibition catalogue], 14-17. New York: The S.R. Guggenheim Foundation, 1965.

Wilson, Mary G. *Edvard Munch: a study of his form language* [thesis, PhD]. Evanston: Northwestern University, 1974.

Wilson, Mary G. "Edvard Munch's Woman in three stages. A source of inspiration for Henrik Ibsens When We Dead Awaken". *The Centennial Review* XXIV, no. 4 (1980): 492-500.

Winter, Gundolf. "Sinnbildlichkeit als Bildsinn. Zum Gestaltungskonzept des frühen Munch". In *Edvard Munch. Liebe, Angst, Tod: Themen und Variationen* [exhibition catalogue], 407-432. Bielefeld: Kunsthalle Bielefeld, 1980.

Woesthoff, Indina. "'... Ihrer Kunst aufrichtig ergeben ...' Die Sammler und Leihgeber der Ausstellung 1929 in Chemnitz". In *Edvard Munch in Chemnitz* [exhibition catalogue], 253-267. Chemnitz: Wienand, 1999.

Woesthoff, Indina. "Edvard Munch und die Deutschen Expressionisten". In *Edvard Munch 1912 in Deutschland* [exhibition catalogue], 51-73. Bielefeld: Kunsthalle Bielefeld, 2002.

Woll, Gerd. *Edvard Munchs arbeiderfrise* [unpublished thesis, magister]. Oslo: Universitetet i Oslo, 1972.

Woll, Gerd. "Nu är det arbetarnas tid". In *Edvard Munch 1863-1944* [exhibition catalogue], 137-141. Stockholm: Liljevalchs, 1977.

Woll, Gerd. "Kunst, krig og revolusjon". In *Die Brücke: Edvard Munch* [exhibition catalogue], 49-56. Oslo: Munchmuseet, 1978 A.

Woll, Gerd. "The Tree of Knowledge of Good and Evil". In *Edvard Munch. Symbols & Images* [exhibition catalogue], 229-248. Washington: National Gallery of Art, 1978 B.

Woll, Gerd. "Angst findet man bei ihm überall". In *Edvard Munch. Liebe, Angst, Tod: Themen und Variationen* [exhibition catalogue], 315-334. Bielefeld: Kunsthalle Bielefeld, 1980.

Woll, Gerd and Arne Eggum. *Edvard Munch. Alfa og Omega* [exhibition catalogue]. Oslo: Oslo kommunes kunstsamlinger, 1981.

Woll, Gerd. *Edvard Munch. Death and Desire. Etchings, Lithographs and Woodcuts from the Munch Museum* [exhibition catalogue]. Adelaide: Art Gallery of South Australia, 1986.

Woll, Gerd. "Edvard Munchs grafikk i tre nordiske samlinger". *Konsthistorisk Tidskrift*, nos. 3-4 (1988): 76-82.

Woll, Gerd. "Der Nordische Katalog zur Graphik von Edvard Munch". In *Edvard Munch/Gustav Schiefler, Briefwechsel*, vol. 2, 9-24. Hamburg: Verlag Verein, 1990.

Woll, Gerd. "Grafikeren". In *Munch og Frankrike* [exhibition catalogue], 240-275. Oslo: Munchmuseet, 1991. [Also published Paris 1991]

Woll, Gerd. "The Frieze of Life. Graphic Works". In *Edvard Munch. The Frieze of Life* [exhibition catalogue], 45-50. London: National Gallery Publications, 1992.

Woll, Gerd. "Fra Aulaen til Rådhuset. Edvard Munchs utsmykningsprosjekter 1909-1930". In *Edvard Munch. Monumentale prosjekter 1909–1930* [exhibition catalogue], 8-105. Lillehammer: Lillehammer Art Museum, 1993.

Woll, Gerd. *Edvard Munch 1895. Første år som grafiker = Edvard Munch 1895. First Year as a Graphic Artist* [exhibition catalogue]. Oslo: Munchmuseet, 1995.

Woll, Gerd. *Edvard Munch. Grafikk fra 1896 = Edvard Munch. Prints from 1896* [exhibition catalogue]. Oslo: Munchmuseet, 1996 A.

Woll, Gerd. "Mon ikke atter kunsten vil bli alles eie?" In *E. Munch. Arbeidets sjel* [exhibition catalogue], 9-52. Rjukan: Norsk Industriarbeidermuseum, 1996 B.

Woll, Gerd. "Byggherren på Ekely". In *Munch og Ekely: 1916-1944* [exhibition catalogue], 93-122. Oslo: Munchmuseet and Labyrinth Press, 1998 A.

Woll, Gerd. "Edvard Munchs grafikk". In *Munch i Munch-museet*, 100-127. Oslo: Messel forlag, 1998 B.

Woll, Gerd. *Fra kunstnerens verksted* [exhibition catalogue]. Oslo: Munchmuseet and Labyrinth Press, 1998 C.

Woll, Gerd. "Fra murer og mekaniker til arbeidere i snø". In *Munch og Warnemünde 1907-1908 = Munch und Warnemünde* [exhibition catalogue], 119-130. Rostock: Kunsthalle Rostock, Oslo: Munchmuseet, 1999 A.

Woll, Gerd. "Kan kunst forandre verden?" In *Engasjert Kunst. Billedkunsten speiler samfunnet* [exhibition catalogue], 91-127. Oslo: Stenersenmuseet and Labyrinth Press, 1999 B.

Woll, Gerd. "Edvard Munch. En evig aktuell samtidskunstner = Edvard Munch. A perennially contemporary artist". In *Skrigets Ekko - Echoes of The Scream* [exhibition catalogue], 104-113. Ishøj: Arken, 2001 A.

Woll, Gerd. *Edvard Munch: The complete graphic work = Edvard Munch: Werkverzeichnis der Graphik*. London: Munchmuseet and Philip Wilson Publishers;

New York: Munchmuseet and Harry N. Abrams Inc. Publ., 2001 B.

Woll, Gerd. "Munchs utstillingsstrategi 'for å få sagt noe' med sine bilder". In *Edvard Munchs Livsfrise. En rekonstruksjon av utstillingen hos Blomqvist 1918* [exhibition catalogue], 37-49. Oslo: Munchmuseet and Labyrinth Press, 2002.

Woll, Gerd. "Papier in Edvard Munchs graphischen Arbeiten". In *Edvard Munch. Thema und Variation = Edvard Munch. Theme and Variation* [exhibition catalogue], 41-52. Vienna: Albertina, 2003 A.

Woll, Gerd. "Stenersens Munch, eller omvendt?" In *Stenersens Munch. Edvard Munch i Stenersenmuseet* [exhibition catalogue], 5-13. Oslo: Stenersenmuseet, 2003 B.

Woll, Gerd. "A good painting never vanishes. The artist and his effects". In *Edvard Munch. The Frieze of Life* [exhibition catalogue], 19-29. Melbourne: National Gallery of Victoria, 2004 A.

Woll, Gerd. "Vita brevis ars longa. Munchs selvportretter som kunstnerisk overlevelsesprosjekt". In *Portrett i Norge* [exhibition catalogue], 38-51. Oslo: Norsk folkemuseum and Labyrinth Press, 2004 B.

Woll, Gerd. "Compiling a catalogue raisonné of Edvard Munchs paintings". In *Edvard Munch. An anthology*, 141-162. Oslo: Unipub, 2006.

Woll, Gerd. "Edvard Munch's Workers' frieze". In *Edvard Munch. The decorative projects* [exhibition catalogue], 189-193. Tokyo: National Museum of Western Art, 2007.

Woll, Gerd. "Bruk og gjenbruk i Munchs tidligste malerier". In *Munch blir "Munch". Kunstneriske strategier 1880-1892 = Munch Becoming "Munch". Artistic Strategies 1880-1892* [exhibition catalogue], 85-101. Oslo: Munchmuseet, 2008 A.

Woll, Gerd. *Edvard Munch. Samlede malerier. Catalogue raisonné*, vols. I–IV. Oslo: Cappelen Damm, 2008 B.

Woll, Gerd. "Recording the waves emitted by society". In *Edvard Munch. The Modern Eye = Der Moderne Blick = L'oeil moderne* [exhibition catalogue], 227-233. London: Tate Publishing, 2012 A. [Also published Paris 2011 and Frankfurt 2012]

Woll, Gerd. *Edvard Munch. Samlede grafiske verk* [revised edition]. Oslo: Orfeus, 2012 B.

Woll, Gerd. "Munch hos Blomqvist, en 40-årig utstillingshistorie". In *Munch og Blomqvist* [exhibition catalogue], 6-56. Oslo: Blomqvist, 2013.

Woll, Gerd. "Edvard Munch's Use and Abuse of Alcohol". *Art in Print* 7, no. 4 (2017): 13-18.

Woll, Gerd. "Munch og Gauguin. Fra Høstutstillingen i 1884 til Sonderbund i 1912 = Munch and Gauguin, from the Autumn Exhibition in 1884 to Sonderbund in 1912". In *Med lukkede øyne. Gauguin og Munch = With Eyes Closed - Gauguin and Munch*

[exhibition catalogue], 127-141. Oslo: Munchmuseet, 2018.

Wylie, Harold W. and Mavis. "'Edvard Munch'. A Study of Narcissism and Artistic Creativity". *American Imago*, no. 4 (1980 A): 413-443.

Wylie, Harold W. and Mavis. "The Creative Relationship of Internal and External Determinants in the Life of an Artist". *The Annual of Psychoanalysis* 17 (1980 B): 73-128.

X

Xani, Kirsten. "Ein Werk für den Menschen - Angst, Krankheit und Tod als Themen des Lebensfrieses". In *Munch revisited. Edvard Munch und die heutige Kunst* [exhibition catalogue], 44-50. Dortmund: Kerber Verlag, 2005.

Y

Yarborough, Tina. *Exhibition strategies and wartime politics in the art and career of Edvard Munch, 1914-1921* [unpublished thesis, PhD]. Chicago: University of Chicago, 1995.

Yarborough, Tina. "Public confrontations and shifting allegiances. Edvard Munch and the art of exhibition". In *Edvard Munch. The modern life of the soul* [exhibition catalogue], 64-77. New York: Museum of Modern Art, 2006 A.

Yarborough, Tina. "The strange case of postmodernism's appropriation of Edvard Munch". In *Edvard Munch. An Anthology*, 191-205. Oslo: Unipub, 2006 B.

Ydstie, Ingebjørg. "Images on the back side of the eye. Perception in Munch's art". In *Edvard Munch. The decorative projects* [exhibition catalogue], 184-188. Tokyo: National Museum of Western Art, 2007.

Ydstie, Ingebjørg. "Dateringen av Munch-museets Skrik = The Dating of the Munch Museum's Scream". In *Skrik = The Scream* [exhibition catalogue], 77-85. Oslo: Vigmostad & Bjørke, 2008.

Ydstie, Ingebjørg. "Åsgårdstrand i Munch og Munch i Åsgårdstrand - Landskapet som mening og sammenheng". In *Kjærlighetens strand. Edvard Munch og Åsgårdstrand* [exhibition catalogue], 39-61. Oslo: Labyrinth Press, 2010.

Ydstie, Ingebjørg. "Akten som felt for ny symboldannelse. Den tapte 1886-versjonen av Munchs motiv for *Pubertet*". In *Edvard Munch: Pubertet = Edvard Munch: Puberty* [exhibition catalogue], 9-29. Oslo: Munchmuseet and Orfeus Publishing, 2012.

Ydstie, Ingebjørg (ed.). *Edvard Munch: Pubertet = Edvard Munch: Puberty* [exhibition catalogue]. Oslo: Munchmuseet and Orfeus Publishing, 2012.

Yvenes, Marianne, Ellen Lerberg and Øystein Ustvedt (eds.). *Edvard Munch i Nasjonalmuseet*. Oslo: Nasjonalmuseet, 2008.

Z

Zarobell, John. "A year in Paris. Edvard Munch's Mermaid". In *Edvard Munch's Mermaid* [exhibition catalogue], 7-23. Philadelphia: Philadelphia Museum of Art and Pennsylvania State University Press, 2005.

Zeiller, Christiane. "'... More or Less My Antipode': The Influence of Edvard Munch on Max Beckmann's Early Work". In *Max Beckmann and Berlin* [exhibition catalogue], 47-54. Berlin: Kerber Verlag, 2015.

Zernichow, U. von. "Malerei in Norwegen". *Die Kunst*, January (1939): 114-124.

Ziemendorff, Stefan. "Edvard Munch y la Momia de un sarcófago de la Cultura Chachapoyas". *Cátedra Villareal* 3, no. 2 (2015): 197-212.

Ø

Østby, Leif. "Edvard Munch". In *Fra naturalisme til nyromantikk: En studie i norsk malerkunst i tiden ca. 1888-1895*, 125-146. Oslo: Gyldendal, 1934.

Østby, Leif. "Et Edvard Munch-motiv". *Kunst og kultur* 49, no. 3 (1966): 151-158.

Øverland, Arnulf. *Edvard Munch*. Kristiania: Berg & Høgh, 1920.

Å

Aarkrog, Tove. *Edvard Munch. Et livsløb af en grænsepersonlighed forstået gennem hans billeder*. Copenhagen: Lundbeck Pharma, 1990.

Archives
Edvard Munchs tekster. Digitalt arkiv, published by Munchmuseet
https://www.emunch.no/
National Library of Norway letters and manuscripts
The National Museum's documentation archive

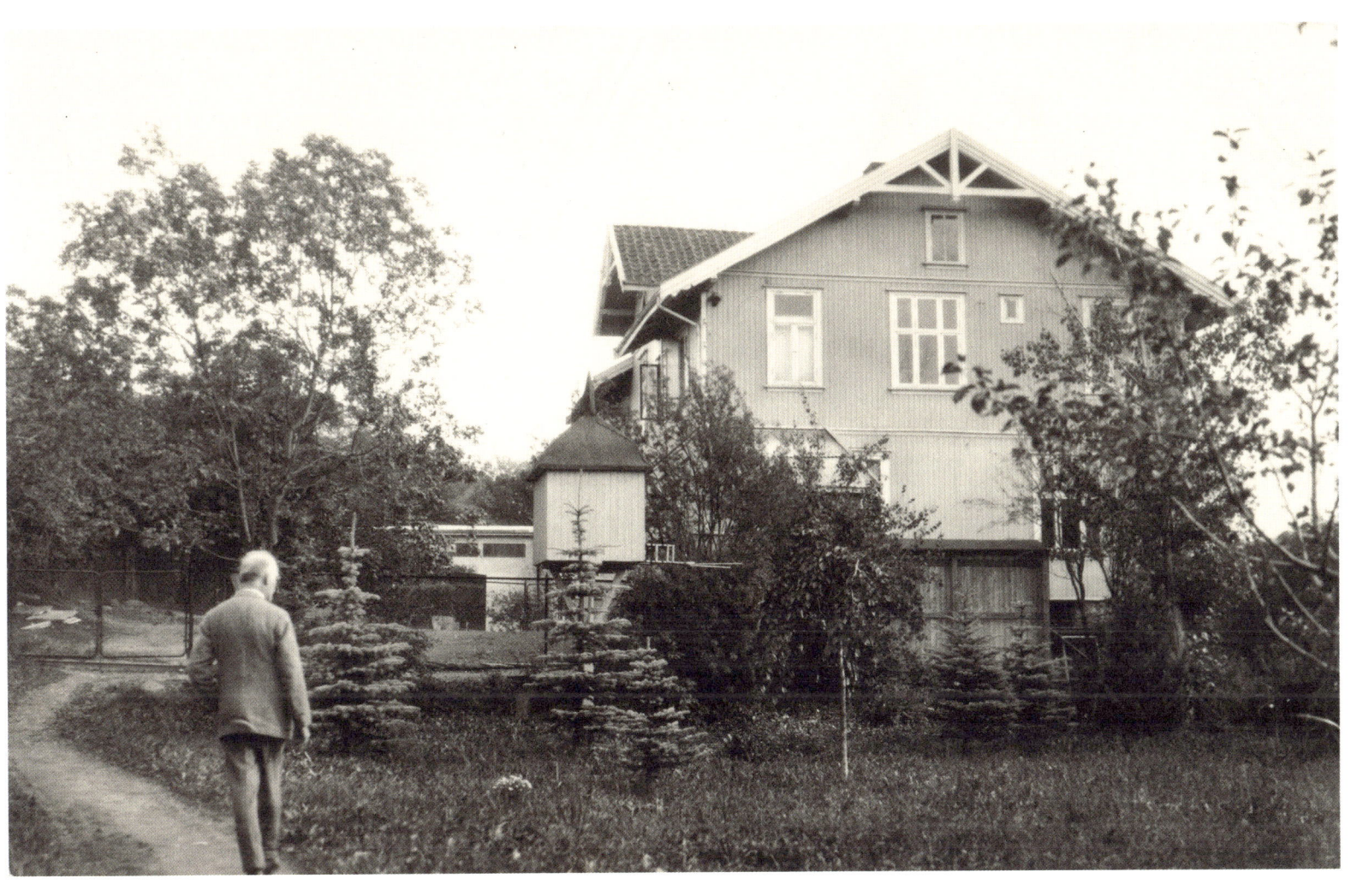

Munch at Ekely, ca. 1932-1933.
MM.D.02469-06
Photo: Munchmuseet/Inger Munch

Edvard Munch in the National Museum. A comprehensive overview

© Nasjonalmuseet for kunst, arkitektur og design
Postboks 7014 St. Olavs plass, 0130 Oslo
Tel. (+ 47) 21 98 20 00
www.nasjonalmuseet.no

1. edition 2022

ISBN 978-82-8154-142-9

Editors: Øystein Ustvedt, Marianne Yvenes
Editorial team: Vibeke Waallann Hansen, Wenche Volle, Sidsel Helliesen, Nils Messel
Picture editors: Beate M. Bang, Therese Husby
Proofreading: Ida Hove Solberg
Bibliography: Trine Nordkvelle, Ida Hove Solberg
Other contributors: Trine Nordkvelle, Frank Høifødt, Gerd Woll
Translation from Norwegian to English (all except Thierry Ford's article): Peter Cripps

The works in the catalogue have been photographed by the museum's photographers:
Nasjonalmuseet / Børre Høstland: Cat. 1-9, 11-33, 35-43, 45-47, 49-57, 119, 226-229
Nasjonalmuseet / Jacques Lathion: Cat. 10, 34, 44, 48
Nasjonalmuseet / Dag A. Ivarsøy: Cat. 58-61, 63-118, 120-225, 230-243

Graphic design: Modest [Rune Døli] and Daniel Bjugård
Repro: JK Morris Production, Sweden
Print: Printer Trento S.r.l., Italy
Paper: 120 gsm Arena Natural Rough, 150 gsm Gardapat Kiara, 115 gsm Sirio Color
Font: Museet Serif

This material is protected by copyright law. Without explicit authorisation, reproduction is
only allowed in so far as it is permitted by law or by agreement with the copyright holders.

Cover:
Edvard Munch, *Self-Portrait with Cigarette*, 1895 (cat. 32)